SPECIAL PROBLEMS IN
CHILD AND ADOLESCENT BEHAVIOR

Edited by

Larry E. Beutler, Ph.D.
Richard Greene, M.A.

©TECHNOMIC Publishing Co., Inc. 1978
265 Post Road West, Westport, CT 06880

SPECIAL PROBLEMS IN
CHILD AND ADOLESCENT BEHAVIOR

a **TECHNOMIC**® publication

TECHNOMIC Publishing Co., Inc.
265 Post Road West, Westport, CT. 06880

Printed in U.S.A.
Library of Congress Card No. 78-56115
I.S.B.N. 87762-253-1

PREFACE

The subject matter of this book is "behaviorism," not the limited behaviorism of a generation ago but a broad ranging social behaviorism under which the psychology of human emotion and personal suffering is included. The current book is designed to draw the reader's attention to the tremendous scope of concepts and problems that are rightly clasified under the term "behaviorism" and which can be aptly applied to a wide spectrum of child and adolescent problems. It is our thesis that the clinical principles of anxiety, motivation, cognitive dysfunction or deficiency and behavior change must be understood within a broader perspective of ecology, social persuasion and cultural values. Hence, we have attempted both to describe many of these general behavioral-ecological concepts and to consider their specific application to younger populations. We trust that you, the reader, will understand therefore, when we say that this is first a book concerning the behavioral-social context of psychopathology and the treatment of psychopathology and then a book of child and adolescent disturbance. Understood in this way, applications of general behavioral principles to children and adolescents require free exchange among professional and conceptual systems, such that the applications selected fit both the individual needs and the social systems of the populations in question.

It should be said that we realize we have taken upon ourselves a large task in our effort to explore the diversity of the field of behaviorism and its applications even to a limited number of child and adolescent problems. Yet, in this effort to apply the various concepts, theories, and therapies of relevance to special problems of child and adolescent behavior, we hope to convey the value of successful exchange among theoretical systems and disciplinary conceptualizations.

This volume is basically an outgrowth of the awesome interest now being shown in the fields of human behavior. The contributing authors represent the diversity of these fields and the diversity of perspectives contained within them. Contributing to this volume are psychologists, physicians, educators, ecologists, sociologists, and social workers, representing both clinicians and basic researchers. The presentation is intended to provide the latest information, techniques and research now available. It is further intended, by its very diversity to provide a comparison and even a marriage among the perspectives and viewpoints represented.

In accordance with the foregoing considerations, we have grouped the authors' selections under two major headings — one devoted to understanding the psychological-social concepts and dynamics which precipitate, perpetuate and maintain behavioral problems and the other to presenting treatment considerations. Each section is further divided into those presentations which emphasize broad based behavioral concepts and those which emphasize more specific applications to select problems of children and adolescents. Our description of the general principles which relate to an understanding of behavioral disturbance include some reflections on the interrelationship between genetics and behavior (Chapter 1), a consideration of the relevance of maturation and cognition to overt behavior (Chapter 2) and a brief but timely presentation of the potentially damaging impact of a social milieu on problem behavior (Chapter 3). Having presented these general principles, there follows a series of more specific discussions on the relationship between these concepts and a multitude of child and adolescent disturbances. For example, the ensuing selections (Chapter 4—8) describe the impact of social and environmental systems, emotions and interpersonal dynamics on delinquent, deficient and excessive behavior.

Under the major division entitled "Altering Problem Behavior" distinctions are made between the usual psychological-behavioral interventions on one hand, and those which emphasize a social-ecological approach on the other. Chapters 9, 10, and 11 provide many of the general concepts from which one can understand the specific applications discussed. For example, concepts relating behavior change to social influence and persuasion (Chapter 9), a description of the diversity and interrelationships of behavioral and traditional approaches (Chapter 10), and an expression of the humanistic and ethical concerns involved with these treatments (Chapter 11) are highlighted. The specific applications to children and adolescents build upon these general principles of broad based behaviorism to provide the reader with a variety of treatment strategies which largely combine principles of social learning, behavioral technology, skill training, and self monitoring (Chapters 12—17).

Finally, the foregoing perspective on altering child and adolescent problem behavior is expanded through a consideration of social and ecological issues. Chapters 18 through 22 reflect the importance of educational systems, community based treatments, institutional milieus, and behavioral architecture on efforts to cope with specific problems and populations.

As one surveys the selections presented in this volume, they will become aware that many of the conceptual divisions appear somewhat arbitrary, and it is hoped that this awareness will sensitize the reader to the relationships existing among the diversity of perspectives represented. It is this diversity, we feel, which makes the current volume unique. While there have been several textbooks written under both single and multiple authorship, which give consideration to behavioral disturbances of children and adolescents, these volumes uniformly have inordinately limited perspectives, approaching the field from a psychological, psychiatric, or limited behavioral viewpoint. It is our opinion that the field is now so specialized and yet varied that it is difficult for one writer or even one discipline to adequately survey the significant developments in the diverse schools and approaches. An interdisciplinary and multi-author approach avoids the pitfalls of a narrow view perceived only through the eyes of an insider. Yet, in a volume such as the present one, every presentation has the advantage of being advanced by an advocate who has indepth knowledge of that about which he or she speaks. The failing of such a broad ranging approach is that the reader is not exposed to the excruciating details of any single theoretical formulation or applied procedure. However, we believe that the exposure presented will give readers sufficient knowledge to direct their search for more depth in those areas where interest is stirred, and will at the same time provide them with sufficient information to allow direct clinical application albeit in a more limited way. With this diversity and intent in mind, this book is directed to all serious minded practitioners and students of the behavioral and social sciences as well as to practicing psychotherapists, psychiatrists, and psychologists. Teachers may find that specific selections are of most use to them and the relative independence of the selections allows their presentation in a manner appropriate to these considerations and preferences.

Many eminent specialists have contributed to this volume. The ideas presented reflect a great deal of creativity on the part of these contributors and also reflect the intensity of effort that these people have made in order to make each contribution a learning experience for the reader. The editors are deeply indebted to this group of outstanding contributors for their insight and perceptive presentations.

Dedicated to

"In loving memory of my father. R. G."

"To my parents and children. L. B."

LIST OF CONTRIBUTORS

Robert C. Beck, Ph.D.
Professor, Department of Psychology
Wake Forest University

Larry E. Beutler, Ph.D.
Associate Professor, Coordinator of Clinical Psychology Training Program
Baylor College of Medicine

Gary G. Brannigan, Ph.D.
Associate Professor of Psychology and Director, Psychological Services Clinic
State University of New York, College at Plattsburgh

Thomas A. Brigham, Ph.D.
Associate Professor, Department of Psychology
Washington State University

Douglas C. Chatfield, Ph.D.
Associate Professor of Psychology
Texas Tech University

Anthony M. D'Agostino, M.D., S.C.
Examiner, Diplomate, American Board of Psychiatry and Neurology
Department of Psychiatry
Strictch School of Medicine
Loyola University of Chicago

Alfred J. Finch, Jr., Ph.D.
Coordinator of Research, Assistant Professor of Psychiatry
Medical College of Virginia

Ben P. Granger, Ph.D.
Dean, School of Social Work
The University of Tennessee

Richard Greene, M. A.
Tenured, Special Education Department Chairman
Madera Unified School District

James Craig Griffin, Ph.D.
Clinical Psychologist
Gulf Coast Regional MHMR Center
Galveston, Texas

Gerald E. Harris, Jr., Ph.D.
Research Associate
Baylor College of Medicine

Philip C. Kendall, Ph.D.
Assistant Professor, Clinical Psychology
University of Minnesota

William F. Landers, Ph.D.
Associate Professor, Department of Psychology
Texas Tech University

Dan Linkenholder, M. A.
Doctoral Candidate, Counseling and Psychological Services
Indiana State University

Bill J. Locke, Ph.D.
Professor and Director of Clinical Training
Department of Psychology
Texas Tech University

Lynne M. McAllister, Ph.D.
Division of Pre-School Programs
Mountain View Public Schools
Mountain View, California

Lawrence T. McCarron, Ph.D.
Associate Professor of Psychology
Indiana State University

Frank J. Menolascino, M.D.
Vice Chairman, Department of Psychiatry, Professor of Psychiatry and Pediatrics
University of Nebraska Medical Center
Clinical Director of Social and Preventive Psychiatry
Nebraska Psychiatric Institute

Harold Michal-Smith, Ph.D.
Professor of Pediatrics & Psychiatry
Director of Psychology and Associate Director of Mental Retardation Institute
New York Medical College

C. H. Patterson, Ph.D.
Professor Emeritus of Educational Psychology
Division of Counseling Psychology
University of Illinois

Earl T. Patterson, Ph.D.
Clinical Psychologist
Veterans Administration Hospital
Dallas, Texas

Stephen Pollack, Ph.D.
Post Doctoral Fellow
University of Rochester College of Medicine

Robert M. Porter — deceased
Superintendent, State Home and Training School
Grand Junction, Colorado

Benjamin D. Singer, Ph.D.
Professor, Department of Sociology
University of Western Ontario

Fred D. Strider, Ph.D.
Associate Professor of Medical Psychology, Department of Psychiatry
University of Nebraska College of Medicine
Chief of the Clinical Psychology Section and Chief of Staff
Nebraska Psychiatric Institute

John M. Throne, Ph.D.
Professor of Psychology, Education and Human Development
University of Kansas

Paul C. Whitehead, Ph.D.
Chairman of the Department of Sociology
University of Western Ontario

Ben J. Williams, Ph.D.
Assistant Professor and chief Child Psychologist
Baylor College of Medicine

Lucille C. Wolf, M. A.
Research Sociologist, CPRI
London, Ontario, Canada

CONTENTS

GENES AND BEHAVIOR:
A RADICAL BEHAVORIST POINT OF VIEW

John M. Throne, Ph. D.
University of Kansas

ABSTRACT

To radical behaviorists, the notion that behavior is a *sign* caused by organismic *significates* is false. Behavior is seen as caused solely by whichever known or knowable environmental stimuli empirically induce it through reinforcement. The radical behaviorist does see genetic and other intraorganismic factors as possibly contributing to the organismic fundament through which the effectiveness of environmental stimuli in inducing behavior must be revealed. However, such factors can only be contingencies, enabling that behavior to occur; in no way can they be its causes, too. This is only to say that genes and other intraorganismic factors cannot be contingencies and causes both: they cannot cause behavior that depends upon themselves.

What *is* the contribution of genetic factors to behavior, from a radical behaviorist point of view? In order to answer this question, the relationship between intraorganismic and extraorganismic factors, as perceived by radical behaviorists, must be clearly understood.

Introduction

To radical behaviorists, whose scientific frame of reference is derived from B.F. Skinner's (1938, 1953), the notion that behavioral responses are caused by factors inside the organism is not true. Behavioral responses are seen as caused by whichever known or knowable environmental stimuli empirically induce them. Radical behaviorists recognize that stimuli causing responses might, in principle, be said to lie inside as well as outside the organism, but the burden is on those who would theorize the locus of causation to be intraorganismic, to prove it empirically. Since the very act of activating an organism to prove the intraorganismic origin of a response attributable to it, would perforce take place in the extraorganismic environment (organisms do not exist in a vacuum), this is a logical impossibility: if environmental input induces organismic output, the former is the cause of the latter regardless of any intraorganismic factors involved. Ultimately, there is simply no getting around the fact that stimuli inducing response occurrences must be extraorganismic.

Jokes about "black boxes" notwithstanding, radical behaviorists are not unaware of the contribution of the organism (the 0 between the S and the R) to its own

1

responses: try imagining a baby *babbling* without a babbling *baby!* However, responding organisms do not explain their own responses: the fact a baby babbles does not account for why (Throne, 1973a). Nor can "interaction," involving impingement of a stimulus upon an organism (whether from within or without), be invoked as the cause of any response. That an organism responds to a stimulus does not indicate the response was caused *by* interaction between the stimulus and the organism, but by the stimulus *in* interaction with the organism (Throne, 1972a).

Reinforcement

What, then, *is* the contribution of intraorganismic, including genetic, factors to behavior, from a radical behaviorist point of view? The radical behaviorist acknowledges that intraorganismic factors do indeed contribute to behavior: but always as contingent, never causal, components of the organismic fundament which must be operative for the function of any stimulus in inducing any response to be revealed. That is, intraorganismic, including genetic, factors may contribute to responses as contingencies sufficient (if not always necessary) to enable their occurrence, but it is *reinforcing* factors in the extraorganismic environment that cause those responses in each instance that they do, in fact, occur (Throne, 1973b).

Reinforcement, as a conceptual invention, is generally accredited to E. L. Thorndike (1911). However, it has most rigorously been operationalized and applied by B. F. Skinner (e.g., 1938, p. 63). (For a brief, up-to-date exposition of Skinner's behavioral model, operant conditioning, including his concept of reinforcement, see Reynolds, 1975.) According to Skinner, stimuli may be said to be reinforcing only a posteriori; that is, only if responses that they follow increase as a function of them. Obversely, only responses followed by reinforcing stimuli may be said to be reinforced. More precisely, responses are reinforced when stimuli following them cause increases in their frequencies, percentages, or rates. Therefore, if stimuli following responses do cause such increases, i.e., are reinforcing, no other variables, genetic factors included, can (or need) be causally credited. But, if stimuli following responses do not cause such increases, i.e., are not reinforcing, no other variables, genetic factors included, can (or need) be causally blamed.

Of course, neither theoretically nor empirically can *nothing* be blamed *even on a contingent basis* for the failure of an event to occur. Failure is a non-event, a nullity. The failure of an event to occur "proves" only that it did not occur, it does not account for why. This principle is embodied in the imperative to reject that is implicit in null hypothesis testing. Even in rejecting the null, one does not prove the experimental hypothesis, only that the probability of occurrence of the occurring event exceeded chance at a certain confidence level. Provided that the experiment yields empirical evidence of a functional relationship between the independent and dependent variables involved, the answer to the question "wherefrom the latter?" is ipso facto resolved. This is the mathematico-logical basis behind the tradition of experiments calculated to reject the null hypothesis rather than accept it; which tradition has led irresistably to a science that is positivistic (even logico-positivistic), and to the reluctance of journal editors to publish negative results, i.e., findings denoting accepted null hypotheses.

The point is, as conceptualized by Skinner, a reinforcing stimulus is always effective to some degree; the null hypothesis is always rejected at some level of confidence, given a reinforcing stimulus. References to "ineffective reinforcing stimuli" are non sequitur; what is (or should be) meant is nonreinforcing stimulus consequences. (Stimulus consequences may also be the reciprocal of reinforcing: they may be extinguishing, as evidenced by subsequent decreases in preceding response frequencies, percentages, or rates.) Thus, Skinner is not only a radical behaviorist par excellence, but one emphasizing the primacy of stimuli that, following responses, function as reinforcers of them; to the neglect, in the opinion of some, of the contingent contribution of stimuli coming prior to those responses. The author has referred to the causal function of stimuli bearing a reinforcing relationship to responses as the *principle of consequential determinism* (Throne, 1970).

Incidentally, the criticism of Skinner, that he neglects the contribution of antecedent contingent stimuli, overlooks the fact that Skinner's references to reinforcement always imply stimuli preceding responses that are reinforced, which stimuli may be (or become) antecedent contingencies of those responses, i.e., discriminative stimuli (see below). However, Skinner may not have taken sufficient pains to make the distinction as clear as he might between the contingent character of discriminative stimuli preceding responses and the causal character of reinforcing stimuli that follow them. In any event, there has been, and remains, much confusion over contingencies and causes by Skinnerians and non-Skinnerians alike (Throne, 1973b).

As Skinner does make clear, responses reinforced in the past will tend to reoccur in the future if stimuli antecedent to them in the past are reintroduced. The reason is not that the antecedent stimuli caused the responses in the past, but, that, when the former did precede the latter previously, the responses, upon occurring, were consequated by stimuli that were reinforcing. When consequential stimuli reinforce responses, stimuli antecedent to them tend to become discriminative: indicate that those responses probably will be reinforced if they occur again (e.g., Skinner, 1953, pp. 107–128). Of course, in the case of past events, this explanation never can be proved directly on an empirical basis. But an empirical basis for proving it indirectly can be provided by demonstrating a functional relationship between *representatives* of the same stimulus and response *classes* in the present. Such proof, it is important to note, always involves independently known or knowable stimulus and response variables; the stimuli are differentiated or differentiable from the responses with which they bear either a discriminative or a reinforcing relationship. Thus, discriminative and reinforcing stimuli are never tautologically inferred, as are, apparently, genes (see below).

Is Reinforcement Tautological?

Reinforcement itself is sometimes charged with being a tautological concept (e.g., by Chomsky, 1959). With respect to Skinner's (if not Thorndike's) concept of it, this is a mistake. A tautology obtains whenever an event is explained on the basis of the event itself. This happens when two statements refer to the same set of facts. Skinner (1953, p. 31) has put it succinctly:

> When we say that a man eats *because* he is hungry, smokes a great deal *because* he has the tobacco habit...or plays the piano well *because* of his musical ability, we seem to be referring to causes. But on analysis these phrases prove to be merely redundant descriptions. A single set of facts is described by the two statements: 'He eats' and 'He is hungry.' A single set of facts is described by the two statements: 'He smokes a great deal' and 'He has the smoking [tobacco] habit.' A single set of facts is described by the two statements: 'He plays well' and 'He has musical ability.'

In Skinnerian terms, however, reinforcement refers to two sets of facts, not one; differentiated or differentiable independent and dependent variables always are involved. A man eats, smokes, plays a musical instrument (dependent variables) not because he is hungry (tautologically inferred from his eating); habituated to tobacco (tautologically inferred from his smoking); or musically inclined (tautologically inferred from his playing); but because reinforcing stimuli (independent variables) following those responses cause them to be maintained or increased. (Even initial responses may be reinforced into being through *shaping*: reinforcing successively closer and closer approximations of them. See, e.g., Skinner, 1953, pp. 91–106.)

Perhaps the critics are confused by the posteriori definition of reinforcement. As indicated above, stimuli may not be defined as reinforcing until increases in the frequencies, percentages, or rates of responses they follow are observed to occur as a function of them (the stimuli). This does not make reinforcement tautological; again, independently known or knowable stimulus and response variables always are involved. Criticisms of Skinner's concept of reinforcement may be right on other grounds, but the charge that it is tautological is simply wrong.

Selective Breeding

The issue of reinforcement aside, our understanding of even the contingent, not to speak of causal, contribution of intraorganismic factors called genes to responses is complicated by the traditional practice among geneticists of adducing functional relationships between genes, or genotypes, and phenotypes on theoretical grounds. Never is a functional relationship between genotypic independent-variable stimuli and phenotypic dependent-variable responses empirically induced. In all genetic experiments on humans and animals alike the reported independent variables are not genotypic but *extra*genotypic; genes, as such, are not empirically in evidence even at the intervening-variable level. Yet, in order to prove that a phenotypic response is caused by a genotypic stimulus on empirical grounds, as opposed to proving it theoretically (that is, via deduction, tautological or otherwise) it is necessary for a functional relationship between them to be empirically induced. Any experiment in which genetic effectiveness is purported to obtain *empirically* in the absence of genes identified independently of their alleged effects is either methodologically flawed or has been misinterpreted. Selective breeding experiments quoted by the controversial psychologist, A.R. Jensen (1969), in support of his genetic-primacy hypothesis to account for differences in standardized intelligence test scores among the races, suffer from one or the other (sometimes both) of these critical shortcomings (Throne, 1975b). (This is not to say that the quoted experimenters are responsible for the totality of uses to which Jensen puts their data, of course.)

For example, Thompson (1954) showed that, after six generations of deliberate and systematic selective breeding in the laboratory, rats starting out in the first generation as equally intelligent in terms of maze-learning ability cleanly divided themselves into "bright" and "dull" categories (Figure 1). Jensen concluded that intraorganismic, that is, genetic, factors were at work despite the fact that the only factors empirically operative were extraorganismic: the environmental machinations inherent in selective breeding, culminating in mating by rats displaying the same levels of the ability in question. (I.e., within each generation, mating rat-pairs were always "intellectually" homogeneous: either "bright" or "dull.") In another experiment quoted by Jensen, Cooper and Zubeck (1958) showed that rats also bred selectively for "brightness" and "dullness" in maze-learning ability performed equally well, markedly unequally, or equally badly depending upon the environmental contingencies prevailing, ranging on a continuum from "stimulating" through "normal" to "restricted" (Figure 2). In "stimulating" environments, both categories of rat ("bright" and "dull") made few errors, in "restricted" environments, many. Only in so-called normal environments midway between "stimulating" and "restricted" — that is, wherein the operative empirical factors were those in which selective breeding was deliberately and systematically manipulated, just as in Thompson's experiment, to produce either "bright" or "dull" rats in such environments (i.e., "normal") — was the number of errors far fewer for the "bright" rats than for the "dull" — as would be expected.

Thus Cooper and Zubek's results indicate that the maze-learning ability of the rats in question varied dramatically from "bright" through "normal" to "dull" as a function of the environmental contingencies prevailing, despite the manipulations through which the rats had been, on a *theoretically* genetic, but *empirically* environmental, basis, selectively bred. Cooper and Zubek's rats proved that the "bright"-"dull" dichotomy in this ability under "normal" environmental contingencies — that is, contingencies neither "stimulating" nor "restricted," as these were defined — could be eradicated under contingencies that were either of these; that maze-learning by those rats could be skewed in one direction or the other by altering or

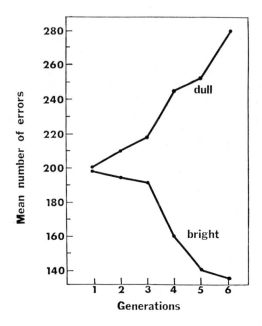

Figure 1. The mean error scores in maze learning for successive generations of selectively bred "Bright" and "dull" rats. (After Thompson, 1954)

adjusting the environmental contingencies. One can reasonably presume a similar potential for Thompson's rats: that even unto the sixth generation and beyond, had they been subjected to environmental contingencies altered or adjusted in the same manner, the same skewing phenomenon would have been exhibited — regardless of how carefully selec*tive* had been their breeding, generation by generation, and, as a consequence (perhaps!), how carefully selec*ted* their genes.

Jensen to the contrary, therefore, "empirical proof" of genetic, intraorganismic contributions to responses supposedly provided by selective breeding experiments like Thompson's and Cooper and Zubek's, turns out to be nothing of the sort: because only environmental, extraorganismic factors were empirically in evidence, whatever the case may have been theoretically. In Cooper and Zubek's experiment explicitly, and in Thompson's implicitly, the very *opposite* of the conclusion drawn by Jensen, that the hypothesis of genetic primacy is supported by the empirical findings of selective breeding experiments, follows logically on the basis of the data that Jensen himself adduces.

To be sure, in the published reports of both the Thompson and the Cooper-Zubek experiments, descriptions of the procedures employed were quite unspecific. They were described very generally, in terms of mere presence or absence of

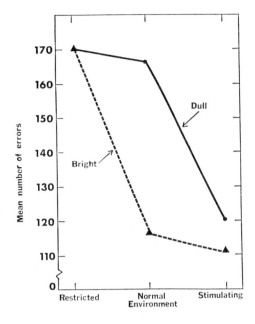

Figure 2. The mean error scores in maze learning by "bright" and "dull" rats raised in restricted," "normal," and "stimulating" environments. (After Cooper & Zubek, 1958)

stimulus materials or elements, not the sequences or other contingencies under which these were delivered or withheld. Therefore, it is impossible in either experiment to point with any exactitude to the functional factors empirically responsible per se, contingently or causally, for the maze-learning ability of either set of rats. Even information about intraorganismic contingencies other than genes that were empirically, or even theoretically, operative in the two experiments is also lacking; such information may be (or have been) available in the raw data, though the unequivocal functionality of those contingencies for the behavior exhibited probably is (or was) not — because of the experimental designs employed. (Variants of analysis of variance, with all factors other than genetic *themselves* theoretically, but not empirically, controlled. See Throne, 1972b, 1975a for arguments against the applicability of the analysis of variance design in research wherein the intention is to answer questions about the effectiveness of certain variables for certain variable effects when the very nature of the research precludes answering those questions if that design is used validly. The same arguments are not explicitly spoken to with respect to selective breeding experiments in the present paper, however, they are implicitly, given the author's understanding of the primacy of reinforcing consequential stimuli in the environment in such experiments.)

7

Thus neither Thompson's nor Cooper and Zubek's experiment can be, or is, referred to by this author in support of the particular environmental thesis, stressing reinforcing environmental consequences (and the operant conditioning model), he has been propounding in this paper. Both experiments are invoked only in support of the *antithetical* argument to the one put forward by those who, with Jensen, regard selective breeding experiments as providing empirical proof (however tentative) of genetic, rather than environmental, primacy on the basis of the data such experiments yield. Empirically, selective breeding experiments indicate that it is environmental factors that are primary in inducing responses in selective breeding experiments, not genes or other intraorganismic factors: that the contribution of all intraorganismic factors to the outcome of thse experiments is entirely theoretical, i.e., superimposed upon the data. In short, the conclusion that there is empirical evidence for the hypothesis of genetic primacy to be drawn from selective breeding experiments, is simply unwarranted.

Genotype and Phenotype

Unwarranted or not, this conclusion seems to stem from the tautological definitions of genes and genotypes. According to one distinguished geneticist, J. Hirsch (1970), a gene is an inference from a selective breeding experiment. According to another, I.I. Gottesman (1958), genotype refers to an organism's genes, phenotype to its physical or chemical characteristics resulting from interaction of the organism and the environment. The problem is, phenotypic characteristics, or effects, can be identified independently of genotypic effectiveness. Genotypic effectiveness, however, can be identified only by phenotypic effects; knowledge of the former depends entirely on knowledge of the latter. To be sure, Gottesman declares that genes exert their influence at a molecular level. How molecular is not certain, but apparently more molecular than that at which enzymes, hormones, and phenotypes, whose sequences, he asserts, define the paths of genes, exert theirs. *That is, evidence of the genes purportedly originating those paths labeled genetic, is not empirically induced; it is theoretically deduced on the basis of tautological reasoning.*

Gottesman proposes that the best way to conceptualize the influence of heredity (for which read: genes) on a phenotype is to think of it as determining a reaction range. (There are no genes *for* any phenotype, he admits.) Within this framework a genotype determines an indefinite but circumscribed assortment of phenotypes, each phenotype corresponding to one of the possible environmental circumstances to which the genotype could be exposed. But vague references to "indefinite" phenotypes and "possible" environmental circumstances would hardly seem to offer firm conceptual foundations to a science. Its vagueness aside, the utility of this entire conceptual mode escapes this author. Logically, a phenotypic, dependent-variable effect y cannot be said to confirm the effectiveness of a genotypic, independent variable x if the two phenomena are operationally indistinguishable (measured by the same procedures). Until phenotypes are able to be operationally distinguished, at least in principle, from genotypes of which they are hypothesized to be a function, neither a causal nor a contingent relationship involving them can logically be even theoretically speculated upon, let along empirically proved.

Environment

Further confusion arises from the way geneticists define environment. According to Gottesman, the environment includes events occurring inside as well as outside the organism. The internal environment includes intrauterine conditions (contingencies) prevailing prior to the organism's birth as well as molecular factors within and between its embryonic cells. Gottesman cautions that since difference genotypes may have the same phenotype and different phenotypes may be displayed by the same genotype a lack of clarity may be perpetuated by a failure to specify the environmental circumstances (contingencies) when describing the phenotype of genes. Conversely, the attribution of a phenotypic effect to an environmental variable may be misleading unless the genotype is specified. But, surely, such warnings can serve little purpose if environments (like genes) refer to factors so molecular as to be known or knowable only through deduction — tautological deduction at that. Only when internal environments, despite their molecularity (and even if molar), can be identified independently of their hypothesized effects, can their effective contribution (like that of genes) to such effects (behavior and other phenotypes) be empirically proved. (Of course, according to the viewpoint being put forward in this paper, this contribution can only be shown to be contingent, never causal.)

Radical Behaviorism and Genetics: Rapprochement

Radical behaviorists would not drive a wedge between the contribution to behavior of genes and other intraorganismic factors, on the one hand, and extraorganismic, or environmental, factors, on the other, but, rather, would render logical the relationship between them. This cannot be done by failing to differentiate unequivocally between empirical and theoretical evidence. Empirical evidence of behavioral causation is rooted, ultimately, in response control. The potential for response control through environmental manipulation implied by the principle of consequential determinism frees radical behaviorists from pursuing any response's causes (even its partial causes) in genes or other intraorganismic factors. It also liberates them from seeking those causes in environmental factors other than consequential stimuli that are reinforcing. The principle of consequential determinism gives radical behaviorists a pragmatic means for trying to change any response of any organism — and to an extent that is indeterminable a priori — regardless of the genetic or other intraorganismic factors that may be operative.

A Down's Syndrome *S* with 47 chromosomes offers an apt example. (Unlike genes, chromosomes — of which genes are reputed to be a part — are identifiable independently of their alleged effects; they and their effectiveness — contingent, but not causal — are beyond empirical dispute.) Consequential stimuli that, given ordinary contingencies, may reinforce normal or supranormal responses by a non-Down's Syndrome *S* may not reinforce such responses by a Down's Syndrome *S*. This is either because, given those ordinary contingencies, the Down's Syndrome *S* typically does not emit sufficient frequencies, percentages, or rates of normal or supranormal responses, or successive approximation of them, to give consequential stimuli the chance to reinforce them; or because he is incapable of thus responding for structural or functional reasons. However, provided extraordinary contingencies are introduced, including antecedent stimuli that are discriminative (e.g., instructions, prompts, models) and/or intraorganismic changes (through medical treatment, for example), the frequencies, percentages, or rates of his normal or supranormal responses, or successive approximations of them, may be increased. If so, the cause of his improved responses is neither those antecedent discriminative stimuli nor those intraorganismic changes; it is the consequential stimuli that those stimuli and/or changes *now* render reinforcing. I.e., even formerly *un*reinforcing consequential stimuli may become reinforcing through the introduction of extraordinary contingencies enhancing their reinforceability or compensating for the *S*'s impaired structural or functional capabilities. Furthermore, if the *absence* of consequential stimuli, previously shown to increase (thus reinforce) some measure of normal or supranormal responses when *present,* subsequently results in their decrease (indicating extinction), an even more convincing empirical basis has been provided for explaining how: normal and supranormal responses increase when they are reinforced, decrease when they are not (i.e., are extinguished). (See Baer, Wolf, and Risley, 1968, for a logical analysis of the general case, which leads the author to this conclusion with respect to the specific case under discussion.)

In short, an *unusual* number of chromosomes (or genes) does not cause a Down's Syndrome *S* to respond subnormally, therefore to function as below average, any more than a *usual* number of these entities causes a non-Down's Syndrome *S* to respond normally or supranormally, therefore to function as average or above. Consequential stimuli that are reinforcing (of course interacting with intraorganismic and other extraorganismic factors) cause the occurrence of all responses by all *S*s. The range of responses a Down's Syndrome *S* with 47 chromosomes, or a non-Down's Syndrome *S* with 46, emits may vary infinitely as a function of the infinite reinforcers that might impinge on those responses in either case: *the principle of behavioral infinitude* (Throne, 1970). Moreover, regardless of the results, they may be modified by modifying the contingencies under which reinforcement occurs. For example, a Down's Syndrome or non-Down's Syndrome *S* previously reinforced for emitting criterion responses, or successive approximations of them, only when certain contingencies are present, now is reinforced for emitting them only when they are not.

Conclusion

As the above example illustrates, radical behaviorists, in denying the causal contribution of intraorganismic, including genetic, factors (and of extraorganismic factors other than reinforcing) to behavior and other phenotypes, do not deny necessarily that they make any contribution at all. Radical behaviorists of course acknowledge the possibility (indeed, in the case of certain such factors — e.g., chromosomes, if not necessarily genes — the probability) of their contribution but only as contingencies through whose agency the causal effectiveness of ordinary or extraordinary reinforcing stimuli may (perhaps must, given the particular instance) be revealed for all phenotypic effects to occur. Radical behaviorists believe, however, that the chances of correctly determing what this contingent contribution is in any given case (certainly empirically but even theoretically) is diminished by geneticists (and psychologists) to the extent they fail to recognize the true and actual contingent, as opposed to causal, character of the putative genes and other intraorganismic factors — and of any non-reinforcing extraorganismic factors — with which reinforcing stimuli may functionally interact. As this author has commented elsewhere, radical behaviorists would not abolish genetic science, they would only radicalize it. Geneticists, too, can be radical behaviorists (Throne, 1972a)!

REFERENCES

Baer, D. M., Wolf M. M., & Risley T. R., Some current dimension of applied behavior anaylsis. *Journal of Applied Behavior Analysis,* 1968, *1,* 91–97.

Cooper, R. and Zubek, J., Effects of enriched and restricted early environments on the learning ability of bright and dull rats. *Canadian Journal of Psychology,* 1958, *12,* 159–164.

Chomsky, N., Review of B. F. Skinner, *Verbal behavior. Language,* 1959, *35,* 26–58.

Gottesman, I. I., Biogenetics of race and class. In M. Deutsch, I. Katz, and A. R. Jensen (Eds.). *Social class, race and psychological development.* New York: Holt, Rinehart and Winston, 1968.

Hirsch, J., Behavior-genetic analysis and its biosocial consequences. *Seminars in Psychiatry,* 1970, *2,* 89–105.

Jensen A. R., How much can we boost IQ and scholastic achievement? *Harvard Educational Review,* 1969, *39,* 1–123.

Reynolds, G. S., *A primer of operant conditioning.* Glenview, Illinois: Scott, Foresman, 1975.

Skinner B. F., *Behavior of organisms.* New York: Appleton-Century-Crofts, 1938.

Skinner, B. F., *Science and human behavior.* New York: Macmillan, 1953.

Thompson, W. R., The inheritance and development of intelligence. *Research and Public Assistance in Nervous and Mental Disorders,* 1954, *33,* 209–331.

Thorndike, E. L., *Animal intelligence: Experimental studies.* New York: Macmillan, 1911.

Throne, J. M., A radical behaviorist approach to diagnosis in mental retardation. *Mental Retardation,* 1970, *8,* 2–5.

Throne J. M., Genetic factors in mental retardation: A radical behaviorist point of view. *Mental Retardation,* 1972, *10,* 32–35. (a)

Throne, J. M., Inferential statistics, operant conditioning, and distinctions between teaching and evaluation. *Educational Technology* 1972, *12,* 29–31. (b)

Throne, J. M., Tautological and pseudological theorizing in linguistic and cognitive research and practice: Chomsky, Piaget and Freud. Paper presented to the convention of the American Association on Mental Deficiency, Atlanta, May—June, 1973. (a)

Throne J. M., Contingency and cause in cognitive research in mental retardation: Zigler, Zeaman and House, Ellis (and Bijou). *Mental Retardation,* 1973 *11,* 45—47. (b)

Throne J. M., The replicability fetish and the Milwaukee Project. *Mental Retardation,* 1975, *13* 14—17. (a)

Throne, J. M., Is the proportion of genetic to total variance in intelligence empirically determined? Socially useful? Individually relevant: *Educational Technology,* 1975, *15,* 9—14. (b)

MOTIVATION, COGNITION, AND BEHAVIORISM*

Robert C. Beck

I. BACKGROUND

Introduction

Behaviorism wears many masks. It presents one face to the Skinnerian, another to the Hullian, a third to the Tolmanite, and still another to the general public. Yet, like the elephant to the blind men, only one face may be taken as the whole. The most "public" view of behaviorism is dominated by statements attributed (erroneously, as often as not) to Watson or Skinner or a fusion of the two. This is readily understood outside the profession. But some considerable lack of communication is indicated when a recent psychology textbook (Ittelson *et al.*, 1974) says: "Behaviorism's leading spokesman today is B. F. Skinner (1953) whose chief contribution has been his studies of operant behavior, in which environmental stimuli evoke responses which lead to reinforcements, positive or negative" (p. 66). Written by respected professionals this sentence nevertheless contains three obvious errors.

First, Skinner is not the leading spokesman for behaviorism in the sense that, say, George Meany is the spokesman for the AFL-CIO. While he certainly and deservedly has attracted a great deal of attention, Skinner nevertheless speaks for Skinner. Second, Skinner has repeated beyond count that operants are emitted, not evoked. He does not hold to an S-R reflex view of behavior. Finally, the caricature of behaviorism quoted implies that behaviorism, Skinnerian or otherwise, is without sophistication or subtlety. Wrong it may be on many particulars, unsophisticated it is not. Few theorists in the last half century have even tried to characterize behavior entirely in terms of specific responses to specific stimuli. The only notable exceptions are Guthrie and Estes, and let him speak who is willing to call Estes' mathematical models unsophisticated. Any form of behaviorism can be as complex as the data justify making it.

At a rather different level, within psychology there has also been an active insurgence against behaviorism by the "humanistic" psychologists, who seem generally disposed against psychology as a science in the usual definition of science. Again, we would take this in large part as a misunderstanding of the role of behaviorism in psychological science.

At the risk of repeating and elaborating what may seem obvious, we shall follow three interrelated themes. First, we shall review briefly the historical reasons for

*The author expresses his appreciation to Deborah Best, Charles Richman, and Frank Wood for readings of earlier drafts and helpful suggestions, many of which have been incorporated in this chapter.

13

what we consider the inevitable rise of behaviorism. Second, we shall look at the problem of motivation, examining a number of theories which vary greatly in the extent to which they *appear* "mechanistic" or "cognitive." Thirdly, we shall examine theoretical approaches to the problems of rewards, particularly to their conceptualizations as reinforcers or as incentives. In general what we shall see is that the theory of motivation, like that of psychology as a whole, has undergone a number of changes. Starting out as "rationalistic," it became "mechanistic" and is now becoming "cognitive." More importantly, however, this is not just circling around; it is more like an outward spiral, wherein we pass certain reference points in each revolution, but are not returning to where we were before.[1]

II. THE RISE OF BEHAVIORISM

Early Psychology and Consciousness

Each man's focal concern is his own life, his own awareness, his own happiness, sadness, elation, and despair. If he can find the means to greater joy he glories in it, and if he cannot he searches for it. Who can seriously doubt that the subject matter of psychology is the mind? What else but the richness of our awareness of ourselves and the world could be called the content of psychology?

When it was decided in the nineteenth century that psychology was going to be a science, it was to be the study of the mind and its structure by which we could account for the richness of our experience. According to the structuralists, mind was the fusion of images and ideas tinted with emotion. Once dissected into its atomic parts, it could be reconstructed into the whole consciousness of the waking man. This was a "commonsense" kind of psychology insofar as it took consciousness as the subject matter of psychology, as any man might do. It did, however, overlay the study of mind on a rigorous physiology.[2]

The structuralist's main dissecting tool was the method of introspection. And herein lay its greatest problem. It assumed that conscious experiences in and of themselves were the fundamental data of psychology. There are probably many reasons for this, not the least of which is the obvious reality of consciousness. But upon being declared a science, psychology was also committed to the same rules that other sciences abide by. These rules, in simplest form, are but two: Objectivity and testability. Objectivity is spuriously simple. We must have two observers agree

---

[1] An additional purpose is to spread the blame for determinism. The most virulent public attacks on Skinner, for example, seem really to be attacks on determinism. They are mostly irrelevant to the details of his system. A book like *Beyond Freedom and Dignity*, for example, is the logical outcome of any deterministic viewpoint. Since psychology as a whole is deterministic, Skinner should hardly have to bear the brunt of the criticism for all of us. In this instance, Skinner *is* psychology's leading spokesman.

[2] It is interesting that in Russia at about the same time the great physiologist Bechterev argued that *physiologists* should be the ones to study the mind because it was they who had the objective methods for doing so (Kimble, 1967). Bechterev also claimed it was the state of mind which was conditioned not just the external behavior manifested.

on what they see. And, indeed, it was here that structuralism was found most wanting. The "trained introspections" of the Titchenerians[3] failed to meet this simple test. In a word, introspection was not objective; it did not meet the criterion of intersubjective reliability. By the same token, of course, testability was also felled. If the data of introspection were not reliable, then they could hardly provide discriminating tests of any theory of mind.

Structuralism after Wundt also fell into debates over what many considered trivial issues. Boring (1946) described a kind of ultimate absurdity in the public confrontation between E. B. Titchener and E. B. Holt over whether green is perceived as a unitary color or as a color with equal amounts of yellow and blue. However engrossing to its participants, such a debate could hardly win disciples to the cause. Indeed, the structuralists did have more objective methods at their disposal (such as reaction times and psychophysical methods) and it may be unfair to characterize the movement as a whole in terms of something like the Titchener-Holt argument. On the other hand, this was how the movement eventually came to be perceived and this perception was very influential.

Finally, although Wundt himself was a devout monist, this early psychology of consciousness tended to be rationalistic. That is, man was considered to make conscious and rational choices between the options open to him and to behave accordingly. Behaviorism and psychoanalysis alike denied that choices are made in such a manner.[4] In particular, Freud produced motivational concepts which bridged the gap between normal and pathological behavior in a way that structuralism never could. The most important concept, of course, was that of an unconscious mind which influences behavior but is not consciously controlling behavior. There was hardly a place for unconscious processes in a psychology dependent on introspection.

It did not take long to see through the fallacies of structuralism. Around the turn of the century the functionalists, with their emphasis on evolutionary adaptation, asserted that introspection was not the only method for studying mind,[5] and shortly thereafter John B. Watson denied that introspection was a respectable psychological method at all. even in Germany, the Gestalt psychologists objected to

---

[3] According to Blumenthal (1975), Wundt has been badly distorted in the histories of psychology and should not be lumped together with Titchener. Wundt's primary phenomenon was what Blumenthal rephrases as "selective volitional attention," an active psychological process. Blumenthal concludes that "Wundt may be more easily understood today than he could have been just a few years ago ....because of the current milieu of modern cognitive psychology and of the recent research on human information processing" (p. 1087). Unfortunately, the bulk of Wundt's work is still in the original German.

[4] The early economists' treatment of rational economic man also fell on hard times as it became painfully obvious that men were not rational in spending their money. Even George Bernard Shaw was moved to write on the "virtue of insurance and the vice of gambling." The paradox, of course is that in the former instance you bet against yourself and in the latter instance you bet for yourself.

[5] Structuralism was akin to the Linnean classificatory approach taken to biology, and functionalism followed from the Darwinian evolutionary-adaptive approach.

the very analytic approach to consciousness taken by their forebears.

The attack on rationalism, consciousness, and introspection came so quickly that, according to Ryan (1970), a commonsense psychology of choice and intentional behavior never had a chance. The behaviorists (including Watson, Pavlov, and Thorndike) so quickly dominated the field that they stifled a reasonable development of commonsense ideas about motivation and cognition. But this is perhaps not an entirely accurate appraisal. After all, before the turn of the century William James could comfortably talk about the stream of consciousness and about the physiology of emotion at the same time and in such a way that he is still widely discussed today. It is perhaps more accurate to suggest that the "mechanists" (read: Behaviorists) held forth because science is concerned with observable data and interpretations which square with what can be seen. Behaviorism flourished because it provided an approach which gave the necessary objectivity to psychological science in a way that structuralism and rationalism could not. Behaviorism is a necessary condition for psychological science. For our purposes we may, however, distinguish between three "kinds" of behaviorism: Naive, descriptive, and methodological.[6]

Naive Behaviorism is the name commonly given to Watson's overzealous attempt to rid psychology of metaphysics. To be sure, Watson (*e.g.,* 1924) was not so "naive" as commonly pictured; he recognized internal and external stimuli of great complexity and responses of either the "muscle twitch" variety or of a complex social nature. Still, he viewed responses as being in essentially a straight-line connection with stimuli and saw no need for inferring anything about the organism other than stimuli and responses. Certainly, he saw no need to discuss consciousness within the context of psychological science, although not denying it as a fact for the individual. In rejecting consciousness as the subject matter of psychology, Watson erred by denying any behaviors which referred to consciousness. This was his naivete. He, as well as many after him, felt that reference to consciousness was too metaphysical for psychology.

Descriptive Behaviorism, or the experimental analysis of behavior, refers to the particular approach taken by Skinner (1938). The concept of the operant response is central. Whereas for Watson a response was a specific muscular or glandular effect and reducible to physiology, for Skinner a response is any behavior that has a particular effect on the environment. (In this respect, he is like Tolman, page 91.) It matters not whether the rat presses the level alternately with pushes of its paw and flicks of its tail, or bites it with his mouth, as long as it has the same effect on the environment. Operants are whatever behaviors are lawfully related to specified conditions, not specific muscle movements. It follows from this concept that it is meaningless to talk about specific stimuli being connected to specific responses

---

[6] Many adjectives have been used with behaviorism. For example, Tolman referred to his variety as molar behaviorism; others have referred to cognitive behaviorism, and so on.

(*i.e.,* S-R reflexes or learned associations) since we are not talking about specific responses. Under certain environmental circumstances, behavior-reinforcement contingencies develop so that the probability of particular behaviors increases or decreases under those conditions.

Methodological Behaviorism defines the subject matter of psychology as behavior and considers that behavior has causes and, given sufficient information, can be predicted. In this sense all scientific psychology is behavioristic, and it is in this broad sense that we discuss behaviorism here. It differs from naive or descriptive behavior in that, being a methodological percept rather than a theory *per se,* it is not restricted with regard to explanatory principles. Its sole limitation is that explanatory concepts be objectively testable, which means testable by observations of behavior. Psychologists using such diverse concepts as anxiety, power motive, need for achievement, need for affiliation, or what have you, are all methodological behaviorists. Each concept is defined in terms of some kind of measurement operation. Watson or Skinner might find little sympathy for such concepts but they are nevertheless legitimate if properly defined.[7] Consciousness itself can be treated as a scientific concept, apart from its use as a personal reference.

Behaviorism and Phenomenology

In recent years there has been a growing interest in phenomenological psychology, particularly with reference to the existential movement in philosophy, clinical psychology, and psychiatry. In this country its particular jumping-off point has been "humanistic" psychology[8] as exemplified in the work of Carl Rogers, Abraham Maslow, and Rollo May.

The essence of the phenomenological view is that each individual must privately come to know himself. At this point no one could argue. There are private experiences which seem to defy verbal description. The richness of my fantasies exceeds my ability to describe them. And that is exactly the point. My fantasies are *not*

---

[7] One guesses that Watson would now be more sympathetic than Skinner. Watson's goal was to purge magic and ghosts from psychology, but he was effectively out of the field before the more sophisticated "neobehavioral" approaches of Hull and Tolman came in. Watson could well be sympathetic toward the hypothetico-deductive method applied to psychology. Skinner, on the other hand has been fully aware of this approach and completely rejects it.

[8] Writers in this area often seem to be asserting that there is some kind of ultimate truth about humans to which only humanistic psychologists have access. This is probably not true of the more sophisticated writers (*e.g.,* Buhler, 1971), but certainly seems implied with greater than chance frequency by others. Two comments will suffice. First, there are many psychologists vitally interested in human concerns who would not otherwise share the outlook of the "humanists." Skinner is one of these; Hull was another. Let it be recalled, for example, that Hull's first two great works were in aptitude testing and hypnosis and that he envisioned the extension of his principles to the solution of social problems. Second, the only way to determine what is uniquely human is the comparative method. Work on language behavior with other primates is beginning to suggest that we may have to rethink the problem of human uniqueness.

data, they are not directly usable in science, and they are not directly open to any clinician or philosopher. They are mine until I *communicate* something of them to somebody. Keen (1975) says: "The phenomenological paradigm rests on the assumption that this level of everyday, non-theoretical self-understanding can be the subject matter of psychology, because it is not random, orderless, or unstructured. The task is merely to find a way to articulate that already existing order and structure explicitly" (p. 128). That is rather like saying that the task of the physicist is *merely* to articulate the existing order and structure of the atom.

According to Brody and Oppenheim (1966), a pure phenomenological psychology would try to study experience "freed, as far as possible, from the encumbrance of any preconceived and theoretical ideas about that which is being investigated" (p. 26). It would deal with nonconceptualized experience. The question is whether such nonconceptualized experience has any scientific value. The value would seem to be in the *discovery* of ideas as opposed to their *verification*. The reason for this is twofold. First, nonconceptualized experience could not, by definition, be put into verbal form and communicated to others. If not communicable, it is not scientifically verifiable. Second, nonconceptualized experience could not provide explanation or prediction of events because both of these require the conceptualization of interrelations among events. The term "explanation" would seem to have no meaning in this context since explanation is relational and relations are conceptualized.

The phenomenologist's answer to the above criticisms is straightforward (Keen, 1975). He is *not interested* in prediction, control, or explanation in the usual sense; he is interested in *understanding*. This understanding is apparently intuitive and self-validating. Two points may be returned here. First, such understanding may be valid, but it does not constitute science. Secondly, if you look at the problems set by themselves, the phenomenologists *are* concerned with prediction. For example, do not self-actualization therapies have a goal? Is it not *prima facie* that existential therapists (a) want their clients to "get better" and (b) believe that their form of therapy will achieve this goal better than some other form of therapy? What grander predictions? "My psychotherapy is better than yours." "Use phenomenology and you will be better." It is not the truth value of such statements which is at question, only their logical structure. They are clearly "If, then ..." statements. That is, they are statements of causal relationship. In sum, then, there may be great therapeutic or other value in self-understanding but a pure phenomenology, unconceptualized and uncommunicated, does not and cannot constitute psychological science.

A Paradigm Shift in Psychology?

In early 1974 two papers of particular interest appeared in the *American Psychologist,* titled respectively "Motivation and the Cognitive Revolution," by William Dember, and "Paradigm Regained? Cognitive Behaviorism Restated" by Alan Boneau. Within at least the first four paragraphs each had referred to Thomas

Kuhn's (1970) term *paradigm*. The general implication of each was that there is in progress a paradigm *shift* in the direction of a more cognitive approach to psychology. It is notable that neither author suggested that behaviorism be scrapped. Boneau specifically says that "...there is no need to deal with concepts such as consciousness in order to get one [cognitive theory] in action" (p. 308). The intended implication of Boneau's title, of course, is that of returning to a cognitive approach, but within the framework of methodological behaviorism. It is also a historical fact that a variety of paradigms (particularly the expectancy-value and the drive-habit) approaches have run in parallel. Any paradigm shift here would then be one of relative ascendancy.

A real paradigm shift, on a grand scale, *would* be from behaviorism to phenomenology. As we have just seen, however, this is not a viable alternative for a scientific psychology since phenomenology lacks the standards by which scientific concepts and evidence are judged. Whether psychology *should* use such standards may be a moot point. Wolman (1971) argues that psychology should develop its own philosophy of science. Until such a philosophy *is* developed, however, we must use the standards available.

If there has been a paradigm shift in psychology it actually occurred a long time ago, with the movement from rationalism to science, and, to a smaller extent, within scientific psychology from structuralism to behaviorism. The behaviorist approach was supposedly mechanistic, invariable responses to invariable stimuli. The paradigm shift that people see occurring now is from mechanism (S-R) to cognition. But what is the distinction between mechanism and cognition? It is our opinion that *there is no distinction to be made between mechanism and cognition.* We assume that all behavior is mechanistic in that it reflects the laws of physics, chemistry and biology, whatever they might be, and that all behavior has causes, however obscure. *The only distinction we find is between the idea of perfect predictability in a closed system where all the variables are known and controlled and the imperfect predictability of an open system where all the variables are not known or controlled.* This is a matter of complexity of subject matter rather than philosophical principle.[9]

---

[9] This statement requires some elaboration. In biology, the concept of vitalism hung on as long as it was believed that if everything tended toward greater entropy there was no basis for increased growth and complexity of organisms. There was then a felt need for some unique "life principle" We now recognize that the second law of thermodynamics holds for closed systems, but within closed systems there can be "islands" of decreasing entropy. Such circumspect areas of a closed system can sustain increasing complexity of the kind found with growth and reproduction but at the expense of the system as a whole. In order to maintain life, which occurs only in open systems with inputs, outputs, and steady states, the environment has to pay an energy cost which does lead to an increase in entropy in the long run.

A slightly different way to look at the same problem is in terms of level of analysis. All the complexities allowed by an open energy system may not be readily discernable. In the extreme, understanding behavior from cellular muscle structure is clearly out of the question right now. This is also true of machinery; understanding of the hardware of a computer enlightens us very little about the nature of the program that happens to be running at the time. Consequently, it is often more feasible to take the conglomerate of muscle movements (which we might call an act, molar behavior, or an operant) and use that as the level of analysis. We assume no little man in the processing unit of the computer and need not assume one (or any mysterious life force) in the processing unit (nervous system) of complex organisms.

The fact that psychology can only make probablistic predictions of behavior (or the relatively crude predictions of inequalities) does not say that behavior is not determined, or not "mechanistic." Early physicists also assumed the world to be orderly, but recognized they themselves were merely human and therefore imperfect in their understanding of it. The language of "cognitive" psychology may in some sense be more "psychologically satisfying" (as opposed to "logically satisfying" [Turner, 1967]) than that of "mechanistic" psychology, but that is a matter of taste. Any real differences between such diverse languages depend on the properties assigned to the terms and their relations with other concepts and observable events. If the properties attributed to expectations and values lead to more accurate and broader-ranging predictions than those attributed to habits and drives, then expectation and value are better concepts. But this is a matter of testability — the blind justice presumed to judge all scientific concepts[10] not a philosophical principle.

III. MOTIVATION AND BEHAVIORISM

In its early period of rationalism, psychology had no concept of motivation *per se* although the topic of emotion was central. Watson also did without a motivational concept, depending on responses to stimuli as his account of behavior. And while Freud introduced motivation, academic psychology was hardly an eager recipient. Instinct theory first came closest to what we would consider contemporary motivation theory, but instincts were so ill-defined and the concept so misused that by the 1920s the instinct concept was virtually abandoned.[11]

The real change in academic psychology came in 1918 when Robert Woodworth put forth the idea of drive, likening behavior to an automobile. The steering mechanism (stimulus) guides the car, but the engine (drive) makes it go. Both are necessary for goal-oriented activity but clearly they are separable components — of the automobile at least. Since that time most psychologists have considered some concept of motivation critical to the understanding of behavior.

In 1925 John F. Dashiell reported that hungry rats explored his checkerboard maze more than did nonhungry rats. This was important to psychologists because it

---

[10] Of course, scientific concepts are not judged in such an even-handed manner. There are partisan loyalties, politics, and fads, and like corporate promotions, concepts may advance only with the deaths of those presently in power. Any concept must be *prepared* to stand the challenge, however, and be communicated with sufficient clarity as to be "blindly" testable.

[11] Contemporary instinct theory is so different from the early 1900s version that we cannot seriously call the new work a revival. We cannot discuss contemporary work in this field here except to note that there is a rapidly increasing interest in species-specific behaviors in many areas of psychology. In particular, present views of learning are shifting from the idea that any behavior can be learned equally well for any situation to the idea that there may be highly specific species dispositions to associating particular stimuli with other stimuli or responses (*e.g.*, see Bolles, 1970, Seligman, 1972).

fit into an evolutionary scheme (survival was more likely if one scurried around for food when hungry), and it suggested physiological mechanisms for the "go" of behavior. That is, drives — like their precessors, instincts — could provide a biological account of activity. It is important to realize that the extant views of the nervous system led us to believe that organisms were quiet unless stimulated, and the drive concept helped us see something of conditions providing the moving force for behavior. Evolutionary theory led us to believe that man was the product of universal mechanistic forces, and it was comforting to have a concept of *individual* behavior compatible with this grand scheme.[12] Following Woodworth, there have been a number of explicit motivational concepts within behavioristic theories. We shall look at just a few of these. The ordering is not entirely chronological, although at some points there is a clearly indicated progression.

Clark Hull

In his early accounts (*e.g.,* 1931) Hull dealt with the problems of purpose and foresight according to the behaviorist principles of the day. That is, his basic units were stimuli and responses, some of which were internal. It was not until the late 1930s that the drive concept entered into his formal theorizing, culminating with his *Principles of Behavior* (Hull, 1943). Hull's main concepts were *habits* (learned S-R associations) and *drives*. A habit was not "operative" unless there was a drive (hunger, thirst, etc.) to activate it. Drives multiplied habits to provide *reaction potential,* which in turn was indexed by some behavioral criterion. Symbolically, Reaction Potential = Habit $\times$ Drive (or $E = H \times D$). For many years, Hull's drive concept has been a major point of departure for discussion of motivation.[13]

Drive was considered a nonspecific energizer, but Hull also argued that drives had stimulus properties which could enter into S-R associations and thus direct behavior. For example, hunger could be an energizer, but internal stimuli specific to hunger could also become associated with particular responses. Hence, an animal would engage in behaviors when hungry that it would not engage in when thirsty, and so on. After 1943, Hull also added an incentive concept to the theory, symbolized by K, so that now the theory said $E = H \times D \times K$.

Two of Hull's students made major changes in the theory. Neal Miller (*e.g.,* 1951) proposed that any intense stimulus could have drive properties, whereas Hull

---

[12] Again, Freud was holding the same deterministic view which came to prevail in all of psychology.

[13] Drive theory has virtually been rejected by every major motivational theorist, for the reason that manipulation of so-called "drive-producing operations" does not produce unitary effects across responses, situations, or species. The results of "general activity" studies, for example, shows that "hunger" and "thirst" have effects so specific to particular experimental procedures, apparatuses, and species, as to defy any such unifying principle as "drive."

had proposed that drives were based on biological needs. Kenneth Spence (*e.g.*, 1956) continued to develop the incentive concept after Hull's death, and gave it a major place in his theorizing.

E. C. Tolman

Like Skinner, Tolman (1932) was concerned with behavioral acts, not specific responses, Similarly, his typical measure of behavior was probabilistic, changes in the frequency of particular choices. Tolman was concerned with purposive behavior but viewed it in what seems a more commonsense way than Hull. Tolman had "learning" and "motivational" concepts, but these were called "expectancies" and "demands."[14] An expectancy was the *anticipation* held by an organism that, under a given set of circumstances, a particular behavior would lead to a certain outcome. Put another way, he had an S_1-R-S_2 theory (McCorquodale and Meehl, 1954) as compared to the S-R theory of Hull. The Ss were environmental events, preceding and following, and behavior was how the organism got from one to another. An expectancy was that one could get from here to there with a certain degree of probability if one performed a certain action. The "demand" was regarding the outcome. An organism might expect ("know") that a certain behavior would produce a certain outcome, but would not engage in the behavior unless there was a demand for that outcome. Demands were determined by both internal and external events. There would be a demand for food, for example, when the organism was hungry but a demand for some things (*e.g.*, sex or highly palatable food) without hunger. Such details have to be worked out for individual incentives. There were also demands against certain outcomes.

What distinguished Tolman as a "cognitive" theorist from the early rationalistic psychologists was Tolman's insistence on working with observable events and inferring expectancies and demands on the basis of these observations. Since his usual subject was the laboratory rat, this was in fact absolutely necessary. Tolman showed that it is possible to talk about purpose, foresight, expectation, or insight, while using objective events as the raw data rather than introspections. Purpose, expectation, and so on were *intervening variables,* explanatory terms inserted between antecedent and consequent conditions. They protect us from the so-called "nominal fallacy" of applying names to things as a means of explanation. For example, if an animal runs fast to food we cannot say it is "hunger-motivated" unless we know independently that it has been without food. To call a fast-running animal "motivated" just because it is fast running is to explain nothing.[15]

---

[14] Tolman was noted for changing his concepts around; we take these two as being central to his general line of thought.

[15] This was also the primary complaint in the "anti-instinct revolt" of the 1920's. Names of instincts were indiscriminately applied as explanation of all kinds of behavior, including complex social acts, without any specification that the instincts existed other than the occurrence of the behaviors in question.

In his classic paper, "The determiners of behavior at a choice point," (1938), Tolman suggested a series of intervening variables, each of which would have separate defining experiments (in which all other variables were held constant), and these would then be interrelated. Two of the intervening variables in his paper (hypotheses, biases) are particularly interesting for they suggest active cognitive influences in dealing with the environment, as opposed to the relatively more passive properties of habits in Hull's system. Indeed, hypotheses were inferred from research indicating that in a problem-solving situation even rats do not act randomly. Rather, they "try out" various alternatives until one is "confirmed" (Krechevsky, 1932). It is clearly possible to do experiments with nonverbal species from which one can infer complex organizing and information-processing properties.

Kurt Lewin and Field Theory

Kurt Lewin (*e.g.,* see Cartwright, 1951) may have been more influential than either Hull or Tolman. He virtually founded the fields of experimental social psychology and group dynamics. Originally a physicist himself, Lewin was very familiar with field theory in physics[16] and carried this over to psychology. The person, he proposed, is part of a "psychological field," and the person's behavior is a function both of himself and the field. That is, Behavior = *f* (person, field). Lewin saw the individual as being acted upon by "field forces," which were interactions between the person and his psychological (perceived) environment. There were valences toward certain goals which depended on such things as expectancy, attractiveness, and psychological distance from the goals. The net field force was a combination of all the field forces acting at a given moment. This was shown particularly in Lewin's treatment of conflict. He also proposed that a force once established persisted until the tension from that force was reduced. This led to the famous Zeignarnik experiment in which incompleted tasks were returned to more readily at a later date than were completed tasks. Always, however, Lewin was working with observable behaviors and his concepts of forces, psychological fields, and so on were inferred from objective events.

Mowrer

Mowrer (1960) tried to combine what he felt were the best aspects of neobehavior theory, expectancy theory, and field theory. He argued that all learning was sign learning and involved emotion. His basic concepts were *fear, hope, relief,* and *disappointment,* all very mentalistic sounding but defined with operational clarity.

---

[16] Wolfgang Kohler, the Gestalt psychologist, was also originally a physicist and his concept of brain-experience isomorphism was based on field-theoretic ideas, as were his interpretations of many perceptual phenomena.

It is assumed that a primary drive state, such as pain, hunger or thirst, has associated with it a conditionable state of fear. A stimulus paired with the onset of a primary drive state comes to arouse fear. Organisms tend not to engage in behaviors which are fear-arousing and to do things which are fear-reducing.

If a fear signal is turned off, the organism is said to experience *relief* (fear reduction). The onset of a safety signal, one which precedes the termination of a primary drive, becomes a conditioned stimulus for fear reduction. This is *hope.* If this safety signal is terminated, the organism is said to experience *disappointment* (fear increment). Relief and hope are therefore *positive* events and approached, whereas fear and disappointment are *negative* events and avoided.

This theory was a radical departure from his previous two-factor theory, most notably in that the concept of any form of learning involving S-R relationships was abandoned. This raised the difficult problem of response selection, which Mowrer handled in terms of emotional (fear increment or decrement) feedback from incipient responses. This has been the most unsatisfactory aspect of the theory. This problem aside, however, the theory was very cognitive in its concepts but behavioral in its specification. One is prone to believe that much of Mowrer's terminology grows out of his own introspections. Even if this is true, however, this is their discovery, not their definition or test. One of Mowrer's outstanding characteristics has been his great capacity and ingenuity at devising behavioral tests of his concepts.

Achievement Motivation

One of the most widely known contemporary social psychological theories is achievement motivation, developed by McClelland and his associates (1953), refined by Atkinson (1964), and recently related to attribution theory (*e.g.,* Weiner, 1972). McClelland *et al.* argued that achievement motivation was acquired through early experiences in which achievement behaviors were followed by positive affective events (*i.e.,* were rewarded). Situational cues then aroused a "redintegration" of these positive events and the specific kinds of behaviors which lead to them. As is well known, individual differences in level of achievement motivation are measured by a standardized scoring scheme for stories people tell in response to specific cue pictures. The relatively permanent level of achievement motivation is thus measured indirectly, but in terms of behavior and with some determinant degree of reliability.

Atkinson generally follows the tradition of Tolman and Lewin, putting achievement theory into the form of so-called "instrumentality" theories (Mitchell and Biglan, 1971). It is assumed that the occurrence of a particular behavior is jointly determined by the *expectancy* that a particular behavior will be *instrumental* in achieving a goal of some *value*. For example, one might engage in a risky business venture (with a low probability of success) if the potential value of the outcome were great enough. Atkinson retained the concept of expectancy or probability of success (symbolized as *Ps*) but divided value into two components: (1) Motivation for success (*Ms*) and (2) incentive value of success (*Is*). Motivation for success is the level of motivation as measured by the McClelland fantasy-scoring procedure. As a special assumption to be applied to achievement behaviors, the incentive value of success is taken to be 1-*Ps*. That is, the lower the probability of success, the greater the incentive value of success. The tendency to engage in success-oriented behavior (*Ts*) then has the following syntax:

$$Ts = Ms \times Ps \times Is$$

One of the victories for Atkinson's theory is accounting for the fact that individuals with high need for achievement tend to be "medium risk-takers." Stated informally, they want success but they also want some feeling of achievement with their success. Therefore, a task is preferred which is neither too difficult nor too easy. Numerous experiments have shown such preferences (*e.g.,* see Atkinson, 1964). In the more precise terms of the theory, however, the medium-risk effect is predicted by the multiplicative formula given above. Simple arithmetic shows that the maximum value of $Ps \times Is$ (that is, $Ps \times 1\text{-}Ps$) is obtained when $Ps = 0.50$. The obtained value of 0.25 (0.50 $\times$ 0.50) is higher than that with any other combination (*e.g.,* 0.10 $\times$ 0.90 = 0.09). There is a symmetrical inverted-U function as values of *Ps* are progressively larger or smaller than 0.50. Inserting different arbitrary values of *Ms* into the complete formula for *Ts* we find that high values of *Ms* produce a *steeper* inverted-U function for *Ts* than do low values of *Ms*. When *Ms* is large, the value of *Ts* at $Ps = 0.50$ is relatively greater than *Ts* at other values of *Ps* as compared to when *Ms* is small. The high-achievement-need individual is thus more likely to take medium risks. (The inverse arguments for individuals with strong motive to avoid failure will not be dealt with here.) This is all summarized in Figure 1. While we can speak intuitively of the individual wanting a feeling of achievement, the theory and its concepts are objectively defined. The theory is "cognitive" in its concepts, but it is not just "rational." The concepts are tied to behaviors.

Weiner (*e.g.,* 1972) and his students have produced an impressive amount of work relating achievement motivation to attribution theory. Weiner argues, first of all, that the single concept of expectancy as the basis of a cognitive theory of behavior is hardly a cognitive theory at all. In relation to achievement motivation Weiner followed Heider (1958) and Rotter (1966). He expanded the concepts of internal and external locus of control to include four attributions applicable to achievement motivation: *Luck, ability, effort,* and *task difficulty.* Each of these is defined in terms of either experimenter manipulations within the research situation or by subjective reports. The main thesis of attribution theory is that people try to make sense out of the world, to look for causal relations. The above-mentioned attributions are four possible causes to which an individual might attribute success or failure.

25

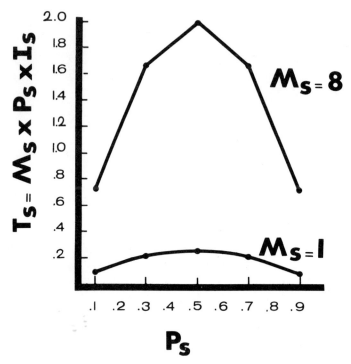

Figure 1. Different values of Ts when Ms = 1 and Ms = 8. With greater values of Ms there is a more pronounced tendency to choose tasks of intermediate difficulty.

The motivational aspect of attribution theory is that people are said to seek causes of events. Such information apparently has incentive value. This formulation is similar to that of Woodworth (1958) who argued that organisms strive to obtain perceptual clarity. Clarification of causal relations (whether or not veridical) would be one form of such clarity.

A second aspect of attributions is their cue value. That is, having perceived a particular attribution for a given situation the person responds differently. For example, James and Rotter (1958) showed that extinction was different depending on whether subjects perceived their task outcome as being primarily due to chance or to skill. Attributions themselves are variously affected by situational factors. For example, success is generally attributed to internal factors and failure to external factors.

Irwin's Intentional Behavior and Motivation

Irwin (1971) deals particularly well with the problem of intentionality and behavior. The essence of his thesis is that: If an organism has equal expectations that Act A will be followed by Outcome A and Act B will be followed by Outcome B, and chooses to perform Act A, we can infer that (1) Outcome A was preferred to B, and (2) Act A was done intentionally. The two act-outcome expectancies and the preference for one outcome over another are called an *interlocking triad* and form the basis for inferring whether any act is intentional. The preference is motivational.

Although couched in cognitive terminology, the defining paradigm is nicely illustrated in Logan's (1960) work on incentives. Rats are given equal exposure to the two arms of a T-maze, each arm having some level of reward. Equal exposure is controlled by forcing the animals to the nonpreferred side following choice trials. This guarantees equal familiarity, and hence equally valid expectancies about outcomes. Incentive values are inferred from the animals' choice behaviors. In Irwin's terms the animals' choices are intentional since the conditions of the interlocking triad are met.

The motivational *concepts* in Irwin's formulation are *desire* and *aversion.* These are intervening variables operationally defined in terms of particular kinds of preferences. Consider the following: A hungry rat is indifferent to the two sides of a T-maze when neither side is baited. Food is now put on one side, and the animal starts going to that side. We would say the food is desirable. If, on the other hand, shock were added to one side rather than food and the animal avoided that side, we would say the shock was aversive. Irwin devotes considerable discussion to the problem of defining neutral outcomes against which to judge whether other outcomes are desirable or aversive. In many real-life situations, of course, we cannot really make such judgments because all we see are preferences. A peference may be for the more desirable of two desirable outcomes (a child may choose ice cream over candy) or for the less aversive of two aversive outcomes (eat your spinach or get spanked). Many possible alternatives produce preferences but are ambiguous with regard to desire and aversion unless more information is available.

Summary of Theoretical Systems

We have discussed eight different theoretical systems with such diverse motivational concepts as drive, demand, fear, hope, relief, disappointment, valence, incentive value of success, need for achievement, luck, ability, desire, and aversion. The reason for this exercise is that — excepting for Freud and the psychoanalytic movement overall, which is simply too large to handle here — the theories described represent about as wide a scope of motivational concepts as one could ask for. By name, they range from very mechanistic (*e.g.,* drive) to very mentalistic (*e.g.,* hope).

Each of these, however, has specific operational procedures for defining the concept as an intervening variable. It is then interesting to compare them more systematically to see their similarities and differences.

For this comparison, let us first distinguish the two standard kinds of intervening variables, S-R and R-R (Spence, 1944). An S-R intervening variable is one in which an experimenter manipulates some antecedent event (such as amount of food deprivation) and observes some consequent behavior (such as speed of running). On the basis of the observed relation, one might infer drive. Unconditioned stimulus intensity is another such antecedent operation, with level of conditioning as the consequent event. An R-R intervening variable is one in which one measure of behavior is related to another measure of behavior. Attitudes and personality characteristics are typically measured with some scale or test providing the antecedent condition, and the score is then related to some other behavior which is the consequent condition. This is a noncircular approach as long as the two behavior samples are independent of each other.

Using the S-R and R-R categorizations, we have summarized in Table 1 the eight theories in terms of their concepts — whether the concepts are S-R or R-R — and the antecedent and consequent conditions typically used. This is not intended as an exhaustive comparison of these systems, but is indicative of how concepts are handled within the systems. Any of the systems could use either S-R or R-R concepts, but some predominantly use one more than the other and hence both are not indicated.

IV. REWARDS: REINFORCERS OR INCENTIVES

Skinner's Descriptive Behaviorism

We have thus far not discussed Skinner's system in any detail because, first, it is dealt with in detail throughout the present volume, and second, because Skinner has eschewed the usefulness of the hypothetical-deductive approach to theorizing in psychology. He has particularly disavowed the use of intervening variables, repeatedly having described them as deceptive and detrimental to the advance of behavioral science. Obviously, a large segment of the profession is in disagreement with him on this point. Miller (1959) has presented a particularly cogent reply to Skinner's general position, pointing out the conditions under which intervening variables are and are not of value.

As mentioned earlier, it is unfortunate that Skinner has been taken by many writers, as well as the general public, as *the* representative of behaviorism. A denial of Skinner, either his system as a whole or any of its parts, is thus taken as evidence against all behavioristic accounts. There *are* certain difficulties with Skinner's approach that should be mentioned at least briefly, however, for as Boneau (1974) has put it: "The Skinnerians achieve a conceptual clarity (and strength) by selectively ignoring much of the subject matter of psychology" (p. 298).

Table 2.1 Comparison of Motivational Concepts in the Systems Discussed (examples, not exhaustive)

System	Motivational Concepts	Type of Concepts	Defining Operations for the Concepts	
			Antecedent Conditions	Consequent Conditions
Hull	Drive	S-R	Food or water deprivation	Running speed
		S-R	Unconditioned stimulus intensity	% or amplitude of conditioned responses
		R-R	Taylor Manifest Anxiety Scale scores	Rate of conditioning
Tolman	Demand	S-R	Deprivation	% choices in a maze
		S-R	Quality of food	% choices in a maze
Lewin	Valence	S-R	Type of goal	Persistence in goal-striving
	Tension	S-R	Interruption of activity	Persistence in returning to original goal
Mowrer	Fear	S-R	Pairing a stimulus with hunger, thirst, pain	Avoidance or escape from fear stimulus
	Hope	S-R	Pairing a stimulus with termination of drive	Approach to the stimulus
Achievement Theory				
A. McClelland	Achievement Motivation	R-R	Thematic Apperception Test stories	Task persistence (*e.g.*, simple repetitive activities). Later job performance.
B. Atkinson	Incentive for Success (Is)	S-R	Experimental manipulation of the probability of success	Persistence in striving toward goal
C. Weiner (Attribution)	Luck, Ability, etc.	S-R	Experimenter informs subjects of degree of luck involved in task	Persistence at task
		R-R	Subjects post-experimental ratings of luck, ability, etc.	Persistence at task
Irwin	Desire	S-R	Type of goal outcome	One outcome preferred to a neutral outcome
	Aversion	S-R	Type of goal outcome	A neutral outcome preferred

Robert C. Beck

Some Difficulties with Descriptive Behaviorism

1. The Problem of Mediation. Consider the following experiment by Mark May (1948). May first trained rats to jump a hurdle to escape shock. He then paired a tone with shock, but without permitting escape. The animals were then put back into the hurdle situation without shock, the tone was sounded, and the animals jumped the hurdle. Since the tone had never previously been paired with hurdling, the tone could not have been directly conditioned as a stimulus for the escape response. The explanation for the results was that: (1) in initial training, shock aroused fear as well as pain, and this fear also became a cue for hurdling; (2) in the second stage the fear was conditioned to the tone; (3) in the final stage the tone aroused the fear which served as a cue to jump the hurdle. In this specific example, fear was a mediator: It served both as a response to shock and the tone and was a stimulus for jumping the hurdle. This can be considered a cognitive account in entirely behavioristic terms. While this particular experiment might be handled within the Skinnerian framework by arguing that what is called fear is simply an internal stimulus which is discriminative for responding in a certain manner, this seems an impoverished argument for *all* kinds of mediation which have been experimentally studied (more are described later). More importantly, perhaps, if one starts *postulating* internal stimuli to any great extent, we have drifted from a purely descriptive behaviorism.

2. Incentive Effects. There have been many varieties of latent learning experiments (Thistlethwaite, 1951). Their common defining characteristic is that animals can learn without apparent reinforcement and that rewards can influence behaviors without being directly contingent on those same behaviors. To take an early example, Bruce (1937) showed that if thirsty rats were given a little water in the goal box before running to water reinforcement, they ran faster on the subsequent running trial. Latent extinction studies, conversely, show that if an animal is trained to run to food and is then put directly in the goal box for a while without food, he subsequently runs slower in extinction than control animals. Here, the lack of food in the goal box affects a later food-getting response without actually following that response. Latent learning and extinct experiments show the same general results as do other incentive shift experiments, but without the subjects' having to perform instrumental responses to find out there has been a shift.

3. Imitation. We continuously see small children copying each other or adults. The question is: Why does the first imitative response occur? Skinner gives no answer: The behavior is simply emitted. Dollard and Miller (1941) argue that it is elicited, but there is no explanation of how it can be elicited without an already established S-R association. Bandura's work on modeling (*e.g.,* 1969) shows clearly that imitation (or observational learning) occurs without prior reinforcement of the specific response sequence involved, and hence he calls it "no-trial learning." Bandura's theory is that either imaginal or verbal response coding occurs during observation and mediates the overt response when retrieved later under appropriate stimulus circumstances.

30

4. Failures of Operant Conditioning. Breland and Breland (1961), working with a wider range of species than anyone else had previously done within the operant conditioning framework, found that in spite of strong reinforcement contingencies particular behaviors either failed to occur or declined. The phrase "instinctive drift" described the shift from reinforced behaviors back to species-specific behaviors. Stadden and Simmelhag (1971) have challenged the ubiquitousness of "superstitious reinforcement" as an explanation of the development of behaviors not obviously given response-contingent reinforcers. The phenomenon of autoshaping, wherein a pigeon will come to peck the response key if it is simply lighted, independently of reinforcement contingencies, is certainly troublesome to reinforcement theory. The response can be maintained even if the bird is specifically *not* reinforced following responses.

5. Verbal Conditioning and Awareness. The early verbal operant experiments were cast in the operant mold for two reasons. First, the frequency of specified verbal responses seemed sensitive to reinforcers, such as the experimenter saying "Uh-huh" or "good." Second, this seemed to occur without the subjects being aware of the contingency. Such an "automatic" reinforcing function seemed to fit well into the operant framework.

As the literature has developed, however, certain problems appear. First, in retrospect, an awkward problem was that subjects did not tend to repeat the identical responses which were reinforced but gave responses within a class, such as plural nouns. It has recently been argued that humans actually *avoid* making responses that have just been reinforced (Freedman, Cohen, and Hennessy, 1974). More attention has been focused, however, on the oft-repeated demonstrations that subjects show an increment in verbal operants only when they are aware of the response-reinforcement contingencies.

The technique for determining awareness has been the use of verbal reports. Such simple questions as "Were you aware of what was going on?" are inadequate to the task, however. A number of appropriately worded questions are necessary. The subject must have ample opportunity to understand what the experimenter is asking without, at the same time, being directed to the preset answer. This issue is discussed insightfully by Spielberger and DeNike (1966) and Dulany (1968). There is thus a kind of return to introspection, but with the explicit recognition that consciousness is to be inferred from verbal behavior.

Every major area of psychology has faced the problem of awareness. Such problems are undoubtedly better phrased not in terms of whether awareness is necessary for learning or behavior, but under what kinds of conditions we learn or behave without being completely aware of the learning, the causes of our behavior, or even of the behavior itself? Just to illustrate the last point, Hefferline (1963) showed that a thumb twitch could become an avoidance response without the subject's being aware of what the effective response was. Awareness is apparently not equally important for all activities and, from a neurological point of view, there is no reason it should be. For our argument, here, however, the point is that awareness presumably does represent some kind of information-processing activity, and this activity is important for some behaviors but not all. Awareness, appropriately defined, can be treated behavioristically like any other concept and can thus contribute to the understanding and prediction of behavior. That is, it is useful for the science.

In summary, then, reinforcement theorists argue that it is the past occurrence of rewards following behavior which makes them effective. As we have seen, however, there are a good many reasons to doubt the generality of reinforcement and to question whether it is the most fruitful concept to account for the effects of rewards.

Incentive theorists, on the other hand, argue that it is the *anticipation* of rewards which accounts for their influence on behavior. The necessary condition for incentive theory is that rewards can influence behavior without necessarily following these behaviors.[17] We have already seen evidence that this is the case. The latent learning experiments of the 1930s and 1940s, the latent extinction research of the 1950s and 1960s, and the goal-box placement experiments of the 1960s and 1970s (dealing with partial reinforcement effects, *e.g.,* Robbins, 1971) all indicate that behavior can be modified by exposing animals to the presence or absence of rewards *when those rewards are not contingent upon responding.* Another kind of interesting specific instance of this is shown in modeling (imitation) experiments where it has been found that the imitation is stronger if the *model* is rewarded for the behavior to be copied (Bandura, 1969). In general, incentive theory can account for effects claimed by reinforcement theories, but the opposite is not true. Therefore, it seems that incentive theory provides the better explanation of the effects of rewards.[18] We then turn to the question: What is it that incentives do?

What Do Incentives Do?

Incentives have often been considered to have physiological *arousal* effects similar to those imputed to drives or emotions. Presently, however, this seems a questionable assertion. Increasing evidence indicates that incentives can arouse behavior without prior independent physiological arousal. For example, a stimulus previously paired with food does not enhance the startle response of the rat (Trapold, 1962) as an incentive-related stimulus might be expected to do if it produced generalized arousal. Furthermore, bar pressing, gross body movement and heart rate of the rat in the Skinner box all increase with higher concentrations of sucrose incentive but heart rate and gross body movement correlate about +.75 (Brillhart, 1975). This fits into a burgeoning literature which indicates that autonomic arousal, heart rate at least, does not occur independently of skeletal activity (*e.g.,* Elliott, 1975; Obrist *et al.,* 1974; Roberts and Young, 1971). The galvanic

---

[17] We deal here primarily with positive incentives. Analogous arguments can be made for negative incentives.

[18] Upon raising the question of such experiments with a strong advocate of descriptive behaviorism, and how operant conditioning would handle such data, the author received the reply "We just wouldn't do such experiments."

skin response may be independent of body activity but there is no uniform evidence that incentives produce "motivational" arousal independently of their effects on skeletal responses. Trapold and Overmeier (1972) believe that incentive motivation may be entirely a mediational phenomenon, without general energizing properties.[19]

It is possible that there may be some incentive arousal during early stages of learning about rewards but not in the later stages. The Solomon and Wynne (1954) work on the autonomic nervous system and avoidance learning may be a general model for incentive motivation. They found that an intact sympathetic nervous system was important for the initial learning of avoidance behavior in the dog, but not for later maintenance of the same behavior. Anyone who has observed the development of avoidance learning knows that animals are less emotional after they have learned the appropriate response and there is much less overt activity. In the case of positive incentives, there may be some "reward value" which is arousing, and perhaps necessary for incentive learning. The cues to incentives may thereafter be non-arousing except as guides to the location or occurrence of incentives. Mandler (1962) speaks of emotions as becoming "representational," following the same kind of model.

Mediation Theory and the Anticipatory Goal Response

An important part of Hull's theory was his concept of the *anticipatory goal response*. In its original form (Hull, 1931) it was conceived as a mechanism to account for purposiveness and foresight in nonmentalistic terms. According to this idea, when an organism reaches some goal and responds to it (*e.g.,* by consuming food) there is a *goal response* (R_G, the consummatory response) and a *fractional goal response* (r_g). This fractional goal response was considered to be a *conditionable* component of R_G and as such could be aroused by stimuli preceding R_G. At the same time, r_g was considered to have stimulus properties (s_g) to which other responses could become attached. Thus, there could develop a sequence of: External Stimuli $\rightarrow$ ($r_g \rightarrow s_g$) $\rightarrow$ Overt Responses. The fractional goal response was a mediating mechanism. This kind of mediation was applied to many different instances.

Osgood (*e.g.,* 1953, 1956) developed his theory of meaning by adopting the fractional goal response principle. He argued that in the presence of a real object (such as a carrot) there is a total response (which might include eating, as well as many other things) and a *fractional* response (r_m), which is conditionable and has stimulus properties (s_m). Multiple r_m's may be conditioned to the same object. If the r_m's from several objects are the same, there is a basis for concept formation.

---

[19]Some recent experiments from our own laboratory (Brillhart & Beck, 1977) and from Lipsitt's laboratory at Brown University (*e.g.,* Crook & Lippsitt, 1976) indicate that in the case of sucrose incentives there may be some autonomic arousal effects (heart rate) separable from activity, either with rats or human infants.

Thus, there are different total responses to beets, carrots, beans, and corn, but there are also common mediating responses, so that we have the following:

Overt Stimuli	Mediating Response	Mediating Stimulus	Overt Response (*e.g.,* verbal)
Carrots Beets Beans Corn	r_m (vegetable)$\rightarrow$	s_m (vegetable)$\rightarrow$	vegetable

A great deal of evidence, of course, supports the idea that some intervening process (called mediation in neobehavioristic theory) is necessary to account for intellectual phenomena. Goss (1961) applied mediation theory to concept formation and Maltzman (1955) to problem solving. The inference for such an intervening process is based on the fact that behaviors occur reliably and predictably under conditions where they have not directly occurred previously. Such mediation accounts for semantic generalization, similar responses to stimuli with common meaning but dissimilar physical properties. In terms of motivation what all this means is that internal "cognitive" (mediating) events could serve to arouse behavior on the basis of specific associations with behaviors. This was Spence's (1956) account of incentive motivation, and it still seems a viable possibility. The vast amount of contemporary work in human learning, involving concepts of stimulus organization, is more complex than the $r_m - s_m$ concept as originally conceived, but not necessarily systematically different.

Cautela (*e.g.,* 1973) has discussed the use of *covert operants* (also called *coverants*) in behavior modification therapeutic situations. He says: "Until recently, covert processes of human beings have not been the subject of speculation or investigation by behavioristically oriented psychologists;; (p. 27). He credits Wolpe (1958) with this "breakthrough." While it does appear to be correct that the therapeutic use of covert behaviors is relatively new, they appear to be in principle traceable to Hull's work with the anticipatory goal response in the 1930s. That is, what Cautela calls covert responses, working within an operant-conditioning framework, appear to be what other behaviorists have called mediating responses. He argues, just as did Hull and Spence, that such covert responses follow the same laws as overt responses. While Cautela, following Wolpe, deals with *imagery* there is nothing the present writer can discern that distinguishes this from, say, Osgood's treatment of representational processes in terms of $r_m - s_m$. This, of course, is not to belittle the development of this area in the therapeutic framework, but only to point out that its conceptual groundwork had been laid a good many years ago.

Transfer of Control Experiments

During the last ten years there has been a revival of Pavlovian concepts in relation to mediation theory. Rescorla and LoLordo (1965) trained dogs to shuttle back and forth in a shock box on a Sidman unsignaled avoidance schedule. The animal can postpone shock for some fixed period of time whenever it shuttles. If it completely fails to respond, it gets shocked at regularly scheduled intervals. A steady rate of shuttling is thus established as a baseline. They then paired one stimulus (CS+) with the onset of electric shock in a different situation, and a second stimulus (CS—) preceded a shock-free interval. Finally, the animals were returned to the shuttle box where they shuttled faster than usual when CS+ was presented and slower than usual when CS— was presented. The interpretation was that CS+ aroused fear and CS— reduced it, hence the greater or lesser activity. The results were couched in terms of Pavlovian excitatory and inhibitory conditioning, later elaborated in considerable detail by Rescorla and Soloman (1967).

The literature in this area has mushroomed, including both appetitive and aversive events. The general notion is that a CS+ preceding food will excite appetitive behavior (*e.g.,* approach to food), but is then harder to make a CS+ in aversive conditioning. On the other hand, a CS— for an appetitive event should be easier to make a CS+ for an aversive event. There are many such possible combinations and the reader is referred to Bolles and Moot (1972) for a detailed literature review. The point here is that these CS+'s and CS—'s are commonly considered to have *informational* properties and this *cue value* is generally more important than any "arousal" properties. Trapold and Overmeier (1972) suggest that such cue value may in fact be equivalent to the Hullian r_g—s_g mechanism. This speculation is based partly on grounds that it has been difficult, as we have already seen, to find energizing properties of incentive stimuli above and beyond those correlated with behavior itself.[20]

---

[20] It should be noted that it has never really been clear whether the r_g—s_g mechanism was an associative (learning) mechanism or a stimulus intensity (motivational) mechanism. This is perhaps mainly a reflection of problems in independently defining learning and motivation. In some cases, such as the Crespi shift, a simple stimulus intensity interpretation would account for the results — a rapid shift in speed of running with a change up or down of incentive magnitude. In the case of latent learning, however, it would appear that an associative mechanism would be required It would be difficult otherwise to see how a change in incentive magnitude (and hence a resulting change in the magnitude of r_g—s_g) would account for a sudden decrease in maze *errors* as the early latent learning experiments showed when food was first introduced into an otherwise familiar maze. Expectancy theory handled this, but simply because it was not specific as to how errors were reduced All it could say was that the animal now anticipated reward and hence ran faster with fewer errors. This is an appealing interpretation but mainly so because it finesses the problem. This is not necessarily bad insofar as it accurately reflects our ignorance of the nature of learning, but neither is it altogether helpful.

Robert C. Beck

Motivation, Cognition and Information

In recent years there has been an increasing tendency (*e.g.,* see Dember, 1965, 1974) to consider the attainment of information as a reinforcing event. Information may be defined informally as finding out something not already known. The greater the uncertainty about an event, the greater the information obtained when the event occurs (Garner, 1962). The more complex a situation is, the greater the uncertainty and hence more information. The evidence indicates, with children or adults, that there is a preference for medium levels of complexity (or information). What constitutes a "medium" level, of course, varies from person to person, depending on a range of variables. Thus, "modern" symphonic music (*e.g.,* Ives, Stravinsky) is *too* novel for many people and hence is disliked. *The Rite of Spring* was considered insulting to its first audiences. As familiarity increases, however, there is a tendency to tolerate or prefer music which departs from Bach, Beethoven, and Brahms.

Dember and Earl (1957) talk about *pace stimuli.* The notion is that people find desirable stimuli that are just a little more complex than those they have become familiar with. This provides the necessary means for organisms to seek out more complex events. If there were no such mechanism, there would be no shift in preference for increasingly more complex events, or in other words, no possibility for intellectual growth.

A large number of experiments have examined the "reinforcing" effects of informational stimuli. Bower, McLean, and Meacham (1966), for example, found that pigeons preferred to peck at a disk which changed color to tell them whether there would be a short or long delay before reinforcement rather than to peck at one which reinforced the same, but did not provide the differential cues. The cues were considered to be entirely informational. The experiments by Egger and Miller (1962, 1963) are well known, showing similar effects. Hendry's (1969) volume on conditioned reinforcement is generally built around the concept that secondary reinforcers are information-providing stimuli. Space prevents a lengthy discussion of secondary reinforcement here, so suffice it to say that the operations for establishing secondary reinforcers and incentive motivation are virtually identical. In that case, we would expect the same trends in the literature to a more cognitive treatment of both concepts.

V. SUMMARY

Where does this leave us. First, it seems clear that methodological behaviorism was an inevitable outcome of psychology becoming a science. A science, by definition, must have observable data and behavior is what psychologists observe.

Second, there are many theories under the behavioristic umbrella, and a large number of motivational concepts. The adequacy or superiority of any of these is to be determined by objective test, not by the particular terms used to name the concepts. Such surplus meanings as are attached to "cognitive" as opposed to "mechanistic," for example, are unfortunate. Cognitive concepts like intention, expectancy or awareness can be objectively defined and used within a completely behavioristic framework.

Third, it is well established that rewards are more important than drives as motivational phenomena. In the overall context of psychology, Skinner's descriptive behaviorism is seen mainly as being concerned with motivational phenomena. His work has been remarkably illuminating, but it is increasingly clear that his system is an incomplete account of either behavior or of motivation.

Fourth, an examination of how rewards operate indicates that they are better conceived as incentives than as reinforcers. Several shortcomings of the reinforcement conceptualization were noted. In large part these hinge around the fact that rewards can influence later behavior without being contingent upon responses. To the contrary, it is the anticipation of rewards under particular conditions which is important.

Fifth, evidence was outlined to indicate that incentives under many circumstances do not produce internal physiological arousal except in conjunction with behavioral arousal. Mediation theory provides an "associationistic" account of incentive action. In the early stages of incentive learning, affective arousal may be necessary but not apparently in later stages.

Sixth, considerable evidence indicates that it is information provided by incentive stimuli which guides behavior. This information has cue functions in the mediational sense. It also has motivational function in that organisms, human and otherwise, have preferences for information-giving stimuli.

In brief, the motivational trend, within a behavioristic framework, is toward more cognitive accounts of motivational phenomena. This is not, hopefully, a cycling back to the rationalistic beginnings of psychology. The difference is that contemporary cognitive accounts utilize concepts objectively definable and testable. Such concepts may be more congruent with common sense, but this congruence is not the test of their usefulness. The data derived from them is the proof.

REFERENCES

Atkinson, J. W., *An introduction to motivation.* New York: Van Nostrand, 1964.

Bandura, A., *Principles of behavior modification.* New York: Holt, Rinehart and Winston, 1969.

Bandura, A., Behavior theory and the models of man. *American Psychologist,* 1974, *29,* 859–869.

Blumenthal, Arthur L., A reappraisal of Wilhelm Wundt. *American Psychologist,* 1975, *30,* 1081–1088.

Bolles R. C., and Moot, S. A., Derived motives. In P. Mussen and M. Rosensweig, (eds.), *Annual Review of Psychology,* 1972, 51–72.

Boneau, C. A., Paradigm regained: cognitive behaviorism restated. *American Psychologist,* 1974, *29,* 297–309

Boring, E. G. Mind and mechanism. *American Journal of Psychology,* 1946, *59,* 173–192.

Robert C. Beck

Bower, G.; McLean, J.; and Meacham, J., Value of knowing when reinforcement is due. *Journal of Comparative and Physiological Psychology,* 1966, *62,* 184–192.

Breland, K., and Breland, M., The misbehavior of organisms. *American Psychologist,* 1961, *16,* 681–684.

Brillhart C. A., *The relationship between heart rate, activity and bar-pressing with varying levels of sucrose incentive.* Unpublished master's thesis, Wake Forest University, 1975.

Brody, N., and Oppenheim, P., Tensions in psychology between the methods of behaviorism and phenomenology. *Psychological Review,* 1966, *73,* 295–305.

Bruce, R. H., An experimental investigation of the thirst drive in rats with especial reference to the goal-gradient hypothesis. *Journal of Genetic Psychology,* 1937, *17,* 49–60.

Buhler, C., Basic theoretical concepts of humanistic psychology. *American Psychologist,* 1971, *29,* 378–386.

Cartwright D. (Ed.) *Field Theory in Social Science.* Selected theoretical papers by Kurt Lewin. New York: Harper & Brothers, 1951.

Crook, C. K. and Lipsitt, L. P., Neonatal nutritive sucking: effects of taste stimulation upon sucking rhythm and heart rate. *Child Development,* 1975, *47,* 518–522.

Cautela J. R., Covert processes and behavior modification. *Journal of Nervous and Mental Disease,* 1973, *157,* 27–36.

Dashiell J. F., A quantitative demonstration of animal drive. *Journal of Comparative Psychology,* 1925, *5,* 205–208.

Dember, W., Motivation and the cognitive revolution. *American Psychologist,* 1974, *29,* 161–174.

Dember W. N., The new look in motivatiion. *American Scientist,* 1965, *53,* 409–427.

Dember, W. N., and Earl, R. W., Analysis of exploratory, manipulative, and curiosity behavior. *Psychological Review,* 1957, *64,* 91–96.

Dulany, D. E., Awareness, rules and propositional control: a confrontation with S-R theory. In T. R. Dixon and D. C. Horton (Eds.), *Verbal Behavior and General Behavior Theory.* Englewood Cliffs: Prentice-Hall, Inc., 1968, 340–387.

Egger, M. D., and Miller, N. E., Secondary reinforcement in rats as a function of information value and reliability of the elements. *Journal of Experimental Psychology,* 1962, *64,* 97–104.

Egger, M. D., and Miller, N. E., When is reward reinforcing?: an experimental study of the information hypothesis. *Journal of Comparative and Physiological Psychology,* 1963, *56,* 132–137.

Elliott, Rogers, Heart rate, activity, and activation in rats. *Psychophysiology,* 1975, *12,* 298–305.

Freedman, P. E.; Cohen, M.; and Hennessy, J., Learning theory: two trials and tribulations. *American Psychologist,* 1974, *29,* 204-206.

Garner, W. G., *Uncertainty and structure as psychological concepts.* New York: Wiley, 1962.

Goss, A., Verbal mediating response and concept formation. *Psychological Review,* 1961, *68,* 248–274.

Hefferline, R. F., Proprioceptive discrimination of a covert operant without its observation by the subject. *Science,* 1963, *139,* 834–835.

Heider, F., *The psychology of interpersonal relations.* New York: Wiley, 1958.

Hendry, Derek, (Ed.) *Conditioned reinforcement.* Dorsey: Homewood, 1969.

Hull, C. L., Goal attraction and directing ideas conceived as habit phenomena. *Psychological Review,* 1931, *38,* 487–506.

Hull, C. L., *Principles of behavior.* New York: Appleton-Century-Crofts, 1943.

Irwin, F., *Intentional behavior and motivation.* New York: Lippincott, 1971.

Ittelson, W. H.; Proshansky, H. M.; Rivlin, L. G.; and Winkel, G., *An introduction to environmental psychology.* New York: Holt, Rinehart and Winston, 1974.

James, W., and Rotter, J. B., Partial and 100 percent reinforcement under choice and skill conditions. *Journal of Experimental Psychology,* 1958, *55,* 397–403.

Keen E., *A primer in phenomenological psychology.* New York: Holt, Rinehart and Winston, 1975

Kimble, G., (Ed.) *Foundations of Conditioning and Learning.* New York: Appleton-Century-Crofts 1967.

Krechevsky, I., 'Hypothesis" in rats. *Psychological Review,* 1932, *39,* 516–532.

Kuhn T., The structure of scientific revolutions. *International Encyclopedia of Unified Science,* 2nd Ed., Enlarged. Chicago: Univ. of Chicago Press, 1970.

Logan F., *Incentive.* New Haven: Yale, 1960.

MacCorquodale, K., and Meehl, P., Edward C. Tolman. In W. K. Estes, S. Koch, K. MacCorquodale, P. E. Meehl, C. G. Mueller, W. N. Schoenfeld, and W. S. Verplanck, *Modern Learning Theory.* New York: Appleton-Century-Crofts, 1954, 177–266.

Maltzman, I., Thinking from a behavioristic point of view. *Psychological Review,* 1955, *62,* 275–286.

Mandler, G., Emotion. In R. Brown, E. Galanter, E. Hess, and G. Mandler. *New Directions in Psychology.* New York: Holt, Rinehart, and Winston, 1962, 267–344.

May, M. A., Experimentally acquired drives. *Journal of Experimental Psychology,* 1948, *38,* 66–77.

McClelland D.; Atkinson J. W.; Clark, R. A.; and Lowell, E. L., *The Achievement Motive.* New York: Appleton-Century-Crofts, 1953.

Meinrath, A. B. and Beck R. C., Heart rate and activity changes during bar pressing and consummatory responding for sucrose incentives in the rat. Paper presented at the 48th Annual Meeting of the Eastern Psychological Association, Boston, Mass., April, 1977.

Miller, N. E., Learnable drives and rewards. In S. S. Stevens (Ed.) *Handbook of Experimental Psychology.* New York: Wiley, 1951.

Miller, N. E., Liberalization of basic S-R concepts: extensions to conflict behavior, motivation and social learning. In S. Koch (Ed.), *Psychology: A Study of a Science.* Vol. 2. New York: McGraw-Hill, 1959, 196–292.

Miller, N. E., and Dollard, J., *Social learning and imitation.* New Haven: Yale University Press, 1941.

Mitchell T., and Biglan, A., Instrumentality theories: current uses in psychology. *Psychological Bulletin,* 1971, *76,* 432–454.

Mowrer O. H., *Learning theory and behavior.* New York: Wiley, 1960.

Obrist, P. A. Howard, J. L.; Lawler, J. E.; Galosy, R. H.; Meyers, K. A.; and Gaebelein, C. J., The cardiac-somatic interaction. In P. A. Obrist, A. H. Block, J. Brener, and L. V. DiCara, (Eds.), *Cardiovascular psychophysiology.* Chicago: Aldine, 1974.

Osgood, C. E., *Method and theory in psychology.* New York: Oxford University Press, 1953.

Osgood, C. E., Motivational dynamics of language behaviors. In M. R. Jones, (Ed.), *Nebraska Symposium in Motivation.* Lincoln: University of Nebraska Press, 1957, 348–423.

Rescorla, R., and LoLordo, V., Inhibition of avoidance behavior. *Journal of Comparative and Physiological Psychology,* 1965, *59* 406–412.

Rescorla R. A., and Solomon, R. L., Two-process learning theory: relationships between Pavlovian conditioning and instrumental learning. *Psychological Review,* 1967, *74,* 151–182.

Roberts, L. E., and Young, R., Electrodermal responses are independent of movement during aversive conditioning in rats, but heart rate is not. *Journal of Comparative and Physiological Psychology,* 1971, *77,* 495–512

Robbins, D., Partial reinforcement: a selective review of the alleyway literature since 1960. *Psychological Bulletin,* 1971, *76,* 412–432.

Rotter, J. B., Generalized expectancies for internal vs. external control of reinforcement. *Psychological Monographs,* 1966, *80,* (1, Whole No. 609), 1–28.

Ryan, T. A., *Intentional Behavior.* New York: Ronald, 1970.

Skinner B. F., *The behavior of organisms.* New York: Appleton-Century-Crofts, 1938.

Skinner B. F., *Science and human behavior.* New York: Macmillan, 1953.

Solomon, r. L., and Wynne, L. C., Avoidance conditioning in normal dogs and in dogs deprived of normal autonomic functioning. *American Psychologist,* 1950, *5* 264 (abstract).

Spence, K. W., The nature of theory constructions in contemporary psychology. *Psychological Review* 1944, *51,* 47- 68.

Spence, K., *Behavior theory and conditioning.* New Haven: Yale University Press, 1956.

Spielberger, C. S., and DeNike L. D., Descriptive behaviorism vs. cognitive theory in verbal operant conditioning. *Psychological Review,* 1966, *73,* 306–326.

Staddon, J. E. R., and Simmelhag, V. L., The "superstition" experiment: a reexamination of its implications for the principles of adaptive behavior. *Psychological Review,* 1971, *78,*3–43.

Thistlethwaite D., A critical review of latent learning and related experiments. *Psychological Bulletin,* 1951 *48* 97–129.

Tolman, E. C., *Purposive behavior in animals and men.* New York: Appleton-Century-Crofts, 1932.

Tolman, E. C., The determiners of behavior at a choice point. *Psychological Review,* 1938, *45,* 1–41.

Trapold, M. A., The effect of incentive motivation on an unrelated startle response. *Journal of Comparative and Physiological Psychology,* 1962, *55,* 1034–1039.

Trapold M. A., and Overmeier, J. B., The second learning process in instrumental learning. In A. H. Black and W. F. Prokasy (Eds.), *Classical conditioning II.* New York: Appleton-Century-Crofts, 1972, 427–452.

Turner M. B., *Philosophy and the science of behavior.* New York: Appleton-Century-Crofts, 1967

Watson, J. B., *Psychology from the standpoint of a behaviorist* (2nd Ed.). Philadelphia: Lippencott, 1924.

Weiner, B., *Theories of motivation.* Chicago: Markham, 1972.

Wolman, B., Does psychology need its own philosophy of science? *American Psychologist,* 1971, *26,* 877–886.

Wolpe, J., *Psychotherapy by reciprocal inhibition.* Stanford, Calif.: Stanford University Press, 1958.

THE NURSING-HOME CURSE FALLS
UPON RESIDENTIAL SCHOOLS

Robert M. Porter

At the time that residential schools for the retarded have their greatest need to provide excellent habilitative programs and a wide variety of services to community agencies, to see that their residents are provided with all their rights and privileges and take a leadership role, many have been struck down with the disease of "Nursing Home Licensure." This irritating malady has affected many state facilities because there is gold in the hills of Medicare. Money that could be used for deposit into general funds instead has been redirected to the institutions. This is not in any direct relationship to the number of Title XIX recipients for whom the institutions were authorized to collect funds, but in accordance with a previously authorized budget document.

To many program-oriented administrations, therefore, the inclusion of their institution under Title XIX did not bring opportunities for improvements but, rather, led to a series of confusing procedures. They were forced to operate, on one hand, under the restrictions of nursing home licensure and, on the other hand, in an attempt to continue their basic beliefs that the mentally retarded are not sick people in need of nursing care, but are citizens who need all the benefits that can be brought to them as the result of modern-day learning and instructional techniques. Furthermore, those institutions that have sincerely attempted to provide small group living situations in as homelike an atmosphere as possible, and permitted their residents to live life as culturally normally as can be provided, find themselves hindered from the construction of residences which will further foster this ideal. They even face the difficulty of modifying excellent existing residential buildings so they can be nursing home facilities.

In my estimation, any facility providing programs for the mentally retarded, based on the illness or disease model, is forced into a role that will continue to lead into considerably more confusion and limitation of programs than one which bases its reason for being on a consideration of mental retardation as a "symptom complex." By making our residential schools false nursing homes for the purpose of qualifying for Medicaid, we have been forced into a regressive position. There is no doubt but that the funds which we receive because of this move are necessary, but hopefully they could be used for the improvement of programs and for facilities, not for the maintenance of current operations. This money should be used to foster the development of programs, hiring of additional personnel, institution of short-term residential treatment programs, preschool developmental programs for younger students, operation of group homes with specialized vocational training to benefit the institution and the community, and correction of those physical or

41

program deficiencies that make it impossible for residential schools to become accredited.

Realizing the need for additional financial support such as that which federal grants provide, and being opposed to the concept of operating nursing home facilities, I proposed a resolution at the 1972 annual convention of the American Association on Mental Deficiency. With the assistance of two of my colleagues, the following resolution was prepared and presented to the administrative section and accepted: "Whereas, mental retardation is no longer considered as a physical illness, the hospital or physical illness model cannot logically be used as a valid basis for the development of either staffing or physical standards for either institutional or community residential units.

Be it therefore resolved, that the standards to be used for the evaluation and licensing of these residential units be those standards developed specifically for the mentally retarded and not be those currently developed for either intermediate or skilled nursing care facilities."

I hope that resolutions such as this may be adopted by other professional organizations within the field of mental retardation and that, eventually, we may once again return to a forward-moving direction that will enable us to have truly habilitative programs. This will be better than trying to operate these programs under the difficulties presented by current financial and political restrictions placed upon us when we qualify for funds made available for licensure as nursing homes, and attempting to get around these restrictions by operating our programs as if they did not exist.

This battle must continue if the mentally retarded students in our residential schools are to receive full benefit from our programs and reach their potential. Under the present system, they are effectively being denied their civil rights. At a meeting of our state's civil rights commission held in our community, I advised the members that, in my opinion, they were not fulfilling one of their major responsibilities. I claimed that many of our state's citizens were being discriminated against because of their limited intelligence and that it was just as wrong to judge people on this basis as it was to discriminate against them because of their race, religion, sex, or economic status. At that time, the commission did not seem to fully appreciate the implications of my statements. Now, however, many members of such organizations are pointing out the fact that the mentally retarded *are* being discriminated against. Hopefully, this contention will become increasingly accepted with the passage of time since we cannot change conditions until we face up to them honestly. The retarded should be judged fairly and without prejudice — as individual citizens and participating members of society.

PSYCHOGENIC MENTAL RETARDATION

Harold Michal-Smith

Over the years, there has been persistent and recurring discussion centered on the existence of a form of mental retardation that etiologically is emotional or psychological in nature rather than organic. The psychologically based retardation is referred to as psychogenic retardation. Adherents of this point of view propose that this type of mental retardation occurs as a consequence of emotional and psychological factors learned early in life and accepted as reality. There are others, though not in full agreement, who at least acknowledge the possibility of such an etiological category. The classification system devised by the AAMD in which psychogenic mental deficiency is placed under the heading of conditions which are due "to uncertain (or presumed psychologic) cause with the functional reaction alone manifested" is a reflection of this view.

The concept of a psychogenic basis for deficiency has led to many hypotheses for consideration. Among these is the belief that in cases of mental retardation of unknown cause, all ambient circumstances must be given consideration and the hypothesis of psychogenic basis is advanced. Another belief inviting consideration is the implication of improvement or reversibility of the condition through therapeutic interventions. This suggests that what has been learned as a function of early life experiences can be replaced by new learning.

Those who contend that mental retardation can have psychogenic bases offer three contributing categories of psychological variables which are as follows:

1. Mental retardation associated with environmental deprivation.
2. Mental retardation associated with emotional disturbance.
3. Mental retardation associated with psychotic disorder.

This psychogenic concept deserves attention. As is generally known, results of some studies of environmental deprivation, which include maternal deprivation, have shown fairly consistent support of the idea that lack of maternal care in infancy and environmental deprivation in general cause a marked lowering of intellectual functioning. Bowlby described the pattern in the following manner: During the first three months of life, there is no specific impairment in development as a consequence of deprivation. The period from four to twelve months is considered critical since there is a marked decrease in the developmental quotient. If the average quotient falls around 100 during the first three months, it drops to around an average of 65 during this crucial period.

Following this period, the average quotient rises to around 90 under the same environmental conditions, although it is still questionable whether permanent intellectual arrest is a consequence of such environmental deprivation. On the other hand, there may be permanent damage in some aspects of personality such as reduced social responsiveness.

Deprivations and trauma related to early parent-child relationships are, of course, less obvious than the inhibitions to optimal growth caused by a hearing loss. Therefore, a major question must be answered. Can emotional starvation early in the life of a particular child engender the kind of adjustment that the child now uses to maintain his homeostasis? What comes to mind are experiences such as enforced separation from the mother in early infancy (incubation of premature babies), surgery early in life, forced restraint of the young infant (tied in bed) to prevent scratching of skin abrasions, child abuse, etc.

What this suggests is that the retardation may be related to *unusual* kinds of experiences occurring at crucial points in the child's life. The symptoms of mental retardation in these instances are considered to be reflections of phenomena as avoidance or repression of painful experiences, or preoccupation with activities and matters which are more gratifying than reality.

While we might build up a hypothetical case for the psychogenesis of this particular retardation, its clinical evaluation continues to be a problem. First of all, even with the best cooperation of parents or parent surrogates, true and significant history is often not obtainable. Secondly, even with a fairly complete history, intelligence tests give little suggestion as to *how* the child's unique history has affected his intelligence and his personality. Projective testing can be of help in this evaluation procedure in single case studies. But more systematic investigations of groups have not produced the startling results that had been hoped for, although the literature does contain studies which report a psychogenic or sociogenic personality disturbance rather than "true" retardation. Unfortunately, the methodology used in some of these studies is debatable even though they are widely cited.

In order to deal with the previously cited problems in evaluating psychogenic retardation, clinical assessment may well have to take a phenomenological approach — that is, to see the world from the child's point of view rather than a behavioristic or objective approach. From this point of view, important determinants of the child's behavior would center on both the child's percept of the world as well as his place in it. What is emphasized here is that a child's style of life, as it is reflected at home, in school or test behavior, is viewed as the culmination of a number of years of living and experience as an individual within an individualized environmental setting; his perceptual world.

Concerning the second category, neurotic and emotional problems, it is easily conceivable that many forms of psychoneurosis are accompanied by an impairment in intellectual functioning and efficiency. It is generally accepted that in these instances mental deficiency represents a partial impairment caused by psychological rather than organic problems. The motivational factors play a central role in the genesis and continuance of the deficits. On a reactive level, a child may develop a defensive maneuver of intellectual immobility in direct reaction to a set of environmental circumstances. An example of this is the case of a very timid child who is intimidated by a dynamic, but overbearing teacher. In her presence he is unable to focus his attention and assimilate what she teaches. With a less overbearing teacher, the timid child is more at ease and able to mobilize his attention and learn.

An illustration of intellectual immaturity due to direct reaction to a set of environmental circumstances can be seen in some children's sensitivity to the stress of socialization. The school, in both direct and indirect fashion, continues and elaborates on the socializing process begun in the home. There are certain standards, school practices, demand for docility and obedience which the child must adhere to completely. All these practices, rituals, and demands induct him into the formalized patterns of social participation with his classmates. To the young child, who recently was much freer in the home, the school's insistence on social control and the use of coercive devices may set up a negative or ambivalent generalization of experience toward the school and symbols of authority. Fearing loss of his freedom, the child may resist participation in school experiences and develop a marked aversion toward school with a consequent diminished capacity for learning. With a change in the precipitating conditions or adjustment to a new set of environmental circumstances, more satisfactory intellectual functioning occurs.

On a deeper level, strong neurotic defenses such as phobias or hysterical reactions may cause poor use of intellectual resources which, if so severely inhibited, may result in functioning at a retarded level. Ordinarily, the average child is very much interested in the world around him and has spent his preschool life in active learning experiences. If the events around him in the course of his explorations have created the concept that the world is a dangerous place, he then may feel that the best safety valve lies in staying with the tried and proved. This attitude interferes with the acquisition of knowledge and new skills, giving the impression of incapacity to learn. Similarly, a child who has learned from experience that mistakes are not to be tolerated may be too frightened to reach out for new experiences. For example, children who are very highly competitive or subserviently fearful of authority figures may react so that these attitudes come between them and the educational information being imparted to them.

The youngster who is neurotically frightened and anxious in many areas may be so apprehensive in carrying out directions that he is in a state of intellectual paralysis. A state of severe dependence may effectively prevent a child from exercising intellectual initiative. Hostility toward a parent who presses for evidences of intellectual achievement may, if deep enough, cut off participation in formal learning situations. Specific learning disabilities have been interpreted similarly and as another example of limited intellectual failure.

Over the years, teachers have become increasingly aware of the young child who is totally uninterested in any formal instruction and engages only in play. He will verbalize his interest in play and pucker up his face in distaste as soon as any subject area is mentioned. Frequently such a child comes from a good socioeconomic background and has intelligent, capable parents. On test evaluation, the child may be pleasant and congenial in informal chatter but highly distractible, politely but firmly negativistic, or resistant in the formal assessment attempts of his abilities.

Exploration and investigation of family background and family relationships show parental misunderstanding of psychological principals. Furthermore, perhaps because of their own immature development they are overpermissive and permit nothing to interfere with the child's immediate gratification of his needs and oral demands. Avoidance of pain, anxiety, and the unpleasant is the guiding rule. Children who have mistakenly been spared from living, in the real sense of the word, usually show an arrested ego development. They have no psychic energy for learning at their disposal, and their desire to learn cannot be easily aroused even by repeated efforts to make the learning process interesting, lively, and animated. To state this phenomenon psychologically, these children have been permitted to operate on the pleasure-pain principle, and have been shielded from pain and anxiety. As a consequence, the development of ego defenses is retarded and nothing that interferes with immediate gratification is tolerated. Such children may learn very little, and, for all interests and purposes, act like retarded individuals.

Proceeding to the third psychological variable, namely mental retardation associated with psychosis, we find that the relationships between childhood schizophrenia and mental retardation remain an unsettled question.

There is general agreement that schizophrenia is frequently found in mentally retarded persons. Estimates of the relationships range from 18 percent to 40 percent. Some of the inconsistencies found in the data about the association of retardation and schizophrenia are due to the differences in the populations studied as well as to the divergence of views on the definitions of both schizophrenia and mental retardation.

In many cases, it is extremely difficult to distinguish between mental retardation and schizophrenia. On the one hand, defective mental functioning may be one of the symptoms of schizophrenia, and on the other, a behavior pattern that appears bizarre for the child's chronological age may also be found in the retarded child. A grossly retarded child may also appear bizarre.

Kanner's diagnostic designation of primary infantile autism has been widely accepted as a specific subgroup in the group of childhood schizophrenias. Descriptions of the condition have pointed out the resemblance of these children to the retarded. Children with the disorder of autism do not respond to the persons caring for them; they do not relate well and are more responsive to objects than to people. Because of this failure to respond, they may not learn to talk and consequently function at a very low intellectual level, despite "good cognitive potentialities."

It was formerly thought that a child's history would clear up some of the diagnostic issues. It was assumed that the retarded child would have a consistently slow development from birth, while the schizophrenic child would have a normal development up to the point at which the symptoms of his abnormality appeared.

It has become increasingly evident, however, that this clear-cut developmental difference is not always present. The histories of many retarded children report average ages for the developmental milestones such as sitting, standing, walking and the onset of speech. On the other hand, as the histories of schizophrenic children are taken more carefully, disturbances in speech, motility, and even hyperirritability in infancy and early childhood are reported. Therefore, diagnosis based on the superficial resemblances of the disturbances to one or the other is of little use in clearing up the perplexing issues.

Certain features of childhood schizophrenia have been described so frequently that the very use of terms such as autism, dissociation, perservation, echolalia, and echopraxia connote schizophrenia. The examiner who uses these terms descriptively may find himself almost bound to make the diagnosis. There is no pathognomonic sympton in schizophrenia. The fact that echolalia is a normal way of learning speech and that it is not unexpected in a retarded child who is mastering speech may easily be forgotten in the reliance on the presumed pathognomonic symptom. Any of the behavior manifestations found in schizophrenic children may also be seen in children with organic disturbances or behavior disorders and in normal children under certain circumstances. For example, intensive pervasive interest in a single activity may indicate constructive preoccupation with a problem; it may also be a signal of brain dysfunction, retardation, or childhood schizophrenia.

The incongruity of normal or near normal physical appearance coupled with aimless running about, repetitive actions, or repetitive speech is very striking. It is often difficult to conjure up in one's mind a physical picture of a little child of the size and appearance that would fit the level of cognition that is demonstrated. If the observed behavior of a retarded child would seem appropriate in a child of eighteen months or three years old, or some other age, then it cannot accurately be called bizarre.

The concept of pseudo mental retardation has frequently been used to account for so-called psychogenic retardation. If the concept of psychogenic factors as a basis for retardation has evoked scepticism, then the concept of pseudo retardation has raised even more doubts and occasional cynicism. As a descriptive term, it has been used to characterize mental retardation with special disabilities, physical and behavioral disturbances. It has also been used to account for psychogenic retardation as well as for errors in diagnosis and prognosis. If the concept of mental retardation is confined to the criteria of a capacity, constitutional basis, and incurability, it follows that a person who does not meet all of these criteria would not fit into the diagnostic category of mental retardation.

The category, pseudo retardation is used to account for similarities between the patient's condition and mental retardation, thus purporting to separate the "true" from the "false."

In conclusion, it should be stated that the concept of a psychogenic basis for mental retardation presented here is in a formative stage. As yet, there has been no conclusive evidence for its existence. However, sympathetic as well as dissenting critics must keep an open mind to this concept. Perhaps our present knowledge of the etiologies of mental deficiency and the available diagnostic equipment have only begun to penetrate the complexity of these problems. It may be that with greater refinement of our approach and tools, what is today only a hypothesis may tomorrow be an actuality.

REFERENCES

Bowlby, J., *Maternal Care and Mental Health.* (Geneva: World Health Organization, 1952)

Grossman, H. J. (Ed.) Manual on Terminology and Classification in Mental Retardation, American Association on Mental Deficiency, Special Publication No. 2, 1973 rev. 180 pgs.

Kanner, L., "Problems of Nosology and Psychodynamics of Early Infantile Autism," *American Journal of Orthopsychiatry,* 1949, 18 pp. 416–426.

Woodward, K. F., Jaffe, N., and Brown, D., Early Psychiatric Intervention for Young Mentally Retarded Children; Psychiatric Approaches to Mental Retardation, (Ed.) Frank J. Menolascino, Basic Books, Inc., Publishers 1970, 276–292.

LABELING THE MENTALLY RETARDED CHILD: AN EXPLORATORY STUDY IN THE SOCIOLOGY OF MENTAL RETARDATION*

Lucille C. Wolf, Paul C. Whitehead and Benjamin D. Singer

Much has been written about the impact of the mentally retarded child on its parents (Farber, 1968; Stone, 1949; Barnard, 1967) and family (Farber and Ryckman, 1965; Schonell and Watts, 1957; Begab, 1958; Farber, 1963; Olshansky, 1962). Aside from their reaction and feelings, there is particular importance in the consequent behavior of parents after they have been informed that their child is retarded, since such behavior may then help determine the child's progress. Such a definition usually comes from a pediatrician, psychologist, or psychiatrist; but it may in some cases represent validation of what parents have suspected for some time, or it may appear to be a judgment that runs counter to what parents actually believe or want to believe. Farber and Ryckman (1965), Barnard (1967), Hellman (1963), Cohen (1962), Michaels and Schucman (1962), among others, have discussed some of the implications of the modes of reacting that are used by parents. Stated in polar terms, parents may either accept or reject the diagnosis. The implications for the future status of the child need more thorough exploration.

Unfortunately, existing research and theory offer contradictory indications as to the factors that are likely to lead to acceptance or rejection of the diagnosis (Farber, 1968; Gerstenberg, 1968). More importantly, the consequences of acceptance and rejection are even less clear even though they are potentially of significant import in determining the possibility of progress or improvement of the mentally retarded child. Rautman (1950) notes the importance of early diagnosis and emotional and intellectual appreciation of the child's assets and liabilities if parents are not to waste time and effort in trying to do the impossible with the inevitable frustrations that result; and he suggests that only after parents have accepted the diagnosis are they able to help the child effectively.

Stoddard (1959) found no significant correlation between parents' awareness and acceptance of the child's defects and the intellectual growth of trainable mentally retarded children. Further, she found that acceptance did not lead to more realistic planning for the child's future. Comprehension of such consequences is also important if guidelines are to be established for those who counsel parents of retarded children in order to achieve a variety of possible goals. However, aggregate data may conceal important subgroups of children and parents for whom there is greater hope.

*This study was supported by the Children's Psychiatric Research Institute (London, Ontario, Canada).

Farber and Ryckman (1965) cite reports of clinical observations of denial of the existence of retardation (*e.g.,* Grebler, 1952; Begab, 1956; Michaels and Schucman, 1962; Auerbach, 1961; Cummings and Stock, 1962). They also mention that there is little in the way of empirical research that assesses the impact of the definition upon parental action (Rautman, 1950; Stone, 1949). This gap in our knowledge is particularly important when coupled with the fact that efforts tend to be devoted toward getting parents to accept the definition of retardation when it is applied by the professional (Smith, 1952; Weingold, 1952; Farber and Ryckman, 1965).

The present paper attempts to assess the way in which the progress of the child may be affected by the socioeconomic status of the parents, acceptance or rejection by the parents of the diagnosis of retardation, stimulation offered to the child, and the variations in such factors as they are related to diagnosis. Examination of those children who exhibited some progress may help to highlight a specific mechanism, limited to certain subgroups or clusters of parent-child systems, or perhaps suggest a general mechanism that explains some or all future states (*e.g.,* those who change and those who do not).

Progress and regression among mentally retarded children, whether in IQ change or some other way, have been attributed to numerous factors. In those areas where research has been conducted the samples have characteristically been small, and there has been heavy reliance on clinical impressions to compensate for inability to test certain crucial alternative hypotheses. Problems related to sample size have also manifested themselves in another area; all too frequently it has not been possible to control for intervening variables. The purpose of these comments is not to present a sweeping critique of all previous research in this area, since even those studies that were based on limited samples and clinical impressions have at times provided insights that spawned further research and proved valuable sources of testable hypotheses. Neither is the present study free of the problems we have been discussing. However, in terms of the limited objectives that we have set for ourselves here, some light may be cast on this problem.

Social Class and Stimulation-Enrichment

There are contradictory suggestions as to whether children from higher-social-class families should manifest greater or lesser IQ changes than children from lower-class families. Part of the controversy, we believe, stems from not taking account of certain intervening variables. One of these is the *stimulation and enrichment* that the child receives. There is, of course, considerable indication that the more stimulation the child receives, the greater is the likelihood of progress. The relationship between social position of parents and the stimulation received by the child is not quite as clear. Some believe that middle-class parents provide greater stimulation for their retarded children and thus expect that children from middle-class homes should show greater improvement than those from lower-class homes (*cf.,* Iano, 1970). However, there is some question as to whether this is really the case (Schucman, 1963; Rautman, 1950). This confusion stems from insufficient consideration of the role played by the second intervening variable in this study; parental acceptance or rejection of the diagnosis of retardation (Sheimo, 1952; Morris, 1955).

Acceptance of Diagnosis

While much has been written on the importance of acceptance or rejection of the diagnosis on the part of parents (Stoddard, 1959; Heilman, 1950), there have been no systematic efforts to relate its relevance to social class, stimulation provided to the child, or progress or regression as measured by IQ change or any other variable.

It is our hypothesis that whatever influence these variables may have would occur in a certain order. Specifically, social position is likely to influence whether parents accept or reject the diagnosis of retardation; acceptance or rejection of the diagnosis will be a determinant of the stimulation received by the child; and the amount of stimulation received will influence the nature and direction of IQ change when it does occur. Each of these possible links is examined in this paper.

METHOD

This study was conducted at The Children's Psychiatric Research Institute, London, Ontario. CPRI has a surrounding area of nineteen counties in southwestern Ontario and has been in operation since 1960. Clinical programs use a multidisciplinary team approach. The team consists of a psychiatrist, pediatrician, psychologist, social worker, nurse, teacher, speech and audio therapists, physiotherapists, and several postgraduate physicians, with either the psychiatrist or pediatrician acting as team coordinator.

To obtain our sample of 161 children, we reviewed all cases born between 1963 and 1967 who fit into the three diagnostic categories noted below. Only those seen at the Children's Psychiatric Research Institute between 1963 and 1971 who had been tested at two points in time were selected. Medical diagnosis determined the placement of the children into three AAMD[1] diagnostic categories:
(1) *78* Encephalopathy associated with prematurity (15 cases)
(2) *79* Encephalopathy, other, due to unknown or uncertain cause with structural reaction manifest (70 cases)
(3) *89* Mental retardation, other, due to uncertain cause with the functional reaction alone manifest (76 cases).
There are 97 males (60.2%) and 64 females (39.8%). IQ levels range from 0

---

[1] AAMD — American Association on Mental Deficiency

(normal) to —5 (profound): 0—4 (2.5%); —1—58 (36.0%); —2—36 (22.4%); —3—3 5 (21.7%); —4—15 (9.3%); —5—13 (8.1%). The progress of the child is measured by IQ change. Children were tested at two points in time with the use of standard IQ tests by psychometrists. Between time one and time two their IQ scores either increased or decreased or remained the same. We have taken note only of changes that involved a change of category in terms of the IQ classification. Those whose scores increased one or two levels[2] were grouped together and those whose scores decreased one or two levels were similarly grouped. Of 161 children who were tested at two points in time, 26 or 16 percent increased, 28 or 17 percent decreased, and 107 or 66 percent remained the same.

The Stanford-Benet is used for young children and WISC for older children and scored as follows:

Stanford-Binet			The WISC	No.	Percent
0	Normal	84—	84	4	2.5
—1	Borderline	68—83	70—83	58	36.0
—2	Mild	52—67	55—69	36	22.4
—3	Moderate	36—51	40—54	35	21.7
—4	Severe	20—39	25—39	15	9.3
—5	Profound	—20	—25	13	8.1

Social class is the sociologists' most often used independent variable. Behavioral patterns are often linked to social position. Here we wish to examine the possible effects of social class on IQ change among retarded children through the intervening variables of acceptance of the diagnosis and stimulation received by the child. We have measured social position through the use of Hollingshead's (1958) two-factor index of social position. The factors are education and occupation which are differently weighted and used to produce composite scores which are then condensed into five classes, from I, the highest, to V, the lowest. Our sample contains relatively few children whose parents score in the higher classes so, for our analysis, classes I, II, and III are combined (N=26; 16.1%) while classes IV (N=83; 51.6%) and V (N=52; 32.3%) remain separate (Table 1).

Data for this study were culled from social case histories taken by social workers, questionnaires filled out by the parent and elaborated on by the team coordinator, as well as the complete case history of each child. There were, of course, problems encountered in obtaining data from the case histories, some of which were completed over an eight-year period. These problems include standardization, while others involve missing or incomplete data such as in the case of the nature of

---

[2] A level is 14 points on the WISC and 15 on the Stanford-Binet

Table 1. Parental Acceptance of the Diagnosis by Index of Social Position

Index of social position	Both parents accept		One or both reject		Both not noted		One accepts, one not noted or 1 parent missing		Total	
	No.	%	No.	%	No.	%	No.	%	No.	%
Class I-III	16	61.5	10	38.5	0	0.0	0	0.0	26	16.1
Class IV	29	34.9	48	57.8	3	3.6	3	3.6	83	51.6
Class V	15	28.8	28	54.8	5	9.6	4	7.7	52	32.3
Total	60	37.3	86	53.4	8	5	7	4.3	161	100

$x^2 = 13.04$, P 0.05, = 6

the stimulation offered the child, which were in some cases unanswered, and these data had to be obtained from pediatricians' interviews, revisit interviews, or failing this, simply coded as "not noted." Each case history was reread on three separate occasions during the period of one year to verify the researcher's decisions on several variables especially parental acceptance or rejection of the diagnosis. Current reports on the child's progress and retest results were also updated.

Stimulation

A stimulation index was developed to assess the stimulation offered to the child. A Likert-type scale of stimulation was constructed consisting of thirteen variables. A score of one was obtained for a "yes" answer, Zero for a "no" answer, and a median value for "not noted." This method was used to correct for the substantial number of "not noted" responses regarding stimulation offered to the child in the case histories and questionnaires filled out by the parents. A median value was established for each of the thirteen variables, and this plus the ones and zeros comprise a total stimulation score for each case. For purposes of analysis the total scores were then divided at the median 9.016 and those cases having a stimulation index of 9.016 and below were termed low stimulation and those above the median were termed high stimulation. There were 81 with "low" stimulation and 80 with "high" stimulation.

The variables that composed the stimulation scale are the following:
(1)   Plays with other children
(2)   Plays with siblings
(3)   Plays with toys and books
(4)   Watches TV
(5)   Goes with family on family outings
(6)   Attends Sunday School
(7)   Participates in sports
(8)   Enjoys music
(9)   Attends nursery school
(10) Is taken for therapy or rehabilitation program
(11) Family is given a home program
(12) Mother spends time enriching the child
(13) Child is included in daily family activity

It should be noted that we are attempting to include not only directed efforts by adults but also the provision of materials and social companionship as part of environmental stimulation.

Acceptance or Rejection of the Diagnosis

Parental attitude toward the diagnosis was obtained from a review of the social case history, physicians' comments, and revisit interviews that are part of the routine documentation on all cases. The rationale for the coding decision was as follows: (1) "Accepting" (a) realized the extent of the retardation and acted accordingly; for example, lowered expectations of the child's performance or seeking a program tailored to the child's difficulty; or (2) "Rejecting" (a) complete unwillingness to accept that there is something wrong with the child; (b) ambivalent, sometimes accepts that the child is retarded and sometimes rejects this notion; or (c) feels that the child is just slow.

RESULTS

Social Position and Acceptance or Rejection of the Diagnosis

Diagnosis

More often, the higher social class families (class I, II, III) accept the diagnosis of retardation (61.5% accept *vs.* 38.5% reject) when compared with social classes IV and V. Only 34.9% accept while 57.8% reject in class IV, and among class V only 28.8% accept and 53.8% reject. (Table 1). These findings are significant at the 0.05 level.

Table 2. Index of Social Position by Stimulation

Social Position	Low Stimulation		High Stimulation		Total	
	No.	%	No.	%	No.	%
I-III	13	50.0	13	50.0	26	16.1
IV	38	45.8	45	54.2	83	51.6
V	30	57.7	22	42.3	52	32.3
Total	81		80		161	100.0

$X^2 = 1.8$ P .05, df = 2.

Social Position and Stimulation

There is no clear pattern of association between social class and stimulation. A greater proportion of children from class IV homes, 54.2%, received high stimulation and 45.8% received low stimulation. Those from classes I–III were evenly divided. Among class V children, 42.3% received high stimulation, and 57.7% low stimulation (Table 2).

Social Position and IQ Change

Approximately two-thirds of the children in each of the social position categories demonstrated no change in IQ between test and retest. The direction of the shift for the one-third that did change displayed more of a tendency for children to move up in IQ in the lower social class positions than was true for social classes I–III. In classes I–III, 25% went up in IQ while 75% went down. In class IV, 57.1% went up and 42.8% down; and in class V, 44.4% went up and 55.5% down (Tables 3 and 4).

Table 3. Index of Social Position by IQ Change For those who Change IQ Change

Index of social	IQ up 1 or 2 levels		IQ down 1 or 2 levels		Total	
	No.	%	No.	%	No.	%
I–III	2	25	6	75	8	14.8
IV	16	57.1	12	42.8	28	51.9
V	8	44.4	10	55.5	18	33.3
Total	26		28		54	100.0

x^2 = 2.7, P 0.05, df = 2.
107 missing as no change in IQ took place.

Table 4. IQ Change by Index of Social Position IQ Change

Index of social position	IQ up 1 or 2 levels		IQ down 1 or 2 levels		No change in IQ		Total	
	No.	%	No.	%	No.	%	No.	%
I–III	2	7.7	6	21.4	18	16.8	26	16.1
IV	16	61.5	12	42.3	55	51.4	83	51.6
V	8	30.8	10	35.7	34	31.8	52	32.3
Total	26	100.0	28	100.0	107	100.0	261	100.0

x^2 = 2.7, P 0.05, df = 4

Acceptance of Diagnosis and Stimulation

The expected significant difference in the proportion of children who receive high or low stimulation when their parents either accept or reject the diagnosis or reject the diagnosis of retardation was not observed (Table 5). The differences tend to be in the direction of those children whose parents accept the diagnosis and receive more stimulation 53.3% high stimulation and 46.7% low stimulation while those whose parents reject the diagnosis receive less stimulation 48.8% high stimulation and 51.2% low stimulation.

Table 5. Parental Acceptance of the Diagnosis by Stimulation

Parental acceptance of the diagnosis	Low Stimulation		High Stimulation		Total	
	No.	%	No.	%	No.	%
Both parents accept the diagnosis	29	46.7	32	53.3	60	37.3
One or both parents reject the diagnosis	44	51.2	42	48.8	86	53.4
Both parents not noted	4	50.0	4	50.0	8	5.0
One accepts one not noted or missing parent	5	71.4	2	28.6	7	4.3
Total	81	50.3	80	49.7	161	100

$x^2 = 1.59$, P 0.05, df = 3

Acceptance of the Diagnosis and IQ Change

Increases in IQ are more characteristic of children who had at least one parent who rejected the diagnosis, than for children who had both their parents accepting the diagnosis of retardation (Table 6). Nearly twice as high a proportion (21.7%) of those whose parents accept the diagnosis go down one or two levels than go up one or two levels (11.7%). Conversely, 19.8% of those with one or more parent rejecting the diagnosis go up compared with 15.1% who go down. Although the cells are small, this suggests further the notion of a parent-child configuration where rejection is productive.

Table 6. IQ Change by Parental Acceptance of the Diagnosis

Parental acceptance of the diagnosis	IQ up 1 or 2 levels		IQ down 1 or 2 levels		No change in IQ		Total	
	No.	%	No.	%	No.	%	No.	%
Both parents accept	7	11.7	13	21.7	40	66.7	60	37.3
One or both parents reject	17	19.8	13	15.1	56	65.1	86	53.4
Both parents not noted	1	12.5	0	0.0	7	87.4	8	5.0
One accepts one not noted or missing	1	14.3	2	28.6	4	57.1	7	4.3
Total	26	26.1	38	17.4	107	66.5	161	100.0

$X_2 = 4.95$, P 0.05, df = 6

Stimulation and IQ Change

There is a positive relationship between stimulation and IQ change among those children whose IQ scores increased (Table 7). Twenty-six children displayed increases in IQ; of these 65.4% received high stimulation. Only 34.6% received low stimulation. Of the twenty-eight children who markedly decreased in IQ test performance, 60.7% received low stimulation and 39.3% received high stimulation.[3] (Table 8 includes the stimulation offered those children who did not change; 51.4% received low stimulation and 48.6% received high stimulation.)

IQ Classification and IQ Change

An important factor to consider when viewing IQ change is that children with IQs of 25 or less are considered custodial and the likelihood of any change is most improbable. Children with an IQ of 25–50 are considered trainable and the likelihood of improvement in IQ is greater, but still not high. It is only with the educable group IQs of 50–75 (or in our study 50–84) that there is an appreciable probability

---

[3] The possibility exists that a process of "feedback" is operative and could account for parents providing more stimulation if they are rewarded with improvement in IQ and providing less stimulation if they see no improvement.

Table 7. Stimulation by IQ Change of Those Who Change IQ Change

Stimulation	IQ up 1 or 2 levels		IQ down 1 or 2 levels		Total	
	No.	%	No.	%	No.	%
Low stimulation	9	34.6	17	65.4	26	48.1
High stimulation	17	60.7	11	39.3	28	51.9
Total	26	100.0	28	100.0	54	100.0

x^2 = 3.68, P 0.05, df = 1

Table 8. Stimulation by IQ Change

Stimulation	IQ up 1 or 2 levels		IQ down 1 or 2 levels		No change in IQ		Total	
	No.	%	No.	%	No.	%	No.	%
Low	9	34.6	17	60.7	55	51.4	81	50.3
High	17	65.4	11	39.3	52	48.6	80	49.7
Total	26	100.0	28	100.0	107	100.0	161	100.0

x^2 = 3.82, P 0.05, df = 2

of change.[4] In the custodial group of 13 cases, 0% went up, 46.2% went down, and 53.8% remained unchanged. In the trainable group of 50 cases, 10% went up, 24% went down, and 66% remained unchanged. In the educable group of 94 cases, 20.2% went up one or two levels, 10.6% went down one or two levels, and 69.1% remained unchanged (Table 9).

Diagnostic Category and IQ Change

Medical diagnostic categories and IQ changes are examined so that diagnosis could possibly be considered as an intervening factor, as perhaps an AAMD 78 which is due to prematurity, and maturation may be at a slower rate. Category 78 indicates encephalopathy associated with prematurity; category 79 encephalopathy, other, due to unknown or uncertain cause with the structural reaction manifest; category 89 mental retardation, other, due to the uncertain cause with the func-

---

[4] According to the classification found in Sarason (1953).

Table 9. IQ Classification and IQ Change

	IQ up 1 or 2 levels		IQ down 1 or 2 levels		No change in IQ		Total
	No.	%	No.	%	No.	%	
Educable (−1, −2)	19	20.2	10	10.6	65	69.1	94
Trainable (−3, −4)	5	10.0	12	24.0	33	66.0	50
Custodial (−5)	0	0.0	6	46.2	7	53.8	13
Total	24		28		105		157

x^2 = 15.6, P 0.05, df = 4
4 cases missing who have borderline IQs (0).

tional reaction along manifest. We note in category 78 (of the 15 cases), 26.7% went up one or two levels, 13.3% went down, and 60% remained unchanged. In category 79 (70 cases), 17.1% went up one or two levels, 20% went down, and 62.9% remained unchanged. In category 89 (76 cases) 13.2% went up one or two levels, 15.8% went down, and 71.1% remained unchanged (Table 10).

Table 10 AAMD* by IQ Change

	DIAGNOSTIC CATEGORY						Total	
IQ Change	78		79		89			
	No.	%	No.	%	No.	%	No.	%
Up 1 or 2 levels	4	26.7	12	17.1	10	13.2	26	16.1
Down 1 or 2 levels	2	13.3	14	20.0	12	15.8	28	17.4
No change	9	60.0	44	62.9	54	71.1	107	66.5
Total	15	100.0	70	100.0	76	100.0	161	100.0

x^2 = 2.4, P 0.05, df = 4
*AAMD Diagnosis from "Manual on Terminology and Classification" in *Mental Retardation. American Journal of Mental Deficiency Supplement* 2nd ed., 1961,

Parents' Acceptance of the Diagnosis and Diagnostic Category

Clearly different manifest conditions elicit different parental responses to the diagnosis. Category 89 indicates only functional reaction manifest, and in this category there are 76 cases. In 67.1% of these one of both parents reject the diagnosis, and in only 26.3% both parents accept it. This is probably because there is no structural reaction manifest as in category 79, and often the diagnosis notes uncertain cause. In category 79, there is a more even distribution of acceptance and rejection of the diagnosis by the parents 50% for the former and 40% for the latter. In the case of category 78 where prematurity was noted, 33.3% of the parents accepted the diagnosis and in 46.7%, one or both rejected it. This possibly indicates a retention of hope of improvement by parents where there is the least physical indication or stigmata (Table 11).

DISCUSSION

In order to investigate the variables which could influence positive IQ change in a group of retarded children, we hypothesized that social class is a factor in parents' acceptance or rejection of the diagnosis of mental retardation, and, further, that rejection of the diagnosis leads to more stimulation offered to the child and consequentially to positive IQ change. Although the data do not support all the hypotheses, the results presented in the previous section indicate an interesting pattern of associations among the variables we have examined. First, parents of higher social position tend to be more accepting of the diagnosis than those of lower social position. Second, high stimulation was most characteristic of class IV homes those in which the diagnosis of retardation was least accepted. Third, class IV children whose parents tended to reject the diagnosis and who tended to receive greater stimulation — had the greatest proportion of positive IQ change; while classes I–III children had the greatest proportion who had negative IQ change. And, fourth, while two-thirds of all children displayed no appreciable change in IQ from the first testing period to the next, those children whose IQs displayed positive change tended to have received high stimulation and those with negative IQ change were characterized by having received low stimulation.

Our findings affirm those of some previous studies and contradict those of others. Iano (1970) also found that there is greater acceptance of the diagnosis among higher socioeconomic status parents (classes I–III) than lower socioeconomic status parents. He found socioeconomic status significantly related to parents' evaluation and estimate of their children's ability, while lower socioeconomic status parents perceived their children as capable and adequate. Schucman (1963) found the opposite situation that parents who had less education had less difficulty accepting the diagnosis. She attributed this to their familiarity with welfare agencies and dependence on others for guidance and direction.

Table 11. AAMD Diagnosis by Parental Acceptance of the Diagnosis

AAMD category	Both accept		One or both reject		Both not noted		One accepts, one not noted or missing		Total	
	No.	%	No.	%	No.	%	No.	%	No.	%
78	5	33.3	7	46.7	1	6.7	2	13.3	15	9.3
79	35	50	28	40	4	5.7	3	4.3	70	43.5
89	20	26.3	51	67.1	3	3.9	2	2.6	76	47.2
Total	68	37.3	86	53.4	8	5	7	4.3	161	100

X^2 = 14.33, P 0.05, df = 6.

While our findings are not as conclusive as one might wish, they are nevertheless suggestive: Positive IQ change may be more likely when one or both parents reject the diagnosis than when they both accept it. What intervenes between acceptance or rejection of the diagnosis and IQ change? We had hypothesized stimulation would be relevant if taken into account within a context of "labeling theory," *e.g.,* that the label the child has been assigned may condition the quality and quantity of stimulation parents provide.

The labeling approach involves a move away from focusing exclusively on the "deviant," in this case, the mentally retarded child; or deviance, mental retardation; to an examination of the interactive process between deviants and nondeviants as part of a social situation and the successful application of the label "deviant" to another person (*cf.* Becker, 1963; 1–6). Successful labeling of one type of deviance may have unanticipated and unwelcome results. For example, "secondary deviance" (Lemert, 1967; 40–64) in the form of enhancing the likelihood of another type of deviance or in the sense of the "self-fulfilling prophecy" (*cf.* Rosenthal and Jacobsen, 1968) where recidivism is the outcome. When children receive low IQ scores or are labeled with a tag saying they have not the means to perform, little is expected of them and they consequently accept the label and act the part.

The label "retardation" carries with it the prognosis of chronicity and hopelessness and the decreased probability that children will achieve positive IQ change. Rejecting such a label, on the other hand, means that the possibility of normality, rather than deviance, is held out. Hence, some parents who reject the diagnosis would tend to provide greater stimulation for their children with the hope of positive IQ change. But our hypothesis that a major role is played by the amount of stimulation received by children of parents who reject the diagnosis does not appear to be borne out since there is no significant difference between the two.

Nevertheless, these findings and the interpretation presented above can be used as the basis for suggesting that perhaps less emphasis should be placed by the physician or psychiatrist on having parents accept the diagnosis of retardation (*cf.* Morris, 1955; Sheimo, 1952; Smith, 1952).

Two cogent questions can be asked and partially answered from our data: First, what are some of the characteristics of families that are likely to be able to cope effectively with a child who is retarded but has not been formally labeled as such; and second, in what ways may the potential of the child best be assessed, *i.e.,* which children are more likely to improve in IQ?

There is apt to be a relationship between social class and the probability of a family operating effectively even though one member's performance may be below average. Evidence from previous research indicates that middle-class families may be least able to cope with a member whose abilities do not measure up to those of other members. In their study of mental patients who return to their homes, Freeman and Simmons (1963) found that patients from middle-class families are the most likely to be rehospitalized. They attribute this phenomenon to the greater expectation and higher levels of performance that operate in middle-class families. In such an environment those whose performance levels are marginal or clearly inferior are likely to be labeled as different or deviant, and this is manifested in terms of higher rates of rehospitalization. Relative to mental retardation we would expect that impaired children from middle-class homes would have their handicaps more readily recognized than children from lower-class homes.

Rautman (1950) notes that retarded children from homes where standards are low, and thus where their retardation is not as conspicuous, have far more favorable educational and adjustment prognosis than children who have equal or less retardation from homes in which their intellectual handicap places them well below the level of family aspirations. By trying to reach these expectations, the children experience frustrations, rejection, and social maladjustment. Michaels and Schucman (1962) note the lesser likelihood of lower-class parents to classify their retarded child as deviant. Therefore, a smaller gap exists between the parents' expectations for the child and the child's ability to achieve. In terms of the above, it would also follow that in families where a high value is placed on performance, subnormal performance would be disruptive; there is therefore a considerable need for a framework within which such deviance can be understood. Hence, we would expect and we did find that middle-class parents would be more likely to accept the diagnosis of retardation than lower-class families.

On the basis of the present findings and previous research it is suggested that initial denial of the diagnosis is not pathological (Farber, 1963) and, further, may be an important defense mechanism for the parents (Sheimo, 1952; Barnard, 1967). Initial acceptance could indicate or lead to resignation and lack of incentive to pursue thereapy (Weingold, 1952). Thus, Rogers (1967) speculates that the absence of a protest reaction to the diagnosis might be considered pathological and represent detachment from the child. In some cases this initial denial of the diagnosis could prove beneficial to the parents as well as the child.

When we address ourselves to the second question, which children are more likely to improve in IQ, we find from the data that they will most probably be from class IV, that the parents will reject the diagnosis of mental retardation and will provide stimulation for them, and lastly, that the medical diagnosis for these children will most probably be AAMD 78 (encephalopathy due to prematurity). Conversely, the children most likely to drop in IQ level will be from classes I–III, the parents will accept the diagnosis and provide little stimulation, and furthermore, the diagnosis will most probably be AAMD 79.

Further investigation is needed to develop a detailed typology of types of families and their assets or liabilities in coping with retarded children, which may provide further determinants of acceptance or rejection as well as stimulation. Some work has been done along these lines by Farber (1968) in the distinction between child-oriented families and career-oriented families. He also notes that a retarded child affects higher-social-class families as a "tragic crisis" and lower class families as a "role-oriented crisis" and all families by a disruption in the "role cycle" in that the retarded child holds back the family cycle by always being considered the youngest regardless of his actual chronological age. We believe that much of this work can be expanded upon and integrated within a larger theoretical framework.

Further work needs to be done on the accurate assessment of the child's potential for improvement. Efforts to combine findings on a child's potential for improvement with the potential for change of his particular diagnosis may prove fruitful as well.

SUMMARY

The present study was designed to investigate the correlation of positive IQ change in 161 retarded children and the four following variables: Socioeconomic status, acceptance or rejection of the diagnosis, stimulation, and diagnostic category.

Significance at the 0.05 level was obtained on (1) parents' acceptance or rejection of the diagnosis and diagnostic category of their child; (2) socioeconomic status and acceptance and rejection of the diagnosis; and (3) stimulation and IQ change.

Significance was not obtained at the 0.05 level on (1) acceptance or rejection of the diagnosis and stimulation, or on (2) IQ change and acceptance or rejection of the diagnosis, as was anticipated.

REFERENCES

Auerbach, A. B., Group education for parents of the handicapped. *Children,* 1961, *8,* 135–140.

Barnard, K., How families react to the crisis of mental retardation. Paper presented to the Canadian Association of Retarded Children. Quebec City, September 1967.

Becker, H. S., *Outsider: Studies in the sociology of deviance.* New York: Free Press, 1963.

Begab, M. J., "Facts on Counselling Parents of Retarded Children," *American Journal of Mental Deficiency,* 1956, *60;* 515–525.

Begab, M. J., "Unmet needs of the mentally retarded in the community," *American Journal of Mental Deficiency,* 1958, *62;* 712–723.

Cohen, P., The impact of the handicapped child on the family. *Social Casework,* 1962, *43,* 137–142.

Cummings, S. T., and Dorothy Stock. Brief group therapy for mothers of retarded children outside the speciality clinic setting. *American Journal of Mental Deficiency,* 1962, *66,* 739–748.

Farber, B., Interaction with retarded siblings and life goals of children. *Marriage and Family Living,* 1963, *25,* 96–98.

Farber, B., and Ryckman, D. B., Effect of severely retarded children on family relationship. *Mental Retardation Abstracts,* 1965, *2,* 1–17.

Farber, B., *Mental retardation: Its social context and social consequences.* Boston: Houghton-Mifflin, 1968.

Farber, B., Report of the conference: The social science of retardation. Bethesda, Maryland, 1968.

Freeman, H. E., and Simmons, O. G., *The mental patient comes home.* New York: Wiley, 1963.

Gerstenberg, M. T., A study of the marital status and attitudes of parents of retarded children in a private residential school in Maryland. *Research Abstracts,* Cardinal Stritch College Issue, 1968, *9,* 61–62.

Grebler, A. M., Parental attitude toward mental retardates. *American Journal of Mental Deficiency,* 1952, *56,* 475–483.

Heilman, A. E., Parental adjustment to the dull handicapped child. *American Journal of Mental Deficiency,* 1950, *54,* 556–560.

Hellman, J., Key problems of parents of the special child: A report of a prospect of parents of self-understanding. New School for Special Children. Seattle, Washington (55-minute tape). Reviewed in *American Journal of Mental Deficiency,* 1963, *68,* 555.

Hollingshead, A. B., and Redlich, F. C., *Social class and mental illness.* New York: Wiley, 1958.

Iano, R. P., Social class and parental evaluation of educable retarded children. *Education and Training of Mentally Retarded,* 1970, *5,* (3), 62–67.

Lemert, E. M., The concept of secondary deviation in *Human deviance, social problems and social control.* Englewood Cliffs, N.J.: Prentice-Hall, 1967, pp. 40–64.

Michaels, J., and Schucman, H., Observations on the psychodynamics of parents of retarded children. *American Journal of Mental Deficiency,* 1962, *66,* 568–573.

Morris, E. F., Counselling parents of retarded children. *American Journal of Mental Deficiency,* 1955, *59,* 510–516.

Olshansky, S., Chronic sorrow: A response to having a mentally defective child. *Social Casework,* 1962, *43,* 190–193.

Rautman, A., Society's first responsibility to the mentally retarded. *American Journal of Mental Deficiency,* 1950, *54,* 152–162.

Rogers, R., Parental attitudes which interfere with utilization of available educational facilities for the mentally handicapped. Address given in California, May 1967.

Rosenthal, R., and Jacobsen, L., *Pygmalian in the classroom.* New York: Holt, Rinehart and Winston, 1968.

Schonell, F. J., and Watts, B. H., First survey of the effects of a subnormal child on the family. *American Journal of Mental Deficiency,* 1957, *61,* 210–219.

Schucman, H., Further observations on the psychodynamics of parents of retarded children. *Training School Bulletin,* 1963, *60,* 70–74.

Sheimo, S. L., Problems in helping parents of mentally defective children. *American Journal of Mental Deficiency,* 1952, *56,* 42–47.

Smith, E. M., Emotional factors as revealed in the intake process. *American Journal of Mental Deficiency,* 1952, *56,* 806–811.

Stoddard, H. M., The relation of parental attitudes and achievements of severely retarded children. *American Journal of Mental Deficiency,* 1959, *63,* 575–598.

Stone, M. M., Parental attitudes to retardation. *American Journal of Mental Deficiency,* 1949, *53,* 363–372.

Weingold, J. T., Parents groups and problems of mental deficiency. *American Journal of Mental Deficiency,* 1952, *56,* 484.

JUVENILE DELINQUENCY AND MENTAL RETARDATION

Dan Linkenhoker

Despite massive rehabilitation efforts, juvenile delinquency remains a social blight. In 1971, for example, over one million juvenile cases, representing 1.9 percent of all children in this country aged ten to seventeen were handled by American juvenile courts (Juvenile Court Statistics, 1971). More importantly, however, juvenile recidivism rates (relapse into crime) are estimated to be between 43 percent to 73 percent of all treated offenders (Arbuckle and Litwack, 1960). The reasons for these rates are not clearly understood. Some authorities (Linkenhoker and McCarron, 1974) have suggested that one reason lies in a failure to recognize and treat the myriad educational, vocational, and behavioral aspects of delinquency. One aspect most often misunderstood is mental retardation and its impact on the adjustment of the juvenile offender.

THE "DEFECTIVE DELINQUENT"

The mentally retarded offender is frequently referred to legally as a "defective delinquent." In 1951, the American Association on Mental Deficiency (AAMD) provided the following definition (Westwell, 1951):

A mentally defective delinquent is any person affected with intellectual impairment from birth, or from an early age, to such an extent that he is incapable of managing himself and his affairs; who is charged with, arraigned for, or convicted of a criminal offense; and who for his own welfare, the welfare of others in the community, requires supervision, control and care; and who is not insane or of unsound mind to such an extent as to require his commitment to an institution for the insane (p. 285).

Unfortunately there is no primary acceptable definition of the mentally retarded delinquent. Various state statutes use the term "defective" to refer to intellectual deficits while others use it to refer to a moral sense, common sense, or both. Many of these statutes also carry with them indeterminate sentences designed to protect society and to maximize treatment intervention. Poorly stated guidelines for defining the defective delinquent may lead either to irreparable mistakes in misplaced institutionalization or to the mistaken release of seriously impaired offenders into the community.

Currently, no court in the United States grants special diminished capacity *by law* for the mentally retarded offender (Giagiari, 1971). Should a sixteen-year-old adolescent with a mental age of ten years, three months, be held responsible for his actions by a court of law? The question is a critical but unresolved issue. Calkins (1967) suggests that if an offender is found to be irresponsible for his actions by reasons of mental retardation, his sentence should be set aside and he should become a ward of the state mental health department. A mentally retarded youth incapable of understanding the charges against him should not be placed in a traditional correctional institution simply because his body is nearly adult and his crime offensive.

It is clear that there is an urgent need to arrive at a more precise, more widely acceptable, and less stigmatizing legal qualification for this exceptionality.

INCIDENCE

Studies that provide data on the incidence of mental retardation in criminal populations are often methodologically flawed by the differences in concept definition and nonspecification of psychometric instruments used in the assessment. Some general information, however, has been complied for this area.

Current estimations of the percentage of the delinquent population that is mentally retarded range from 0.5 percent to 55 percent (Beier, 1964). Several authors have noted gradual mean IQ score increases in the delinquent population over the past several years. These changes went from a mean IQ score of 71 in 1931 to 92 in 1950 (Woodward, 1955) and finally to 95 in 1973 (Mauser, 1973). The reasons for this increase might be partially attributed to the effect of poor research methodology in previous studies and to an overall basic increase in the caliber of American educational endeavors.

Although there has been a noticeable increase in IQ scores in this group, and since most researchers conclude that mental retardation is a complicating factor rather than a direct cause of delinquency (Giagiari, 1971), it might be simple to conclude that the problem is relatively nonsignificant. There is, however, a large proportion of delinquents that are mentally retarded and in need of special program considerations. The Atlanta Association for Retarded Children (1973), for example, has found in their recent survey that nearly 50 percent of the adolescent offenders in the Georgia state penal system fall into the mentally retarded range. Other states have reported similar findings; a Wisconsin survey (1971) revealed that among 831 male and 256 female first admissions to juvenile correctional programs, 20.8 percent of the male population were dull normal, 14.2 percent borderline, and 7.3 percent defective. Among the girls 21.1 percent were dull normal, 10.9 percent borderline, and 3.1 percent were defective.

Although the magnitude of this problem is significantly large, there are other complicating factors characteristic of the retarded offender and his situation that makes this issue ever more demanding of immediate intervention.

CHARACTERISTICS OF THE MENTALLY RETARDED OFFENDER

Offenses

Youths under the age of eighteen referred to juvenile courts constitute approximately one-fourth of all persons charged with rape, one-third of all persons charged with robbery one-half of all persons charged with burglary and larceny, and more than one-half of all persons charged with auto theft (Wenk, 1974). Although no data are available on the number of retarded youths arrested on criminal charges each year, there is some information to indicate that retarded offenders as a group commit proportionately a greater number of more dangerous crimes (Boslow and Kandel, 1965).

Youthful retarded offenders usually commit offenses that include arson, property destruction, sexual offenses, and even homicide. Brown, Courtless and Silber (1970), for example, found in their study of a group of retarded offenders that 26.8 percent committed homicide and 59 percent committed other offenses against the person.

Lacking the inner resources for adequate control and understanding of potentially violent situations and being incapable often to anticipate the consequences of his behavior, the retarded offender often finds himself the perpetrator of violent crimes.

Family Structure

The function of the family cannot be overemphasized in its role as the primary socializing agent in the child's life. Delinquency has been related to early forms of family disturbance including parental rejection, parental loss, emotional deprivation, and inconsistent disciplinary techniques. It is likely, however, as Oltman and Friedman (1967) point out, that parental deprivation per se is of less importance in producing antisocial behavior than are the emotional and physical disturbances that precede the physical departure of the parents. In fact, many retarded delinquents who come from the lower socioeconomic group have often been found to have suffered psychological or physical abuse and neglect (Dennis, 1966).

The presence of a retarded child can have a serious impact on family stability. Marital integration often suffers when a retarded child lives with the family. This poor integration tends to be even more pronounced when the child is male and when the family is lower class (Farber, 1959). This impact is reflected also in adjustment difficulties with the retardate's siblings. Girls are more affected by the presence of a retarded sibling at home, but maladjustment is greater in male siblings when the retardate is institutionalized (Farber, 1959). In a family where instability is already present, the introduction of a mentally retarded child can be tremendously destructive. Parent and sibling instability increases, parental ineffectiveness increases, and the probabilities of the retardate's involvement is delinquent behavior also greatly increases.

The manner in which the retardate's parents deal with the emotional climate produced by the child's presence in the family has a great impact upon the child's future development. Many mentally retarded children suffer more from emotional problems than from their intellectual deficits. In those cases where parents are insensitive to the child's frustrations, anxieties, and humiliations from sources at home and in the community there exists the greater chance that these feelings will be expressed in delinquent or asocial behavior.

The need for intensive counseling in the families of retarded offenders is evident. Not only must the objective reality of the child's retardation be examined but also the subjective reality of the parents' feeling of personal responsibility must be probed. In many cases parents must also be provided with parental effectiveness training to teach them behavioral techniques for successful child management. Learning how to accept, to manage, and to be more consistent with discipline can help the parents deter the retarded child from delinquency.

Educational Provisions

When the family structure fails as the first-line defense against delinquency, the school system must then assume the role of a major socializing agent in the child's life. The school environment, in fact, appears to be one of the most critical functions that determine a youth's successful or unsuccessful adaptation in the community. (Wenk, 1974). Public schools, however, have failed to teach the social skills and responsibilities that aid students in achieving personal growth. They have, in this sense, contributed to the delinquent process.

Retarded delinquents in particular are often the victims of inappropriate school provisions. They not only fail to receive adequate socializing experiences for interpersonal growth but they frequently do not receive the quality educational experiences consistent with their abilities and needs. They must live not only with the stigmatizing label of "delinquent," but they must also cope with the label "mentally retarded." When combined with the frustrations and anxieties of being forced into some classroom situations poorly designed for their needs, these factors can only add to their adjustment difficulties. Disruptive and asocial behaviors then become a by-product of the school's neglect for the child's needs. Mukerjee (1971) has in fact found that the delinquent behavior of boys was higher while they attended school and significantly lower after they dropped out. In this sense, dropping out would seem to be a rather healthy response to a perceived desperate situation. The retarded offender is placed in a double-bind situation. Remaining in school may continue to provoke his frustrations, anxieties, and delinquent behavior; dropping out, however, guarantees a loss of whatever socialization and vocational opportunities exist at school.

The problems encountered by the retarded and nonretarded delinquent in the educational system are not inevitable. The manner in which educational officials react to the child's misconduct at school may determine whether it will be followed by delinquency (*Task Force Report: Juvenile Delinquency and Youth Crime,* 1967). Wenk (1974) believes that the most effective, long-range protection of society from crime and delinquency will come from reformation and innovative designs in the public school. He recommends programs aimed at primary action, primary prevention, treatment, and rehabilitation. Children in need of assistance must be located but not stigmatized with labels; teachers must be made aware of the relationship between the child's self-concept, his social adjustment, and resulting behavior; and educational systems must be overhauled to foster responsibility, social development, and effective problem-solving skills. New programs must be provided especially for the retarded offender. The effects of dual labeling and poor vocational and poor social skills preparation make the situation demanding of quick intervention.

Employment and Street Survival Skills

Very closely related to the various academic and social problems experienced by retarded delinquents are deficits in the knowledge required for successful day-to-day living in the community and for adequate vocational adjustment.

Street survival skills involve such things as being able to read and understand want ads, to understand the yellow and the white pages of the telephone book, to make bank deposits and withdrawals, or to be able to recognize signs and warnings for personal protection. Such skills, however, are usually sparsely developed in the delinquent population and even more lacking in the retarded offender group. With improper vocational and educational preparation, inadequate street survival skills, and the stigmatizing effects of a delinquent and retarded label, retarded offenders are not well suited for immediate entrance into the job market.

In those fortunate situations where retarded offenders are the recipients of adequate prevocational preparation and efficient placement services, entry into the job stream is more successful. Halpern (1973) has shown that although it is difficult for mentally retarded persons new in the labor market to find jobs during periods of high community unemployment, well-structured vocational training programs can locate adequate job placement in many cases regardless of community unemployment levels. Most correctional institutions, however, do not have the specialized training facilities and placement services to guarantee a coordinated effort to employ the retarded offender. Without such services, the individual's work record reflects unemployment, job nomadism, or marginal employment; his legal record likely reflects more delinquent activity.

Since the average age of referral to juvenile court is 12.6 years (Giagiari, 1971), it has been recommended that programs of vocational training should begin no later than age twelve or at least at the point of first contact with the juvenile justice system (Connecticut Mental Retardation Office, 1966). Separate and specialized facilities, small enough to deal with the youth's educational and vocational needs, should be established in each state. Training programs must teach improved interpersonal skills that facilitate appropriate work-supervisor and work-peer relationships. Specific programs should prepare the offender for local industrial needs and for general street survival. Placement services and on-the-job counseling would then assist the individual with maintenance and growth on the job. The retarded offender might then begin to become a fully functioning citizen in his community.

Diagnosis, Treatment, and Adjustment

The retarded offender would also seem to require a greater proportion of therapeutic time than the nonretarded offender. His unresponsiveness to many traditional intervention approaches and a lack of community placement alternatives makes the process of treatment a difficult and complex task. The Patuxent study (Boslow and Kandel, 1965) demonstrated that retarded delinquents caused more behavioral incidents within the institution, remained committed longer than the nonretarded, and were responsible for a larger share of the recidivism rate during post-program adjustment.

Basic research suggests that the highly verbal-oriented therapies with emphasis on insight have shown consistently poor results when used with retarded delinquents (Sternlight, 1966), while nonverbal approaches such as behavior modification, play therapy, modeling, and psychodrama have shown the best behavioral results. In addition to behavioral intervention, specific educational and vocational training arrangements such as sheltered workshops, speech therapy, and multisensory training approaches are required as part of the overall intervention techniques. In some cases, chemotherapy and more specialized medical approaches such as treatment of blood-related problems or neurological surgery are required.

Proper and adequate treatment should be based on adequate diagnostic procedures. Frequently, however, there is a failure to identify the retarded offender before he is sentenced either because of a lack of referral agencies or because of the juvenile judge's overzealous desire to protect the community. An adequate diagnosis should be performed by a multidisciplinary team composed of professionals who can speak about the child's intellectual, educational, vocational, adaptive, and medical problems. Once the primary cause and the level of retardation are determined, appropriate treatment schemes and recommendations can be provided for the court.

Even in those cases where diagnostic services are available, many states unfortunately do not have adequate facilities and alternatives for handling such special cases. The retarded delinquent is frequently placed in large correctional programs with older and hardened offenders where a paucity of specialized intervention approaches exist. The staff is not trained or prepared to deal with the peculiar problems of this group and tends to become disenchanted with its own ineffectiveness. In many cases where probation exists as an alternative to institutionalization, probation officers are not adequately trained to handle such specialized caseloads, or else have such large caseloads that they simply do not have time for the retarded offender and his needs.

There is a need to provide quality diagnostic services that will help guarantee improved justice and individual treatment for the retarded offender at this first contact with the juvenile justice system. The problems of obtaining such services are, however, quite large given the increasing numbers of juveniles entering the court system. Innovative diagnostic programs utilizing high-speed computers have the potential of providing quick, reliable assessment procedures with recommendations to probation officers, parents, and teachers on the special problems of juvenile delinquency (Linkenhoker and McCarron, 1974).

In addition to providing improved diagnostic services, there must be special treatment facilities geared to handle the problems of mentally retarded offenders. The general consensus among most authorities is that separate facilities be established apart from traditional correctional institutions to handle this group of youthful offenders. Several states (e.g., Maryland, New Jersey, and California) have been moving in this direction for some time; other states, however, have been less successful and must soon implement new programming in order to meet the needs of the retarded delinquent.

Summary

Giagiari (1971) has described the retarded offender as the "forgotten man" in the justice system. A serious shortage of correctional services and opportunities combined with intellectual deficits, inadequate street survival skills, and the duality of labels has greatly contributed to this unjust situation.

The need to continue basic research and to develop model codes for the identification and treatment for the retarded offender is critical. Programs to guarantee improved delivery of social services to the family, to the school, and to the individual offender are necessary before any significant impact will be felt in this problem area.

REFERENCES

Arbuckle, D., and Litwack, L., A study of recidivism among juvenile offenders. *Federal Probation,* 1960, *24,* 44–46.46.

Atlanta Association for Retarded Children. Annual report of the Atlanta Association for Retarded Children. *Corrections Digest,* 1973, *4,* (25), 3–5.

Beier, D. C., Behavioral disturbance in the mentally retarded. In H. Stevens and R. Heber, (Eds.), *Mental retardation: a review of research.* Chicago: University of Chicago Press, 1964, 453–487.

Boslow H., and Kandel, A., Psychiatric aspects of dangerous behavior: the retarded offender. *American Journal of Psychiatry,* 1965, *122* (6), 646–656.

Brown B. S.; Courtless, T. F.; and Silber, D. E., Fantasy and force: a study of the dynamics of mentally retarded offender. *Journal of Criminal Law, Criminology and Police Science,* 1970, *61* (1), 71–77

Calkins, L., The mentally retarded offender. *Correctional Psychologist,* 1967, *3* (2), 17–20.

Connecticut Mental Retardation Office. *Miles to go.* Hartford, 1966.

Dennis F., *The mentally retarded public offender and the law.* Tallahassee: Florida Press, 1966.

Farber B., The effects of a severely retarded child on family integration. *Monograph of Social Research and Child Development,* 1959, 71.

Giagiari, S., The mentally retarded offender. *Crime and Delinquency Literature,* 1971, *3* (4), 559–574.

Halpern A., General employment and vocational opportunities for EMR individuals. *American Journal of Mental Deficiency,* 1973, *78* (2), 123–127.

Juvenile Court Statistics-1971, Washington, D. C., 1971, DHEW publication number (2RS), 73-03452.

Linkenhoker, D., and McCarron, L., Computerized assessment programming (CAP): a prescriptive strategy for delinquents. *Behavioral Science,* 1974 (in press).

Mauser, A., The remediation of learning disabilities in juvenile delinquent youth. Paper presented at the 10th International Conference of ACLD, Detroit, 1973.

Mukerjee, S., *A typological study of school status and delinquency.* Ann Arbor, Mich.: University Microfilsm, 1971.

Oltman J., and Friedman, S., Parental deprivation in psychiatric conditions. *Diseases of the Nervous System,* 1967, *28,* 298–303.

Sternlight M., Treatment approaches to delinquent retardates. *International Journal of Group Psychotherapy* 1966, *16* (1), 91–93.

Task force report: juvenile delinquency and youth crime. Washington, D. C.: U.S. Government Printing Office, 1967

Wenk E., Schools and delinquency prevention. *Crime and Delinquency Literature,* 1974, *6*(2), 236–258.

Westwell, A. E., The defective delinquent. *American Journal of Mental Deficiency,* 1951, *56,* 283–289.

Woodward M., The role of low intelligence in delinquency *British Journal of Delinquency,* 1955 *5* (3), 281–300

Wisconsin Division of Corrections. *Admissions to juvenile institutions - calendar 1970,* Madison, Wis., 1971.

ANXIETY IN CHILDREN: THEORETICAL VIEWS AND RESEARCH FINDINGS*

A. J. Finch, Jr. and Philip C. Kendall

Probably no other emotion has received as much attention or captured as much interest within the general public as has anxiety, and this is particularly true with children. Parents speak of their young children feeling anxious or not anxious when they meet strangers, go to school, play with other children, ride a pony, await a dental appointment, or visit their grandparents. Later, children speak of themselves as feeling anxious when their teacher watches them work, when their parents correct them, when they talk with a member of the opposite sex, when learning to drive a car, or when they read a paper before their classmates. Indeed, anxiety is an emotional condition aroused by many and varied environmental situations. Moreover, inasmuch as Aristotle discussed the subject, anxiety can be said to have deep historical roots and, probably, to have been a problem for generations of people.

In an attempt to better understand the nature of anxiety, numerous individuals, both literary and scientific, have posited a theory of anxiety. Initially, the present paper will give a brief review of the psychological theories relating to anxiety. Among the issues emerging from these theories are the difficulty and importance of the measurement of anxiety which are also discussed within this paper. Lastly, a report of our research into the nature and experience of anxiety in children is presented.

THEORETICAL VIEWS

Freud

Historically, the underpinnings of anxiety theory can be traced to Freud (1924) who, according to Spielberger (1966), regarded anxiety as "something felt," an unpleasant state of the organism, and "all that is covered by the word nervousness." Freud considered anxiety to be related to one's personality in that it is affected by the necessity to gratify the individual's basic needs. Originally, Freud thought of anxiety as dammed-up or frustrated sexual excitement, but later he began to view anxiety as a more complex phenomenon stemming from both internal and external

*The writing of this material and portions of the actual research were supported by the Small Grants Program of the School of Medicine of Virginia Commonwealth University awarded to the first author and by the National Institute of Mental Health Predoctoral Research Fellowship (#1 F31 MH05270-01) awarded to the second author.

The authors wish to thank the staff of the Virginia Treatment Center for Children for their cooperation during the inconvenience and extra work that these projects caused.

threats (Hall and Lindzey, 1970). The role of the surrounding environment is related to the desire for gratification in that it decreases anxiety by providing means for satisfaction (e.g., the hungry organism with food) or by containing dangerous and threatening conditions which, by preventing satisfaction, increase anxiety. The individual's response to external threats is to become afraid or overwhelmed with excessive stimulation which is what Freud calls anxiety. The function of anxiety is to warn the person of impending danger. It is considered by Freud to be a signal or indicator that something is not going well in the life of the individual.

To clarify the complex nature of anxiety, three forms were identified by Freud (Hall 1954): (1) objective anxiety, (2) moral anxiety, and (3) neurotic anxiety. Objective anxiety, also called reality anxiety, is an appropriate response to a dangerous stimulus as was suggested by the "signal" function discussed previously.

Realistic anxiety strikes us as something very rational and intelligible. We may say of it that it is a reaction to the perception of an external danger, that is, of an injury which is expected and foreseen (Freud, 1963, p. 393).

Moral anxiety is fear of one's conscience. It is the feeling of a sense of guilt when one does something, or even thinks of doing something, against the moral code by which the individual was raised. Similar to objective anxiety, moral anxiety can be considered to have a realistic basis since the person has probably been punished in the past for breaking the moral code.

Neurotic anxiety is associated with the dread of being overwhelmed by one's internal drives or being attacked as a function of having these drives. Hall (1954) points out that although Freud distinguished between neurotic, objective, and moral anxiety, he did not consider them to differ qualitatively. They were all thought to have the quality of unpleasantness.

In his final position, Freud surmised that anxiety is a psychological reaction to a threat. The major threat for the individual was being overwhelmed by a flood of physical stimulation, and the goal was to reduce the stimulation to a state of tranquility. Thus, when anxiety is aroused it motivates the person to do something to relieve the unpleasantness. The individual may flee from the situation which threatened him, inhibit the threatening impulse, or follow the direction of his conscience. When anxiety is not coped with by rational methods, the individual falls back on unrealistic methods called the defense mechanisms.

The Freudian theoretical analysis of the concept of anxiety, while serving as a major portion of our understanding today, has remained stagnated at the theoretical level because of a lack of measurement instruments. It is this lack of a measure for Freud's "anxieties" which prevented further investigation in a more scientific and systematic fashion.

Neo-Freudian Theory: Horney

The Neo-Freudian theorist Karen Horney proposed a more social-psychological theory of anxiety. A clear difference between the Neo-Freudian and Freudian theories lies in the degree of importance which they attach to environmental influences, with the Neo-Freudians seeing the environment as playing a more important role than intrapsychic influences.

Horney's conception of anxiety (1939), which attempts to escape Freud's attachment to genetic or instinctive psychology, concerns the feeling of being isolated and helpless in a potentially hostile world. A broad band of emotional factors is seen as related to the development of anxiety, and thus Horney makes an elaborate set of environmental circumstances basic to the concept of anxiety. Stated generally, anything that disturbs the security of a child in his relation to his parents produces basic anxiety. It is theorized that this leads the individual to develop neurotic solutions to the basic disturbance.

Although the Neo-Freudian viewpoint successfully emphasized environmental influences and advanced our understanding, few empirical investigations of anxiety worked from the Neo-Freudian notions. Thus, little experimental evidence is available to support or refute the Neo-Freudian theoretical position.

Dollard and Miller

The works of Dollard and Miller (1950) centered on their desire "to combine the vitality of psychoanalysis with the rigor of the natural-science laboratory, and the facts of the culture" (1950, p. 3). The transformation of some of Freud's concepts into independent variables provided at least some sense of objectivity. Essentially, Dollard and Miller postulate that a generalized fear arising from a specific set of stimuli is definitive of anxiety. Such a trend toward an overt behavioristic explanation was designed to improve rigorous investigation.

Dollard and Miller (1950) argue that learning is a function of a stimulus (drive) being reduced as a consequence of some response. Drive reduction following a response reinforces that response. Fear is classified as an extremely important learned drive, and anxiety is a form of fear in which the stimulus source of the fear is obscured. According to Dollard and Miller, the stimulus source of the fear becomes obscured from conditions of neurotic conflict. Conflict over the expression of basic needs (e.g., dealing with feelings, toilet and sex training) develops into intense anxiety. Anxiety proneness is thus the result of intense conflict in early life. Unfortunately, their trend toward relating anxiety to empirical psychology never went beyond analogue studies with rats.

Existentialists: Kierkegaard and Heidegger

Existentialists (e.g., Kierkegaard, 1944; Heidegger, 1963) include among their discourses on man some discussion of the concept of anxiety. Anxiety is not the sole topic of existential philosophy nor is existential thought absolutely necessary in a discussion of anxiety. Yet the existential viewpoint is somewhat unique, interesting, and representative of a nonempirical approach.

Kierkegaard (1944) believes that man is different from all other animals in that he faces "possibilities." Man is caught between freedom and the necessity to make his life what he will and, at the same time, his capability of being acutely aware of the possibilities for freedom. Actualizing certain possibilities is the goal and man strives for this by reflecting on his situation, confronting his options, selecting and realizing his responsibility for the selection of possibilities. According to Kierkegaard, anxiety is in the gap that exists between comprehending the possibilities and the choice which leads to actualization of these possibilities. Kierkegaard (1944) states that anxiety "is to be found in the movement from 'I might' to 'I will and am responsible for'" (p. 38). He continues to describe anxiety as the self-awareness of the possibility of freedom, ..."anxiety (dread) is freedom's reality as possibility for possibility" (p. 38).

Kierkegaard appears somewhat unique among anxiety theorists by noting that anxiety is necessary for personal growth. On the other hand, he is consistent with other anxiety theorists in distinguishing between fear and anxiety. Kierkegaard writes that in fear there is a definite object and a direction to move to avoid it, but in anxiety the object is unclear and the person's reaction is nondirectional. Thus, the person is anxious about uncertainty.

Heidegger's writings about anxiety are concerned with his notion of man's being, called "Dasein," and the typical modes of being of Dasein. Anxiety and fear are both dispositional modes of being and affective states. While Heidegger does not explicitly distinguish between dispositional and affective states, he did contrast fear and anxiety. According to Heidegger (Richardson, 1963), fear is concerned with a specific entity whereas anxiety

is not any being within the world at all, nor is it injurious in any determined or determinable way, nor is it here nor there nor anywhere (p. 72).

Fear and anxiety are both uncomfortable for the individual, but fear is object related while anxiety is related to the meaninglessness of the world. Indeed, the existential philosophy has a literary quality. However, the messages of Kierkegaard and Heidegger have not been clarified theoretically nor evaluated scientifically.

Drive Theory: Taylor

Janet Taylor (Spence) is most noted for her research efforts on anxiety as a drive. The central role assigned to anxiety as a drive has been as a personality variable in a series of investigations concerned with learning and conditioning in the Hullian (1943) framework. Taylor (1953), by operationalizing the notion of anxiety in the Manifest Anxiety Scale (MAS), played a major part in the enhancement of a systematic evaluation of individuals differing in level of anxiety. Taylor considers anxiety as an important drive and, therefore, individuals differing in level of anxiety should also differ in drive level. This conceptualization led to much research with humans dealing with Hull's concept of drive.

Within the drive theory it was assumed that the dominant response, that response with the greatest habit strength, has the greatest probability of occurrence under conditions of drive or anxiousness. This assumption led researchers to speculate about the effects of anxiety on the performance of intellectual tasks. Hypotheses generated from the Taylor-Spence theory stated (1) high anxious subjects should perform better than low anxious subjects when the dominant response is correct, and when the dominant response is incorrect, low anxious subjects would be initially expected to be superior in performance; (2) anxiety should facilitate simple task performance and interfere with complex tasks. Evidence for (Spence, 1964; Goulet, 1968) and against (Wiener, 1959; Maltzman, Eisman, and Morrisett, 1961; Pyke and Agnew, 1963) these hypotheses with adults have been found. Indeed, the drive theory approach to anxiety stimulated much research. Unfortunately, this research was conducted without making a state-trait conceptualization which is discussed further in a later section.

Physiology of Anxiety

Cannon, as early as 1916, discussed the interaction of the cerebral cortex and the adrenal medulla in various control pathways in the genesis of anxiety (Hoch and Zubin, 1964). More recently, Selye (1950, 1956) developed the role of the pituitary-adrenocortical axis in the body's response to the stress of anxiety. While these men have made significant contributions to our understanding, there is still an apparent sense of disagreement among the various physiological theorists. What has been chosen to be presented here incorporates the areas of general agreement in the literature, and yet, the fact that diverse variables have been hypothesized to function within anxiety is noted.

Generally speaking, when the cerebral cortex perceives threat or stress it sends a message which starts a series of complex body reactions. The hypothalamus, with its ascending and descending pathways, is considered to mediate emotional expression including anxiety (Gutman and Benson, 1971). The hypothalamus stimulates the anterior pituitary to secrete adrenocorticotrophin. Adrenocorticotrophin is related to the release of cortisol which initiates the process of glycogenolysis and also the mobilization of free fatty acids. The hypothalamus also has direct connection with the adrenal medulla and can stimulate a release of the catecholamines, epinephrine and norepinephrine, into the blood stream. The autonomic nervous system (ANS) is involved also with hypothalamic functioning. Stimulation of the sympathetic division of the ANS causes the release of norepinephrine while parasympathetic activation causes the release of acetylcholine. The complex body reactions stated here are considered to be related to an individual's perception of threat.

The body reacts to the perceived threat and subsequent hypothalamic activation. The internal processes provide the skeletal musculature with a large blood supply, the heart beats faster and stronger, and blood is shunted from the skin. The increased heart rate further directs blood and nutrients to the skeletal muscles. The individual finds himself in a state of arousal.

The symptomatology of the chronically or acutely anxious patient appears related to the above mechanisms. The fast pulse (and sometimes palpitations) is related to increased heart rate activity and circulating epinephrine. The sweating is related to the shunting of blood from the skin, and tremors are related to activation of the skeletal muscles.

At this point, the physiology of anxiety has a quality of definitiveness. However, while there does appear to be considerable agreement on the role of the hypothalamus (Guyton, 1971; Lader, 1974), the adrenals (Kendall and Mikulka[1] Mason, 1968), the cerebral cortex, the autonomic nervous system, the pituitiary gland (Lader, 1974), and circulating catecholamines (Gentry and Williams, 1975; Edmondson, 1972; Lader, 1974) in the experience of anxiety, there are numerous hypothesized relationships which as yet are not sufficiently supported.

Interestingly, the physiology of anxiety is similar to that of fear. They are said to share similar physiological manifestations and are generated by similar mechanisms. It is the recognition, or lack of recognition, of the threat or danger which is distinguishing between the two for the physiologist. Researchers in the area of physiology and emotion have realized the complexity of emotional phenomena and have decided, justifiably, to study individual emotions. Indeed, specificity is the desired trend if we are to advance our understandings. Presently, our knowledge about the emotional state of anxiety and related bodily reactions is rapidly growing.

Operant Theory: Skinner

Although some writers have called B. F. Skinner atheoretical, his efforts to understand behavior through operant procedures does entail a theoretical point of view. Skinner's (1972) notions about behavior are quantitative and deal with aspects of the rate of a behavior. Thus, Skinner would posit quantitative properties of anxiety.

Perhaps the two main properties of anxiety are that (1) it is an emotional state, resembling fear (a conditioned emotional response), and (2) the stimulus which initiates the emotional state does not precede or accompany the state but is "anticipated" in the future. The operant theorist believes that behavior is lawful and thus the "anticipation" of anxiety can be explained.

An anxiety response is defined as a reaction to a stimulus. The response, however, is not to the stimulus itself but to the history of that stimulus preceding a second stimulus condition (an aversive stimulus). The first stimulus signals that the second stimulus condition is approaching which initiates the anxiety state. While the second condition is being anticipated, a change in the rate of behavior can be

---

[1] Kendall, P.C., and Mikulka, P.J. The effects of noise stress on the physiology of mice. Paper presented at the Southeastern Psychological Association Convention, New Orleans, April, 1973.

observed and this change is indicative of anxiety. In considering anxiety as a change in the rate of performance, the operant theory of anxiety is clearly operational and consequently subject to verification.

Operant theory can be said to have influenced a great deal of present-day psychological research including the area of anxiety. Initially, the efforts to substantiate the operant approach used the animal analogue approach. More recently, operant theory has been successfully translated into treatment procedures for anxious individuals. The precision of measurement within the operant theory and the subsequent adaption to treatment have been valuable advances.

Factor-analytic Theory: Cattell

Cattell's lifelong work with factor analysis, and anxiety in particular, has been quite productive. Most noteworthy are the advances in the definition of anxiety (Cattell and Scheier, 1958; 1961) through the operation of factor analysis. Cattell (1966) describes the history of confused research on anxiety as being the result of an inability to discover, define, and measure the anxiety or anxieties which may exist. His undertakings have clarified the research on anxiety and greatly advanced our definition of the term.

Cattell and Scheier (1958, 1961) have made successful use of both P technique (use of one's. individual's scores on a set of different measures with comparisons for different occasions) and d-R technique (use of a large number of individuals measured twice, factoring the difference scores) in the examination of anxiety. P technique has shown how manifestations of anxiety vary within an individual, showing patterns across individuals which are best described in terms of the anxiety state. Factoring difference scores between occasions for a large number of subjects, d-R technique, produces a common pattern roughly similar to averaging the patterns of individuals. Cattel questions whether this anxiety is different from or anything more than the frozen measurement of an anxiety state. Scheier and Cattell (1962) investigate such a notion by retesting individuals over various time intervals and report a sufficient stability coefficient (.8 for 2–4 weeks) to attest to the idea of *more* than a frozen state, perhaps the anxiety *trait*.

Cattell and Scheier (1961) applied multivariate techniques to phenomenological and physiological variables and found that variables contributing to their state factor have different loadings on their trait factor. These authors hypothesized that it should be possible to assess both state and trait anxiety from a single personality questionnaire. Indeed, Cattell and Shceier are to be credited with contributing the state-anxiety/trait-anxiety distinction.

The factor analytic approach has provided a valuable advance in the study of anxiety by distinguishing between anxiety "states" and anxiety "traits." Research efforts which preceded this conceptual distinction (e.g., early work with the Manifest Anxiety Scale and Children's Manifest Anxiety Scale was frought with related problems.

State-Trait Theory: Speilberger

Thorne (1966) considers personality states as cross-sections of life that exist at a given moment in time. In contrast to the transitory nature of personality states, personality traits are considered as enduring individual tendencies or predispositions to react in a certain way.

Much of the equivocal evidence and related controversy concerning research on anxiety is considered to be the result of the conceptual ambiguity of the term. Cattell and Scheier's (1961) identification of "state" and "trait" anxiety has been vital to the advancement of our understanding. Indeed, Spielberger (1966; 1972) considers the controversy and confusion within the anxiety literature to be a result of the failure of most investigators to distinguish conceptually and empirically between the state and trait anxiety constructs.

In most previous investigations, "anxiety" denoted a transitory condition (a state) in some reports and a description of an individual difference in a predisposition to respond in an anxious fashion (a trait) in still others. Spielberger has attempted to clarify this distinction by specifying the characteristics of both state and trait anxiety. Spielberger (1966) conceptualizes state anxiety as the emotional reaction

consisting of unpleasant, consciously perceived feelings of tension and apprehension, with associated activation or arousal of the autonomic nervous system (p. 29).

In addition to anxiety states, Spielberger (1966) contends that individuals differ on a dimension of anxiety proneness — the individual's anxiety trait — which he describes as

differences between individuals in the probability that anxiety states will be manifested under circumstances involving degrees of stress (p. 15).

Spielberger goes on to describe traits as reflecting the frequencies and the intensity with which certain emotional states have been manifested in the past, as well as in the future.

The state-trait theory of anxiety is firmly based upon the conceptual framework of anxiety states (A-State) and anxiety traits (A-Trait). Within the state-trait theory, anxiety is part of a process that is initiated by internal or external stimuli that are perceived as threatening by the individual. The major task of researchers in anxiety, according to Spielberger (1972), is to

describe and specify the characteristics of stressor stimuli that evoke differential levels of A-State in persons who differ in A-Trait (p. 39).

The state-trait theory states that persons high in trait anxiety tend to perceive a larger number of situations as dangerous or threatening than persons who are low in trait anxiety, and they are expected to respond to threatening situations with state anxiety elevations of greater intensity. Essentially, Spielberger views trait anxiety as the measure to indicate anxiety proneness, and from which predictions of state anxiety reactions can be made. Indeed, the state-trait distinction and its related theory has advanced our conceptualization of anxiety.

Multidimensional Trait Anxiety Theory

What is suggested by the term multidimensional is that trait anxiety is many faceted, that the various facets or dimensions can be identified, and that the dimensions are, for the most part, respectably unrelated to each other. Identification of the specific dimensions is thus an important function of research. Likewise, establishing measuring instruments for each trait dimension and testing their independence are equally important.

The recent interaction model of anxiety (Endler, 1975; Shedletsky and Endler, 1974) is one multidimensional trait anxiety theory. It is basically derived from the rationale which was used to develop the original S-R Inventory of Anxiousness (Endler, Hunt and Rosenstein, 1962) and its revisions (Endler and Okada, 1975). These authors contend that the tendency to exhibit a particular personality trait is dependent upon four factors: (1) the situation, (2) the number and type of responses, (3) the response intensity and duration, (4) the provocativeness of the situations in arousing specific responses (Endler et al., 1962). The major point that consider each source of variability — i.e., individual differences, the responses that characterize anxiety, and the *situations* which are likely to arouse anxiety reactions. Endler and Hunt (1966) provided support for the relative importance of the sources of variability examining the amount of variation accounted for by each of the sources. That data, basically a reanalysis of the Endler et al. (1962) study, suggested that the variations were most accounted for by the person by situation interaction. It is the person by situation contribution to the variance which portrays the interaction model.

Recently, Endler (1975) has viewed the situational component as *vital* for predicting state anxiety reactions. This position is clear when he states

if one wants to examine the interaction of physical threat and A-Trait on state anxiety, it is necessary to assess physical danger A-Trait independent of other facets of A-Trait (Endler, 1975, p. 161).

Although not explicit in the term *multidimensional trait anxiety (MTA),* an important premise within MTA theory is that of a state-trait relationship. The state-trait relationship is essentially similar to that of state-trait theory with one exception; trait anxiety is multidimensional and not unidimensional. MTA theory and state-trait theory agree that subjects high in trait anxiety will show greater state anxiety reactions under stress than will subjects low in trait anxiety. Where MTA theory differs from state-trait theory is in the specificity of the trait measure needed to make the differential state predictions. While state-trait theory would use one trait measure as a predictor of state anxiety, MTA theory postulates the need for a trait measure which is consistent or congruent with the particular stress under investigation. For example, subjects differing on a specific trait measure of *concentration* anxiety should show differential state reactions in an attention or short-term memory task while subjects differing on an overall, unidimensional measure of trait anxiety may not.

83

Regarding the theories of anxiety discussed thus far, most have dichotomized, or at least separated, fear and anxiety (the noted exceptions are the physiology of anxiety and the operant approach). MTA theory contends that fear and anxiety are not as dissimilar as some past theories would suggest. The traditional fear/anxiety distinction can be capsuled as follows: fear is stimulus specific; anxiety is nonspecific. Yet, if state anxiety reactions can be predicted from specific stress-related trait anxiety measures, as MTA theory states, the nonspecificity of anxiety could indeed be questioned. That is, the anxiety trait would no longer be properly conceived of as unrelated to any stimulus or stimulus condition, but rather as a disposition which has specifiable precursors.

Throughout the theories of anxiety that have been considered there is the consistent notion of anxiety being related to stress of impending danger. Notwithstanding that earlier conceptualizations of anxiety have been confused by the failure to recognize and utilize the distinction between states and traits, the global term *anxiety* has been regarded as part of a stress system. MTA theory contends that individuals do indeed experience anxiety as stress related, and their reported subjective feelings of anxiety are stress related. Indeed, it is the stress-related nature of the feeling and report of anxiety that links the predictions of differential state reactions to stress-related measures.

Consider the individual who, throughout his life, has done moderately well in school but has consistently disappointed his parents. Each time this individual arrives at school for an examination he becomes stressed and finds himself becoming quite anxious. It is likely, after years of school, that the trait of evaluation anxiety would be high, and a state anxiety reaction in an evaluation setting would be predicted. On the other hand, the individual would not necessarily be expected to get anxious before dental surgery where an evaluation would be absent. Measuring the level of an individual's trait anxiety must therefore take into account the nature of the situation or stress.

Clearly the most current theoretical approach to the study of anxiety, multidimensional trait theory has a short history and an open future. By including the valuable state-trait distinction, and by specifying the trait according to situation, the multidimensional trait theory appears to have incorporated two valuable ideas into its framework. With assessment tools that are designed along the multidimensional-trait anxiety theoretical approach, much should be clarified.

Summary

Anxiety has been discussed from many theoretical viewpoints in its psychological history. Due to the pervasiveness of anxiety there is hardly a global psychological theorist who has not written about it. Having considered these varied theories, some general points are noteworthy. First, a theory should provide an impetus to empirical verification, and when theories lack a measurement device they do not fulfill this need. Thus, theories which have not been examined scientifically are still theories and will always be theories. Second, little attention has been directed toward a theory of anxiety in children. Implicitly, it can be assumed that the concept of anxiety is similar for both children and adults. Is this the case? Hopefully, the summary of our research efforts will provide empirical information from which some conclusions can be drawn.

ANXIETY MEASUREMENT

Despite the early interest in anxiety, the term appeared primarily in clinical practice and nonempirical publications until the 1950s. Several explanations for this fact have been offered. For example, Levy (1961) suggests that the increased use of the term *anxiety* in experimental research closely parallels the development of instruments to measure it. On the other hand Spielberger (1966) suggests that the increased interest in anxiety since 1950 represents the increased and renewed interest in anxiety as an emotion. Whatever the cause of this increase, it has been remarkable. Spielberger (1966) presents the results of a search of *Psychological Abstracts* for the use of the term *anxiety*. By 1963 the percentage of studies relating to anxiety has increased eightfold over the number in 1930.

Certainly the introduction of Taylor's (1953) Manifest Anxiety Scale helps to stimulate interest in anxiety since it helped to operationalize the construct and thus permitted the investigator to evaluate the role of anxiety in psychological phenomena. In order to aid in the investigation of anxiety in children, Casteneda, McCandless, and Palermo (1956) introduced the Children's Form of the Manifest Anxiety Scale (CMAS). The CMAS consists of forty-two anxiety items and eleven additional items which constitute a Lie scale. Children are required to indicate whether or not an item is true of them.

Spielberger (1973) developed the State-Trait Anxiety Inventory for Children (STAIC) as a research tool for the study of anxiety in elementary school children. Relfecting Spielberger's conceptualization of anxiety, the STAIC is composed of two separate self-report scales for measuring state anxiety (A-State) and trait anxiety (A-Trait). The STAIC A-State scale contains twenty statements that require the child to report how he feels at a *particular moment in time.* On the other hand, the STAIC A-Trait scale contains twenty statements that require the child to report how he generally feels.

The remainder of this chapter reports the result of a research program conducted at the Virginia Treatment Center for Children into the nature and measurement of anxiety in emotionally disturbed children in residential treatment. Each study has involved the Children's Manifest Anxiety Scale (CMAS) and/or the State-Trait Anxiety Scale for Children (STAIC). The group of studies presented represents approximately three parts of research in the area and reflects the development of our conceptualization about anxiety in children.

RESEARCH FINDINGS

Reliability

One of the first tasks required when any phenomenon is being investigated is the determination of how reliably the instrument measures that phenomenon. Does the instrument yield consistent scores on the same individual when retested? At the beginning of our project, the CMAS was the only instrument we were considering. A review of the literature indicated that reliability with normal children ranged from .65 to .86. However, no known investigation of its reliability with emotionally distrubed children was available. Our first study (Finch, Montgomery, and Deardorff, 1974a) involved a test-retest investigation of the reliability of the CMAS with emotionally disturbed children. At the beginning and end of a three-month period thirty children in residential psychiatric treatment were individually administered the CMAS. Since many of the children had difficulty reading, it was decided that the test should be read to all children. This practice has been employed in all of our subsequent research. The mean raw score on the anxiety portion of the CMAS was 22.33 with a standard deviation of 9.94 on the initial administration and 23.67 with a standard deviation of 9.68 on the second. The resulting correlation was highly significant (r=.77; $p < .001$) and the t-value between the means of the first and second administration nonsignificant. For the Lie scale of the CMAS the mean raw score was 2.97 with a standard deviation of 2.30 on the initial administration and 2.43 with a standard deviation of 2.65 on the second. Again the resulting correlation was significant (r=.80; $p < .001$) and the t-value nonsignificant. These results were felt to indicate that the CMAS yields a reliable measure with emotionally disturbed children.

At approximately the middle of the three-month period of the CMAS reliability study the STAIC was published. Reliability data for the STAIC scales was reported by Spielberger (1973) to be moderate while the internal consistency of these scales was good for normal children. However, no data were available for emotionally disturbed children. Therefore in Finch, Montgomery, and Deardorff (1974b), thirty emotionally disturbed children were administered the STAIC at the beginning and end of a second three-month period. The mean raw score on the initial A-State scale was 36.03 (82nd percentile) with a standard deviation of 9.90 and 34.06 (75th percentile) with a standard deviation of 9.90 on the second administration. The test-retest correlation was significant (r=.63; $p < 0.2$) and the t-value nonsignificant. The A-Trait mean raw score was 4.90 (73rd percentile) with a standard deviation of 8.93 on the initial administration and 42.77 (77th percentile) with a standard deviation of 8.79 on the second. Again the correlation coefficient was significant (r=.44; $p < 0.2$) and the resulting t-test nonsignificant. Measures of internal consistency for the two scales were good.

Despite indicating good internal consistency of both the STAIC A-State and A-Trait scales, there were certain differences between the results obtained with emotionally disturbed children and those found with normal children. A-State Anxiety was more reliable with emotionally disturbed children than was A-Trait anxiety while the opposite was true for normal children. Finch, Montgomery, and Deardorff (1974b) suggested that some difference between the experiencing and/or reporting of anxiety in these two populations might be responsible.

Following these investigations, it was felt that both measures of anxiety in children (CMAS, STAIC) were reliable enough to be acceptable for further study. Given the acceptability of the reliability of the two scales, some indication of their respective validity was felt to be essential.

Validity

The most important aspect of any psychological test is its validity. Does the test actually measure what it purports to measure? One of the problems with a hypothetical construct such as anxiety is defining how to determine validity since the actual level of anxiety is primarily a private event. Montgomery and Finch (1974) reasoned that since high levels of anxiety are generally associated with emotional disturbance, children in residential psychiatric treatment should obtain significantly higher levels of anxiety than children in public schools with no known history of emotional disturbance. Likewise, since both the CMAS and STAIC (A-Trait) reportedly measure the same construct, there should be a high correlation between scores on these measures. They administered both the STAIC and CMAS to a group of sixty emotionally disturbed and sixty normal children matched on sex and mental age. They found that the emotionally disturbed group obtained significantly higher scores on A-State, A-Trait, and CMAS anxiety than did the normal group while the normal group obtained a significantly higher score on the CMAS Lie scale. These findings tend to support the validity of the anxiety scales for children.

In order to determine the ability of the scores obtained on these anxiety scales to correctly identify the individuals with emotional disturbance, Montgomery and Finch (1974) established optional cutoff scores for the CMAS, A-State, and A-Trait anxiety scales as well as a score obtained by combining the two STAIC scores. With these optional cutoff scores they were able to correctly identify 62% of the emotionally disturbed group with the CMAS, 65% with the A-State, 63% with the A-Trait, and 65% with the two STAIC scores combined while misclassifying 33%, 29%, 37%, and 35% of the normals respectively. The authors interpreted their results as supporting the validity of the CMAS and STAIC.

Montgomery and Finch (1974) support the validity of the STAIC and CMAS scales in general but the validity of the STAIC A-State and A-Trait scales also rests on the ability to reflect changes in momentary (A-State) anxiety changes while A- Trait remains unchanged. In order to evaluate the effects of psychological testing on A-State and A-Trait anxiety in emotionally disturbed children, Sitarz[2] varied the degree of structure of the test and whether or not the examiner was present while the child took the test. She found that A-State remained constant during all conditions while A-Trait increased during an unstructured test with the examiner absent. These results are in contrast to Newmark, Nelson, Newmark, and Stabler (1975) who found variations in A-State but not A-Trait with normal children. Sitarz[2] suggests that the emotionally disturbed children might have had difficulty with the conceptualization of anxiety required by the STAIC (i.e., the now "state" and the in general "trait") or that the emotionally disturbed children might differ in their experiencing of anxiety.

In order to determine further the sensitivity of the STAIC to changes in anxiety, Finch, Kendall, Montgomery, and Morris (1975) assigned thirty-six emotionally disturbed children to either a failure group, a failure plus ego-involving instructions group, or a test-retest control group. The actual task was a series of anagrams ranging from difficult to impossible. These authors found a significant increase in both A-State and A-Trait Anxiety. They hypothesized that emotionally disturbed children might have been unable to distinguish between state and trait anxiety; that is, the emotionally disturbed children's feelings at any given moment (state) superseded his previous history of feelings (trait) and thus both A-State and A-Trait were vulnerable to situational stress. Another possibility is that personality traits are not as firmly established in emotionally disturbed children.

Our investigation into the validity of both the CMAS and STAIC continues. It would appear that both are effective in discriminating between high and low anxious subjects. However, whether the A-State portion of the STAIC varies as a function of situational stress while the A-Trait portion remains constant, as it is supposed to, seems to be seriously in question with emotionally disturbed children.

Behavior Correlates of Anxiety

The next portion of our research was designed to investigate those behaviors which are associated with anxiety. These studies represent a mixture of interests and are tied together only by their looking at some form of behavior in relation to anxiety.

In the first study Deardorff, Finch, and Royal (1974) reasoned that children who bite their fingernails would be expected to endorse more anxiety items than children who do not. In order to test this hypothesis they administered the CMAS to 90 seventh- and eighth-grade children and then examined their fingernails to determine if they were bitten. They found no difference in anxiety scores between the nails bitten/not bitten groups. The results were considered in terms of other

---

[2] Sitarz, A.M. Effects for psychological testing on state-trait anxiety in emotionally disturbed children. Unpublished master's thesis, Virginia Commonwealth University, 1974.

possible causes of nail-biting behavior such as repressed hositility and in terms of the population employed (lower socioeconomic status as opposed to middle-class children).

Finch and Nelson (1974a) investigated the relationship between anxiety and locus of conflict with emotionally disturbed children. Locus of conflict refers to the type of behavioral manifestation which results in the child being called emotionally disturbed. In internalization of conflict, the main conflict is between impulses and their inhibitions. Subsequently behaviors are rigidly controlled, and the child experiences subjective discomfort. In externalization of conflict, the conflict is between the child's actions and the reactions that they bring about in others. The behavior manifestations are freely discharged into the surrounding environment and society suffers. Previous factors in analytic work (Quay, 1972) had suggested that internalization of conflict should be more closely associated with anxiety than externalization of conflict.

To test this hypothesis with emotionally disturbed children, Finch and Nelson (1974a) individually administered the CMAS and STAIC to fifty children and had their special education teachers complete ratings on locus of conflict. These authors found no significant relationship between either internalization of conflict or externalization of conflict and anxiety. They postulated that with extremely anxious populations, such as emotionally disturbed children, the relationship might break down. However, they did find some interesting differences between males and females. That is, boys were rated as exhibiting more internalization of conflict, more externalization of conflict, and more maladjustment than did girls. However, girls reported more anxiety on the CMAS and the A-Trait portion of the STAIC. These findings were interpreted as providing some indication as to why more boys are referred for psychiatric treatment than girls. While the behavioral manifestations of disturbances in boys are more pervasive and obvious, emotionally disturbed girls reported more subjective anxiety.

In order to extend the body of research on the relationship between locus of conflict and anxiety, Nelson, Kendall, Finch, Kendall, and Nelson (1974) individually administered the STAIC and CMAS to fifty-four delinquents in a state training school and obtained ratings on locus of conflict from their teachers. Again neither CMAS nor A-Trait anxiety were significantly related to locus of conflict. However with this delinquent population A-State anxiety was significantly related to internalization of conflict. The authors suggest that with delinquents internationalization of conflict is more related to fluctuating situational anxiety than to stable individual differences in anxiety proneness.

As with emotionally disturbed children, it was found that boys were rated as exhibiting more internalization and externalization of conflict as well as more maladjustment than girls. Likewise girls again reported more subjective anxiety than boys. As in the previous study, relatively high anxiety scores were obtained and the authors suggested that these may have served to erode the relationship.

Nelson, Finch, Kendall, and Gordon[3] investigated the relationship between anxiety and locus of conflict with normal children. Sixty-three public school children were administered the CMAS, and locus of conflict ratings were obtained from their teachers. They found that both internalization and externalization of conflict as well as the total maladjustment index were correlated with CMAS anxiety but not with A-Trait anxiety. A-State anxiety correlated only with the total maladjustment index. They did not find any significant difference between boys and girls in either their anxiety scores or their ratings. These findings suggest that high levels of anxiety were significantly related to locus of conflict and maladjustment, as rated by the child's teacher, but that there were no differences between normal boys and girls in their self-reported anxiety or in their rated locus of conflict and maladjustment. Thus, it would appear that anxiety is related to internalization and externalization of conflict as well as maladjustment with normal children but that with high anxious groups (i.e., emotionally disturbed and delinquent) this relationship tends to be eroded.

Several theories have suggested that personal space, the spacing that humans and animals maintain between themselves and others, is a function of anxiety. High anxious individuals would be expected to require more space between themselves and another individual than would low anxious people according to this position. In order to test this hypothesis, Kendall, Deardorff, Finch, and Graham, (in press) obtained STAIC anxiety measures on twenty emotionally disturbed and twenty normal boys and then obtained in vivo personal space measures. Interestingly, they found that emotionally disturbed boys require significantly more personal space than do normals but that anxiety was not related to personal space requirements. Kendall et al. (in press) state the need for additional research in this area before a definite conclusion about these findings can be made.

Another area which has been reported to be related to anxiety is locus of control. Locus of control refers to whether the individual perceives both positive and negative outcomes as contingent on his own behavior — i.e., internally controlled — or the result of luck, fate, or other individuals — i.e., externally controlled. Previous research with adults suggested that a feeling of lack of control over the environment and the outcome of one's actions (external locus of control) was associated with anxiety. Finch and Nelson (1974b) investigated whether locus of control was associated with anxiety in a group of emotionally disturbed children. They administered two measures of locus of control and two measures of anxiety (CMAS and STAIC) to a group of children in residential treatment. Anxiety, as measured by the CMAS, was significantly related to external locus of control on the two measures but neither A-State nor A-Trait portions of the STAIC were significantly related to locus of control. These results would suggest that with

---

[3] Nelson, W.M., III; Finch, A.J., Jr.; Kendall, P.C.; and Gordon, R.H. Anxiety and locus of conflict in normal children. Unpublished manuscript, Virginia Treatment Center for Children, 1976.

emotionally disturbed children a feeling of not being in control of what happens to oneself is related to anxiety, at least as measured by the CMAS. Why the A-State and A-Trait measures of anxiety were not related to locus of control is difficult to determine but may suggest some difference in the type of anxiety measured by the CMAS and STAIC.

In this section we have examined various correlates of anxiety. In summary, we have determined that whether or not an individual bites his fingernails is not related to his level of anxiety; whether an emotionally disturbed child acts out his symptoms or internalizes them is not related to his anxiety level; with delinquents, internalization of conflicts is associated with A-State anxiety; with normal children anxiety is significantly related to both internalization and externalization of conflict as well as the total maladjustment index; personal space requirements are not related to anxiety in either emotionally disturbed or normal children; and an external locus of control is related to anxiety as measured by the CMAS.

Factor Analytic Investigations

Since several investigators have argued that anxiety is a multidimensional construct rather than a unitary one, Finch, Kendall, and Montgomery (1974) subjected the responses of 245 children to the CMAS to one principal components factor analysis using an indirect oblimin oblique rotation. They found three anxiety factors and two Lie factors. Factor I was called *Anxiety: Worry and Oversensitivity* and composed of six items from the anxiety portion of the CMAS which were related to excessive worry and the tendency to allow one's feelings to be hurt with the slightest provocation. Factor II was called Lie: *Social Impeccability* and composed of six items from the Lie portion of the CMAS which were related to those perfect characteristics which at best are only closely approximated by even the "best behaved" child. Factor III was called *Anxiety: Physiological* and composed of five items from the anxiety portion which were related to physiological processes such as swallowing, digestion, bowel movements, and breathing. Factor IV was called *Anxiety: Concentration* and composed of four items from the anxiety portion of the inventory which were related to distractibility and uncertainty. The fifth factor, called *Lie: Over Self-Control,* was represented in three items from the Lie portion which reflect an ability, again which is at best only approximated, to maintain self-control.

Finch, et al. (1974) conclude that the three anxiety factors correspond to the types of anxiety manifestations encountered in clinical practice and that the distinction between them is valid. They continue by stating that different predictions would be made as to the behavioral manifestation exhibited by subjects scoring high on various of these factors. We will return to a consideration of this point in a later portion of this paper when we discuss the effects of anxiety on higher mental processes.

After having contrasted the findings of Sitarz[4] and Finch et al. (1975) (that A-Trait also may vary as a function of stress with emotionally disturbed children) with those of Newmark et al. (1975) and Spielberger (1973), who reported only A-State changes with normal children, Finch, Kendall, and Montgomery (in press) asked to what extent is one entitled to interpret scores on a particular inventory as reflecting the same construct for different subject groups, especially when one group is a "disturbed" one. In order to determine if a qualitative difference exists between anxiety in emotionally disturbed and normal children and in order to further investigate the state-trait distinction, Finch et al. (in press) compared the factor structure of the STAIC for a group of emotionally disturbed children with that obtained with a group of normal children.

For the emotionally disturbed group four factors were obtained with two of the factors containing only A-State items while the other two contained A-Trait items. The two A-State factors accounted for significantly more variance than the two A-Trait factors.

For the normal group six factors were obtained with two of the factors containing only A-Trait items while four factors contained only A-State items. There was no significant difference in the amount of variance accounted for by the A-Trait and A-State factors with normal children.

Finch et al. (in press) conclude that their results support the state-trait anxiety distinction since in neither of the analyses did A-State and A-Trait items load on the same factors. In addition they stressed the importance of considering the subject population being employed when discussing the state-trait distinction and related research since it would appear that in addition to a quantitative difference, a qualitative difference from various subject groups may affect the construct or internal structure of the particular inventory and thus could affect the resulting scores. Also, they state that the greater amount of variance accounted for by state factors for emotionally disturbed children suggests that traits are not firmly established with this group. On the other hand, with normal children an equal amount of variance was accounted for by state and trait factors. This difference quite possibly accounts for many of the differences in the results of our work with emotionally disturbed children and that of other investigators with normal children.

In comparing the results of the factor structure of the CMAS with the STAIC, certain differences and similarities are evident. Since the CMAS is a trait measure of anxiety, it should have more in common with the A-Trait portion of the STAIC which the results showed. The two A-Trait factors obtained with emotionally disturbed children as well as the two with the normal group have many very similar items to those found on the three CMAS factors. It is apparent that a very similar construct should be inferred from the answers to these items. However, it is obvious that the CMAS is a more multidimensional measure of trait anxiety than is the

---

[4] Sitarz, A.M.

A-Trait portion of the STAIC. The CMAS has more of the items that loaded on the *Physiological* factor and the *Concentration* factors while the A-Trait is primarily composed of items similar to the *Worry* and *Oversensitivity* factor. One direction which our present research is taking is attempting to make differential predictions based on scores obtained on the various factors. One such study will be reported later in this paper.

Anxiety and Higher Mental Processes

The studies in this section deal with the relationship between anxiety and higher mental processes. Specifically, achievement, short-term memory, and verbal learning were explained in relation to anxiety with various degrees of success.

Finch, Montgomery, Kendall, and Nelson[5] investigated the relationship between anxiety and academic achievement in emotionally disturbed children in three separate studies. In their first one they individually administered the STAIC and standard achievement tests to forty-one children. Previous research with normal children suggested that a negative correlation exists between anxiety and achievement. However, they failed to find a significant relationship between either A-State or A-Trait and academic achievement.

In their second study they individually administered the CMAS and standard achievement tests to thirty-seven emotionally disturbed children. With the CMAS they found the predicted inverse relationship between anxiety and achievement with higher anxiety scores corresponding with lower achievement scores.

In the third study they speculated that, based on previous findings, emotionally disturbed children may have difficulty conceptualizing anxiety along a continuum as was required by the STAIC. They modified the STAIC to a true-false format, administered this modified STAIC and standard achievement tests to a group of forty-five emotionally disturbed children, and found no significant relationship between achievement and either A-State or A-Trait anxiety.

They concluded that some difference exists between the type or nature of anxiety as measured by the CMAS and the STAIC. For example, the CMAS is a multidimensional measure of trait anxiety while the STAIC trait measure is not. If there were no differences one would have anticipated a similar relationship between achievement and anxiety as measured by both scales. Finally, the importance of being aware of how anxiety is being measured when discussing anxiety and its relationship to the other variables was stressed.

Finch, Anderson, and Kendall (in press) investigated the relationship between anxiety and short-term memory as measured by a digit span task. Previous research had suggested that with adults digit span performance was more significantly

---

[5] Finch, A.J., Jr.; Montgomery, L.E.; Kendall, P.C.; and Nelson, W.M., III. Anxiety and academic achievement in emotionally disturbed children. Unpublished manuscript, Virginia Treatment Center for Children, 1976.

related to A-State anxiety. However, Finch et al. (in press) reasoned that if the *Anxiety: Concentration* factor obtained from the factor analysis of the CMAS was valid, an inverse relationship between scores on this factor and digit span performance would be expected. They administered the entire CMAS and a digit span task to thirty-eight emotionally disturbed children. Subjects were divided into high and low groups according to their scores on the CMAS and each of the three anxiety factors Worry and Oversensitivity, Physiological, and Concentration), and their performance on the digit span task were compared. Specifically, it was predicted that high and low groups would not differ for the total CMAS score or the *Worry and Oversensitivity* and *Physiological* factor scores. However for the *Concentration groups,* it was predicted that the high group would obtain significantly lower scores than the low group. Their findings were as predicted and the results were interpreted as supporting the validity of the *Concentration* factor and as supporting a multidimensional theory of trait anxiety.

Finch, Kendall, Dannenburg, and Morgan[6] investigated the anxiety-producing effects of learning a difficult versus an easy list of nonsense syllables as a function of age in a group of thirty emotionally disturbed children. They employed one list (difficult) composed of randomly selected three-letter nonsense syllables from a list of zero percent meaningfulness and another list (easy) composed of randomly selected three-letter nonsense syllables from a list of one-hundred percent meaningfulness. Children were presented each of the two lists ten times and asked to learn them. Measures of A-State and A-Trait were obtained before the presentation of the list and then immediately after the completion of that list. They found a decrease in A-State anxiety following the easy list and an increase following the difficult list for the older children but no difference in changes in anxiety according to list difficulty for the younger group. Analysis of actual performance data added clarity to these findings. While the older group made significantly higher scores on the easy list than on the difficult one, there was no difference for the younger group. For the younger children both lists were equally difficult. In fact the task was almost impossible for them and all the young children's scores were very low. Finch et al.[6] conclude that their findings indicate a success experience (easy list with older children) successfully reduces anxiety while failure on a task which is perceived as possible (difficult list with older children) results in an increase in anxiety. On the other hand failure on a task perceived as impossible (both easy and difficult list with younger children) has no effect on one's anxiety level.

---

[6] Finch, A.J., Jr.; Kendall, P.C.; Dannenburg, M.; and Morgan, J.R. The effects of task difficulty on anxiety of different aged emotionally disturbed children. Unpublished manuscript, Virginia Treatment Center for Children, 1976.

SUMMARY AND CONCLUSIONS

What have we learned about anxiety in emotionally disturbed children from all of this research? The most important conclusions that we can draw is that, when talking about anxiety in children, the exact population employed and the exact way anxiety is being measured definitely should be stated. Our research has raised many questions along these lines. The results we have obtained with emotionally disturbed children have differed considerably from those other investigators have found with normal children. A-State anxiety was more reliable than A-Trait; A-Trait varied rather than A-State in response to an unstructured psychological test with the examiner present; both A-State and A-Trait anxiety increased as a function of failure; A-State and A-Trait anxiety were related to internalization and externalization of conflict as well as the total maladjustment index with normals but not with emotionally disturbed children; and the factor structure of the STAIC varied as a function of the population employed. Likewise, our findings tended to vary as a function of which instrument was employed; A-State anxiety was significantly correlated with internalization of conflict with delinquents while neither A-Trait nor CMAS anxiety were related; internal locus of control was significantly negatively correlated with CMAS anxiety but not with either A-State or A-Trait anxiety; CMAS anxiety was significantly negatively correlated with achievement but neither A-State nor A-Trait were; and digit span was significantly influenced by *Anxiety: Concentration* scores from the CMAS but not by the total CMAS score or scores on any of the other factors. We feel these results clearly illustrate the need to carefully specify both the population being employed and the instrument being used when discussing anxiety in children.

How do our findings contribute to the various theories of anxiety discussed earlier? Unfortunately, most of the theories regarding anxiety are low on verifiability and do not generate predictions which can be tested readily; therefore, it is not possible to make conclusive statements about their viability. In addition, the same results are sometimes interpretable by different people as both supporting and not supporting a certain theory. Furthermore, most theories of anxiety are derived from work with adults and all of our research has been with children. Despite these difficulties we feel that our findings tend to add support to some aspects of certain theories while generating certain new information which needs to be incorporated.

First, the conceptualization of anxiety "states" and "traits" was an important advance for both theory and research. The dichotomy of these anxiety constructs has been supported in work with normal and emotionally disturbed children. However, the sensitivity of the A-State scale to transient feelings and the utility of the A-Trait measure as an indication of a relatively inflexible anxiety proneness are supported with normal but not with emotionally disturbed children. In addition, "state anxiety" appears more important for the emotionally disturbed children. Despite the questionable nature of states and traits in emotionally disturbed children, the state-trait theory has been both a theoretical and psychometric advance for the study of anxiety.

Second, the assumption that the anxiety trait is unidimensional would appear tenuous. Several of our research findings suggest that the anxiety trait is multidimensional and that these various dimensions can be isolated and identified. In addition, there is evidence to support the validity of the separate dimensions of trait anxiety. The most promising theory in the study of anxiety in children at this time is a multidimensional trait approach which accepts the state-trait distinction. That is, subjects with the predisposition to respond in a certain fashion (trait) can be organized into trait classes. These trait classes represent the multidimensional nature of trait anxiety. A trait class such as *Concentration* anxiety includes the predisposition to anxiety in condition of immediate memory, focusing thoughts, or paying careful attention. On the other hand, a *Worry and Oversensitivity* trait class includes predispositions to be self-depreciating and easily upset. Yet another trait class, physical threat, might be said to include the individual's tendency to become anxious under conditions such as waiting for the dentist, avoiding rough athletics, or shock avoidance.

The trait classes are a most promising advance for the study of anxiety in children. They allow subjects to be measured for each trait class and thus enhance predictions regarding subsequent behavior. It is suggested that careful measurement of a given trait class will augment the predictions of anxiety states. Although stating the population being investigated remains an important issue, assessing trait classes may clarify the dilemma of anxiety measurement.

Our research efforts within the area of anxiety in children have dealt with reliability, validity, behavior correlates, factor analyses, and the role of anxiety in higher mental processes. These investigations have clarified our understanding of the phenomena and of the children involved in the projects. At this point we are interested in originating a research program designed to examine various methods of treatment for anxious children. With an understanding of the phenomena in question, with some information concerning its antecedents and consequences, and with appropriate methodologies, the evaluation of the efficacy of treatments for anxious children should prove beneficial.

REFERENCES

Castaneda, A.; McCandless, B.R.; and Palermo, D.S., The children's form of the manifest anxiety scale. *Child Development,* 1956, *27 ,* 317–326.

Cattell, R.B., and Scheier, I.H., The nature of anxiety: A review of 13 multivariate analyses comparing 814 variables. *Psychological Reports,* Monograph Supplement, 1958, *5,* 351–388.

Cattell, R.B., and Scheier, I.H., *The meaning and measurement of neuroticism and anxiety.* New York: Ronald Press, 1961.

Cattell, R.B., Patterns of change: Measurement in relation to state-dimension, trait change, liability and process concepts. *Handbook of multivariate experimental psychology.* Chicago: Rand McNally, 1966.

Deardorff, P.A.; Finch, A.J., Jr.; and Royall, L.R., Manifest anxiety and nail-biting. *Journal of Clinical Psychology,* 1974, *30,* 378.

Dollard, J., and Miller, N., *Personality and psychotherapy.* New York: McGraw-Hill, 1950.

Edmondson, H.D., Biochemical evidence of anxiety in dental patients. *British Medical Journal,* 1972, *4* 7–9.

Endler N. S.; Hunt, J. McV.; and Rosenstein, A. J., An S-R Inventory of Anxiousness. *Psychological Monographs,* 1962, *76,* No. 17 (Wole No. 536), 1–33.

Endler, N. S., and Hunt, J. McV., Sources of behavioral variance as measured by the S-R Inventory of Anxiousness. *Psychological Bulletin,* 1966, *65,* 336–346.

Endler N. S., and Okada, M., A multidimensional measure of trait anxiety: The S-R Inventory of General Trait Anxiousness. *Journal of Consulting and Clinical Psychology,* 1975, *43,* 319–329.

Endler N. S., A person-situation interaction model for anxiety. In C. D. Spielberger and I. G. Sarason (Eds.), *Stress and anxiety* (vol. 1). Washington, D. C.: Hemisphere Publication (Wiley), 1975.

Finch A. J., Jr., Anderson, J.; and Kendall, P. C., Anxiety and digit span performance in emotionally disturbed children. *Journal of Consulting and Clinical Psychology* (in press).

Finch A. J., Jr.; Kendall, P. C.; and Montgomery, L. E., Multi-dimensionality of children's anxiety: Factor structure of the Children's Manifest Anxiety Scale. *Journal of Abnormal Child Psychology,* 1974, *2,* 331–336.

Finch A. J., Jr.; Kendall, P. C.; and Montgomery, L. E., Qualitative difference in the experience of state-trait anxiety in emotionally disturbed and normal children. *Journal of Personality Assessment* (in press).

Finch, A. J., Jr.; Kendall, P. C.; Montgomery, L. E.; and Morris, J., Effects of two types of failure on anxiety in emotionally disturbed children. *Journal of Abnormal Psychology,* 1975, *84,* 583–585.

Finch, A. J., Jr.; Montgomery, L. E.; and Deardorff, P. A., Children's Manifest Anxiety Scale: Reliability with emotionally disturbed children. *Psychological Reports,* 1974, *34,* 658. (a)

Finch, A. J., Jr., Montgomery, L. E.; and Deardorff, P. A., Reliability of state-trait anxiety with emotionally disturbed children. *Journal of Abnormal Child Psychology,* 1974, *2,* 67–69. (b)

Finch A. J., Jr., and Nelson, W. M., III, Anxiety and locus of conflict in emotionally disturbed children. *Journal of Abnormal Child Psychology,* 1974, *2,* 33–37. (a)

Finch A. J., Jr., and Nelson, W. M., III, Locus of control and anxiety in emotionally disturbed children. *Psychological Reports,* 1974, *35,* 469–470. (b)

Freud S., *Collected papers* (vol. 1). London: Hogarth Press, 1924.

Freud, S., Introductory lectures on psychoanalysis (quoted text written in 1927). In the *Standard edition of the complete psychological works of Sigmund Freud,* (vol. XVI). Translated by James Strachey. London: Hogarth Press, 1963.

Gentry, W. D., and Williams, R.B., *Psychological aspects of myocardial infarction and coronary care.* St. Louis: C. V. Mosby, 1975.

Goulet L. R., Anxiety (drive) and verbal learning: Implications for research and some methodological considerations. *Psychological Bulletin,* 1968, *69,* 235–247.

Gutman W., and Benson, H., Interaction of environmental factors and systemic arterial blood pressure: A review. *Medicine,* 1971, *50,* 543–570.

Guyton, A. C., *Textbook of medical physiology.* Philadelphia: Saunders, 1971.

Hall C. S., *A primer of Freudian psychology.* New York: World Publishing, 1954.

Hall C. S., and Lindzey G., *Theories of personality.* 2nd ed. New York: 1970.

Heidegger M., *Being and time* (translated from Seih and Zeit, Erste Halfte, Jahrbuch fur Philosophic and Pehnomenologische Forschung, vol. viii [1927], pp. 1–438, by John Macquarrie and Edward Robinson). New York: Harper & Row, 1963.

Hoch, P. H., and Zubin, J., (Eds.) *Anxiety.* New York: Hafner Publishing, 1964.

Horney, K., *New ways in psychoanalysis:* New York: Norton, 1939.

Hull, C. L., *Principles of Behavior.* New York: Appleton, 1943.

Kendall, P. C. ; Deardorff, P. A.; Finch, A. J., Jr.; and Graham, L., Proxemics, locus of control anxiety and type of movement in emotionally disturbed and normal children. *Journal of Abnormal Child Psychology* (in press).

Kierkegaard, S., *The concept of dread* (original text written in 1844 translation, with introduction by Walter Lowsie). Princeton: Princeton University Press, 1944.

Lader M., The peripheral and control role of the catecholamines in the mechanism of anxiety. *Internation Pharmacopsychiatry,* 1974, *9,* 125–137.

Levy, L. H., Anxiety and behavior scientist's behavior. *American Psychologist,* 1961, *16,* 66–68.

Maltzman, I.; Eisman, E.; and Morrisett, L., Rational learning under manifest and induced anxiety. *Psychological Reports,* 1961, *8,* 357–366.

Mason, J.W., A review of psychoendocrine research on the sympathetic adrenal medullary system. *Psychosomatic Medicine,* 1968, *30,* 631–645.

Montgomery, L. E., and Finch, A. J., Jr., Validity of two measures of anxiety in children. *Journal of Abnormal Child Psychology,* 1974, *2,* 293–298.

Nelson, W. M., III; Kendall, P. C.; Finch, A. J., Jr.; Kendall, M. S.; and Nelson, S. B., Anxiety and locus of conflict in delinquents. *Journal of Abnormal Child Psychology,* 1974, *2,* 275–279.

Newmark, C. S.; Nelson, D.; Newmark, L.; and Stabler, B.,Test-included anxiety with children. *Journal of Personality Assessment,* 1975, *39,*409–413.

Pyke, S., and Agnew, N., Digit span performance as a function of noxious stimulation. *Journal of Consulting Psychology,* 1963, *27,* 281.

Quay, H. C., Patterns of aggression, withdrawal, and immaturity. In H. C. Quay and J. S. Werry (Eds.) *Psychopathological disorders of childhood.* New York: Wiley, 1972.

Richardson, S. J. Wm., *Heidegger: through pehenomenology to thought.* The Hague: Martinus Nijhoff, 1963.

Scheier, I. H., and Cattell, R. B., *The IPAT 8-parallel form anxiety battery.* Champaign, III.: IPAT, 1962.

Selye, H., *The Physiology and Pathology of Exposure to Stress.* Montreal: Acta, 1950.

Selye, H., *The Stress of Life.* New York: McGraw-Hill, 1956.

Shedletsky, R., and Endler, N. S., Anxiety: The state-trait model and the interaction model. *Journal of Personality,* 1974, *42,* 511–527.

Skinner, B. F., *Cumulative record.* New York: Appleton-Century-Crofts, 1972.

Spence, K. W., Anxiety (drive) level and performance in eyelid conditioning. *Psychological Bulletin,* 1964, *61,* 129–139.

Spielberger, C. D., The effects of anxiety on complex learning and academic achievement. In C. D. Spielberger (Ed.), *Anxiety and behavior.* New York: Academic Press, 1966.

Spielberger, C. D., Anxiety as an emotional state (ch. 2). In C. D. Spielberger (Ed.), *Anxiety: Current trends in theory and research* (vol. I). New York: Academic Press, 1972.

Spielberger, C. D., *Preliminary manual for the State-Trait Anxiety Inventory for Children ("How I Feel Questionnaire").* Palo Alto, Calif.: Consulting Psychologists Press, 1973.

Taylor, J. A., A personality scale of manifest anxiety. *Journal of Abnormal and Social Psychology,* 1953, *48,* 285–390.

Thorne, F. C., Theory of the psychological state. *Journal of Clinical Psychology,* 1966, *22,* 127–135.

Wiener, G., The interaction among anxiety, stress instructions, and difficulty. *Journal of Consulting Psychology,* 1959, *23,* 224–228.

MODELS OF HYPERACTIVITY

Gerald Harris, Stephen Pollack and Ben Williams

Introduction

Hyperactivity is one of the most prevalent childhood disorders. Estimates vary from 3% to 20%, but the most likely overall rate is between 5% and 7% of the elementary school age population (Cantwell, 1975; Stewart, 1973; Huessey, 1967). The large range of these incidence figures may be partly attributable to actual differences in the populations surveyed. Unsystematically varying populations would result in widely divergent estimates of prevalence. A second factor in the reported variance could be inconsistency in the definition or measurement techniques of hyperactivity. Different diagnostic criteria or methods of investigation will also affect such estimates. For example, they tend to be higher with teacher ratings than with direct observation of behavior (Kenney et. al., 71), and these methods typically use somewhat different criterion behaviors. Even the most conservative estimates, however, suggest that hyperactivity is a cause for concern to many parents, teacher, and professionals.

While it is generally agreed that hyperactivity is a problem of considerable proportion, there is no consensus as to how it should be conceptualized. Some investigators view hyperactivity as a non-specific symptom which can occur in many different medical and behavioral disorders, such as mental retardation, brain injuries, and emotional disturbance (eg. Ney, 74, Howell et. al. 72). From this viewpoint, hyperactivity can have a variety of possible etiologies. Hyperactivity can also be considered the "core" symptom of a hyperactive behavior disorder (eg. Dubros and Daniels, 1966). In this case, hyperactivity may be the major presenting symptom, but other symptoms often accompany it, such as short attention span and impulsivity. This class of inappropriate behaviors is typically considered to be caused, or at least maintained, by a variety of social and non-social factors. Other investigators, often those who approach the phenomena from a medical perspective, see hyperactivity as one major symptom of a specific symdrome. (eg. Clements, 1966; Wender, 1971; Stewart, et. al., 1966). This viewpoint suggests a specific etiology for the hyperactive behavior and those symptoms associated with it. Research to date has not resolved the discrepancies between the above viewpoints, and they continue to be associated with different approaches to the investigations and management of hyperactivity.

The degree of confusion in conceptualizing hyperactivity does not extend to the clinical descriptions of a hyperactive child. In fact, there is remarkable agreement on the most common, and most central, behavioral manifestations. These are high levels of sustained motor activity, distractibility, short attention span, impulsivity, and poor academic performance in spite of normal or above intelligence (eg. Werry,

1972). Other frequently reported symptoms include emotional liability, poor peer relationships, low self-esteem, and anti-social behaviors (Clements, 1966; Laufer and Denhoff, 1957; Safer and Allen, 1976). Although the specific pattern of symptoms may vary from child to child, these are considered characteristic of hyperactives in general.

Children who are judged to exhibit significant quantity or frequency of the above symptoms are likely to be referred for professional help. In the case of a preschool age child, the parents are typically the referring agents and the clinician is usually a pediatrician. Extreme overactivity and impulsivity are often of more concern at this age than are attentional difficulties. By the time a child reaches school age, his ability to attend and to inhibit behavior becomes more important. The majority of hyperactives are identified at this time, primarily because of difficulties in school. Although the parents may be the referring agents, they usually do so at the urging of school officials. Elementary school teachers, who have both the experience and the opportunity to do so, are often the first to identify the hyperactive child (Harlin, 1972). Identification within the school setting is more likely to result in referrals to child guidance clinics or other non-medical agencies, although medical treatment of some sort is still most often applied.

Current estimates are that at least 150,000 children are being given stimulants for behavior or learning problems (Sroufe, 1975). Some of the issues concerning the appropriateness and effectiveness of the medical management of hyperactivity will be examined later, within the context of the medical model. A second class of treatments often used for hyperactivity involves behavior modification. The use of these techniques to change the child's behavior and cognitive functioning will be discussed in the behavioral and cognitive sections. There is some support for the short-term effectiveness of these treatments, but the long term outlook for hyperactives is still not good. Early investigators of hyperactivity felt the child would "outgrow" his symptoms as he matured into adolescence (Laufer and Denhoff, 1957; Bradley, 1957; Bakwin and Bakwin, 1966; Eisenberg, 1966). While it is true that activity level often decreases with maturity (Shaffer, et al, 1975; Cromwell, Baumeister, and Hawkins, 1963), follow-up studies indicate that hyperactive children are prone to develop other significant psychological and behavioral abnormalities.

Adolescence appears to be a particularly difficult time for the hyperactive. Activity level may be diminished, but other problems, such as disorders of attention and chronic underachievement, remain (Weiss, Minde, and Werry, 1971; Laufer, 1962). Difficulties in school continue to plague the adolescent previously labeled hyperactive. One study (Hoy, Weiss, Minde, and Cohen, 1972) attempted to determine the causal factors of such poor academic achievement. They compared hyperactive and normal children's performance on tests requiring a variety of academic skills. Their results suggested that hyperactives can perform as well as normals under optimal conditions, but not in non-optimal everyday situations. Douglas (1974) has reported results which support this contention. In addition to academic difficulties, psychological problems are also prominent in adolescence. Several studies (Anderson and Plymate, 1962; Weiss, Minde, and Werry, 1971; Mendelson, Johnson, and Stewart, 1971; Huessey, Metoyer, and Townsend, 1974) have reported finding low self-esteem, anti-social behavior, agressiveness, and depression. These, and other studies, also report greater than average legal trouble, peer and family relation problems, and psychiatric institutionalization.

The clinical picture is not as clear in adulthood but still looks poor. There is some evidence for continued psychological and behavioral problems, but the scarcity of follow-up data, and some conflicting results, leave many questions unanswered. The first long term follow-up of hyperactive children (based on retrospective diagnosis) resulted in rather pessimistic findings (Menkes, et al 1967). Although some of the subjects were self-supporting, several were institutionalized, or had been for psychiatric problems. There were still symptoms of neurological abnormality, restlessness, and distractibility. Other research (Morrison and Stewart, 1971; Cantwell, 1972) suggests that hyperactivity in childhood may be a precursor of some psychiatric disorders in adulthood. Their findings indicate that hyperactivity bears a familial relationship to the adult disorders of alcoholism, hysteria, and sociopathy. Cantwell (1975) suggests that hyperactives may be at risk for these types of problems. It must be emphasized, however, that more research is needed in order to make any definitive statements about the adult status of hyperactives. In particular, the effect of treatment on long term prognosis is uncertain. The lack of specification of treatment variables, and the heterogeneity of subjects, in the follow-up studies done to present prevents the determination of long-term treatment effects.

The major issue confronting hyperactivity researchers today is subject selection. As mentioned previously, the term hyperactivity is used to denote a wide variety of children. Terms such as Minimal Brain Damage, Minimal Brain Dysfunction, Learning Disabled, and Hyperkinetic Behavior Disorders are often used interchangeably. Considered under these labels are children who have known brain damage, mental retardation, specific learning disabilities, and primary emotional disturbance, as well as children who exhibit no etiologically suggestive factors. This heterogeneity hinders the generalization of research findings beyond the specific group studied. Many professionals have recognized this problem (Wender, 1971; Bax and MacKeith, 1963; Cantwell, 1975), and have called for a delineation of homogenous hyperactive subgroups.

Attempts to define distinct subgroups have not fared well. Etiology is the most frequent basis for separating hyperactives. Many of the earlier studies emphasized an organic-nonorganic dichotomy (Still, 1902; Cruickshank, et al, 1961). Bender (1953) posited three etiological subgroups; constitutional, organic, and environmental. Chess (1960) proposed four categories of hyperactives, and others have suggested divisions into several classes (Ney, 1974; Lesser, 1970; McMahon, et al, 1970). However, research is scarce in this area and there is relatively little convincing evidence for specific subgroups within hyperactivity (Langhorne, 1976).

The following sections will examine hyperactivity from the viewpoint of the three major approaches, the medical, behavioral and cognitive. The theoretical orientation of each model will be discussed in relation to its application to assessment or diagnosis, considerations of etiology, and management of hyperactivity. While each model has been derived from the available literature, in practice most professionals integrate some components from each, and so would not subscribe to one particular model.

The Medical Model

The medical community has traditionally dominated both theoretical and practical work in the area of hyperactivity. The earliest investigations of hyperactivity are attributed to an English pediatrician, Still (1902). The three cardinal features of today's medical view of hyperactivity are essentially identical to those introduced by Still. He emphasized the diagnosis of hyperactive children (although he described them as children with "defects of moral control") based on etiological factors. He considered the major causes to be physiological in nature, resulting from either brain damage or brain dysfunction in the absence of demonstrable injury or lesion. Regardless of etiology, Still's choice of treatment was medication and hospitalization. These components of Still's work; emphasis on diagnosis, internal etiology, and medication, continue to be central to the medical approach to hyperactivity.

The medical diagnosis of hyperactivity is typically comprised of four steps. The first is an interview with the parents and with the child. During the interview it is important to note whether there were difficulties in birth, or other early signals of possible brain damage, and if there is evidence of hyperactive behavior dating back to the child's early years. Indications for the various symptoms associated with hyperactivity from either the parents or child are also important. Behavior checklists or rating scales, such as the Conners (1960) Teacher Questionnaire, may be used to determine what symptoms the child displays in the classroom. Report cards are useful in determining whether academic performance is low, and to suggest the presence of learning disabilities, often considered a diagnostically positive sign. A physical exam should be essentially normal, although there may be some minor physical anomolies, such as widely spaced eyes or a curved fifth finger (Waldrop and Haverson, 1971; Rapaport, et al, 1974). A neurological exam is often given in order to detect major or minor neurological abnormalities. Thus, the medical diagnosis of hyperactivity depends in large part upon evidence of brain damage or brain dysfunction.

Research linking hyperactive behavior to actual brain damage began in earnest soon after Still's early theorizing. Some investigators (Ebaugh, 1923; Rosenfeld and

Bradley, 1948) reported hyperactivity resulting from damage to the brain sustained during severe illness or injury. Studies of adults with head injuries, and ablation studies with animals (French and Harlow, 1955) also supported brain damage as a causal factor. However, there still remained a large group of hyperactives who did not demonstrate any brain damage. To accommodate these children, the concept of minimal brain damage or dysfunction was proposed (Tregold, 1908; Smith, 1926; Clements, 1966). Several studies appeared to support the concept of minimal brain damage by relating hyperactivity to mild neurological, perceptual, and sensory-motor abnormalities, or histories suggestive of brain damage (Burks, 1960; Rosenfeld and Bradley, 1948; Laufer et al, 1957; Werry, Weiss, and Douglas, 1964). However, the neurological significance of minor abnormalities is contentious (Wender, 1971). Also, as Werry and Sprague (1970) point out, the results of several studies which began by diagnosing subjects as brain damaged by neurological signs do not show hyperactivity to be any more frequent in the brain damaged group than in the control group. Results are much the same with regard to histories suggestive of brain damage. In contrast to the studies mentioned above, some investigators (Stewart, et al, 1966; Schacter and Apgan, 1959) have found no difference between normal and hyperactive groups in the number of historical events that would indicate a possibility of brain damage. Thus, there is no firm evidence at present for brain damage as the major etiological factor in hyper-activity.

There is more support for an internal etiology based on genetic factors. Although a specific analysis of the interaction between environment and genetic predispositions may be impossible (Omenn, 1973), research has suggested that genetic factors play an important part in the origin of hyperactivity. Two studies (Cantwell, 1972; Morrison and Stewart, 1971) indicate hyperactivity to be a familial disorder. They do not however, answer the question of whether trans-mission is genetic or environmental. Twin studies should be more effective in deter-mining the genetic component of transmission, but the one twin study using diagnosed hyperactive children (Lopez, 1965) is generally considered uninterpret-able due to sex differences in the monozygotic and dizygotic twin pairs (Omenn, 1973). Other twin studies have demonstrated a substantial genetic component to activity level (Willerman, 1973; Vandenberg, 1962; Scarr, 1966). Adoption studies (Morrison and Stewart, 1973; Safer, 1973) have supported the argument for a hereditary factor in hyperactivity which works in combination with environmental factors. Wender (1971) and Morrison and Stewart (1973) propose a polygenetic mode of transmission, which seems to account for the available data. This mode of transmission implies that the hyperactive child is born with a genetic predisposition, and the specific outward manifestations will depend on the environmental factors he encounters. Morrison and Stewart (1973, 1973a) reported some findings to support the hypothesis of polygenetic transmission. In sum, there is some very suggestive evidence for the importance of genetic factors in hyperactivity. However, metholdological weaknesses in existing research, and the absence of critical segregation and linkage studies still leave room for question.

Stimulants are the most popular medication for hyperactivity. For example, a survey of the public schools in Baltimore County in 1973 revealed that 59% of the children receiving medication were taking Ritalin (methylphenidate) and 29% were taking Dexedrine (Dextroamphetamine) (Krager and Safer, 1974). One theory concerning the action of stimulants is that hyperactive children are underaroused anatomically, and are thus unable to inhibit movement and attending to inappropriate stimuli (Sroufe and Stewart, 1973). Stimulants are believed to increase the arousal of the inhibitory system and thus allow the child to inhibit and control his behavior. There is little experimental evidence to support this view of a paradoxical effect. Available evidence indicates that rather than calming the child, stimulants prompt more appropriate and well integrated responses in settings characterized by high demands for compliance (Conners, 1972; Werry, 1968; Werry and Sprague, 1970). A more recent theory, in line with the previous findings, is that stimulants work on hyperactive children much as they do on adults. They increase motivation and the ability to concentrate, and reduce the effects of such factors as fatigue (Sroufe and Stewart, 1973; Weiss and Laties, 1962). Additional evidence showing that hyperactive children on stimulants are not less active in informal settings supports this contention (Ellis et al, 1974; Whalen, and Henker, 1976).

Stimulants have been proven to have potent short-term experimental effects that are seen as beneficial by clinicians, parents, and teachers (Sroufe, 1975; Clements, 1966; Sroufe and Stewart, 1973). Both social behavior and performance on various laboratory tasks are enhanced. Increases are seen in attention span, perception, motivation, the ability to inhibit responding, accuracy, and motor steadiness. Decreases are noted in response latency, variability of response time, impulsivity, and irrelevant behavior in task performance settings. Unfortunately, there is a lack of reliable data concerning the effects of stimulants on problem solving, reasoning, and non-rote learning. There is also an absence of studies on long-term effects, despite the questions raised over possible side effects of stimulants. The only investigations relevant to long term effects are some early follow-up studies which indicate a poor outcome for hyperactives treated primarily with drugs (Weiss, et al, 1971; Mendelson, et al, 1971).

Apart from effectiveness, the major issues in drug treatment are possible side effects, problems in discontinuing medication, and the possibility of state dependent learning. Since stimulants are the most widely used class of drugs, there is considerable information concerning their negative side effects (Whalen, and Henker 1976; Sroufe, 1975). The most common side effects at low dosage levels (.2 to .5 mg/kg) are insomnia, loss of appetite, increased heart rate and blood pressure, irritability, and sadness. At higher dosage levels (.6–1.0 mg/kg) side effects may include stomach aches and suppression of height and weight gain (Safer, et al, 1972; Safer and Allen, 1973). The side effects seen at lower dosages often seem to disappear after a few days or weeks (Eisenberg, 1972), but those resulting from higher dosages may not. Suppression of body growth is potentially very serious, but recent work (McNutt, 1976) has indicated that there may not be any differences in growth between hyperactives on medication and those that are not. The issue is not settled however, since there is evidence that amphetamines do affect the release of growth hormone (Sroufe and Stewart, 1973).

Cessation of stimulant drug intake does not produce physical withdrawal in children or adults when dosages have been kept at maintenance levels. There may be some increase in lethargy and need for sleep (Small et al, 1971) but these effects do not appear to be very strong or persistent. Behavioral gains are typically not maintained, however, when the drug is discontinued. This has often been pointed out as evidence of the drugs effectiveness. Post-drug treatment is considered to be comparable to the third phase of a behavioral ABA single case research design and thus a demonstration of the child's need for medication in order to behave appropriately. However, a more recent theory suggests that regression upon discontinuation may be evidence of behavioral dependence (Sroufe, 1975). In other words, the child has learned that he is expected to behave correctly only when he has taken the drug.

The issue of state dependent learning is also relevant to the medical treatment of hyperactivity. The central question is whether children will retain, in a non-drug condition, things they have learned in a drug condition. Current research on animals and adults suggests that some habits learned under drugs do not carry over to non-drug states (Sroufe and Stewart, 1973). Whether or not this happens in children using drugs prescribed for hyperactivity is still questionable. Some studies with children using Ritalin and Mellaril have shown no evidence for state dependent learning on laboratory tests of short term memory, paired associate learning, and motor performance (Sprague and Sleator, 1973). However, Sprague, et al, (1970) report an unpublished study which did show "less remembering" in children when transferring from a drug (Ritalin) condition to a non-drug condition. As is the case with many other issues concerning drug treatment, a lack of research does not allow the drawing of any definite conclusions.

In summary, medical treatment has been shown to improve some types of behavior. Serious questions remain, however, concerning the relation of these improvements to actual academic and social performance, the long term outcome of treatment, and the possibility of serious negative side effects. These issues are critical to the proper use of drugs in treating hyperactive children, and the present lack of knowledge dictates some caution.

The Behavioral Model

The behavioral view of hyperactivity is based on traditional learning theory. The primary assumption is that deviant behavior is learned and/or maintained through the mechanism of environmental contingencies. Behaviors are seen as lawful phenomena, which can be predictably controlled without reference to hypothetical internal variables. The main features of the behavioral view are the emphasis on observable behavior, and the use of a scientific methodology in assessing, manipulating, and evaluating changes in behavior. Assessment in this model focuses on observable behavior in the natural setting. There are three primary methods of obtaining data on the child's behavior. The first and most popular is rating scales or behavioral checklists, such as Conners Teacher Rating Scale or Parent Rating Scale (1969, 1970). These scales are simple, take little time to complete, and give fairly detailed information about the child's behavior, as seen by parents or teachers. Direct observation of the child's behavior is another mode of assessment often used. The child is observed in his normal activities, and his behavior is coded according to pre-selected categories (Werry and Quay, 1969). While this strategy is more objective in that a neutral observer can record the frequency and rate of behavior more accurately, it is also more costly and time consuming. Both of these methods use criterion scores of deviant behavior to assess hyperactivity. A third type of measurement, used primarily in research, is mechanical. Several devices have been developed to measure motor activity, one of the most reliable being the stabilimetric chair (Sprague and Topp, 1966). These mechanical measures are limited to a quantitative assessment of behavior however, and so cannot distinguish between appropriate and inappropriate behavior. All of the above have one thing in common, they assess observable behavior.

Behaviors characteristic of hyperactivity can be acquired through reinforcement or observational learning. Since children do differ in activity level in the early days of life (Kessen, et al, 1961), those exhibiting a high activity level might attract more attention from adults. This could strengthen the behavior pattern so that it would occur more frequently in later years. As hyperactive behaviors become more prominent in the child's reportoire, he will more frequently be reinforced for them, by either positive or negative attention. At some point in this process, the child may be identified as hyperactive and referred for special help. Support for the observational learning of hyperactivity comes from the genetic investigations discussed earlier. The findings that parents of hyperactive children were often hyperactive themselves is consistent with a social etiology. Since research has demonstrated that children exposed to active models are themselves more active (Bandura, Ross, and Ross, 1961, 1963; Kaspar and Lowenstein, 1971), it is reasonable to suspect that children raised by active adults would be likely to become unusually active themselves.

Even though mechanisms are known by which hyperactive behavior can be learned, the behavioral view of etiology is not completely incompatible with the idea of internal physical causation. A child could be constitutionally pre-disposed to hyperactive behavior and yet only develop it under the right environmental conditions. However, even if there is a substantial genetic contribution to the development of hyperactivity, it is not at all clear what implications there would be, if any, for treatment programs. The behavioral view is that while original causal factors are neither determinable nor manipulable, present environmental factors are.

Behaviorial treatment is intentionally systematic, though behaviors targeted for change may vary from child to child. The first step in designing a treatment program is to identify and define those behaviors to be changed, the target behaviors. Inadequate or imprecise specification here can make even the most carefully designed program useless. Target behaviors should be selected by consensual agreement, and particular attention paid to ensuring that the behaviors are defined in observable terms. Early behavioral treatments often focused on suppressing the inappropriate behaviors of the child, thus leading to charges that behavior modification was being used to create "zombies" for the benefit of school personnel. Current studies, however, tend to focus on increasing appropriate behaviors, which encourages the use of positive techniques. Both of these goals, increasing appropriate and decreasing inappropriate behavior, can be accomplished by selecting appropriate behaviors to increase that are incompatible with the undesired behaviors. As Mann (1972) points out, it is possible to increase the frequency of a desired behavior, but undesired behavior may continue to operate at a high frequency also unless it is incompatible with the desired behavior. An example of this strategy is reported by Parks (1975), in which the appropriate academic performance of hyperactive children was positively reinforced. Teachers later reported a decrease in hyperactive behaviors incompatible with the children's improved academic performance.

After selecting and defining the target behaviors, observational analyses of the environmental stimuli acting on the child's behavior must be made. Those stimuli, or events, associated with the elicitation of the inappropriate behavior are noted, as well as those which appear to be reinforcing the behavior. For example, the teacher's presence may be an eliciting stimuli for a child's out of seat behavior and her attention the reinforcing event. Natural contingencies must be determined before they can be manipulated in order to gain the desired results.

Selection of a reinforcement scheme is next. Reinforcers are those things which serve to increase behaviors contingent upon them, and may be primary (candy, free play time, etc.) or secondary (points, tokens, etc.). Reinforcement can also result from the cessation or avoidance of negative stimuli, but most argue that punishment should be avoided if possible. Punishment is effective in temporarily suppressing unwanted behaviors, but it may have undesirable side effects, such as emotional reactions or suppression of desirable behavior. In the case of exceptionally obnoxious or dangerous behavior, time out, the absence of any positive reinforcement, is often effective without the side effects of punishment. The scheduling of reinforcements is especially important in hyperactivity since there is some suggestion that these children respond differently than normals (Douglas, 1974, 1975). Continuous reinforcement, with some mild negative feedback, seems to be more advantageous for hyperactives than partial reinforcement or only positive feedback. Consideration should also be given to fading out artificial reinforcers in favor of natural and social reinforcers in order to ensure persistence of the new behaviors.

Those instruments used to assess hyperactivity, such as rating scales, are also used to evaluate treatment effects. The measurements obtained prior to treatment are considered the baseline, or normal behavior for that child. Additional measurements are often taken during and after treatment and allow close tracking of changes in the child's behavior. Changes can thus be instituted in the treatment program at the first signs of failure of the behavior to change in the planned direction.

Considerable research has been done on the effectiveness of behavioral treatment in changing activity level, attentional behaviors, social behaviors, and academic performance (chapter 8). In terms of activity level, it has been shown that significant control can be achieved (Edelson and Sprague, 1974). However, there is some question as to the clinical significance of reduced activity level. Douglas (1974) has found that increases in academic performance may be accompanied by increased activity. Similarly, short term effectiveness in improving attentional behavior has been demonstrated (Patterson, et al, 1965), but questions remain concerning the overall academic significance of the behavior. The effectiveness in shaping social behavior and academic performance also looks promising (Parks, 1975; Hall et al, 1968), although more work is needed in this area. Behavioral techniques may be effective in changing the major behavioral symptoms of hyperactivity, but questions of long term outcome have not been addressed.

Issues related to treatment outcome include the maintenance of the changes in behavior and the generalization of the changes to other than treatment settings. The question of maintenance, or persistence, of behavioral changes has typically not been addressed in behavioral research. Techniques have been proposed to ensure the maintenance of new behavior, but few follow-up studies have actually been carried out. The follow-up studies which have been done are of very short duration. For example, two studies (Frazier and Schneider, 1975; Rosenbaum, O'Leary, and Jacob, 1975) followed up changes in social behavior after a period of approximately one month. Results were positive, but one month is an inadequate time interval for investigating long term maintenance effects.

The issue of generalization has received more research attention, but methodological problems and lack of replication still do not permit the drawing of any firm conclusions. Several studies (Meichenbaum, Bowers, and Ross, 1968; O'Leary, et al, 1968; Walker, Hops, and Johnson, 1974) have failed to show any positive generalization from educational, or institutional, to similar settings. One study (Martin,, 1967) has demonstrated some positive generalization from the home to a school setting, but others (Wahler, 1969; Skinrud, 1972) have not. In fact, there is some evidence to support the concept of behavioral contrast. This refers to the fact that positive behavior changes in one setting may adversely affect behavior in another setting. Several studies have reported such behavioral contrast (Walker, Hops, and Johnson, 1974; Wahler, 1974; Meichenbaum, Bowers, and Ross, 1968; Johnson, Bolstad, and Lobitz, 1974). These studies are by no means conclusive, but the results are certainly interesting, and suggest the need for a more ecological approach to treatment evaluation.

The Cognitive Model

The cognitive approach to hyperactivity is based primarily on studies of cognitive style (Kagan, Moss, and Sigal, 1963; Kagan, et al, 1964; Witkin, et al, 1962) and principles of cognitive control (Gardner, et al, 1959). Emphasis is on the cognitive functioning of the hyperactive child as it relates to academic and social performance. Learning theory provides the techniques by which inefficient information processing behaviors or strategies are changed.

The poor academic performance of hyperactive children has prompted investigations of their intellectual functioning as compared to normals. Early studies supported the idea of difficulty in school for many hyperactives (Clements and Peters, 1962; Laufer, Denhoff, and Riverside, 1957; Laufer, Denhoff, and Solomons, 1957), but did not separate the factors of ability and performance. Data comparing hyperactives with normal children of similar I.Q. level suggest that the hyperactive does not perform at a rate consistent with his I.Q. (Minde, et al, 1971; Cantwell, 1975). Other studies have compared I.Q. levels of normal and hyperactive children and found that hyperactives do not initially have lower I.Q. levels (Burks, 1960; Loney, 1974; Prinz and Loney, 1974) but do after several years in school (Palkes and Stewart, 1972; Miller, Palkes, and Stewart, 1973). Indications are then that hyperactives have a normal intellectual capacity, but are unable to take full advantage of learning situations in school.

Several factors have been postulated to account for these findings. One is that hyperactive children are deficient in their conceptual abilities (Burks, 1960; Clements and Peters, 1962; Rosenfeld and Bradley, 1948). However, two studies that addressed this issue (Friebergs, 1965; Friebergs and Douglas, 1969) found no differences in conceptual ability of hyperactives and normals when attentional factors were held constant.

The inability to inhibit motor behavior has also been proposed as a factor (Patterson, 1965; Doubros and Daniels, 1966). Studies in this area have suggested that hyperactives do exhibit more irrelvant behavior in the classroom, but they do not differ from normals in the overall amount of activity (Schliefer, et al, 1975; Douglas, Weiss, and Minde, 1969; Sroufe, et al, 1973). Additional findings on motor inhibition are that decreases in activity level are not always accompanied by improved concentration or behavior control (Millichap and Boldrey, 1967; Sprague, Werry, and Scott, 1969). In fact, there are indications that improved performance in hyperactives may be related to increased extraneous movement (Cohen and Douglas, 1972).

Investigations of distractibility have proven similarly disappointing. The idea that hyperactive children are more distractible, and thus perform better under minimally stimulating conditions, was developed by Strauss and Lehtinen (1947). Several studies have used this approach in an attempt to improve performance with negative results (Cruickshank, et al, 1961; Haring and Phillips, 1962; Shores and Haubrick, 1969). Further, direct comparisons of hyperactives and controls on distractibility measures have found no differences (Douglas, 1972, 1974; Browning, 1967; Worland, et al, 1973). There is support, however for the idea of improved performance and reduced activity level under highly stimulating conditions (Cleland, 1961; Scott, 1970; Turnure, 1970, 1971; Cromwell, Banneister, and Hawkins, 1963; and Gardner, Cromwell, and Fosher, 1959).

Thus there is little support for the importance of conceptual ability, motor inhibition, or distractibility in the hyperactive's poor performance. The next factors to be considered were attention and impulsivity. These two factors are often observed concurrently (Burks, 1960; Knobel, Wolman, and Mason, 1959; Stewart, et al, 1966) in hyperactive children. Various investigators (Sykes, Douglas, and Morgenstern, 1973; Sykes, et al, 1971) have pointed to the major role and importance of these factors in hyperactivity, and Douglas (1974) presents evidence linking them to the two cognitive styles of reflection-impulsivity (Kagan, et al, 1964; Kagan and Kagan, 1970) and field dependence-independence (Witkins, et al, 1962). These cognitive styles appear to be a good way of conceptualizing the behavioral manifestations of hyperactivity. The dimension of reflection-impulsivity refers to the child's tendency to respond slowly or rapidly when confronted with a problem solving situation in which there is ambiguity due to the possibility of several alternative solutions. Field dependence-independence reflects individual differences in the ability to separate an item from the field in which it is embedded, and the degree to which perception is global or analytic.

Measures of these cognitive styles differentiated hyperactive and normal children, with the hyperactives scoring significantly higher on both field dependence and impulsivity (Campbell, Douglas, and Morgenstern, 1971; Douglas, 1972; Cohen, Weiss, and Minde, 1972). The instrument used in these studies to measure reflection-impulsivity is Kagan's Matching Familiar Figures Test. The reflective pole is characterized by long latencies and few errors on a series of match-to-standard items, while the impulsive pole is reflected in short latencies and more errors. To assess field dependence-independence, the Children's Embedded Figures Test was used. The field dependent child has more trouble overcoming a confusing context when isolating figure from ground than does the field independent, and also tends to perceive things more globally.

In terms of assessment methods, Douglas (1974) has proposed dropping existing diagnostic labels in favor of evaluating children on the basis of attentional and impulse control problems. She envisions the development of a battery of well-standardized, valid, and reliable measures. This battery would probably include those tests which have been shown to discriminate between hyperactives and normals and which are sensitive to drug effects, for example, the MFF and Children's Embedded Figures Tests. Other candidates might be the Continuous Performance Test or the Delayed Reaction Time Test. However, these instruments have not been standardized and further development would be needed to produce a battery such as Douglas describes.

The cognitive view of etiology revolves around information processing behavior. The possibility of a physiological origin of the hyperactive pattern is accepted as is the possibility that learning is the responsible factor. The emphasis, however, is on the current status of the child, and the manner in which his inefficient cognitive functioning interferes with both learning and performance. Like the behaviorists, they feel that hyperactivity can best be treated through the manipulation of external contingencies.

The cognitive treatment of hyperactivity focuses on altering the child's information processing behaviors through learning principles. Three strategies are typically used, reinforcement, direct instruction, and modeling. Reinforcement procedures are often used to effect changes in the indices of cognitive functioning, such as number of errors or response latencies on the MFF. An impulsive child would be rewarded for an increased response latency or for each correct response. Several studies have shown some success in using these methods (Kagan, 1966; Friebergs and Douglas, 1969; Douglas, 1975). Results from these studies also suggest that hyperactive children respond differently to reinforcement contingencies than do normals. Noncontingent reinforcement seems to result in improvement in normal's performance and deterioration in the performance of hyperactives. Contingent reinforcement improves the performance of both groups. Hyperactive children also performed worse under partial reinforcement conditions, and better under continuous reinforcement. Mild negative feedback also appeared to be helpful with hyperactives.

Direct instruction techniques have also been used with some success. This technique involves instructing the child in the use of more efficient cognitive strategies. For example, a child might be instructed to take his time and carefully consider each alternative before responding. One study has used this method to change both latency to response and accuracy scores on a matching-to-standard task (Kagan, et al, 1966).

The use of modeling is the most popular strategy. Effective cognitive strategies are modeled by an adult before the child attempts them himself. The procedure can be varied by having the child also verbalize the correct strategy, and then shifting from overt to covert verbalization across training sessions. This allows the child to internalize the appropriate behavioral controls. Palkes and her colleagues (1968, 1972) have demonstrated that training hyperactives to use self-directed verbal commands results in significant improvement in performance. Other investigators (Meichenbaum and Goodman, 1971; Ridberg, Parke, and Hetherington, 1971) have also shown that training the child to internalize efficient cognitive strategies is both possible and effective in improving performance.

Although these results look promising, there are some methodological and conceptual issues raised concerning cognitive treatments. There is a lack of long term follow-ups in the research, which is unfortunate. There are also problems internal to many research studies to date. For example, Ault and co-workers (Ault, et al, 1976) discuss the methodological problems associated with the use of the MFF Test, which could result in reinterpretation of many findings. Denney, (1972) also raises an interesting conceptual issue. That is, how to determine if there is true cognitive change, as opposed to merely learning task specific behaviors. He suggests some criteria for assuming cognitive change: the ability of the child to explain the changes, persistence of the changes, and generalization of the changes to other stimuli and responses. This issue has not been addressed by other researchers, however, and so remains just an interesting proposal. These issues suggest a need for more systematic research in the area of cognition before any definite conclusions can be drawn as to the validity of the cognitive approach.

Summary

The heterogeneity of the group of children called hyperactive makes any direct comparison of theoretical orientation impossible. Research within and across the models discussed in this paper is difficult to integrate due to the differences in subject selection and other methodological issues. While the perspective of each model may be appropriate for certain subgroups of hyperactive children, there is no research to say what characteristics define those subgroups.

Each of the models has demonstrated some effectiveness in differentiating hyperactives from controls and in treating some of the behaviors associated with hyperactivity. However, none of the models have shown any long term benefits for the hyperactive child, even though hyperactivity has been shown to have serious consequences throughout the child's lifetime.

After considering the present state of knowledge concerning hyperactivity, it appears that any or all of the approaches discussed may be relevant to an individual child. Thus, until future research is able to answer the questions that have been raised, a multi-modal approach to the management of hyperactivity seems to be the only reasonable solution.

REFERENCES

Anderson, C. M., and Plymate, H. B., Management of the brain-damaged adolescent. *American Journal of Orthopsychiatry,* 1962, *32,* 492–500.

Ault, R., Mitchell, C., and Hartmann, D., Some methodological problems in reflection-impulsivity research. *Child Development,* 1976, *47,* 3 227–231.

Bandura, A., Ross, D., and Ross, S. A., Transmission of aggression through imitation of aggressive models. *Journal of Abnormal and Social Psychology,* 1961, *63,* 575–582.

Bandura, A., Ross, D., and Ross, S. A., Imitation of film-mediated aggressive models. *Journal of Abnormal and Social Psychology,* 1963, *66,* 3–11.

Bakwin, H., and Bakwin, R. M., *Clinical management of behavior disorders in children.* Philadelphia: Saunders, 1966.

Bax, M., and MacKeith, R. (Eds.), Minimal cerebral dysfunction. *Little Club Clinics in Developmental Medicine,* 1963, *10,* London: Heineman.

Models of Hyperactivity

Bender, L., *Aggression, hostility, and anxiety in children.* Springfield, Illinois: Thomas, 1953.

Bradley, C., Characteristics and management of children with behavior problems associated with organic brain damage. *Pediatric Clinics of North America,* 1957, *4,* 1049–1060.

Browning, R., Effect of irrelevant peripheral visual stimuli on discrimination learning in minimally brain-damaged children. *Journal of Consulting Psychology,* 1967, *31,* 371–376.

Burks, H. F., The hyperkinetic child. *Exceptional Children,* 1960, *21* (1), 18–26.

Campbell, S. B., Douglas, V. I., and Morgenstern, G., Cognitive styles in hyperactive children and the effect of methylphenidate. *Journal of Child Psychology and Psychiatry,* 1971, *12,* 55–67.

Cantwell, D. P., Psychiatric illness in the families of hyperactive children. Archives of General Psychiatry, 1972, *27,* 414–417.

Cantwell, D. P., (Ed.) *The hyperactive child.* New York: Spectrum, 1975.

Chess, S., Diagnosis and treatment of the hyperactive child. *New York State Journal of Medicine,* 1960, *60,* 2379–2385.

Cleland, C. C., Severe retardation: Program suggestions. Presented to Council on Exceptional Children, Austin, Texas, 1961.

Clements, S. D., *Task Force One: Minimal brain dysfunction in children.* National Institute of Neurological Diseases and Blindness, Monograph No. 3, U. S. Department of Health, Education, and Welfare, 1966.

Cohen, N. J., Weiss, G., and Minde, K., Cognitive styles in adolescents previously diagnosed as hyperactive. *Journal of Child Psychology and Psychiatry,* 1972, *13,* 203–209.

Cohen, N. J., and Douglas, V. I., Characteristics of the orienting response in hyperactive and normal children. *Psychophysiology,* 1972, *9,* 238–245.

Conners, C. K., A teacher rating scale for use in drug studies with children. *American Journal of Psychiatry,* 1969, *126,* 884–888.

Conners, C. K., Symptom patterns in hyperkinetic, neurotic, and normal children. Child Development, 1970, *41,* 667–682.

Conners, C. K., Symposium: Behavior modification by drugs. II. Psychological effects of stimulant drugs in children with minimal brain dysfunction. *Pediatrics,* 1972, *49,* 702–708.

Cromwell, R. L., Baumeister, A., and Hawkins, W. F., Research in activity level. In N. R. Ellis (Ed.), Handbook of mental deficiency. New York: McGraw-Hill, 1963, pp. 632–663.

Cruickshank, W. M., Bentzen, F. A., Ratzeburg, F. H., and Tannhauser, M. T., *A teaching method for brain injured and hyperactive children.* Syracuse, N. Y..: Syracuse University Press, 1961.

Denney, D. R., Modification of children's information processing behaviors through learning: A review of the literature. Unpublished manuscript, 1972.

Doubros, S. G., and Daniels, G. J., An experimental approach to the reduction of overactive behavior. *Behavior Research and Therapy,* 1966, *4,* 251–258.

Douglas, V. I., Weiss, G., and Minde, K., Learning disabilities in hyperactive children and the effect of methylphenidate. *Canadian Psychology,* 1969, *10,* 201–210.

Douglas, V. I., Stop, look, and listen: The problem of sustained attention and impulse control in hyperactive and normal children. *Canadian Journal of Behavioral Science,* 1972, *4,* 259–282.

Douglas, V. I., Sustained attention and impulse control: Implications for the handicapped child. In J. A. Swets and L. I. Elliot (Eds.), *Psychology and the handicapped child.* Washington, D. C.: U. S. Department of Health, Education, and Welfare, DHEW Pub. No. (OE) 73-05000, 1974.

Douglas, V. I., Are drugs enough? — To treat or train the hyperactive child. *International Journal of Mental Healtth,* 1975, *4,* No. 1–2, 199–212.

Ebaugh, F. G., Neuropsychiatric sequelae of acute epidemic encephalitis in children. *American Journal of Diseases of Children,* 1923, *25,* 89–97.

Edelson, R. I., and Sprague, R. L., Conditioning of activity level in a classroom with institutionalized retarded boys. *American Journal of Mental Deficiency,* 1974, *78,* 384–388.

Eisenberg, L., The management of the hyperkinetic child. *Developmental Medicine and Child Neurology,* 1966, *8,* 593–632.

Eisenberg, L., The hyperkinetic child and stimulant drugs. *New England Journal of Medicine,* 1972, *287,* 249–250.

Ellis, M. J., Witt, P. A., Reynolds, R., and Sprague, R. L., Methylphenidate and the activity of hyperactives in the informal setting. *Child Development,* 1974, *45,* 217–220.

Frazier, J., and Schnieder, H., Parental management of inappropriate hyperactivity. *Journal of Beahvior Therapy and Experimental Psychiatry,* 1975, *6,* 246–7.

French, G. M., and Harlow, H. F., Locomotor reaction decrement in normal and brain damaged Rhesus monkeys. *Journal of Comparative and Physiological Psychology,* 1955, *47,* 496–501.

Freibergs, Vaira, *Concept learning in hyperactive and normal children.* Unpublished Ph. D. thesis. McgGill University, 1965.

Freibergs, V., and Douglas, V. I., Concept learning in hyperactive and normal children. *Journal of Abnormal Psychology,* 1969, *74,* 388–395.

Gardner, W. I., Cromwell, R. L., and Foshee, J. G., Studies in activity level: II. Effects of distal visual stimulation in organics, familials, hyperactives, and hypoactives. *American Journal of Mental Deficiency,* 1959, *63,* 1028–1033.

Hall, R. V., Panyan, M., Rabson, D., and Broden, M., Instructing beginning teachers in reinforcment procedures which improve classroom control. *Journal of Applied Behavior Analysis,* 1968, *1,* 215–322.

Haring, N. G., and Phillips, E. L., *Educating emotionally disturbed children.* New York: McGraw-Hill, 1962.

Harlin, V. K., Help for the hyperkinetic child in school. *Journal of School Health,* 1972, *42,* 587–592.

Howell, M. C., Rener, G. W., Scholl, M. L., Towbridge, F., and Rutledge, A., Hyperactivity in children, Types, diagnosis, drug therapy, approaches to management. *Clinical Pediatrics,* 1972, *11,* 30–39.

Hoy, E., Weiss, G., Minde, K., and Cohen, N. J., Characteristics of cognitive and emotional functioning in adolescents previously diagnosed as hyperactive. Unpublished manuscript, McGill University, 1972.

Huessey, H. R., Metoyer, M., and Townsend, M., 8–10 year follow-up of 84 children treated for behavior disorder in rural Vermont. *Acta Paedopsychiatrica,* 1974, *40,* 230–235.

Huessey, H. R., Study of the prevalence and therapy of the choreatiform syndrome or hyperkinesis in rural of Vermont. *Acta Paedopsychiatrica,* 1967, *34,* 130–135.

Johnson, S. M., Bolstad, O. D., and Lobitz, G. K., Generalization and contrast phenomena in behavior modification with children. Paper presented at the Sixth Annual Banff International Conference on Behavior Modification, March–April, 1974.

Kagan, Jerome, Relfection-impulsivity: the generality and dynamics of conceptual tempo. *Journal of Abnormal Psychology,* 1966, *7,* 17–24.

Kagan, Jerome, Moss, Howard, A., and Sigel, I. E., Conceptual styles and the use of affect labels. *Merrill-Palmer Quarterly,* 1960, *6,* 261–276.

Kagan, Jerome, Rosman, B. L., Kay, Deborah, et. al. Information processing in the child: significance of analytic and reflective attitudes. *Psychological Monographs: General and applied,* 78 (1, Whole No. 578), 1964, 1–37.

Kagan, Jerome, Pearson, Leslie, Welch, Lois, The modifiability of an impulsive tempo. *Journal of Educational Psychology,* 1966, *57,* 359–365.

Kagan, J., and Kagan, N., Individuality and cognitive performance. In P. H. Mussen (Ed.), *Carmichael's manual of child psychology* (3rd ed., Vol. I). New York, Wiley, 1970.

Kasper, J. C., and Lowenstein, R., The effect of social interaction on activity level in six-to-eight-year-old boys. *Child Development,* 1971, *42,* 1294–1298.

Kenney, T. J., Clemmens, R. L., Hudson, B., Lentz, G. A., Jr., Cicci, R., and Nair, P., Characteristics of children referred because of hyperactivity, *Journal of Pediatrics,* 1971, *79,* 618–622.

Kessen, W., Hendry, L. S., and Leutzendorff, A., Measurement of movement in the human newborn. *Child Development,* 1961, *32,* 95–105.

Knoble, M., Wolman, M. B., and Mason, E., Hyperkinesis and organicity in children. *Archives of General Psychiatry,* 1959, *1,* 310–321.

Krager, J. M., and Safer, D. J., Type and prevalence of medication used in the treatment of hyperactive children. *New England Journal of Medicine,* 1974, *291,* 1118–1120.

Langhorne, J. E., Jr., Loney, J., Paternite, C. E., and Bechtold, H. P., Child hyperkinesis: A return to the source. *Journal of Abnormal Psychology,* 1976, *85,* 201–209.

Laufer, M. W., Cerebral dysfunction and behavior disorders in adolescents. *American Journal of Orthopsychiatry,* 1962, *32,* 501–506.

Laufer, M. W., and Denhoff, E., Hyperkinetic behavior syndrome in children. *Journal of Pediatrics,* 1957, *50,* 463–474.

Laufer, M. W., Denhoff, E., Riverside, R. I.,Hyperkinetic behavior syndrome in children. *Journal of Pediatrics,* 1957, *50* (4), 463–474.

Laufer, M., Denhoff, E., and Solomons, G., Hyperkinetic impulse disorders in children's behavior problems. *Psychosomatic Medicine,* 1957, *19,* 38–49.

Lesser, L. I., Hyperkinesis in children. *Clinical Pediatrics* (Philadelphia), 1970, *9,* 548–554.

Loney, J., The intellectual functioning of hyperactive elementary school boys: a cross-sectional investigation. *American Journal of Orthopsychiatry,* 1974, *44,* 754–762.

Lopez, R. E., Hyperactivity in twins. *Canadian Psychiatric Association Journal,* 1965, *10,* 421.

Mann, Jay, Vicarious desensitizaiton of test anxiety through observation of video taped treatment. *Journal of Counseling Psychology,* 1972, *19,* 1–7.

Martin, D. M., Hyperkinetic behavior disorders in children. *Western Medicine,* 1967, January, 23–27.

McMahon, S., Deem, M. A., and Greenberg, L. M., The hyperactive child *Clinical Proceedings of Children's Hospital,* 1970, *26,* 295–316.

McNutt, B. A., Boileau, R. A., Cohen, M. N., Sprague, R. L., Von Newmann, B., The effects of long term stimulant medication on the growth and body composition of hyperactive children: II Report on two years. Paper presented at the meeting of Early Clinical Drug Evaluation Unit of NIMH, Key Biscayne, Florida, May, 1976.

Meichenbaum, D. H., Bowers, K. S., and Ross, R. R., Modification of classroom behavior of institutionalized female adolescent offenders. *Behavior Research and Therapy,* 1968, *6,* 343–353.

Meichenbaum, D. H., and Goodman, J., Training impulsive children to talk to themselves: A means of developing self-control. *Journal of Abnormal Psychology,* 1971, *77,* 115–126.

Mendelson, W., Johnson, N., Stewart, M. A., Hyperactive children as teenagers: A follow-up study. *Journal of Nervous and Mental Diseases,* 1971, *153,* 273–279.

Menkes, M. M., Rowe, J. S., and Menkes, J. H., A twenty-five year follow-up study on the hyperkinetic child with minimal brain dysfunction. *Pediatrics,* 1967, *39,* 393–399.

Miller, R. G., Palkes, H. S., and Stewart, M. A., Hyperactive children in suburban elementary schools. *Child Psychiatry and Human Development,* 1973, *4,* 121–127.

Millichap, J. G., and Boldrey, E. E., Studies in hyperkinetic behavior. II Laboratory and clinical evaluations of drug treatments. *Neurology,* 1967, *17,* 467–471, 519.

Minde, K., Lewin, D., Weiss, G., Laviguer, H., Douglas, V., and Sykes, E., The hyperactives child in elementary school: A 5 year controlled follow-up. *Exceptional Children,* 1971, *38,* 215–221.

Morrison, J. r., and Stewart, M. A., A family study of the hyperactive child syndrome. *Biological Psychiatry,* 1971, *3,* 189–195.

Morrison, J. R., and Stewart, M. A., The psychiatric status of the legal families of adopted hyperactive children. *Archives of General Psychiatry,* 1973, *28,* 888–891.

Morrison, J. R., and Stewart, M. A., Evidence for polygenetic inheritance in the hyperactive child syndrome. *American Journal of Psychiatry,* 1973a, 130–7, 791–792.

Ney, P. G., Four types of hyperkinesis. *Canadian Psychiatric Association Journal,* 1974, *19,* 543–550.

O'Leary, K. D., Becker, W. C., Evans, M., and Saudargas, R. A., A token reinforcement program in a public school: A replication and systematic analysis. *Journal of Applied Behavior Analysis,* 1968, *2,* 3–13.

Omenn, G. S., Genetic issues in the syndrome of minimal brain dysfunction. *Seminars in Psychiatry,* 1973, *5,* 5–17.

Palkes, H., and Stewart, M., Intellectual ability and performance of hyperactive children. *American Journal of Orthopsychiatry,* 1972, *42,* 35–39.

Palkes, H., Stewart, M., and Kahana, B., Porteus Maze performance of hyperactive boys after training in self-directed verbal commands. *Child Development,* 1968, *39,* 817–826.

Palkes, H., Stewart, M., and Freedman, J., Improvement in maze performance of hyperactive boys as a function of verbal-training procedures. *Journal of Special Education,* 1972, *5,* 337–342.

Patterson, G. R., Jones, R., Whittier, J., and Wright, M. A., A behavior modification technique for the hyperactive child. *Behavior Research and Therapy,* 1965, *2,* 217–226.

Prinz, R., and Loney, J., Teacher-rated hyperactive elementary school girls: An exploratory developmental study. *Child Psychiatry and Human Development,* 1974, *4,* 246–257.

Rapaport, J. L., Quinn, P. O., and Lamprecht, F., Minor physical anomolies and plasma dopamine-beta-hydroxylase activity in hyperactive boys. *American Journal of Psychiatry,* 1974, *131,* 386–390.

Ridberg, E. H., Parke, R. D., and Hetherington, E. M., Modification of impulsive and reflective cognitive styles through observation of film-mediated models. *Developmental Psychology,* 1971, *5,* 369–377.

Rosenbaum, A., O:Leary, K., and Jacobe, R., Behavioral Intervention with hyperactive children: Group consequences as a supplement to individual contingencies. *Behavior Therapy,* 1975, *6,* 315–323.

Rosenfeld, George B., and Bradley, Charles. Childhood behavior sequelae of asphyxia in infancy, with special reference to pertussia and asphyxia neonatorium. *Pediatrics,* 1948, *2,* 74–84.

Safer, D. J., A familial factor in minimal brain dysfunction. Behavior Genetics, 1973, *3,* 175–186.

Safer, D. J., and Allen, R. P., Factors influencing the suppressant effects of two stimulant drugs on the growth of hyperactive children. *Pediatrics,* 1973, *51.* 660–667.

Safer, D. J., Allen, R. P., *Hyperactive children.* Diagnosis and management. Baltimore: University Park Press, 1976.

Safer, D., Allen, R., and Barr, E., Depression of growth in hyperactive children on stimulant drugs. *New England Journal of Medicine,* 1972, *287,* 217–220.

Scarr, S., Genetic factors in activity motivation. *Child Development,* 1966, *37,* 663–673.

Schachter, F. F., and Apgar, Virginia, Perinatal asphxia and psychological signs of brain damage in childhood. *Pediatrics,* 1959, *24,* 1016–1025.

Schleifer, M., Weiss, G., Cohen, N., Elman, M., Cvejic, H., and Krueger, E., Hyperactivity in preschoolers and the effect of methylphenidate. *American Journal of Orthopsychiatry,* 1975, *45,* 38–50.

Scott, T. J., The use of music to reduce hyperactivity in children. *American Journal of Orthopsychiatry,* 1970, *40,* 667–680.

Shaffer, D., McNamara, N. E., Princus, J. H., controlled observations on patterns of activity, attention, and impulsivity in brain-damaged and psychiatrically disturbed boys. *Psychological Medicine,* 1974, *4,* 2–18.

Shores, R. E., and Haubrick, P. A., Effect of cubicles in educating emotionally disturbed children. *Exceptional Children,* 1969, *36,* 21–24.

Skinrud, K., Generalization of treatment effects from home to school settings. Unpublished manuscript, Oregon Research Institute, Eugene, 1972.

Small, A., Hibi, S., Feinberg, I., Effects of dextroamphetamines sulfate on EEG sleep patterns of hyperactive children. *Archives of General Psychiatry,* 1971, *25,* 369–380.

Smith, G. B., Cerebral accidents of childhood and their relationships to mental deficiency. *Welfare Magazine,* 1926, *17,* 18–33.

Sprague, R. L., and Toppe, L. K., Relationship between activity level and delay of reinforcement in the retarded. *Journal of Experimental Child Psychology,* 1966, *3,* 390–397.

Sprague, R. L., and Sleator, E. K., Effects of psychopharacologic agents on learning disorders. *Pediatric Clinics of North America,* 1973, *20,* 719–735.

Sprague, R. L., Werry, J. S., and Scott, K. G., Drug effects on activity level and learning in retarded children. Unpublished manuscript, 1969.

Sprague, R. L., Barnes, K. R., and Werry, J. S., Methylphenidate and thioridazine: Learning, activity, and behavior in emotionally disturbed boys. *American Journal of Orthopsychiatry,* 1970, *40,* 615–628.

Sroufe, L. A., and Stewart, M. A., Treating problem children with stimulant drugs. *New England Journal of Medicine,* 1973, *289,* 407–413.

Sroufe, L. A., Drug treatment of children with behavior problems. In F. Horowitz (Ed.), *Review of Child Development Research,* Vol. 4, Chicago: University of Chicago Press, 1975.

Sroufe, L. A.,Sonies, B. C., West, W. D., and Wright, F. S., Anticipatory heart rate decleration and reaction time in children with and without referral for learning disability. *Child Development,* 1973, *44,* 267–273.

Stewart, M. A., Hyperactive children. *American Journal of Psychiatry,* 1973, *94,* 577–585.

Stewart, M. A., Pitts, F. N., Craig, A. G., and Dieruf, W., The hyperactive child syndrome. *American Journal of Orthopsychiatry,* 1966, *36,* 861–867.

Still, G. F., The Coulstonian Lectures on some abnormal physical conditions in children. *Lancet,* 1902, *1,* 1008–1012, 1077–1082, 1163–1168.

Strauss, A.A., and Lehtinen, L. E., *Psychopathology and education of the brain-injured child.* New York: Grune and Stratton, 1947.

Sykes, D. H., Douglas, V. I., and Morgenstern, G., Sustained attention in hyperactive children. *Journal of Child Psychology and Psychiatry,* 1973, *14,* 213–220.

Sykes, D. H., Douglas, V. I., Weiss, Gabrielle, et. al. Attention in hyperactive children and the effect of methylphenidate (Ritalin). *Journal of Child Psychology and Psychiatry,* 1971, *12,* 213–220.

Tregold, C. H., Mental Deficiency (amentia) (1st ed.) New York: Wood, 1908.

Turnure, J. E., Children's reaction to distractors in a learning situation. *Developmental Psychology,* 1970, *2,* 115–122.

Turnure, J. E.,Control of orienting behavior in children under five years of age. *Developmental Psychology,* 1971, *4,* 16–24.

Vandenberg, S. G., The heredity abilities study: Heredity components in a psychological test battery. *American Journal of Human Genetics,* 1962, *14,* 220–237.

Wahler, R. G., Setting enerality: Some specific and general effects of child behavior therapy. *Journal of Applied Behavior Analysis,* 1969, *2,* 239–246.

Wahler, R. G., some structural aspects of deviant child behavior. Unpublished manuscript, University of Tennessee, 1974.

Waldrop, M. F., and Halverson, C. F., Minor physical anomolies: Their incidence and relation to behavior in a normal and deviant sample. In R. C. Smart and M. S. Smart (Eds.) *Readings in development and relationships,* New York: MacMillan, 1971.

Walker, H. M., Hops, H., Johnson, S. M., Generalization and maintenance of classroom treatment effects. *Behavior Therapy,* 1974, *3,* 214–220.

Weiss, B., and Laties, V. G., Enhancement of human performance by caffiene and the amphetamines. *Pharmocological Reviews,* 1962, *14,* 1–36.

Weiss, G., Minde, K., Werry, J. S., Douglas, V., and Nenneth,E., Studies on the hyperactive child: VIII. Five-year follow-up. *Archives of General Psychiatry,* 1971, *24,* 409–414.

Weiss, G., Minde, K., Douglas, V., Werry, J., and Sykes, D., Comparison of the effects of chlorpromazine, dextroamphetamine, and methylphenidate on the behavior and intellectual functioning of hyperactive children. *Canadian Medical Association Journal,* 1971, *104,* 20–25.

Wender, P. H., *Minimal brain dysfunction in children.* New York: Wiley-Interscience, 1971.

Werry, J. S., Developmental hyperactivity. *Pediatric Clinics of North America,* 1968, *15,* 581–599.

Werry, J. S., Organic factors in childhood psychopathology. In: Quary, A. C. and Werry, J. S. (Eds.), *Psychopathological disorders of childhood.* New York: Wiley-Interscience, 1972, 83–121.

Werry, J. S., and Sprague, R. L., Hyperactivity. In C. G. Costello (Ed.), *Symptoms of psychopathology.* New York: Wiley-Interscience, 1972, 83–121.

Werry, J. S., and Sprague, R. L., Hyperactivity. In C. G. Costello (Ed.), *Symptoms of psychopathology.* New York, Wiley, 1970, 397–417.

Werry, J. S., and Quay, H. C., Observing the classroom behavior of elementary classroom children. *Exceptional Children,* 1969, *35,* 461–470.

Werry, J. S., Weiss, G., and Douglas, V., Studies on the hyperactive child. I. Some preliminary findings. *Canadian Psychiatric Association Journal,* 1964, *9,* 120–130.

Whalen, C., and Henker, B., Psychostimulants and Children: A review and analysis. *Psychological Bulletin,* 1976.

Witkin, H. A., Dyk, R. B., Fattuson, H. F., Goodenough, D. R., and Karp, S. A., *Psychological Differentiation: Studies of development* New York: Wiley, 1962.

Worland, J., North-Jones, M., and Stern, J. A., Performance and activity of hyperactive and normal boys as a function of distraction and reward. *Journal of Abnormal Child Psychology,* 1973, *1,* 363, 377.

PSYCHOTHERAPY AND PERSUASION

Larry E. Beutler
Baylor College of Medicine

Psychotherapy is an interpersonal relationship which parallels in many ways those studied in the social psychology laboratory. Many authors (Beutler, 1973; Goldstein, 1966; Pepinsky and Karst, 1964; Strupp, 1973; Raimy, 1975) have found common forces in interpersonal persuasion research and psychotherapy. Although this parallelism has been obvious to many for some period of time, psychotherapists long resisted the systematic application of social psychological principles. While some (Ellis and Harper, 1961; Murphy, 1955; Samler, 1960) advocated that attitude change be a psychotherapeutic goal, most authors still hesitate to recognize attitude or value change either as a central therapeutic ingredient or process.

Reactions to Eysenck's (1952) criticisms of psychotherapy highlighted the weak scientific foundation of traditional clinical practice and underlined the observation that psychotherapists have not traditionally welcomed the scientific influence. Although the prevalent training model has long stressed that the clinician should be both a scientist and a practitioner, arising as it did from two independent and hostile influences — the "art" of psychotherapy and the "science" of behavior influence — the scientst-professional has from the beginning been an animal at odds with himself. With the advent of behavior modification and behavior therapy, however, the influence of the psychological laboratory was at last felt in the psychiatric clinic and hospital. This advent signaled a significant success in reconciling the scientist and professional aspects of training and practice. Paradoxically, in the midst of loud criticisms of the prevalent training model, the potential for a true scientist-professional became a reality.

In the last decade the psychotherapist has been inundated both with "scientific" data extolling applications of learning theory to clinical practice and with exponential increases of propaganda from new psychotherapy theories. The thoughtful clinician is torn between claims of "empirical findings" from the learning laboratory on the one hand, and unresearched but rationally attractive theoretical propaganda on the other. This state of conflict is exacerbated by the observation (e.g., Bergin, 1975; Breger and McGaugh, 1965) that therapy techniques based upon "learning theory" are probably not so clearly founded as the proponents would suggest. In the barrage of speculative theories on the one hand and "scientific data" on the other, it is understandable that most clinicians lose sight of the fact that data from the learning laboratory represents only a portion of the applicable laboratory-derived knowledge that is available to them.

Because psychotherapy research lags behind theory application, it is not always clear how or, indeed, if the findings of laboratory experiments relate to clinical activities. In an attempt to include more of the experimentally derived concepts in the clinician's armamentarium, a number of researchers over the past decade have undertaken to evaluate principles of interpersonal persuasion or attitude and value change as applied to clinical diagnosis, counseling, and psychotherapy (Beutler, 1971c; Beutler et al., 1972a; 1973b; Goldstein, 1966; 1971; Goldstein and Simonson, 1971). From these efforts it now seems possible to assess many of the persuasive forces which may distinguish effective from ineffective therapy.

This chapter is devoted to a review of the parallel between social persuasion on the one hand, and psychotherapy on the other. Although the review of literature presented is limited, it is representative both of the findings available from the social psychology laboratory and those obtained by psychotherapy researchers.

PSYCHOTHERAPY AND VALUE CHANGE

It was not long ago in the history of psychotherapy and psychotherapists that religious, economic, and evaluative or moral attitudes were considered off-limits. Some practitioners (e.g., Mowrer, 1953) even argued that moral values could not be altered by psychotherapy and state legislators proposed laws refusing to allow a person to change his concept of God or his religious beliefs while in psychotherapy. Though admitting that attitudes about such things as sex and aggression are often at the root of a patient's difficulties, even Freud (1958) believed that moral problems were beyond the competence and interest of psychoanalysis.

Horney (1939), among others of Freud's students, broke this early tradition and maintained that since values and moral convictions are often crucial and unrecognized forces in influencing a patient, they must receive attention in the therapeutic process. Horney asserted that the patient's morals in part resulted from and in part contributed to neurotic conflicts; hence, the analyst was of necessity interested in value dilemmas. Two decades ago it became apparent that the therapist's theoretical values are reflected in what he calls "good adjustment," and that therapists from different schools differ essentially in the values which they "teach" their patients during psychotherapy (Bergum, 1957; Glad, 1955; 1959; Glad, Lewis, Page, and Jeffers, 1953; Wolff, 1954). In recent years, both clinicians and researchers (e.g., Beutler, 1971b; Korner, 1956; London, 1964; Murphy, 1955; Bergum, 1957; Buhler, 1962; Patterson, 1973, Smith, 1961; Szasz, 1960; Watson, 1958) have attempted to come to grips with the intuitive truth that a therapist's personal and moral values, as well as his theoretical ones, cannot go unrevealed in the therapeutic relationship.

Today, it is virtually impossible to find a textbook on counseling or psychotherapy that does not deal with the question of the therapist's values and personal attitudes as potential or "real" variables in the therapeutic relationship. London (1974) goes so far as to maintain that the question of whether or not a therapist's values influence his patients is no longer an issue. The therapist's choice, according to London, is confined to the dilemma of how to best allow these values to impact the therapeutic environment. With this awareness has come an increasing emphasis upon psychotherapy as an interpersonal persuasion process, and research has been growing rapidly in support of this point of view. Today, literally hundreds of research studies exist which apply concepts from interpersonal persuasion to the psychotherapy relationship. This condition is in contrast to the situation scarcely more than a decade ago wherein Ehrlich and Weiner (1961) were able to find only two studies that dealt directly with the issue of attitude influence.

Since Wolff's (1954) demonstration that a large proportion of leading psychotherapists believed that their personal value systems tended to be adopted by their patients during successful treatment, many studies have investigated this possibility. For example, Rosenthal (1955) administered a moral value scale — designed to measure attitudes towards sex, aggression, and authority — to twelve beginning, long-term psychotherapy patients and their therapists. At the time of each patient's termination of therapy, ranging from six months to three years, he was readministered this value scale with the demonstration that "successful treatment" was highest among those patients who had acquired the value stance of their therapists. An additionally interesting, if not statistically significant observation was that among half of Rosenthal's patients, moral attitudes became less like those of their therapists, and these patients tended to be judged as unimproved or worse.

At least some subsequent studies (Parloff, Iflund, and Goldstein, 1960; Nawas and Landfield, 1963; Landfield and Nawas, 1964; Welkowitz, Cohen, and Ortmeyer, 1967) have continued to find a generalized tendency for successful patients to acquire certain values of their therapists. Other findings (e.g., Beutler, 1971c; Beutler, Jobe, and Elkins, 1974; Beutler, Johnson, Neville, Elkins, and Jobe, 1975) suggest that this relationship is more complex than originally supposed, but support the general concensus that the concept of value-free psychotherapy is a myth (Garfield, 1974; Strupp, 1973; 1974; Frank, 1973).

The position to be taken in this chapter is that psychotherapy is a process of interpersonal persuasion, and that a therapist's persuasiveness relates complexly to his effectivenss. We will attempt to support this thesis by delineating forces found to be significant in attitude and value change and assessing their similarity to variables found to be significant in psychotherapy process and outcome. The forces likely to be influential in changing the cognitive, affective, or behavioral dispositions of another person (e.g., his attitudes and values) can be arbitrarily conceptualized under three titles: (1) persuader attributes, (2) characteristics of the communication, and (3) characteristics of the listener.

For our purposes, discussion of persuader characteristics will be limited to a consideration of persuader credibility, attractiveness, and bias. Our presentation of communication variables, however, includes some which could easily have been listed as persuader variables. Since both the persuasive attributes and the values of a communicator are inferred as a listener assesses persuader similarity, dissimilarity, and acceptability of basic beliefs, personal communication *styles* are as important to the persuasion process as the more obvious *techniques* which the persuader may devise. While personal styles of communication are highly individualized, techniques can be applied without regard to the personality of the communicator. Whereas the former establishes the communicator's credibility, attractiveness, and biases, the latter is the dimension on which theoretical approaches to psychotherapy are assumed to differ. In our presentation we will discuss both interpersonal styles and techniques under the heading of communicator variables.

Listener characteristics are important for predicting (1) the compatibility of the persuader's basic values to that of the listener, and (2) whether or not persuasive characteristics will be attributed to the communicator. Even if persuader-listener compatibility is high, different methods of persuasion are not equally effective with all people, however. Assessing which technique is appropriate with whom is of ultimate concern to the psychotherapy enterprise.

In considering the forces of persuasion in psychotherapy, the following material will assume an analogy between therapist and persuader, on the one hand, and between patient and listener on the other. A comparision of persuader, communication, and listener variables of significance both in the social psychology laboratory and in the psychotherapist's office is suggestive of the degree to which psychotherapy can be conceptualized as a powerful, attitudinal, and value persuasion process.

FORCES IN INTERPERSONAL PERSUASION

Persuader Attributes

Strong (1968) has delineated some similarities between persuasive forces and therapeutic conditions. Extending this point, the following will present data suggesting that both therapeutic and attitudinal change occurs as a similar function of persuader/therapist credibility, attractiveness, and bias.

Credibility

A. A persuader's credibility is a combination of his presumed expertness and trustworthiness (Middlebrook, 1974). Generally speaking, experts produce greater influence over attitude change than nonexperts (Aronson, Turner, and Carlsmith, 1963; Bergin, 1962; Topavola, 1974). There are conditions, however, under which the effect of expertness is attenuated. For example, when a communication is highly personal and ego involving, persuader expertness may not influence the degree to which one changes in order to accommodate negative feedback (Johnson and Steiner, 1968). Secondly, there are conditions under which a low status communicator can produce greater influence than a high status communicator. For example, Walster, Aronson, and Abrahams (1966) have demonstrated that if a low status communicator argues a position seen as contrary to his personal interests, he is likely to be more persuasive and more influential than a high status communicator arguing a position for what may be ulterior motives. From such data it appears that the increase in trust which accrues as a result of a communicator's perceived "consistency" outweighs his expert status in producing influence on others.

In an effort to delineate conditions under which credibility may increase persuasiveness, Jones and Gerard (1967) hypothesize that attitudes contain both a belief and a value premise. An expert who is assumed to have superior knowledge may be more influential in affecting the belief premise of an attitude, whereas a peer may have greater power in affecting the value premise. It is the position of Jones and Gerard (1967) that one must take account of both the expert and peer status of a persuader in order to predict the effects of his credibility on attitude change.

The hypothesis of Jones and Gerard (1967) has received some support. Connolly, Green and Kaufman (1973) have found that a person's beliefs change more when the persuasive source is objectively dissimilar but perceived as an expert, whereas the values one holds tend to change more if the source is perceived as a peer and is both objectively and subjectively similar to the listener.

The possibility that interpersonal similarity interacts with credibility in the persuasion process has received additional research both by Aronson, Turner, and Carlsmith (1963); by Topavola (1974), and by Bergin (1962). In the first study it was found that if an opinion is presented as coming from a highly credible source (T. S. Elliot), increasing discrepancy between the communicated opinion and the initial opinion of the subject produces similar increases in the subject's tendency to change in the direction advocated. On the other hand, a source who is perceived as having low credibility in the evaluation of poetry (e.g., a fellow student) produces attitude change only among those who initially have views that are moderately similar to the position advocated. In a similar vein, Bergin (1962) found that among attitudes toward one's own sexual adjustment, discrepant feedback from a highly credible source produced change proportional to the degree of initial communicator-recipient difference. However, feedback from a low credibility source, in this case a high school student, produced little change when the discrepancy between feedback and self-opinion was great.

Apparently, a recipient of a persuasive communication first decides if the issue is one on which the persuader is likely to have relevant knowledge (i.e., credibility) and only then will the communicator be persuasive. Similarity between persuader and listener interacts with credibility to produce a persuasive impact, a point to which we will return shortly in reference to interpersonal attractiveness.

B. In the psychotherapy literature, credibility is found to be an equally important variable to that determined in the social psychology laboratory. Unfortunately, however, most of the studies relevant to psychotherapy have been conducted in analogue situations rather than in truly clinical settings. Among such studies, that by Browning (1966) and those by Strong and his colleagues (Keierleber, Matross, and Strong, 1974; Meland, Matross, and Strong, 1974) stand out.

Browning investigated a therapist's "prestige" on a patient's ability to accept "therapeutic interpretations." Nonpsychotic college student volunteers were assigned either to high or low status "therapists." The results demonstrated that with high expert therapists, "patients" were more accepting of interpretations which represented a large discrepancy from their own belief systems as compared to "patients" who were subjected to interpretations from inexpert therapists. On the other hand, although failing to find a clear-cut superiority of expert interviewers in producing change of self-rated achievement motivation, Strong and his colleagues (Keierleber, Matross, and Strong, 1974; Meland, Matross, and Strong, 1974) suggest that the perceived status of an interviewer interacts significantly with idiosyncratic variables. Whereas one interviewer may have greater influence when perceived as an expert than when perceived as a nonexpert, other interviewers may have their greatest influence when they are perceived as nonexperts rather than experts. These findings underline the relative complexity of attitudes and values.

As further testament to the potential effect of credibility on psychotherapy, Strong and Schmidt (1970) demonstrate that upward variations of patient trust produce increased influence on attitudes of personal reference. Similarly, Strong and Dixon (1971) have demonstrated that expertness interacts with attractiveness in changing self-attitudes. When an interviewer is attractive, his expert status alone has little influence, but when the interviewer is unattractive, "patients" are likely to rely with greater weight on the interviewer's expertness. This interactive effect is not surprising in view of the fact, to be illustrated in the next section, that interpersonal similarity is an element in interpersonal attraction as well as in perceived credibility.

Two studies have undertaken to evaluate the impact of therapist credibility on treatment outcome in a clinical population. Beutler, Johnson, Neville, Elkins, and Jobe (1975) assessed the role of therapist credibility on subsequent patient attitude change and rating of improvement. The results suggest that while a patient's initial perception of his therapist's credibility is not a strong determiner of subsequent attitude change, it does significantly influence his self-evaluation of therapeutic gain.

Truax, Fine, Moravec, and Millis (1968) have investigated psychotherapy improvement as a function of "persuasive potency," a concept whose description appears analogous to therapist credibility. The results support the Beutler et al. (1975) suggestion that a therapist's power, as perceived by his patient, is significantly related to various criteria of improvement.

In addition to expertness, a highly credible source is also perceived as trustworthy. As discussed earlier, trustworthiness seems to be in large part based upon the consistency of the communicator's position and an evaluation of whether his expressed position is in line with internal motives (e.g., Hovland and Mandell,

1952). In psychotherapy literature, consistency appears under the label of "congruence" or "genuineness" (Truax and Carkhuff, 1967), and research provides ample support for the importance of this "trust" variable in the psychotherapy relationship. Truax and Mitchell (1971), for example, review eight studies of both individual and group psychotherapy, utilizing 564 patients with a preponderance of data strongly indicative of genuineness as a pervasive variable in producing positive therapy change. Similarly, Mitchell, Truax, Bozarth, and Krauft (1974) provide data suggesting that even in non-Rogerian therapy, lack of genuineness mitigates against successful treatment. Perhaps even in psychotherapy (or especially in psychotherapy) as in the social influence laboratory, the presence of trust (e.g., Walster et al., 1966) bolsters the influence even of a low prestige therapist.

The foregoing results suggest the importance of credibility, expertness, and trustworthiness in producing influence both in the social psychology laboratory and the psychotherapy office. Although it is not clear from these findings that credibility consistently produces attendant attitude change or persuasion in psychotherapy, the data do suggest that the therapist's credibility is associated with diverse ratings of patient improvement and is interactive with other interpersonal variables such as similarity and trust. Credibility is a complex variable, as demonstrated in the foregoing discussion, and can probably best be understood by evaluating the related concept of attractiveness and considering at greater length the effect of interpersonal similarity on psychotherapy outcome and persuasiveness.

Attractiveness

A. Like credibility, attractiveness is a complex phenomenon. Numerous authors (Bryne, Griffitt, and Golightly, 1966; Simons, Berkowtiz, and Moyer, 1970) have pointed out that attractiveness, credibility, and value similarity are closely related. Concepts of credibility and attractiveness are by no means interchangeable, however. In fact, there appear to be situations in which attractiveness is increased when fallibility or credibility is decreased (e.g., Feldman-Summers, 1974). Interpersonal similarity, on the other hand, as mentioned heretofore, is related in diverse ways both to credibility (Bergin, 1962) and to attractiveness (Simons et al., 1970).

A persuader's attractiveness promises to have a potential, though not always direct, influence, on his persuasiveness (e.g., Scott and Cherrington, 1974) and is a function of the persuader's perceived values and social similarity to the listener (e.g., Byrne, Griffitt, and Golightly, 1966; Simons et al., 1970). For example, pairs of subjects whose attractiveness to each other is experimentally enhanced are consistently found both to make more effort to influence each other and to be more influenced by each other than are subjects who are induced to have less interpersonal attraction (Back, 1951). In turn, attraction between persons is increased when a sense of cooperation is induced (Scott and Cherrington, 1974) and subjects perceive themselves as similar on important value (Anderson, 1975; Nowicki, Nelson, and Ettinger, 1974), attitude (Asher, 1973), or background dimensions (Brock, 1965).

Social psychological literature, however, is not universal in suggesting that either interpersonal attractiveness or attitude similarity is directly related to persuasion. For example, physical appeal is often a stronger component of interperson influence than is perceived in attitudinal similarity (Kleck and Rubenstein, 1975). Additionally, increased similarity is not necessarily related either to increased attraction (Johnson, 1974) or to increased influence (Simons et al., 1970). Apparently, both similarity between partners and attendant attraction only exert a direct effect on persuasiveness when seen as relevant to the issues at hand (Berscheid, 1966). Although interpersonal similarity may provide a basis for attractiveness which is necessary to initiate a cohesive and efficient interpersonal process, other variables apparently enter into maintaining interpersonal attraction once the process is initiated (Anderson, 1975).

At least initially, similarity of values and attitudes (Asher, 1973), needs (Nowicki et al., 1974), and background (Brock, 1975) may play a significant role in establishing relationships in which one may produce influence upon another. Under some conditions, however, dissimilarity rather than similarity may be most influential (Simons et al., 1970). Concern over when interpersonal similarity is more conducive to persuasion than is dissimilarity has given rise to numerous theories of interpersonal influence. For example, dissonance theory (Festinger, 1957) suggests that if other conditions are held constant, large discrepancies between a persuader and a listener will produce maximal cognitive dissonance and hence maximal change. If, however, the persuader presents an unattractive image (Abelson and Miller, 1967) or is untrustworthy (Simons et al., 1970), changes in a direction away from those advocated by the persuader may occur under conditions of interpersonal discrepancy. The difficulty with dissonance formulations is that such "boomerang effects" are difficult to predict on an *a priori* basis (Aronson, 1969; Sherif, 1970; Tedeschi, Schlenker, and Bonom, 1971). This weakness in dissonance theory has led to the development of theories which are designed specifically to predict the types of persuader-listener relationship that will result in negative as well as positive influence.

Sherif and Hovland (1961) have proposed social judgment theory as a viable alternative to dissonance theory. They speculate that attitude acceptability is a better predictor both of positive and negative attitude change than is simple persuader-listener dissimilarity. Simply put, social judgment theory holds that if a persuader's preferred position lies within the listener's latitude of acceptance — that range of possible viewpoints found to be acceptable — the listener will both evaluate the persuader's position as being more similar to his own than it is in actuality (assimilation effect) and will change his own position accordingly. If, on the other hand, the persuader's opinion lies within the listener's latitude of rejection — that range of possible positions which is objectionable — it is predicted that the listener will both estimate the persuader's position as being less like his own than it is in actuality (contrast effect) and will produce very little or even negative attitude change in response to the persuader's communication. Social judgment theory has potential advantages over dissonance theory in being able to predict, *a priori,* negative changes as well as positive ones, and has been supported by considerable research (e.g., Hovland, 1965; Sherif, Sherif and Nebergall, 1965; Peterson and Koulack, 1969). The effectiveness of this approach may in part reside in the fact that it takes into account both the listener's ego involvement, as measured by the number of alternative positions a subject finds acceptable, and the perceived discrepancy between the position advocated by a persuader and that held by a listener.

The foregoing suggest that the role of attractiveness in interpersonal persuasion is influenced by numerous variables. When one specifies similarity as an antecedent to interpersonal attraction he must necessarily specify the type of similarity discussed — value similarity, attitudinal similarity, social class similarity, etc. Furthermore, although apparently representing a potent force in interpersonal influence, both interpersonal similarity and attractiveness are viable only as mediators to the influence process. Attraction in and of itself, though setting the stage for interpersonal persuasion, does not necessarily produce it, and by the same token similarity on irrelevant dimensions produces little persuasive potency. Hence, the arguments of Jones and Gerard (1967) may again be highlighted in suggesting that when the issue is one of knowledge, divergence between the persuader and the listener's position may be most advantageous to persuasion, whereas if the focal topic is one of values, similarity may be most influential.

B. The complexity of the psychotherapy relationship can be seen quite clearly by assessing the effects of attractiveness on psychotherapeutic process and outcome. Goldstein (Goldstein, 1971; Goldstein and Simonson, 1971; Goldstein, Heller and Sechrest, 1966), among others (e.g., Wilkins, in press), has aptly reviewed a number of studies pertinent to interpersonal attraction as influencing the therapeutic process. Since attractiveness is not consistently related to beneficial therapy outcome (e.g., Bednar and Mobley, 1971; Jobe, Beutler, Johnson, Neville, and Workman, 1973), however, Goldstein has taken the tact of investigating attractiveness as a catalyst which may influence many of the variables considered to be important in the therapeutic exchange. Goldstein's assessment of interpersonal attraction as having an indirect effect upon outcome appears consistent with findings from the social psychology laboratory. In a series of psychotherapy studies evaluating interpersonal attraction, Goldstein (Goldstein and Simonson, 1971) has ascertained that when patients are highly attracted to their therapists, they are conversely rated as more attractive by their therapists, thus supporting the reciprocity effect noted in the social psychology literature (e.g., Johnson, 1974). The value of therapist warmth and regard have been advocated (e.g., Goldstein, 1966; Goldstein and McGinnie, 1964) as facilitators of perceived therapist attractiveness, and in other research these variables have been found to be significantly implicated in therapeutic outcome (Traux and Carkhuff, 1967).

Strong and his colleagues (e.g., Strong and Dixon, 1971; Strong, 1968; Schmidt and Strong, 1971) have further illuminated the potential role of therapist attractiveness in producing therapeutic change. These therapy analogue studies suggest that therapist attractiveness has potent influence in the modification of self-related attitudes (Schmidt and Strong, 1971), and may even partially compensate for deficiencies in perceived "expertness" (Strong and Dixon, 1971).

In turn, several authros (Schmidt and Strong, 1971; Mehrabian and Williams, 1969) observe that if interviewers emphasize their liking for a "patient," areas of similarity, and emit "friendly" comments, "warm" postural-gestural cues, and maintain eye contact, the persuasiveness and attractiveness of the therapist is substantially increased. Traux and Carkhuff (1967), as well as their colleagues (Traux and Mitchell, 1971), aptly illustrate the therapeutic value of such attraction-inducing qualities as warmth and empathetic interest. Whereas therapist congruence or consistency is clearly related to credibility and trust, empathy and warmth are apparently precipitators of interpersonal attraction. In turn, matching patients and therapists for maximal success suggest that such attraction-inducing qualities as empathy, acceptance, and nurturanance are viable components in successful matches (Berzins, 1974; Beutler, Johnson, Neville, and Workman, 1972a; Beutler, Johnson, Neville, Workman and Elkins, 1973).

The role of interpersonal similarity in promoting therapeutic attractiveness has also been studied. Garfield (1971) has convincingly suggested that therapists tend to select as patients those who are similar to themselves on socioeconomic indices. Taking this point further, Holzman (1962) demonstrates that such similarity promotes beneficial therapy outcome. Schofield (1964) has noted that young, attractive, verbal, intelligent, and successful patients (the YAVIS patient) are those with whom most therapists prefer to work. However, neither the therapist's social class (Pettit, Pettit, and Welkowitz, 1974), nor value similarity to his patients (Beutler, 1971c; Beutler et al., 1974) has the power to reliably predict a patient's likelihood of prematurely dropping out of psychotherapy.

In an effort to evaluate the relative efficacy of dissonance theory and social judgment theory for predicting dropout, attitude change, and improvement in psychotherapy, Beutler (1971c) initially evaluated sixty-four mental health clinic outpatients seen by sixteen therapists. Treatment consisted of either individual psychotherapy, family therapy, or group therapy. Therapist ratings of improvement were assessed as well as changes in patients' sexual, aggressive, and relationship values. After three months of psychotherapy, it was ascertained that large discrepancies in initial patient-therapist moral values were highly predictive ($r = .64$) of subsequent patient value change regardless of treatment modality.

From the foregoing and subsequent studies of individual, marital, and group psychotherapy a number of consistent suggestions emerge: (1) Initial value discrepancy between patient and therapist is associated with proportional changes in the patient's expressed beliefs toward those held by the therapist (Beutler, 1971c; Beutler et al., 1974; Beutler et al., 1975). (2) Even large value discrepancies are not reliable predictors of dropout in psychotherapy (Beutler, 1971c; Beutler et al., 1974), though personality dissimilarity might fare better in this regard (Mendelsohn and Geller, 1963, Mendelsohn, 1966). (3) Patient improvement is often associated with the degree of acceptability but not necessarily with the degree of similarity between patient and therapist values (Beutler, 1971c; Beutler et al., 1974). (4) At least under some circumstances ratings of patient improvement may be associated with the patient's adoption of certain of his therapist's values (Nawas and Landfield, 1963; Landfield and Nawas, 1964). And, (5) there is some evidence to suggest that value similarity and change among patients and their spouses are important correlates of success in marital therapy (Beutler, 1971a; Gurman, 1974).

As with relationships between patient and therapist values, complementariness on certain global personality dimensions also seems to be conducive to successful outcome. For example, Berzins, Freidman and Seidman (1969) have demonstrated that therapists tend to resemble in mode of adjustment those patients with whom they might be expected to be least effective, and Wogan (1970) has demonstrated that high degrees of personality similarity between a patient and his therapist both decrease the therapists's attractiveness and slow the rate of therapeutic progress. Similarly, dominant and independent therapists, when paired with submissive and dependent patients (their opposites), produce the most significant therapeutic effects (Jobe, Beutler, Johnson, Neville, and Workman, 1973; Berzins, 1974; Pettit, Pettit, and Welkowitz, 1974). However, conflicting data is present on whether or not personality similarity increases through the course of successful psychotherapy (Carson and Heine, 1962; Carson and Llewellyn, 1966; Carr, 1970) in the manner that value similarity may increase.

In view of the functional complexity of perceived attractiveness, and credibility in influencing therapy outcome, we must assume that these persuader variables serve only as a basis for facilitating a therapeutic relationship and are not necessarily a direct contributor to therapeutic change. Reciprocal attractiveness may be necessary for the establishment of a therapeutic alliance in which both patient and therapist work together in a mutually desired and equitable relationship (e.g., Orlinsky and Howard, 1975).

Apparently, while similarity on dimensions such as social class and liking for one another, are facilitative of interpersonal attraction, dissimilarity of values and certain personality dimensions are often more conducive to relevant change in psychotherapy. The complexity of these variables is exacerbated when one remembers that amount of attitude persuasion and therapeutic improvement are not isomorphically related, and acceptability of the therapist's expressed values is a more viable contributor to beneficial outcome than is amount of actual .similarity or dissimilarity. Some degree of value acceptability as well as divergence seems necessary to promote both effective therapeutic progress and persuasion.

Expectancy effects

A. Since the classic work of Rosenthal and Jacobson (1968) on experimenter bias, subtle ways in which a leader may unknowingly communicate his attitudes and expectancies to a recipient in the process of inducing change have been given a primary place in persuasion investigation. Although Rosenthal and Jacobson originally reported that teacher expectancies of pupil achievement substantially effected subsequent gains in IQ, it now appears clear that these findings were exaggerated by methodological difficulties (Hersh, 1971; Sattler and Winget, 1970). The strong experimental bias effect noted originally by Rosenthal and Jacobson (1968) apparently occurs only under prescribed circumstances, as for example when teachers are familiar with the specific outcome measures to be used and coach specific test responses (Pellegrini and Hicks, 1972). The subject's observed behavior has greater impact on subsequent teacher ratings than does prior teacher expectancy (Sattler and Winget, 1970).

Subtle movements, gestures, and comments all seem to be implicated as means through which one's expectancies of other persons may be conveyed to them. If these gestures and comments are accompanied by the implicit or explicit communication of approval, contingent upon change, communicator expectancies become powerful persuaders. The subtle means by which covert attitudes and values are communicated will be discussed in a later section, but in the meantime a brief recollection of so-called *verbal conditioning* (e.g., Verplanck, 1955) seems relevant for providing an illustration of how communicator bias may influence a subject's responses.

Verbal conditioning is a procedure whereby certain verbal expressions are altered by making positive or negative gestures contingent upon them. By making "approving" or "disapproving" nods or sounds immediately contingent on verbal expressions, the frequency of these expressions tends to increase or decrease, respectively, even when neither the recipient nor the communicator is aware of the existent contingency. Through this means, both word categories (Greenspoon, 1955) and expression of attitudes (Verplanck, 1955) can be altered. Since verbal conditioning can occur without the communicator himself being aware of the contingencies which he creates, this process may be significantly implicated in the layman's observation that people tend to respond as others expect them to.

A large volume of literature now exists on "self-fulfilling prophecy" as it applies to interpersonal interactions and need not be elaborated on presently. Suffice it to say that subtle expectancies on the part of the communicator may, under prescribed circumstances, have significant influence on the behavior and beliefs of a recipient. Although not as strong as originally hypothesized, the influence is nonetheless significant and bears investigation in clinical settings.

B. The necessity of evaluating therapist expectancies in the psychotherapy relationship is underlined by three findings. First, therapists are more likely to provide treatment to those for whom they have the highest expectations of success (Garfield and Affleck, 1961). Second, therapist expectancies regarding the degree and nature of patient involvement in therapy seem to partially determine the nature and speed of the involvement (Lennard and Bernstein, 1966). And third, patient satisfaction with therapy may be more a function of whether or not he fulfills the therapist's expectancies than whether or not he attains his own initial therapy aims (Hill, 1969).

Investigations of expectancy effects in clinical settings suggest that an inter-action occurs between the personal styles of clinicians and patients. For example, schizophrenic patients who have poor social skills are more influenced by the social expectancies of *affect-oriented* therapists as opposed to task-oriented therapists. On the other hand, the expectancies of *task-oriented* therapists exert more influence on the performance of high socially skilled schizophrenics than similar expectancies held by their affect-oriented counterparts (Trattner and Howard, 1970). In a manner analogous to verbal conditioning, the subtle effects of postures and gestures (Mehrabian and Williams, 1969) in shaping attitudinal expressions in clinical-like situations has been implicated in understanding expectancy effects. And no less than in the laboratory, the clinician's expectations may have an influence on patient change (Goldstein, 1971; 1960; Leonard and Burnstein, 1966; Heller and Goldstein, 1961).

Therapist expectancy in part determines the manner in which patients learn to evaluate their improvement. Patients tend to evaluate their growth by criteria held by their therapists (Hill, 1969), and therapists of patients who come to feel im-proved seem to have higher initial expectations of success than do therapists of patients who feel themselves becoming worse during the course of psychotherapy (Goldstein, 1960). The effects of the therapist's expectations may be mediated and tempered by other variables, however, and hence may often produce only an indi-rect effect on outcome. For example, as in laboratory studies of persuasion, high levels of therapist attractiveness (Heller and Goldstein, 1961) and the presence of behavior which is markedly inconsistent with initial expectations (Kumar and Pepinsky, 1970) tend to override the effect of pretreatment bias. Unfortunately, the effects of therapist expectations have been less investigated than those of patient expectations and, consequently, their precise effects are less predictable. Judging from the foregoing data, however, there are parallels between experimenter bias and self-fulfilling prophecy, on the one hand, and therapist expectancy effects on the other.

Summary

In this section we have reviewed the major psychotherapeutic impact of variables which are known to be central to the process of persuading another person to change values and beliefs. The findings presented in this section suggest that therapist credibility and trustworthiness, interpersonal attractiveness and similarity, and prior biases and expectancies for psychotherapy process and outcome, all significantly influence progress toward therapeutic goals, usually in a manner analogous to their influence on values and beliefs. To be maximally effective, a therapist, like an advocate of attitude or value change, will be perceived as highly credible, trustworthy, interpersonally attractive, and will hold a strong and positive expectation for the success of the techniques and procedures he uses.

We have seen that in both psychotherapy improvement and in attitude persuasion, interpersonal similarity interacts with variables of credibility and attractiveness to produce the desired effect. Therapists' attractiveness, credibility, and acceptability are all mediated by various dimensions of interpersonal similarity and have significant impact both upon value change and improvement in personal adjustment which occurs during the course of psychotherapy. The role of value dissimilarity in the therapeutic environment parallels the relationship between persuader and listener value dissimilarity in the laboratory and is suggestive of a dissonance resolution process in which patients evaluate their beliefs in contrast to those presented by their therapist. If, in this process, they also determine that their therapist's values are compatible with those they already hold, improvement is more likely to occur.

Therapist expectancies, like experimenter expectancies, appear to be subtly communicated to patients and have a subsequent effect on observed change. As will be seen in the following section, the subtle gestural and postural cues by which these expectancies are communicated may themselves influence therapeutic change and can be utilized to increase the potency of therapy techniques.

Characteristics of the Communication

It is not always easy to discriminate between characteristics of the communication and those of the communicator. It is through communication styles that the listener comes to perceive the persuader as credible and attractive. This is only possible because the manner in which a persuasive communication is presented is heavily influenced by relatively stable characteristics of the source. Human beings operate on the assumption, true or not, that they can infer stable personal qualities as well as moods and emotions of another person by observing his appearance and manner (Middlebrook, 1974).

Some communicators utilize certain persuasive styles more than others, but this phenomenon is little investigated outside of the rather rational speculations relating psychotherapy style to therapist theoretical position. Hence, to some extent a discussion of communication characteristics must be considered somewhat arbitrarily and artificially differentiated from persuader characteristics.

In this section, we will discriminate between differences of *style* and differences of *technique*. We will reserve the term *technique* for those procedures which are typically manipulated for effect by the persuader. *Style* variables, on the other hand, refer to those characteristics which are not usually manipulated systematically, and which are assumed to reflect more basic attitudes, values and attributes of the communicator than those contained in the manifest message.

Communication Styles

Voice. A. Through verbal and nonverbal styles, a communicator discloses his beliefs and feelings. A growing body of research testifies that these styles can be powerful forces both in the persuasion and in the psychotherapy process. Early, it was found that verbal messages are more powerful persuaders than are written messages (Cantril and Allport, 1935). Within this context, qualities of a persuader's voice have been found to consistently imply reliable personality and emotional states (Phillis, 1970; Kramer, 1963; Scherer, 1971), and altering these qualities produces corollary changes in persuasiveness (Bettinghaus, 1961). Beginning in childhood, a person learns to relate a loud voice to "bad," ominous, and threatening persons (Phillis, 1970) and this attribution of personality characteristics through voice quality seems to continue throughout adulthood (Scherer, 1971). Regardless of the accuracy of these attributions, overwhelming intersubject consistency (Kramer, 1963) in the inferences suggests their power in human communication.

B. Although a specific relationship between voice quality and psychotherapy outcome has not been ascertained, there is some tentative suggestion that therapists may be differentiated on the basis of certain voice parameters (Franco and Kulberg, 1975). Perhaps more to the point, however, are the findings which suggest that inferences of therapeutic warmth and acceptance are related to characteristics of the therapist's speech (Welkowitz and Kuc, 1973). Unfortunately, voice quality as it relates either to interpersonal persuasion or to therapeutic process and outcome is not well researched. The current literature is only sufficient to suggest that: (1) Voice quality has a significant impact both on the processes of attitude communication and change. (2) There are consistent attributions of personality and emotional states which occur as a function of defined speech patterns. And (3) some of the personal characteristics which are attributed to a person on the basis of his voice have been demonstrated to be facilitative of psychotherapeutic change.

Nonverbal. A. A second category of persuasive styles has been popularized as "body language." The observation that postural, gestural, and facial expression belie a person's basic values and opinions has received notoriety in the popular press (e.g. Nierenberg and Calero, 1971). These popularized notions suggest social-clinical applications, however, and have been systematically researched (Mehrabian, 1972). In empirical literature, body language has been evaluated by assessing the impact of various types of specific body cues on an observer's interpersonal impression. Although the total body posture appears to convey more accurate information about a person than does face alone (e.g., Ekman, 1964; Ekman and Friesen, 1969), under certain circumstances just a person's face conveys a great deal of relatively accurate information about his feelings and mood (e.g., Howell and Jorgensen, 1970).

Studies evaluating the persuasive potency of postural and gestural styles implicate body cues in the process of conveying acceptance, approval, and other significant attitudes of importance to persuasion. For example, body and facial cues convey the impression that the communicator is secure and comfortable (Tankard, 1970; Le Compte and Rosenfeld, 1971), that he likes the subject (Mehrabian, 1967), and that he is credible and reliable (Mehrabian and Williams, 1969). Additionally, body language increases the persuader's attractiveness (Kleinke, Staneski, and Berger, 1975) and increases the power, both of negative and positive statements during the persuasive process (Ellsworth and Carlsmith, 1968). Whether or not facial-body cues convey accurate information about the communicator, it may be enough to know that the subject believes that such information is accurate and responds to it accordingly. In view of the consensus of meaning attributed to facial and gestural cues (Kozel and Gitter, 1968; Kozel, 1969), it seems logical to assume that such communications will have a potent influence regardless of their accuracy. Hence, relating as they do to forces which exaggerate the power of a communication, body-postural cues appear to be potent catalysts in interpersonal persuasion (e.g., Middlebrook, 1974).

B. Most efforts to discuss the significance of body language suggest their clinical utility. Aside from analogue research (e.g., Mehrabian, 1967; Mehrabian and Williams, 1969; Kleinke et al., 1975), however, little direct work has been done in analyzing body language in the psychotherapy relationship. Nevertheless, the potential impact of postural-gestural variables has such intuitive appeal that numerous authors (e.g., Brammer and Shostrom, 1969; Polster and Polster, 1973) have described their therapeutic use, and therapeutic techniques have even been formulated around them (Pearls, Heferline, and Goodman, 1951; Reich, 1945). The tentative data available suggests that different therapists have characteristic postural-gestural styles which may relate to their differential effectiveness (Novick, 1967) and which assist in conveying the therapist's interest to the patient (Smith, 1972). In marital relationships, improving a spouse's accuracy in reading body cues may increase the likelihood of a successful marital adjustment (Kahn, 1970).

Self-Disclosure. Personal self-disclosure is a function both of a communicator's verbal and nonverbal style of communication. Self-disclosure is usually discussed either as a listener-patient variable (e.g., Egan, 1970) or as a listener variable which reciprocates persuader-therapist disclosure (e.g., Jourard, 1969; Chittick, and Himelstein, 1967; McAllister and Kiesler, 1975). Nevertheless, as a characteristic of the therapist or persuader, personal self-disclosure has power for producing some of those characteristics found important both to the attitude change process and to psychotherapy outcome. In view of the shaded boundary between clinical and social research in this area, however, we will observe the importance of this variable both to clinical and social research without making a precise distinction between them.

The degree either of experimenter (Jourard, 1969) or therapist (Jourard and

Jaffe, 1970) self-disclosure precipitates a similar disclosure level in subjects and patients. This finding has relevance in the present context because it implies that persuader-therapist self-disclosure promotes a sense of trust on the part of the patient or listener. This implication has received direct research support (Chaiken, Derlega, Bayma, and Shaw, 1975).

The willingness of a persuader to disclose himself, by his facial expression, eye contact, or words and voice quality, determines the degree to which a listener attributes to him those characteristics which are therapeutically and persuasively potent. Through these means, both listeners and patients come to perceive their persuader and therapist as trustworthy, credible, and attractive.

Communication Techniques

In contrast to communicative styles, which are assumed to be reflective of basic communicator attitudinal traits, communication *techniques* are under a good deal of volitional control by the communicator. Communication techniques can be sub-classed into the following categories: (1) language content, (2) interpersonal distance, (3) modeling or role playing, and (4) coercion. These categories reflect many of the dimensions on which psychotherapy techniques vary.

Techniques are designed to have a direct influence on specific attitudes, values, and behaviors. Research in this area has been more directly devoted to understanding attitudinal influence than has that applied to interpersonal style. The latter research focus has been upon determining the processes of communication and attribution which influence the persuasion process rather indirectly.

Language Content. A. Categories of verbal responses, their relative frequency, and the arousal they induce are all related to the persuasive power of a communication. For example, rhetorical questions as opposed to factual statements produce maximal persuasion (Zillman, 1972). Similarly, repetition and interpretation of a point (e.g., Wilson and Miller, 1968; Hovland and Mandell, 1952) increases the persuasive potency of a message. The relative persuasive impact of verbal techniques is apparently related to the amount of provocation or affect arousal potentiated by them. Although the exact effect of arousal on persuasion is not entirely clear, there is little doubt of its potency. While some studies have demonstrated that low arousal is accompanied by greater persuasiveness than comparatively high arousal (e.g., Janis and Feschbach, 1954), others have demonstrated that a high level of arousal induces maximal persuasion (Leventhal and Singer, 1966). Apparently arousal increases the power of a communication both for positive and negative persuasion.

The differential persuasive effects induced by arousal depend on variables such as the motivation and dominant defense strategy of the subject. Janis (1967) hypothesizes that if one is fearful of arousal, arousing communications may simply increase defensiveness. Hence, both excessive and insufficient arousal may be ineffective whereas moderate arousal may produce maximal persuasiveness. Any procedure which serves to decrease defensive tendencies while maintaining arousal is likely to produce a corollary adoption of the persuasive message (e.g., Janis and Feschbach, 1954). Extrapolating from persuasion to psychotherapy literature, we would expect that verbal techniques which induce moderate arousal will be maximally effective.

B. To set the stage for this discussion, let us draw attention to the work of Berenson and his colleagues (Berenson, Mitchell, and Laney, 1968; Berenson, Mitchell, and Moravec, 1968) who have reliably demonstrated that therapists who offer high levels of therapeutic empathy, warmth, and regard also tend to be more interpretative and confrontive in relationships with their patients. Within the broad dimension of confrontation and interpretation, however, high and low functioning therapists can be differentiated. Therapists who represent high levels of the therapeutic conditions, described by Truax and Carkhuff (1967), are more prone than their less effective counterparts both to confront discrepancies between their own and their patient's perceptions of the patient and to focus their interpretations more upon strengths than upon weaknesses. In contrast, therapists who produce little empathy, warmth, or genuineness tend to focus upon weakness and less upon the discrepancies between the patient's and therapist's perception of the relationship.

Clarifying the relationship between these psychotherapy process findings and interpersonal persuasion necessitates a consideration of verbally induced arousal in effective psychotherapy. Much work has been done on psychophysiological correlates of psychotherapy content (e.g., Lacey, 1959; McCarron and Appel, 1971). It is a typical demonstration that mean arousal decreases as repetition of a topic increases. Keeping in mind that decreases in at least subjective arousal levels is associated with therapeutic gain (e.g., Johnson and Matross, 1975), this outcome finding is not unlike that obtained between repetition and persuasion.

The affective arousal induced by different categories of therapist statements is consistent (McCarron and Appel, 1971). Confrontive statements, interpretative statements, interrogative statements, and reflective statements are found, as a general rule, to produce decreasing levels of arousal, respectively. However, even though experienced therapists engage in more confrontation and interpretation than ineffective ones, they are able to do so while producing only moderate degrees of arousal (similar to that obtained with interrogation) whereas confrontations with student therapists produce higher and less effective arousal (McCarron and Appel, 1971). A parallel effect exists between the inverted U function observed between verbally induced arousal and attitude influence, on the one hand, and verbally induced arousal and outcome in effective psychotherapy, on the other.

Segal's (1970) analysis of 2,347 therapists' verbalizations suggests that the differential effectiveness of psychotherapy may in part reflect stable differences in use of arousal-inducing verbalizations. So-called B-type therapists Whitehorn and Betz, 1960) who are effective with highly anxious, neurotic patients (McNair, Callahan, and Lorr, 1962) use fewer anxiety-inducing techniques than their A-type counterparts, whose therapeutic forte may be in the treatment of less affect-ridden schizophrenics. Apparently both personality characteristics (e.g., Franco and Kulberg, 1975) and experience serve to make the therapist skilled at maintaining moderate rather than either very high or low arousal levels in psychotherapy.

Interpersonal Distance. A. Proxemics and interpersonal distance, like face and body gestures, are variables with some power for influencing a listener's perception of the persuader and for conveying the persuader's values and attitudes. Sommer (1969), for example, maintains that implicit norms exist for interpersonal distance, and anxiety increases if these norms are violated. Other things being equal, anxiety can be increased as the communicator moves closer to the listener. In the persuasion process, however, close physical arrangements may be preferred. When the relationship is an intimate one, rather than being threatening, a close physical arrangement precipitates the listener's attribution of the communicator's warmth, interest (Felipe and Sommer, 1966), self-confidence, and friendliness (Evans and Howard, 1973).

In contrast to physical closeness, physical distance conveys rejection and dislike (Hall, 1964; Kleinke, Staneski, and Berger, 1975) and feelings of isolation (Spinetta, Rigler, and Karon, 1974). When a listener finds a persuader unattractive, he tends to establish greater interpersonal distance than when the persuader is seen as attractive (Kleinke et al., 1975). Hence, physical closeness reflects both degree of interest and desire for affiliation, while at the same time potentiating the perception of attractiveness and warmth. When a persuader establishes himself at a close distance, he conveys his desire for a deeper relationship and his interpersonal interest. It is only when the distance established is inconsistent with the listener's expectancy of intimacy in the relationship that closeness becomes aversive (Felipe and Sommer, 1966).

B. In the intimate relationship of psychotherapy, one might expect, on the basis of the foregoing, to find that close interpersonal distances are likely to convey personal attitudes and attributes of the therapist which are more attractive and therapeutic than those conveyed by greater distances. The potential impact of interpersonal distance and posture has been speculated by numerous theorists (e.g., Brammer and Shostrom, 1960) and has been supported in some psychotherapy and psychotherapy analogue research. For example, Mehrabian (1968) has found that interpersonal liking for a communicator increases in relationships maintained within three feet and with a forward balanced posture when compared with interpersonal distance of seven feet and a relaxed, backward balanced posture. Leaning forward and close physical distance tends to convey the therapeutic attitudes of interest and regard, which as we have seen are both potent therapeutic variables.

In contrast to the fear-arousing potential of intimate distance applied in nonintimate relationships (Sommer, 1969), in the intimacy of psychotherapy the greatest countertherapeutic fear of self-disclosure accrues from distances beyond three feet (Quinlan and Janis, 1975). This therapeutic finding is similar to that of Felipe and Sommer (1966) wherein maximum attitudinal influence was maintained in an intimate relationship with close interpersonal distance.

Role Playing. A. Another persuasive technique is *role-playing* a dissonant attitude (e.g., Culbertson, 1957; Janis and King, 1954). Even the anticipation of playing a role consistent with one's own position tends to intensify the strength of a subject's attitudinal stance (Jellison and Mills, 1969), attesting to the cognitive as well as the behavioral mechanisms involved in role playing. Having once decided to make a change in behavior, one's total perspective of a situation is likely to be reevaluated and changed accordingly (e.g., Brehm, 1956); hence, the claim (e.g., Brehm and Cohen, 1962; Cohen, 1964) that the attitudinal influence of role playing can be understood in terms of dissonance resolution. Essentially, this position maintains that a person, having once decided upon or initiated a behavior which is contrary to his preferred position, is in a state of cognitive dissonance. This dissonance may be resolved either by investing that behavior with increased value, at the expense of the original position, or by finding an external rationalization for having made the decision to behave. Hence, role playing which is coerced or forced rather than chosen may not produce the attitude change which follows voluntary role playing because of its susceptibility to rationalization (Kelman, 1961).

The effectiveness of role playing in inducing dissonance may be seen in the amount of arousal instigated by such a procedure. Such arousal if not too extreme, can motivate dissonance resolution (Brehm and Cohen, 1962). For example, Mann and Janis (1968) demonstrate that when smokers role-play patients with terminal lung cancer, both anxiety-fear arousal and persuasiveness increase.

It is important to point out that cognition is an important aspect of role playing. Although attitude-persuasion research demonstrates that behavioral rehearsal or role playing produces more persuasion than cognitive rehearsal, covert rehearsal in situations where behavior role playing is impractical may, nonetheless, be effective (e.g., Cialdini, 1971; Watts, 1967); significant and reliable therapeutic effect (e.g., Kazdin, 1974a; 1974b; Marshall, Boutlier, and Minnes, 1974). Not only does such covert role playing produce therapeutic behavioral benefits, but it also modifies attitudes (e.g., Kazdin, 1974b). As if in support of the similarity of forces underlying overt and covert role rehearsal, Kazdin (1974b) suggests that covertly observing oneself perform a behavior may have greater impact than covertly observing a dissimilar, other performing the same behavior.

The beneficial effects of covert rehearsal underlines the cognitive aspects of role playing, and in this regard bears a similarity to classic modeling. Modeling is defined as observing another's behavior and then rehearsing the same behavior (e.g., Rachman, 1972). The clinical effectiveness of modeling can be partially attributed to the cognitive process of covert rehearsal (e.g., Rachman, 1972; Bandura, 1969;

1971). Such certainly seems to be the case in those instances wherein therapeutic gains are maximized by allowing a patient to observe growth-producing therapy behavior prior to the initiation of psychotherapy (e.g., Truax, Shapiro, and Wargo, 1969; Strupp and Bloxom, 1973).

Coercion. A. Although both overt and covert role playing can be precipitators of attitude change, the amount of *coercion* brought to bear on the listener attenuates or exaggerates the persuasive force of role playing. If one is coerced to behave in a manner contrary to his wishes, he may comply publicly to avoid repercussions without changing his cognitive beliefs (e.g., Kelman, 1961). When a subject feels that his freedom to choose a behavior or attitude is threatened, he tends to resist attitudinal influence (Steiner, 1970). This tendency to react against persuasive forces is called *reactance* (Brehm, 1966), and may vary as a function of personality.

By this point it may be seen that the response to coercion parallels in many ways a subject's response to fear arousal. Perhaps this similarity suggests that reactance is keyed by fear of losing control over one's behavior or attitudes. Messages tend to produce reactance when they are framed in a manner that ostensibly limits choice and demands compliance (Pollack and Heller, 1971). For example, when a persuader asserts, "you must believe ..." or "you can't help but believe ...", reactance is generated.

From this perspective, reactance can be conceptually linked to Rotter's (1966) perceived *locus of control* concept. Locus of control refers to a person's tendency either to perceive himself as controlled by external events, institutions, or fate (external locus of control) or to perceive himself as the principal cause of events which happen to him (internal locus of control). Although perceived locus of control usually describes a personality dimension (Joe, 1971), there are times when the listener's perceptions are systematically manipulated. When studied as a dimension of personality, externally controlled subjects are more, rather than less, susceptible to interpersonal influence attempts (e.g., Getter, 1966; Strickland, 1965; Biardo and Macdonald, 1971). When external locus of control is induced by the state of the environment, however, the listener's action parallels Brehm's (1966) concept of reactance. For example, confronting a situation which one is helpless to change induces an externalized perception of control (e.g., Gorman, 1968; McArthur, 1970), and such externality may result in social resistence (Crawford and Naditch, 1970) and social protest (Silverman and Nakamura, 1972).

B. In regard to choice and psychotherapy, Strong and Matross (1973) observe that patients often generate forces to repell and resist change, and this resistance is likely to increase when the therapist is perceived as demanding change. Hence, a paradoxical effect is created in psychotherapy in which the greater the therapist's demand for improvement, the less the likelihood of change. However, as in the persuasion process, a patient-listener's perception of control may vary as a function of the treatment provided. Treatments which encourage a patient to interpret his change as deriving from internal forces produce more long-lasting therapeutic change than procedures which encourage the patient to perceive his change as coerced (Davidson and Valins, 1969). For example, Davidson, Tsujimoto, and Glaros (1973) have demonstrated that even drug induced improvement in initial insomniacs is better maintained when the patient is led to believe that those changes occurred because of psychological reasons rather than the drug he ingested. Apparently, resistance to initiating or maintaing change is lessened if the message, either implicitly or explicitly, avoids limiting choice.

The foregoing suggests that a parallel exists between coerced social-attitudinal change, on the one hand, and coerced therapeutic change, on the other. Inducing a sense of freedom or internal control is effective in producing desired effects, be it attitude change or therapeutic improvement.

Summary

Our review of communication variables has focused both upon those which are relatively intrinsic to the communicator and those which are easily controllable by the communicator. Through this analysis we have seen that qualitative styles of voice and body language are influential in revealing a persuader's attitudes and values, and self-disclosure is correspondingly influential in effecting therapeutic change.

The persuasive techniques — such as the method in which a message is presented, the interpersonal distance at which the message is delivered, the degree to which the recipient overtly or covertly places himself in an alternate role, and the degree to which the listener feels manipulated or coerced by the advocate-therapist — are all found to be significant both in altering attitudes and pathological behaviors in the desired direction. Role playing, for example, when accompanied with a perception of freedom, is apparently able to facilitate both attitudinal change and therapeutic gain through its dissonance-inducing properties. Similarly, persuasive or therapeutic techniques which produce perceived restrictions in freedom result in resistance both to attitudinal and therapeutic influence.

Listener Characteristics

Numerous listener characteristics influence susceptibility to persuasion. At least in psychotherapy, however, these characteristics seem to be secondary to those associated with the therapist-persuader. Berzins (1974), for example, reports that there are more indicators of improvement associated with therapist variables than there are with patient variables, Nevertheless, both state conditions, as in transitory expectancies, and trait characteristics, as in personality and demographic variables, produce a significant influence on the degree of persuasibility and on one's sus-ceptibility to improvement.

Although demographic variables may be significant both to interpersonal per-suasion (Hyman and Sheatsley, 1947; Janis and Field, 1959) and to the psycho-therapy process (Orlinsky and Howard, 1975), they will not be considered in the present comparison. Both in psychotherapy and in persuasion research we have principally studied the young, intelligent, and educated individual, and while this restriction makes the populations somewhat comparable, it mitigates against determining the stable effects of demographic variables in either population or comparing them. Socioeconomic status, intelligence, and education often determine the therapist's interest in treating a given patient (Anzel, 1970; Schofield, 1964; Stein, Green, and Stone, 1972; Garfield, 1971), but within the restricted population offered psychotherapy there is some doubt whether demographic variables further determine a patient's response to treatment (Wogan, 1970). In a similar way, the tendency to study university freshmen restricts the range of demographic variables represented in the persuasion research. Hence, the following discussion will attend to variables that are relatively well represented both in attitude influence literature and in clinical research.

For the following presentation, listener-patient characteristics are categorized under two headings: (1) *Listener Expectancies,* which includes both expectancy to disclose oneself and expectancy for external control; and (2) *Effort Expended* in the course of the influence process. Parallel effects between these variables in clinical and laboratory environments will be considered.

Listener Expectancies

Process Expectancy. A. There are two kinds of listener expectations which are critical to the understanding of interpersonal persuasion. First, *state* expectations may differ as to the behaviors which will be required in a specific relationship. Secondly, expectations may be considered from the standpoint of personality *traits,* representing a generalized expectation of one's environment.

As one anticipates a defined interpersonal state, positive or negative expectancies serve to increase or decrease the power of a persuasive message. For example, in social psychology literature, efforts to innoculate a person against subsequent influence attempts demonstrate consistently (e.g., McGuire and Papageorgis, 1961; Lewan and Stotland, 1961) that strengthening one's expectancy by providing information which is consistent with one's pretreatment attitude or belief efficiently inhibits subsequent opinion change.

On the other hand, changing one's expectancy results in significant changes in one's response to interpersonal situations. These changes represent changes of attitudes in their own right, and have potent effect in determining the effectiveness of future influence attempts. For example, Wilson and Rappaport (1974) have demonstrated that in talking to an interviewer, a listener's expectancy to self-disclose significantly influences the amount of subsequent self-disclosure evidenced. In this study, expectancy of self-disclosure was altered by providing "feedback" from a credible source, suggesting that the subject was the type of person for whom self-disclosure would either be easy or difficult. As the intimacy of the topic under discussion increased, more self-disclosure was noted as a function of these predesigned expectancies. As attitudes in their own right, however, such generalized expectancies are heavily influenced by the behavior of the persuader. For example, the presentation of personal information by one member of a dyad produces reciprocal amounts of personal revelation from the recipient (e.g., Chittick and Himelstein, 1967; Jourard, 1969; Jourard and Jaffe, 1970).

B. In the therapeutic environment, expectancy has been investigated both as a nonspecific and a specific change variable. By altering patient expectancies, both global improvement (McGlynn and Williams, 1970) and therapy process (Egan, 1964; Goldstein, 1966) are facilitated. Patient expectancies of psychotherapy are so potent a variable in influencing therapeutic process (e.g., Marcia, Rubin, and Efran, 1969) that some go so far as to suggest that much of what passes for psychotherapy may be nothing more than a nonspecific placebo treatment (Shapiro, 1971). There is some doubt, however, whether patient expectancy effects have been adequately analyzed apart from therapist expectancy to draw definitive conclusions in this regard (e.g., Wilkins, 1973, in press).

One method of studying specific expectancy effects in psychotherapy is to systematically present information, prior to treatment, which is designed to create an attitudinal set as to "appropriate" therapy behaviors and realistic gains (e.g., Hoehn-Saric, Frank, Imber, Nash, Stone, and Battle, 1964; Strupp and Bloxom, 1973). In view of the efficiency of these procedures in maintaining the therapeutic relationship and facilitating therapy change, Strupp and Bloxom (1973) argue that inducing therapy expectancies may be particularly valuable when treating low income, undesirable, and poorly motivated patients who otherwise hold expectations which are widely divergent from middle-class therapists.

Expectancies of self-disclosure are ordinarily studied in the therapy environment as trait dimensions. That is, one's attitudinal set to disclose oneself in interpersonal relationships is evaluated as a corollary to certain therapy processes. Considered in such a way, expectancy of self-disclosure has received considerable discussion in the literature as it applies to psychotherapy (e.g., Egan, 1964). As in persuasion research, reciprocity of self-disclosure is indicated in the therapy environment. In a clinical population, however, expectancy of self-disclosure seems closely related to other significant variables. For example, the generalized disclosure expectancies of neurotic patients seem relatively untempered either by the intimacy of the topic or the self-disclosure of the therapist (Chaiken, Derlega, Bayma, and Shaw, 1975).

In a similar manner, the tendency to self-disclose is affected by other pretreatment expectancies. For example, if a patient has a low expectancy of favorable outcome, he tends to become markedly more guarded and reluctant to disclose personal information than if he has a high expectancy of improvement (Kopfstein, 1974). Because of this relationship of self-disclosure expectancy to generalized expectancy of therapeutic gain, the tendency to disclose oneself is not universally associated with therapeutic improvement. In behavior modification programs, for example, where degree of intimacy is relatively low, high levels of patient disclosure may be followed by feelings of vulnerability, defensive reactiveness, and lack of cooperation (Quinlin and Janis, 1975).

Locus of Control. A. A second aspect of listener expectancy to be considered in this section is the listener's generalized anticipation of how or from whence efforts to control him will derive. Rotter (1966) has defined internal and external generalized expectancies of reinforcement or control, and demonstrated that these represent significant and stable attitudes which are a strong determining feature of the person's response to interpersonal influence. Although people in general tend to react against external forces which restrict their alternatives (e.g., Biando and MacDonald, 1971), those who characteristically expect external control are more susceptible to such influence than are those who characteristically expect their control to derive from internal sources (e.g., Crowne and Liverant, 1963; Julian, Lichtman, and Rykman, 1968). It is no surprise to find that externally dependent people are more susceptible to the subtle interpersonal forces which produce even unintended social influence (Smith and Flenning, 1971), and that they are highly susceptible to subtle verbal conditioning procedures (Getter, 1966; Alegre and Murray, 1974) which may occur without their awareness. This effect is exaggerated the more the persuader is perceived as competent, independent, and internally controlled (Julian and Katz, 1968).

This persuasive susceptibility of "external" subjects seems to occur in part because such subjects are highly attentive to the potential of interpersonal evaluation in social situations (Bellak and Tillman, 1974). To the extent that an externalized, interpersonal focus is reflective of needs for social approval, logic suggests that such people may be highly susceptible to influence from the subtle biases of a persuader. This hypothesis has received some research support in the work of Smith and Flenning (1971) who demonstrate that when need for approval is relatively high among experimental subjects, the experimenter's biases regarding the expected outcome of the experiment are significantly more likely to influence the results. As a result, people with external expectancies are less effective in dealing with their environment (e.g., Phares, 1968), avoid evaluative feedback of their performance, and have little social opportunity to improve their ability to handle difficult problem situations (Holmes and Jackson, 1975). In competitive situations, subjects with external expectancies of control tend to team themselves with those of known inferiority, thus insuring against negative comparisions even at the expense of team failure (Ryckman and Sherman, 1974).

The foregoing suggests that an expectancy of external control is an indicator of relatively poor social and interpersonal adjustment. Hence, with an eye toward treatment, the question arises as to the feasibility of changing these generalized expectancies. Eisman (1972) evaluated this possibility in the laboratory environment, and suggests that an experimenter-manipulated conditioning process may be effective in producing increased internal expectations. In his procedure, Eisman provided reinforcements for verbal expressions of internal control and demonstrated a more generalized change in the experimental subjects' acquisition of an internal expectancy.

B. Clinical research on generalized expectancies of external and internal control has focused on two aspects of the problem. First, efforts have been made to evaluate the effects of various psychotherapy procedures on patients with these two generalized expectancies. Second, efforts have been made to empirically relate internal and external expectancies of control to other personality characteristics. In regard to the first line of research, one would expect from laboratory findings that subjects with internal expectancies will react more negatively to high potency, directive therapy attempts, whereas subjects with external expectancies will be more susceptible to directive and coercive approaches. This hypothesis has in fact been supported in clinical literature. For example, Abramowitz, Abramowitz, Roback, and Jackson (1974) demonstrate that with midly depressed, externally oriented patients, a directive therapeutic procedure produces more improvement in patients' ratings of self-esteem, anxiety, and affectional needs, than when treated with a relatively passive, nondirective therapy regime. Patients with internal expectancies, on the other hand, gained the greatest benefit from a low profile, nondirective influence procedure. This general tendency has been replicated in other research (e.g., Friedman and Dies, 1974) and extended to self-directed behavior therapy (Balch and Ross, 1975) and biofeedback procedures (Johnson and Meyer, 1974).

The results of such studies as the foregoing are consistent with laboratory findings which suggest that highly directive and powerful influence efforts are rejected by those who maintain an internal attitudinal expectancy of control, whereas those with an external expectancy are highly susceptible to controlling and coercive influence.

A second body of clinical research suggests that in clinical populations, as in laboratory populations, an external expectation of control is associated with pathological characteristics (Duke and Mullens, 1973). An external expectancy of control tends to produce both increased defensiveness to internal threat (Lipp, Kolstoe, James, and Randall, 1968) and heightened sensitivity to negative evaluations (Phares, Ritchie, and Davis, 1968). Those with an external expectancy who react to failure by blaming and developing externalized defenses — as opposed to internalizing anxiety like those with an internal expectancy do (Phares and Lamiell, 1974) — tend to distance themselves from other people (Duke and Mullens, 1973).

Transitory changes in external or internal expectancies of control may produce somewhat different types of psychopathology, however. For example, it may be speculated that if circumstances combine to produce a sense of helplessness in one's environment, one may become both more expectant of external control and more depressed. The concept of depression has been rationally related to acute feelings of helplessness (e.g., Hiroto, 1974; Miller and Seligman, 1975; Seligman, 1975), but there is some data to suggest that although a relationship exists between depression and external expectancy of control, it is relatively small (Naditch, Gargan, and Michael, 1975).

The apparent association between external expectancy of control and psychological difficulty brings us once again to the question of how generalized expectancy of control may be altered by psychotherapy procedures. Following the lead of Eisman (1972), several authors (e.g., Reimanis, 1974; Smith, 1970) have demonstrated that internal perceptions of control may increase with psychological treatment regimes. While no direct evidence exists that therapy-induced change in such generalized expectancies approximate the expectancies held by their therapists, there is suggestive data that the degree and probability of this change is apparently facilitated by more experienced psychotherapists (Diamond and Shapiro, 1973) and does not occur in a therapist-absent group. These data are suggestive both that changes in expectancy of control are a positive index of therapy improvement (e.g., Gillis and Jessor, 1970) and that patients may make these expectancy changes in reference to their therapist's attitude of internal control.

Effort Expended

A. From a perspective of dissonance theory (Festinger, 1957), a listener's attitude about a given object may change proportional to the amount of effort expended in relation to that object. For example, if one sees himself expending a great deal of effort in a disliked activity, he may justify his effort and restore consonance by changing his negative opinion. This is the principle upon which initiation into fraternities, sororities, clubs, and religious groups is based.

In support of this point of view, Festinger and Carlsmith (1959) found that the amount of money one receives for undertaking a boring task was inversely proportional to the amount of liking for that task. Participants apparently rationalized their willingness to undertake the task for minimal pay by exaggerating the desirability of the task itself. Translating these findings into physical effort, Aronson and Mills (1959) evaluated the manner in which initiation rites affect a person's subsequent liking for a group. They demonstrated in a sample of sorority girls that if one suffers to join a group the value of the group increases. This finding has been replicated in other situations (e.g., Hautaluom and Spurgin, 1974). Extending these findings more directly to classical persuasibility, Zimbardo (1965) has demonstrated that if one has to expend more effort in order to hear a persuasive speech, the persuasive potency of the speech is exacerbated above the level obtained when one has to exert little effort to hear.

B. In psychotherapy, research has failed to confirm the linear relationship between effort expended and either attitude change or improvement which would be expected from the foregoing. Goldstein (1971) manipulated three levels of effort between sessions and measured patients' resultant attraction to psychotherapy. Minimal effort subjects simply attended psychotherapy sessions in the regular manner. Moderate effort subjects, on the other hand, were asked to return to the therapist's office in order to listen to a recording of one session before undertaking another. Maximal effort subjects were also required to listen to the last session before undergoing the next but their effort was compounded by introducing white noise into the therapy tapes, thus making listening more difficult. Repeatedly, throughout the therapeutic experience, the patient's attraction both to therapy and to the therapist was measured. The results suggest that increased attractiveness is a function of effort expended, at least early in therapy. Surprisingly, however, moderate effort produced greater attractiveness than either relatively low or high expended effort. There was no evidence to suggest that patients' perception of the relevance of the effort altered the effect.

From a similar perspective, Beutler, Johnson, Neville, and Workman (1972b) evaluated the relationship between distance voluntarily traveled to obtain treatment at a private psychiatric hospital both on a patient's evaluation of his therapist and his therapist's ratings of improvement. After ruling out systematic bias in age, education, and degree of disturbance, the results are analogous to those obtained by Goldstein (1971). Though not suggesting that effort expended has a direct influence on a patient's perception of his therapist, moderate levels of effort expended (i.e. distance traveled) tended to produce higher improvement ratings than either high or low levels of effort expenditure.

While not producing results precisely equivalent to those obtained in the social psychology laboratory, the foregoing findings do suggest that a patient's evaluation and attraction to his therapist may be effected by the amount of effort expended to undergo treatment. Though it appears that in a clinical population large amounts of effort expended in seeking treatment may have negative effects, the data suggest that effort is a potent variable in the treatment process.

Summary

In our analysis of listener characteristics, we have chosen not to discuss demographic variables because of their restricted range in populations used to study both psychotherapy and interpersonal persuasion. Instead, we have focused our attention upon generalized listener expectancies and effort expended as variables which may be more or less differentiated from characteristics of the communication.

The foregoing review, although brief, has demonstrated that one's expectancy of his role in an interpersonal situation tends to exert a substantial influence on how he actually behaves in that situation. Inducing changes in these expectations can influence the amount both of attitudinal and therapeutic change incurred. For example, one's expectancy to disclose himself tends to become self-fulfilling. In a similar manner, a patient's generalized expectancy to look to external as opposed to internal sources for direction seems to influence the degree of his responsiveness to structured, persuader-controlled influences. A trait of external expectancy seems to make one more responsive to highly directive influence attempts than if one has a trait of internal expectancy. This characteristic seems to hold whether the variable being discussed is attitude change or more broadly conceived estimates of therapeutic change. A trait of external expectancy, however, is associated with certain maladaptive and even pathological characteristics; and specific psychological techniques have been shown to exert both an effect upon the expectancy attitude in the persuasion laboratory, and on specific indices of therapeutic growth.

Our evaluation of the effort a listener expends in listening to a persuasive or therapeutic communication does not produce results which are precisely parallel in the two situations. Whereas effort expended seems rather linearly related to amount of subsequent attitude change in the persuasion laboratory, moderate effort seems to be associated with greater therapeutic progress in the clinical environment. Perhaps effort expended in psychotherapy does not produce precisely the same effects as in the persuasion laboratory because of an emphasis on affect dominant attitudes in the former, and cognitive dominant attitudes in the latter. Argyris (1969) argues that different variables mediate affectively laden and cognitively laden attitudes and values. While variables such as effort expended, expectancy, and communicator characteristics may be equally potent both in persuasion of cognitive and affective attitudes, the parameters which describe the effect of these variables may differ substantially in the two situations.

CONCLUSIONS

In the preceding review of psychotherapy and interpersonal persuasion, we have seen that many of the variables which result in effective persuasion also result in beneficial response to psychological treatment. For example, attributing high levels of credibility, attractiveness, and positive expectancy either to a therapist or a persuader tends to maximize the amount of influence which he exerts upon a listener's attitudes, values, and/or therapeutic improvement.

While a good deal of parallelism exists between interpersonal persuasion and psychotherapy outcome, there are at least two areas in which there are notable inconsistencies. First, we have seen several cases in which degree of persuasiveness in psychotherapy was related to attitudinal and value discrepancy of patient and therapist, whereas persuasion and various ratings of improvement were not so related. Second, while persuasion literature suggests that attitude change may be linearly related to the amount of effort expended in the persuasion process, psychotherapy research suggests that process and outcome are complexly, and usually curvilinearly related to effort expended in treatment.

We must conclude that while interpersonal persuasion and psychotherapy may be analogous processes, psychotherapy as an attitude or value change process is somewhat different than the usual laboratory, interpersonal persuasion process. Attitudes are classically defined as behavioral, cognitive, and affective predispositions for response to an object or idea. The cognitive attitude component is more frequently studied than either the behavioral or affective components in the usual laboratory situation, however. On the other hand, the affective component may be more heavily involved in psychotherapy (e.g., Argyris, 1969). Hence, certain variables, though significant in both endeavors, may operate differently in each; and this distinction may account for the areas in which variables in persuasive influence produce different effects upon improvement ratings and attitude change, respectively.

We have presented evidence that attitude-value change occurs consistently through the course of both individual, family, and group psychotherapy (Beutler, 1971c; Beutler et al., 1974; Beutler et al., 1975). Not only are patients able to quickly and accurately perceive their therapists' values (Beutler, 1971b), but there is a consistent and strong tendency for the amount of initial disparity existing between patient and therapist values to be significantly related to the way in which values change during the course of psychotherapy. That is, patients become increasingly more similar to their therapist as a product of the amount of initial value disagreement.

Since dissonance theory (Festinger, 1957) predicts that other things being equal the amount of attitude discrepancy between the communicator and the recipient is linearly predictive of the amount of attitude change resultant, one might interpret the foregoing results as demonstrating that cognitive dissonance is a significant factor in the therapeutic value change process. Hence, psychotherapy must be considered an attitude influence process. At the current state of our knowledge, however, the relationship between value or attitude change and improvement is very complex. Until we can specifiy what values are important in therapeutic growth, we are best confined to our attempts to influence the usual outcome criteria by systematically manipulating the conditions under which specific persuasive forces, such as credibility, attractiveness, and persuasive power, are invoked. When in the state of our knowledge we can specify and reliably measure the attitudes and values of significance to various criteria of improvement, we may then be able to exert a direct influence on these attitudes and values through more precise therapeutic techniques and, at the same time, utilize measurements of these values as a more direct improvement criterion than the global measures currently in vogue.

As we have analyzed the characteristics of persuasive communication, it may have become apparent that therapeutic approaches can be conceptualized as differing along the dimensions presented. That is, different therapeutic techniques emphasize different forms of verbal content and variations in interpersonal distance and posture, place different emphasis upon role playing or behavioral rehearsal, and exercise different levels and kinds of coercion or direction. For example, client-centered therapy emphasizes the use of reflection, as opposed to interpretation, admonishes the therapist to maintain close interpersonal distance, and minimizes both role playing and external direction. In contrast, psychoanalytic therapy emphasizes interpretation and confrontation, and "objective" interpersonal distance, while continuing to deemphasize role playing and external coercion. In a similar way, behavioral therapies as well as specific subtypes of cognitive, affective, and behavioral approaches may be distinguished on the basis of the relative weight given to each of these communication variables. Future research must consider the implications of this analysis at greater lengths in preparation for defining the appropriate application of various approaches.

REFERENCES

Abelson R., and Miller, J., Negative persuasion via personal insult. *Journal of Experimental and Social Psychology,* 1967, *3,* 321–333.

Abramowitz C. V., Abramowitz, S. I., Roback, H. B., and Jackson, C., Differential effectiveness of directive and nondirective group therapies as a function of client internal-external control. *Journal of Consulting and Clinical Psychology,* 1974, *42,* 849–853.

Alegre, C., and Murray, E. J., Locus of Control, behavioral intention, and verbal conditioning. *Journal of Personality* 1974, *42,* 668–681.

Anderson, A. B., Combined effects of interpersonal attraction and goal path clarity on the cohesiveness of task oriented groups. *Journal of Personality and Social Psychology,* 1975, *31,* 68–75.

Anzel Anne Smith, A-B typing and patient socioeconomic and personality characteristics in a quasi-therapeutic situation. *Journal of Consulting and Clinical Psychology,* 1970, *35,* 1, 102–115.

Argyris, C., The incompleteness of social-psychological consistency, and attribution research. *American Psychologist,* 1969, *24,* 893–908.

Aronson, E., The theory of cognitive dissonance: A current perspective. In L. Berkowitz (Ed.), *Advances in Experimental Social Psychology, Vol. 4,* New York: Academic Press, 1969, pp. 1–34.

Aronson E., and Mills, V., The effects of severity of initiation on liking for a group. *Journal of Abnormal and Social Psychology,* 1959, *59,* 177–181.

Aronson, E., Turner V., and Carlsmith, M., Communicator credibility and communicator discrepancy as determinors of opinion change. *Journal of Abnormal and Social Psychology,* 1963, *67,* 31–36.

Asher, N. W., Manipulating attraction toward the disabled: An application of the similarity-attractiveness model. *Rehabilitation Psychology,* 1973, *20,* 156–164.

Back K. W., Influence through social communication. *Journal of Abnormal and Social Psychology,* 1951, *46,* 9–23.

Balch, P., and Ross, A. W., Predicting success in weight reduction as a function of locus of control: A unidimensional study. *Journal of Consulting and Clinical Psychology,* 1975, *43,* 119.

Bandura, A., *Principles of Behavior Modification.* New York: Holt, Rinehart & Winston, 1969.

Bandura, A., Psychotherapy based upon modeling principles. In A. E. Bergin and S. L. Garfield (Eds.), *Handbook of Psychotherapy and Behavior Change.* New York: Wiley, 1971, pp. 653–709.

Bandura, A., Blanchard, E. B., and Ritter, B., The relative efficacy of desensitization and modeling approaches for inducing behavioral, affective and attitudinal changes. *Journal of Personality and Social Psychology,* 1969, *13,* 173–199.

Bednar, R. L., and Mobley, M. J., A-B therapist perceptions and preferences for schizophrenic and psychoneurotic clients. *Journal of Abnormal Psychology,* 1971, *78,* 2, 192–197.

Bellack, A. S., and Tillman, W., Effects of task and experimenter feedback on the self reinforcement behavior of internals and externals. *Journal of Consulting and Clinical Psychology,* 1974, *42,* 330–336.

Berenson, B. G., Mitchell, K. M., and Laney, R., Level of therapist functioning, types of confrontation, and type of patient. *Journal of Clinical Psychology,* 1968, *24,* 111–114.

Berenson, B. G., Mitchell, K. M., and Moravec, J. A., Level of therapist functioning, type of confrontation, and patient depth of self-exploration. *Journal of Counseling Psychology,* 1968, *15,* 136–139.

Bergin, A. E., Some implications of psychotherapy research for therapeutic practice: A 10-year follow up. Presidential address given at the 6th annual meeting of the Society for Psychotherapy Research, Boston, June, 1975.

Bergin, A. E., The effect of dissonant persuasive communications upon changes in a self referring attitude. *Journal of Personality,* 1962, 423–438.

Bergum, M., Values and some technical problems in psychotherapy. *American Journal of Orthopsychiatry,* 1957, *27,* 338–348.

Berscheid E., Opinion change and communicator communicatee similarity and dissimilarity. *Journal of Personality and Social Psychology,* 1966, *4,* 670–680.

Berzins, J. I., Matching patients with therapists: Conceptual, empirical, and pragmatic perspectives. A paper presented at the 5th annual meeting of the Society for Psychotherapy Research, Denver, June, 1974.

Berzins, J. I., Friedman, W. H., and Seidman, E., Relationship of the A-B variable to patient symptomatology and psychotherapy expectancies. *Journal of Abnormal Psychology,* 1969, *74,* 119–125

Bettinghaus, E., Operation of congruity in an oral communication setting. *Speech Monographs,* 1961, *28,* 131–142.

Beutler, L. E., Attitude similarity in marital therapy. *Journal of Consulting and Clinical Psychology,* 1971a, *37,* 298–301.

Beutler, L. E., Perceived patient-therapist similarity and patient change in psychotherapy. Paper presented at the meeting of the Southeastern Psychological Association, Miami Beach, May, 1971b .

Beutler, L. E., Predicting outcomes of psychotherapy: A comparison of predictions from two attitude therories. *Journal of Consulting and Clinical Psychology,* 1971c, *37,* 411–416.

Beutler, L. E., Value and attitude change in psychotherapy: A case for dyadic assessment. *Psychotherapy: Theory, Research and Practice,* 1972, *9,* 362–367.

Beutler, L. E., The therapy dyad: Yet another look at diagnostic assessment. *Journal of Personality Assessment,* 1973, *37,* 303–308.

Beutler, L. E., Jobe, A. M., and Elkins, D., Outcomes in group psychotherapy: Using persuasion theory to increase treatment efficiency. *Journal of Consulting and Clinical Psychology,* 1974, *42,* 547–553.

Beutler, L. E., Johnson, D. T., Neville, C. W., Jr., Elkins, D., and Jobe, A. M., Attitude similarity and therapist credibility as predictors of attitude change and improvement in psychotherapy. *Journal of Consulting and Clinical Psychology,* 1975.

Beutler, L. E., Johnson D. T., Neville, C. W., Jr., and Workman, S. N., "Accurate Empathy" and the A-B dichotomy. *Journal of Consulting and Clinical Psychology,* 1972a, *38,* 362–376 .

Beutler, L. E., Johnson, D. T., Neville, C. W., Jr., and Workman, S. N., Effort expended as a determiner of treatment evaluation and outcome: The honor of a prophet in his own country. *Journal of Consulting and Clinical Psychology,* 1972b, *39,* 495–500.

Beutler, L. E., Johnson D. T., Neville, C. W., Jr., Workman, S. N., and Elkins, D., The A-B therapy type distinction, accurate empathy, nonpossessive warmth, and genuineness in psychotherapy. *Journal of American Psychiatry,* 1973, *32,* 273–277.

Biondo J., and MacDonald, A. P., Jr., Internal-external locus of control and response to influence attempts. *Journal of Personality,* 1971, *39,* 407–419.

Brammer, L. M., and Shostrom, E. L., *Therapeutic Psychology.* Englewood Cliffs, New Jersey: Prentice-Hall, 1960.

Breger, L., and McGaugh, J. L., Critique and reformulation of "learning theory" approaches to psychotherapy. *Psychology Bulletin,* 1965, *63,* 338–358.

Breham, J., *A Theory of Psychological Reactance.* New York: Academic Press, 1966.

Brehm, J., and Cohen, A. R., *Explorations in Cognitive Dissonance.* New York: Wiley, 1962.

Breham, J., Post decision changes in desirability of alternatives. *Journal of Abnormal and Social Psychology,* 1956, *52* 384–389.

Brock T., Communicator-recipient similarity and decision change. *Journal of Personality and Social Psychology* 1965, *1,* 650–654.

Browning, G. J., An analysis of the effects of therapist prestige and levels of interpretation on client response in the initial phase of psychotherapy. *Dissertation Abstracts,* 1966, *26,* 4803.

Buhler, C., *Values in Psychotherapy.* New York: Free Press, 1962.

Byrne. D., Griffitt, W., and Golightly, C., Prestige as a factor in determining the effect of attitude similarity dissimilarity on attraction. *Journal of Personality,* 1966, *34,* 434–444.

Cantril, H., and Allport, G., *The Psychology of Radio.* New York: Harper, 1935.

Carr, John E., Differentiation similarity of patient and therapist and the outcome of psychotherapy. *Journal of Abnormal Psychology,* 1970, *76,* 3, 361–369.

Carson, R. C., and Heine, R. W., Similarity and success in therapeutic dyads. *Journal of Consulting Psychology,* 1962, *26,* 38–43.

Carson R. C., and Llewellyn, C. E., Jr., Similarity in therapeutic dyads: A revaluation. *Journal of Consulting Psychology,* 1966, *30,* 458.

Chaiken A. L., Derlega, V. J., Bayma, B., and Shaw, J., Neuroticism and disclosure reciprocity. *Journal of Consulting and Clinical Psychology,* 1975, *43,* 13–19.

Chittick E. V., and Himelstein, P., Manipulation of self-disclosure. *Journal of Psychology,* 1967 *65* 117–121.

Cialdini, R., Attitudinal advocacy in the verbal conditioner. *Journal of Personality and Social Psychology* 1971, *17,* 350–358.

Cohen, A. R., *Attitude change and social influence.* New York: Basic Books, 1964.

Conolley, E. S., Green, D., and Kaufman, A., Interpersonal similarity and persuasiveness: The message is the medium. Unpublished Manuscript, University of California, 1973.

Corsini, R. J., *Roleplaying in Psychotherapy: A Manual,* Chicago: Aldine, 1966.

Crawford, T. J., and Naditch, M., Relative deprivation, powerlessness, and militancy: The psychology of social protest. *Psychiatry,* 1970, *33,* 265–281.

Crowe D., and Liverant, S., Conformity under varying conditions of personal commitment. *Journal of Abnormal and Social Psychology,* 1963, *66,* 574–555.

Culbertson F., Modification of an emotionally held attitude through role playing. *Journal of Abnormal and Social Psychology,* 1957, *54,* 230–234.

Davison G. C., Tsujimoto, R. N., and Glaros, A. G., Attribution and the maintenance of behavior change in falling asleep. *Journal of Abnormal Psychology,* 1973, *82,* 1, 124–133.

Davison G. C., and Valins, S., Maintenance of self attributed and drug attributed behavior change. *Journal of Personality and Social Psychology,* 1969, *11,* 25–33.

Diamond, M. J., and Shapiro, J. L., Changes in locus of control as a function of encounter group experiences: A study and replication. *Journal of Abnormal Psychology,* 1973, *82,* 514–518.

Duke, M. P., and Mullens, M. C., Preferred interpersonal distance as a function of locus of control orientation in chronic schizophrenics, non-schizophrenic patients and normals. *Journal of Consulting and Clinical Psychology,* 1973, *41,* 230–234.

Egan, G., *Encounter.* New York: Brooks-Cole, 1970.

Ehrlich D., and Wiener, D. N., The measurement of values in psychotherapeutic settings. *Journal of General Psychology,* 1961, *64,* 359–372.

Eisenman, R., Experience in experiments and change in internal-external control scores. *Journal of Consulting and Clinical Psychology,* 1972, *39,* 434–435.

Ekman, P., Body position, facial expression and verbal behavior during interviews. *Journal of Abnormal and Social Psychology*, 1964, *68*, 295–301.

Ekman, P., and Friesen, W., Nonverbal leakage and clues to deception. *Psychiatry*, 1969, *32*, 88–106.

Ellis, A., and Harper, R. A., *A Guide to Rational Living*. Englewood Cliffs, New Jersey: Prentice-Hall 1961.

Ellsworth P., and Carlsmith, J., Effects of eye contact and verbal content on affective response to a dyadic interaction. *Journal of Personality and Social Psychology*, 1968, *10*, 15–20.

Evans, G. W., and Howard, R. B., Personal space. *Psychological Bulletin*, 1973, *80*, 334–344.

Eysenck, H. J., The effects of psychotherapy: An evaluation. *Journal of Consulting Psychology*, 1952, *16*, 319–324.

Feldman-Summers, s. A., Blunders and interpersonal attraction under conditions of dependency. *Journal of Abnormal Psychology*, 1974, *83*, 3, 323–326.

Felipe, N., and sommer, R., Invasions of personal space. *Social Problems*, 1966, *14*, 206–214.

Festinger, L., *A Theory of Cognitive Dissonance*. Stanford: Stanford University Press, 1957.

Festinger, L., and Carlsmith J., Cognitive consequences of forced compliance. *Journal of Abnormal and Social Psychology*, 1959, *58*, 203–310.

Franco, E. A., and Kulberg, G. E., Content analysis of the natural language of A & B males in a dyadic interaction. *Journal of Consulting and Clinical Psychology*, 1975, *43*, 345–349.

Frank, J. D., *Persuasion and Healing*. Baltimore: Johns Hopkins University Press, 1973 (2nd Edition).

Freud, S., (Collected writings) In J. Strachey (Ed.), *The Standard Edition of the Complete Psychological Works of Sigmund Freud*. London: Hogarth Press, 1958, 24 Vols.

Friedman, M. I., and Dies, r. R., Reactions of internal and external test anxious students to counseling and behavior therapies. *Journal of Consulting and Clinical Psychology*, 1974, *42*, 921.

Garfield, S. L., Research on client variables in psychotherapy. In A. E. Bergin and S. L. Garfield (Eds.) *Handbook of Psychotherapy and Behavior Change*. New York: Wiley, 1971, pp. 271–298.

Garfield, S. L., Values: An issue in psychotherapy: Comments on a case study. *Journal of Abnormal Psychology*, 1974, *83*, 202–203.

Garfield, S. L., and Affleck, D. C., Therapists' judgments concerning patients considered for psychotherapy. *Journal of Consulting Psychology*, 1961, *25*, 505–509.

Getter, H., A personality determinant of verbal conditioning. *Journal of Personality*, 1966, *34*, 397–405.

Gillis, J. S., and Jessor, R., Effects of brief psychotherapy on belief in internal control: An exploratory study. *Psychotherapy: Theory, Research, & Practice*, 1970, *7*, 135–137.

Glad, D. D., *Operational Values in Psychotherapy*. New York: Oxford University Press, 1959.

Glad, D. D., Theories, operations and behavioral feedbacks in interview process research. *Journal of Colorado Wyoming Academy of Science*, 1955, *4*, 56–57.

Glad, D. D., Lewis, R. T., Page, C. W., and Jeffers, J. R., Improvement in psychotherapy. A function of therapy methods and performance measures. *Journal of Colorado-Wyoming Academy of Science*, 1953, *4*, 49–50.

Goldstein, A. P., Psychotherapy research by extrapolation from social psychology. *Journal of Counseling Psychology*, 1966, *13*, 38–45.

Goldstein, A. P., *Psychotherapeutic attraction*, New York: Pergamon, 1971.

Goldstein, A. P., Therapist and client expectation of personality change in psychotherapy. *Journal of Counseling Psychology*, 1960, *7*, 180–184.

Goldstein, I., and McGinies, E., Compliance and attitude change under conditions of differential social reinforcement. *Journal of Abnormal and Social Psychology*, 1964, *68*, 567–570.

Goldstein, A. P., Simonson, N. R., Social psychological approaches to psychotherapy research. In A. E. Bergin & S. L. Garfield (Eds.) *Handbook of Psychotherapy and Behavior Change.* New York: Wiley, 1971, pp. 154–195.

Goldstein, A. P., Heller, K., & Sechrest, L. B., *Psychotherapy and the Psychology of Behavior Change.* New York: Wiley, 1966.

Gorman, B. S., An observation of altered locus of control following political disappointment. *Psychological Reports,* 1968, *23,* 1094.

Greenspoon, J., The reinforcing effect of two spoken sounds on the frequency of two responses. *American Journal of Psychology,* 1955, *68,* 409–416.

Gurman, A. S., Attitude change in marital cotherapy. *Journal of Family Counseling,* 1974, *2,* 50–54.

Hall, E. T., Silent assumptions in social communication. *Disorders of Communication,* 1964, *42,* 41–55.

Hautaluom, J. E., and Spungin, H., Effects of initiation severity and interest on group attitudes. *Journal of Social Psychology,* 1974, *93,* 245–259.

Heller, K., and Goldstein. A. P., Client dependency and therapist expectancy as relationship maintaining variables in psychotherapy. *Journal of Consulting Psychology,* 1961, *25,* 371–375.

Hersh J. B., Effects of referral information on testers. *Journal of Consulting and Clinical Psychology,* 1971, *37,* 116–122.

Hill, J. A., Therapist goals patient aims, and patient satisfaction in therapy. *Journal of Clinical Psychology,* 1969, *25,* 455–459.

Hiroto, D. S., Locus of Control and learned helplessness. *Journal of Experimental Psychology,* 1974, *102,* 187–193.

Hoehn-Saric, R., Frank, J. D., Imber, S. D., Nash, E. H., Stone, A. R., and Battle, C. C., Systematic preparation of patients for psychotherapy: I. Effects on therapy behavior and outcome. *Journal of Psychiatric Research,* 1964, *2,* 267–281.

Holmes, D. S., and Jackson, T. H., Influence of locus of control on interpersonal attraction and affective reactions in situations involving reward and punishment. *Journal of Personality and Social Psychology,* 1975, *31,* 132–136.

Holzman M. S., The significance of value systems of patient and therapist for outcome in psychotherapy. *Dissertation Abstracts,* 1962, *22,* 4073.

Horney, K., *New Ways in Psychoanalysis.* New York: Norton, 1939.

Hovland, C. I., Reconsiling conflicting results derived from experimental and survey studies of attitude change. In I. D. Steiner & M. Fishbein (Eds.) *Current Studies in Social Psychology.* New York: Holt, Rinehart, & Winston, 1965, pp. 173–186.

Hovland, C., and Mandell, W., An experimental comparison of conclusion drawing by communicator and the audience. *Journal of Abnormal and Social Psychology,* 1952, *47,* 581–588.

Howell, R., and Jorgenson, E., Accuracy of judging emotional behavior in a natural setting: A replication. *Journal of Social Psychology,* 1970, *81,* 269–270.

Hyman, H., and Sheatsley P., "The authoritarian personality": A methodological critique. In R. Christie and M. Jahodo (Eds.) *Studies in the Scope and Method of "The Authoritarian Personality".* New York: Free Press, 1954, pp. 50–122.

Janis, I., Effects of fear arousal on attitude change: Recent developments in theory and experimental research. In L. Berkowitz (Ed.,), *Advances in Experimental Social Psychology, Vol. 3.* New York: Academic Press, 1967, pp. 167– 224.

Janis, I., and Feshbach, S., Personality differences associated with responsiveness to fear-arousing communications. *Journal of Personality,* 1954, *23,* 154–166.

Janis, I., and Field, P., Sex differences and personality factors related to persuasability. In C. Hovland and I. Janis (Eds.) *Personality and Persuasability.* New Haven: Yale University, 1959, pp 55–68.

Janis, I., and King, B., The influence of role playing on opinion change. *Journal of Abnormal and Social Psychology* 1954, *49,* 211–218.

Jellison, J., and Mills, J., Effect of public commitment upon opinions. *Journal of Experimental Social Psychology,* 1969 *5,* 340–346.

Jobe, A. M., Beutler, L. E., Johnson, D. T., Neville, C. W., Jr. and Workman, S. N., Psychotherapy outcome as a function of cognitive style and the A-B dichotomy. Paper presented at the meeting of the Southwestern Psychological Association, Dallas, April, 1973.

Joe, V. C., A review of the internal-external control construct as a personality variable. *Psychological Reports,* 1971, *28,* 619–640.

Johnson, C. D., Competance motivation and interpersonal evaluation. *Bulletin of the Psychognomic Society,* 1974, *4,* 199–200.

Johnson, D. W., and Matross, R. P., Attitude modification methods of helping people change. In F. H., Kanfer & A. P. Goldstein (Eds.) *Helping people change: Methods & Materials.* Elmsford, New York: Pergamon, 1975.

Johnson H., and Steiner, I., The effects of source on responses to negative information about one's self. *Journal of Social Psychology,* 1968, *74,* 215–224.

Johnson, R. K., and Meyer, R. G., The locus of control construct in EEG alpha rhythm feedback. *Journal of Consulting and Clinical Psychology,* 1974, *42,* 913.

Jones E. E., and Gerard, H. B., *Foundations of Social Psychology.* New York: Wiley, 1967.

Jourard, S. M., Effects of experimenter's self disclosure on subjects' behavior. In C. D. Spielberger (Ed.), *Current topics in clinical and community psychology, Vol. 1,* New York: Academic Press, 1969.

Jourard, S. M., and Jaffe, P., Influence of an interviewer's disclosure on the self-disclosing behavior of interviewees. *Journal of Counseling Psychology,* 1970, *17,* 252–257.

Julian, J. W., and Katz, S. B., Internal vs external control and the value of reinforcement. *Journal of Personality and Social Psychology,* 1968, *8,* 89–94.

Julian, J. W., Lichtman, C., and Rykman, R. M., Internal-external control and the need to control. *Journal of Social Psychology,* 1968, *76,* 43–48.

Kahn M., Nonverbal communication as a factor in marital satisfaction. *Dissertation Abstracts International,* 1970, *30* (10-B), 4794.

Kazdin, A. E., Covert modeling, model similarity, and reduction of avoidance behavior. *Behavior Therapy,* 1974a, *5,* 325–340.

Kazdin, A. E., The effect of model identity and fear relevant similarity on covert modeling. *Behavior Therapy* 1974b, *5,* 624–635.

Keierleber, D. L., Matross, R. P., and Strong, S. R., Expertness, type of appeal, and influence in counseling. *University of Minnesota Research Bulletin,* July, 1974, *15,* 3, 1–11.

Kelman H., Processes of opinion change. *Public Opinion Quarterly,* 1961, *25,* 57–78.

Kleck, R. E., and Rubenstein, C., Physical attractiveness, perceived attitude similarity and interpersonal attraction in opposite sex encounter. *Journal of Personality and Social Psychology,* 1975 *31,* 107–114.

Kleinke C. L., Stanesk, R. A., and Berger, D. E., Evaluation of an interviewer as a function of interviewer gaze, reinforcement of subject gaze, and interviewer attractiveness. *Journal of Personality and Social Psychology* 1975, *31,* 115–122.

Kopfstein, J. H., Relation of personality, expectancy, and situational variables to self-disclosure behavior. *Journal of Consulting and Clinical Psychology,* 1974, *42,* 703.

Korner, I. N., Of values, value lag and mental health. *American Psychologist,* 1956, *11,* 543–546.

Kozel, N., Perception of emotion: Race of expressor, sex of perceiver, and mode of presentation. *Proceedings of 77th Annual Convention of the American Psychological Association,* 1969, *4* (pt. 1), 39–40.

Kozel, N., and Gitter, A., Perception of emotion: Differences in mode of presentation, sex of perceiver, and role of expressor. *Technical Report,* No. 18, Boston University, 1968.

Kramer, E., Judgment of personal characteristics and emotions from nonverbal properties of speech. *Psychology Bulletin,* 1963, *60,* 408–420.

Kumar, U., and Pepinsky, H. B., Counselor expectancies and therapeutic evaluations. *Proceedings of the 73rd Annual Convention of the American Psychological Association,* 1965, *1,* 357–358.

Lacey, J. I., Psychophysiological approaches to the evaluation of psychotherapeutic process and outcome. In A. E. Rubinstein and M. B. Parloff (Eds.) *Research in psychotherapy.* Washington, D. C.: National Publishing, 1959.

Landfield, A. W., and Nawas, M. M., Psychotherapeutic improvement as a function of communication and adoption of therapist's values. *Journal of Counseling Psychology,* 1964, *11,* 336–341.

Lazarus, A. A., Behavior rehearsal vs nondirective therapy vs. advice in effecting behavior change. *Behavioral Research & Therapy,* 1966, *4,* 209–211.

Le Compte, W., and Rosenfeld H., Effects of minimal eye contact in the instruction period on impressions of the experimenter. *Journal of Experimental and Social Psychology,* 1971, *7,* 211–220.

Lennard, H. L. and Bernstein A., Expectations and behavior in therapy. In B. J. Biddle & E. J. Thomas (Eds.) *Role Theory: Concepts and Research.* New York: Wiley, 1966.

Leventhal, H., and Singer, R., Affect arousal and positioning of recommendations in persuasive communications. *Journal of Personality and Social Psychology,* 1966, *4,* 137–146.

Lewan, P. C., Stotland E., The effects of prior information on susceptibility to emotional appeal. *Journal of Abnormal and Social Psychology,* 1961, *62,* 450–453.

Lipp, L., Kolstoe R., James, W., and Randall, H., Denial of disability and internal control of reinforcement: A study using a perceptual defense paradigm. *Journal of Consulting and Clinical Psychology,* 1968, *32,* 72–75.

London P., Communication of values in psychotherapy. Symposium presented at the 86th annual meeting of the American Psychological Association, New Orleans, 1974.

London, P., *The Modes and Morals of Psychotherapy.* New York: Holt, Rinehart, & Winston, 1964.

Mann, L., and Janis I., A follow up study on the long term effects of emotional role playing. *Journal of Personality and Social Psychology,* 1968, *8,* 339–342.

Mann, J. H., and Mann C., The effect of role playing experience on self ratings of personal adjustment. *Group Psychotherapy,* 1968, *11,* 27–32.

Marcia, J. E., Rubin B. M., and Efran, J. S., Systematic desensitization: Expectancy change or counter conditioning? *Journal of Abnormal Psychology,* 1969, *74,* 382–387.

Marshall, W. L., Boutilier, J., and Minnes, P., The modification of phobic behavior by covert reinforcement. *Behavior Therapy,* 1974, *5,* 469–480.

Mcallister, A., and Kiesler, D. J., Interviewee disclosure as a function of interpersonal trust, task modeling and interviewer self disclosure. *Journal of Consulting and Clinical Psychology,* 1975, *43,* 428.

McArthur, L. A., Luck is alive and well in New Haven: A serendipitous finding on perceived control of reinforcement after the draft lottery. *Journal of Personality and Social Psychology,* 1970, *16,* 316–318.

McCarron, L. t., Appel, V. H., Categories of therapist verbalizations and patient-therapist autonomic response. *Journal of Consulting and Clinical Psychology,* 1971, *37,* 123–134.

McGlynn, F. D., and Williams, C. W., Systematic desensitization of snake-avoidance under three conditions of suggestion. *Journal of Behavior Therapy and Experimental psychology,* 1970, *1,* 97–101.

McGuire, W., and Papageorgis, D., The relative efficacy of various types of prior belief-defense in producing immunity against persuasion. *Journal of Abnormal and Social Psychology,* 1961, *62*, 327–337.

McNair, C. M., Callahan, D. M., and Lorr, M., Therapist "type" and patient response to psychotherapy. *Journal of Consulting Psychology,* 1962, *26,* 425–429.

Mehrabian A., Inference of attitude from the posture, orientation, and distance of a communicator. *Journal of Consulting and Clinical Psychology,* 1968, *32,* 296–308.

Mehrabian, A., *Nonverbal Communication.* Chicago: Aldine-Atherton, 1972.

Mehrabian A., Orientation behaviors and nonverbal attitude communication. *Journal of Communication,* 1967, *17,* 324–332.

Mehrabian, A., and Williams, M., Nonverbal communication of perceived and intended persuasiveness. *Journal of Personality and Social Psychology,* 1969, *13,* 37–58.

Meland, J. A., Matross, R. P., and Strong, S. R., Counter influence and counselor effectiveness. *University of Minnesota Research Bulletin,* 1974, *14,* 1–7.

Mendelsohn, G. A., Effects of client personality and client similarity on the duration of counseling: A replication and extension. *Journal of Counseling Psychology,* 1966, *13,* 228–234.

Mendelsohn, G. A., and Geller M. H., Effects of counselor-client similarity on the outcome of counseling. *Journal of Counseling Psychology,* 1963, *10,* 71–77.

Middlebrook, *Social Psychology and Modern Life.* New York: Alfred A. Knopf, 1974.

Miller W. R., and Seligman, M. E. P., Depression and learned helplessness in man. *Journal of Abnormal Psychology,* 1976, *84* 228–238.

Mitchell, K. M., Truax, C. B., Bozarth, J. D., and Krauft, C. C., Antecedents to psychotherapeutic outcome. Paper presented at the 20th annual meeting of the Southeastern Psychological Association. Hollywood, Florida, May, 1974.

Moreno J. L., Psychodrama In S. Arieti (Ed.) *American Handbook of Psychiatry, Vol. 2.* New York: Basic Books, 1959, 00. 1375–1396.

Mowrer, O. H., Neurosis and psychotherapy as interpersonal processes: A synopsis. In O. H. Mowrer (Ed.) *Psychotherapy: Theory and Research.* New York: Ronald, 1953, pp. 69–94.

Murphy, G., The cultural context of guidance. *Personnel and Guidance Journal,* 1955, *34,* 4–9.

Naditch, M. P., Gargan, M. A., and Michael, L. B., Denial, anxiety, locus of control, and the discrepancy between aspirations and achievements as components of depression. *Journal of Abnormal Psychology,* 1975, *84,* 1, 1–9.

Nawas, M. M., and Landfield, A. W., Improvement in psychotherapy and adoption of the therapist's meaning system. *Psychological Reports,* 1963, *13,* 97–98.

Nierenberg, G., and Calero, H., *How to Read a Person Like a Book.* New York: Hawthorn Books, 1971.

Nowicki, S., Nelson, D. A., and Ettinger, R. F., The role of need for social approval in initial attractiveness. *Journal of Social Psychology,* 1974, *94,* 149–150.

Orlinsky, D. E., and Howard, K. I., *Varieties of Therapy Experience.* New York: Teachers College Press, 1975..

Pallack, M., and Heller, J., Interactive effects of commitment to future interaction and therapist attitudinal freedom. *Journal of Personality and Social Psychology,* 1971, *17,* 325–331.

Parloff, M. B., Iflund, B., and Goldstein, N., Communication of "therapy values" between therapist and schizophrenic patients. *Journal of Nervous and Mental Disorders,* 1960, *130,* 193–199.

Patterson, C. H., *Theories of Counseling and Psychotherapy* (2nd Ed.) New York: Harper & Row, 1973.

Pellegrini, R. J., and Hicks, R. A., Prophecy effects and tutorial instruction for the disadvantaged child. *American Educational Research Journal,* 1972, *9,* 413–419.

Pepinsky, H. B., and Karst, T. C., Convergence: A phenomenon in counseling and in psychotherapy. *American Psychologist,* 1964, *19,* 333–338.

Perls, F., Hefferline, R. F., and Goodman, P., *Gestalt Therapy,* New York: Julian Press, 1951.

Peterson, P. D., and Koulack, D., Attitude change as a function of latitudes of acceptance and rejection. *Journal of Personality and Social Psychology,* 1969, *11,* 4, 309–311.

Pettit, I. B., Pettit, T. F., and Welkowitz, J., Relationship between values, social class, and duration of psychotherapy. *Journal of Consulting and Clinical Psychology,* 1974, *42,* 4, 482–490.

Phares, D., Differential utilization of information as a function of internal-external control. *Journal of Personality,* 1968, *36* 649–662.

Phares, E. J., and Lamiell, J. T., Relationship of internal-external control to defensive preference. *Journal of Consulting and Clinical Psychology,* 1974, *42,* 872–878.

Phares E. J., Ritchie D. E., and Davis, W. L., Internal-external control and reaction to threat. *Journal of Personality and Social Psychology,* 1968, *10,* 402–405.

Phillis, J., Children's judgments of personality on the basis of voice quality. *Developmental Psychology,* 1970, *3* (3, pt. 1), 411.

Polster E., and Polster, M., *Gestalt Therapy Integrated.* New York: Brunner/Mazel, 1973.

Quinlan D. M., and Janis, I. L., Optimal level of contact in counselor-client dyads. Paper presented at the 6th annual meeting of the Society for Psychotherapy Research, Boston, 1975.

Rachman S., Clinical applications of observational learning, imitation, and modeling. *Behavior Therapy,* 1972, *3,* 379–397.

Raimy, V., *Misunderstandings of the Self.* San Francisco: Jossey-Bass, 1975.

Reich W., *Character analysis.* New York: Orgone Institute, 1945.

Reimanis, G., Effects of locus of reinforcement control modification procedures in early graders and college students. *Journal of Educational Research,* 1974, *68,* 124–127.

Rosenthal, D., Changes in some moral values following psychotherapy. *Journal of Consulting Psychology,* 1955, *19,* 431–436.

Rosenthal, R., and Jacobson, L., *Pygmalion in the Classroom: Teacher Expectation and Pupils' Intellectual Development.* New York: Holt, Rinehart, & Winston, 1968.

Rotter J. B., Generalized expectancies for internal vs external control of reinforcement *Psychological Monographs: General and Applied,* 1966, *80,* Whole No. 609.

Ryckman, R. M., and Sherman, M. F., Locus of control and perceived ability level as determinants of partner and opponent choice. *Journal of Social Psychology,* 1974, *94,* 103–110.

Samler, J., Change in values: A goal in counseling. *Journal of Counseling Psychology,* 1960, *7,* 32–39

Sattler, J. M., and Winget, B. M., Intellectual testing procedure as affected by expectancy and IQ. *Journal of Clinical Psychology,* 1970, *26,* 446–448.

Scherer, D., Attribution of personality from voice: A cross cultural study on interpersonal perception. Proceedings of 79th Annual Convention of the American Psychological Association, 1971, *6* (pt. 1), 351–352.

Schmidt, L. D., and Strong, S. R., Attractiveness and influence in counseling. *Journal of Counseling Psychology,* 1971, *18,* 348–351.

Schofield, W., *Psychotherapy, the purchase of friendship.* Englewood Cliffs, N.J.: Prentice-Hall, 1964.

Scott, W. E., and Cherrington, D. J., Effects of competitive, cooperative, and individualistic reinforcement contingencies. *Journal of Personality and Social Psychology,* 1974, *30,* 748–758.

Segal, B., A-B distinction and therapeutic interaction. *Journal of Consulting and Clinical Psychology,* 1970, *34,* 442–446.

Seligman, M. E. P., *Helplessness: On Depression, Development and Death.* San Francisco: W. H. Freeman, 1975.

Shapiro, A. K., Placebo effects in medicine, psychotherapy and psychoanalysis. In A. E. Bergin and S. L. Garfield (Eds.), *Handbook of psychotherapy and behavior change.* New York: Wiley 1971, pp. 439–473.

Sherif, C. W., Sherif, M., and Nebergall, R. E., *Attitude and attitude change.* Philadelphia: Saunders, 1965.

Sherif, M., On the relevance of social psychology. *American Psychology,* 1970, *25,* 144–156.

Sherif, M., and Hovland, C. I., *Social Judgment.* New Haven: Yale University, 1961.

Silverman, L. E., and Nakamura, C. Y., Powerlessness, social-political action, social-political views: Their interrelation among college students. *Journal of Social Issues,* 1972, *27,* 137–157.

Simons, H. W., Berkowitz, N. N., and Moyer, R. J., Similarity, credibility, and attitude change: A review and theory. *Psychology Bulletin,* 1970, *73,* 1–16.

Smith, E. W. L., Postural and gestural communication of A and B "therapist types" during dyadic interviews. *Journal of Consulting and Clinical Psychology,* 1972, *39,* 29–36.

Smith, M. B., Mental health reconsidered: A special case of the problem of values in psychology. *American Psychology,* 1961, *16,* 299–306.

Smith, R. E., Changes in locus of control as a function of life crisis resolution. *Journal of Abnormal Psychology,* 1970, *75,* 328–332.

Smith, R. E., and Flenning, F., Need for approval and susceptibility to unintended social influence, *Journal of Consulting and Clinical Psychology,* 1971, *36,* 383–385.

Sommer, R., *Personal space: The behavioral basis of design.* Englewood Cliffs, N. J.: Prentice-Hall, 1969.

Spinetta, J. J., Rigler, D., and Karon, M., Personal space as a measure of a dying child's sense of isolation. *Journal of Consulting and Clinical Psychology,* 1974, *42,* 751–756.

Stein, L. S., Green, B. L., and Stone, W. N., Therapist attitudes as influenced by A-B therapist type, patient diagnosis, and social class. *Journal of Consulting and Clinical Psychology,* 1972, *39,* 2, 301–307.

Steiner, I., Perceived freedom. In L. Berkowitz (Ed.) *Advances in Experimental Social Psychology, Vol. 5,* New York: Academic Press, 1970, pp. 187–248.

Strickland, B. R., The prediction of social action from a dimension of internal-external control. *Journal of Social Psychology,* 1965, *66,* 353–358.

Strong, S. R., Counseling: An interpersonal influence process. *Journal of Counseling Psychology,* 1968, *15,* 3, 215–224.

Strong, S. R., and Dixon, D. N., Expertness, attractiveness and influence in counseling. *Journal of Counseling Psychology,* 1971, *18,* 562–570.

Strong, S. R., and Matross, R. P., A study of attribution techniques in the interview. *Research Bulletin,* Minneapolis: University Minnesota, 1974, 15.

Strong, S. R., and Schmidt, L. D., Trustworthiness and influence in counseling. *Journal of Counseling Psychology,* 1970, *17,* 197–204.

Strupp, H. H., Some observations on the fallacy of value-free psychotherapy and the empty organism. *Journal of Abnormal Psychology,* 1974, *83,* 199–201.

Strupp, H. H., Toward a reformulation of the psychotherapeutic influence. Presidential address delivered at the 4th annual meeting of the Society for Psychotherapy Research, Philadelphia, June, 1973.

Strupp, H. H., and Bloxom, A. L., Preparing lower class patients for group psychotherapy: Development and evaluation of a role-induction film. *Journal of Consulting and Clinical Psychology,* 1973, *41,* 373–384.

Szasz, T., The myth of mental illness. *American Psychology,* 1960, *15,* 113–118.

Tankard, J., Effects of eye position on personal perception. *Perceptual and Motor Skills,* 1970, *31,* 883–893.

Tedeschi J. T., Schlenker B. R., and Bonom, T. V., Cognitive dissonance: Private ratiocination or public spectacle? *American Psychology,* 1971, *26,* 685–696.

Topalova, V., Credibility of information source. *Polish Psychological Bulletin,* 1974, *5,* 73–80.

Trattner, J. H., and Howard, K. I., A preliminary investigation of covert communication expectancies to schizophrenics. *Journal of Abnormal Psychology,* 1970, *75,* 245–247.

Truax, C. B., and Carkhuff, R. R., *Toward Effective Counseling and Psychotherapy: Training and Practice* Chicago: Aldine, 1967.

Truax, C. B., Fine H., Moravec, J., and Millis, W., Effects of therapist persuasive potency in individual psychotherapy. *Journal of Clinical Psychology,* 1968, *24,* 359–362.

Traux, C. B., and Mitchell, K. M., Research on certain therapist interpersonal skills in relation to process and outcome. In A. E. Bergin and S. L. Garfield (Eds.), *Handbook of Psychotherapy and Behavior Change.* New York: Wiley, 1971, pp. 299–344.

Truax, C. B., Shapiro J. G., and Wargo, D. G., The effects of alternate sessions and vicarious therapy pretraining on group psychotherapy. *International Journal of Group Psychotherapy,* 1968, *18,* 186–198.

Verplanck W. S., The control of content of conversation: Reinforcement of statements of opinion. *Journal of Abnormal and Social Psychology,* 1955, *51* 668–676.

Walster, E., Aronson, J., and Abrahams, D., On increasing the persuasiveness of a low prestige communicator. *Journal of Experimental Social Psychology,* 1966, *2,* 325–342.

Watson G., Moral issues in psychotherapy. *American Psychology,* 1958, *13,* 574–575.

Watts, W., Relative persistence of opinion change induced by active compared to passive participation. *Journal of Personality and Social Psychology,* 1967, *5,* 4–15.

Welkowitz, J., Cohen, J., and Ortmeyer, D., Value systems similarity: Investigation of patient-therapist dyads. *Journal of Consulting Psychology,* 1966, *2,* 48–55.

Welkowitz, J. and Kuc, M., Interrelationships among warmth, genuineness, empathy, and temporal speech patterns in interpersonal interaction. *Journal of Consulting and Clinical Psychology,* 1973, *41,* 472–473.

Wilkins, W., Expectancies in Applied Settings. In A. S. Gurman & A. N. Razin (Eds.) *The Therapist's Contribution to Effective Psychotherapy.* New York: Pergamon, in press.

Wilkins, W., Expectancy of therapeutic gain. An empirical and conceptual critique. *Journal of Consulting and Clinical Psychology,* 1973, *40,* 69–77..

Wilson, M. N., and Rappaport, J., Personal self disclosure: Expertness and situational effects. *Journal of Consulting and Clinical Psychology,* 1974, *42,* 901–908.

Wilson W., and Miller, H., Repetition, order of presentation, and timing of arguments and measures as determiners of opinion change. *Journal of Personality and Social Psychology,* 1968, *9,* 184–188

Wogan, M., Effect of therapist-patient personality variables on therapeutic outcome. *Journal of Consulting and Clinical Psychology,* 1970, *35,* 3, 356–361.

Wolff W., Fact and value in psychotherapy. *American Journal of Psychotherapy,* 1954, *8,* 466–486.

Zillman D., Rhetorical elicitation of agreement in persuasion. *Journal of Personality and Social Psychology,* 1972, *21,* 159–165.

Zimbardo, The effect of effort and improvisation on self persuasion produced by role playing. *Journal of Experimental Social Psychology,* 1965, *1,* 103–120.

BEHAVIOR: ITS MODIFICATION AND THERAPIES

Richard Greene

This chapter is an attempt to describe in one context, two diverse schools of psychological thought, the school of behaviorism and the school of psychoanalysis. The objective is to demonstrate that in combination, the effectiveness of these two approaches is enhanced.

THE ORIGINS OF BEHAVIORISM

The psychological schools are merging, particularly in the area of psychotherapy. Today, it is nearly impossible to talk of schools of psychological thought. The field of psychology is much too broad and inter-related.

As originally formulated, John B. Watson's school of behaviorism had two specific objectives, the first was to predict an organism's response, from an observation of the stimulus and the second was to predict the stimulus, by observing the response. Accordingly, the major postulates of Watsonian behaviorism were as follows:

1. Behavior is composed of response elements and can be successfully analyzed by standard scientific methods.
2. Behavior is composed entirely of glandular secretions and muscular movements, and these are ultimately reducable to physiochemical processes.
3. There is always an immediate response, of some variety, to every effective stimulus, and conversely, every response has an associated stimulus. In other words, there is a strict cause-effect relationship in behavior.
4. Conscious processes, if indeed they exist at all, cannot be successfully, scientifically studied; allegations concerning consciousness represent supernatural tendencies, and are carryovers from either prescientific or theoretical formulations which must be ignored.

An assumption made by Watson was that a large number of inherited reactions have stimulus properties and almost immediate modification of these occurs, through the processes of "conditioning," into more and more complicated and individualistic but differentiated tendencies. Watson stated that one of the major problems of behaviorism was the ever-increasing range of stimuli to which an individual responds. Thus, it becomes increasingly difficult to predict either the response or its accompanying stimuli. The school of Watsonian behaviorism further maintained that the selection of responses and of a sufficient stimulus depends strictly upon innate and acquired stimulus-response connections.

The school of Watsonian behaviorism also offered several arguments against the existence of consciousness:

1. The stimulus is the important element in introspection, not the alleged conscious correlation. Introspection is simply the way of reporting what has been learned by language training.
2. The assumption of nonphysical events (consciousness) interacting with physical systems (the organism) violates the conservation-of-energy principle. All energy within a physical system can be accounted for physically; none is gained or lost to any nonphysical system. If conscious events affected the body physiologically, they would have to do this by adding or subtracting energy or mass, an impossibility according to laws of physics and the principle of the conservation of energy.

The Watsonian behaviorist would also argue; if there is a conscious mind, then it must either affect behavior (interactionism) or not affect behavior (parallelism). If mind affects behavior, then the law of conservation of energy in physics is violated. If mind does not affect behavior, then one must believe that all things are coincidental.

The Watsonian behaviorist resorted to a strict physical monism, according to which "mental" is merely a description of the way physical events function and consciousness has no independent or unique existence. Other early behaviorists modified and expanded Watson's views. For example, Alpert P. Weiss saw behavior as ultimately reducible to physiochemical terms and maintained that psychology was a new branch of physics. Weiss regarded psychology as a biosocial discipline because of the nature of the variables with which it was concerned.

Additionally, Walter S. Hunter made some very important methodological contributions to the field of animal learning. Hunter developed and maintained a small but active department of experimentally oriented psychologists. Methodological innovations for which Hunter is responsible include the delayed response procedure and double alternation tasks, both of which pave the way to investigate symbolic abilities in animals.

Karl S. Lashley, a physiological psychologist who ventured occasionally into learning patterns, is known for research that expanded knowledge in brain-behavior relationships. Lashley's two famous principles of *equipotentiality* and *mass action* are generalizations based on brain extirpation. The first principle states that one part of the cortex is essentially equal to another with respect to its contribution to performance tasks like maze learning. The second principle states that the efficiency of learning depends upon the total mass of cortex left functioning. Although both principles have been revised and refined, they stand as major contributions to the development of an integrated behavioral psychology.

Floyd H. Allport popularized the behavioristic concepts of the circular conditioned reflex theory of language development. Allport extended behaviorism to the realm of social psychology. Elsewhere in this book we have discussed the interrelation of these latter principles to clinical practice. Allport was a major contributor to later developments in cognitive, social psychology.

Richard Greene

While the foregoing writers extended behavioral principles to related areas of science, other theorists within behavioral schools refined Watson's formulations. It is far too broad a task, however, to explicate in detail the work of such as E. C. Tolman, E. R. Gutherie, C. L. Hull, B. F. Skinner, and D. O. Hebb. Some of these names will arise again, however, as this chapter evolves.

CONTEMPORARY BEHAVIORISM

The principles of learning that behavior therapy brings to light suggest there are two basic kinds of conditioning that affect the establishment and elimination of responses. They are (1) respondent conditioning, and (2) operant conditioning.

Respondent conditioning

Pavlovian conditioning or classical conditioning, as it is sometimes called, involves the modification of responses that the organism is innately capable of making by substituting a conditioned stimulus for the natural or unconditioned stimulus. A distinct aspect of respondent conditioning is an innate response that is elicited by a potent, environmental stimulus preceding and to which the organism passively responds. Wolpe and others who treat maladjustment and maladaptive reactions by what they have called "counter-conditioning" or "reciprocal inhibition" produce a decrement of a conditioned response by eliciting an incompatible response to the same conditioned response.

Operant conditioning

The psychologist whose name is most synonomous with contemporary operant behaviorism is B. F. Skinner. Every psychological theory, hypothesis, or law must come to rest on a set of beliefs that are part of a technical concept. The understanding of these beliefs is of utmost importance in grasping the essential flavor of the theory. Indeed, this is the case with B. F. Skinner's operant behaviorism. The basic axims and corrolaries of this system are:

1. There exists a set of systematic and functional relationships between behavior and the environment.

2. Before a useful science of behavior can be established, a discovery of these relationships is necessary.

3. The psychological data should be representative of agreement among all independent observers.

4. It is misleading and totally unnecessary to speculate on what is happening within a person in order to explain behavior, unless, of course, the psychologist is ready to make the necessary observations to test the truthfulness of his speculations.

5. A science of behavior should be developed by first observing behavior, identi-

fying relationships between patterns of responses and environmental conditions. Inductive as well as deductive reasoning needs to be part of a science of behavior.

6. Every organism beloning to each different species shares some basic similarities.

7. A science of human behavior will generate a technology that is useful for dealing with a wide variety of practical problems.

8. Organisms are capable of multiple forms of action in any given situation.

9. Environment is affected by and in turn affects an individual's overt behavior.

Some basic assumptions used in the operant modification of behavior include the notion that a response can be strengthened by presenting a positive reinforcer immediately after the response is emitted and can be eliminated by terminating the response reinforcement contingency. Furthermore, since behavior is maintained through reinforcement it can be additionally modified either by changing the schedule of reinforcement or by modifying aversive stimuli. Regarding the latter, for example, a response can be strengthened by removing an aversive stimulus immediately after the response is emitted. A response can also be suppressed through punishment. In the instance of punishment, a response is suppressed when it is immediately followed by the presentation of aversive stimuli.

Finally, the probability of a response can be increased by first depriving the organism of a relevant stimulus. Alternatively, the probability of a response can be decreased by first satiating the organism with a relevant stimulus. Similarly, one can increase the probability of a response by presenting a discriminative stimulus and can decrease the probability of a response by removing the discriminative stimuls (Wenrick, 1970).

Many popular conceptions have developed about Skinnerian behaviorism. Often these are exaggerations and misinterpretations that cast Skinner and his ideas in an unfavorable light. The misconceptions include:

1. Skinner places humans in the same category as the machines.

2. Skinnerian behaviorism views human behavior as no more complex than that of the rat.

3. Skinner has regarded himself as the supreme authority in determining what people should and should not do.

4. Absolute stimulus determinism is treated as a proven principle of unlimited scope.

5. Skinner believes that private feelings have no place in the realm of human learning.

6. Stimulus-response psychology and operant behaviorism are one and the same.

As is the case with every theory or hypothesis put forth in the field of psychology, there are weaknesses in B. F. Skinner's operant behaviorism. For example, the Skinnerian analysis of complex human behavior sometimes extends beyond the limits of experimental verification. Hence, the relationship between theory and practice is often not clear, and particularly in the area of language many claim that limited relevance is attached to Skinner's experimental model. Skinner has failed to adequately extend the model to principles and functions which are unique to human behavior.

On the other hand, Skinner's operant behaviorism has derived basic principles which are firmly rooted in empirical fact. Furthermore, operant behaviorism is not cluttered with concepts. The basic principles are relevant to much of human behavior, particularly that which is observable, and concrete. Hence, the theory provides a useful criterion for appraising the practical value of other approaches.

Skinner has proposed a behavioral based and controlled society, the main features of which are:

1. In the operant community, the general pace of living would be slower.

2. Dependence on threats or coercion for controlling behaviors would be minimized.

3. The shaping of altruistic behavior patterns would be accomplished through positive operant child-training methods.

4. In order to reduce monotony and boredom, jobs would be redesigned to produce more job satisfaction.

5. A reversal in the present trend toward fragmentation of moral codes would be accomplished by the consistent application of operant techniques.

6. An effort would be made to strengthen the awareness of interdependence through a strong social and mutual reinforcement pattern in the family, school, and business world.

7. A streamlining and simplification of the present legal structure would be accomplished by placing less dependence upon the written law. Common law would predominate.

In Skinner's system, social change would be preceded by the use of operant analysis so as to determine socially desirable behavior patterns and then, through the application of operant principles, behavior would be shaped in accordance with these objectives (Carpenter, 1974). It is Skinner's thesis that the key to understanding, controlling, and predicting the behavior of individuals lies in identifying and arranging the events that follow the behavior in question. The term "positive reinforcer" is almost synonymous with the more common term "reward;" a reward may or may not be a positive reinforcer. Only those events or objects that follow a behavior and increase the frequency of that behavior are defined as positive reinforcers. However, an event which is positively reinforcing in one situation is assumed to be similarly reinforcing in another. If an object or behavior is to become a positive reinforcer, it must immediately follow the response to be conditioned, and be temporally contiguous with an established reinforcer.

As set of responses that *have* something in common is called a "response class." Hence, any change in a response may ultimately be so pervasive as to modify much of the observable character of the individual. This is true because the conditioning of one response may have the indirect effect of altering any or all other responses in the class. The more established and fundamental the response altered, the more pervasive the generalized change.

Response differentiation comes when one member of a response class is reinforced, and the other members of the response class are not reinforced. The process of reinforcing one response and neglecting to reinforce other responses in that same class is called "differential reinforcement."

Extinction consists of withholding reinforcement of a conditioned response until it occurs no more often than it did before conditioning. Forgetting, in contrast, results when a response is not emitted for a period of time. Forgetting behavior is evidenced by a decrease in the rate of response following a period when the response did not occur. Forgetting and extinction are similar in that they are both manifest by a decrease in the response rate. However, the process of forgetting involves the prevention of a response, whereas, in extinction the response occurs but without reinforcement.

Classically, behavior modifiers have been ideographic in their approach both in the laboratory and in clinical practice. That is, they have avoided pooled statistical research designs (nomothetic approaches) in favor of the single organism approaches. They have argued that research designed to yield results in terms of means and standard deviations obscures functional relationships and often substitutes probabilistic ignorance of precision. Increasingly, however, nomothetic approaches have been emerging in behavioral literature.

The behavior modifer's case study approach to treatment is different than that of the usual therapy. The behavior modifier has given more attention to inquiries into the individual's reinforcement history, making careful, precise, and quantifiable observations of rates of various behaviors until a stable base rate for these behaviors has become established. Then, the operant behaviorist intervenes with a program that attaches reinforcement contingencies to the behavior, maintaining careful observations of the behavior in order to evaluate the efficacy of the program.

Positive reinforcement may not only alter the frequency of established responses, but may be employed to bring about new responses in an individual's behavior. One procedure by which they may be accomplished is known as the "method of successive approximations" or "response shaping." The term, "shaping" refers more to the actions of the experimenter, whereas the term "successive approximation" emphasizes the general behavior of the responder. By either term, the procedure involves the use of positive reinforcers contingent on behavior which may at first only faintly resemble the terminal behavior which the experimenter desires. It is through a gradual process of applying reinforcement to responses which increasingly resemble the terminal behavior, which in itself is finally conditioned (Whaley, 1971).

Behavior modification is a purely psychological approach and as such discounts most considerations of behaviors as "illnesses." Some behavioral practitioners would like to abandon such terms as "pathology," "deviant," "cure," and "neurotic." These concepts would be replaced with terms such as "training," "conditioning procedures," and "problem solving." With or without such terms, behavior modification methods can be effectively utilized in a wide variety of settings including traditional hospitals and clinics, classrooms, homes, children's camps, therapists' offices, and playgrounds. Since its application is not dependent upon either medical or extensive psychological training, the application of behavior modification promises to extend to the layman, the power to help others. The psychologist who embraces behavior therapy is confronted with only three questions when a patient seeks help: (1) What specifically is the behavior to be modified? (2) What are the stimuli currently maintaining behavior? (3) What are the variables which will produce the appropriate behavior modifications?

From an operant behavioral perspective, psychological disorders can be classified into two groups: (1) deficient behavior, and (2) maladaptive behavior. Deficient behavior occurs when the child has failed to learn certain responses. The therapeutic task in this case is to teach the child adaptive responses. In contrast, maladaptive behavior occurs when the child has learned inappropriate responses. The therapeutic task is to modify the child's responses so as to make his or her behavior more adaptive to the demands of the environment. In either deficient or maladaptive behavior the treatment involves learning, unlearning, and relearning. Hence, behavior therapy demands a detailed and intensive assessment of the conditions under which the behavior in question takes place or fails to take place. The behavioral task is then to modify these conditions or the client's reaction to these conditions.

BEHAVIORAL ADAPTATIONS TO THERAPY

Behavioral theory rests on the premise that psychological disorders represent learned behaviors and that the principles of learning can be applied to the modification of these disorders. Although Shoben (1949), Mowrer (1950), and Dollard and Miller (1950) made early attempts to translate psychoanalytic constructs into learning theory terms, it was not until Skinner (1953), Eysenck (1957), Wolpe (1958), and Bandura (1961) that it became possible to apply laboratory-derived and tested, operant methods to the modification of psychological disorders.

In contrast, a prototype of the application of classical learning principles to the alleviation of a child's psychological problems was proposed in 1924 when Mary Cover Jones published the case of Peter, whose generalized fear of furry objects was treated by applying the principles of classical conditioning. Later, Krasnogoski (1925), Ivanov-Smolenski (1927), and Gessell (1938) also showed the relevance of Pavlovian conditioning to the treatment of psychological disorders, and when Wolpe rediscovered the work of Jones in 1938, behavioral approaches to treatment rapidly gained wider acceptance.

When the problem is maladaptive or excessive behavior, the problem behavior can be modified or replaced through adaptive behavior. Treatment involves learning (conditioning); regardless of whether the respondent or the operant paradigm is to guide the treatment. The procedures selected depends in part, on whether the response in question is skeletal-motor-muscular (voluntary), or vascular-visceral-autonomic (involuntary). Behavior therapists generally assume that the operant paradigm is best suited for modification of responses in the skeletal-motor realm, while the respondent paradigm is best suited when fear, anxiety or related autonomic responses are the focus of treatment.

When the respondent paradigm guides the treatment, behavior therapy will have to present stimuli to the child that are intended to elicit responses which are incompatible with fear so that these can be paired with stimuli to which the child had been responding with fear. In contrast, when the operant conditioning paradigm guides the treatment approach, the child is a very active participant because he or she engages in an operation that does something to the environment. The therapist arranges the environment in such a way as to ensure that the child's operant responses occur under particular conditions and are followed by planned consequences. This contingency management requires that the therapist have some control over the stimulus and reinforcement conditions that the child will encounter. The level of possible control will determine the effectiveness with which the treatment can be conducted. In order for therapists to conduct this type of treatment in a nonresidential setting, they need to obtain the close cooperation of parents, and teachers since these people are in a better position to manage reinforcement contingencies than the therapist who only has occasional contact with the child.

The foregoing distinctions among treatment approaches exist in theory, but in reality, all treatment approaches entail both operant and respondent aspects. When a given response constellation is being learned, it is rarely possible to identify the exact principles involved (Ross, 1972). Moreoever, the relationship between behavior therapy and learning theory is controversial. Kanfer and Sasklow (1969) still insist that behavior therapy should be based exclusively on knowledge of experimentally established principles of learning against a background of physiology while others (e.g., Bucher & Lovaas, 1970; Lang, 1970; Lazarus, 1971; Yates, 1970) insist that learning theory is too equivocal to provide a defining characteristic upon which to base therapy. Lang (1970) cites a number of difficulties which have led to a reevaluation of the relationship between behavior theory and learning theory. In order to examine some aspects of the influence of learning theory on behavior theory, the following should be considered.

1. The stimulus, organism, response (SOR) model of behavior emphasizes interaction between the organism and its environment. This model is an input-internal processing-output model which recognizes that internal processing is mostly unobservable and that inputs and outputs are often observable.

2. Great amounts of emphasis are placed on the value of publicly observed behaviors by those within the behaviorist learning tradition.

Desensitization

A therapeutic procedure discussed earlier called "desensitization" was developed largely by Wolpe who now claims successful application of the procedure to a variety of neurotic disorders. As indicated, the procedure is derived mainly from a concept of reciprocal inhibition. The origin of reciprocal inhibition comes from neurophysiology where the term refers to suppressive effects upon one nerve unit by a second antagonistic nerve unit. Wolpe contends that there are naturally antagonistic emotional responses that cannot exist together. For example, one cannot feel anxious and relaxed at the same time. Neuroses are considered nothing more than maladaptive behaviors reflecting disordered learning and producing anxiety. Phobic behavior can be considered as one type of avoidance behavior in that it leads to distancing in time or space from some contingency. Phobic patients have learned to avoid situations which result in an excessive anxiety response. The therapeutic task is to relieve the inappropriate anxiety response and by so doing, to thereby relieve the phobia. The anxiety response is relieved by eliciting a concurrent relaxation response that reciprocally inhibits the elicitation of anxiety.

The therapeutic treatment then for phobia begins by instituting a procedure designed to teach the patient to relax. The therapist counterconditions the neurotic anxiety by pairing the previously conditioned relaxation-eliciting stimulus with a representation of the anxiety-eliciting stimulus. Sexual inhibitions and problems with self-assertion can also be considered types of avoidance behavior; desensitization can be applied to them with slight modifications.

Wolpe (1958, 1969: Wolpe & Lazarus, 1966) describe *reciprocal* inhibition as a group of behavior therapies which rely on techniques of counterconditioning. Among the therapy derivations are assertive training, response substitution and Systematic Desensitization. Of all the behavior therapies, Systematic Desensitization has one of the broadest empirical bases of support and is the most widely used.

At the heart of Wolpe's Systematic Desensitization approach is the principle of reciprocal inhibition, which states that if a response inhibitory of anxiety can be made to occur in the presence of anxiety-evoking stimuli, it will weaken the bond between these stimuli and the anxiety. In Systematic Desensitization the response inhibitory of anxiety is usually complete relaxation and the anxiety-evoking stimuli are the fears and phobias which the patient brings to the clinic. In therapy the elimination of these fears and phobias is accomplished through reconditioning former anxiety, eliciting stimuli to the responses associated with complete relaxation. Hence, the process of Systematic Desensitization must involve several operations: (1) training in deep muscle relaxation; (2) the construction of anxiety hierarchies and (3) counterposing relaxation and anxiety-evoking stimuli from the hierarchies.

The first operation, similar to the method of relaxation developed by Jacobson (1938) but with modifications by Wolpe requires only a few interviews for its completion. The patient is instructed regarding the nature of muscle relaxation, after which he or she is trained in progressive relaxation involving various part of the body until complete relaxation is achieved.

The most difficult aspect of systematic desensitization is the construction of anxiety hierarchies, a task which is required in order to extinguish the fear response and to recondition relaxation responses to the stimuli which evoke anxiety.

A unique application of a counterconditioning model in conjunction with analytic methodology has been reported by Wilson and Smith (1968) in a study of diffuse, nonspecific anxiety (pan-anxiety). In contrast to the desensitization preliminaries in which the therapist constructs a hierarchy, the procedure used in this study was to involve the use of "free association" as a means of building and working on one or more anxiety hierarchies in each session. Wilson and Smith hypothesized that free association, used in conjunction with muscle relaxation, would be an efficient means simultaneously to define and countercondition complexes of anxiety-mediating stimuli. In this application of counterconditioning, the therapist assumed that the patient's association would begin with the stimuli somewhat distant from the anxiety focus and that the deconditioning of these associations would generalize to the more important stimuli. As the extinction generalized, the patient would be able to move closer and closer to the anxiety-focused stimuli in the progress of therapy.

Implosive therapy

Stampfl and Levis (1967) state that the objective of implosive therapy is to have the patient imagine and verbalize important dynamic and symptom-contingent cues in the absence of primary reinforcement. These cues are conditioned stimuli which the therapist has surmised or ascertained as motivating the patient's problem behavior. These cues are either selected from real life experiences of the patient or are based on psychodynamic speculations. Prior to presenting these stimuli, the therapist establishes an avoidance serial cue hierarchy (ASCH). That is, the therapist simply ranks those cues associated with a particular disturbance. A cue is selected to elicit a great deal of anxiety and is presented in fantasy until the reaction is "worked through."

One of the first experimental reports on the successful application of implosive therapy was by Hogan and Kirchner (1967) and dealt with the extinction of rat fears. Other studies by Hogan in 1960 and by Levis and Carrera in 1967 have supported the value of this technique and extended its usefulness to clinical populations.

Implosive therapists believe that their technique is applicable and appropriate to the treatment of a variety of behavior problems. Among the problems mentioned are phobias, obsessive-compulsive disorders, depressive reactions, and psychotic disorders including affective schizophrenic and paranoid reactions. It is also believed that Implosive Therapy holds promise for the treatment of those with personality disorders including homosexuality, alcoholism, and speech disorders.

For the modification of aversively conditioned emotional reactions, both implosive and systematic desensitization therapies have several advantages over nonbehavior therapies. For example, both therapies are relatively brief and economical thus making treatment available and feasible. An even more significant advantage of behavior therapy over other forms of treatment, however, is the goal of modifying reactions that are objective, readily identifiable and easily measurable. This goal eventually leads to a well-defined criterion of therapeutic progress and success. While nonbehavior therapies speak of helping the individual actuate potential, realize a better self-image, resolve an Oedipus complex or put one's id, ego, and super-ego in better harmony, to most behavior therapists, these goals are largely irrelevant.

Operant therapy

Behavior modification refers to techniques which are broadly related to the field of learning, but learning with a particular clinical intent. Major variables include operant conditioning (a term used by B. F. Skinner and his followers); behavior therapy (whose most vocal spokesman is H. J. Eysenck); and psychotherapy based on reciprocal inhibition (a designation preferred by J. Wolpe). The emphasis of these approaches rests on behavior.

The working operant behavior therapist is likely to ask three questions:

1. What behavior is maladaptive?
2. What environmental contingencies support the subject's behavior?
3. What environmental stimuli changes usually reinforcing stimuli may be manipulated to alter the subject's behavior?

The most typical operant therapy refers to behavior modification through the application of differential reinforcement from the patient's interpersonal environment. Operant therapy has come into wide acceptance in the treatment of neurotic and psychotic behavioral disorders, in the education of the mentally retarded, and more broadly in the field of education.

The behavioral therapist has rejected standard classification of psychiatric diagnoses, but has offered constructive guidelines to an alternative approach. The term "functional analysis" specifies the causes of behavior as a form of environmental manipulation, the variables of which can be objectively identified and are potentially controlled. Unlike desensitization and aversion therapy, operant therapy need not approach the patient in a stereotyped fashion. functional analysis varies with different patients and with different behaviors by the same patient. Therefore, therapeutic programs, in order to be effective, need varying degrees of tailoring to meet the individual requirements. Operant therapy, thus far, has had its greatest success on psychiatric inpatient units. Whether operant therapy can effectively be adapted to meet the demands of a wide range of problems encountered in outpatient treatment remains to be investigated (Moss, 1969). Operant therapy draws on an array of techniques which include assertive training (Ludwig & Lazarus, 1972); aversive conditioning (Rachman, Teasdale, 1969); a variety of operant approaches (Krasner, 1971); Systematic Desensitization (Marquis et al., 1971 Paul, 1966), and many others (Bond, 1974).

Recent research on behavior modification can be summarized thusly:

1. Behavior therapies derive most of their power and effect from nonspecific place effects.

2. In a noncoercive situation the subject must be made aware of and cooperate with the therapists; thus the subject has ultimate control.

3. Coercive techniques produce little change beyond that which is delegated to the therapist and there is little generalization. Hence, these results suggest that behavior modification has great potential, it does not now provide the psychologist with as new and powerful a method of control as originally hoped.

Other non-coercive conditioning methods

Noncoercive conditioning occurs in situations that most resemble normal everyday activities. In noncoercive conditioning the subject is frequently neither seeking to have his behavior changed nor is in a situation which has strong authoritative constraints.

Verbal conditioning will be used in the current context as a model for all noncoercive conditioning. In examining verbal conditioning, however, we should note that the procedures are far from being completely successful. There now have been more than 1,000 studies and several thorough reviews done on verbal conditioning. Consequently, many of the essential aspects of verbal conditioning are clear. It is known, for example, that verbal conditioning is important in insight or evocative psychotherapy, but the fact does remain that some verbal conditioning takes place during evocative psychotherapy. Verbal conditioning can give vital information concerning the influence of the therapeutic relationship in evocative psychotherapy as well as in normal, interpersonal situations in an open society.

The conclusions derived from studies in verbal conditioning and relationship influence in evocative psychotherapy have a vital impact on the long-standing contention of behaviorists that psychotherapists are covertly controlling their patients. It is clear that even in client-centered psychotherapy, the therapist engages in the prediction, the influencing, and even the direct control of behavior. The process that occurs in therapy situations can at most be called "influencing." In the influencing process, the therapist makes statements which in effect give the client various options. The client then may either accept, reject or ignore the therapist's suggestions. The point here is that the client and only the client decides on whether or accept the therapist's suggestions on what to tell the therapist and even whether to stay in therapy. Hence, the client ultimately controls the entire situation.

171

There is also another principle of importance to understanding operant behavior. The Hawthorne effect is an improvement in general behavior of a group due to nonspecific sources produced by any form of treatment which gives attention or encouragement to people. This improvement in general behavior is undoubtedly due to suggestion. Marks, Sonoda, and Schalock (1968) compared a token program treatment with relationship therapy by using 11 matched pairs of schizophrenic patients in the reinforcement group. They were included in the planning of treatment and received some personal encouragement, which is a basic condition for the Hawthorne effect. The matching group received relationship therapy for an equal length of time. Both groups demonstrated improvements. The data suggest that relationships and expectancies are a major element in treatment and may have a powerful effect as the operant elements of token economies.

When there is no specific generalization due to operant techniques, one may expect no therapeutic or behavior control that lasts beyond the specific operant procedures. In most situations there is a lack of generalization in verbal conditioning and in operant methods as applied to children.

Aversion therapy

To complement desensitization therapy, there is aversion therapy. While in desensitization the main goal is to overcome avoidance behavior; in aversion therapy, the goal is to induce avoidance behavior. Aversion treatment involves the application of an aversive stimulus to a maladaptive behavior. Clinically, the procedures are either respondent or operant. In the respondent approach, the aversive stimulus acts as an unconditioned stimulus and is paired with a stimulus previously associated with maladaptive behavior. In the operant approach, the clinical paradigm could be considered a sort of "punishment therapy."

In aversion therapy there are procedural problems in the application of aversive control to maladaptive behavior. A deficiency inherent in both desensitization and aversion therapy is that there is little literature to suggest that any attention is being given to the environmental variable supporting maladaptive behavior.

In coercive behavioristic methods, another area that warrants more examination is "brainwashing." Brainwashing is defined as *methods to affect people when applied in severely coercive conditions, as for example, in the Korean War.* It was during the frenzy of the Korean War that the American people came to believe that powerful behavior techniques had been developed which would reverse moral and ethical beliefs. Jerome Franks' book *Persuasion and Healing* assumed that brainwashing techniques were extremely powerful (Russell, 1974).

Self-generated aversive consequences

Two essentially different types of self-generated aversive consequences which can be used to control behavior are self-punishment and self-reinforcement. They differ in that self-punishment is aimed at interrupting or deaccelerating a response while in negative reinforcement a response in increased. In negative reinforcement or conditioning an unpleasant stimulus is escaped or avoided by increasing or engaging in an alternative or competing behavior. An example of self-administered punishment is the use of aversive conditional reinforcers in the "thought-stopping technique." In this technique, the client is asked to think about some internal process that needs to be deaccelerated. When the client is well into this behavior he raises his finger and a helper shouts "STOP" loudly enough to evoke a startle response. When continued, this method is effective in eliminating disturbing thoughts. A related procedure, "covert sensitization" is a procedure where the client is trained to imagine an unpleasant event and to make this unpleasant event's removal contingent upon carrying out the desired behavior.

Still another form of self-administered punishment is called "satiation." In satiation, the subject is asked to deliberately repeat a behavior even when the client no longer wants to do it. "Covert conditioning" is also a widely used technique of behavior modification. This procedure of anxiety reduction utilizes self-presented imagery as a substitute for reproducing the actual physical conditions under which a client experienced the intense fear. Contingent "covert reinforcement" may be applied and is thought to parallel the procedure of overt self-reinforcement. Covert self-reinforcement differs from overt self-reinforcement only in that it requires the self-presentation of an imagined object or scene rather than an overt object or verbal statement. The client is trained to imagine a well-practiced scene which is subjectively experienced as happy or pleasant.

In covert negative reinforcement, the procedure is to have the client imagine an unpleasant situation which can later be used in the place of other aversive reinforcers. It has been suggested that covert negative reinforcement can be used as a noxius stimulus for escape conditioning. In turn, in "escape conditioning," the client first imagines the rehearsed unpleasant scene and then imagines escape through performing the response which is to be increased. A related procedure, "covert extinction" runs parallel to operant extinction. In this procedure the client is asked to present himself with the target response to be decreased and to imagine a neutral effect, rather than the usual pleasant consequences.

A variation of the foregoing is "covert modeling," wherein imagined stimuli are substituted for live or film models in the reduction of fearful behavior. The patient is then asked to actively superimpose his idealized self-image on his current image and observe the gradual enhancement of his self-image. This feeling is then used to motivate efforts to acomplish the set goal.

Another cognitive management technique, similar to Ellis' rational emotive therapy, is "systematic rational restructuring." After exposure to imagined anxiety-provoking situations the client is asked to label the degree of arousal and to put the anxiety states to use in exploring and describing his or her self-defeating attitudes or expectations about the fear arousing situation. Goldfriend, Decenteceo, and Weinberg have described this procedure of systematic rational restructuring as one in which clients learn to control anxiety by modifying the cognitions with which they approach potentially upsetting situations (Kanfer, 1975).

Other coercive control methods

A coercive situation may be defined as any authoritarian program where participation by the subject is involuntary. In this type of situation, the control of all aspects of the environment is placed in the hands of the behavior therapist by persons who are already in authority over the subject. This very effectively removes all but the most drastic countercontrol methods from the subject. The problem of operant, coercive behavior control as in a token economy, demonstrates the effectiveness of behavior control methods when therapists have been given extensive control of the environmental conditions prior to the application of behavior methods. If behavior methods do not increase the effectiveness of traditional coercive methods, they they would hardly be effective in a free situation.

In this presentation the reader may wonder at our inclusion of token economies under "coercive techniques." It should be emphasized that, contrary both to operant literature and Skinnerian concepts, token economies are constructed on aversive foundations. Hence, token programs are far from being pure reward situations. In some cases, both reward and punishment are directly utilized. When reward is used, for example, the subjects first must be deprived of certain basic needs, including food, either by placing them in a closed ward or by using an institutional facility which has previously deprived inmates of basic needs. These procedures are necessitated because operant token programs require methods of preventing subjects from acquiring tokens, privileges, or money from a nonexperimental source. While behaviorists may not consider the foregoing an aversive situation, there is little doubt that inmates do. They resent it and this increases the interpersonal distance between inmates and ward personnel.

FOUNDATIONS OF ANALYTIC THERAPY

Since our immediate concern is with developing a relationship between basic behavioral principles and psychoanalytic thought, let us turn now to the founding of the latter school.

The school of psychoanalysis was developed by Sigmund Freud. Freud believed the understanding of behavior was to be found in the interplay of conscious and unconscious forces. Different kinds of laws were thought to determine what happens in these two states. In theory, the unconscious operates on the principle of what Freud called "the primary process and the conscious on the principle of the "secondary process." The actions and meanings mediated through dreams were attributed to the action of primary process. In dreams, meanings were thought to be clouded by the condensation of several thoughts into symbols and the displacement of an impulse from one symbol to another.

The individual's motivation was explained by the concept of "libido" which was the mind source of biological tensions. The most important aspect of this energy, insofar as mental economy was concerned, was considered to be sexual. The id, on the other hand, was the reservoir of this energy, and was an unconscious mental apparatus which operated in accordance with the pleasure principle, demanding immediate gratification and remaining oblivious to reality or social constraints. The part of the mind that complements the id is the "ego" which operates according to the secondary process and is attentive to the demands of reality.

A third part of the mental machinery, according to Freud, was the "superego." Unlike the ego which serves the pleasure principle and only postpones gratification, the superego attempts to halt the pleasure principle completely. The operation of the superego was thought to be largely unconscious. Interplays between the hypermoralistic superego and amoral id were modulated and regulated by ego functions.

It is important to note, that many have contributed to expanding psychoanalytic thought to a broader scientific base. We will discuss these theorists, however, only as they interface with the propositions of "behaviorism." Indeed, although divergent, theoretically, Watsonian behaviorism took cognizance of analytic thought, particularly when it came to issues of sex. Through a misunderstanding of Freud's theory of the Oedipus complex, Watson developed a mechanical way of handling infants in order to avoid Oedipal involvements. Similarly, it would seem that Freudian influence was not overly impeded by the anti-instinct trend, in Watsonian behaviorism. Floyd Allport, in spite of behavioristic leanings, did not jetison the idea of instinct and E. C. Tolman was as much affected as Floyd Allport by the Freudian theory of instincts.

Toman's encounter with psychoanalysis while in Vienna actually served to quiet some of his doubts about behaviorism. Tolman considered his stay in Vienna to have made him more receptive to psychoanalysis and generally testifies to his lack of arrogance and his tolerance of a variety of points of view. In his autobiography, Tolman wrote that he had gained from Freud the understanding, later incorporated into his behavioral theory, that the determiners of much behavior are not to be found in introspective consciousness. He also attributed to Freud his notions of drives, the means (i.e., cathexes) by which objects obtain a value; an appreciation for the validity of defense mechanisms, and a feeling that such mechanisms must somehow fit into a general theory of learning, lack of learning, distortion of learning, and so forth. Finally, Tolman gained from psychoanalysis a growing conviction that there are some important differences between preceptions, expectancies, beliefs, and motives which get into consciousness and those which do not get into consciousness (Shakow and Rapport, 1964).

John Watsons' early behaviorism initiated a denial of the unconscious, a denial which psychoanalysts were prone to describe as the result of unconscious defenses. To even the modern-day behaviorist, the "unconscious" can be formulated in more commonsense terms referring to habits or habit systems. As behaviorism became influential after 1913, many psychologists and a few psychoanalysts, in an unsuccessful integrative move, hope to reduce the unconscious to an aspect of neurological functioning.

Also along the road of integration, Horace W. Fink and William A. White borrowed the language of behaviorism to make the concept of transference credible. Meanwhile, behaviorism's founder, John Watson became interested in psychoanalysis through Adolf Myer at Johns Hopkins University in 1910. Watson became convinced of the relevance and facts of Freud's work, but felt that the terminology of the psychoanalysts must be discarded. Freud himself thought of the possibility of dropping the terminology, and just adhering to the facts and "truths" of psychoanalysis.

Freud's distilled central truth is also one common to hard shell behaviorism. Namely, that youthful, outgrown, and partially discarded habits and reactions can and do influence the forthcoming functioning of the adult system of reactions. To a certain extent, this formulation includes the possibility of forming those habit systems which we reasonably expect to form. Congealed, both viewpoints would argue that "habit systems" are pathological disturbances.

Analytic "transference neurosis" to the behaviorist school could be explained in terms of "conditioning" and generalization. The unconscious, which had been made into a "metaphysical" entity by Freud and his followers may merely signify a group of habits to behaviorists.

Horace Fink, assuming a behaviorist viewpoint, argued that the transference phenomena is plausible through animal conditioning. A thesis offered by Fink stated that just as Pavlov's dog's gastric juices were conditioned to flow at the sound of a bell and the sound of a bell became the stimulus which set off the entire pattern; so a person in a patient's past could set off preconditioned reactions that belonged to the past. By making the patient aware of the origins of the habits, which were reenacted for the physician, the patient's "adaptive flexibility" was enhanced.

Fink was an assimilated psychoanalyst, a sort of hybrid behaviorist derived from the schools of Pavlov, Irwin Bissell Holt, and John Watson. Fink made a special point of the relativity of sexual morals and may have been more permissive about sexual conduct than many, more traditional psychoanalysts. Fink believed that sexuality held great potential for happiness and good. Since the sexual instinct was the most natural instinct, only warped and deformed by society, the analyst's job was to help the patient accept sexuality more rationally. Therapy was designed to help promote a free flow of instinctual energy and foster more satisfactory sublimation of parental and infantile tendencies.

Fink invoked behaviorism to explain why and how psychoanalysis affected a process Freud had said little about. Namely, the memory gaps in neurosis. Fink argued that it was possible to define Freud's unconscious as the "instinct" of the Watsonian behaviorist. The behaviorist's "habit" became the equivalent of the

Freudian "foreconscious," the locus wherein was acquired resistance and controls over instincts. It is these controls which Fink believed create memory gaps in neuroses. Behavioristic analysis focused on the awareness of habitual behaviors or reactions. In order to help patients fill in memory gaps, behavioral analysis reconstructed the exact historical origin of each habit and the circumstances under which the neurosis was originally formed. Thus, the behavioral analysts fostered mature decisions adapted to reality, rejected or modified so that wishes and desires once expressed in habitual symptoms could be either sublimated or fulfilled within the demands of society (Hale, 1971).

The Finch and Cain formulation of etiological factors in childhood psychological disorders induces not only the very basic concepts of fixation, regression and trauma, but also the following:

1. Constitutional elements (e.g., marked hyperactivity, low pain threshold, aberrant drive endowment, or those behaviors which interfere with needs, interaction patterns, and style of relating to primary objects in the dhild's environment).

2. The lack of necessary stimuli and experience for ego formation and development.

3. Prolonged repetitive patterning of interactional experiences of minor frustrations due to unbound tensions.

4. The organism has a history of overloading with internal and external tasks at a given point.

Child psychoanalysis both as a subspeciality and as a specific theory has been and remains grossly underdeveloped. Years ago Anna Freud noted a series of crucial problems faced in the diagnostic assessment of childhood psychological disorders which often have been exacerbated by our limited conception of what psychological normality, adaption or health is in children. There is currently no adequate nosological system. A major difficulty exists in assessing an organism still highly fluid and amidst rapid physical and psychological changes; and who lacks fully extended evidence of cumulative patterned behavior. Existing norms are incomplete for development at various stages, and the openness of children render them immediately responsive to numerous potent influences in their environment.

In the psychoanalysis of children the role of the parents is placed under scrutiny. Two relevant questions are: "What types of intervention with parents, if any, does a given case require in order to permit a facilitated view of a particular child?" and "What effects are such interventions likely to have on the analytic processes with a given child?"

The nature of analytic contact with parents will depend on the type of disorder, the degree to which conflicts are internalized, the child's age, the nature of marital interactions, parental relationships to the child's disturbance, situational variables and the phase of treatment (Finch and Cain, 1968).

Melanie Klein's psychoanalytic technique adheres to formal Freudian concepts.

The setting is the same as in a classical Freudian analysis. The role of the analyst is confined to interpreting the patient's verbal material and all criticism, advice, encouragement, and reassurance are vigorously avoided. Interventions are centered on the transference situation and problems are impartially taken as manifestations of positive and negative transference.

An understanding of Klein's use of fantasy is necessary in order to understand her approach to resistance. It should be pointed out that in Kleinian technique, resistance is synonymous with defenses against insight. A Kleinian analyst interprets the content of conscious fantasy and neglects the analysis of defenses (Segal, 1967).

ANALYTIC ADAPTATIONS TO THERAPY

Daseinanalysis

Existential psychoanalysis is a term applied to all those theoretical and practical deviations from classical psychoanalysis which replace the libido and psychic apparatus theories with an emphasis on immediately apprensible human existence. Existential psychoanalysis bases its knowledge of the nature of human beings on the insights of existential philosophy, particularly on the work of the German philosopher Martin Heidegger. The key term of Heidegger and his followers is *Dasein,* popularly translated as "existence." Melard Boss, in order to avoid confusion with other, so-called existential psychoanalytical schools, called the Heidegger approach "Daseinanalytic." Daseinanalysis does not and cannot teach any particular new phrases or concepts that might serve to formulate reflections on or investigations into psychotherapy or psychopathology. This approach limits the psychotherapist to the description and investigation of all immediately observable moods of human behavior and their perceptable underlying moods, confining the therapist to speak of the patient in everyday language. The Daseinanalytic therapist understands that man is essentially one whose meaning involves disclosing relationships. Because the Daseinanalytic therapist realizes that the meaning and context of everything that comes his way shows itself directly, he has no need either to destroy what he actively sees and hears from the patient or to replace it with assumed forces supposedly underlying the patient's behavior and perception. The therapist is free to discard psychoanalytic theory as well as the labored psychoanalytic interpretations of symbols, both of which are considered obstacles to an immediate understanding between physician and patient. The therapist, instead, devotes himself fully to the patient. The therapist does not approach the patient from the point of view of scientific theory; nor is the therapist distracted by the observation of assumed anonymous forces within the patient. The therapist's behavior rests on the insight that, being human, he is called upon to disclose both things and men. This knowledge increases the therapist's sensitivity to all obstacles which generally reduce potential relationships of a patient to a few rigid and unauthentic modes of behavior.

Daseinanalysis imbues the therapist with a deep respect for everything he encounters. Such nonpartiality is of great practical importance and eliminates the so-called unbreakable transference. The Daseinanalytic attitude toward the patient's feelings in the transference situation is characteristic of his attitude toward all happenings during analytic treatment. Whatever belongs either to the creature realm or the divine is permitted to remain just that. Hence, so-called transference does not transfer anything. The Daseinanalytic therapist does not try to persuade the patient that much of what he feels and means is only a cloak for opposite wishes and tendencies, either in terms of transference or other areas of experience (Boss & Concrau, 1967)

Short-term psychotherapy

In short-term psychotherapy, the effort is primarily directed at:

1. Modifying or removing and relieving suffering.

2. Reviving a level of adaptive functioning that the patient possessed prior to the outbreak of the illness.

3. Promoting an understanding of obvious problems that underlie symptoms, sabatoge, functioning, and interfere with a complete enjoyment of life.

4. Presenting ideas on how to recognize these problems at their inception.

5. Providing some immediate way of dealing with problem patterns and their effects.

A brief summary of effective tactics used in short-term psychotherapy are:

1. At the first session an attempt is made to establish a working relationship while getting complete information about the patient.

2. At the end of the first session, patients are given some explanation for the symptoms.

3. It is emphasized that the treatment period will be limited and that results depend on how well the patient applies himself to the guidance.

4. During succeeding visits an attempt is made to establish patterns which have been operating and causing stress.

5. An exploration is made to see if these patterns have their roots in early childhood and have a relationship to parents and siblings.

6. Through pointed questioning, the patient is encouraged to put the pieces together for himself or herself.

7. An exploration is made as to why patients are unable to work out their present difficulty, bringing them to an awareness of how and why they are resisting or are unable to resolve their troubles.

8. Patients are encouraged in self-observation and taught how to relate symptoms to precipitating happiness in their present environment as well as to resolving conflicts within themselves.

9. In the event that tension or depression are too severe, tranquilizers or energizing drugs are temporarily utilized.

10. Hypnosis may be introduced when adaptional collapse is present or resistance is evident.

11. In the case of phobic symptoms which do not resolve with interpretation, behavior therapy may be emphasized.

12. Dream exploration may be instituted where advantageous.

13. Patients are actively aided to have insight into actions and to desensitize themselves to painful situations.

14. Patients are encouraged to develop a cooperative life philosophy.

15. Therapy is terminated with recognition of immediate   accomplishments which may be modest, but with continued application of self-understanding will help bring about more sustained changes (Wolberg, 1968).

Group therapy

In addition to individual therapy, group therapy is often a treatment of choice. There are three basic approaches to group psychotherapy:

1. *The Intrapersonalist* approach is applied by group psychotherapists who appear to have transposed their views of the individual treatment process to the group setting. The intrapersonalist therapist maintains that the main focus is on the individual and seeks to effect changes in intrapsychic structure and the subject's internal balance. Supporters of this approach to treatment usually insist that methods are best adapted to analytic methods.

2. *The Transactionalist (Interpersonalist)* is a label given to those who attempt to focus on the dyad or subgroup. The transactionalist deals primarily with interpersonal relationships in a group setting. The transactionalist views include those held by Frank (1957), Bach (1954), and Berne (1966). All perceive the group as providing stimuli which permit the individual member to demonstrate his or her idiosyncratic modes of relating and responding to a broad range of individuals.

Transactionalists believe that the patient's behavior in the group may be understood in part as a manifestation of properties of the group. Transactionalists are as much concerned with the personality characteristics of the patient as with the dynamics of the total group. The transactionalists appear to have certain advantages in group psychotherapy, since this medium permits the study of the individual as he responds to a number of other individuals and provides the opportunity for therapeutic change by means of the relationship effected.

3. *The Integralist* is a term applied to the group psychotherapist who places major emphasis on group processes. It is the belief of the integralist that the study of the group as an entity reveals the functioning of the individual member in his full complexity. It is further assumed that all group activity reflects overt or covert aspects of the individual's behavior. The integralists believe that the primary determiner of the patient's problem is his inability to be an effective member of a task-oriented group (Parloff, 1968).

ANALYTIC THERAPY AS A LEARNING PROCESS

Some basic learning experiences which occur in psycholanalytic therapy are:

1. The therapist sets an example of acceptance, respect, tolerance, nonpermissiveness, reliability, trustworthiness, punctuality, nonretaliation, evenness of temper, truth, and predictability.

2. The therapist sets limits. He limits the time devoted to each client and expects punctuality respect for property rights, privacy, and independence.

3. Through the foregoing the therapist teaches tolerance of delay by regulated frustration, and nonanticipation of dependency, such as terminating the sessions by the clock, rather than by the client's wishes.

The emotional learning which occurs during psychoanalytic psychotherapy can be reduced to a basic model:

1. The therapist provides a good climate in which the client can come to recognize a safe positive environment.

2. The patient is consciously willing to engage the therapist in the collaborative venture of psychotherapy.

3. The task of the therapist is to convince the patient of the irrationality, futility and self-defeating aspects of his defensive maneuvers.

Thus, the therapist encourages the abandonment of old beliefs and the substituting of new attitudes, beliefs, values, etc., as a model for interpersonal collaboration. Behavior modification is aimed at eliminating or modifying the maladaptive responses. This is contrary to psychoanalytic therapy which views any behavioral act as a complex resultant of inner motivational forces. Behavior therapy respects all intrapsychic determinants hypothesized by analytic therapy, however, behavior therapists have attacked psychoanalytic therapy, because of its inordinate length, expense, narrow range of applicability, and its ineffectiveness (Strupp, 1968).

It seems that two particular issues hinder communications between behavior modification experts and traditional clinical psychologists. The issues are (1) symptom specific treatment emphasis in behavior modification, and (2) the relative perspective on ethical issues attendant on behavior control techniques. In regards to the first, behavior modifiers have historically deemphasized classical etiology. Instead they argue that it is the current rather than past behavior that is making people miserable, and hence that current behavior needs to be changed. Further, they equate cause-and-effect concepts with reinforcement history and current rates of behavior emission. In most cases, they believe it is unscientific to speculate about mediation processes that cannot be observed and understood and that the reinforcement paradigm is a more economical explanatory tool. It is noteworthy, however, that currently an increasing emphasis is being placed on cognitive factors, signaling a significant change in behavior modification. Nevertheless, the behavior modifier feels that current behavior has been shaped lawfully by principles of

181

reinforcement and extinction and these principles are thought to explain maladaptive as well as adaptive behaviors.

Behavioral conceptualizations of the maintenance of symptoms by consequences are very similary to the psychoanalytic concept of secondary gain. Symptom removal is seen as doing more than just removing the symptom; it also provides the occasion for the acquisition of new socially adaptable behavior. This process is facilitated either by extinguishing unwanted behavior through the cessation of reinforcement, or by having the unwanted behavior followed by aversive consequences. To accomplish either of these ends, the behavior modifier has to be at least partially in control of the patient's environment; hence, the concern with ethical issues.

The ethical concern with regard to behavior modification has been heightened because behavioral techniques seem to be very powerful tools in many circumstances. The behavior modifier feels that control cannot be avoided or eliminated; that in fact everybody is under the control of other people (teachers, parents, employers, professors, etc.). Hence, the ethical issue becomes one of *who* controls and for what reinforcers. The behavior modifier admits that he *does* control although, ideally, this control is exerted for the good of the patient (Nevringer, 1970). In addition it is well to observe the following distinguishes behavior therapy and both psychoanalysis and client-centered therapy:

1. Learning theory emphasizes a variety of aspects of human functioning which might be involved in problematic behavior, neurophysiological, physiological-motor, verbal, perceptual, and cognitive. Both psychoanalytic and client-centered therapy place an unblanaced stress on mental processes, usually ignoring the possibilities that behavior could have nonpsychological meanings. While psychoanalysis focuses on ideas, memories, and feelings, client-centered therapy emphasizes feelings and their verbal expression.

2. Behavioral views emphasize problem manifestation within the everyday environment as opposed to manifestation only within an interview. Psychoanalytic and client-centered therapy usually limit themselves to verbal reports, and even these are usually limited to the therapy session. This is partly due to the fact that the report is based almost solely on the data of the interview.

Traditional psychoanalytic and client-centered therapy seldom pay systematic attention to the aspects of everyday situations where the client's difficulty occurs. Behavior therapy, on the other hand, pays close attention to the specific aspects of environment where the client experiences problems; and it has been consistently concerned with how therapy activity is going to affect changes in ordinary life situations. Indeed, operant approaches (Goldiamond, 1965; Krasner, 1971) often focus on careful analysis of discriminative stimuli and the reward-punishment aspects of the environment. Operant approaches also often train the client to manipulate relevant aspects of everyday situations.

An obvious limitation of the psychoanalytic and client-centered approaches is their almost complete dependence upon a single mode of treatment often without effective regard for the great variety of problems presented by their clients. Behavior therapy, on the other hand, begins with a flexible and inclusive model (S-O-R) which focuses on a thorough description of the problem and then devises a treatment strategy adequate to modify behavior in the desired manner. Psychoanalysis is marked by an unmistakable neglect of the task of specifying and systematizing its techniques.

Pioneering attempts at translating psychotherapy into learning theory terms has, up to this point, focused largely upon reinterpreting traditional psychotherapy practices in terms of a different language system. The recent emergence of behavior therapy has been an implementation of a learning theory based on a didactic or overt intervention approach. Behavior therapy enhances the effectiveness of traditional psychotherapy. A therapist who combines behavioral strategies with high levels of empathy, warmth and genuineness may be more effective than either the usual psycho- or behavior therapist. Such a therapist may provide a potent reinforcer and elicit a positive affect, which increase the level of the subject's positive self-reinforcement. This tends to decrease anxiety and increase the level of a positive effect communicated to others. In contrast, therapists who are low in communicated empathy, nonpossessiveness, warmth, and genuineness are generally ineffective in producing change in the patient (Truax, 1966). It is suggested here that conditioning techniques do not replace traditional interviewing techniques and that the results of conditioning research be applied to two areas of practice:

1. To provide rules for the control of the therapeutic interview. To date, there are few practical uses of the verbal conditioning research.

2. To provide an integrated technique for behavior modification. A combination of conditioning therapies and interview techniques could maximize the scope and flexibility of treatment approaches and extend the areas of the counselor's effectiveness.

Someday, therapists may publicly differentiate between two types of services which the therapist can offer:

1. Behavior therapy for the treatment of the socially crippling behavior disorders associated with specific socially inadequate responses.

2. Friendship therapy for the counsel and guidance of the uncertain, confused, but socially adequate person.

The progress toward a broader application of learning principles in psychotherapy and construction of a technology of behavior therapy has been thwarted by a failure to combine interview and conditioning techniques. The combination is essential because conditioning provides a methodology and approach for processes of treatment. The interview provides for methods permitting the collection of life-history data and provides opportunities for observation of interactional behaviors. A combination of interview and conditioning theories lies in a technique called "instigation therapy." Instigation therapy rests heavily on the utilization of the client's verbal repertoire and self-regulatory behaviors. It consists, in essence, of teaching the client to arrange optimal conditions for his own behavior change in his daily environment. This approach relies heavily on interviews, as well as conditioning sessions. Through an extension of instigation therapy, behavior changes have been obtained not only by direct contact with the client himself, but by working with people who can regulate the client's environment for him (Kanfer, 1966).

BEHAVIORIALISM: AN INTEGRATED SYSTEM

Textbooks still define behavior modification as a psychotherapy or educational intervention based on either Skinnerian principles or other related laboratory-derived learning principles. At its inception behavior modification was an expanding form of intervention which is now being applied by a wide range of personnel, in public schools, private offices, state schools, hospitals, and prisons. Most likely the bulk of behavior modification projects have criteria and techniques that are part of behavior modification terminology but otherwise are without theoretical foundation. This understanding of current behavior modification can provide fundamental growth in theory, research and practice. Indeed, a formal distinction can be made between "behaviorism" and "behavioralism." A behavioralist develops alternative theories and practices which are no longer restricted by customary allegiances to the behavior terminologies, consideration, and philosophical assumptions. The term "behavioralism" is geared to explicit openness and to theoretical understandings of behavior which are idealistic but not necessarily scientific. The behavioralist takes a comprehensive focus on ongoing behavior in life, rather than confining his observations to laboratory parameters.

Behavioralism's methods and descriptions are consensual, requiring all persons to be able to reach agreement about the appearance of a phenomenon within a specified situation. This description and context of the phenomenon can be refined until a total consensus is reached. Behavioralists agree with behaviorists that psychological data should be observable behavior and that environment is an essential component in the unit. However, the behavioralist is also open to the possibility that behavior may embody such uniquely human phenomena as consciousness, perception, purposefulness, and dialectical relations between the current environment and the future. Behavioralism's goal is not only to predict or control behavior but to aim for understanding, sharing, providing direction and unilateral intervention (Fischer 1973).

Psychotherapy clearly has arisen in order to bring about a change in the human condition. The many disparate models illustrate the range of creative energy devoted to this process. As seen in the foregoing, methods vary from those which stress unconscious mental processes that need to be elucidated in order to understand the patient's symptoms to those which regard neurotic symptoms as conditioned habits mediated by anxiety. Similarly, emphases vary from heavy reliance on the use of external reinforcement to control and shape behavior and to concern with the therapist's personal attitudes in the relationship (e.g., empathy, regard and liking for the client). The various schools of psychotherapy, however, seem to have in common a relationship between client and therapist; conversational content and formalized verbal techniques which provide reward and punishment.

In formal psychoanalysis, it is expected that the client has feelings about the therapist which are derived in part from the client's previous emotional experiences. In behavior therapy, such feelings facilitate reciprocal inhibition. In short, psychotherapists of whatever persuasion use both positive and negative reinforcement in a variety of ways, slowly shaping both verbal and overt behavior. It is chiefly in their technical aspects that therapies differ, but all may, at a particular level, approach the same goals in a different manner. It is now apparent that the greatest barrier to integration of present-day therapies lies in their different theoretical assumptions. Perhaps empirical research will provide the forum out of which may come the psychotherapy of tomorrow (Sloane, 1969).

REFERENCES

Bond, J. A., Behavior therapy, learning theory and scientific method. *Psychotherapy: Theory Research and Practice,* 1974, *3* (2), 118—131.

Boss M., and Condrau, G., Existential psychoanalysis. In B. Wolman, (Ed.), *Psychoanalytic technique — a handbook for the practicing psychoanalyst.* New York: Baser Books, 1967, 443—467.

Carpenter, F., *The Skinner primer beyond freedom and dignity.* New York: Free Press, 1974.

Finch S. M., and Cain, A. C., Psychoanalysis of children: problems of etiology and treatment. In J. Marinor (Ed.), *Modern psychoanalysis — new directions and perspectives.* New York: Basic Books, 1968, 424—454.

Fischer, C. T., Behaviorism and behavioralism. *Journal of Psychotherapy: Theory Research and Practice,* 1973, *10* (1), 2—4.

Hale, N. G., *Freud and the American — the beginning of psychoanalysis in the United States 1876—1917.* New York: Oxford University Press, 1971.

Kanfer, F. H., Implications of conditioning techniques for interview therapy. *Journal of Counseling Psychology* 1966, *13* (2), 171—177.

Kanfer, F. H., Self-management methods. In F. M. Kanfer and A.P. Goldstein (Eds.), *Helping people change.* New York: Pergamon Presss, 1975, 1—78.

Mark, M. H., and Hillix, W. A., *Systems and theories in psychology* (2nd ed.). New York: McGraw-Hill 1927

Moss, G. R., An outline of the behavior therapies. *International Journal of Psychiatry,* 1969, *8* (6), 883—894.

Neuringer, C., Behavior modification as the clinical psychologist views it. In C. Neuringer and J. Michael (eds.), *Behavior modification in clinical psychology.* New York: Appleton-Century-Crofts 1970, 1—10.

Parloff, M. B., Analytic group psychotherapy. In J. Marmor (Ed.), *Modern Psychoanalysis — new directions and perspectives.* New York: Basic Books, 1968, 492—531.

Ross, A. R., Behavior therapy. In B. Wolman (Ed.), *Manual of child psychopathology.* New York: McGraw-Hill, 1972, 900—925.

Russell, E. W., The power of behavior control: a critique of behavior modification methods. *Journal of Clinical Psychology,* 1974, *30* (2), 111—137.

Segal, H., Melanie Klein's technique. In B. Wolman (Ed.), *Psychoanalytic technique — a handbook for the practicing psychoanalyst.* New York: Basic Books, 1967, 168–190.

Shakow, D., and Rapport, D., The influence of Freud on American psychology. *Psychological Issues, 4* (1). (Monograph 13, International Universities Press, New York, 1964, pp. 148–150.

Sloan, B. R., The converging paths of behavior therapy and psychotherapy. *International Journal of Psychiatry,* 1969, *7*(7), 493–501.

Strupp, H. H., Psychoanalytic therapy of the individual. In J. Marmor (Ed.), *Modern psychoanalysis — new directions and perspectives.* New York: Basic Books, 1968, 293–342.

Traux, C. B., Some implications of behavior therapy for psychotherapy. *Journal of Counseling Psychology,* 1966, *13* (2), 166–170.

Wenrick W. W., *A primer of behavior modification.* Belmont, Calif.: Brooks/Cole, 1970.

Whaley, D. L., and Mallott, R., *Elementary principles of behavior.* New York: Appleton-Century-Crofts, 1971.

Wolberg, L. R., Short-term psychotherapy. In J. Marmor (Ed.), *Modern psychoanalysis — new directions and perspectives.* New York: Basic Books, 1968, 343–354.

HUMANISTIC CONCERNS AND BEHAVIOR MODIFICATION

C. H. Patterson
University of Illinois, Urbana-Champaign

INTRODUCTION

We seem to be moving into a new social era in regard to moral and ethical behavior. Before I am misunderstood to be referring to the morality of Watergate and the apparent loosening of sexual morals, let me state that these represent the end of an era. It is the reaction against the political morality of Watergate which represents the new era. Other elements of the new ethic include the concern about the invasion of privacy by Government agencies, the movement to recognize the consumer in business and credit agencies, the Buckley amendment giving individuals the right to information in their academic records, and concern about the administration of the Freedom of Information Act. Closer to psychology are the court cases involving the right to treatment of patients in institutions for the emotionally disturbed and the mentally retarded, and the furor over the use of behavior modification in correctional institutions. Within psychology itself we see the new ethics manifested in the Ethical Principles in the Conduct of Research with Human Participants.

This social change has come none too soon, if Watergate is any indication of the state of morality in the nation's politics. It has been said by historians that a civilization or a nation in which corruption becomes widespread is doomed to destruction either from within or without.

It would of course be interesting to know the sources or social antecedents of this change. Not being a sociologist or even a social psychologist, I am not competent to deal with this question. However, it appears that professionals in the behavioral sciences, including psychologists, have not been in the forefront. Journalists, the traditional muckrakers, have been involved in uncovering the corruption of morals in public life. Lawyers concerned about civil liberties and civil rights have been involved with many of the legal challenges to individual rights and freedom. But there seems to be an underlying wave of public concern, indignation, and demand for higher standards of ethics and morality. Where or how did this originate and develop?

I think it is important to point out that the ethical and moral standards being demanded are not new. No new system of ethics has been developed or proposed. What is being demanded is that the long accepted principles of ethical and moral

Presented at a conference on "Moral and Ethical Implications of Behavior Modification," University of Wisconsin-Madison, March 20–21, 1975.

conduct be practiced. These principles are part of our culture. They are promulgated and taught in our religious and educational institutions.

Henry Steele Commager (1975), the historian, in a recent article entitled "The School as Surrogate Conscience," writes that "increasingly, schools are required to take on the function of a moral safety valve. The more virtuous the sentiments and standards of conduct they inculcate, the more effectively they perform the function of a surrogate conscience permitting society to follow its own bent while consoling itself with the assurance that they are training up a generation that will do better.... Thus society rejoices when schools teach that all men are created equal and entitled to life, liberty and happiness, but has no intention of applying that noble principle to the ordinary affairs of business and government. Thus society applauds the principle of racial equality but does not itself provide the young an example of such equality — knowing instinctively that the example is more dangerous than the admonition. Thus society rewards pupils who can recite the Bill of Rights but has no serious interest in the application of these rights to the tiresome minority groups who clamor for them." Commager then states that this method is ineffective: "Rarely, if ever in the history of education have so many been exposed to so much with results so meager. To judge by results — the results of the past 40 years or so — this whole enterprise of relying on schools to reform society by direct teaching has been an unmitigated failure."

I suggest that this may be a premature judgment. Perhaps the schools have been more successful than we realize. It just may be that the public concern about social ethics and morality is, at least in part, an outcome of the teachings of our educational system.

IS BEHAVIOR MODIFICATION EFFECTIVE?

But our concern here is not with the sociological analysis of the developing public concern with ethics. Nor is it with the public concern about governmental and political morality. Our focus is upon the ethical implications of the control of behavior, specifically with the methods of control collectively designated by the term behavior modification. It has been pointed out that the current interest in the ethics of behavior modification and in regulation or control of the controllers is an indication that psychology has become important and relevant because it is actually able to control human behavior (e.g., Robinson, 1973). If one reads the recent research on behavior modification, however, there is certainly room for questioning the ability of the behaviorists to control human behavior. The situation seems to be much more complicated, involving many more variables, than is suggested by the optimism of behaviorists a few years ago. The control of the behavior of pigeons and rats, and even of human beings, in the laboratory is a far cry from the control of human behavior in social situations (Reppucci and Saunders, 1974). The extent, and particularly the persistence, of the control achieved by behavior modification are questioned by research which involves longer time periods than the earlier studies.

If the behaviorists are subject to the influence of reinforcement, or the consequences of their own behavior, one can predict a precipitous decline in the application of techniques of behavior modification. It appears that much of the short term
effect may be due to variables which relate to the social psychology or the demand
characteristics of the experiments, the Hawthorne and placebo effects (Davison,
1968), or to the genuine interest and concern of experimenters for their subjects.
The A P A *Monitor* (November, 1974) headline for its report of Professor Bandura's
presidential address (Bandura, 1974) states the situation succinctly: "Psychology's
power exaggerated, says Bandura."

At least one behavior therapist has modified his approach almost to the point of
abandoning behavior modification, as a result of his follow-up of his patients
(Lazarus, 1971). Lazarus obtained a 95 percent return to a questionnaire sent to a
random sample of his clients, and interviewed personally or by telephone additional
members of the random sample which totalled 112 cases. Forty-one had relapsed in
from one week to six years after treatment, usually because of new stress-producing
situations, according to Lazarus. Successful cases suggested that improvements were
related to adoption of a different outlook and increased self-esteem. On an adjec-
tive checklist, the words most frequently used to describe him (sensitive, gentle,
honest) refer to humanistic characteristics rather than to behavioristic techniques.

In my opinion there are other methods of behavior control more dangerous than
behavior modification. The methods employed by some of those involved in groups
are highly manipulating. The transactional analysts are, in my opinion, particularly
pernicious, since they disdain any responsibility for their clients. While the extreme
behaviorists (e.g., Skinner) state that behavior is completely determined by the
environment, the transactional analysts deny that the environment — or other
people, including themselves — has any influence on their clients. Yet at the same
time they engage in the most blatant manipulation of their clients.

BEHAVIOR CAN BE INFLUENCED

But whether the methods of behavior modification are effective, and thus
potentially dangerous or subject to abuse, it is the issue of the control of some
persons by others, by whatever methods, which is of concern. There is no question
that behavior is influenced, or, in some instances controlled, by others, and it is the
general recognition and resistance to such influence and control which has raised, or
is raising, questions about the ethics which are involved. The fact of influence and
control has of course always been present. The nature and sources of political
power have been continuing issues in society. The difference between the present
and the past lies in the fact that now psychology is beginning to develop some
understanding of how influence and control operates, thus making it possible to
more effectively influence and control behavior. As indicated above, the extent of
this knowledge is exaggerated, not only in the minds of the public but in the minds
of some psychologists. But it is clear that knowledge and understanding of human

189

behavior, and consequently the possibility of prediction and control, will increase. The issue of the objectives of such control, with its value and ethical implications, will become increasingly important. As we become better able to control human behavior, we cannot avoid facing the question of what kind of person we want to develop. Do we want to attempt to create the kind of persons who inhabit Walden Two (Skinner 1948), people who, although they are completely controlled, are unaware of it, but who feel free, and are productive and happy?While I do not believe that it will be possible to create such a society — this is one of the exaggerations of psychologists which has led to the public having an exaggereated idea of the power of psychology — it is a possible goal to be worked toward. If this is not an acceptable goal, what would be? What are the criteria for the acceptance of a goal for human behavior? Most practicing behaviorists have not considered this question. They have been satisfied with rather simple, concrete, immediate goals — reducing disruptive behavior in classrooms, reducing anxiety and eliminating phobias in college students or clients, etc., etc. It is assumed that these are desirable ends in themselves. But on what bases are they considered desirable? What is the criterion for accepting or rejecting specific objectives or goals of behavior modification?

ETHICS OF BEHAVIOR MODIFICATION

Until recently, the behaviorists in general have been little concerned about the ethical implications of their activities. (Leonard Krasner [1962] has been a notable exception.) They have avoided discussion of values as related to their goals. The general position has been that they are technicians. As such they have not been concerned about ethical or value aspects of their objectives, failing to recognize that, as Bandura (1969) has noted, the specification of objectives or goals involves a value system, implicitly if not explicitly. Technology is always related to goals, and exists in a situation where ethics are of concern.

Other behaviorists have accepted the goals and values of their clients, or of society in general. Thus, Michael and Meyerson wrote in 1962 that "In schools, no one questions that it is better for children to learn school subject matter than not to learn it; it is desirable to get along with other children and with adults without excessive conflicts; more is to be gained by staying in school than by dropping out; very early marriage of school children is unwise; law abiding behavior is better than delinquent behavior.... If the drop-out problem is a serious one; if we really believe that our society and economy require an educated population; and if the monetary and social costs of large numbers of uneducated and undereducated persons are great; there should be no hesitation in taking advantage of scientific principles of learning to apply effective extrinsic reinforcers to help shape desirable behavior. Some problems of juvenile delinquency and its behavioral treatment can be considered in the same way" (Michael and Meyerson, 1962).

A similar approach has been taken to the treatment of patients in mental hospitals, represented by the statement of Leonard Ullmann in a class lecture to the effect that no one in our society has a right to be a patient in a mental hospital, and therefore anything necessary to get him out is justified. James V. McConnell is quoted from "Psychology Today" in the A P A *Monitor* (Trotter and Warren, 1974) as saying: "I don't believe the Constitution of the United States gives you the right to commit a crime if you want to; therefore, the Constitution does not guarantee you the right to maintain inviolable the personality it forced on you in the first place — if and when the personality manifests strongly anti-social behavior."

Beit-Hallahmi (1974), referring to this group, writes: "We should commend our colleagues who practice behavior modification for their honesty in stating their value preferences. Most of them are quite open about the fact that they work to enforce social norms and prevent deviance.... Their starting point is always what is socially desirable and socially acceptable."

This approach to the ethics of behavior modification assumes that the ends justify the means. It furthermore assumes that there is really no problem of values or goals, since society has already agreed upon these. It is an approach which puts society before the individual. As such it is more in keeping with an authoritarian society such as Russia than with a democracy. Moreover, it has become apparent that society, as represented by individuals subjected to such arbitrary treatment and their representatives — the lawyers and journalists concerned with human rights — is not in agreement about these goals or the ethics implicit in the means to them.

It is impossible for those who influence the behavior of others to abdicate responsibility for the ethical and moral aspects of their methods. Anyone who is in a position of influencing others has a responsibility to be aware of, and to be ready to defend or justify, the ethical bases or principles on which he operates. If one can influence or control behavior, an ethical problem is involved in deciding whether or not to do so and in what way or to what ends. What is "good" or desirable behavior? It is not sufficient to claim that one is a technician in the service of society; that is what the professionals in Germany became during the Nazi regime with no support from world opinion and the postwar Nuremberg trials. Neither is it adequate to claim that one is a scientist, and that science is only concerned with empirical relationships between methods of influence and outcomes, and that values or ethics are not involved. In spite of claims to the contrary, science is not value free. Science itself represents a value. Moreover, the value of a science which claims to be value free, and not concerned about the social effects or utility of its efforts, is being questioned.

ETHICAL AND VALUE SYSTEMS

We face the problem of finding a generally acceptable system of ethics or set of values, if such exists. The general conclusion of most of those who have been concerned with this problem is that no generally acceptable or universal system of values or ethics exists. Values and ethics, it is claimed, are relative. Or the position may be taken that there are a number of different systems, with no adequate basis for choosing among them. Lowe (1959), for example, identifies four different categories of value systems: naturalism, culturalism, theism, and humanism. Since these systems, it is stated, involved differences which cannot be resolved, Lowe concludes that "there is no single professional standard to which his [the psychologist's] values can conform." Psychology, he says, cannot accept one of these sets of values because it then would no longer be a science but would become a social movement.

There are several apparent flaws in this argument. In the first place, as already indicated, science is not above values and ethics, and cannot be if it is to be an inherent part of society. Its goals are its values, and must also be accepted as values by society. Second, it may be questioned whether there are numerous different sets or systems of ethics and values. The four categories of Lowe may be reduced to two: natural or humanistic and supernatural or theistic. Third, these categories are simply presumed sources of values. In the one case it is assumed that values arise naturally from the experience of human beings living together. In the second case it is assumed that systems of ethics or values are revealed, supernaturally, to man, as in the stone tablets given to Moses or the gold tablets given to Joseph Smith. Fourth, the systems of ethics arising at different times in different societies, or revealed at different times to seers, prophets or other religious leaders are not basically different or in unresolvable conflict. While it is true that there are some values which vary at different times and among different cultures, there are also some basic universal values upon which the religious leaders and philosophers of all times and cultures appear to agree.

Two questions follow from the above. First, what are the basic or universal values, and what is their origin and bases? Second, what is the relation of these values to a science of psychology?

There appear to be at least two basic values which transcend time and cultures. There no doubt have been certain brief times and certain (small) groups where these values have been absent, and of course there have been and are individuals who ignore or fail to subscribe to them. But these values appear to have been subscribed to by the major religions and philosophies of all times and cultures. The first of these is respect for the individual. In its ultimate form it is respect for human life; in its broader form it is respect for the human person. Aspects of this respect include respect for the rights of the individual to autonomy, freedom of choice, and freedom to act within the context of the rights of others, and freedom from invasion of privacy. In a positive sense respect involves a concern for others, a caring and compassion. In its highest form it is manifested in love, or agape.

The second value is a basic honesty in human relations. All ethical systems appear to include the condemnation of deception, dishonesty, trickery. In our current philosophy of existentialism the term authenticity is used. Others speak of transparency (Jourard, 1964).

These values are not simply the product of the thought of religious leaders and philosophers. They are the products of the experience of men living together in society. Without the observance of these values, or their implementation at least at a minimal level, society could not survive. Respect for life, in some degree and in some situations, is necessary for the survival of the race. The infant needs someone to provide him with a minimal degree of caring or love for his physical survival. The individual needs a minimum of caring and love from others if he is to become a person or develop a self. If there is not a minimal level of honesty in a society, a basis for trust in others, the social order would collapse.

Skinner appears to accept the survival of the group or culture as the ultimate goal. He writes: "If a science of behavior can discover those conditions of life which make for the ultimate strength of men, it may provide a set of 'moral values' which, because they are independent of the history and culture of any one group, may be generally accepted" (1953, p. 445). Again, he says: "Eventually the practices which make for the greatest biological and psychological strength of the group will survive" (Skinner, 1955).

VALUES AND SCIENCE

Bronowski, in "Science and Human Values" (1955) proposes that values develop from science. Science is the pursuit of truth, which implies honesty. It requires independence and freedom, and the right to dissent. It implies democracy, including tolerance and respect for others and their views. Thus, he writes, "The values of science turn out to be the recognizably human values" (Bronowski, 1955, p. 32). For Bronowski, these values derive from the methods of science. It is no doubt true that they can be derived from science, in that they are necessary for its methods. But this does not mean that they originated from science. These values arose before the development of the scientific method, and make possible the existence of science.

The relationship of science to human values is complex. From one point of view, values are outside of science. They are chosen by society in some manner, directly or indirectly, at various levels or by various groups. Thus the employers or supporters of science determine the objectives of scientific research, and thus set the values of scientific endeavor. It might appear that at an ultimate level there is agreement that the survival of the race is generally or universally accepted as the objective of science. But it is conceivable that this could be rejected and the annihilation of man would be the objective of science. Further, physical survival is a minimal objective. The quality of life must be considered. In "Walden Two" everyone is productive and happy, though (except for the controller) completely controlled without being aware of it. For Skinner, this is utopia. Many would not agree that this is utopia. Certainly there are other possibilities. Presumably man is flexible and can be changed or molded into a variety of forms, both biologically and psychologically. How do we decide what man will become, and who decides? Are there no limits to what he can become? Is there nothing inherent in man's nature which influences, if not determines, what he should become?

VALUES AND HUMANISM

This suggests another point of view regarding human values. Man's nature, including his potentialities, may be a source from which values can be derived. Certain values may be inherent in man's biological and psychological nature and needs. Whatever is necessary to meet man's need or drive for biological survival becomes a value. Even for physical survival of the individual the care or love of another human being is necessary, as indicated earlier. It is relatively simple to determine what is needed for physical survival, and these become values to the individual and to society. The need for survival is an inherent characteristic of the organism. A society which chose to frustrate this drive, or to annihilate itself, would be denying the inherent nature of man.

At the psychological level it is not so obvious what the inherent nature, needs, and potentials of man are. What is the psychological equivalent to the physical drive to survive and to nurture the growth and development of the body? If man has a physical nature doesn't he also have a psychological nature, and if so, what is it?

Clearly, we do not have agreement on this. Is it inherent in man to strive for happiness or productivity? But if there is a drive to develop the potentials of the physical organism through activity, isn't there also a drive in man to develop his psychological potentials? And if there is, then what are these potentials?

Here we come, finally, to humanistic psychology, which has been concerned with these questions. Humanistic psychology is not a homogeneous discipline, or perhaps even a discipline in its present stage of development, certainly not as behavior modification is — or at least was until quite recently, since it appears that behaviorism has been changing so much (cf. Bandura, 1974) that it probably no longer should be called behaviorism if the word is to have any historical meaning. Thus, while I am apparently identified as humanistic in my orientation, as indicated by my being asked to present the humanistic position, and while I do consider myself as a humanistic psychologist, I wish to enter a disclaimer that I represent humanistic psychology.

Humanistic psychology assumes that as there is a drive in the organism to develop its physical potential, so there is a corresponding drive to develop its psychological potential. Indeed, these may be only two manifestations of a single drive — to preserve and enhance the self, of which the body is a part (Combs and Snygg, 1959). Several terms have been used to refer to the person who is moving towards the enhancement of the self or of the process of self-enhancement. These include self-realization, self-fulfillment, the fully functioning person and, most widely used, self-actualization, a term apparently first used in this context by Goldstein (1939). It would appear that if we could reach agreement on the nature of this process or the description of a self-actualizing person we would achieve two important things: (1) we would have a statement of a goal which would be more than a theoretical, philosophical or theological construct, but would be anchored in the biological nature of man, and (2) this goal would be a criterion against which we could measure the desirability or acceptability of man's behavior toward man. Acceptable and desirable behaviors would be those which facilitate the self-actualization of other persons.

There appears to be some agreement, at least among humanistically oriented psychologists, about the nature of the self-actualizing process or at least about the characteristics of self-actualizing persons.

SELF-ACTUALIZATION AS A VALUE

The description of the adequate self or personality given by Combs and Snygg (1959, p. 246) provides a basis for a description of a self-actualizing person. Such a person perceives himself in positive ways (as competent?); he has a positive self-concept. He accepts himself. He also accepts others. The adequate person is open to his experiences, and is able to accept into awareness all his perceptions, without distortion or rejection. Behaviorally he manifests more efficient behavior, since he is not handicapped by defensiveness. Being secure, he can take chances, and is thus capable of spontaneous and creative behavior. He is independent, finding that his own feelings, beliefs and attitudes are adequate guides to his behavior. Finally, Combs and Snygg describe the adequate person as compassionate: not being defensive, he can relate closely to others without hostility and fear.

Rogers' concept of the fully functioning person (Rogers, 1959, 1961) is similar to the adequate person of Combs and Snygg. The fully functioning person has three main characterisitcs: (a) he is open to his experience, to all stimuli, external and internal, and does not have to be defensive or to distort his experience, (b) he lives existentially — that is, he is constantly in process, and is flexible and adaptable; (c) his behavior is determined from within — the locus of control is internal. Since the fully functioning person is open to his experience, all relevant available data influences his behavior. Some relevant data may be missing, so that behavior is not always perfect, but the presence of constant feedback leads to correction.

Maslow has provided the most extensive description of the self-actualizing person. While his work is well known, it would appear that many writers who refer to it have perhaps not recently read it, since it often appears to be misrepresented. It therefore appears to be desirable to summarize it in some detail.

Maslow, on the basis of a study of persons (living and dead) selected as being self-actualizing persons on the basis of a general definition, described the self-

---

actualizing person as follows, as compared to ordinary or average people (Maslow, 1956):

1. *More efficient perception of reality and more comfortable relations with it.* This characteristic includes the detection of the phoney and dishonest person and the accurate perception of what exists rather than a distortion of perception by one's needs. *Self-actualizing people are more aware of their environment,* both human and nonhuman. They are not afraid of the unknown and can tolerate the doubt, uncertainty, and tentativeness accompanying the perception of the new and unfamiliar. This is clearly the characteristic described by Combs and Snygg and Rogers as awareness of perceptions or openness to experience.

2. *Acceptance of self, others, and nature.* Self-actualizing persons are not ashamed or guilty about their human nature, with its shortcoming, imperfections, frailties, and weaknesses. Nor are they critical of these aspects of other people. *They respect and esteem themselves and others.* Moreover, they are *honest, open, genuine, without pose or facade.* They are not, however, self-satisfied but are concerned about discrepancies between what is and what might be or should be in themselves, others, and society. Again, these characteristics are those which Kelly, Rogers, and Combs and Snygg include in their descriptions.

3. *Spontaneity.* Self-actualizing persons are not hampered by convention, but they do not flout it. *They are not conformists,* but neither are they anti-conformist for the sake of being so. They are not externally motivated or even goal-directed — rather their motivation is the internal one of growth and development, the actualization of themselves and their potentialities. Rogers and Kelly both speak of growth, development and maturation, change and fluidity.

4. *Problem-centering.* Self-actualizing persons are not ego-centered but focus on problems outside themselves. They are *mission-oriented,* often on the basis of a sense of *responsibility, duty, or obligation* rather than personal choice. This characteristic would appear to be related to the security and lack of defensiveness leading to compassionateness emphasized by Combs and Snygg.

5. *The quality of detachment; the need for privacy. The self-actualizing person enjoys solitude and privacy.* It is possible for him to remain unruffled and undisturbed by what upsets others. He may even appear to be asocial. This is a characteristic that does not appear in other descriptions. It is perhaps related to a sense of security and self-sufficiency.

6. *Autonomy, independence of culture and environment.* Self-actualizing persons, though dependent on others for the satisfaction of the basic needs of love, safety, respect and belongingness, "are not dependent for their main satisfactions on the real world, or other people or culture or means-to-ends, or in general, on extrinsic satisfactions. *Rather they are dependent for their own development and continued growth upon their own potentialities* and latent resources." Combs and Snygg and Rogers include independence in their descriptions, and Rogers also speaks of an internal locus of control.

7. *Continued freshness of appreciation.* Self-actualizing persons repeatedly, though not continuously, experience awe, pleasure, and wonder in their everyday world.

8. *The mystic experience, the oceanic feeling.* In varying degrees and with varying frequencies, *self-actualizing persons have experiences of ecstasy, awe, and wonder* with feelings of limitless horizons opening up, followed by the conviction that the experience was important and had a carry-over into everyday life. This and the preceding characteristic appear to be related and to add something not in other descriptions, except perhaps as it may be included in the existential living of Rogers.

9. *Gemeinschaftsgefuhl.* *Self-actualizing persons have a deep feeling of empathy, sympathy, or compassion for human beings in general.* This feeling is, in a sense, unconditional in that it exists along with the recognition of the existence in others of negative qualities that provoke occasional anger, impatience, and disgust. Although empathy is not specifically listed by others (Combs and Snygg include compassion), it would seem to be implicit in other descriptions including acceptance and respect.

10. *Interpersonal relations.* *Self-actualizing people have deep interpersonal relations with others.* They are selective, however, and their circle of friends may be small, usually consisting of other self-actualizing persons, but the capacity is there. They attract others to them as admirers or disciples. This characteristic, again, is at least implicit in the formulations of others.

11. *The democratic character structure.* *The self-actualizing person does not discriminate* on the basis of class, education, race, or color. He is humble in his recognition of what he knows in comparision with what could be known, and he is ready and willing to learn from anyone. *He respects everyone* as potential contributors to his knowledge, merely because they are human beings.

12. *Means and ends.* Self-actualizing persons are highly ethical. *They clearly distinguish between means and ends* and subordinate means to ends.

13. *Philosophical, unhostile sense of humor.* Although the self-actualizing persons studied by Maslow had a sense of humor, it was not of the ordinary type. Their sense of humor was the spontaneous, thoughtful type, intrinsic to the situation. Their humor did not involve hostility, superiority, or sarcasm. Many have noted that a sense of humor characterizes people who could be described as self-actualizing persons, though it is not mentioned by those cited here.

14. *Creativeness.* All of Maslow's subjects were judged to be creative, each in his own way. The creativity involved here is not special-talent creativeness. It is a creativeness potentially inherent in everyone but usually suffocated by acculturation. *It is a fresh, naive, direct way of looking at things.* Creativeness is a characteristic most would agree to as characterizing self-actualizing persons.

The resistance of some writers to the concept of self-actualization appears to be related to some misconceptions or misunderstanding regarding its nature or meaning.

One objection to self-actualization appears to be the belief that it is inimical to individuality. This view would seem to represent the self-actualizing person as a collection of traits, which are the same for all self-actualizing persons, and which manifest themselves in standard, identical behaviors. It is true that self-actualizing persons have many common characteristics or behaviors. Since it involves the actualization of individual potentials, it allows for the fact that different individuals have different potentials, as well as different interests. More will be said about this later. As Maslow (1962, p. 196) noted, since self-actualization is the actualization of a self, and since no two selves are alike, individuals actualize themselves in different ways.

A second widespread notion is that a self-actualizing person is antisocial, or at least asocial or self-centered.

The idea that the self-actualizing person is, or can be, antisocial was stated in 1958 by E. G. Williamson. Pointing out that human nature is potentially both good and evil, and that "man seems to be capable both of becoming his 'best' bestial and debasing self, as well as those forms of 'the best' that are of high excellence," he contends that it cannot be accepted that "the nature or form of one's full potential and self-actualization will thus be the 'best possible' or the 'good' form of human nature" (Williamson, 1965, p. 195). While one could contend that counseling would provide conditions for the actualizing of one's "best" potential, Williamson questions the "implicit assumption that the 'best' potentiality will be actualized under optimum counseling relationships" (Williamson, 1963). He appears to believe that counseling, by accepting self-actualization as its goal, is in danger of encouraging "growth through demolishing all barriers restricting free development in any and all directions, irresponsibly and without regard for the development of others" (Williamson, 1950). He questions the assumptions that "any and all forms of growth contain within themselves their own, and sufficient, justification," and asks "Do we believe that the fullest growth of the individual inevitably enhances the fullest growth of all other individuals?" (Williamson, 1958).

Skinner (1975) assumes that self-actualization is a selfish process: "We see a concern for the aggrandizement of the individual, for the maximizing of credit due him, in the self-actualization of so-called humanistic psychology...."

Bandura (1974) also presents a negative view of self-actualization: "Behavioral theorists, however, recognize that 'self-actualization' is by no means confined to human virtues. People have numerous potentialities that can be actualized for good or ill. Over the years, man has suffered considerably at the hands of self-actualized tyrants. A self-centered ethic of self-realization must therefore be tempered by concern for the social consequences of one's conduct."

Some humanistically oriented psychologists appear to share this view.

Maddi (1973a), criticizing self-actualization as the good life, writes "Actualization will tend to take place without the aid of socialization. Indeed, society is usually regarded, in this view, as an obstruction, because it forces individuals into molds, roles, conventions that have little to do with their own unique potentialities. The best thing society can do is impinge upon the individual as little as possible." In another place (Maddi, 1973b), he writes: "According to Rogers.... what blocks individuals is society, in the form of persons and institutions reacting with conditional positive regard and therefore being too judgmental to be facilitative of self-actualization... The definition of the good life involved emphasizes spontaneity rather than planfulness, openness rather than critical judgment, continual change rather than stability, and an unreflective sense of well being. Enacting this, one would more likely live in the woods than enter public life."

Smith (1973) sees self-actualization as including undesirable, or antisocial, behaviors: "and the problem of evil remains: people may realize their potentialities in ways that are humanly destructive, of others if not of themselves."

Even White (1973) views self-actualization as self-centered or selfish. Recognizing that Maslow included "focusing on problems outside oneself and being concerned with the common welfare" in the concept of self-actualization he questions its inclusion: "To call working for the common welfare 'self-actualization' instantly falsifies it into something done for one's own satisfaction." Thus it is apparent that he views self-actualization as self, or selfish, satisfaction. "I ask readers to observe carefully," he writes, "whether or not self-actualization, in its current use by psychological counselors and others, is being made to imply anything more than adolescent preoccupation with oneself and one's impulses." This, in my opinion is an unfair and unwarranted characterization of counselors who accept the concept of self-actualization.

The implicit assumption in this conception of self-actualization is that there is an inevitable conflict between the individual and society, and that the full development (or self-actualization) of individuals is inimical to the self-actualization of other individuals.

The formulations by Rogers of the self-actualizing person deal with this issue. Individuals live, and must live, in a society composed of other individuals. He can actualize himself only in interaction with others. Selfish and self-centered behavior would not lead to experiences which would be self-actualizing (or satisfying) in nature. The self-actualizing person "will live with others in maximum possible harmony, because of the rewarding character of reciprocal positive regard" (Rogers, 1959, pp. 234–236). "We do not need to ask who will socialize him, for one of his own deepest needs is for affiliation and communication with others. As he becomes more fully himself, he will become more realistically socialized" (Rogers, 1961, p. 194). He is more mature, more socialized in terms of the goal of social evolution, though he may not be conventional or socially adjusted in a conforming sense. "We do not need to ask who will control his aggressive impulses, for when he is open to all his impulses, his need to be liked by others and his tendency to give affection are as strong as his impulses to strike out or to seize for himself. He will be aggressive in situations in which aggression is realistically appropriate, but there will be no runaway need for aggression" (Rogers, 1959, p. 291). The self-actualizing person needs to live in harmony with others, to love and to be loved, to meet his own needs, to be a self-actualizing person. Thus, the self-actualizing person provides the conditions for the self-actualization of others, rather than being a negative social influence.

It would appear that some of this confusion about the nature of self-actualization is a matter of semantics. But is also in part a matter of how one views the nature of man. If man is viewed as innately bad or depraved, then self-actualization would involve the development of socially negative characteristics. If man is viewed as innately good, then this would not occur. If man is viewed as neither, or if he is viewed as essentially good but with potential for evil — for selfishness, for hurting others, for aggression — then it becomes important to know the conditions which lead to the expression of such behaviors on the one hand, and on the other hand those conditions which lead to the development of positive behaviors which facilitate the development of the positive self-actualizing behaviors in others.

Aggression has long been considered an instinct. Adler originally proposed that aggression was the single basic motive or instinct of man (Ansbacher and Ansbacher, 1956, p. 34). The strength and practical universality of aggression argue for its innateness. However, many have questioned its innateness or instinctiveness. Anthropologists have found societies with little trace or evidence of aggression. Ashley Montagu writes:

> My own interpretation of the evidence, strictly within the domain of science, leads me to the conclusion that man is born good and is organized in such a manner from birth as to need to grow and develop his potentialities for goodness.... (The view that aggressiveness is inherited) is not scientifically corroborated. In fact, *all* the available evidence gathered by competent investigators indicates that man is born without a trace of aggressiveness (Montagu, 1962).

He refers to Lauretta Bender's finding that hostility in the child is a symptom complex resulting from deprivation in development. Charlotte Buhler, in her studies of infants, also found that there is "evidence of a primary orientation toward 'reality' into which the baby moves with a positive anticipation of good things to be found. Only when this reality appears to be hurtful or overwhelming does the reaction become one of withdrawal or defense" (Buhler, 1961, p. 71). Maslow also declares that impulses of hate, jealousy, hostility, and so on are acquired. "More and more," he writes, "aggression is coming to be regarded as a technique or mode of compelling attention to the satisfaction of one's need" (Maslow, 1949). There is no instinct of aggression that seeks expression or discharge without provocation or without regard to circumstances.

In other words, aggression is not primary but is a reaction to deprivation, threat, or frustration. This is the frustration-aggression hypothesis put forward in 1939 by the Yale anthropologist Dollard and his psychologist associates (Dollard, et al.,

1939). A more general term for the stimuli that provoke aggression is threat. Aggression is universal because threat, in some form or other, is universal. The psychoanalyst Bibring, in criticizing Freud's theories, questions "whether there are any phenomena of aggression at all outside the field of the ego-preservative functions" and notes "the empirical fact that aggressiveness appears only or almost only when the life instincts or the ego instincts are exposed to harm" (Bibring, 1958). A popular novel purporting to demonstrate the innateness of aggressiveness in man inadvertently supports the view that aggression is the result of threat, since the development of aggression in the group of castaway boys occurs under conditions of fear and feelings of being threatened (Golding, 1955).

There is evidence that man is inherently good in the continual striving toward an ideal society, with the repeated and independent development of essentially similar religious and ethical systems whose ideals have withstood the test of time. In spite of deprivation, threat, and frustration, these ideals have been held and practiced by many individuals. Mankind has developed systems of government and law that, though imperfectly, especially in their applications, represent these ideals.

It might actually be argued that goodness or cooperation has a survival value (Montagu, 1950), and that innate aggression would be selectively eliminated by evolution. If there were not an inherent drive toward good in man, or if aggression were innate, it is difficult to understand how the human race could have continued to survive. The potential for good has survived in the face of continued threat and frustration. When we can reduce deprivation and threat, the manifestations of good will increase and aggression will decrease. It is important to add that aggression does not include assertive behavior, initiative behavior, nor even much of competitive behavior. The confusion of these kinds of behavior with aggression has perhaps contributed to the belief that aggression is innate.

THE CONDITIONS FOR SELF-ACTUALIZATION

If aggressive behaviors are the result of threat, then the absence of threat should lead to the expression of positive behaviors towards others. Here we can find some suggestions from experience and research in counseling or psychotherapy, particularly what is called client-centered or relationship therapy, since this approach accepts as its goal the development of more self-actualizing persons and appears to have developed at least some of the conditions which lead to this goal.

Three conditions which have been identified and studied are empathic understanding, respect, warmth, concern, or caring, and therapeutic genuineness. These conditions hardly need to be elaborated upon, since they have become so well known through the writing of client-centered therapists and researchers. Extensive research (see Truax and Carkhuff, 1967, Carkhuff, 1969, Truax and Mitchell, 1971) indicates that these conditions, when provided at an adequate level in the psychotherapy relationship, are related to a wide variety of positive outcomes which include the aspects of self-actualization. Included among these outcomes appear to be the conditions themselves. Thus, persons who are treated with empathic under-standing, respect, and therapeutic genuineness or honesty respond with similar behaviors.

The operation of such influences on others can be viewed, at least in part, from a behavioristic frame of reference. The process clearly involves modeling, which is claimed by the behaviorists as a behavioristic method. The process may also be viewed as involving reinforcement. The conditions can be considered to be the reinforcers of the similar behavior, or more broadly, of a wide variety of positive behaviors (Patterson, 1974, pp. 131–141). It can be argued that, in behavioristic terms, the most potent reinforcer of human behavior is a good human relationship.

If this is so, then is there not the possibility of the human relationship – of empathy, respect and honesty – to control and manipulate others for selfish pur-poses against the best interests of others? However, there appears to be an inbuilt protection in the nature of a good human relationship against excessive control or manipulation. The conditions of a good human relationship are not effective, at least in the long run, unless they are real and genuine. Real respect for another is inconsistent with the exploiting of the other for one's own selfish purposes. In addition, when there is the awareness that another is attempting to manipulate, that another is lacking in respect, then resistance to being controlled or changed arises. Thus respect for another prevents one from attempting to manipulate another, and awareness of lack of respect in another prevents one from being manipulated.

SUMMARY

Our objective has been the attempt to develop a basis for evaluating efforts to influence and control human behavior. Currently those who are engaged in behavior modification are under scrutiny. But there are other behavior influencers whose behaviors also have serious ethical implications, including those active in the group movement. The increasing concern about ethical practices and the rights of individ-uals appears to signal the beginning of a new social era, in which the individual or person is coming into his own.

Most of those behaviorists who are concerned about the ethical justification of their objectives accept presumed social norms as criteria. This is an inadequate or unacceptable criterion. It accepts the status quo, and attempts to induce con-formity to it. This attitude is the basis for the contention that counseling or psychotherapy is an instrument of social control for maintaining the establishment (Halleck, 1971).

The problem is to derive bases for, and a statement of, a generally acceptable set of values or ethical system by which we can evaluate psychological methods or techniques for influencing or changing behavior. The argument that there are no universal values and that all values are relative is rejected. It is argued that there are some values which are not time or culture bound, and that these relate to the nature of man and the conditions for his survival and development. Two such basic values are respect and honesty. These values derive from the experience of men living together, and presumably could be supported by scientific study of groups and societies. These values are not only necessary for physical survival and development, but for psychological survival and development. The concept of self-actualization is developed to encompass the individual's development and exercise of his psychological potentials. Some misconceptions of the nature of self-actualization are noted.

The adherence to the two basic values of respect and honesty, together with empathic understanding, are necessary conditions for the development of self-actualizing persons. It is noted that there is considerable support for this statement in research in counseling or psychotherapy.

We thus have a concept which provides a criterion for a system of ethics, and a goal toward which the influence of human behavior can be directed. Specific methods of control can be evaluated in terms of their consistency with the desired outcome. Thus, for example, since autonomy is a characteristic of self-actualizing persons, then methods which take over the control of the individual's behavior and deny him autonomy or independence and responsibility for his own behavior are unacceptable, except in cases where the person has clearly demonstrated his inability to be responsible for his own behavior and interferes with the rights and autonomy of others.

It is not asserted that a complete basis for a system of ethics has been provided. It is only suggested that a foundation has been provided for a system which should be acceptable not only to humanistic psychologists but to those who accept science as a value.

REFERENCES

Ansbacher, H. L., and Ansbacher, R. (Eds.), *The individual psychology of Alfred Adler*. New York: Basic Books, 1956.

Bandura, A., *Principles of behavior modification*. New York: Holt, Rinehart and Winston, 1969.

Bandura, A., Behavior theory and the models of man. *American Psychologist,* 1974, *29,* 859–869.

Beit-Hallahmi, B., Salvation and its vicissitudes: Clinical psychology and political values. *American Psychologist,* 1974 *29,* 124–129.

Bibring, E., The development and problems of the theory of instincts. In Stacy, C. L. and Martino, M. F. (Eds.) *Understanding Human Motivation.* Cleveland: Howard Allen, 1958, 474–498.

Bronowski, J., *Science and human values.* New York: Julian Messner, 1956, Harper and Row Torchbooks, 1959.

Buhler, C., *Values in psychotherapy.* New York: Macmillan-Free Press, 1961.

Carkhuff R. R., *Helping and human relations,* Vol. I; *Selection and training,* Vol. II; *Practice and research.* New York: Holt, Rinehart and Winston, 1969.

Cattell, R. B., Ethics and the social sciences. *American Psychologist,* 1948, *3,* 193–198.

Combs, A. W., and Snygg, D., *Individual behavior.* 2nd Ed. New York: Harper and Row, 1959.

Commager, H. S. The school as surrogate conscience. *Saturday Review,* January 11, 1975, 54–57.

Creegan, R. F., Concerning professional ethics. *American Psychologist,* 1958, *13,* 272–275.

Davison, G. C., Systematic desensitization as a counterconditioning process. *Journal of Abnormal and Social Psychology,* 1968, *73,* 91–99.

Dollard, J., Doob, L. W., Miller, N. E., Mowrer, O. H., and Sears, R. R., *Frustration and aggression.* New Haven: Yale University Press, 1939.

Golding, W., *Lord of the flies.* New York: Coward McCann, 1955.

Goldstein, K., *The organism.* New York: American Book, 1939. (Boston: Beacon Press, 1963.)

Halleck, S. L., *The politics of therapy.* New York: Science House, 1971.

Jourard, S. M., *The transparent self.* New York: Van Nostrand Reinhold, 1964.

Krasner, L., Behavior control and social responsibility. *American Psychologist,* 1962, *17,* 199–204.

Lazarus, A., *Behavior therapy and beyond.* New York: McGraw-Hill, 1971, 15–23.

Lowe, C. M., Value orientations: An ethical dilemma. *American Psychologist,* 1959, *14,* 687–693.

Maddi, S., Creativity is strenuous. *The University of Chicago Magazine,* 1973, September–October, 18–23, (a).

Maddi, S., Ethics and psychotherapy: Remarks stimulated by White's paper. *The Counseling Psychologist,* 1973, *4* (2), 26–26, (b).

Maslow, A., Our maligned human nature. *Journal of psychology,* 1949, *20,* 273–278.

Maslow, A. H., Self-actualizing people: A study of psychological health. In C. E. Moustakas (Ed.) *The self: Explorations in personal growth.* New York: Harper and Row, 1956.

Michael, J., and Meyerson, L., A behavioral approach to counseling and guidance. *Harvard Educational Review,* 1962, *32,* 382–402.

Montagu, A., *On being human.* New York: Henry Schuman, 1950.

Montagu, A., *The humanization of man.* Cleveland: World Publishing, 1962.

Muller, H. J., Human values in relation to evolution. *Science,* 1958, *127,* 625–629.

Patterson, C. H., *Relationship counseling and psychotherapy.* New York: Harper and Row, 1974.

Reppucci, N. D., and Saunders, J. T., Social psychology of behavior modifification: Problems of implementation in natural settings. *American Psychologist,* 1974, *29,* 649–660.

Robinson, D. N., Therapies: A clear and present danger. *American Psychologist,* 1973, *28,* 129–133.

Rogers, C. R., A theory of therapy, personality, and interpersonal relationships as developed in the client-centered framework. In S. Koch (Ed.) *Psychology: A study of a science: Vol 3, Formulations of the person and the social context.* New York: McGraw-Hill, 1969, 184–256.

Rogers, C. R., *On becoming a person.* Boston: Houghton Mifflin, 1961.

Skinner, B. F., *Walden Two.* New York: Macmillan, 1948.

Skinner, B. F., *Science and human behavior.* New York: Macmillan, 1953.

Skinner, B. F., *The control of human behavior.* Transactions of the New York Academy of Sciences, 1955, *17,* 547–551.

Skinner, B. F., The steep and thorny way to a science of behavior. *American Psychologist,* 1975, *30,* 42–49.

Smith, M. B., Comment on White's paper. *The Counseling Psychologist,* 1973, *4,* (2) 48–50.

Trotter, S., and Warren, J., Behavior modification under fire. *A P A Monitor,* 1974, *5* (4), 1.

Truax, C. B., and Carkhuff, R. R., *Toward effective counseling and psychotherapy.* Chicago: Aldine, 1967.

Truax, C. B., and Mitchell, K. M., Research on certain therapist interpersonal skills. In Bergin, A. E. and Garfield, S. L. (Eds.) *Handbook of psychotherapy and behavior change: An empirical analysis.* New York: Wiley, 1971.

White, R. W., The concept of healthy personality: What do we really mean? *The Counseling Psychologist,* 1973, *4* (2), 3–12 67–69.

Williamson, E. G., A concept of counseling. *Occupations,* 1950, *29,* 182–189.

Williamson, E. G., Value orientation in counseling. *Personnel and Guidance Journal,* 1958, *37,* 520–528.

SOCIAL LEARNING AND ADOLESCENT PSYCHOTHERAPY

Gary G. Brannigan

Adolescent psychotherapy, in the social learning framework, is primarily concerned with changing expectancies. Maladaptive behavior, whether it be avoidant behavior in the sense of avoiding some previously experienced specific punishment or a learned, direct way to obtain gratification with a history of reinforcement, is interpretated in terms of expectancy for future reinforcement. This process requires maximum use of the adolescent's own experiences and optimally would concentrate on lowering the expectancy that maladaptive behavior will lead to gratification, and increasing the expectancy that alternative or new behaviors will lead to greater gratification in the same situation.

Rotter (1954) has suggested five methods of increasing the expectancy for gratification for new behaviors. (1) The most direct way of increasing behavior potential or probability is through direct reinforcement. In his contacts with the patient, the therapist has the opportunity to respond, either positively or negatively, to the behavior of the patient. However, the relative effectiveness of reinforcement is related to the degree to which an individual feels that what happens to him will be contingent on his own behavior or is independent of his own behavior. Patients having a belief in "external" control, being less susceptible to the influence of positive reinforcement, may require an analysis of this attitude before change can take place. (2) The therapist can place the patient in, or help him to find and enter, situations where he may observe in others alternative behaviors and their consequences, or where by discussion and interpretation he can try to understand the behavior of others retrospectively. (3) The therapist may deal with the patient's history of alternative behaviors, reducing his expectancy that they will now result in negative reinforcements as they did in the past, and verbally increasing his expectancy that these alternative behaviors will now lead to gratification. (4) The therapist may discuss possible alternatives, showing how the behaviors are carried out and creating an expectancy that they may lead to gratification. (5) The therapist can create and reinforce an expectancy that the client may solve his problems more effectively by looking for and trying out alternative solutions or behaviors.

Rotter (1954) also states that when a client does not display behavior that the therapist might directly reinforce, alternative methods of behaving might be discussed with him so that he will attempt new behaviors or, at least, behaviors that he has not used in these situations before or may not have used for some time. He may also be made aware of how others use different behaviors. More recently, Bandura, (1965) has emphasized the effectiveness of "modeling" procedures in transmitting new response patterns in children. Bandura (1965) further suggests the use of modeling in a hierarchic progression. Such a procedure would be similar to Wolpe's

(1958) use of the behavioral hierarchy in systematic desensitization. Both methods involve taking an individual through a series of progressively more difficult behaviors. In modeling, a person views an adequate handling of these situations, while in desensitization he associates a more adjustive response to the stimulus situations.

Bandura and Walters (1963) have indicated three major effects of modeling: (1) the observer may acquire new responses that did not exist in his behavior repertoire, (2) exposure to models may also strengthen or weaken (depending on the desired outcome) inhibitory responses in the observer, and (3) the behavior of models may elicit previously learned responses that match precisely or bear some resemblance to those exhibited by the model. Bandura (1965) suggests further that the acquisition of matching responses takes place through contiguity, whereas reinforcements administered to a model exact their major influence on the performance of imitatively learned responses. Research, relevant to these points, has been clearly illustrated in several investigations (e.g., Bandura, Ross, and Ross; 1961; 1963) designed to explore the social transmission of novel aggressive responses. In these studies, nursery school children were exposed to either aggressive adult models or to models who displayed inhibited and nonaggressive behavior. For the aggressive-model group the model exhibited unusual forms of physical and verbal aggression toward a large inflated plastic doll (Bobo). After exposure to their respective models, all children were mildly frustrated and then tested for the amount of imitative and nonmatching aggressive behavior they would exhibit in the situation. The results of these experiments show that children who observed the aggressive model displayed a greater number of precisely imitative aggressive responses, whereas such responses rarely occurred in the nonaggressive-model group. Furthermore, children in the nonaggressive-model group displayed the inhibited behavior characteristic of their model to a greater extent than did the control children.

Subsequent studies (Bandura, Grusec, and Menlove, 1967; and Bandura and Menlove, 1968) suggest that well-established fears can be eliminated by having fearful children observe a graduated sequence of modeling activities beginning with presentations that are easily tolerated. Children who were shown to be fearful of dogs participated in eight therapy sessions in which they observed a fearless peer model exhibit progressively longer, closer, and more intimate interactions with a dog. Following completion of the treatment series, two-thirds of the children overcame their fear of dogs completely, as shown by the fact that they were willing to remain alone in a room confined with a dog in a playpen.

A third research project (Bandura, Blanchard, and Ritter, 1968) was designed to assess the comparative efficacy of modeling and desensitization treatment approaches for producing behavioral, affective, and attitudinal changes in adolescents and adults suffering from snake phobias. All patients were administered a behavioral test and an inventory measuring the strength of their avoidance of snakes. Participants were assigned to one of three conditions or an untreated control group. One group participated in a self-administered symbolic modeling treatment in which they observed a film depicting young children, adolescents, and adults engaging in progressively threatening interactions with a large snake. A second group of subjects received a form of treatment combining graduated modeling with guided participation. The treatment consisted in a model demonstrating the desired behavior under secure observational conditions, after which subjects were aided through further demonstration and joint performance to execute progressively more difficult responses. Whenever subjects were unable to perform a given behavior after demonstration alone, they enacted the feared activities concurrently with the model. Physical guidance was gradually reduced until they were able to perform the behavior alone. A third group received the standard form of desensitization treatment devised by Wolpe (1958).

Upon completion of the treatment series the assessment procedures were readministered to all subjects. The results showed that the control subjects remained unchanged in avoidance behavior; symbolic modeling and desensitization produced substantial reductions; and live modeling combined with guided participation eliminated snake phobias in over 90 percent of the subjects. Similar results were found on the attitude measure, with the modeling-participation treatment effecting the greatest change. Although both modeling procedures neutralized the anxiety-arousing properties of the phobic stimuli, the desensitization group experienced less emotional arousal while performing snake-approach responses.

The research of Bandura and his associates on modeling behavior offers an important step in applying the principles of social learning theory. Bandura (1969) states that

"Behavioral enactment methods are frequently utilized for a wide variety of purposes in which people who want to develop new competencies are provided with actual or symbolic models of desired behavior. They are given opportunities to perform these patterns initially under nonthreatening conditions before they are encouraged to apply them in their everyday lives. Since, in modeling approaches, a person observes and practices alternate ways of behaving under lifelike conditions, transfer of learning to naturalistic situations is greatly facilitated" (p. 163).

Therefore, the modeling approach appears to be an effective means of bringing about expectancy change. This expectancy change may be further enhanced by the adolescent's observing the reinforcing consequences of both the model's behavior and his own attempts.

Structuring Therapy

The term *structuring* refers to the discussion between patient and therapist, about the purposes and goals of therapy, the plans of the therapist, the respective roles and responsibilities of the patient and therapist, and the attitudes both have toward the therapy at any time. Rotter (1954) suggests that structuring is of the utmost importance in therapy involving rational techniques, verbal communication, and insight, but is of less importance in therapy consisting of direct reinforcement.

One of the primary purposes of structuring is to keep the patient's motivation for change high. In other words, the adolescent's behavior of seeking help and coming to therapy must be reinforced so that the expectancy that it will lead to satisfaction is maintained at a high level. In order to accomplish this, it may be necessary that the adolescent experience some early success in therapy (i.e., that it is possible to change and to get greater gratification or less punishment from a new behavior or a new way of approaching a problem). One way of doing this may be to select problems, early in therapy, with expectancies that can be most easily changed.

Relationship and Transference

Rotter (1954) discusses the relationship between the client and therapist in terms of "acceptance," "reassurance," and "transference." The terms *acceptance* and *reassurance* refer to the therapist's attitude toward the adolescent and his problems. In other words the therapist must accept the adolescent as an individual by indicating his interest and his desire to understand his problems, as well as avoiding criticism, blame, or moral judgment of his behavior or attitudes. The therapist should also reassure the adolescent that his problems are genuine and that his attempt to do something about them, by seeking psychological therapy, is justified. He should further reassure the adolescent that he is capable of accomplishing specific goals and changing himself (i.e., that therapy can be successful).

Transference refers to the degree of involvement the adolescent feels toward the therapist, and is a direct function of the amount of reinforcement that the adolescent either has received or has expectations of receiving from the therapist.

Since the therapist may affect changes in the adolescent's behavior through his own direct reinforcements, his effectiveness is a function of his reinforcement value to the patient. Therefore, one of the prime effects of acceptance, reassurance, and transference is that they increase the therapist's value to the adolescent as a reinforcer.

Catharsis and Insight

Rotter (1954) and Bandura and Walters (1963) suggest that catharsis may produce more harm than good, yet in some cases and under certain conditions it may be useful. Catharsis refers to the individual's discussing his past history and experiences, problems, wishes, and fears. There is no dramatic recall of long repressed experiences or vivid reliving of previous emotional reactions. Catharsis is helpful to the degree to which the adolescent acquires new insights into his own behavior, thereby reducing the behavior potential of present maladaptive behaviors.

Gary G. Brannigan

Interpretation

Social learning theory implies a quite active role on the part of the therapist. Since therapy is a learning situation, it is important to provide new experiences and ideas for the adolescent in order for him to learn new behaviors. Rotter (1954) refers to interpretation as "what the therapist does verbally to help the patient see new relationships or to clarify relationships" (p. 380).

Interpretation is usually minimal during the early stages of therapy, but as the therapist learns more and more about the adolescent, he becomes more active in helping him to see new relationships for his behavior. These relationships might deal with the adolescent's goals or motivations, with the reinforcements that follow behavior, with the effects of previous experience on present behavior, or with present behaviors and future outcomes.

The therapist's early attempts at interpretations are somewhat nondirective in nature, but gradually they become more and more assertive and positive. However, they never exceed the level of "I think this is probably ...", or "It seems to me ...", since it would force the adolescent into a position of either accepting the statement or rejecting the therapist. Some resistance to interpretation should be expected, since the interpretation that is readily accepted may not be needed. Interpretation that is helpful and provides some new insight for the adolescent may in fact have to be presented a number of times and supported by different experiences of the patient before it is accepted.

In concluding, Rotter (1954) states that "therapy takes place not only as a function of what happens in the therapy room but also as a result of new experiences in life situations, obtained concurrently with therapy, that occur to the patient as a result of trying out new or alternative behaviors" (p. 398).

Case Study

In keeping with the social learning viewpoint Brannigan and Young (1978) described a successful method of developing social skills in an adolescent with minimal brain dysfunction. The procedure involved maximum use of the adolescent's own experience, and focused on rebuilding a damaged self-image by identifying maladaptive behavior patterns and providing adequate alternatives.

The client was a thirteen-year-old male. Presenting problems included: poor school and social adjustment, attention-seeking, poor emotional control, and nervous habits. Initial therapy sessions were devoted to exploring the relationship between the subject's behavior and his self-concept. The negative connotation which he had attached to being labeled as "hyperactive" was discussed at some length. He had little confidence in his ability to improve or regulate his own behavior. Consequently, an effort was made to help the subject reevaluate his attitude toward himself. The therapist attempted to consistently point out situations in which the subject had demonstrated his ability to control his behavior. The

210

subject's problems were discussed as "bad habits" which he had developed when he was much younger. The point was emphasized that now that he was older people would and should expect him to behave in a more mature fashion. The training in social skills development was presented as a new opportunity for him to learn to better regulate his own conduct by building upon his positive qualities.

Directive Training in Social Skills Development

1. Specific problem areas were identified, based on information provided by the subject and his parents during the initial interviews. For example, he had no friends at school and refused to go out of the classroom during recess.

2. Recordings which described problem situations in detail were played to the subject. He was instructed to close his eyes and imagine that the situation being described was really happening, and that he should respond in his typical manner at the end of the taped description.

3. Following the description and the subject's response, the recording was played back and discussed. The therapist provided extensive feedback to him in the form of social reinforcement for appropriate behaviors in addition to offering and modeling alternatives to inappropriate behaviors.

4. Role-playing and coaching were also used to help him practice these new responses.

5. The subject was encouraged to practice these new responses at home and in school. Discussions of these experiences also provided opportunities for feedback and social reinforcement for appropriate behaviors.

Parental Counseling

Consultations on modifying child management practices were held in order to help the parents deal with the subject's problem behaviors at home in a consistent fashion. The emphasis was placed on initiating positive contacts with their child through reinforcing his appropriate behaviors.

Discussion

Immature and inappropriate behaviors were reduced in frequency to the point where both the subject and his parents felt that these behavior patterns no longer presented a management problem. Emotional outbursts occur less frequently and with less intensity. School behavior in both social and academic areas has improved considerably.

REFERENCES

Bandura, A., Behavioral modifications through modeling procedures. In L. Krasner and L. P. Ullmann (Eds.), *Research in behavior modification.* New York: Holt, Rinehart and Winston, 1965, pp. 310–340.

Gary G. Brannigan

Bandura, A., *Principles of behavior modification.* New York: Holt, Rinehart and Winston, 1969.

Bandura, A.; Blanchard, E. B.; and Ritter, B., The relative efficacy of desensitization and modeling approaches for inducing behavioral, affective, and attitudinal changes. Unpublished manuscript, Stanford University, 1968.

Bandura, A.; Grusec, J. E.; and Menlove, F. L., Vicarious extinction of avoidance behavior. *Journal of Personality and Social Psychology,* 1967, *5,* 16–23.

Bandura., and Menlove, F. L., Factors determining vicarious extinction of avoidance behavior through symbolic modeling. *Journal of Personality and Social Psychology,* 1968, *8,* 99–108.

Bandura, A.; Ross, D.; and Ross, S. A., Transmission of aggression through imitation of aggressive models. *Journal of Abnormal and Social Psychology,* 1961, *63,* 575–582.

Bandura, A.; Ross, D.; and Ross, S. A., Imitation of film-mediated aggressive models. *Journal of Abnormal and Social Psychology,* 1963, *66,* 3–11.

Bandura, A., and Walters, R. H., *Social learning and personality development.* New York: Holt, Rinehart and Winston, 1963.

Brannigan, G. G., and Young, R. G., Social skills training with the adolescent with minimal brain dysfunction: a case study. *Academic Therapy,* 1978 (in press).

Rotter, J. B., *Social learning and clinical psychology.* Englewood Cliffs, N.J.: Prentice-Hall, 1954.

Wolpe, J., *Psychotherapy by reciprocal inhibition.* Stanford, Calif.: Stanford University Press, 1958.

REFLECTION-IMPULSIVITY: IMPLICATIONS AND TREATMENT STRATEGIES FOR CHILD PSYCHOPATHOLOGY

A. J. Finch, Jr. and Philip C. Kendall

INTRODUCTION

One of the most common problems resulting in children being referred for mental health services is behavior involving a lack of inhibitory control and a tendency to respond quickly without thorough deliberation. These "impulsive" children have been described as hyperactive, distractible, and unable to tolerate delay. Such behaviors result in the child presenting behavioral problems in the regular school classroom since most teachers expect a child to remain in his seat, complete assignments, work independently, and seek relatively long-term goals. When the impulsive child is unable to meet these demands the regular classroom teacher, because of her responsibility to the other children in the classroom, cannot provide the additional attention and structure which this child seems to need. A similar pattern occurs at home, where the impulsive, overactive child can wear thin the patience of even the best of parents. The impulsive child becomes an aversive stimulus for the teacher, parent, and other children who then begin to emit a number of control strategies designed to reduce the impulsive behaviors (e.g., ignoring, punishing, etc.). Unfortunately, the impulsive child emits an exceptional number of behaviors since he spends less time deliberating each response, and teachers or parents attempting to extinguish these disruptive behaviors by ignoring them will reach their tolerance point rather quickly. When this happens they will be forced to attend to, and thus intermittently reinforce, the behavior. Another teacher or parent attempting to reduce the inappropriate behaviors continuously reprimands the child for each disruptive behavior and thus could be reinforcing the very behavior he or she wishes to decrease. The teacher or parent, by providing contingent attention, or by continual punishment, could suppress an entire repetoire of behaviors (both desirable and undesirable). On the other hand, the teacher or parent might attempt to shape the impulsive child to emit more reflective behaviors. However, since the impulsive child has difficulty delaying gratification and since the teacher or parent has other children and responsibilities, it is rare that a program designed to deal with impulsive behaviors works satisfactorily. The outcome is generally the same. The impulsive child's aversive stimulus value to the adult eventually reaches such an intensity that the child is expelled from school, referred to the local mental health clinic or school psychologist, or placed in special classes.

Despite the magnitude of the problem presented by the impulsive child, mental health professionals generally do not have much better success with such children than do the teachers or parents who referred them. To paraphrase an old saying, "what mental health professionals need is a good impulsive behavior treatment."

The present paper presents the preliminary results of a developing research program designed to investigate some of the causes of impulsive behavior and to devise a treatment package paradigm for the impulsive child. For the sake of clarity and to facilitate reading, a narrative writing style as opposed to a technical one will be employed.

BACKGROUND

After having initiated a behavior modification program with a group of brain-damaged youngsters and having compiled some impressive-looking data as to changes in target behaviors, it was somewhat disconcerting when one of the special education teachers began to complain that some of the children remained "careless" in their work. Feeling an intense need to quiet this insurrection in an otherwise "tight" behavioral program, diligent observations of these "careless" children were made. It soon became apparent that what was meant by the teacher's description of "careless" was an impulsive task approach. These children appeared to respond immediately when faced with a new situation and apparently did not attend to all of the available discriminative stimuli that would increase the probability of their making a more appropriate response. For example, they frequently did not attend to the operation sign in arithmetic problems so that they performed the incorrect operation; they frequently would read words by attending to only a part of them such as "bedroom" being read as "bathroom"; instructions were rarely read and much less followed; entire portions of assignments were skipped; sentences were begun but not completed, and so forth.

The similarity of the behavior in these "careless" children and the children described by Kagan (1966) as impulsive within his reflection-impulsivity cognitive model was immediately noted. Reflection-impulsivity is the cognitive dimension employed by Kagan and his colleagues (Kagan, 1965a; 1965b; 1965c; Kagan and Kogan, 1970; Kagan, Pearson, and Welch, 1966) to describe differences in children's approaches to problem solving. Whenever a number of response alternatives are simultaneously available and uncertainty as to correct response is high, some children (reflectives) delay responding until all alternatives have been considered carefully and they have a high probability of being correct. On the other hand, other children (impulsives) respond quickly with less thorough evaluation of the various possibilities and consequently make more mistakes. The "carelessness" exhibited by the group of brain-damaged children appeared to be on the impulsive end of the reflection-impulsivity dimension.

It seemed logical to believe that if the determinants of an impulsive cognitive style could be found, this would provide some information about the causes of impulsive behavior. In order to investigate the relationship between an impulsive cognitive style and impulsive behavior a series of studies were conducted.

COGNITIVE IMPULSIVITY AND IMPULSIVE BEHAVIOR

Despite the apparent similarity between an impulsive cognitive style and impulsive behavior it was felt that a relationship between an impulsive cognitive style and impulsive behavior would have to be demonstrated. To this end, Ollendick and Finch (1973) examined the performance of a nonretarded, brain-damaged sample and a group of normal children of the same mental age on Kagan's (1966) Matching Familiar Figures Test (MFF). This test has generally been used in studies investigating the reflection-impulsivity dimension. The MFF is a twelve-item matching to sample task in which the child is shown a single picture of a familiar object and is instructed to select from an array of six variants the one picture which is identical to the stimulus picture. The latency to the first response and the number of errors are the usual measure.

It was predicted by Ollendick and Finch (1973) that the group of brain-damaged boys would respond more quickly and make more errors than the group of normal boys since brain-damaged children are generally described as more hyperactive and impulsive than normal children. The results supported their prediction and indicated that a clinically more impulsive population was cognitively more impulsive than a normal one.

In an attempt to extend the generality of these results, Montgomery (1974) compared responses of sixty emotionally disturbed children with sixty normal children matched on mental age. He found that although the emotionally disturbed group did not differ from the normal group on their latency to first response, they did make significantly more errors. A number of possible explanations can be considered, but of prime importance for this discussion was the finding that a group of emotionally disturbed children *not* selected because of their impulsive behavior were found to differ on one of the two measures on the MFF used to determine cognitive impulsivity. It seems likely that a group of emotionally disturbed children would contain some who were overly inhibited as well as some who were more likely to act out. Thus, it would be anticipated that those children who were more impulsive would be more likely to act out while those who were more inhibited would be more likely to be reflective.

In order to further investigate this hypothesized relationship between reflection-impulsivity and behavior, Montgomery and Finch (1975) obtained ratings of locus of conflict on impulsive and reflective emotionally disturbed children. They reasoned that, to the extent that children's conflicts in interpersonal relations resembled problem-solving tasks, a child's cognitive style would be expected to affect his locus of conflict. In internalization of conflict a child's impulses are highly controlled, and the conflict is between impulses and their inhibitions. In externalization of conflict impulses are freely discharged into the surrounding environment, and the conflict is between the behaviors of the child and the reactions they bring about in others. These authors postulated that a reflective cognitive style

215

would play a major causative role in a child's ability to resist freely discharging impulses and to control their external expression. They continued by reasoning that an impulsive cognitive style would lead to freely discharging impulses into the environment without regard for their consequences. In comparing the ratings for locus of conflict of thirteen impulsive and thirteen reflective emotionally disturbed children in residential treatment Montgomery and Finch (1975) found that children with an impulsive cognitive style were more likely to be rated as exhibiting externalization of conflict while those with a reflective cognitive style were more likely to be rated as internalizers. These results are consistent with the predictions and are indicative of the importance of cognitive style in determining behavior.

Extending the investigation of the relationship between cognitive style and behavior, Finch and Nelson (1976) made observations on a group of impulsive and reflective children and then made predictions as to how parents would rate their son's behavior. They found that impulsive boys were more likely than reflectives to talk of others blaming them unfairly, threaten to injure themselves, hit and bully other children, and be excessively rough in play. On the other hand, reflective emotionally disturbed boys were more reluctant to talk with adults outside of the family. These results provide additional support to the relationship between cognitive impulsivity and impulsive behaviors.

Finch, Kendall Deardorff Anderson, and Sitarz (1975) hypothesized that cognitively impulsive children would exhibit less persistence behavior than would reflective children. In order to investigate this hypothesis, they administered the Matching Familiar Figures Test and a persistence task to seventy-eight emotionally disturbed children in residential treatment. They found a significant relationship between latency to responding to the MFF and duration of persistence behavior. Stated somewhat differently, the impulsive children tended to be less likely to apply themselves in a persevering or industrious fashion. This finding also would tend to support the relationship between cognitive impulsivity and impulsive behavior.

A final study which contributed to the ascribed relationship of the reflection-impulsivity dimension and behavior is one which relates more by inference than actual findings. Finch, Pezzuti, Montgomery, and Kemp (1974) reasoned that to the extent that academic attainment involves one's self-application to a task and problem solving, a child's cognitive style would be expected to affect his academic achievement. Since many academic tasks require that the child make decisions and choose between response alternatives, the hypothesis that whether a child is reflective or impulsive in this approach should influence his rate of academic attainment seemed acceptable. To investigate this possibility, the MFF and standard achievement tests were administered to sixty-five children. The hypothesized relationship between whether the child was reflective or impulsive and his academic achievement was not found since all the children were achieving below grade expectancy. However, when the actual grade placements were compared for these reflective and impulsive children who did not differ as to achievement, it was found that the reflective group was placed two grade levels above the impulsive group. Indeed, the groups did not differ as to achievement scores, allowing Finch et al. (1974) to suggest that some classroom behavioral characteristics must account for the obtained difference.

The results of the research reviewed in this section is considered to be consistent with the hypothesis that a child's cognitive style is a significant factor in determining his behaviors.

DETERMINANTS OF AN IMPULSIVE COGNITIVE STYLE

What determines whether a child is reflective or impulsive? Kagan and Kogan (1970) suggest that the tendency to be reflective or impulsive is most likely to be under the services of several different forces. The dynamic which they feel is best supported by the literature is fear of failure. They suggest that the greater the fear of making a mistake, the more reflectively the child responds. Reflective children were felt to be concerned excessively with making a mistake and appeared to avoid an error at all cost. On the other hand, Kagan and Kogan (1970) state that impulsive children appear minimally concerned about errors and consequently respond quickly. Fear of failure has also been postulated as an important variable in trait anxiety (Atkinson, 1964; Spielberger, 1966; 1972). The greater the individual's fear of failure and the larger the number of situations which evoke his fear-of-failure responses, the higher the individual trait anxiety level is likely to be (according to the state-trait theory of anxiety, Spielberger, 1966; 1972).

Considering the importance given to fear of failure in the explanation of both the reflection-impulsivity dimension and the state-trait theory of anxiety, Montgomery (1974) hypothesized that reflective children would be more anxious than impulsive ones. In order to test this hypothesis he compared the level of state anxiety, trait anxiety, and manifest anxiety in impulsive and reflective normal and emotionally disturbed children. He found that for both populations, reflective children were no more anxious on any of the measures than were the impulsive ones. In addition, a comparison of the responses of impulsive and reflective children to the statement "I worry about making mistakes" (from the State-Trait Anxiety Inventory for Children, Spielberger, 1973) indicated that they did not differ significantly.

Since anxiety had not proven to be an important factor in a child's cognitive style, other determining factors needed to be investigated. After having observed the behavior of impulsive and reflective children and having noted that reflective children employed more verbalizations than impulsives, Finch and Montgomery (1973) hypothesized that reflective children employed a more mature form of thinking than did impulsive children. In order to test this hypothesis they compared a group of thirteen impulsive and thirteen reflective children on an information-seeking task designed to indicate the type of thinking used by the child. As predicted, the results showed that impulsives think in pictures while reflectives think with words (the more mature thinking approach).

In an attempt to extend the generality of Finch and Montgomery's (1973) findings that impulsives think with pictures while reflectives think with words, Stein, Finch, Hooke, Montgomery, and Nelson (1975) employed an equivalence task which was designed to assess children's thinking. Although their results were somewhat less clear-cut than the Finch and Montgomery (1973) study, they generally support the hypothesis that reflective and impulsive children employ different types of thinking. While reflective children think symbolically by using words, impulsive children tend to think iconically by employing pictures.

In an attempt to find what other variables might be important in determining whether a child was reflective or impulsive, Finch, Nelson, Montgomery, and Stein (1974) reasoned that a child with an internal locus of control would be expected to assume more responsibility for his behavior and therefore would be likely to exhibit a reflective cognitive style. To test this hypothesis they administered the Nowicki-Strickland Locus of Control Scale for Children (Nowicki and Strickland, 1973) to ten impulsive and ten reflective emotionally disturbed children. Although the difference was in the predicted direction, these authors did not find a significant difference in the locus of control of reflective and impulsive children. An obvious problem with the Finch, Nelson, Montgomery, and Stein (1974) study is the relatively small number of subjects that were employed. To rectify this shortcoming Finch et al (1975) obtained MFF scores and locus of control scores on seventy-eight emotionally disturbed children. They found a significant relationship between the internal-external locus of control dimension and the reflection-impulsivity dimension with reflectives tending to be more internal within locus of control while impulsives are more external.

Another child characteristic — need for achievement — would be expected to affect a child's motivation and be related to whether a child was impulsive or reflective. Finch, Crandell and Deardorff (1976) hypothesized that individuals with a high need for achievement would be more reflective than would individuals with a low achievement need. To test this hypothesis, they obtained need for achievement and MFF scores on thirty-six emotionally disturbed children. They found a difference between high- and low-need children on their latencies on the MFF with high-need children delaying longer, but not a significant difference on the number of errors.

The research reviewed in this section suggests that anxiety is not related to whether a child is impulsive or reflective (Montgomery, 1974); that whether a child uses words when he thinks is related to the number of errors he makes on the MFF (Finch and Montgomery, 1973; Stein et al. 1975) and to the length of time he delays before responding in one study (Finch and Montgomery, 1973) but not in another (Stein et al., 1975); that whether or not he feels in control of the good- and bad-event outcomes that affect him is related to his impulsiveness with impulsives feeling less internal in their control; and that a high need for achievement affects latencies on the MFF but not error rate (Finch, Crandell, and Deardorff 1976).

MODIFICATION OF IMPULSIVE COGNITIVE STYLE

The group of studies within the present section deals with attempts to modify an impulsive cognitive style and reflects the changing views of our perception of impulsivity during the course of our investigations into its causes.

In the previous section the importance placed on fear of failure by Kagan and Kogan (1970) was discussed. Accepting the contention that the greater the fear of failure the more reflective the child should respond, Montgomery (1974) hypothesized that impulsive children would be more reflective following a failure experience. In order to test this hypothesis, he exposed fifteen emotionally disturbed and fifteen normal impulsive children to a failure experience and then readministered the MFF. The failure experience apparently had no affect on cognitive style since there was not a significant difference following the failure experience. Montgomery (1974) concluded that increasing one's fear of failure did not modify cognitive style.

Drawing from the finding that impulsives do not employ thinking with words (symbolic representation), Finch, Wilkinson, Nelson, and Montgomery (1975) reasoned that training in verbal self-instructions should maximize the likelihood of helping the children respond more reflectively. Modeling their treatment strategy after the paradigm employed by Meichenbaum and Goodman (1971), Finch et al. (1975) assigned fifteen impulsive emotionally disturbed boys to one of three groups: (1) cognitive training; (2) delay training; and (3) control.

In the *cognitive training group* each subject was seen individually for six one-half hour sessions distributed over a three-week period. In the first session the experimenter performed one of the training tasks and talked aloud to himself. Specific step-by-step self-instructions were verbalized and repeated frequently. An error was deliberately made, and the trainer stated to herself that she should have proceeded more carefully. After the experimenter completed the task, the subject was asked to perform the task and to verbalize the self-instructions to himself. If any difficulty was encountered, the subject was assisted in self-instructing. During sessions five and six, subjects were instructed to continue giving themselves self-instructions but to do so covertly. The day following the sixth training session the subjects were readministered the MFF.

In the *delay training group* the subjects had the same number of sessions, were exposed to the identical materials, and engaged in the same activities as the cognitive training group. However, this group did not receive training in verbal self-instructions, but rather were instructed to respond slowly. Again, following the sixth session, the MFF was readministered.

The *control group* was a simple test-retest control group which was administered the MFF at the beginning and end of a five-week period which corresponded to the passage of time in the other two groups. No contact with the experimenter took place between test administrations.

The results indicated that the *cognitive training* procedure which emphasized verbal self-instructions resulted in a significant modification in cognitive style with both an increase in latencies and a decrease in errors being obtained. In the *delay training group*, which emphasized delaying before responding during training, an increase in latencies was found but not a corresponding decrease in the number of errors. No significant changes were found with the *control group*. Finch et al. (1975) interpreted their results as indicating the potential usefulness of cognitive training in verbal self-instructions to reduce impulsivity in emotionally disturbed children. However, they also indicated a need to examine other factors to determine the maximal effectiveness of this treatment procedure.

Viewing the reflection-impulsivity dimension as having a motivation-for-success component as well as a fear-of-failure one, Nelson, Finch, and Hooke (1975) suggested that the impulsive child already has within his repetoire the ability to respond reflectively, but that he lacks motivation to do so. They suggest that a comparison of the effectiveness of a response-cost and reinforcement procedure should provide a test of the relative merits of the fear-of-failure versus the success-seeking explanation of the reflection-impulsivity dimension. They continue by saying that response-cost can be viewed as maximizing fear of failure since the child can avoid losing reinforcers only by avoiding mistakes. On the other hand, positive reinforcement should maximize success-seeking behavior because he is reinforced only after making a correct response. Nelson et al. (1975) state that the fear-of-failure hypothesis would predict a more reflective approach under a reinforcement condition. In order to test this hypothesis, forty emotionally disturbed boys were administered the MFF and randomly assigned to either a response-cost, reinforcement or control condition. Approximately two and a half weeks later, subjects were retested. In the response-cost condition subjects were given a number of tokens which could be traded in for prizes and instructed that they would lose a chip each time they made a mistake on the MFF. In the reinforcement group, children were informed that they would receive a token for each correct response and subjects in the control group were simply readministered the MFF. The results indicated that both reinforcement and response-cost resulted in an increase in latencies and a decrease in errors while there was no change for the control group on either variable. In order to compare the effectiveness of the conditions for reflective and impulsive subjects, separate analyses were performed. These analyses indicated that while reinforcement and response-cost both increased latencies and decreased errors, the response-cost procedure was more effective with impulsive children. These authors point out that although the performance of the impulsive boys was greatly enhanced by the response-cost and reinforcement procedure, their performance remained more impulsive than the original reflective group. This finding would tend to support the existence of other important variables in addition to motivational ones in the determination of cognitive style.

The positive outcome of both the verbal self-instruction training and the response-cost procedure demonstrates the modifiability of an impulsive style. What is proposed then is that perhaps the optimal approach in modifying impulsive responding might be one that integrates both verbal self-instructions and response-cost, or in more general terms an integration of procedures to increase motivation with cognitive training and/or modeling.

A CASE ILLUSTRATION

In order to examine the efficacy of the combined verbal self-instructions and response-cost procedures Kendall and Finch (1976) undertook an intensive single-subject investigation. The patient was a nine-year-old boy who was seen on an out-patient basis. A history of classroom behavior problems had culminated with the child being demoted just prior to the initiation of this case study. Observations of the patient revealed a pattern of hurrying and constant movement. The patient would climb in and out of his seat, talk rapidly about many topics, and change the direction and purpose of his behavior without apparent reason. Initial testing on the MFF resulted in a mean latency of 4.59 seconds with 9 errors. The observed behavior, along with this set of MFF scores, clearly placed the child within the "impulsive" category.

Prior to the beginning of therapy it was decided that specific behaviors, performance on the MFF, and the generalizability of the results would be systematically evaluated. The specific behaviors that were targeted were the inappropriate and untimely "switches" in (1) topics of conversation, (2) games played with, and (3) rules of play. The evaluation strategy for these behaviors was a multiple baseline design. MFF performance was evaluated at post-treatment and at six-month follow-up. Lastly, the generalizability of the therapy procedure was assessed by recording behavioral switches while varying the context or situation of the treatment. Three variations were applied: (1) the therapy room was changed; (2) the array of games was changed (available games had been held constant); and (3) with the new games another therapist administered the program.

Before the application of the treatment program, base-line data was recorded. This entailed a systematic frequency count of the natural occurring incidences of the targeted behavior "switches." During base-line, and throughout, recording units of ten minutes were used. In addition, care was taken to talk and play with the patient without a specific therapy strategy and to prevent the patient from receiving feedback about his behavior by avoiding the recording of "switches" just following the emitted behavior. Having recorded base-line for seven 10-minute segments of therapy, treatment was implemented.

At the start of each therapy session, the therapist provided training in verbal

221

self-instructions (modeled after Meichenbaum and Goodman, 1971).
According to Kendall and Finch (1976) the training proceeded as follows:
First the therapist modeled performance of the task (mazes, Wechsler, 1949) and talked aloud to himself while the patient observed; then the patient performed the task instructing himself aloud; next the therapist performed the task whispering to himself; and lastly the patient performed the task with the instruction to talk to himself (covert self-instructions). The self-instructions were step-by-step verbalizations concerning the problem definition, problem approach, focusing of attention, and coping statements. The coping statements were programmed in following a deliberately made error by the therapist (e.g., "I should have gone slower and thought and been more careful.") When difficulty was encountered the patient was assisted in self-instructing. After this training in general self-instructions, the use of self-instructions for the target behavior(s) was rehearsed. An example is the tailored self-instruction for topics.

"What should I remember? I'm to finish talking about what I start to talk about. O.K. I should think before I talk and remember not to switch. If I complete what I'm talking about before I start another topic I get to keep my dimes. I can look at this card (cue) to remind me."

During the treatment sessions a training-aid card was used as a cue to help the patient remember to think before responding. The cue was a 5" X 7" card with "STOP, LISTEN, LOOK, and THINK before I answer" presented in both written and picture form and was originally employed by Palkes, Stewart and Kahana (1968).

The response-cost component of treatment concerned five dimes which were given to the patient at the beginning of each session. The client was told that these dimes were his to keep but that he could lose one each time he "switched" in the middle of talking about something (playing or changing a rule depending on the phase of the multiple base-line). An example was given to the patient, and he reported a clear understanding of the contingency. For incidences when the patient lost a dime for an inappropriate "switch," his behavior was labeled and stated as the reason for the loss of a dime.

The results of this treatment combination were most favorable. The frequency of switches in topics of conversation, games played with, and rules for play across ten-minute segments of the therapy sessions are presented in Figure 7-1. The success of the treatment procedure is evident in the changes in the target behaviors which occur systematically following treatment installation.

Results of a post-treatment administration of the MFF yielded a mean latency of 18.73 seconds and 5 errors. This performance, when compared with both his initial test latency of 4.59 seconds and 9 errors, and previous experience, is *not* considered impulsive and represents a "reflective" cognitive style. In addition, Kendall and

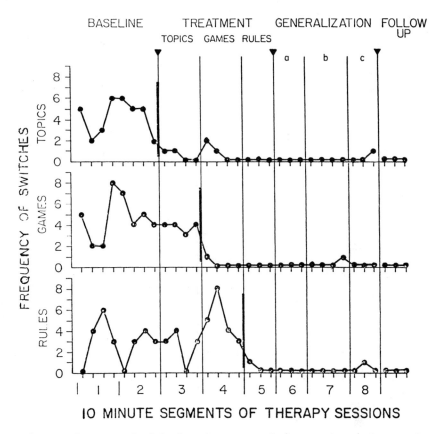

Figure 1. Frequency of switches in topics, games, and rules across ten-minute segments of therapy sessions as a function of treatment and generalization tests.

Finch (1976) report that during the post-testing the patient volunteered his "strategy" for the task (e.g., "the reason it's this one is 'cause — see, this one is the way and so is that one"). This statement was verbalized after the performance of the task suggesting that he had problem-solved in a self-instructional fashion.

A summary of the patient's report card from his regular classroom teacher is presented in Table 7-1. As can be seen in Table 7-1, the study skills categories of "listens attentively," "completes work on time," "uses spare time well," and "begins promptly," all went from I (needs improvement) to S (satisfactory). Of particular noteworthiness is that the change in classroom behavior occurred concomitantly with treatment. In addition to study-skill changes, the pretreatment comments made by the teacher which were negative were replaced by progressively improving comments such as "working harder" and "participates often."

Table 7-1. Summary of School Behavior from Report Card*

Report no.	Study Skills Category						
	Listens attentively	Follows directions	Completes work on time	Works carefully	Uses spare time well	Begins promptly	Considerate of others
1. (pretreatment)	I	S	I	S	I	I	S
2.	S	S	S ("better")	S	S ("better")	I	S
3.	S	S	S	S	S	S	S
4.	S	S	S	S	S	S	S

Teachers' Overall Comments

1. (pretreatment) ... not attentive, not participating.
2. ... has been more attentive.
3. ... continues to improve.
4. ... working harder, participates often

*I and S were the only two grading codes available for use in the reporting of behavior. I = needs improvement, S = satisfactory.

Results of the assessment of generalization produced a most favorable outcome (a, b, and c of Figure 7-1). The durable change in behavior when a different room, new toys, and even a new and different therapist were involved in the program is strong evidence for generalization. Kendall and Finch (1976) point out that both stimulus generalization (a, b, and c of Figure 7-1) and response generalization (as evidenced in the class report data) appear to have occurred.

An additional administration of the MFF and the verbal self-instructions and response-cost procedure was conducted at a six-month follow-up. MFF performance remained reflective with a mean latency of 24.7 seconds and only 4 errors. The behavioral recordings of switches presented in Figure 7-1 for the follow-up period indicate the total absence of inappropriate switches.

The application of verbal self-instructions and response-cost procedures, a cognitive-behavioral program, appears to have been an effective treatment procedure to reduce inappropriate behavioral switches and to alter cognitive style. Noteworthy here is that both latency and error measures were altered in the desired direction. This is similar to the findings of Meichenbaum and Goodman (1971) and Finch, Wilkinson, Nelson, and Montgomery (1975) who used solely a verbal self-instruction procedure. In addition to demonstrating successful reduction of cognitive impulsivity, the present case study is evidence for the usefulness of this treatment procedure to reduce impulsive, overactive behaviors.

Indeed, when one considers the behavioral changes, cognitive style modification, and the generalization of the effect, the combined treatment program appears quite promising.

FUTURE DIRECTIONS

At this point the reader should be aware of the stimulus value of a research project. The findings of a given research endeavor often raise more questions than they answer and, thus, produce additional projects. Likewise, one of the functions of a single-subject investigation is to provide a source of hypothesis for later investigation (Kendall and Nay, in press). Based upon the literature we have discussed, including the case illustration, several implications for the future research become apparent. What is the *relative* efficacy of the treatment components? That is, notwithstanding that they have been separately evaluated in group studies, the direct and specific comparision of impulsive children treated with (1) self-instruction, (2) response-cost, (3) self-instructions and response-cost, and (4) an attention control group, would be most informative. Also, what role did the "cue card" play in reminding the client? Did it serve to provide a moderate degree of external pacing?

Based upon the reply of the patient in the case illustration to a query concerning therapy, an interesting hypothesis was generated. The patient was asked to state what it was that he could lose a dime for? His response was only somewhat correct in that he stated a "concrete" example. This was thought to have been related to the concrete labeling used by the therapist. Perhaps, the use of *conceptual* labeling, in which a diverse set of behaviors would be included, would aid the behavior change. Would this conceptual labeling aid in mental development? Can young children benefit from abstract contingencies? The research work begins, it does not end, with the completion of one study.

At present, our understanding of impulsivity is certainly incomplete. A total understanding with empirically derived treatment strategies remains our goal. The possibility of this ocurring is constantly a source of motivation.

REFERENCES

Atkinson, J. W., *An introduction to motivation.* Princeton, N.J.: Van Nostrand-Reinhold, 1964.

Finch, A. J., Jr., and Montgomery, L. E., Reflection-impulsivity and information seeking in emotionally disturbed children. *Journal of Abnormal Child Psychology,* 1973, *1,* 358–362.

Finch, A. J., Jr.; Nelson, W. M., III; Montgomery, L. E.; and Stein, A. B., Reflection-impulsivity and locus of control in emotionally disturbed children. *Journal of Genetic Psychology,* 1974, *125,* 273–275.

Finch A. J., Jr.; Pezzuti, K. A.; Montgomery, L. E.; and Kemp, S. R., Reflection-impulsivity and academic attainment in emotionally disturbed children. *Journal of Abnormal Child Psychology* 1974, *2,* 71–74.

Finch, A. J., Jr.; Wilkinson, M. D.; Nelson, W. M., III; and Montgomery, L. E., Modification of an impulsive cognitive tempo in emotionally disturbed boys. *Journal of Abnormal Child Psychology,* 1975, *3,* 47–51.

Finch, A. J., Jr.; Kendall, P. C.; Deardorff, P. A.; Anderson, J.; and Sitarz, A. M., Reflection-impulsivity, persistence behavior, and locus of control in emotionally disturbed children. *Journal of Consulting and Clinical Psychology,* 1975, *45,* 748.

Finch, A. J., Jr.; Crandell, C.; and Deardorff, P. A., Reflection-impulsivity and need for achievement in emotionally disturbed children. *Journal of Genetic Psychology,* 1976, *129,* 329–331.

Finch, A. J., Jr., and Nelson, W. M., III, Reflection-impulsivity and behavior problems in emotionally disturbed boys. *Journal of Genetic Psychology,* 1976, *128,* 271–274.

Kagan, J., Reflection-impulsivity; the generality and dynamics of conceptual tempo. *Journal of Abnormal Psychology,* 1966, *71,* 17–24..

Kagan, J., A developmental approach to conceptual growth. In H. J. Klausmeier and C. W. Harris (eds.), *Analysis of concept learning.* New York: Academic Press, 1965. (a).

Kagan, J., Individual differences in the resolution of response uncertainty. *Journal of Personality and Social Psychology,* 1965, *2,* 154–160. (b)

Kagan, J., Impulsive and reflective children: significance of conceptual tempo. In J. D. Krumboltz (ed.), *Learning and the education process.* Chicago: Rand McNally, 1965. (c)

Kagan, J., and Kogan, N., Individual variation in cognitive processes. In P. H. Mussen (ed.), *Carmichael's manual of child psychology.* New York: Wiley, 1970.

Kagan, J.; Pearson, L.; and Welch, L., Conceptual impulsivity and inductive reasoning. *Child Development,* 1966, *34,* 583–594.

Kendall, P. C. and Finch, A. J., Jr., A cognitive-behavioral treatment for impulse control: A case study. *Journal of Consulting and Clinical Psychology,* 1976, *44,* 852–857.

Kendall, P. C., and Nay, W. R., Treatment evaluation strategies. Chapter in preparation for W. Robert Nay, *Behavioral Assessment Strategies.* New York: Gardner Press (in press).

Meichenbaum, D. H., and Goodman, J., Training impulsive children to talk to themselves: a means of developing self-control. *Journal of Abnormal Psychology,* 1971, *77,* 115–126.

Montgomery, L. E., Reflection-impulsivity in emotionally disturbed and normal children. Unpublished doctoral dissertation, University of Southern Mississippi, 1974.

Montgomery, L. E., and Finch, A. J., Jr., Reflection-impulsivity and locus of conflict in emotionally disturbed children. *Journal of Genetic Psychology,* 1975, *126,* 89–91.

Nelson W. M., III; Finch, A. J., Jr.; and Hooke, J. F., Effects of reinforcement and response-cost on cognitive style in emotionally disturbed boys. *Journal of Abnormal Psychology,* 1975, *84,* 426–428.

Nowicki, S., Jr., and Strickland, B. L., A locus of control scale for children. *Journal of Consulting and Clinical Psychology,* 1973, *43,* 148–154.

Ollendick T. H., and Finch, A. J., Jr., Reflection-impulsivity in brain-damaged and normal children. *Perceptual and Motor Skills,* 1973, *36,* 654.

Palkes, H.; Stewart, M.; and Kahana, B., Porteus Maze performance of hyperactive boys after training in self-directed verbal commands. *Child Development,* 1968, *39,* 817–829.

Spielberger, C. D., Anxiety as an emotional state. In C. D. Spielberger (ed.), *Anxiety: current trends in theory and research.* Vol. 1. New York: Academic Press, 1972.

Spielberger, C. D., Theory and research on anxiety. In C. D. Spielberger (ed.), *Anxiety and behavior* New York: Academic Press, 1966.

Spielberger, C. D., *Preliminary manual for the State-Trait Anxiety Inventory for Children ("How I Feel Questionnaire")* Palo Alto, Calif.: Consulting Psychologists Press, 1973..

Stein, A. B.; Finch, A. J., Jr.; Hooke, J. F.; Montgomery, L. E.; and Nelson, W. M., III., Cognitive tempo and the mode of representation in emotionally disturbed and normal children. *Journal of Psychology,* 1975, *90,* 197–201.

CHILDHOOD PSYCHOSIS, MENTAL RETARDATION, AND THE DEVELOPMENT OF BEHAVIOR THERAPY

Anthony M. D'Agostino

CHILDHOOD PSYCHOSIS AND MENTAL RETARDATION

The concept of psychosis in childhood is unique to the twentieth century. Prior to 1900 there are few reports of insanity in school-age children, and the belief was that mental disturbances occurring at these ages were due to brain damage, disease, or mental retardation. This may have been because of the fact that children did not become the object of scientific study until after the French Revolution with its ideas concerning the inherent worth of the individual and the industrial revolution with the ensuing laws regarding child labor and juvenile crime. The turn of the century saw a number of people studying the experiences of childhood, with Freud, Montessorir, Binet, and Piaget as leaders in their respective fields.

Historical Perspectives

Probably the earliest paper in the medical literature to address itself to the issue of psychosis in childhood was published in 1906 by an Italian psychiatrist, DeSanctis (DeSanctis, 1971 translation). This paper was unique in that it departed from the accepted thinking of the time which considered that psychoses either did not exist at all before puberty, or when they did, did not differ appreciably from the more common adolescent or adult varieties. DeSanctis felt that there were some children who presented early as mentally retarded but who, at puberty or after, developed the typical picture of dementia praecox (schizophrenia). He referred to the syndrome as "dementia praecocissinia" (very precocious insanity).

In 1930 Heller (Heller, 1971 translation) published a paper describing children who, in their third or fourth year, suddenly began to regress developmentally and intellectually. These reversals were without focal central nervous system symptoms, and motor functions were undisturbed. Heller called this syndrome "dementia infantalis" and felt it was definitely not schizophrenia, stating that in thirty-five years of practice he had seen only one definite case of schizophrenia in early childhood. His paper is important, however, because of the similarity in histories obtained in his cases and those obtained in generally agreed-upon cases of childhood psychoses of whatever variety. Some cases of "dementia infantalis" have died since the original paper, and the presence of a central nervous system degenerative process has been definitely established by autopsy in several instances (Kanner, 1972). At the present time, many in the medical profession still refer to behavioral and cognitive deterioration occurring in a child under age six as "Heller disease," usually with the assumption of an underlying degeneration of brain tissue.

Potter (1933) studed six children whom he diagnosed as schizophrenic. These cases were characterized by: (1) lack of interest in environment; (2) dereistic feelings and thoughts; (3) schizophrenic-like thought disturbance (blocking, symbolization, mutism); (4) impaired emotional rapport; (5) affect disturbances; (6) behavior change. The emphasis here was on the similarity between his sample and adult schizophrenia, the differences being attributed to the earlier developmental level of the children when the process manifested itself.

Kanner (1948) in a report on eleven children, felt he had identified a unique syndrome which he thought would ultimately prove to be related to schizophrenia. These "autistic disturbances of affective contact" were characterized by an inability to "relate themselves in the ordinary way to people and situations from the beginning of life." He felt that, although they scored low on psychometric tests, there was good reason to believe that cognitive potentialities were simply being masked by the basic disorder. Importantly, Kanner believed the "basic disorder" to be affective in nature with cognitive capacities impaired secondarily. The syndrome later came to be known as Early Infantile Autism or, in Europe, Kanner's Syndrome. Since Kanner was so sure that autism could be differentiated from mental retardation, and since autism was thought to be basically affective (emotional), many psychiatrists and educators have opted to refer to all autistic children categorically as *not* retarded regardless of their cognitive capacities.

Mahler et al. (1949; 1959; 1968) described an apparently psychotic disorder in childhood which appeared to be a less severe version of Kanner's autistic children. The Mahler children were characterized by an inability to separate themselves from the mother lest serious panic reactions ensue. Mahler felt that these children often presented as autistic, and she introduced the concept of primary versus secondary autism. Primary autism was the syndrome described by Kanner. Secondary autism referred to the autistic symptoms seen in basically "symbiotic" children. As a defense against the fear of separation from the mother, the child with a "symbiotic psychosis" would secondarily adopt an autistic posture. Symbiotic psychosis was felt to be less severe since it represented a developmentally more advanced process. In the primarily autistic child the arrest in development was much earlier, in what Mahler called the ''normal autistic phase.'' In symbiotic children the arrest occurred during the stage of "separation-individuation." While Mahler's 1949 paper refers to a "constitutional defect" as probable since the basic disorder is so severe, the bulk of her writings and the particulars of her treatment program clearly emphasize the importance of psychoanalytically oriented psychotherapy of both the child and the mother.

Bergmann and Escalona (1949) described "unusual sensitivities" in young children, and Rank (1949) developed the concept of the "atypical child." To varying degrees these were apparently psychotic children who presented clinical pictures which varied somewhat from the syndromes described up to that point.

Loretta Bender (1947; 1956) is the name most frequently associated with the term "childhood schizophrenia." According to her, schizophrenic children manifest disturbances in "every patterned functioning field of behavior." The picture was one of developmental lags of varying degrees affecting reality testing, self-world differentiation, and body image. She regarded the basic disorder to be a type of encephalopathy, but felt the process was often precipitated by severe psychological stress; e.g., separation from a parent, birth of a sibling, etc. Bender also called attention to the fact that the age at onset may vary consinderably, from the first two years to age 11½. While all of these children showed language abnormalities, only those whose onset appeared during the first two years of life ever presented with no language at all.

Clinical Features

Given the early descriptions touched upon above, as well as a number of others not described here it should be apparent that the clinical features of childhood psychoses vary considerably. On the one hand, there are the late onset age group of Bender (1947; 1956) whose clinical features differ little from the picture of schizophrenia as seen in adolescents and adults. These children may present with basically neurotic features such as anxiety and obsessive-compulsive reactions. They tend to evolve persecutory systems and may often be delinquent — what Bender has called "pseudopsychopathic schizophrenia." Cognitive skills are often highly developed as one might expect with onset so near the end of the developmental period. At the other end of the spectrum are the children first described by Kanner (1943). These children often show no language at all and are believed to be abnormal from birth. They often do not relate to humans at all, preferring inanimate objects. They do not tolerate changes in the environment and often do not allow changes in diet during infancy, remaining on milk or formula exclusively for an extended period. They do not engage in "peek-a-boo" or "pat-a-cake" games or other social interactions common during the first year. They may show peculiar gestures and mannerisms, posturing, toe-walking, unusual sensitivity to noise, and inappropriate use of toys. Eye contact is often actively avoided. Lack of speech or peculiarities of speech, e.g., pronoun-reversal echolalia, or appropriate words in inappropriate contexts (delayed echolalia) often form the basis for the initial referral to neurologist or psychiatrist. When speech does not develop, hearing difficulties or mental retardation are often considered.

In an attempt to develop some generally agreed-upon criteria for the diagnosis of psychosis in childhood, a British working party under Creak (1963; 1964) proposed the now famous nine points:
1. Gross and sustained impairment of emotional relationships with people.
2. Apparent lack of awareness of personal identity
3. Pathological preoccupation with certain objects in nonfunctional manner
4. Sustained resistance to change in the environment
5. Abnormal perceptive experience, especially unusual responses to sensory stimuli

6. Acute, excessive, seemingly illogical anxiety
7. Disturbed speech
8. Disturbed motility patterns
9. General retardation with islets of normal or exceptional skill

As one might expect, these criteria have not been found acceptable by everyone concerned with these children. The late onset psychoses certainly would be lacking many of the above features. But for the majority of those labeled "autistic," as well as for Bender's 3-to-4½-year-old age of onset group (the most common according to Bender), the criteria would apply. In contrast to the later onset group (over age six), these children do not show a remitting course, and do not respond to drugs, electroconvulsive therapy, or psychotherapy. On psychometric tests these children often test in the retarded range.

Etiology

Theories of etiology are of some importance in that treatment programs may differ radically in what they do with the child and what they do with the parents. These differences usually have to do with whether one views psychosis as caused by environmental (parental) or biological (genetic, biochemical, physical, or chemical trauma, etc.) factors.

The most ardent proponents of the parental etiology of childhood psychoses are Szurek (1956), Boatman and Szurek (1960), and Bettelheim (1956; 1967). Bettelheim sees autism as a reaction of the essentially normal infant to a con-centration-camp-like experience with the mother during the first year of life. He calls this the "extreme situation" to which the child reacts with the autistic with-drawal. The psychological trauma is subtle and has to do with the unconscious rejection of the child by the mother which the child picks up in the mother's lack of warmth and spontaneity, giving rise to fears of annihilation. Bettelheim openly states that his theory is influenced by his own concentration camp experiences where he saw people withdraw emotionally in the "extreme situation" of the camp. Prolonged psychotherapy on a residential basis is seen as imperative since the child cannot be left with the parents unless and until they themselves have had extensive therapy. Boatman and Szurek (1960) recommend prolonged and intensive therapy of both child and mother using a psychoanalytic model. Severe psychopathology in the parents is felt to be a universal finding with psychosis in the child being a defense against unconscious hostility and rejection by parents. King (1975) pro-poses that the mother "double-binds" the child during the first month or so of life with often devastating consequences. Psychotherapy for the mother is always important. Mahler (1949; 1959; 1968) sees symbiotic, disturbed mothers as important etiologic agents in the development of symbiotic psychotic children. While suggesting a possible constitutional factor, the treatment involves conjoint therapy of mother and child.

Eisenberg and Kanner (1956) suggest a combination of psychological and biological factors and have described the parents as cold and obsessive. However, Kanner (1973) has apparently changed somewhat and in fact states that he has always believed biological factors as primary. Moreover, his treatment approaches have advocated educational over psychotherapeutic interventions.

Bender (1947; 1956) sees psychoses in children as an encephalopathy with psychological implications. Bender's student and colleague Fish (1960; 1961) has studied children at high risk for schizophrenia and reports on evidence of CNS dysfunction from early infancy. Their treatments involve antipsychotic drugs, convulsive therapy, as well as psychotherapy for support. A host of other writers have found evidence of CNS dysfunction in psychotic children (Gittelmann and Birch, 1967; Goldfarb, 1961; Chess, 1971, Creak, 1963, 1964; Taft and Goldfarb, 1964). Rimland (1964) sees the mid-brain reticular activating system as the site of the disorder although he feels, at least in autism, the problem is transmitted genetically as a personality trait which appears in milder form in the parents, usually the father. Kallmann and Roth (1956) published on genetic aspects of "preadolescent schizophrenia." Studying twins, they reported a concordance rate of 70.6% for monozygotic twins (one-egg) and 17.1% for dizygotic (two-egg) twins. Kringlen (1966) did another genetic study which attempted to avoid some of the problems in selection of the Kallmann studies and came out with lower overall concordance rates for monozygotic (28–38%) and dizygotic (5–14%) twins. These latter figures are now generally considered the more accurate and raise the question of why there is not greater concordance in the monozygotic group if the problem is principally genetic. Pollin et al. (1966) have addressed themselves to this issue and report a higher incidence of demonstrable CNS dysfunction in the schizophrenic as opposed to the nonschizophrenic twin, suggesting an interplay between genetic and traumatic factors. Ornitz and Ritvo (1968) suggest that some forms of psychosis may be symptomatic of brain vestibular dysfunction resulting in poorly modulated sensory input – the syndrome of "perceptual inconstancy."

Finally, Goldfarb (1961) has proposed that there are two kinds of childhood schizophrenia: (1) organic and (2) nonorganic. In the organic group evidence of brain damage is clear, and the parents are normal. In the nonorganic group, the parents exhibit "perplexity" and are presumed important in the disorder (Meyers and Goldfarb, 1962). This model has some problems which may become apparent later.

The scientific evidence at this point is highly suggestive of a biological etiology for all forms of childhood psychosis in the opinion of the present writer. Even Szurek (Berlin and Szurek, 1973) has begun to question the usefulness of a completely environmental model, and Schachter et al. (1962) and Weiland (1971) have written on their experiences with psychotherapy in childhood psychotics and their reevaluation of the usefulness of that modality.

Schizophrenia or Autism

The most ardent proponent of maintaining the distinction between these entities is Rimland (1964). He makes a strong case for seeing autism as essentially the opposite of schizophrenia. He uses Kanner's data (Kanner, 1973) on family history to argue that autistics have a very low incidence of major mental illness in their relatives, whereas schizophrenics show the opposite. Autistics do not develop hallucinations or delusions, do not interact socially, show normal EEGs, and generally have good health and general appearance. Schizophrenics develop hallucinations and delusions, are very dependent on adults, show EEG abnormalities, and are often sickly. Because they appear as polar opposites, Rimland argues that perhaps the genes which influence obsessiveness, intelligence, and personality are involved in both entities but represent opposite extremes of phenotypic expression of the genotype. Considerable weight is given to Kanner's description of the parents as cold and obsessive (Kanner, 1943; Eisenberg and Kanner, 1956; Kanner, 1973). Rimland sees the child as the more extreme expression of a milder disorder in the parents, especially the father. Rimland regards these children as exceptionally intelligent, on theoretical grounds alone. This is based on supposed high intelligence and high scientific and artistic accomplishments of parents and blood relatives (Kanner, 1972; 1973). Some degree of corroboration of this view is given by Lotter (1967) and Treffert (1970). Both found higher educational levels in parents of autistic as opposed to parents of children with other types of psychoses. Rutter and Lockyer (1967) report an excess of autistics in social class I (highest in Britain) and a significant lack in social classes IV and V, using nonpsychotic but disturbed children from the same clinic as controls. A more recent study (Ritvo et al., 1971) reports no social class differences in an autistic-nonautistic clinic population. The issue is not yet closed and may hinge on differences in definition of autism or in kinds of children referred to a particular clinic, although the Lotter and Treffert studies were not based on referrals to a particular clinic and were carefully done.

Other arguments for a distinction between autism and schizophrenia derive from clinical outcome and sex ratios. Rutter et al. (1967) report that by late adolescence children diagnosed autistic rarely showed delusions or hallucinations as seen in schizophrenics. In addition, the sex ratio for autistics, 4.25/1, is different than seen in schizophrenia which approximates 1/1 (Treffert, 1970; Lotter, 1967). Rutter (1968) mentions that this may be due to age of onset but finds the sex, social class, and family history differences difficult to explain in this way. Bender (1970) followed up fifty cases of autism using Kanner's criteria. She reported that many do develop the rather typical adult-like schizophrenic picture. Bender, however, does not define her population as carefully as does Rutter and talks about some children as having "schizophrenia with autism" early in life. Menolascino and Eaton (1965) and Menolascino (1971) argue against the concept of autism as a distinct entity based on their experiences in a mental retardation clinic, and will be discussed later.

From the point of view of the present writer, what can be said at this time is that there are a good many children who present as psychotic who do not show the features described by Kanner as "autistic." On the other hand, there are a few children who present with the history and findings characteristic of classical Kannerian autism who appear in no way schizophrenic in the sense that we observe in adults. Nevertheless, the largest group is made up of children in whom the clinical findings are quite varied and often confounding. From a treatment perspective, the differences may well be merely academic and may have to with varying etiologies or degrees of severity. Childhood psychosis must still be looked upon as syndrome rather than disease, although perhaps one day the various subtypings may point more clearly to etiology.

Psychosis or Mental Retardation

"Mental deficiency is the condition most readily confused with childhood psychosis, and indeed they have much in common. The psychotic child, while in the early withdrawal stage of his illness, is the most ineducable of any, and conversely, one meets among retarded patients odd skills, obsessional drives to no very obvious purpose, active withdrawal from social contacts, and many instances of bizarre behavior. The distinction where there are psychotic children, or examples of psychotic behavior in severely retarded children, is almost an academic one. Such children function at a grossly retarded level, even if it often seems that it is the emotional isolation that closes the doors of learning to them. These cases show that even with reasonable care and long-term oversight, it is still possible to be in the dark as to the real diagnosis. Greater precision in diagnosis should be possible, and the nine points were designated to help in this. We will always probably be faced with the problem: 'Is he mad because he is limited or limited because he is mad?' — to put it crudely" (Creak, 1963).

This pithy quotation summarizes the problem which often confronts both physician and educator. Only recently have data become available which shed some light on the problem, although it is here that one's theoretical orientation will most acutely affect treatment or educational planning. Kanner (1943; 1972; 1973), Rimland (1964), and Bettelheim (1956; 1967) have presented arguments concerning the supposed high intelligence of at least autistic children, and Anthony (1958) cautions against accepting the results of psychometric testing in childhood psychoses, voicing the common clinical belief that intellectual capacities are merely being masked by the psychotic process. Presumably, should treatment be successful, one would be able to demonstrate IQ gains over the years, or at least significant variation between different testings. Rutter and Lockyer (1967) and Lockyer and Rutter (1969) found that more than half the autistic children in their study tested in the retarded range and found no variation in IQ with changes in clinical state. As a rule, IQ scores at ages five or six predicted IQs obtained in adolescence and even remained the same in that small group who recovered or improved significantly.

Rutter (1969) states that the mental retardation seen in autistic children is as "real" as in any other child where retardation is part of the clinical picture. What must be highlighted, however, is that between 25% and 35% of autistic children test in the normal range (Rutter and Lockyer, 1967). Since the behavioral characteristics were similar for both retarded and nonretarded autistics, mental retardation alone is insufficient explanation for autism. Rutter points out further that IQ differs according to intellectual function examined. Autistics do very poorly on verbal tasks and those requiring abstract capacities and much better on visuo-spatial tasks like object assembly and block design. Rutter concludes that to some extent the autistic's low intelligence may be related to specific language deficits rather than global intellectual deficiency (Rutter, 1969).

As mentioned earlier in the chapter, however, the absence of references to psychoses in children prior to 1900 begs the question: where were these children prior to the twentieth century? A most likely explanation is that they were felt to be retarded and, as Rutter suggests, they are in fact retarded whatever else they may be. Knobloch and Pasamanick (1974) make reference to an article which appeared in the 1941 edition of Gesell and Amatruda's *Developmental Diagnosis*. There was described a syndrome highly suggestive of autism as originally set forth by Kanner in 1943. Gesell and Amatruda used the term "pseudosymptomatic retardation" to refer to the observation that the bizarre nature of the behavior often fostered attribution of a psychogenic eitology. "The parents, fearing a diagnosis of mental subnormality as suggestive of hopelessness, were at times ready to accept any other explanation. They would point to what appeared to be precocious feats of memory and other features which they believed were inconsistent with the diagnosis." It was Gesell's impression that these children were retarded despite the unusual findings. Knobloch and Pasamanick go on to point out that psychotic behavior is not unusual among mentally retarded people and report that in the first 1,900 patients seen by their developmental service (85% less than twenty-four months of age), sixty-four (3.4%) warranted a diagnosis of "autism" using Kanner's criteria. Of patients who had phenylketonuria (PKU), fourteen of seventeen showed psychotic behavior. These were excluded from their study, and the remaining fifty compared to the next fifty children who showed central nervous system abnormalities without psychosis. Another group of fifty children were studied who showed no neuropsychiatric problems, being seen for adoption or teaching purposes. Both abnormal groups differed significantly from the normals but not from each other on the variables examined: prenatal and paranatal complications, sociocultural factors, motor and intellectual deficits or associated disorders. One-fifth of the autistics were of low birth weight (premature); one-half of these pregnancies were associated with bleeding, toxemia, or neonatal complications. Only ten autistics had developmental quotients (DQs) above 75 (normal, 100) and 50% had DQs less than 50. A total of 75% had seizures, 50% had strabismus, 50% had cerebral palsy or other specifically diagnosed central nervous system disorders — obstructive hydrocephalus, Schilder's disseminated sclerosis, Hurler's disease, trisomy 21, encephalitis, meningitis, etc. The fifty abnormal but nonpsychotic children showed a similar spectrum of disorders.

At follow-up of the fifty autistics, three to ten years with a mean of five years, the autistic symptoms were variable. Five children died of organic pathology. In 75% of the patients the autistic symptoms disappeared with age. It should be recalled here that 35% of the children were under twenty-four months when first seen. Of those under one year at referral, all lost their autistic symptoms. If the child was over three years old at the first visit, the autistic symptoms persisted. In all cases the initial mental deficiency was not a function of psychotic withdrawal. At follow-up, 60% were functioning and testing at below 35 IQ. Language function was related to IQ. As in many mentally retarded individuals, language behavior was often more retarded than adaptive behavior. Echolalia and pronoun reversals were common as in normal twenty-one to thirty-month-old children.

The above study can be easily criticized as being composed of many children in whom the diagnosis of "autism" may have been premature or incorrect by virtue of the high numbers of neurologically damaged children. Nevertheless, it calls attention to the fact that autistic or psychotic behaviors do occur in such children and casts serious doubt on theories which suggest that autism is a unitary condition characterized by, among other features, normal or high intelligence, and an absence of CNS pathology. Moreover, inability to find discrete lesions is certainly not evidence of psychogenicity where the behavior is often indistinguishable from those having known organic disease. Creak (1963) reports on two cases of childhood psychoses without neurological findings who died and at autopsy were found to have an unsuspected disorder of neurolipid metabolism. Havelkova (1968) reports similar experiences and Chess (1971), in a study of 243 children with congenital rubella, found no less than eighteen presenting with the clinical picture of autism.

Menolascino and Eaton (1967) describe their experience in a mental retardation clinic. Of 616 children examined for mental retardation, thirty-four presented with symptoms of autism. Of these, only two could be called early infantile autism using Kanner's criteria. Five were diagnosed as childhood schizophrenia and twenty-two labeled organic brain syndrome with psychosis. The others were either not psychotic at all or could not be labeled. They confirmed Eisenberg's (1956) finding that the better the language the less the retardation (see also Rutter, 1967; Lotter, 1967). Outcome was generally poor despite discrepancies between verbal and motor performance scores which suggested higher intellectual potential. These discrepancies often led to false optimism in parents and professionals alike. The number of neurological findings tended to increase with age and the earlier "soft" (nonspecific) neurological findings tended to get "hard" (specific, localized) with eventual deterioration in some cases.

Menolascino (1971) sees no evidence for autism as a unique syndrome with unique etiology. Discrete clinical entities such as infantile autims, childhood schizophrenia, and organic brain syndrome with psychosis depend on age at onset, and a variety of factors eventuate in one final common pathway. Multiple-handicapped children may show "affect inaccessibility" which may appear psychotic. Affective responses depend upon the "raw data" of sensory input. Therefore, brain-damaged children are particularly prone to personality decompensation which may be the result of unstable, inconsistent, or rejecting parents. Too often mentally retarded children are thought to have uniform behaviors as though mental retardation itself were some specific condition rather than a generic label for a variety of conditions. The present writer has seen a number of obviously retarded, brain-damaged children referred because the child showed autistic behaviors which in some circles automatically voids the retardation and brain damage. The implication is clearly that the presence of autistic symptoms equals "emotional" disorder; hence the medical, psychological, social, and educational expectations need revamping. The end result is often unwarranted expectations and needless financial outlay.

THE DEVELOPMENT OF BEHAVIOR THERAPY
WITH PSYCHOTIC CHILDREN

The application of laboratory-derived theories and practices to the treatment of psychotic children began approximately fifteen years ago under the suggestive influence of C. B. Ferster (1961). In this paper Ferster presented his theoretical formulation of how early infantile autism might be produced by parents through the inappropriate reinforcement (or more properly, nonreinforcement) of an infant's behavior. Suggesting that autism was the result of environmental contingencies, Ferster apparently was influenced by the intellectual and scientific climate of that period which saw the child as essentially normal at birth and the autism as reaction to parental behavior. Therefore, if the autistic child's behavior could be established along more appropriate lines, then perhaps this most obstinate of disorders might be "cured," since the problem was disordered behavior and nothing more.

In several papers Ferster and DeMyer (1961; 1962) reported on experiments using the principles of learning theory to study the performances of autistic children in an automatically controlled environment. They were able to demonstrate that the performance curves of these children followed expected laws and were therefore under operant control. They reported rather limited behavioral repertoires but were able to develop more complex forms of behavior.

DeMyer and Ferster (1962) also reported on a more clinically oriented study. They worked on teaching social behavior to eight psychotic children, ages two through ten, by instructing the ward staff of a children's service in the basic techniques of behavior modification. Reinforcers were based on whatever the children seemed to like best after a period of observation on the unit. They demonstrated that relatively untrained nonprofessional workers could be quite effective in changing the behavior of these children. The study also utilized a practical approach without complex pieces of equipment used in more elegant research units.

Anthony M. D'Agostino

Wolf, Risley, and Mees (1964) reported the case of Dickey, a 3½-year-old psychotic child who needed to wear glasses to preserve his vision but could not be made to do so. In addition, he had frequent tantrums with self-injurious behavior, and bedtime rituals requiring the presence of one parent in the room during the night. He threw his glasses, had no normal social and verbal repertoires, and had eating problems.

The temper tantrums were dealt with by using a combination of mild punishment and extinction procedures. With each tantrum Dickey was placed in his room with the door closed until the tantrum subsided. Self-injurious behavior dropped off quickly, with milder tantrum behavior superceding, and eventually controlled. Bedtime problems were controlled in similar fashion by using an open door as reward for returning to bed when ordered to do so. The door was closed if he did not comply. After five nights of severe tantrums following door closing, bedtime ceased to be a serious problem.

A shaping procedure was used for wearing glasses. A conditioned reinforcer in the form of a click from a noisemaker was used. The click became a discriminative stimulus (SD) after which small amounts of candy would appear in a bowl. Through successive approximation, an attempt was made to have Dickey wear glassless frames for increasing periods of time and eventually introduce the glass into the frames. Things did not go as planned, however, and Dickey would not wear the glasses properly and would not allow anyone to touch any part of his head. Candy and fruit proved weak reinforcers since the ward staff were reluctant to use food deprivation. After five weeks without success, Dickey began to approximate the desired glass-wearing behavior following a long day with very little to eat. Once established, proper wearing became easy to differentially reinforce, and progress thereafter was rapid. When, sometime later, throwing of the glasses became a problem, he was put in his room for ten minutes for each throw or tantrum. Throwing decreased to zero in five days.

Although able to speak, speech was not used for communication and was rarely appropriate. Using breakfast and lunch as training sessions, Dickey gradually learned to respond appropriately to pictures, then objects, and finally to remote events; e.g., "Where are you going tonight?" Once established, speech could be maintained using weaker conditioned reinforcers like attention and approval.

Food throwing, food stealing, and eating with his hands were met with removal of the food with verbal stimuli "no" or "stop that." After a few minutes the food was returned to be removed permanently if the undesirable behavior recurred. Soon these verbal stimuli alone were sufficient to suppress these undesirable behaviors.

Developing Verbal Behavior

The earliest follow-up studies of autistic children were published by Eisenberg (1956; 1957). He highlighted the interesting observation that those psychotic children who had developed useful speech have the best prognosis. These children

238

usually had such verbal behavior in evidence by about five to six years of age. Instating verbal behavior therefore seemed to be an important priority.

It is of some interest that the first reference to the use of behavioral techniques for language acquisition in psychotic children appeared in *The Psychoanalytic Study of the Child* (Weiland and Rudnick, 1961). The problem is that they were not referred to as "behavioral." The report is on eight-year-old Nelson "who had developed a symbioticlike relationship with the child-care staff following three years of psychotherapy...," but had no speech! Departing from analytic theory which suggests that the psychotic child cannot tolerate frustration, Weiland and Rudnick decided to withhold Nelson's favorite toy (a ball) until he said "ball." Twelve weeks later he said "ball," and continued to use the word appropriately when he wanted the ball. Encouraged, they began requiring other words, this time using doughnuts to "learn to talk as the result of the 'teasing' behavior of the workers." He soon developed a vocabulary of several dozen words and used them seemingly with great pleasure. He also learned to sing simple songs with apparent pleasure. In Nelson's case it seems that the act of naming had become reinforcing for its own sake, and perhaps his greater communication skill facilitated his finding staff (people) more reinforcing.

Hewitt (1965) developed an approach involving four phases. Phase one was introductory wherein the child learned to work for rewards in a specially designed speech-training box. When he appeared comfortable with environment, apparatus, and teacher, he went on to the next phase. In phase two, social *imitation* occurred. The child learned to follow verbal commands and imitate the teacher's hand movement e g., pointing to the head after the teacher pointed to his head. During phase three, speech training occurred by first reinforcing all random verbalizations, and then later, through successive approximations, gradually shaping simple words to build a vocabulary. In phase four an attempt was made to transfer from teaching booth to hospital ward. This was done by requiring the child to utter appropriate words for the objects and things he desired.

Lovaas et al. (1966) described a program involving four basic steps: (1) The child is rewarded for all vocalizations until he is responding every five seconds and looking at an adult's mouth. (2) The child is rewarded if he responds verbally within six seconds of an adult's verbalization. (3) Step 3 is similar to step 2 except the child has to match the adult's word. In this case it was felt to be useful to use words which could be prompted initially, then faded, then, using a musical stimulus, requiring the child to initiate the word himself. An example is teaching the "b" sound. Training here involved three stages: (1) Adult emits "b" and prompts by holding child's lips and suddenly letting go when the child exhales; (2) Prompt is faded by gradual removal of fingers from lips to cheek and jaw; (3) Adult says "b" without prompt. It was found that children were better able to imitate sounds with obvious visual components like the consonant "m" or the vowel "a". Gutturals like "k" and "g" proved quite difficult.

Step 4 was step 3 all over but with a new sound. Sounds of step 3 were presented occasionally to see that the child was truly imitating. When the experimenters switched from a response-contingent method of reward to rewards given on a time-lapsed-since-previous-reward basis, imitative behavior deteriorated. To see whether or not the children might be able to acquire new behaviors on their own, Norwegian words were uttered which were not rewarded. The children ostensibly improved in their uttering of Norwegian words also. Lovaas felt this kind of response generalization held particularly strong therapeutic potential.

Risley and Wolf (1967) describe techniques for establishing functional speech in echolalic children. They begin by using shaping and imitation training, then fade in new stimuli with gradual fading out of prompts to transfer from imitative control to control by appropriate stimulus conditions. They used extinction and time out to reduce inappropriate behavior with differential reinforcement of appropriate responses incompatible with inappropriate behavior. This latter technique will be referred to in a later section.

While the work of the authors quoted above suggests that considerable improvement can be attained in the speech of at least these severely afflicted psychotic children, there still remains the important question of whether or not what is being taught can be considered true language. Weiss and Born (1967) argue that language behavior differs from speech behavior and that psychotic children are often incapable of the former due to an inherent inability to generalize. Certainly this has been the experience of the present writer and others (Churchill, 1969; Lovaas et al., 1974; Weiland, 1971).

Many of these children develop impressive verbal performances which appear to be utilized by the child in an appropriate manner for communicative purposes. But remove the child from the treatment milieu and the child behaves as though he had never learned how to appropriately ask for a glass of milk, etc. Lovaas (1974) suggests that a solution may lie in specifically teaching the child *to generalize.* Hewitt (1965) has apparently shown that speech taught through operant techniques could generalize to new situations, but the final chapter has not yet been written on this issue. There would be no problem if psychotic children simply could not generalize at all under any circumstances. Not only do these children differ widely in this capacity, however, but they change as they get older — generally for the better — much as do retarded and normal children, regardless of the particular theoretical orientation of the treatment program. Whether the successes related in the teaching of abstract language capacities reported by Hewitt (1965) and Lovaas et al. (1966; 1967; 1973; 1974) presage developments which will one day lead to more definitive treatment of these language disabilities remains to be seen. What one can say at this point is that behavioral techniques are the fastest and most efficient means of teaching speech to nonverbal children, whatever the ceiling on their cognitive capacities may be.

Developing Social and Interpersonal Behavior

In most descriptions of psychotic children, and especially those children re-garded as autistic, the problem of social or interpersonal unavailability is high-lighted. Kanner's (1943) original paper described the "extreme autistic aloneness" which, along with the need for "sameness," he regarded as a primary feature of the psychotic process. This interpersonal deficit is also viewed as primary in all psycho-dynamic theorizing and is the starting point in therapies both psychodynamic and behavioral (Bettleheim, 1967; Wenar et al., 1967; Szurek, 1956; Boatman and Szurek, 1960; Rank, 1949; Mahler et al., 1949; Churchill, 1969; Ruttenberg, 1971; Lovaas et al., 1965). Since the often stark absence of appropriate social behavior results in decreased social contact, the process of acquiring social skills is thereby further retarded. To learn social behaviors, the child must first attend. Once attend-ing is established, the specific behaviors which are adjudged as lacking must be developed.

DeMyer and Ferster (1962) reported on work with eight schizophrenic children aged two through ten. Using a good deal of body contact and tangible reinforcers the children seemed to like best, nonprofessional ward staff were able to stimulate a wide variety of social behaviors after a limited amount of instruction in behavioral principles.

Hingten et al. (1965) attempted to stimulate peer interaction in six psychotic children. They trained the children to operate a lever to obtain coins for a vending machine. Later they set up a situation in which one child had to work with another by alternately pressing a single lever, then adding a second lever to be pressed alternately in order to obtain reinforcement. It was unclear if this kind of "coopera-tive" behavior generalized in any way to extraexperimental situations. Lovaas et al. (1965) reported on the use of aversive conditioning in the development of social behavior. They used an electric floor grid to apply an aversive stimulus, attempting to get the children to approach adults. The model was development of a condi-tioned avoidance response to pain with approaching of adults required for escape. They reported that, initially, the children did not know what to do when shocked. Eventually they did learn the escape procedure. After training, it was reported that when hurt in any manner they would seek out adults (nurses). They even became affectionate toward those adults who manipulated the painful stimuli. Use of the word "no" with shock resulted in the acquisition of punishing properties by that word alone, and shock could eventually be withdrawn.

Risley (1968) reported on some interesting "side effects" of aversive stimulation for dangerous, self-injurious behavior. When time-out, extinction procedures, and reinforcement of incompatible behaviors failed to eliminate dangerous behavior, electric shock was used only to eliminate dangerous behavior. Moreover, they re-ported increases in eye contact, affectionate behavior toward staff, and other desirable social behaviors. He suggests there may be a "functional incompatibility" between stereotyped behaviors and socially productive behavior. "Symptom substitution" appears to have occurred, only in a seemingly desirable direction.

Simmons and Lovaas (1969) and Simmons and Reed (1969) discuss at length the theoretical and clinical application of aversive stimulation in the treatment of psychotic children. They review the psychological literature which up to that point had suggested that punishment was not useful for three reasons:

1. It is less effective than other alternatives, especially the use of positive reinforcement.
2. It produces undesirable side effects.
3. It is unkind to the individual.

Their conclusions, drawn from literature review as well as their own research, were:

1. Aversive stimulation does suppress responsiveness and the greater the intensity of the stimulus, the greater the suppression.
2. If pains were taken to make the aversion response contingent, there followed greater suppression of the undesirable response and little suppression of non-punished responses.
3. Where more than one response is available, punishing the "wrong" response facilitates response differentiation.
4. An inverse relationship exists between the amount of response reduction and time between response and punishment. The shorter the internal, the greater the response reduction.

They devised a hierarchy of aversion from: (1) saying "no," to (2) slap, to (3) shock. Like Risley (1968) they also found that shock facilitated the development of social responsiveness if used only to decrease specific behaviors and if the punisher also was the provider of positive reinforcements.

Churchill (1969) describes a comprehensive program which does not utilize aversive stimulation in the manner described by Lovaas and Simmons (1969) but admits that escape from a possibly aversive confinement may be an important component. He begins by isolating the child completely for three weeks. During that time a single person works with the child in areas of (1) general body imitation, (2) use of objects, and (3) imitative vocalization. An "imitative set" is felt to be established when the child can imitate new models on the first presentation. Cutting with scissors, building with blocks, using a dart gun, and writing on a blackboard are then established. Eventually speech is developed, initially by reinforcing all spontaneous vocalizations, then differentially reinforcing open and closed mouth sounds. Lastly, sounds are shaped in imitation of adults. During these three weeks children generally become attentive, cooperative, and highly motivated. Churchill points out, however, that even with high motivational state, the child is often unable to perform certain tasks. He feels that this lack of ability to perform results in the bizarre negative behavior. As the child's psychotic appearance recedes, he becomes more spontaneous. If failure on a task occurs, the rituals and negativisms return.

Churchill calls symptoms "the results of unrelieved frustration and inevitable failure in an incomprehensible world." His explanation is, in many ways, like the explanations and insights into the psychotic process described by members of the psychoanalytic school (Bettelheim, 1967; Szurek, 1956; Boatman and Szurek, 1960). The difference, however, is that the emphasis in the behavioral school is on the disability rather than on the motivation, which Churchill has demonstrated is *not* lacking in psychotic children.

Controlling Self-Destructive and Self- Stimulatory Behavior

While of theoretical importance only in the psychoanalytic school (Bettelheim, 1967), self-destructive behavior is often a reality which must be dealt with whatever one's orientation. Many of these children are capable of doing great harm to themselves physically and to their parents and caretakers emotionally. It takes an unusual person to be able to cope with and love a child who, week after week and month after month, rewards one's most devoted efforts with bitten flesh and battered skull and "love" takes the form of leather restraints.

Lovaas et al. (1965) and Lovaas and Simmons (1969) discuss the role of environmental stimuli in the maintenance of self-mutilation. They were able to demonstrate that sympathetic remarks and reassurances increased the frequency of self-destructive behavior. Using an extinction technique, the children were isolated and within several days the behavior decreased markedly. Following a typical extinction curve, the behavior increased initially and during this phase the potential for serious tissue damage was a problem. In addition, they found that the extinction procedure worked in the isolation room but did not always generalize to other areas. Their postulate is that these behaviors may have to undergo extinction in a variety of places and situations in order to be adequately controlled. Because of these difficulties and the potential for serious injury, they decided on a punishment study using electric shock applied to the skin contingent upon self-injurious behavior. Within a relatively short time the frequency of these behaviors fell to zero. Reverting to the previous conditions without aversive stimulation and with attention, the behaviors in question were quickly reinstated. An interesting corollary to the use of reversive stimulation is their report that generalized affects appeared in a clinically desirable direction. Eye contact increased and socially more desirable behavior appeared to fill the void left by the absence of self-destructive behavior.

Tate and Baroff (1966) report on a two-part study of a nine-year-old blind, psychotic boy. In the first study, self-injurious activity was decreased by using withdrawal of physical contact. The decrease was of significant proportion but did not occur as quickly as in the second study where aversive shock was used. Following shock, the authors report a generalized improvement which did not follow upon the first study using only withdrawal of physical contact. They postulate that aversive stimulation produces central nervous system arousal, with increased attention to the environment provided by virtue of decreased self-destructive behavior being more reinforcing to more desirable behaviors.

243

Wolf and Risley (1967) described a training procedure for substituting self-patting for self-pinching behavior. They hoped to decrease pinching by substituting the less injurious patting. While they report success in developing patting, the pinching did not decrease.

Jones et al. (1974) report failure of a program of responsive-contingent shock. In this study shock resulted in increased self-destructive responding, complete suppression of self-feeding, and necessity for constant restraint. The new program was essentially an extinction procedure using twenty-four weeks of twice daily two-hour sessions of noncontingent social isolation. They attribute reports of failure with this technique to session lengths of less than 1½ hours per day for less than twelve days, since in this study no significant change in response rate occurred until week two. This study is an interesting departure from those mentioned above since the reasons for their reported success are unclear. It appears that, in contrast to previous studies, the patient's self-destructive behavior was not noticeably under social control at the beginning of the study, and an adult's entrance into the isolation room appeared to have no effect on the rate of self-destructive behavior. They speculated that these behaviors may have been under partial stimulus control of restraints. With restraints, self-destructive behavior did not occur; without them it began immediately. As the behavior decreased in isolation, the stimulus control excited by the restraints may have been lost. At the completion of the study, the patient refused to wear restraints. Since the patient's behavior clearly generalized to other areas of the ward, this study stands in contrast to one quoted above (Lovaas and Simmons, 1969). They suggest that noncontingent social isolation may in fact be more broadly applicable than contingent aversive control.

Lovaas et al. (1965, 1971) and Risley (1968) report on the control of stereotyped behaviors (self-stimulation, autoerotism) which were not necessarily self-destructive. These are behaviors such as rocking, twirling, finger-flicking, etc. They felt that elimination of such behaviors results in greater social responsiveness and readiness for learning. The specific procedures are similar to those described above for elimination of self-destructive behavior and involve contingent aversive stimuli (shock). Most clinicians view self-stimulatory behavior as undesirable and attempt control either by aversive means or by attempting to develop incompatible behaviors which, in practice, usually translates to giving the child specific tasks to complete and engaging him in human social interactions.

Imitation and Generalization

Speech is the most obvious example of imitation (verbal imitation) but will not be discussed here (see above). Lovaas (1967, 1974) cites the universal observation that autistic children are profoundly deficient in imitative behavior and appear to learn little through observation. In their 1967 paper, Lovaas et al. point out that simply providing a model is not sufficient in establishing nonverbal imitation. Reinforcers, usually primary reinforcers, are most often required. Using a wide variety of tasks, they were able to establish imitative behavior, some of which appeared to become naturally reinforcing. They demonstrated that control of newly acquired imitative behavior could be shifted from nonverbal to verbal control and ultimately to subject control. Areas where imitation training appears to have generalized included swimming, self-care and grooming, drawing, and playing games by the rules. These activities, once established, often do not require continuance of primary reinforcers, the children ostensibly enjoying them for their own sake.

Hingten et al. (1965) describes training in imitation of two mute autistic children. Using the model described above (Churchill, 1969), the children were each isolated for three weeks and trained in imitative behavior on (1) general use of body (2) use of objects, and (3) vocalizations. During the teaching of approximately 200 responses and a number of words, they noted that about 25% could be imitated on first presentation, suggesting the spontaneous generalization of the imitative act.

These studies suggest that many of these children are capable of higher-level performances than was thought formerly to be the case. Given these rather basic skills, many children are able to progress independently up to certain limits.

Lovaas et al. (1973) present data on stimulus generalization, response generalization, and generalization over time on the first ten children treated. Four children went to an institution and six returned home to their parents. Those sent to the institution rapidly lost almost all of what they had learned, while those trained in behavioral methods who were sent home to parents maintained gains or improved. Also reported were gains in Stanford-Binet IQ and Vineland Social Quotient, although children were not trained on these tests.

In the original follow-up studies of Eisenberg (1956, 1957), the rather poor outcome of the group as a whole was highlighted. Lovaas (1974) also reports limited overall progress in these children with behavior modification procedures. In addition, a "natural" environment usually does not suffice to maintain gains, and the child requires some extension of the training milieu. Lovaas emphasizes that while development up to this point has relied heavily on animal-laboratory derived principles of learning theory generally, the future would appear to belong to research designed specifically to investigate the special deficits of psychotic children and methods to circumvent these specific deficits.

One of the more cogent criticisms of the use of behavioral concepts in the treatment of psychotic children and beyond comes from Breger (1965) who argues that the autistic child lacks the ability to generalize and hence is the ideal subject for experiments in stimulus-response learning. Nevertheless, as soon as one's subject gets, or is already, beyond that juncture, significant problems arise which cannot be explained by traditional animal-laboratory derived approaches. Breger and McGaugh (1965) suggest a reformulation of learning theory in which the learning process is viewed as acquisition and storage of information, and emphasize the role of central processes (thinking, feeling, etc.) as the child moves up the developmental ladder. Leff (1971), in a review of the behavioral literature, also concludes that cognitive concepts will most likely need to be integrated at some level, but how, where, and how much remains to be seen.

Certianly psychotic children may be able to benefit from approaches which attempt to understand their confused perceptions of the world and reach out in a humane manner. Certainly there are parents who, largely through lack of information and not a little frustration, will respond inappropriately at times and generate some of the symptomatology. Nevertheless, the concept that these disturbed children got this way primarily through parental behavior is untenable, and developments in behavior theory and therapy have contributed significantly to the demonstration of this thesis. (For an interesting study bearing upon child-rearing attitudes of mothers of psychotic children, see Pitfield and Oppenheim, 1964.)

CURRENT STATUS OF TREATMENT IN CHILDHOOD PSYCHOSES

To a considerable extent, treatment remains a function of theoretical persuasion. Bettelheim (1967; 1974) states categorically that about 80% of children achieve a fair-to-good outcome after extensive treatment in his program No other report in the literature gives anywhere near this figure for favorable outcome. No one has yet reproduced this figure even in other psychoanalytically oriented programs. Certainly no reports of outcome with behavior therapy have attained this figure so far as the present writer is aware. Bettelheim operates on the "extreme situation" hypothesis as alluded to earlier in the chapter, and therapy and milieu are oriented toward helping the child to overcome his emotional and behavioral responses to this aversive early experience. Where and how the other obvious cognitive deficiences come into play is difficult to discern. Is selection of patients random, or is there a selective process operating which may explain outcome? Were the original diagnoses correct? Were they made on medical-descriptive grounds, behavior, or psychodynamics? Some psychoanalytic writers tend to dilute the concept of psychosis to include any number of "atypical" (Rank, 1949) children who may be improperly classified as psychotic. Szurek (1956) proposes a gradient of disorder from neurosis through autism and schizophrenia. Such a loose conception of psychosis leads to overdiagnosis and, if one can select one's cases for treatment, the possibility is strong that less-severe or misdiagnosed cases may be included, leading to incorrect suppositions regarding the treatment program. Betz (1947), Mahler (1949, 1959, 1968), and Ruttenberg (1971) give descriptions of psychoanalytic treatment approaches but do not give treatment results.

Weiland and Rudnik (1961) do not give specific treatment results, but they adequately convey their sense of frustration at their limited success. They feel that treatment can result in a child who is no longer psychotic but rather is "developmentally arrested (retarded?)." This is similar to the findings of Churchill (1969) who reports quick improvement in a behavioral program only to be stymied by the "learning disability." In an assessment of psychoanalytic and behavioral treatment programs, Weiland (1971) finds both approaches lacking but feels that behavior therapy takes less time to bring a given child to his highest level of improvement and that the child is in no way worse off because of the experience. This view is in contrast to psychoanalytic views (Bettelheim, 1967; Mahler et al., 1959; Ruttenberg, 1971) which hold that forced contact with a child and active manipulation of his behavior can result in withdrawal and increased autism (Bettelheim, 1967; Ruttenberg, 1971).

Another recent treatment approach which is gaining in popularity is that of Delacato (1974). Here the view is that the child is basically brain-damaged, and the treatment approach follows the idea that the various behaviors of the child are expressions of the child's need for contact and the specific channel or modality (learning, vision, tactile) which is defective is hinted at by the symptoms. Treatments entail the elaborate stimulation and development of these sensory deficits. Unfortunately, Delacato does not make any attempt to compare his approach with any other except to say that he succeeds where others fail and that they expect their children to approximate normal with greater frequency than those treated by other methods. His book is quite specific about how to treat these children, however, and should be a comfort to those who cannot abide the ambiguity and uncertainty which pervades the field.

The behavioral approaches usually involve treatment along lines similar to Lovaas (1971, 1974) or Churchill (1969). These approaches have utilized controlled studies and applied scientific method to explore the potentials of psychotic children in a manner far in excess of that attempted by any other school. Certainly the improvement in specific behavior is undoubted and well demonstrated. As an educational method, behavior modification appears emperically superior to other methods. Nevertheless, we are still left with a good deal of uncertainty as to its ultimate benefit to the individually afflicted child. The question yet to be answered is: will the behavioral approach prove superior in the long term?

The answer would appear to depend on adequate follow-up. There have been several follow-up studies reported in the literature (Eisenberg, 1956, 1957; Kanner, 1971; Havelkova, 1968; Bender, 1970; Lockyer and Rutter, 1969; Lotter, 1974; DeMyer et al., 1973; Rutter et al., 1967). Eisenberg (1957) studied the group of children identified by Kanner and himself at the Johns Hopkins Clinic as autistic or schizophrenic. He reported that among the group with the best overall outcome, there was a high percentage of children who had developed useful speech by about age five. Among the somewhat larger group in which there developed a more malignant course, only very few had any speech in evidence by age five. These children, by the way, had received essentially no "treatment" in the usual sense. There were no special programs developed at the time, and the children were often tutored specially or were institutionalized. Few could attend regular schools. This report is doubly significant, however, in that it is not only the first such report, but also provides something of a control group against which later studies might be compared. If treatment A or treatment B is superior to simple humane care, they

247

would have to achieve results significantly better than Eisenberg's untreated group in which 2% or 3% were "almost normal," 30% "fair-good" in the sense of being able to function with considerable close support, and the remainder requiring custodial care in an institution or at home.

Rutter (1967) found four factors related to outcome: (1) testable IQ; (2) speech development; (3) severity of the process; and (4) schooling.

1. *IQ.* There is a widespread attitude among clinicians that psychotic children are "highly intelligent" despite low performance on standard IQ tests (Kanner, 1972; Rimland, 1964; Anthony, 1958). This attitude has led to the exclusion of psychotic children from classes for the retarded based on what appear to be false premises. The exclusion itself would not be so bad were it not for the fact that these children are then given no formal education at all. Many states, in their zeal to prevent nonretarded children from being placed in classes for the retarded, have gone so far as to believe that all psychotic children, by virtue of that diagnosis, are not retarded. Rutter shows that IQ testing at age five or six correlates highly with outcome. In this study of sixty-three psychotic and sixty-three nonpsychotic but disturbed controls, eighteen or nineteen psychotic "untestable" children were found to have "very poor" outcome at follow-up. All of the children with a better outcome had testable IQs greater than 60. Moreover, the academic achievements of psychotic children were similar to the nonpsychotic controls of the same age, sex, and IQ. The study demonstrates that psychotic children, like normal children, tend to show stable IQs from age six.

2. *Speech.* Lack of speech development is often a symptom of retarded development. Rutter also found results similar to Eisenberg in that a child who was thought possibly deaf and who had no useful speech predicted poor outcome. Speed here appears to have been a function of intelligence.

3. *Severity of the Process.* The more flagrant the symptoms of psychosis, the worse the prognosis. In general, those children with the lowest IQs and the poorest speech also showed the most flagrant psychotic behavior.

4. *Schooling.* Children able to get an education had much better outcome than those who had little or no schooling. This finding has relevance for educators and clinicians in that it suggests that education can make a significant difference in outcome. Behavioral approaches may in this area have the greatest potential. Still, ability to be educated is a function of IQ, and ability to tolerate education in the Rutter study may speak more to the intelligence of the child and severity of the process, rather than the education per se, as critical to outcome. Lotter (1974) reports similar findings.

Finally, DeMyer et al. (1973) report on a twelve-year-follow-up of 120 autistic children treated largely with behavior therapy. Their results: 1–2% recovery to normal; 5–15% borderline; 16–25% fair; and 60–75% poor. The best predictor of functional capacity was rating at intake. Performance IQ and severity of illness were next.

What these studies indicate is that no single approach to date has been convincingly demonstrated as superior to any other in affecting ultimate outcome in childhood psychosis. Behavior modification approaches appear to be superior in developing specific behaviors in a relatively short period of time, but may not affect ultimate prognosis. The treatment of choice for the most severely disturbed of these children is, therefore, special education with strong emphasis on behavior modification techniques. For children less severely afflicted (Rutter's below 60 IQ group), a variety of approaches may well be useful so long as close support and quality instruction are provided.

Little has been said regarding the use of drugs in the treatment of these children. Needless to say, a variety of drugs and somatic treatments, including convulsive therapies, have been tried. Bender (1956) reports good response to convulsive therapy only in the late-onset schizophrenic group and not in the early-onset type which has been the subject of this article. Ferster and DeMyer (1961) reported superiority over placebo of perchlorperazine given psychotic children required to perform a matching-to-sample discrimination task. Rimland (1964) reports improvement with the drug Deanol, but little has been heard of this drug in the past ten years in the therapy of autism. Drugs are useful, however, in managing specific target behaviors, and psychotics and nonpsychotics often respond in similar fashion to their administration. Ritalin (methylphenidate) and d-amphetamine can be used for the hyperactivity of psychotic as well as nonpsychotic children. So-called major tranquilizers (Thorazine, Mellaril, Taractan, Stelazine, Navane, Moban, etc.) are also used to control hyperactivity, aggression, and impulsivity. These drugs are useful adjuncts and will continue to be used into the near future. They generally cannot be expected to affect ultimate outcome. Sedatives are not advised and often worsen the undesirable behavior. Drugs are all potentially dangerous, should be used judiciously, and should not be used as a substitute for other techniques described in this chapter.

The evidence to date indicates that childhood psychoses are syndromes of central nervous system dysfunction. It is likely that only research in neurochemistry can hope to eventually discover the causes and suggest specific treatments. In the meantime we should avail ourselves of whatever proves effective in medicine, education, and rehabilitation to maximize potentials for whatever the future may bring.

REFERENCES

Anthony E. J., An experimental approach to the psychopathology of childhood autism. *British Journal of Medical Psychology*, 1958, *31*, 211–225.

Bender, L., Childhood schizophrenia, a clinical study of 100 schizophrenic children. *American Journal of Orthopsychiatry*, 1947, *17*, 40–56.

Bender, L., Schizophrenia in childhood — its recognition, description, and treatment. *American Journal of Orthopsychiatry*, 1956, *26*, 499–506.

Bender, L., The life course of children with autism and mental retardation. In F. J. Menolascino, (ed), *Psychiatric aspects of mental retardation*, New York: Basic Books, 1970.

Bergmann, P., and Escalona, S., Unusual sensitivies in very young children. *Psychoanalytic Study of the child,* 1949, *3–4,* 333–352.

Berlin, I. N., and Szurek S. A., *Clinical studies in childhood psychoses.* New York: Brunney/ Mazel, 1973.

Bettelheim, B., Schizophrenia as a reaction to extreme situations. *American Journal of Orthopsychiatry,* 1956, *26,* 507–519.

Bettelheim, B., *The empty fortress.* New York: Free Press, 1967.

Bettelheim, B., *A home for the heart.* New York: Knopi, 1974.

Betz, B., Study of tactics for resolving the autistic behavior in the psychotherapy of the schizophrenic personality. *American Journal of Psychiatry,* 1947, *104,* 267–273.

Boatman, M. J., and Szurek, S. A., A clinical study of childhood schizophrenia. In D. D. Jackson (ed.), *The etiology of schizophrenia,* New York: Basic Books, 1969.

Breger L., Comments on "Building social behavior in autistic children by use of electric shock." *Journal of Experimental Research in Personality,* 1965, *1,* 110–113.

Breger, I., and McGaugh, J., Critique and reformation of "learning theory" approaches to psychotherapy and neurosis. *Psychological Bulletin,* 1965, *63,* 338–358.

Chess, S., Autism in children with congenital rubella. *Journal of Autism and Childhood Schizophrenia,* 1971, *1,* 33–47.

Churchill, D. W., Psychotic children and behavior modification. *American Journal of Psychiatry,* 1969, *125,* 1585–1590.

Creak, M., Childhood psychosis: a review of 100 cases. *British Journal of Psychiatry,* 1963, *109,* 84–89.

Creak, M., Schizophrenic syndrome in childhood. *Developmental Medicine and Child Neurology,* 1964, *6,* 530–535.

Creak, M., Diagnostic and treatment variations in child psychoses and mental retardatiion. In F. J. Menolascino (ed.), *Psychiatric approaches to mental retardation,* New York: Basic Books, 1970.

Delacato, C., *The ultimate stranger.* New York: Doubleday, 1974.

DeMyer, M. K., and Ferster, C. B., Teaching new social behavior to schizophrenic children. *Jouranl of the American Academy of Child Psychiatry,* 1962, *1,* 443–461.

DeMyer, M. K.; Barton, S.; DeMyer, W. E.; Norton, J. A.; Allen, J.; Steele, R., Prognosis in autism: a follow-up study. *Journal of Autism and Childhood Schizophrenia,* 1973, *3,* 199–246.

DeSanctis, S., On some varieties of dementia praecox. In John Howells (ed.), *Modern Perspective in International Child Psychiatry,* New York: Brunner/Mazel, 1971.

Eisenberg, L., The autistic child in adolescence. *American Journal of Psychiatry,* 1956, *112,* 607–612.

Eisenberg, L., and Kanner, I., Early infantile autism 1943–1955. *American Journal of Orthopsychiatry,* 1956, *26* 554–556.

Eisenberg, L., The course of childhood schizophrenia. *Archives of Neurology and Psychiatry,* 1958, *78,* 69–83.

Fenickel, C., Special education as the basic therapeutic tool in treatment of severely disturbed children. *Journal Autism and Childhood Schizophrenia,* 1974, *4,* 177–186.

Ferster, C. B., Positive reinforcement and behavioral effect of autistic children. *Child Development,* 1961, *32,* 437–456.

Ferster, C. B., and DeMyer, M., The development of performances in autistic children in an automatically controlled environment. *Journal of Chronic Disease,* 1961, *13,* 312–345.

Ferster, C. B., and DeMyer, M. K., Increased performances of an autistic child with prechlorperazine administration. *Journal of Experimental Analysis of Behavior,* 1961, *4,* 84–89.

Ferster, C. B., and DeMyer, M. K., A method for the experimental analysis of the behavior of autistic children. *American Journal of Orthopsychiatry*, 1962, *32*, 89–98.

Fish, B., Involvements of the C.N.S. in infants with schizophrenia. *A.M.A. Archives of Neurology*, 1960, *2*, 115–122.

Fish, B., The study of motor development in infancy and its relationship to psychological functioning. *American Journal of Psychiatry*, 1961, *117*, 1113–1118.

Gittelmann, M., and Birch, H. G., Childhood schizophrenia intellect, neurologic status, perinatal risk, prognosis, and family pathology. *Archives of General Psychiatry*, 1967, *17*, 16–25.

Goldfarb, W., *Childhood schizophrenia*. Cambridge: Harvard Press, 1961.

Havelkova, M., Follow-up study of 71 children diagnosed as psychotic in pre-school age. *American Journal of Orthopsychiatry*, 1968, *38*, 846–856.

Heller, T., About dementia infantalis (translation of article originally published in 1930). In J. Houcils (ed.), *Modern perspectives in international child psychiatry*. New York: Brunner/Mazel, 1971.

Hewitt, F., Teaching speech to an autistic child through operant conditioning. *American Journal of Orthopsychiatry*, 1965, *35*, 927–936.

Hingten, J. N.; Sanders, B. J.; and DeMyer, M. K., Shaping cooperative responses in early childhood schizophrenic. In L. P. Ullmann and L. Krasner, (eds.), *Case studies in behavior modification*. New York: Holt, 1965.

Hingten, J. N., and Churchill, D. W., Differential effects of behavior modification in four mute autistic boys. In D. W. Churchill, G. D. Alpern, and M. K. DeMyer, (eds.) *Infantile autism*. Springfield, Ill.: Charles Thomas, 1971.

Jones, F. H.; Simmons, J. Q.; and Frankel, F., An extinction procedure for eliminating self-destructive behavior in a nine-year-old autistic girl. *Journal of Autism and Childhood Schizophrenia*, 1974, *4*, 241–250.

Kallmann, F., and Roth, B., Genetic aspects of preadolescent schizophrenia. *American Journal of Psychiatry*, 1956, *112*, 599–606.

Kanner, L., Autistic disturbances of affective contact. *The Nervous Child*, 1943, *2*, 217–250.

Kanner, L., Follow-up study of eleven autistic children originally reported in 1943. *Journal of Autism and Childhood Schizophrenia*, 1971, *1*, 119–145.

Kanner, L., *Child psychiatry*, 4th ed. Springfield, Ill.: Charles Thomas, 1972.

Kanner, L., *Childhood psychosis: initial studies and new insights*. Washington, D.C.: Winston, 1973.

King, P., Early infantile autism and schizophrenia. Paper read at 128th annual meeting of the American Psychiatric Association. Anaheim, California, May 5–9, 1975.

Knobloch H., and Pasamanick B., *Developmental diagnosis*, 3rd ed. New York: Harper & Row, 1974.

Kraepelin E., *Dementia praecox*. Translated by M. Barclay. Edinburgh: Livingston, 1919.

Kringlen, E., Schizophrenia in twins: an epidemiologic study. *Psychiatry*, 1966, *29*, (2).

Leff, R., Behavior modification and childhood psychosis. In A. Gragiano (ed.). *Behavior therapy with children* 1971, Chicago: Aldine-Atherton.

Lockyer, L., and Rutter, M., A five-to-fifteen year follow-up study of infantile psychosis in psychological aspects. *British Journal of Psychiatry*, 1963, *115*, 865–882.

Lotter, V., Epidemiology of autistic conditions in young children — part 1: prevalance. *Social Psychiatry*, 1966, *1*, 3, 124–137.

Lotter, V., Epidemiology of autistic conditions in young children. In: some characteristics of parents and children. *Social Psychiatry*, 1967, *1*, 163–173.

Lotter, V., Factors related to outcome in autistic children. *Journal of Autism and Childhood Schizophrenia*, 1974, *4*, 263–277.

Lovaas, O. I.; Schaeffer, B.; and Simmons, J. Q., Experimental studies in childhood schizophrenia: building social behavior using electric shock. *Journal of Experimental Research in Personality*, 1965, *1*, 99–109.

Lovaas, O. I.; Freitag, G.; Gold, V. J.; Kassorla, I. C., Experimental studies in childhood schizophrenia: analysis of self-destructive behavior. *Journal of Experimental Child Psychology*, 1965, *2*, 67–34.

Lovaas, O. I.; Berberick J. P.; Perloff B. F.; and Schaeffer, B., Acquisition of imitative speech by schizophrenic children. *Science* 1966, *151*, 705–707.

Lovaas O. I.; Freitas L.; Nelson, K.; and Whalen, C., The establishment of imitation and its use for the development of complex behavior in schizophrenic children. *Behavior Research and Therapy*, 1967, *5*, 171–181.

Lovaas O. I. and Simmons, J. Q., Manipulation of self-destruction in three retarded children. *Journal of Applied Behavior Analysis*, 1969, *2*, 143–157.

Lovaas, O. I.; Litrownik, A.; and Mann, R., Response latencies to auditory stimuli in autistic children engaged in self-stimulatory behavior. *Behavior Research and Therapy*, 1971, *9*, 39–49.

Lovaas O. I., Considerations in the development of a behavioral treatment program for psychotic children. In D. Churchill, et al (eds.), *Infantile autism*. Springfield, Ill.: Charles Thomas, 1971.

Lovaas, O. I.; Schreibman, L.; Koegel, R.; and Rehm, R., Selective responding by austic children to multiple sensory input. *Journal of Abnormal Psychology*, 1971, *77*, 211–222.

Lovaas, O. I.; Koegel, R.; Simmons, J. Q.; and Long, J. S., Some generalization and follow-up measures on autistic children in behavior therapy. *Journal of Applied Behavior Analysis*, 1973, *6*, 131–166.

Lovaas, O. I.; Schreibman, L.; and Koegel, R. L., A behavior modification approach to the trreatment of autistic children. *Journal of Autism and Childhood Schizophrenia*, 1974, *4*, 111–129.

Mahler, M.; Ross, J.; and DeFries, Z., Clinical studies in benign and malignant cases of childhood psychosis. *American Journal of Orthopsychiatry*, 1949, *19*, 295–305.

Mahler, M. S.; Furer, M.; and Lettlage, C. F., Severe emotional disturbances in childhood: psychosis. In S. Arietis (ed.), *American handbook of psychiatry*, New York: Basic Books, 1959

Mahler, M., *On human symbiosis and the vicissitudes of individuation*, Vol. 1, New York: International Universities Press, 1967.

Menolascino, F. J., and Eaton, L., Psychoses of childhood. A five year follow-up study of experiences in a mental retardation clinic. *American Journal of Mental Deficiency*, 1967, *72*, 370–380.

Menolascino, F. J., The description and classification of infantile autism. In D. W. Churchill; C. D. Alpern, and M. K. DeMyer (eds.), *Infantile autism*. Springfield, Ill.: Charles Thomas, 1971.

Meyers, D., and Goldfarb, W., Psychiatric appraisal of parents and siblings of schizophrenic children. *American Journal of Psychiatry*, 1962, *118*, 902–915.

Ornitz, E., and Ritvo, E., Perceptual inconstancy in early infantile autism. *Archives of General Psychiatry*, 1968, *18*, 79–98.

Pitfield M., and Oppneheim, A. N., Child rearing attitudes of mothers of psychotic children. *Journal of Child Psychology and Psychiatry*, 1964, *5*, 51–57.

Pollin, W.; Stabener, J. R.; Masher, L.; and Tupin, J., Life history differences in identical twins discordant for schizophrenia. *American Journal of Orthopsysychiatry*, 1966, *36*, 492–501.

Potter, H. W., Schizophrenia in children. *American Journal of Psychiatry*, 1933, *89*, 1253–1269.

Rank, Beata Adaptation of the psychoanalytic technique for the treatment of young children with atypical development. *American Journal of Orthopsychiatry*, 1949, *19*, 130–139.

Rimland, B., *Infantile autism*, New York: Appleton-Century-Crofts, 1964.

Risley, T. and Wolf. M., Establishing functional speech in echolalic children. *Behavior Research & Therapy.* 1967, *5,* 73–88

Risley, T., The Effects and Side Effects of Punishing the Autistic Behaviors of a Defiant Child. *Journal of Applied Behavior Analysis,* 1968, *1,* 21–34.

Ritvo, E.; Cantwell, D.; Johnson, E.; Clements, M.; Benbrook, F.; Slagle, S.; Kelly, P., Ritz, M., Social class factors in autism. *Journal of Autism and Childhood Schizophrenia,* 1971, *1,* 297–310.

Ruttenberg, B. A., A psychoanalytic understanding of infantile autism and its treatment. In D. W. Churchill; Alpern, C. D., and DeMyer, M. K., (eds.), *Infantile autism,* 1971, Springfield, III : Charles Thomas.

Rutter, M. Medical aspects of the education of psychotic (autistic) children. In P.T.B. Western (ed), *Some approaches to teaching autistic children,* Oxford, Eng.: Pergamon Press, 1965.

Rutter, M., Greenfield, D., and Lockyer, L., A five-to-fifteen year follow-up study of infantile psychosis: II., Social and behavioral outcome. *British Journal of Psychiatry,* 1967, *113,* 1183–1199.

Rutter, M , and Lockyer, L., A five-to fifteen year follow-up study of infantile psychosis: I., Description of the sample. *British Journal of Psychiatry,* 1967. *113.*

Rutter, M., Concepts of autism: a review of research. In Chess and Thomas (eds.), *Annual progress in child psychiatry and child development,* New York; Brunner/Mazel, 1969.

Rutter, M., and Bartak, I., Causes of infantile autism: some considerations from recent research. *Journal of Autism and Childhood Schizophrenia,* 1971, Vol. 1.

Schachter, F.; Meyer, L. R.; and Loomis, E. A., Childhood schizophrenia and mental retardation: differential diagnosis before and after one year of psychotherapy. *American Journal of Orthopsychiatry,* 1962, *32,* 584–595.

A STRATEGY FOR THE DEVELOPMENT
OF MOTOR TRAINING ACTIVITIES

Lawrence T. McCarron, Ph.D.

The normal child's neuromuscular development proceeds in a predictable sequence. In the infant's first three months of life he shows reflexive responses such as sucking, startle and grasping reflexes. As the infant matures, the reflexive responses are extinguished and motor activities become progressively more integrated with purposeful movements under cortical control. At one year the child intentionally manipulates objects using his thumb and index finger in a pincer grasp and his balance ability improves from a sitting to a standing position. By the time the preschool child is four years of age, he can run, balance himself on one foot, jump a distance of several feet and assumes considerable mastery in handling objects. His muscle tonus has developed as a consequence of more vigorous participation in play activities. Precision and accuracy of movement become regulated by cortical control. When the normal child enters first grade, he has progressed through a sequence of developmental stages and has considerable mastery in motor skills.

Many educators contend that motor behaviors play an essential role in the learning process (Barsch, 1967, Cratty, 1968, Early, 1969, Frostig and Maslow, 1970, Getman et al., 1968, Kephart, 1971). The assumption that sensory-motor skills are related to learning skills tends to be supported by the fact that the majority of children who have special learning problems such as mental retardation or neurological dysfunction have measurable delays in motor development. Educators have observed that coordination skills are particularly important in learning. Barsch; (1967) and Kephart (1971) recommend that education curriculum for children with learning disabilities should be based on sensory-motor activities which can foster kinesthetic and body awareness as well as visual perception. While the interaction between sensory-motor skills and educational skills has been asserted, there is relatively little information concerning the specific function that sensory-motor skills play in the learning process. The thesis that sensory-motor abilities are essential to cognitive development and subsequent school performance is tenable, but research on the efficacy of visual-motor training to improve academic skills has not yet been demonstrated (Hammill, Goodman, and Wiederholt, 1973). In view of the purported importance that sensory-motor skills play in the educational process, there is a definite need to develop and evaluate a comprehensive program of motor training activities.

There are at least three major factors which might account for the limited advances in relating sensory-motor behaviors to educational performance.
1. There is a need for a systematic, theoretical position that defines the problem and specifies the role that sensory and neuromuscular skills play in the learning process.

2. There is a need for valid and standardized measures of sensory-motor abilities.
3. There is a need to develop a comprehensive curriculum of sensory-motor activities based on a theoretical model. The theoretical model provides the basis for selecting and sequencing particular motor training activities. Controlled studies can then evaluate the effectiveness of the compensatory programs in remediating specific problems in the learning process.

The purpose of the present paper is to briefly review some of the theoretical positions which attempt to define the problem and suggest various approaches to training motor skills. Secondly, a standardized measure of neuromuscular development which is based on a clinical neuropsychological perspective of motor development provides a method of evaluating each child's fine and gross motor skills. A case study is then presented to demonstrate a profile analysis of motor problems. The deficits indicated by the profile are used to compile motor training activities which are suited to the needs of the particular child.

Movigenic Theory

A movigenic or space-oriented approach to learning has been postulated by Barsch (1967). In the child's exploration of terrestrial space he acquires movement efficiency. Of particular importance is the development of gross motor movements of muscular strength, dynamic balance, body, spatial, and temporal awareness. The movigenic theory considers the relationship of movement development to learning efficiency. The learning experiences derived from physical movements as well as spatial and temporal awareness have a direct bearing on cognitive experiences and learning. Man is physiologically equipped for movement and experiences life through movement.

The movigenic perspective suggests a curriculum guide based on observations and evaluations of the learner's performance efficiency. Since all behavior, including reading, writing arithmetic and spelling can be considered to involve spatial and temporal orientation, the child's total experiences with his environment are to be observed and then structured to provide useful learning experiences from which the child builds a more complex level of behavior. While the movigenic perspective has heuristic value, it does not provide a systematic curriculum of motor training.

Internalized Organization

The perceptual training programs outlined by Early (1969), Kephart (1971) and Dunsing and Kephart (1965) are based on the assumption that a child can experience perceptual confusion and learning disabilities if he lacks internal organization and structure. A child needs an internalized organization or a structured motor base in order to handle incoming information from the environment. There is an interaction between the child's internalized structure or organized self awareness and the way he copes with his experiences. A functioning inner structure is instrumental in helping the child organize his perceptions and experiences in the world. If a child experiences inner confusion, he has difficulty handling the incoming environmental experiences which result in perceptual distortions and behavioral confusion.

The internal organization starts in infancy with total body movements. The developmental experiences help the child to become aware of and to differentiate body parts and functions. Body awareness and differentiation proceed in two directions (1) the proximodistal direction from the center of the body outward and (2) the cephalocaudal direction from the head to toe. From this theoretical perspective, the child first becomes aware of the center of the body including his trunk and shoulders. Body awareness proceeds to the outer extremities of elbows, forearms, wrists, hands, and fingers. In the cephalocaudal sequence, he first differentiates musculature in the neck area which allows movement of the arms, and evolves downward to the hips, legs and feet. The child initially has gross motor movements and gradually refines his movements to become more precise with control of complex movements. Motor training activities are designed to follow the proximodistal and cephalocuadal direction of development.

Sensory-Motor Training

The writings of Frostig and Maslow (1970) emphasize the importance of sensory motor skills and self-awareness in development. Retarded development may occur because of dysfunctions in the nervous system, environmental deprivation, as well as poorly integrated sensory motor experiences. The child's development of abilities is considered to follow a definite sequence. The first developmental stage is the sensory-motor phase with maximum development in the first two years of life. During this early phase of development there are four groups of sensory motor skills: (1) perceptual recognition of the environment (2) awareness of self as distinct from his environment (3) increased mastery in gross motor motility and (4) the development of finger and hand dexterity in grasping, releasing and manipulating objects. "The mastery of these four sensory-motor skills constitutes the child's first steps toward independence, ability to adapt to the demands of the environment, and toward future learning. Training in sensory-motor abilities is therefore a most important aspect of education" (p. 26). The earlier visual-motor training programs designed by Frostig and Horne (1964) emphasized perceptual and fine motor activities such as form recognition and drawing lines through a maze. This relatively structured program of perceptual and fine motor activities has been used rather extensively in schools, but the effectiveness of such activities in helping the learning disabled child remains questionable.

A recent emphasis by Frostig and Maslow (1970) is to help the child integrate gross motor activities. In a comparision of factor analytic studies Frostig and Maslow suggest that there are six common factors found in motor educational programs. The six factors include: (1) coordination and rhythm (2) speed and agility (3) flexibility (4) strength (5) balance and (6) endurance. A series of exercises such as "crab walk," "hot potato," etc., provide gross motor exercises for each of the six attributes of movement. The types of exercises described by Frostig and Maslow are frequently used by special education teachers working with youngsters with developmental problems.

Physiological Integration

An understanding of human behavior can be approached by viewing life functions as interrelated dynamic systems. The human body is composed of highly specialized organ systems which function as an integrated entity. A remarkable example of the specialized, yet integrated body functions is the pumping action of the heart to circulate blood which supplies oxygen and removes waste from the cells, while the kidney functions to cleanse the blood. The principle of physiological integration is also demonstrated by the functional relationship between muscles, bones and nerves. Skeletal muscles function by an arrangement of agonistic-antagonistic pairs. Movement involves the contraction and increased tonus of one muscle with the simultaneous relaxation and decreased tonus of the other. The smooth coordinations of movement requires the interaction and reciprocity of muscle systems. There is also an important relationship between muscles and bone structure. The muscle tonus exerts essential forces upon the growing bone. A balanced stimuli of muscle stressors is necessary for normal bone formation. When there is an imbalance in muscle tonus, the bones and limbs become malformed or do not grow properly. The muscles, in turn, are regulated by the nervous system. Motor acts are not entirely regulated by a narrowly circumscribed area of the cerebral cortex, but are controlled by a dynamic, interrelated structural organization of brain systems. A particular motor act involves several brain structures including the premotor cortex, cerebellum and basal ganglia. The concept of a dynamic, interrelated functional system explains the clinical observation that a local brain lesion does not result in a total loss of a function, but rather a disorganization of that function (Luria, 1966). Similarly, the remarkable neurophysiology of the brain has the capacity to structurally reorganize the connective pathways of cortex systems which account for the often observed recovery of impaired functions due to brain injury.

The dynamically related physiological and behavioral functions might be taken into consideration when teaching children with learning disabilities. The capacity to perform an academic task such as reading or writing involves multiple sensory modalities and highly integrated sensory-motor systems. Inability to perform a particular academic task can be the result of an impairment of a primary sensory-motor function, such as poor eye sight or hearing loss. Initial steps in the remediation of academic dysfunctions then, would consist of correcting the sensory impairment with glasses or a hearing aid as required. Of equal importance when assessing a child with a handicap condition is an analysis of the extent to which there is disorganization in the functioning of dynamically related neurophysiological systems. A systematic assessment of brain-behavior relationships provides a basis for formulating strategies of habilitation. Remediation consists of helping the child to organize and integrate his underlying neurological and physiological systems. The central concern of the educator is to provide the necessary sequence of experiences that assist the child to integrate neurophychological functions in order to perform relatively complex human behaviors.

Process Verses Task

There are several alternative approaches which can be used to help the child with a learning problem. Special educators often approach a problem from either a process or a task orientation. The process teacher asks the question "What's wrong with the child?" The assumption is that defective visual-motor or emotional processes are the underlying cause of the learning difficulty. It is assumed, for example, that the reading problem cannot be significantly improved until the underlying problems are resolved. The objectives of the process specialist are to isolate and remediate the perceptual-motor processes underlying the learning disability. Diagnostic and remedial tools consist of the Illinois Test of Psycholinguistic Abilities, the Frostig materials and exercises, and the Purdue Motor Programs.

The task oriented specialist, on the other hand, asks the question, "What's wrong with the child's reading?" The problem is defined in terms such as reading comprehension and phonic analysis. The task oriented specialist views the child at a performance level of behavior and is concerned with the specific academic task that is a problem for the child. The tools of his trade are the Durrell Analysis of Reading Difficulty, Gray Oral Reading Test, the Slingerland Screening Test for Learning Disabilities and other academic tests. If the child is found to have a reading difficulty, the specialist focuses upon the immediate task of teaching the child to read.

Whether one approaches learning disabilities from a process or a task orientation, an appropriate learning experience can help the child integrate his physiological and behavioral systems. Perhaps the main distinction between the process and task oriented specialist is the degree of behavioral complexity they attend to. When a child has only a mild impairment, the restructuring of experiences may not be required. His level of mastery and organization is sufficient to allow him to focus on the specific reading task. However, when there is a marked impairment and the reading task requires a level of difficulty and organization that is beyond the child's experience, he may require a more structured sequence of activities. The seriously impaired child needs more intensive and structured sensory-motor experiences to establish integration and organizational capacity. Before he can be expected to perform effectively on many educational tasks which require a relatively high level of functioning, he must first master rudimentary behaviors and neuropsychological processes. An educator's identification as a process or a task specialist may depend more upon the disability level of the children he works with, than upon any inherent advantage of one approach over the other.

Children with learning disabilities frequently have multiple dysfunctions, the way they process sensory and motor information, or in their expressive behaviors. When a child has a special problem in organizing his sensory-motor skills, a sequence of learning experiences with specific objectives may be designed. The following case study illustrates how a standardized-assessment procedure can be used to describe a child's neuromuscular abilities. The information derived from the assessment procedure is then used to suggest appropriate methods of remediation.

Case Study

Bill was jaundiced at birth following a prolonged labor and delivery time of 72 hours. The delivery was unusually difficult. His eating behavior was appropriate but he was described by the parents as a difficult and fussy baby. Bill was a very active infant and slept on the average only 5 hours each day. He crawled at 5 months, began walking at 11 months, but did not begin to vocalize until around 18 months and then only in monosyllables. He was still being toilet trained at age 4 years.

When Bill was first enrolled in kindergarten he was an extremely hyperactive child with excessive movement, distractibility and constant talking. He became easily frustrated and would clinch his fist and shake. Unfortunately, the parents were reportedly told by the teacher that he was "hopelessly retarded and would never fit into a public school system." He was referred to a community mental health and mental retardation center for evaluation. The mother's primary concern was what could be done to improve his extreme hyperactive, clumsy, and at times impulsive behavior.

Psychological testing was performed to determine Bill's level of intellectual and emotional functioning and to prescribe a program of treatment for the boy. The following tests were administered: Peabody Picture Vocabulary Test, Wechsler Intelligence Scale for Children, Draw-a-person, Bender Visual Motor Gestalt Test, Rorschach, Devereux Child Behavior Rating Scale, and the McCarron Assessment of Neuromuscular Development.

On the Peabody Picture Vocabulary Test Bill obtained a mental age of 8 years and a resulting Intelligence Quotient of 110. These results clearly contradict the subjective opinion of a "hopelessly retarded child" and indicate the need for a more comprehensive intellectual assessment. The Wechsler Intelligence Scale for Children revealed a Verbal Scale of IQ of 80 and a performance Scale IQ of 113 and a resulting Full Scale IQ of 95. Such a wide discrepancy between the verbal and performance scale are often indicative of specific learning disabilities, possibly attributed to minor neurological dysfunctions. His greatest deficits were in the areas requiring attention, auditory memory and the integration of perceptual-motor skills. Expressive verbal skills, while marked with poor articulation and slurring, were not noticeably deficient. The results of both the Peabody Picture Vocabulary Test and the Wechsler Intelligence Scale for Children supported the observation of appropriate receptive and expressive verbal skills, but suggested specific deficiencies in the auditory and perceptual motor areas.

259

Bill's reproductions of the Bender Visual-Motor Gestalt designs also indicated specific problems in perceptual confusion, perservation, poor spatial awareness and difficulties in integrating perceptual-motor skills. The quality of the drawings also suggested the need for further examination by an ophthamologist. Subsequently, visual problems were identified and corrected. The projective Rorschach and Draw-a-person tests revealed numerous confabulations, color naming, perserverations and distortions. The Draw-a-person was poorly executed with overlapping and heavily-drawn lines. In addition, emotional indicators suggested poor impulse control and heightened but poorly modulated affect which are frequently associated with an organically impaired youngster. The psychometric profile of verbal-cognitive skills was used to generate a prescriptive program of learning activities for Bill. Specific educational activities were recommended to the teacher from the Computerized Assessment Programming (CAP) system (Linkenhoker and McCarron 1974).

Assessment of Motor Skills

The McCarron Assessment of Neuromuscular Development (MAND) (McCarron, 1976) was used to provide a profile analysis of Bill's neuromuscular skills and generate suggestions for a motor training program. The assessment procedure consists of ten motor tasks that are carefully observed and objectively scored. The five fine motor tasks include: (1) Placing beads in a box, (2) Placing beads on a rod, (3) Rapid finger tapping, (4) Turning a bolt into a nut, and (5) Sliding a peg on a rod as slowly as possible. The five gross motor tasks include: (6) Dynamic hand strength, (7) Finger-nose-finger movements, (8) Jumping, (9) Tandum heel to toe walk, and (10) Standing on one foot. A factor analysis of these tasks has revealed that the test measures essentially four motor factors: (I) Persistent Control, (II) Muscle Power, (III) Kinesthetic Integration and (IV) Bimanual Dexterity. A profile of Bill's fine and gross motor skills and scores for each of the four factors is presented in Figure 1.

Persistent Control

The first factor, Persistent Control, involves the consistent regulation of a pattern of motor movements. A continuous maintenance and regulated control of muscle systems is required while moving a peg as slowly as possible and in the synchronized movement of alternately touching the tip of the nose and tip of the finger. An underlying behavior for each of these tasks is controlled eye-hand coordination. The tasks require the ability to focus attention while inhibiting extranious motor movements. In addition to the integration of perceptual-motor skills, proprioceptive feedback also assists in the maintenance of spatial relationships and in the continuous regulation of movement. The repeated sequence of body motions such as eating or walking involve a particular pattern and sequence of body motions. The sequenced pattern of movement is learned with practice and neurologically inte-

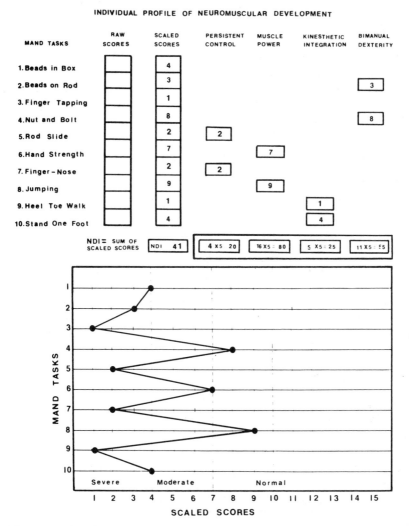

Figure 1. Profile of neuromuscular development for a hyperactive, learning disabled child.

grated in the premotor cortex and cerebellum. With continued learning and experience the pattern of movements becomes more precise.

The important distinction to be made between a normal child and a child with developmental problems, specifically when there is a dysfunction in the premotor cortex or cerebellum, is a loss in coordinating a pattern of movements; but not a loss of single discrete movements of the muscles. The difficulties emerge when the individual is required to integrate several muscle groups into a smooth sequence of

261

movements or have simultaneous functioning of several muscle groups. The child may have acceptable performance with segmented tasks, but has difficulty integrating the more complex sequence of movements that require diverse muscle groups.

The inadvertant teaching of splinter skills is a related problem. A splinter skill is a motor behavior which has been learned to accomplish a specific task, but which has little generalization to related activities. The child has simply learned an isolated segment of motor acts. He performs discrete, highly circumscribed movements in order to accomplish a designated task; but he fails to integrate these localized motor acts as part of his generalized movement pattern.

Muscle Power

The second factor which emerged can be considered a muscle power dimension. In the upper extremities the tasks involve dynamic hand strength. In the lower extremities the tasks involve the dynamic extension of the leg muscles in jumping. The healthy functioning of the skeletal muscles are reflected in the power factor. The greatest muscle power is achieved when the muscles are contracted simultaneously. Weak dynamic muscle strength can be due to poor coordination in the simultaneous contraction of muscle units. Additional causes might include inadequate diet, physical fatigue, or a lack of development and use of skeletal muscles. It is conjectured that improved diet and opportunities for motor activities can result in improved power motor skills.

Kinesthetic Integration

The third factor generated from the matrix can be interpreted as a kinesthetic integration dimension. A basic function of the cerebellum and vestibular system is the smooth coordination of muscular movements and the maintenance of posture. The control of balance and orientation of the body in space is derived from positional cues and from body sensations in the muscles, tendons and joints. The maintenance of equilibrium and movement is a common denominator to the gross motor behaviors of walking heel to toe and balancing on one foot. The cerebellum integrates information from the motor cortex as well as proprioceptive feedback from muscles, tendons and joints. When the body is in motion, a function of the cerebellum is to anticipate the spatial position of the body. Balance and equilibrium can be maintained through the cerebellum which has a function in the anticipation of body position and integration of the corrective signals to retain balance. The cerebellum and motor areas of the cortex are therefore involved in the synthesis and coordination of motor systems. Dysfunction of the vestibular system and cerebellum result in a loss of ability to anticipate spatial position of the body with falling or slow movements to compensate for the defect.

The purkinje cells of the cerebellum are particularly sensitive to damage by an anoxic condition. Children with a medical history of marked anoxia (a sustained lack of oxygen to the brain cells) often evidence problems of disequilibrium or swaying, falling and problems in perceiving spatial relationships. The effects of a marked anoxic condition may be indicated at birth with APGAR scores of 5 or less. The physician obtains an APGAR score by observing the infants vital signs at birth. Healthy vital signs include a fast heart rate, active respiration, pink skin color, good muscle tone, and reflexes. Children who have sustained a prolonged anoxic condition at birth, or who have been subjected to infections and harmonal dysfunction in the prenatal period have a much higher probability of experiencing learning disorders and delayed neuromuscular development.

Bimanual Dexterity

The fourth factor can be considered as a bimanual dexterity factor. The tasks include the use of both hands for manipulation of nuts and bolts, and in placing beads on a rod. Efficiency of performance is measured by a standard unit of time. The task involves the coordinated use of both hands for efficient and rapid manipulation of the materials. Individuals with hemiparesis or a weakness to one side of the body can often experience difficulties with these tasks.

Curriculum Recommendations

The results of the individual's profile of motor abilities are used to plan a strategy of motor training activities and intervention techniques for each of the four primary motor factors. When an educator has limited training and experience in formulating motor training curricula, the professional consultation from a physical therapist or person with skills in adaptive physical education for the handicapped can often be extremely helpful. Using the case study as a guide, let us review some of the possible intervention techniques that can be of help to this particular child. An initial inspection of the entire motor profile presented in Figure 1 indicates significant problems in general neuromuscular development. A moderate degree of neuromuscular disability is represented by the neuromuscular development index (NDI) of 41. It can be noted that the raw scores for each of the motor tasks has been converted to scaled scores from age related tables of norms provided in the MAND manual. The sum of the scaled scores for reach of the ten tasks provides the neuromuscular development index. A normal child can be expected to obtain an NDI of 100. Similarly, the factor scores for a normal individual can also be expected to be 100. Scores between 40 and 70 represent moderate disabilities, while scores of 39 and below represent severe disabilities. Bill's profile is at least one, and in most instances two standard deviations below the mean for his age and the profile can be interpreted as indicating significant delays in neuromuscular development. The particular profile configuration, with an NDI of less than 50, and an elevation in muscle power skills above 70 while the other factors are low is frequently encountered with children who have a paradoxical response to stimulant medication and are variously described as manifesting hyperkinetic behaviors and learning disabilities. A program of motor training for this child would require activities in each of the four areas. When the MAND scores are used as input data with the Computerized Assessment Programming (CAP) Systems, (Linkenhoker and McCarron, 1974) the following statements and intervention suggestions may be printed out for the teacher or educational diagnostician. Several of these suggestions are based on the work of Kephart (1971), Frostig (1964, 1970) as well as activities currently used in special education programs.

DIAGNOSTIC STATEMENT
ASSESSMENT OF NEUROMUSCULAR DEVELOPMENT

Persistent Control

This individual demonstrates poor ability to persistently control and visually monitor a pattern of motor movements. His movements are awkward and impulsive, with poor coordination in the sequencing of a pattern of repeated movements.

Intervention Suggestions

Staff teacher and parental counseling recommentations:
Training tips: Activities should be structured to allow the child to increase his attention span and persistence with a task. The activities can be varied, changing from one activity to another, in order to accommodate the child's tolerance for persistence with a particular task. A variety of activities are initially presented for a short period of time and then systematically increased in duration. This behavioral engineering approach is particularly effective with hyperactive, distracted children. The duration of a task is gradually increased to retain his interest and persistence. The suggested tasks are intended only as representative examples of activities. The teacher is encouraged to devise and select a variety of activities which involve similar behavioral components of integrating patterns of motor movements.

The persistent control and integration of a pattern of movements involve ocular pursuit skills. In the following ocular pursuit training exercises it is crucially important that the child receive the necessary feedback to know when he is performing adequately. If during training, the child loses the target, stop the movment of the target and ask the child to re-fixate on it. Such remarks, as "Where is it?", "Where did it go?" will usually catch the child's attention and cause him to fixate again.

Always make sure that the child's eyes are centered on the target. Begin with a large ball such as a beach ball and gradually decrease the size as the child improves. The child places both hands against the ball while the teacher moves the ball. The ball is now held between two sets of hands. Move the ball in a pattern and provide as much resistance and kinesthetic information as desired by pressing against the

264

ball. Continue to observe the child's behavior and after several short sessions proceed to alternative activities.

Marsden ball exercises: This technique requires the child to follow a moving target and respond to it in terms of its position, it requires accurate timing and a good synthesis between the visual and motor systems. When a child has serious visual-motor problems the teacher should begin with basic procedures and gradually increase the complexity of the task. The child visually tracks the ball while his hands move with the ball. The additional proprioceptive cues help the child compensate for his difficulty in visual tracking. Eventually the child can learn to visually track the large ball without the use of his hands. A small size ball is used while the speed of movement is progressively increased and a variety of movement patterns are introduced. The Marsden ball exercises require that the child follow a moving target and respond to it in terms of positional and spatial relationships. It requires accurate timing and a good synthesis between the visual and motor systems.

A soft ball (tennis ball size) is suspended by a string from the ceiling. (Attach the string to the ball by putting a small cup hook into the rubber as a fastener.) The ball can be swung laterally or in a circular motion about the child. By alternating the length of the string, the timing of the swing can be slowed or increased.

The child stands at one side about an arms length from the ball with the pivet string directly in front of him. Let the ball swing in front of him by its own weight; there is no need to push or strike it. As the ball passes in front of him, he is instructed to reach out and contact the ball in one movement. He cannot put his finger in the path of the ball and wait for it to touch him. He is given different starting points for his finger each time he thrusts out with a definite movement. Begin first at shoulder height, then at eye level and finally at hip level. He is always to thrust out in one steady movement, not in a searching manner.

The child starts the ball in motion and each time the ball returns to him he hits the ball with a designated part of the body such as shoulder, elbow, hip, etc. Two children may participate in the activity by hitting the ball back and forth to each other. If the ball is suspended a few feet away from a wall, the child can bounce the ball off the wall and try to dodge the ball so it does not hit him. These activities are enjoyable and initiate spontaneity of movement in the children.

DIAGNOSTIC STATEMENT: FINE AND GROSS MOTOR ASSESSMENT

Muscle Power

This individual demonstrates weak muscle power. His muscle tonus is poor and he has limited stamina. Vigorous play activities are usually avoided and he may appear listless and tired at times.

Intervention Suggestions

Staff, Teachers and Parental Counseling Recommendations

Training Tips: Weak muscle power may be due to an inadequate diet, physical fatigue, a lack of development and use of skeletal muscles or poor coordination in the simultaneous contraction of muscle units. Very low muscle strength is also observed in various syndromes of mental retardation and in muscular dystrophy. It is important to determine if the child's diet is adequate. Many disadvantaged youngsters do not receive sufficient nutrition and provision should be made to assure that a child has had breakfast and lunch either at home or in the school.

Attention span and educational motivation will often increase substantially when the nutritional needs of the child are met.

The child's sleeping habits should also be determined. Interruptions, excessive noise, parental conflicts, and other environmental factors can contribute to poor sleep. In exceptional cases, a depressed child with emotional stress in the home will have difficulty sleeping as well as other depressive symptoms such as somatic complaints, poor appetite, excessive worry and acting out behavior. If depressive symptoms are evidenced referal of the family to a community mental health center is appropriate.

If the child does not have circulatory or cardiac problems and poor muscle strength is the result of a lack of development and inadequate use of skeletal muscles, he should be encouraged to participate in play activities as well as the compensatory training program. Use the activities described under kinesthetic integration as well as supervised trampoline exercises, wresting, gymnastics and swimming.

DIAGNOSTIC STATEMENT: FINE AND GROSS MOTOR ASSESSMENT

Bimanual Dexterity

This individual demonstrates poor eye-hand coordination and manual dexterity and is slow in tasks that require well developed fine motor coordination. He has difficulty in controlling fine motor activities that involve the use of both hands.

Intervention Suggestions

Staff, Teacher and Parental Counseling Recommendations.

In the classroom, watch the child's performance. If, when he is writing or drawing and the shoulder and arm are stiff and rigid or just the reverse, if they are limp and without tonus, these are indications that fine motor activity may not be integrated with his other activities. In this event, it is a good idea to temporarily stress the gross motor exercises until there is a good balance between the fine and gross motor skills. The intent is to help the child integrate patterns of gross motor activities. Gradually introduce fine motor skills to be integrated with his accomplished gross motor activities. Appropriate activities include finger painting in which the child is allowed the freedom for large body movements as well as more refined movements. The repetition of designs such as circles & spirals which are progressively decreased in size help integrate body movement and spatial awareness. Working in clay with squeezing, pulling, rolling, and pounding are enjoyable activities and help develop integration. As the child's skills improve he can be encouraged to make objects and animals.

Training Tips: Have the child pick up small objects such as pennies, marbles, beans, and straight pins. Manipulate the objects with both hands and place them through a small opening in a box. The size of the opening can be made progressively smaller. Begin with these exercises untimed and later have the child increase his speed in a race against the clock. Competitive exercises of this type can also be used in the classroom between individuals or groups of children. (1) The child closes his hands into tight fists and then opens them widely. Repeat the exercise several times. (2) Holding his hands up, palms facing each other, have the child move his thumbs in and out. Have him move his fingers up and down. This should be done alternating each finger. (3) Have the child manipulate blocks, puzzles and other construction objects with both hands. Structure various construction tasks which require the coordinated use of both hands.

Place a half sheet of newspaper in front of him. With one hand the child crumbles the paper into a tight ball. When the paper disappears into his hands allow him to smooth it out with both hands and repeat the task with the other hand. This task may be continued as long as the paper and the child's interest will allow.

Have a number of children sit in a circle on the floor. Give one child a ping-pong ball. Move the ball about the circle by: (1) flipping the ball, using thumbs and pointer fingers. (2) batting the ball with the front or back of the hands. (3) toss the ball back and forth between the hands.

In the development of eye-hand coordination, the initial developmental stage involves teaching the eyes to follow the hand. Training should then involve tasks in which the hand moves in a controlled fashion and the child watches his hand as it moves. The following recommendations are fashioned around this approach:

Provide the child with a large sheet of (butcher) wrapping paper and pencil and encourage him to scribble. Scribbling provides a good bridge between a simple perceptual-motor match where the eyes follows the hand and the more complex perceptual activities. Begin the exercise with large movements to emphasize the relationship between the fine motor activity of the fingers and hands and the overall motor activities of the body. The child should be encouraged to watch his hand and to attend to the perceptual information created by the scribbling.

To a piece of ¾ inch dowel, 12 inches to 18 inches long, attach a narrow streamer of crepe paper ribbon. The child grasps the dowel with both hands and moves his hands in a circular pattern. The streamer follows the pattern of the movement and sets up a similar pattern as it moves through the air. The child's attention is drawn to the movement of his hands and he visually follows the target stimulus.

The use of templates offers external guides and tactual-kinesthetic cues for the hand. A template is a pattern cut out of cardboard or similar materials. Simple forms (circles, squares, triangles, etc.) are frequently used. The child inserts his finger, a pencil, chalk, etc. in the cutout and runs it around the boundaries of the form. The teacher should pay particular attention to the control of the movement and provide feedback for the child on his performance.

Dexterity and Motor Speed

A board drilled with holes through which bolts of various sizes are permanently inserted and fitted with free turning nuts is very useful for training dexterity and motor speed. The child is required to screw the nuts onto and off the bolts in timed and untimed exercises. Encourage him to use wrist action; discourage turning the arm at the shoulder. This device also helps train size judgments and size matching.

Prepare a gadget board with extensive series of locks, latches, plugs, zippers, levers and varied buttons and snaps of all kinds. Go through timed and untimed exercises until the child masters the board in an acceptable period of time. Alternate between the right and left hand and the use of both hands. Provide pick-up sticks or marble games and puzzles for the child to manipulate.

DIAGNOSTIC STATEMENT: FINE AND GROSS MOTOR ASSESSMENT

Kinesthetic Integration

This individual demonstrates poor performance on tasks requiring balance and the coordination of large muscle systems in the legs and trunk. His walking gait and posture may appear awkward. The child has difficulties in gross motor activities and in body spatial relationships.

Intervention Suggestions

Staff, Teacher and Parental Counseling Recommendations:
Training Tips: It is important to insure that the child learns gross perceptual motor skills in terms of his entire body before proceeding to finer motor control skills. The learning sequence begins with overall body activities and is gradually focused on integrating fine motor skills so that perceptual motor control remains related to the child's total body movements.

Basic Body Movements

Elephant-walk: Have the child bend forward from the waist, allowing his arms to hang limply with hands clasped. Walk forward by taking big steps.
Crab-walk: Have the child sit on the floor, placing his hands on the floor behind him. Have him raise his body so that he is standing on his hands and feet. Have him walk on his hands and feet in a backward direction. Move slowly.

Back-twins: Two children stand back to back with elbows linked. From this position they attempt to sit down slowly and then try to stand again.

Yo-Yo bounce: The child stretches his arms out in front, bends his knees and lowers himself to a squatting position. He then straightens out his legs and stands.

Leg-crossover: Have the child lie on his back. Keeping the right leg in place, have him cross the left over the right and place the foot flat on the floor. Alternate legs.

Scissors: Have the child lie on his back. Keeping legs straight, have him raise one leg and lower to the floor. Repeat with the other leg.

Bicycle: Have the child lie on his back with his feet in the air. Imitate the riding of a bicycle in the air by holding one leg in the air, while the other is lowered toward the chest. Knees are bent when lowering. Alternate the legs.

Have the child practice walking. Make sure that arms and legs alternate and swing freely. Alternate walking patterns: Have the child walk backwards on tiptoes with arms overhead. Have him go up and down on the tips of his toes. The activities can be performed with music and rhythm. A balance beam (walking board) four by four inches and ten feet in length can be used with a variety of exercises. The children walk forward and backward looking at a spot on the wall. They walk using special steps such as kneeling, deep knee bends, sitting, etc.

Boys particularly enjoy balance boards which are simply made of a one foot square plank fastened to a four inch square. Balance and agility are improved with these tasks.

The use of hula hoops allow a variety of gross motor and integrated visual-motor exercises. Have the children "find as many ways to use your hoop as you can." The hoop can be swirled, rolled, used to jump through while rolling or swung with the hand.

Have the children jump on and off a very large inflated truck tire tube. Several children can hold hands and jump on the tube together. These activities develop muscle strength. Rubber balls can be thrown against the tire tube and caught. A variety of games can be improvised for a pair of children. The aforementioned activities are a small sample of tasks which serve to demonstrate the basic motor behaviors which can be included in a motor training curriculum.

Principles of Learning

The computer printout of recommendations and training tips provides only a limited sample of possible motor training activities. Careful observation of the child's behavior with continued evaluation of his progress will suggest the appropriate activities to be introduced each day. The teacher can expand upon and improvise activities to match the particular needs of each child. In addition to identifying a profile of neuromuscular abilities and improvising a program of motor activities there are a few basic principles of learning which the teacher may find useful in working with the children. The three principles of learning to be considered are reinforcement, transference, and level of difficulty.

Reinforcement

The child's motivation and ego involvement in the activities are facilitated by positive reinforcement. The teacher's assertive and encouraging compliments focus on the desirable behaviors, while minimal attention is given to undesirable behaviors. The shaping of desirable behaviors is accomplished by giving the child positive feedback immediately following his performance. Reinforce any small step toward the desired behavior, but have realistic expectations and don't insist on 100% perfect performance on the first series of trials. Immediate reinforcement following the child's response is particularly important in teaching new tasks. During the early learning stages, reinforce every concrete response. As the child improves and the responses become more consistent, require more correct responses before reinforcement. Enjoy the activities with the child and encourage him to participate according to his own style and capability.

Transference

Transference of learning is facilitated when the new task has similar elements found in a previously learned skill. The ease with which a new task is mastered depends upon the overlap of elements between the new task and previously learned skills. The intent is to structure the curriculum so that the new activities involve many of the previously learned skills. The teacher systematically extends the level of difficulty and diversity of the required skills. For example, the placement of objects in a container is made progressively more difficult by decreasing the size of the opening, introducing different shaped objects and requiring the child to use alternate hands. Although variations and more complex motor activities are introduced, the essential pattern of movements underlying the task is repeated and integrated in a variety of activities. The repetition of diverse motor activities helps establish the necessary pattern of movement.

Level of Difficulty

Motivation and positive anticipation can be retained by selecting activities that are within the ability range and can be successfully performed by the child. There will be some day to day variability in the child's interest, so allow a flexible program of activities. The program of activities is developed with the objectives of improving sensory motor performance as well as enhancing the child's self concept. Intermittently introduce a motor activity with a relatively high degree of difficulty to challenge the child, but avoid frustrating experiences. Allow the child sufficient freedom and flexibility to enjoy the spontaneity of the activities, but at the same time provide sufficient structure and set limits for acceptable behavior. During a motor training session it is preferable to simultaneously work on improving several body areas such as legs, arms and eye-hand tracking, rather than restrict activities to have an isolated focus. A variety of motor activities which involve different muscle systems of the body help retain interest and allow spontaneity in the children.

A child may have different rates of development in different parts of his neuromuscular system. This variability in a child's rate of development should be taken into consideration when designing a program of activities for him. The child's emotional development should also be taken into consideration. For example, if a child has a short attention span, is hyperactive and impulsive, select a varied sequence of activities. In order to retain interest each activity is scheduled for a short duration and the next activity is introduced according to the child's tempo and interest. With reinforcement, the child's attention span can be gradually and systematically increased. Quite often attention should be focused on remediating the child's emotional problems. The effective management of a child during motor training activities can contribute substantially to the remediation of emotional as well as motor problems.

The described method of evaluating a child's neuromuscular development and suggested strategy for improvising motor training activities is intended to serve only as a guide to educators. The maturation of neuromuscular systems and the relationship of these systems to learning skills involves complex processes. Considerable research remains to be done in this essential, yet relatively unexplored, dimension of human development. One of the most crucial questions remains unanswered, mainly, "What is the specific relationship between sensory-motor behaviors and dysfunctions in the learning process?" "When we identify a specific sensory-motor dysfunction, are the proposed activities helpful in remediating the sensory-motor deficit as well as remediating an associated learning problem?" The systematic deliniation of cognitive, sensory-motor and behavioral factors involved in the process of learning would appear to be a necessary step in our exploration of these problems.

SOME SELF-MANAGEMENT TECHNIQUES
FOR PRESCHOOL CHILDREN

Thomas Armon Brigham and Lynne Margaret McAllister

ABSTRACT

Children in a preschool class with moderate to high rates of disruptive behavior during group activities were taught self-management techniques in an attempt to reduce the level of their disruptive behavior. The self-management procedures were introduced sequentially with two children at a time in a multiple baseline across subjects.

Following the self-management training, the children used the following self-administered procedures: assessment, recording, discrimination of the availability of reward and delivery of reward. The self-management procedures reduced the level of disruptive behavior during group activities. The use of these procedures also produced a substantial increase from base line in the percentage of days the children caused no disruptive behavior.

INTRODUCTION

Contingency management techniques have been widely used to modify children's problem behaviors in preschool settings. It has been shown that the disruptive behavior of preschool children can be effectively controlled by teacher-managed reinforcement systems, e.g., Harris, Johnston, Kelley and Wolf (1964) and Hart, Allen, Buell, Harris, and Wolf (1964). Since then, many other investigators have demonstrated similar effective changes in children's behavior. The present study was designed to investigate whether a self-management system could produce significant changes in preschool children's inappropriate behavior and thus provide an alternative to teacher-managed reinforcement systems.

Bolstad and Johnson (1972) demonstrated that elementary school children could successfully use self-management techniques to decrease their rate of disruptive classroom behavior They found that first and second graders were able to self-observe accurately and that the use of self-management procedures resulted in consistently lower rates of disruptive behavior. The successful use of self-management techniques with first and second graders indicates that such procedures may also be appropriate for use at the preschool level.

---

*This study was supported in part by NIMH Grant R01MH26084-01. Requests for reprints should be sent to: T. A. Brigham, Department of Psychology, Washington State University Pullman, WA 99163.

Much of the previous work done with self-management procedures has involved children with serious behavior problems or those in special classes, e.g., Kaufman and O'Leary (1972). McLaughlin (1976) has pointed out the need for investigating the effects of the use of self-control procedures with children in a regular classroom. The current study used normal preschool children and attempted to deal with everyday discipline problems in the preschool classroom. The target behaviors were chosen and defined to reflect typical teacher expectations of the children's behavior in the group activities of the class session.

It was expected that the use of self management procedures would greatly reduce the children's rates of inappropriate behavior and that self-managed contingencies would be shown to be a viable alternative to the teacher-managed contingencies previously used with preschool children.

METHOD

Subjects

Five boys and one girl, between four and five years old, who attended a university laboratory preschool, participated in the study. The children could be described as middle class; five were white, one black, All had attended the preschool the previous semester.

These children were selected to participate in the study because they displayed sufficient amounts of inappropriate behavior during the group activities of the class session for the teachers to consider their behavior a problem. They frequently interrupted the teacher while she/he was talking during circle activity and behaved in such a manner that they required teacher intervention or correction at circle or snack time. Further, they consistently failed to clean up after the snack; did not replace their chair at the table; or did not throw their paper cup and napkin in the wastebasket after the snack.

Setting

Fifteen children attended the preschool session which ran from nine to twelve o'clock, four days a week. The schedule included free play, circle activity, snack time, story reading, and outdoor play. Experimental manipulations and recording were done during the regularly scheduled activities of the class session. Two consecutive activities — the circle and snack time, where all the children participated as a group — were used as the target periods. Circle time included singing, fingerplays, and games. The teachers introduced new concepts and asked the children questions about what they had learned. After the circle, the children were dismissed to snack, where they ate together in small groups.

Thomas Armon Brigham and Lynne Margaret McAllister

General Procedures

The procedures were carried out by a graduate student and eight undergraduate assistants who served as observers, monitored the token exchange, and supervised the reward activities.

Observer training was conducted along the lines suggested by Bijou (1969). The observers memorized the behavioral definitions of the target behaviors and the code used in recording. Then in pairs they recorded the behavior of the same two children in the same time interval and discussed behavior rating criteria and compared target behavior rate totals until they attained agreement.

When the study began, five of the assistants were designated as regular observers. Each observed the same two children throughout the study. The other three served as reliability observers. Reliability checks were made approximately twice a week across conditions. Reliability between observers was calculated in terms of numbers of agreements divided by the number of agreements plus the number of disagreements. The average percentage agreement between regular and reliability observers over the entire study was 90 percent.

The observers also served as monitors at the token exchange. They were trained to teach the children how to use the tokens. Each received and memorized written instructions consisting of a step-by-step statement of the procedures to be used and a "script" of what they were to say to the children during each stage of the training. The "script" was used so that the training instructions would be approximately the same for each child.

Self-management Procedures

A simplified token system was used in which the children could earn tokens for a zero rate of each target behavior during two consecutive activities — the circle and the snack. These two activities were separate but the teacher-related target behaviors were the same for each: correction by the teacher. Child-related target behaviors were interrupting the teacher for the circle activity, not pushing the chair up to the table after snack, and not throwing the paper cup and napkin in the wastebasket after snack for the snack period.

The children reported to the token exchange after both the circle and the snack to report his/her count of the target behaviors and to receive their tokens. Each child could earn a total of ten tokens during the half-hour circle and snack period. A zero frequency of each target behavior earned two tokens with two target behaviors for circle and three for snack. A total of ten was used because all the subjects could count to ten. Round plastic chips were used for tokens. Each could be exchanged for one minute of a reward activity which was chosen from games and toys that were frequently played with in the preschool.

Research Design

The self-management procedures were introduced sequentially to two children at a time in a multiple baseline across subjects. Subjects 1 and 2 went from baseline to self-management training while the other four children remained in the baseline condition. Subjects 3, 4, 5, and 6 did not go directly into the self-management training; instead a noncontingent token condition was introduced. Subjects 5 and 6 remained in the noncontingent token condition when subjects 3 and 4 were given the self-management training. Finally, subjects 5 and 6 were given the self-management training, and all six children used the self-management procedures for the last two weeks of the study. The noncontingent token condition was introduced as a control for any possible effects of simply receiving tokens after the circle and snack periods. The sequence of experimental conditions and the number of sessions in each condition for each child are summarized in Table 6-1.

Table 6-1. Sequence of Conditions and Sessions per Condition for Individual Subjects

	Session numbers in order by condition			
Subject	Base Line	Noncontingent tokens	Self-management training	Self-management
1	1–14	None	15–19	20–38
2	1–14	None	15–22	23–38
3	1–18	19–23	24–27	28–38
4	1–18	19–23	24–28	29–38
5	1–18	19–29	30–33	34–38
6	1–18	19–29	30–33	34–38

Baseline

Frequencies of the target behaviors were recorded for a period of fourteen days, during which there were no experimental manipulations. The children participating in the study received no feedback from the experimenters on the rates of their behavior. Throughout the study the preschool staff continued to remind all the children in the class of their inappropriate behaviors at circle and snack.

Noncontingent Tokens

Noncontingent tokens were introduced after the baseline with subjects 3, 4, 5, and 6. Every day following circle, the children were dismissed to the token exchange. The experimenters told them, "It is your turn to get your tokens this way today." The experimenters then gave each child five tokens, half the maximum total it would be possible to earn on contingent tokens. Next, all the children in the class went to snack. After the snack, the children were called to the token exchange where they again received five tokens in the same way, making a total of ten tokens for each child. Each child received ten tokens every day regardless of their target behavior rate. As in the baseline, the children were given no feedback on their rates of inappropriate behavior.

The children began giving themselves the tokens twice each day as soon as they could answer accurately when the experimenters asked: "How many tokens do you get each time?" "When do you get your tokens?" The experimenters then asked only: "Did you give yourself your tokens today?" and checked for accuracy.

Experimenters told the children that ten tokens could be traded for ten minutes of play with a reward activity. A selection of reward activities was offered every day, and the children traded their tokens for the activities of their choice.

Self-management Training

During the class session before the target period began, the experimenters told the first two children (subjects 1 and 2): "We are going to do something new today. You will be able to earn tokens by remembering what to do at circle and snack. You will then be able to trade the tokens for special playtime." Then the experimenter taught each child individually to recognize and observe the target behaviors for circle and snack. When self-management training began for subjects 3, 4, 5, and 6 they were given slightly different instructions since they had already received noncontingent tokens. These instructions emphasized that the children could now earn the tokens by changing their behavior.

The children were taught simple behavioral definitions and were asked to repeat them back. In addition, each incidence of a target behavior was pointed out and defined to the children at the token exchange. The following is an example of teaching the target behaviors for circle: "Today at circle you were wrestling with Billy and the teacher had to ask you to stop. You can earn two tokens if the teacher does not have to ask you to stop what you are doing. So you did not earn any tokens for that today. You did not talk about something different from what the teacher was talking about, or talk while she was talking at circle. When you do not interrupt the teacher, you can earn two tokens. You earned two tokens at circle today." The target behaviors for snack were taught in a similar manner.

During the training the children were asked the following questions: "When can you earn tokens?" "What can you earn tokens for?" "How many tokens can you earn?" When a child answered the questions accurately, he/she began learning to count the target behaviors.

Next the children were told "Today at circle and snack time, watch carefully and remember what to do to earn tokens. Watch what you do very carefully, it is important to remember just right." When the children reported to the token exchange, they were asked about the target behaviors, one at a time, e.g.: "Did you push your chair up to the table after snack today?" If the child answered yes, the adult responded: "Then you earned two tokens." Children's inaccurate responses were noted and corrected. For example: "I think that you had a race to the bookcase with Suzy as you were leaving the snack table and you forgot to push in your chair, so you don't earn any tokens for that today. Do you remember now? Think carefully when you tell me what you did to earn your tokens. It is important to remember it just right." Accurate responses were praised and the importance of accuracy was stressed. As each target behavior was named, the child placed two tokens in his/her cup if there had been no occurrence of that behavior.

When the children could recall their behavior and accurately repeat procedures, they began to observe and report completely on their own. The children were told: "Now every day you will watch and remember what you did to earn your tokens by yourself, and you will give yourself the tokens that you earn. We'll help you learn how." When children reported to the token exchange, they were asked: "How many tokens did you earn at circle today? As you count them out, say what you earned them for." Any inaccuracies were pointed out and corrected. Finally, the experimenters simply watched at the token exchange and made corrections for accuracy when necessary. At this point, subjects 1 and 2 were using the self-control procedures completely on their own. Self-control training for subjects 3, 4, 5, and 6 followed the same pattern.

Self-management

Daily, the children watched for incidences of target behaviors. After circle, they were dismissed to the token table where they counted out the number of tokens they had earned. The class then went to snack. During snack, the children again observed their own behavior. As the children finished snack, they again went to the token table and gave themselves the appropriate number of tokens.

After the children had their tokens, the experimenters named the reward activities available that day, and the children each exchanged their tokens for the activity of their choice. The class then went to storytime. When the children finished their stories, they went to the area of the classroom where their chosen activity was offered and participated for the length of time they had earned. The experimenters made corrections for accuracy as necessary at the token exchange. They supervised the reward activities, telling each child when his time was up. Except for performing these two functions, the experimenters did nothing but watch as the children carried out the self-management procedures.

RESULTS

The number of inappropriate behaviors per session decreased for all children in the study from the base line to the self-control condition. The frequency of target behaviors per session for individual subjects is presented in Figure 6-1. As can be seen, the level of inappropriate behaviors per session was consistently lower overall when the self-control procedures were in effect with five of the six children displaying zero frequencies by the end of the study.

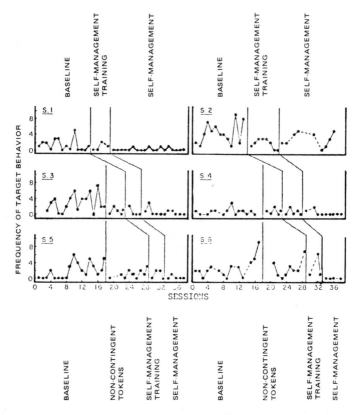

Figure 6-1. Frequency of target behaviors per session for individual subjects. Dashed lines within individual graphs indicate absence.

The general results of the study may be summarized by examining subject 5's data. Subject 5 displayed a pattern of increasing disruptive behavior during baseline. There was an immediate decrease in frequency when the noncontingent token procedures were introduced. Subjects 3 and 6 showed a similar decrease in target behaviors in the noncontingent token condition. However, as this condition continued subject 5's frequency of inappropriate responses again increased to baseline levels as did subject 6's, while subject 3 remained low. It then required four sessions for subject 5 to learn the self-management procedures (four sessions was the median number), after which the child was responsible for carrying out the self-management procedures. During the five sessions of self-management, only one inappropriate response occurred. All of the other children, with the exception of subject 2, displayed similar results.

Subject 2 had the highest base line frequency of target behaviors. In addition, his responses were often of longer duration and a more serious nature, i.e., hitting, screaming, and use of abusive language. The self-management training appeared to reduce the level of these behaviors, and for the last two sessions of training the child did not emit any disruptive responses. This reduction was not maintained during the self-management condition. The child's frequency of inappropriate behavior fluctuated up and down but was clearly increasing when he was removed from school.

Although systematic data collection was discontinued after thirty-eight sessions, the self-management procedures were continued for the rest of the year at a less rigorous level by the second author. During the final week of school the five children who were still attending were each observed at least twice, and there was only one occurrence for the entire group of a target behavior.

DISCUSSION

Use of self-management procedures in the present study resulted in clear and important changes in the children's rates of inappropriate behavior. There were reductions in the number of inappropriate behaviors per session for five of the six children in the study, and the number of days at zero frequency of the target behaviors increased for all the children participating. The results of the present study support the hypothesis that self-management programs can successfully reduce the rate of inappropriate behavior of preschool children and thus provide an effective alternative to teacher-managed programs for behavior management in preschool settings.

The self-management procedures had little effect on the behavior of subject 2. Although there was a generally lower rate of inappropriate behavior in the self-management training, there was no consistent trend toward improved behavior in the final condition. His relatively high frequency of target behavior for the self-management condition may reflect an interactive effect between the program and the attempts of the preschool staff to deal with his disruptive behavior. The teachers considered him to be a major problem and attended to each inappropriate behavior. It may be that the teacher's attention was more effective in maintaining the inappropriate behavior than the consequences provided by the self-management program. Alternatively, it may be that the procedures used in this study were not appropriate for this child's problems. (See Santogrossi, O'Leary, Romanczyk, and Kaufman [1973] for a discussion of this issue.)

The self-management procedures used in this study can be viewed as an educational program to develop independent or autonomous behavior. This is a commonly stated goal for preschool programs (e.g., Love and Osborne, 1971; Spodek, 1972, 19773; Weber, 1970). It is possible that self-management could be successfully integrated with preschool program goals for the development of independent behavior. The self-management of disruptive classroom behavior and the increase of independently managed appropriate social behavior produced by the current program would seem to be congruent with the goals of most preschool teachers. Although the research involved a large number of people, their participation was a function of scientific needs rather than a requirement to run the program. The second author continued the program on her own after the formal data collection period had ended, with no apparent loss in effectiveness. Since most preschools operate with low student-to-teacher ratios, it is likely that programs similar to the one used in the current study could be implemented as an educational component of preschool programs.

The self-management program used in this study involved four distinct components, all of which were self-administered: observation, recording, discrimination of the availability of reward, and delivery of reward. Since the objective of the current research was to develop a program which would teach children to effectively manage their own behavior, no attempt was made to experimentally evaluate the role of each component in the results.

In discussing the components of the program, the label *reward* has been used rather than *reinforcement*. These procedures are very similar to ones which have been labeled reinforcement in the literature, e.g. Bandura and Perloff, 1967; Glynn, Thomas and Shee, 1973. However, Skinner (1953) and Catania (1976) have questioned whether these self-administered procedures are analogous to the positive reinforcement process. Rather, the process appears to be one where the subject learns to discriminate when a reinforcer is available. This was true of the procedures used in the current study where the children's token delivery was corrected if they inaccurately reported their behaviors. Studies of self-reinforcement have frequently used similar correction procedures if the self-reinforcement was not appropriate (e.g. Mahoney and Bandura, 1972; and Johnston and Martin, 1972).

Both Brigham (1977) and Catania (1976) have raised additional conceptual difficulties with the idea of self-reinforcement. Until such questions are answered, it may be more appropriate to use the term *self-delivered reward* which does not have theoretical implications of self-reinforcement as a label for these procedures.

REFERENCES

Bandura, A., and Perloff, B., Relative efficacy of self-monitored and externally imposed reinforcement systems. *Journal of Personality and Social Psychology*, 1967, *7*, 111–116.

Bijou, S., Methodology for experimental studies of young children in natural settings. *Psychological Record, 19*, 1969.

Bolstad, O., D., and Johnson, S. M., Self-regulation in the modification of disruptive classroom behavior. *Journal of Applied Behavior Analysis*, 1972, *5*, 443–454.

Brigham, T. A., Some speculations about self-control. In T. A. Brigham and A. C. Catania (eds.), *Applied behavioral research: the analysis of social and educational processes*. New York: Irvington Press/John Wiley, 1977.

Some Self-Management Techniques for Preschool Children

Bushell, D., Wroebel, P. A., and Michaelis, M. L., Applying "group" contingencies to the classroom study behavior of preschool children. *Journal of Applied Behavior Analysis,* 1968, *1*, 55–61.

Catania, A. C., The myth of self-reinforcement. In T. A. Brigham, R. Hawkins, R. J. Scott, and T. F. McLaughlin (eds.), *Behavior analysis in education: self-control and reading.* Dubuque, Ia.: Kendall/Hunt, 1976.

Glynn, E. L., Thomas, J. D., and Shee, S. M., Behavioral self-control of on-task behavior in an elementary classroom. *Journal of Applied Behavior Analysis,* 1973, *6,* 105–113.

Harris, F. R.; Johnson, M. K.; Kelley, C. S.; and Wolf, M. M., Effects of positive social reinforcement on regressed crawling of a nursery school child. *Journal of Educational Psychology,* 1964, *55,* 35–41.

Hart, B. M., Allen, K. E., Buell, J. S., Harris, R. R., and Wolf, M. M., Effects of social reinforcement on operant crying. *Journal of Experimental Child Psychology,* 1964, *1,* 145–153.

Johnson, S. M., and Martin, S., Developing self-evaluation as a conditioned reinforcer. In B. Ashem and E. G. Poser (eds.), *Behavior modification with children.* New York: Pergamon, 1972.

Kaufman K. F., and O'Leary, K. D., Reward, cost, and self-evaluation procedures for disruptive adolescents in a psychiatric hospital school. *Journal of Applied Behavior Analysis,* 1972, *5,* 293–309.

Love, H. D., and Osborne W. H., *Early childhood education.* Springfield, Ill.: Charles C. Thomas, 1971.

Mahoney, M. J., and Bandura, A., Self-reinforcement in pigeons. *Learning and Motivation,* 1972, *3,* 293–303.

McLaughlin, T. F., Self-control in the classroom: A review. *Review of Educational Research.* Winter, 1976.

Moore, S. G., and Kilmer, S., *Contemporary preschool education: a program for young children.* New York: John Wiley, 1973.

Santogrossi, D. S., O'Leary, K. D., Romanczyk, R. G., and Kaufman, K. F., Self-evaluation by adolescents in a psychiatric hospital school token program. *Journal of Applied Behavior Analysis,* 1973, *6,* 277–288.

Skinner B. F., *Science and human behavior.* New York: Macmillan, 1953.

Spodek, B., *Teaching in the early years.* Englewood Cliffs, N. J.: Prentice-Hall, 1972.

Spodek, B., *Early childhood education.* Englewood Cliffs, N.J.: Prentice-Hall, 1973.

ALTERNATIVES TO MEDICATION IN THE TREATMENT OF HYPERACTIVITY: A REVIEW OF BEHAVIORAL RESEARCH

Stephen Pollack, Gerald Harris, and Ben J. Williams

INTRODUCTION

Considerable public and professional interst has been focused recently on hyperactive children, their problems, and the problems they create for those around them. Interested individuals can now easily obtain surveys which document current thinking on the nature and etiology of hyperactive behavior (e.g., Cantwell, 1974), the broad range of available research evaluating the effectiveness of drug (e.g., Lipman, 1976) and non-drug (e.g., Ross and Ross, 1976) treatments, as well as more practical manuals for the implementation of treatment programs (e.g., Safer and Allen, 1976).

This review will examine the *quality* of empirical support for use of the available non-drug treatments with children considered hyperactive. This is an attempt to systematically examine the evolving data bases for each of the major treatments in light of methodological considerations. Certainly the entire spectrum of research issues relevant to the study of treatment effectiveness is beyond the ken of any single chapter (cf., Bergin and Garfield, 1971), yet some significant issues with particular relevance to the "psychological" treatment of hyperactivity can be approached. For instance,

(1) *Who should receive the treatment?*

From a research standpoint, this is the question of subject selection. In general, one needs to develop valid means to identify that portion of the population which is both suited for and willing to undergo treatment. The disagreements over the nature of hyperactivity (e.g., Conrad, 1976) create special problems in this area which will be discussed in detail later. For the moment, however, we can examine some rather divergent notions. On one hand, hyperactivity has been viewed as a medical syndrome defined by a constellation of behaviors exhibited by a group of afflicted individuals (Strauss and Lehtinen, 1947) and alternatively as a set of behaviors emitted by individuals under specific conditions (Werry and Sprague, 1970). With the former, one is faced with the task of circumscribing that array of attributes which are characteristic of the syndrome and then developing instruments to establish group membership. The behavior view, on the other hand, necessitates determining what form behavior must take (e.g., *high rates* of gross motor activity in settings where such behavior is incompatible with appropriate responding) to warrant treatment and techniques to validate that; relative to the rest of the population, those who receive treatment exhibit criterion behaviors.

(2) *Under what conditions is the treatment effective?*
This question subsumes a wide variety of issues. On the most global level, is there sufficient suggestive evidence for the efficacy of the procedures to merit examination, use and further research? Moving to the more precise, what are the "active ingredients" of the treatment regime, and under what conditions are they most effectively delivered? One must also determine if a particular type of therapist or some subset of the treatable population tends to have better outcomes with the procedures. How does the treatment compare with other available treatments in terms of its cost, communicability, ethics, and effectiveness? Finally, do beneficial treatment effects persist and generalize to situations other than those at which treatment was aimed?

(3) *Are the measures of treatment effectiveness valid?*
Again, such a question encompasses an overwhelming number of issues which can only be approached in this context. One subset concerns the quality of measures utilized to demonstrate treatment effects. Within the treatment-outcome literature, one can find largely *inferential* techniques like projective tests, personality inventories, global rating scales, clinical interviews, examinations and diagnoses, and even anecdotal reports in addition to more *direct* measures of behavior such as systematic independent observation, self-monitoring and physiological measurements. Though absolute verification is out of reach, each of these procedures must convincingly document its accuracy, reliability, and validity, as well as the possible sources of contamination and how to minimize them.

Another subset of issues raised by this question concerns the adequacy and appropriateness of the analytical tools, typically statistical techniques, used to assert that the changes reflected in dependent measurements are significant. Even when appropriate statistical manipulations are performed and mathematically significant results obtained, one must question whether the results reflect change which would be considered meaningful to the clinician who delivers the treatment or the society which sanctions such procedures (Barlow and Hersen, 1973).

The final research considerations are the relative strengths and weaknesses of the various experimental designs available for experimental tests of treatments. In his influential article, Gordon Paul (1969) refers to this as concern over the "possible level of product which may be obtained through different levels of design." This idea of the "possible level of product" is an extension of Campbell and Stanley's (1966) notion of internal validity; that is, the power of a design to demonstrate that the treatment, and not uncontrolled factors, produced the obtained dependent measure changes. Paul arrays the available designs from the least to the most potent: (1) single case study; (2) nonfactorial single-group design; (3) nonfactorial group design with untreated controls (i.e., treated subjects vs. no-treatment controls); (4) factorial group design with untreated and nonspecific-treatment controls; and (5) laboratory-based designs. Though there are appropriate applications for each of these certainly one must be at the factorial group-design level if one hopes

Stephen Pollack, Gerald Harris and Ben J. Williams

to specify not only cause and effect relationships, but also the relative impact of therapist, patient and setting attributes. Paul, like Lazarus and Davison (1971) and Leitenberg (1973), views single case methodology as a weak tool, valuable only in the earliest phases of outcome research primarily to develop and crudely test new hypotheses.

To be sure, this critical view of single case methodology has been challenged, most notably by Hersen and Barlow (1976). They, too, eschew the "clinical" case study (i.e., without measurement of some sort), but argue that direct replications with pre- and post-treatment assessments as well as replications systematically varied across clients, therapists and settings can be used to establish casual relationships as compelling as those obtained with factorial group designs.

Though somewhat at odds, these two viewpoints can be reconciled. If one chooses single-case designs, perhaps to avoid obscuring the variability of individual subjects (Sidman, 1960), one must implement both direct and systematically-varied $n=1$ studies to show functional relationships between independent and dependent variables. The choice of the group comparison approach, for example, to compare the potencies of two different treatments (Hersen and Barlow, 1976), ultimately necessitates factorial designs. Clearly, both designs can be fruitfully applied to investigations of treatment effectiveness.

In sum, documenting treatment effectiveness is a complex task that demands that one attend to questions regarding the selection of appropriate subjects, those conditions which promote positive outcomes which then generalize and persist, and the use of adequate experimental tests. Certainly no single study can investigate all of these issues. Series of studies, consistently developed to build on prior research, are needed to replicate, refine and extend promising treatments.

The remainder of this paper examines the series of reported studies on treatments targeted at hyperactivity-related behaviors in a manner calculated to point out the major strengths and weakness of existing research. Unfortunately, this inquiry revealed methodological concerns so substantial that one must question whether use of these techniques can be considered empirically warranted. Although many factors could account for this, some special issues concerning the interface between behavioral treatments (i.e., the class of treatments which have been most extensively investigated) and hyperactivity seem to have potently influenced the course of research. A brief, concluding section will discuss these issues and some ideas from the philosophy of science, particularly those of Kuhn (1962), which seem to account for what has happened in hyperactivity treatment research.

NON-DRUG TREATMENT OF HYPERACTIVE BEHAVIOR

Recent literature is replete with reports of novel treatments and modifications of existing procedures, all targeted at changing the behavior of the hyperactive child. The vast majority of these cannot presently be considered as having sufficient empirical support to warrant their use. Typically, this stems from methodologically unsound experimental tests, lack of replication, or a complete absence of empirical examination. Relatively novel treatments include breathing control training (Simpson and Nelson, 1974), contingent background music (Scott, 1970; Reid, Hill, Rawers and Montegar, 1975), physical therapy (Smith and Phillips, 1970), massage for relaxation of muscle tension (Henderson, Dahlin, Partridge and Engelsing, 1973), and modification of sleep habits (Bergman, 1976). Existing treatment procedures like role-playing, fixed-role therapy, brief therapy and transactional analysis have also been proposed (Ross and Ross, 1976). Informational feedback on cognitive tasks (Ozolins and Anderson, 1976) and biofeedback training (Nall, 1973; Mulholland, 1974; Simpson and Nelson, 1974; Braud, Lupin and Braud, 1975) are promising new approaches, although they target behaviors with an uncertain relationship to the hyperactivity phenomenon.

At least some comment must be made concerning the efficacy of traditional individual psychotherapy with hyperactive children. Though several well-known volumes on the management of hyperactivity completely dismiss such procedures as ineffective (Stewart and Olds, 1973; Wender, 1971), the only available tests (Cytrin, Gilbert and Eisenberg, 1960; Eisenberg, Gilbert, Cytrin and Molling, 1961) are methodologically unsound to the point of being inconclusive. We must agree with Ross and Ross (1976) that the usefulness of individual psychotherapy in treating the hyperactive's difficulties remains to be proven or disproven.

By far the largest number of published studies in non-drug treatments of hyperactivity fall in the behavior therapy domain. At about the same time, the researchers at Johns Hopkins begin to test methylphenidate (i.e., Ritalin) with emotionally disturbed children (Eisenberg *et al,* 1963), the first reports on the application of behavioral technology also appeared. Patterson's (1964) automated "work box" device for conditioning attentional behavior attracted the most interest and replication, while several other early studies went largely unnoticed (Anderson, 1964; James, 1963). The subsequent research on the potentcy of behavioral treatments is the focus of the next section of this paper.

Behavioral Treatment of Hyperactive Behavior

Virtually all of the published reports on the behavioral treatment of hyperactivity fall in the operant conditioning domain. While the general considerations for implementing operant procedures (Safer and Allen, 1976) and evaluating them (Sidman, 1960) have been documented elsewhere, the prototypical experimental design is worthy of brief review. Most operant work examines the changes in behavior over time of a single subject. Typically, an intervention is evaluated with the ABA design where baseline observations (A) are followed by treatments (B) which are followed by a reinstatement of baseline conditions (A). In such a design, dramatic behavioral changes during the treatment phase are directly attributable to treatments only when the final baseline condition ultimately promotes extinction (i.e., behavior returns to initial baseline levels). Thus, the subject serves as his own control and the withdrawal of treatment constitutes a test to see if the treatment is the controlling factor of the observed behavioral changes. Inclusion of an additional treatment condition, the ABAB design, allows one to both overcome the ethical issues raised by discontinuing a beneficial treatment and obtain an additional evaluative test. In lieu of statistical analysis, visual examination of graphed data, in the form of *rates* of behavior, is used to document significant changes in dependent measures. Observations of behavior or obtained scores on a relevant task most often constitute the dependent measure data.

Outcome research of this variety entails questions and problems over and above those enumerated earlier. For example, one must adequately operationalize target behaviors and effectively select and schedule reinforcers. Confounding can arise from a variety of sources like unstable baseline rates, differing lengths of experimental phases, interference from multiple treatments, and, when more than one treatment is delivered, sequence effects (see Hersen and Barlow, 1976, for a more detailed discussion). In light of growing concerns within the behavior therapy area (e.g , Wahler, 1969), questions concerning the generalization and maintenance of treatment effects seem to merit special attention.

Research on the operant conditioning of hyperactive behavior has proceeded such that sub-domains of specific procedures and classes of target behaviors can be identified and the course of replication and extension examined. In the succeeding section, we examine the quality of empirical support for the use of the various operant technologies in changing four often associated components of hyperactivity: (1) attentional behavior; (2) activity level; (3) social behavior; and (4) academic performance. Each of these areas are further subdivided into automated and non-automated treatment packages. Although this is not a theoretically meaningful dimension, automated treatment procedures do differ from non-automated ones in terms of their expense and ease of implementation as well as their potential for precise treatment delivery and data collection.

Operant Conditioning of Attentional Behavior – As noted earlier, Patterson's (1964) report of successful shaping of increased attentional behavior was the first behavioral treatment study of hyperactivity to earn research attention. Central to the procedure was an experimenter-controlled, automated apparatus which sat on the subject's desk and signalled the ocurrence of appropriate behavior and reinforcement. A practical implementation manual for the "work box" technology is available (Ray, Shaw and Cobb, 1970). It is interesting that the majority of investigations concerned with the operant shaping of attention similarly relied on automated devices which are seen here as constituting a sub-domain of the operant conditioning area.

Patterson's single subject was a clinic-referred, nine-year-old boy who presented with an array of neurological, psychological and intellectual impairments, including hyperactivity. The intervention involved the "work box" and a set of instructions for what has come to be called a "group contingency" (Rosenbaum, O'Leary and

Jacobs, 1975). With a group contingency program, the experimenter (or teacher) announces to the whole class that a specific target child will be earning reinforcers for everyone. The intention here is to program the social world of the treated child to support the desired behavioral changes and thus enhance the maintenance of treatment-produced effects. Using the work box, reinforcements were delivered continuously for each 10-second period during which no interfering, deviant behavior occurred. Appropriate attentional behavior was defined only as the absence of behaviors which would interfere with attention to class tasks. The fact that a calm, appropriately oriented, though totally unproductive, child, would be considered to be attending with such a response definition is a critical flaw. Patterson reported dramatic success in increasing attending behavior (i.e., actually reducing non-attending), although it is impossible to know if such gains reached the point of being "clinically" significant from the perspective of the classroom teacher. Some attempt was made to secure anecdotal follow-up information from parents and teachers which, at 4 months, suggested that the behavioral changes had been maintained. Though this early $n=1$ study was flawed, it certainly was an adequate beginning.

This automated, operant technology for shaping attentional behavior was replicated, refined and extended over the following 10 years. Instead of pursuing direct replication as a means to establish the applicability of the treatment across a class of subjects, Patterson and his colleagues (1965) next reported on a modified version of the procedure. The target child was grossly comparable to the previous one, and his pre- and post-treatment behavior ratings were evaluated relative to those of clinically-matched, "no treatment" control child. Using the same apparatus and dependent measures, the intervention was modified as follows: (1) the observer was unobtrusive; (2) the time of day was varied to sample both morning and afternoon class periods; (3) four experimental phases were programmed — baseline, adaptation, classroom conditioning and extinction; and (4) individually-tailored reinforcers were adminstered on a continuous schedule for the first 5 days, after which a switch was made to the variable interval schedule which increased to 30 seconds over the remaining trials. Though such modifications constituted potential improvements in the procedure, they were derived from general behavior therapy considerations rather than from obtained results with hyperactive children. Had the reinforcement scheduling component been investigated systematically with hyperactives at this point, they might have uncovered the fact that hyperactives do respond differently to schedules of reinforcement than would be expected based on general behavioral theory (Douglas, 1975).

Patterson again reported success in decreasing (mean) non-attending behaviors, though the inclusion of a control allowed him to demonstrate that these gains were significant relative to an untreated hyperactive. Finer examination of the data obtained during the final baseline condition reveals that some of the dependent behaviors extinguished rapidly while others did not, raising a somewhat thorny issue as to the interpretation of such results. In the classic interpretation of an ABA treatment study, rapid extinction following cessation of conditioning was considered a desirable result in that it suggested that the behavior changes observed during the conditioning phase were a function of the shaping procedures alone. A failure to extinguish, on the other hand, suggested that other factors were controlling behavior. Werry and Sprague (1974) suggest another perspective when they argue that behavior changes which are not resistant to extinction may be of little practical value, particularly to those who implement them in settings where unforeseen circumstance is likely to interfere with pre-programmed treatments. Similarly, when conditioning alters the social presentation of a subject, one would expect the social environment to change in ways which would maintain treatment-produced changes. Finally, general learning theory dictates that extinction rates vary as a function of reinforcement schedules. Without careful examination of each of these issues, the interpretation of extinction data will continue to be a matter of opinion.

Finally, Patterson *et al* question the internal validity of their design because the observer also functioned as the experimenter during the conditioning trials. The likelihood of independent-dependent measure confounding mediated by experimenter expectancy effects (Rosenthal, 1969) is increased in such instances. The pervasiveness of this critical design problem in the behavioral treatment literature has not been determined and, in fact, is quite rarely discussed.

The next significant step came with the publication of a modified replication of the procedure by Doubros and Daniels (1966). At the outset they noted several weaknesses of the earliest Patterson research: (1) informing an entire class created opportunities for uncontrolled and unmeasurable social reinforcement; and (2) the target child's awareness of contingencies enhanced placebo-type effects. Doubros and Daniels worked with six institutionalized, retarded boys who were considered on the basis of clinical data to be hyperactive. All observations and interventions were made with individual children in a clinic playroom setting. The ABA design was modified to include an additional "phase out" condition (i.e. considerable increases in amount of attending needed to get reinforcement) between the conditioning and extinction phases. Individual conditioning was used to mitigate social reinforcement effects while instructions which explained only the process of earning reinforcement (and not which behaviors would earn them) were used to eliminate conditioning awareness effects. Further, the utilization of a group design allowed for the collection of outcome data across a variety of retarded, hyperactive children.

As with the Patterson work, the results were impressive: (1) in terms of the absolute frequency of response, the rate of non-attending decreased across the conditioning trials and remained below pre-conditioning levels during extinction; (2) the variability of responding followed the same pattern suggesting that the hyperactives had attained a relatively stable rate of responding; and (3) those with the higest ratings on a hyperactivity checklist developed for the study showed the greatest response to treatment. While such data augment the argument that it is the reinforcers themselves, that are responsible for the behavioral improvements obtained with the "work box" technology, the use of the severely retarded as subjects limits the generalizability of these findings as they seem to constitute only a small subset of the hyperactive population. Also, the addition of a novel "phase out" condition obscures determination of the "active ingredients" of the process.

Walker and Buckley (1968) continued the inquiry in a $n=1$ study where the shaping program ultimately was transferred to the regular classroom teacher. Several design factors merit special attention. The authors report that conditioning was not begun until a stable baseline on graphed behavior observation data was observed. Though visual examination of graphed behavior rates is not an empirically adequate technique, it is at least an attempt to tackle this critical design issue. Another modification in the Walker and Buckley study was the instruction that attending to the counter indicating reinforcement constituted a distraction which would result in a loss of points exchangeable for a toy. A behavioral coding system comprised the dependent measures, although it differed from earlier work in that it specified not only non-attending but also a set of desirable attending behaviors derived from a little-noted, though valuable, operant conditioning analysis of attention (Martin and Powers, 1967). An increasing fixed interval schedule, from 30 seconds to 10 minutes, was used in the initial laboratory conditioning phase. Again, the intervention was potent, reducing both the frequency and duration of non-attending while increasing the rate of attending. Both rapidly returned to baseline levels during extinction. In the classroom conditioning phase that followed, all procedures were identical except that the teacher was reinforced with a 30-minute variable interval schedule, presumably to streamline implementation. In this setting, rates of attending behavior again rose quickly.

In light of the inconsistent extinction data, an examination of the "active ingredients," perhaps the scheduling variable, which produced varying extinction and maintenance effects would have been appropriate. Instead, Quay, Werry, Sprague and McQueen (1967) applied comparable procedures to a group of five hyperactive children. A single experimenter sat next to the classroom teacher randomly observing each child and delivering reinforcement via a light box on each desk for every 10 seconds of attentional behavior. With such a procedure, the delivery schedule for reinforcement of visual orientation to the teacher is characterizable only as not continuous. Edible and social reinforcers were earned, the latter in the form of "pats on the head." Quay *et al* departed from the norm by submitting their pre- and post-treatment observations of subjects attending to an analysis of variance test which, in fact, revealed significant treatment effects. A number of authors have challenged the use of this statistic, particularly in *n=1 studies,* with time-sampled behavioral data (Glass, Gottman and Wilson, 1973; Hersen and Barlow, 1976) due to the serial dependency problem (i.e., the level of observed behavior at one point is correlated with the next observed level, hence violating the ANOVA requirement of independence). Such problems do not necessarily indicate that the treatment is ineffective, only that the method used to document effectiveness is inappropriate.

Alabiso (1975) produced the most recent study of an automated operant procedure for modifying attentional behavior. Like Doubros and Daniels (1966), he worked with a special subset of the hyperactive population, the institutionalized retardate. Unfortunately, the eight children who underwent conditioning were also concurrently on unspecified medication, thus creating confounding which obscures the relative and interactive contributions of the multiple treatments. (Note: This problem of multiple treatment interference also arises with strictly behavioral interventions like that of Novy *et al* (1973) who used a "work box" procedure in a class run on a token economy.)

Alabiso defined attention in terms of three components: (1) *span*=time in seat; (2) *focus*=productivity on a very simple task; and (3) *selectivity*=ability to make certain visual discriminations. Certainly this was an attempt at dependent measure refinement. Each subject was conditioned individually in a laboratory using continuous, then increasing fixed interval, and finally increasing variable interval reinforcement delivery schedules. Extinction and generalization phases were also included. Alabiso presented absolutely no data though he stated that it showed rapid acceleration with treatment and subsequent resistance to extinction on all three components of attention.

Though automated devices allow precision monitoring as well as immediate and systematic reinforcement, they are somewhat impractical, particularly for the regular classroom teacher. Several non-automated studies which relied on teachers to discriminate and reinforce appropriate attending constitute another subset of operant treatment. First, James (1963) and then Broden *et al* (1970) simply trained teachers to distinguish and reinforce desired behavior while extinguishing problematic behaviors. Such techniques are grossly referred to as "DRO" procedures; that is, differential reinforcement for other behavior. One interesting variation of the Borden design was the investigation of the effects of teacher attention as a reinforcer for one child on the behavior of another child seated at an adjacent desk. A minimally obtrusive observer coded alternating 5-second intervals of attending and non-attending behaviors for each child as well as frequency of teacher attention. Like Alabiso, their dependent measure of attending was refined to include both appropriate postural orientation and productivity on class assignments. Experimental phases included; (1) baseline; (2) teacher reinforces one subject; (3) teacher reinforces other subject; (4) baseline; and (5) reinforcement for both subjects. Graphically represented data indicated not only that the teacher brought about great increments in the amount of attending of the targeted child but that such an intervention promoted moderate increases in an adjacent child. This study sheds no light on the mechanisms responsible for such "unintended" effects, but it does demonstrate their potential potency in group or classroom situations. Obviously, those obtained here were beneficial, but our lack of understanding of how such effects come about leaves open the possibility for undesirable results. Since no subsequent reports of the differential reinforcement of attentional behavior have appeared, this question and many others remain unanswered.

In sum, only research on the automated, operant treatment of hyperactivity-related attentional problems approaches the pattern of replication and increasing refinement needed to validate a treatment. Unfortunately, this has not been duplicated in other research areas.

Operant Conditioning of Activity Level — Given the widespread belief that excessive motoric activity is a fundamental characteristic of hyperactivity, a surprisingly small number of reports have appeared to document the effectiveness of behavioral techniques in modifying activity levels. In 1967, Pihl used an automated operant procedure to increase sitting in a single 14-year-old subject with a variety of psychological and neurological complaints, including hyperactivity. Using a light box to indicate reinforcement (exchangeable for money and home privileges) earned for each 25 seconds of sitting still, Pihl was able to gain stimulus control over the boy's activity in only five 45-minute laboratory sessions.

Edelson and Sprague (1974) were concerned with the application of these automated shaping techniques to groups of hyperactive subjects. With three sessions per week over a 4 week period, sixteen institutionalized retarded boys were trained in groups of four in a laboratory setting. The setting approached comparability to a classroom as a filmstrip and an accompanying multiple-choice quiz were presented during all trials. Subjects were also informed that a blinking light on their desk would indicate correct responding in a "sit-in-your-seat game" with money as prizes. The dependent variable was the number of movements per 30-second interval as measured by a stabilometic cushion. This cushion is placed on the seat of a chair and is equipped with micro-switches sensitive to buttocks movement and is attached to a counter and a visible red light. Such an instrument is unique in this literature as it is a truly direct and non-inferential way to assess behavior changes. Subjects were randomly divided in half, each group then was subjected to several baseline and two different experimental conditions. The order of the two treatments was varied for the groups to control for sequential treatment confounding. The two conditions differed as to whether increased or decreased seat movement was shaped, though the change in contingencies between conditions was not discussed with the children. Reinforcement criteria were individually calculated such that the time interval of desired behavior increased for every subject. As Pihl had found, stimulus control of activity was quickly gained, yet Edelson and Sprague were able to both increase and decrease it relative to baseline levels. Such demonstrated potency in modifying the direction of behavior lends considerable credence to such procedures. Surprisingly, individual correlations between mean seat movements per trial and quiz scores were insignificant, suggesting that buttocks movements (or their absence) may not be a determining factor in performance on class tasks. Certainly, this raises questions over the value of this admittedly potent technology.

This issue of subject selection also merits attention here. With a group design, subjects must be matched along relevant variables prior to treatment and some means utilized to establish how members of the group differ from those who do not belong. Clinical judgments were used to establish group membership in the Edelson and Sprague study. Their procedure must be challenged, however, since the *baseline* levels of seat activity for one of the randomly constituted groups appears, by visual examination, to be three times higher than that of the other. Utilization of behavior rating scales intended to tap hyperactivity which were available at the time (e.g., Conners, 1969) would have allowed an independent means to establish group membership and document that one had obtained two meaningfully homogeneous sets of subjects.

Quite recently, Ball and Irwin (1976) extended the technology with a portable, automated device which could be worn by a subject in virtually any setting and used to reinforce the "postural orientation associated with in-seat behavior." Although no scores were reported, the single subject was chosen on the basis of high rating of overactivity and distractibility on Miller, Palkes and Stewart's (1973) questionnarie for hyperactivity. Behavioral observations of "in-seat" and "tilting" were collected every 10 seconds across the seven experimental phases: (1) baseline; (2) orientation-familiarization with device prior to intervention; (3) reinforcement for each 2-minute period of sitting still; (4) a single "reversal" session when standing was reinforced; (5) reinforcement for 6.5 minute intervals of sitting; (6) removal of the device and substitution of a kitchen timer now set to a 20-minute criterion interval; and (7) removal of the kitchen timer. As with both of the preceeding reports, activity conditioned quickly, but, where Edelson and Sprague produced changes with little resistance to extinction, Ball and Irwin found that treatment gains were maintained after the intervention was stopped. The poverty of systematic replication in this area rendors such curious results inexplicable.

Several studies have evaluated differential reinforcement strategies used by adults to shape components of motor behavior without the aid of mechanical monitoring and reinforcement devices. Such interventions, though desirable from a practical standpoint, are quite difficult to equate across published reports. Perhaps the most unique report came from Miklich (1973), who applied relaxation training and then systematic desensitization to calm a 6-year-old hyperactive referred for panic reactions during asthmatic attacks.

Whitman, Caponigri and Mercurio (1971) shaped in-seat behavior in a severely retarded 6-year-old girl who roamed her "special" classroom almost continuously in spite of her teacher's frequent commands to "sit down." Training began outside the classroom, first with the experimenter reinforcing brief periods of sitting and then increasingly longer intervals and greater (unspecified) distractions. Whereas heightened responsiveness to distracting stimuli is a commonly discussed characteristic of hyperactivity (e.g., Strauss and Lehtinen, 1947) in descriptive and theoretical literature, rarely is it integrated into treatment research. On the tenth day, training was moved into the child's regular classroom, again proceeding from brief to increasingly longer criterion intervals. A fixed-ratio, partial reinforcement schedule was eventually introduced. Comparison of pre- and post-treatment mean scores on a set of classroom observation codes reveals an impressive drop in both the number of teacher sitting commands and the latency of the child's sitting response as well as a six fold increase in the time spent in-seat. Still, the child was only remaining seated for about 6 minutes of the 30-minute observation periods per day. Of course, this rate of in-seat behavior would be intolerable in many classrooms; yet in the present study the relative increase was taken to indicate considerable success.

Certainly, research on *in vivo* treatments necessitates the collection of data on how settings differ. Information on structural and perceived aspects of classrooms and other naturalistic treatment settings must be developed and integrated. Hochschild and Levine (1977), for example, have shown how certain types of classroom environments are related to student deviant behavior. Using a structured observation and interview format to determine where an elementary school classroom falls on the "open" to "traditional" dimension, they obtained an inverse relation between "open" classroom ratings and rates of student maladjustment. Such information has obvious relevance to the treatment of maladaptive behavior in these settings and such a rating scale offers a meaningful way to equate or differentiate classroom environments.

The final study discussed in this section (Twardoz and Sajwaj, 1972) again raises questions about the "unintended" effects of operant procedures, a phenomenon which had begun to surface elsewhere in the literature (e.g., Buell, Stoddard, Harris and Baer, 1968; Lovaas and Simmons, 1969; Risley, 1968; Wahler *et al*, 1970). Twardoz and Sajwaj chose a severely retarded 4-year-old boy whose behavioral repertoire consisted almost exclusively of either lying on the floor or squirming and jumping around. The teacher conducted the program during half-hour free play periods by seating the subject at a table and giving him tokens (exchangeable for candy or toys) and praise for "about" every 10 seconds of sitting. This criterion interval was eventually increased to 1 minute. Although this procedure was quite simple and the desired response rather gross, examination of experimental condition means evidenced great success in increasing sitting behavior as well as toy usage and proximity to classmates. Once again, these unintended effects are desirable ones. However, examination of graphs of daily observations suggest that their reliance on mean scores to demonstrate treatment effects may actually have obscured considerable within-condition variability. The fact that baseline rates of several dependent behaviors appear to be quite unstable prior to the initiation of treatment constitutes a potentially serious problem. Many of the single-subject treatment studies would be enhanced by the use of time-series statistics (Box and Jenkins, 1970) to evaluate such troubling data.

In general, behavioral programs can be designed to gain control over rates of motor behavior. The limited number of studies and the unsystematic pattern of replication have left many questions unanswered, however. In addition to ther pervasive problem concerning the maintenance of treatment effects, the "clinical" significance or value of the reported changes in the various measures of activity seems to be especially critical.

Operant Conditioning of Social Behavior — Research on modifying the "deviant" social behavior of the hyperactive began with *teaching others* to implement the procedures. It may not have seemed necessary to demonstrate the effectiveness of such interventions by a professional in an artificially constructed situation because of the large amount of pre-existing research documenting the power of behavioral techniques in modifying social behaviors. Interestingly, the use of precision mechanical monitoring has, with the exception of videotaped observation and feedback (e.g., Bernal *et al* 1968), not found a place in the operant research on the hyperactive's problematic social behaviors.

Hall and Broden (1967) first reported three replications of a procedure involving the training of parents and teachers in general and case-specific operant techniques. Target behaviors were individually-tailored to presenting social behavior problems, and immediate social reinforcers (i.e., praise and proximity) were delivered for each occurrence of desired behavior. An independent observer monitored both target social behaviors (e.g., social play) and reinforcements on a daily basis which, when reviewed, allowed the prompt modification of programs when declining rates of desired behaviors first appeared. On-going program changes such as these cannot easily be evaluated empirically so that treatments are equated, but they do allow for checks on what is actually being done with consequent opportunities for correction of misdirected applications. Results of the Hall and Broden study indicated that significant adults were able to gain control over a variety of social behaviors, control which persisted at follow-up observations 3 months after the termination of treatment. Certainly the collection of such maintenance data across three comparable subjects, demonstrating at least some generalizability across hyperactive children, constituted a solid foundation for research in the area.

Several years later, Salzinger, Portnoy and Feldman (1970) reported some of the results of an ambitious project aimed at a population comparable to those in the Hall and Broden study. From a roster of an association for brain-inured children, almost 500 families were contacted and asked to give some descriptive behavioral information and to indicate whether they were interested in participating in a treatment study. Review of returned questionnaires allowed the generation of profiles of participants and non-participants in the program. For example, eventual participants tended to indicate "hyperactivity" as a general presenting problem as well as specific difficulties coping with tantrums and physical and verbal abuse.

Based on reported data, no matching for diagnosis or specific complaints was attempted, and no child was excluded for prior or concurrent medication (or treatment). The actual program, however, contained some interesting elements. Following an initial interview regarding the child, parents received direct training in observational skills. Virtually all clinicians know the import and potency of accurate observation as well as the time and effort needed to develop it, yet few have taken the time to teach such skills to parents or teachers. Salzinger *et al* also assessed parents' reading abilities, a relevant dimension given the program's reliance on written instructional materials to explain operant principles. In lieu of data, the authors discuss one treatment success in considerable detail. They do note that, of the 15 families who enrolled, only four carried out their operant program *exactly* as it was designed with consequent "considerable or complete success." For reasons which Salzinger *et al* find difficult to specify, the remainder did not carry out at least part of their programs with correspondingly limited success. An additional finding was that "successful" parents tended to have higher comprehension scores and more education than "unsuccessful" ones. It is encouraging to see even a small attempt to determine which people respond positively to such programs. Salzinger *et al* suggest that more direct demonstration and *in vivo* training with "unsuccessful" parents might have lowered their rather high rate of treatment "failures."

As if heeding this last suggestion, Wiltz and Gordon (1974) moved the entire family of a 9-year-old "hyperactive, aggressive" boy into "apartment-like" experimental living quarters for five days of training. The intention here was to facilitate generalization to the setting (i.e., the family home) where problems actually occurred. Parents first received training in general operant principles and behavioral observation as well as opportunities for rehearsal of specific procedures. The experimenters prompted and modeled correct reinforcement techniques and, during parent rehearsal sessions, gave corrective feedback.

In addition to the strategies for differentially reinforcing appropriate social behaviors, parents were instructed in the use of time out with highly abusive behaviors. Reports on the use of time out with children not considered hyperactive suggest that this intervention may have particular value in dealing with the extremes of behavior (Sachs, 1973; Firestone, 1976). Following the fifth day of training, the family returned home continuing the program with telephone supervision by one of the authors. The treatment package produced considerable reductions in parent commands and child-initiated destructive and non-compliant acts. These gains were maintained, by parent report, at a one month follow-up conversation. Certainly Wiltz and Gordon's attempts to program and monitor generalization through a brief post treatment period were laudable, yet parent verbal report is not the strongest basis on which to demonstrate such effects (Hawkins *et al,* 1966). The authors also documented the number of professional man-hours required to implement the program. Their figures suggested that the program is relatively inexpensive, with the cost of the experimental apartment.

Going one step further, Frazier and Schneider (1975) actually worked in the home of a 3-year-old mentally retarded, hyperactive boy. A welcome addition was the use of a standardized hyperactivity rating scale, the Werry-Weiss-Peters Activity Scale (Werry, 1968) and a behavioral assessment of hyperactivity with norms for observed activity scores (Routh *et al,* 1974). On both of these instruments, the child's scores fell above the 98th percentile for 3-year-olds. The actual reinforcement techniques paralleled those of Wiltz and Gordon, although the experimenters did all of the training in the home. Based on parent behavior ratings, the program promoted effective control of the child's behavior (e.g., reduced food refusal) which was maintained at 35 days after the cessation of treatment. Frazier and Schneider also sent an independent observer to the home during the follow-up phase to make periodic spot checks on the reliability of parent observations. Although such a procedure is not without its pitfalls (Bolstad and Johnson, 1973), it does enhance the quality of parent-collected, follow-up observations.

The final study of this section is one of the few sophisticated group designs in the hyperactivity treatment literature. To put it in context, one must look back to Patterson's earliest study which used a "group reward for individual contingencies" to shape attentional behavior. Individual contingencies with individual rewards were used in many subsequent studies without recognition of the difference between the two types of programs. Rosenbaum, O'Leary and Jacob (1975) used a factorial group design to pit individual against group rewards in a teacher-implemented operant program. Relative to other research in the area, the most impressive aspect of the study was the subject selection process. Candidates for the study were identified via teacher referral, though inclusion resulted only when referrals were corroborated by criterion rating scores on the abbreviated Conners' Teacher Rating Scale, a standardized instrument with published norms (Sprague and Sleator, 1973). Subsequently, subjects were assigned to one of the two treatment groups, matched "as closely as possible" with respect to age, grade and Conners' ratings. The experimenter and the teachers worked together to develop lists of individually tailored target behaviors which included both social (e.g., no fighting, stay in seat, etc.) and academic goals (e.g., completed classwork). In the individual reward program, teachers privately explained the nature of contingencies, target behavior goals, and available rewards. An explanation of the group reward program was given to the entire class, patterned after Patterson's (1964) instructions, and class rewards were charted on the blackboard. Teachers in the individual reward group rated the child on each of the selected target behaviors (i.e., the Problem Behavior Report) at the end of each hour and gave a candy reward, if earned, at the end of the day. Twenty children (in 20 different classrooms) received 4 weeks of daily treatment, followed by a 4-week withdrawal period to assess the persistence of obtained effects. Pre- and post-treatment comparisons of the abbreviated Conners' and the Problem Behavior Reports indicated significant beneficial treatment effects across both programs. Group differences were non-significant, yet consistently favored the group-reward program. Further an attitudinal measure of teacher satisfaction revealed that the group program was the more popular of the two. That either was very popular is somewhat surprising because, though mean hyperactivity ratings were significantly lower at post-test, they still fell over the hyperactivity criterion on the Conners'. In other words, teachers were pleased with methods that left them with children who could still be considered hyperactive.

Certainly, there is evidence of systematic refinement in subject selection and treatment maintenance and generalization in research on the differential reinforcement of the hyperactive's social behaviors. Still, there is reason to question whether the reported treatments have been equivalent and, consequently, whether general conclusions can presently be supported.

Operant Conditioning of Academic Performance — Virtually all of the preceeding studies targeted those behavioral difficulties of the hyperactive child that can be viewed as interfering with adequate academic performance. The presumption seems to have been that removing or lessening such inhibiting factors would somehow free up the child to perform well on class tasks. These last two studies took an alternative view that shaping up academic behavior should then inhibit unproductive or deviant behaviors.

O'Leary, Pelham, Rosenbaum and Price (1975) developed sets of individual target behaviors which included primarily academic and pro-social goals. As in the Rosenbaum *et al* (1975) study, children were selected whose scores exceeded the criterion for hyperactivity on the abbreviated Conners'. Half of these were then randomly assigned to a "no-treatment" control group. An even more impressive aspect of the design was the use of independent observers in the classroom to rate the hyperactives and randomly selected same-sex peers in terms of locomotion, fidgeting and not attending to task. The significantly higher, average rating received by the hyperactives across all three behaviors offered some convergent validation for the teacher ratings on the Conners's.

The actual treatment utilized a novel home reward program and consisted of five phases: (1) teacher specification of daily goals; (2) teacher praise for success as occurs; (3) end-of-day evaluation of progress; (4) progress report on meeting goals sent to parents; and (5) when earned, parent delivery of reinforcements. On both the Conners' and the Problem Behavior Report, only the treated group had significantly lower scores at the end of treatment. Unlike the previous study, Conners' scores did not fall in the hyperactive range. Unfortunately, no follow-up or generalization data were reported.

Like O'Leary *et al* (1975), Ayllon and Roberts (1974) had found that shaping increased academic performance tended to eliminate incompatible classroom misbehavior. Ayllon, Layman and Kandel (1975) took an even more careful look at this phenomenon in a multiple-baseline study of three clinically diagnosed, hyperactive children. Treatment proceeded as follows: (1) baseline-on Ritalin; (2) baseline-off medication; (3) reinforcement for successfully completed math work only; (4) reinforcement of both math and reading performance. An independent-observer time sampled each child's behavior throughout the study, rating math and reading performance as well as hyperactive behaviors (i.e., a coding system developed by Becker *et al,* 1967). Though academic performance scores were near zero during *both* of the baseline phases, the rapid acceleration in hyperactivity ratings during the off-medication baseline suggested that the Ritalin was effective in inhibiting disruptive behavior. While rewarding math work produced behavioral and academic gains only during math period, reinforcement of both types of work produced behavioral ratings comparable to those obtained in the on-medication phase and increases in academic output far surpassing those obtained with Ritalin. Although far more research will be needed to scrutinize and extend these findings, they offer considerable promise. An additional positive aspect of such techniques is that by training teachers to modify academic behavior, one circumvents the ethical issues often raised when teachers are taught to control other aspects of behavior or when drugs are used for similar purposes.

Summary: Only the research on behavioral treatment of attentional behavior, where automated devices were relied on for treatment delivery and data acquisition, approach the pattern of direct and systematically varied replications earlier described as necessary to document the potency of a particular procedure. One can say that automated, attentional treatments have demonstrated short-term effectiveness across a range of clinically selected hyperactives. Still, questions linger concerning generalization, those therapist and patient variables associated with the best outcomes, the "clinical significance" of obtained behavioral gains, and, finally, the "active ingredients" which produce changes in behavior.

The differential reinforcement of appropriate social behavior by adults has also been shown to be effective across a range of hyperactive subjects, but the actual treatments applied have been, at best, only grossly comparable. Within this area, we have also seen refinements in subject selection, program monitoring, and the planning and evaluation of maintenance and generalization effects. Further, suggestive data on subject variables associated with positive outcomes and the relative potencies of different treatments has been gathered.

Empirical support for the remaining areas is severely weakened, typically due to inadequate or unsystematic replication. Though we know, for example, that significant control can be gained over rates of motor activity, we do not know whether lower activity levels will alter the social presentation of a hyperactive child, particularly in the elementary school classroom. Similarly, rather sophisticated experimental designs have yielded promising data on the differential reinforcement of academic behavior which now sorely begs for replication.

Overall, empirical support for the behavioral treatment of hyperactivity-related behaviors can be characterized as checkered in that the numerous reports of positive outcomes seem to be matched by an equally impressive set of unanswered questions. The following section of this paper is an attempt to explain this disturbing state of affairs.

At this point, let us venture into some notions usually associated with the philosophy of science, particularly the ideas of Thomas Kuhn (1962). Kuhn is best known for his delineation of the concept of the *paradigm* in science which will be discussed briefly here. Although Kuhn's discussion of this concept has attracted considerable criticism (e.g., Masterman, 1970), Lachman (1976) seems to capture the essence of it when he states, "A paradigm is a scientific community, with a common technical language, similar research problems and methods, a common data base, and a common view of reality as it is reflected in and reflects the subject matter." Implicit in such a conception is that domains in science are comprised of two components: (1) a *rational* component consisting of the tradition of formal theory, relevant research questions, methods and data base; and (2) a *conventional* or non-empirical component comprised of a whole system or pre-theoretical beliefs which, though not derived from theory or data, exert considerable influence on the course of scientific developments. Though not the first or only proponent of such a view, Kuhn did establish the value of examination of ideological premises when attempting to understand the course of scientific inquiry within any scientific domain.

Lachman has also specified six criteria for distinguishing paradigms: intellectual antecedents, pre-theoretical ideas, preferred analogies, subject matter of interest, technical language, and instrumentation. The first three of these form a guide for examining the implicit premises within any research domain while the remainder are more formal, empirical factors.

In sum, research within any particular scientific area must be viewed in light of theoretical and empirical developments as well as the ideologies of the community of scientists producing the research. Without claiming paradigm status for either, this perspective can be applied to the research on both the concept of hyperactivity and behavioral treatment. Hopefully, this will illuminate the major factors responsible for the inadequate empirical support for the behavioral treatment of hyperactivity.

The Evolution of the Concept of Hyperactivity — As was discussed in the preceeding section, the history of thought in a particular scientific domain is one of several factors which can actively influence contemporary inquiries. Tracing the evolution of the concept of hyperactivity should then illuminate a portion of the context within which current research discussion proceeds. In this section, we will briefly trace this history, relying heavily on the excellent review provided by Ross and Ross (1976), and then examine the present status of theoretical discussion of the concept.

Although serious discussion of hyperactivity did not begin until the first years of this century, several authors (Stewart, 1960; Cantwell, 1974) have located the first description of a hyperactive-like child in a children's poem written by Heinrich Hoffman in 1845. Curiously enough, Hoffman was a German physician. George Still, a London pediatrician, opened more formal discussion with a series of lectures on children with "defects in moral control" (i.e., their clinical descriptions are remarkably similar to those of present-day hyperactives) given to the Royal College of Physicians in 1902. Although Still speculated on a variety of possible causes, some organic and some linked with childrearing practices, he argued that medication was always the treatment of choice. Interestingly, Still also seems to have anticipated the concept of *minimal brain dysfunction,* which did not receive specific diagnostic recognition until much later (Clements, 1966). Referring to children who now would be described as retarded and hyperactive, Still hypothesized that the cause of the hyperactive component was "to be sought not in any gross lesion or gross failure of development but in some *much finer physical abnormality"* (p. 1012). Both the preference for medication as a treatment and the notion of an underlying but nonspecific organic etiology enjoy current professional approval.

Ross and Ross pinpoint the next critical development in thinking about hyperactivity in the period following the encephalitis epidemic of 1918. During this period, clinical descriptions were published to document hyperactivity as a secondary effect of this and other physical diseases like epilepsy. The notion that hyperactive behavior could be linked with non-demonstrable brain injury continued to appear.

It was not until the late 1940's that Strauss formally identified a "hyperkinetic syndrome" which he linked with infections, traumas and other physical injuries to the nervous system (Strauss and Lehtinen, 1947). In a sense, Strauss reiterated earlier conclusions as this hyperkinetic syndrome was identified in a population of brain-injured retarded children comparable to that examined by Still. As Ross and Ross have noted, Strauss ultimately elevated hyperactivity to the category of hard neurological signs (Strauss and Kephart, 1955).

Laufer and his colleagues took the next step when they suggested the specific diagnostic category of "hyperkinetic impulse disorder" (Laufer, Denhoff and Solomons, 1957). By this time, there was a considerable amount of evidence available which challenged the link between hyperactivity and even minimal CNS injury. The concept of *minimal brain dysfunction* was developed in response to such evidence, and it enjoys considerable professional usage to this day. As Clements (1966) stated, the notion of dysfunction maintains the link between hyperactivity and organic etiology.

In reviewing hyperactivity research of the last decade, Ross and Ross concluded that hyperactivity has changed "from a medical to a behavioral problem." Although behavioral descriptions of the nature and etiology of hyperactivity have been proposed (e.g., Werry and Sprague, 1970), the preponderance of the evidence suggests that the traditional medical construction of hyperactivity persists to this day. Organic etiologies are still most often inferred, and medication is still the treatment of choice (Ross and Ross, 1976; Conrad, 1976). The preference for medication in treating hyperactivity is curious because it persists in the face of serious concern over demonstrated adverse side effects (Cohen, Douglas and Morganstern, 1971; Safer and Allen, 1973; Safer Allen and Barr, 1975), mounting ethical challenges (e.g , Schrag and Divory, 1975), and critical questions regarding the lack of adequate methodology in the majority of drug treatment studies (Grant, 1962;

Freeman, 1966; Eisenberg and Conners, 1971; Sroufe, 1975). One can only conclude that the prevailing conception of hyperactivity has ventured little from that proposed by Still in 1902. It remains a medical concept and a medical problem, consistently linked to an organic ethiology and most often treated by physicians with medication. In a sense, these ideas constitute the implicit premises of the hyperactivity research community.

In a slightly different context, Conrad (1976) cites three factors, external to the mainstream of hyperactivity research, that have potently shaped the course of inquiry; (1) pharmaceutical companies have for some forty years increasingly expanded both the production and sale of psychoactive drugs; (2) the medical community has come to use medication with the spectrum of behavior problems and only recently has come to regard child psychiatry as an area of critical import; and (3) actions taken by government agencies and special interest groups like Association for Children with Learning Disabilities, have generally served to perpetuate medical approaches to hyperactivity. Certainly, recent cutbacks in government research funding and the consequent need for researchers to obtain support from the private sector in general and pharmaceutical companies in particular have similarly influenced the kinds of questions asked about hyperactivity.

Although we argue that the *implicit* premises in hyperactivity research have remained relatively unchanged over the years, this is not meant to imply that *explicit* theoretical discussion has followed a similar course. In fact, hyperactivity-related phenomena have been given at least 40 different labels (Mercer and Bower, 1975), with as many as 99 defining behaviors (Clements, 1966) variously construed as sets of weakly related "symptoms" or components of unitary "syndromes." Obviously, formal theorizing on hyperactivity is in disarray.

The Status of Behavior Therapy and the Interface with Hyperactivity — In an earlier section of this paper, research on the operant conditioning of hyperactive behaviors was reviewed and the argument put forward that empirical support for such treatments was inadequate. Now let us look at the larger domains of behavior therapy and behavioristic psychology as other aspects of the context within which the operant treatments of hyperactivity have been developed.

Few would disagree with the assertion that behavioristic psychology is a domain of psychological inquiry that is meaingfully distinct from the illness or medical approach to conceptualizing behavior. This is not to say that either or both of these perspectives have attained that status of a paradigm, but rather to beg this hotly debated question (cf., Weimar and Palermo, 1973) and simply assert that the differences in both formal theory and implicit premises are significant. Both Price (1972) and Ullmann and Krasner (1969) have detailed the critical differences in both the rational and conventional components of these two systems, and their efforts will not be duplicated here.

Kuhn asserts that theoretical perspectives (including those which attain paradigm status) that differ particularly in their ideological commitments are largely *incom-*

mensurable. To appreciate this concept, one must consider that Kuhn was trying to explain what transpired during the period of "revolution" or "paradigm clash." Such periods always occur early in the development of a new scientific domain (i.e., before the first dominent paradigm arises) and in the periods following the fall of a dominant paradigm, usually due to the discovery of unexpected experimental "anomalies." Kuhn argues that during such periods, proponents of available theoretical perspectives engage in something like competition which ends only when one view comes to dominate the field. Since the competing perspectives are paritially composed of implicit ideological premises, the theoretical debates can never be resolved solely on the basis of empirical findings. Incommensurability then refers to the absence of a mutually-acceptable basis for comparison between competing perspectives due to implicit disagreements concerning relevant questions, acceptable concepts, analogies, and even language, etc.

If incommensurability between clashing perspectives inhibits communication and prevents empirical decision-making, then it is a small step to suggest similar adverse effects when attempts are made to blend or integrate theoretically distinct domains. Following Kuhn's thinking, the conceptual work necessary to find common theoretical and terminological ground, to develop mutually-acceptable models and analogies, and to decide on relevant research questions and how to answer them will at best be incomplete. We propose that this is exactly what occurred when attempts were made to use operant treatments with hyperactive children. Operant conditioning grew out of the behavioristic tradition in psychology and its use reflects commitments to a particular set of orienting attitudes (e.g., learning as a central concept; the import of operationalizing concepts which can be subjected to controlled empirical test; the use of the laws of conditioning to explain behavior change; the rejection of mentalistic concepts; and so on). Hyperactivity, on the other hand, is essentially a medical concept which evolved within a different framework and set of commitments (e.g., disease as the basic metaphor; an orientation which dictates the need to search for organic causes of "symptoms, syndromes, illnesses or disorders;" priority on medical treatments, etc.). These underlying differences are critical as the resultant difficulties in translating concepts prevent the kind of consensual agreement necessary for extended, systematic research. In such instances, one finds varying arrays of concepts, interventions, experimental designs, analytic and interpretive tools, and, in general, a pattern of unsystematic replication like that found in the research on treating hyperactive behaviors with behavioral techniques.

Several other factors must be implicated as contributing to the unsatisfactory course of research on the behavioral treatment of hyperactivity. First, the entire behavioral paradigm has come under considerable attack. with some suggesting that we are witnessing its final decline (Weimar and Palermo, 1970; Segal and Lachman, 1972). Further, behavior therapy is currently the subject of heated theoretical debate (e.g., Meichenbaum, 1975; Wolpe, 1976) and also faced with potent empirical anomalies concerning the lack of generalization and maintenance of treatment effects (e.g., Wahler, 1969; Walker and Buckley, 1972).

In sum, we have pinpointed both the theoretical disarray within the behavior therapy and hyperactivity areas as well as their conceptual incompatibility as the primary factors responsible for the unsatisfactory course of outcome research on the behavioral treatment of hyperactivity. Clearly, our argument attributes considerable potency to intangible factors which many might consider more subtle. Further, the means to resolving the hypothesized conceptual impasse are difficult to envision. It is interesting that the non-drug treatments which currently garner the most research attention, do not fall strictly in either the behavioral or medical domains. For example, there is a class of treatments that might be considered "cognitive" in that they target the "impulsive" information processing strategies often found in hyperactive children (e.g., Kagan, Pearson and Welch, 1966; Denney, 1972; Finch and Kendall, 1977). Also, there are treatments designed to foster "self-control" with impulsive, hyperactive children that, though developed within the behavioral framework, are now considered by some to fall outside the behavioral realm (e.g., Goldiamond, 1976). Self-control treatments typically involve training hyperactives either to self-monitor and self-reinforce (e.g., Johnson and Martin, 1973; Drabman, Spitalnik and O'Leary, 1973; Parks, 1975) or to produce internal, self-directed commands which the child can use to inhibit impulsive behavior (e.g., Palkes, Stewart and Kahana, 1968; Meichenbaum and Cameron, 1974).

REFERENCES

Alabiso F., Operant control of attentional behavior: A treatment for hyperactivity. *Behavior Therapy*, 1975, *6*, 39–42.

Anderson, D., Application of behavior modification technique to the control of a hyperactive child. Unpublished M.A. thesis, University of Oregon, 1964.

Ayllon. T., Layman, D. and Kandel, H., A behavioral-educational alternative to drug control of hyperactive children. *J. of Applied Behavior Analysis,* 1975, *8,* 137–146.

Ayllon, T. and Roberts, D., Eliminating discipline problems by strengthening academic performance. *J. of Applied Behavior Analysis,* 1974, *7,* (1), 71–76.

Ball, T. and Irwin, A., A portable automated device applied to training a hyperactive child. *J. of Behavior Therapy and Experimental Psychiatry,* 1976, *7* (2), 185–188.

Barlow, D. and Hersen, M., Single-case experimental designs: Uses in applied clinical research. *Archives of General Psychiatry,* 1973, *29* (3), 319–325.

Becker, W., Madsen, C., Arnold, C. and Thomas, D., The contingent use of teacher attention and praise in reducing classroom misbehavior problems. *J. of Special Education,* 1967, *1,* 287–307.

Bergin, A. and Garfield, S. (Eds.), *Handbook of psychotherapy and behavior change.* New York: Wiley, 1971.

Bergman, R., Treatment of childhood insommia diagnosed as "hyperactivity." *J. of Behavior Therapy and Experimental Psychiatry,* 1976, *7* (2), 199.

Bernal, M., Duryee, J., Pruett, H. and Burns, B., Behavior modifications and the brat syndrome. *J. of Consulting and Clinical Psychology,* 1968, *32,* 447–455.

Stephen Pollack, Gerald Harris and Ben J. Williams

Box, G. and Jenkins, G., *Time series analysis: Forecasting and control*. San Francisco: Holden-Day, 1970.

Braud, L., Lupin, M. and Braud, W., The use of electromyographic biofeedback in the control of hyperactivity. *J. of Learning Disabilities,* 1975, *8,* 420–425.

Broden, M., Bruce, M., Mitchell, M., Carter, V. and Hall, R., Effects of teacher attention on attending behavior of two boys at adjacent desks. *J. of Applied Behavior Analysis,* 1970, *3,* 199–203.

Buell, J., Stoddard, P., Harris, F. and Barr, D., Collateral social development accompanying reinforcement of outdoor play in a preschool child. *J. of Applied Behavior Analysis,* 1968, *1* (2), 167–173.

Campbell, D. and Stanley, J., *Experimental and Quasi-experimental designs for research.* Chicago: Rand-McNally, 1966.

Cantwell, D. (Ed.), *The hyperactive child: Diagnosis, management, current research.* New York: Spectrum, 1974.

Clements, S., Task Force I: Minimal brain dysfunction in children. National Institute of Neurological Diseases and Blindness, Monograph No. 3, U.S. Department of Health, Education and Welfare, 1966.

Cohen, N., Douglas, V. and Morganstern, G., The effect of methylphenidate on attentive behavior and autonomic activity in hyperactive children. *Psychopharmacologia,* 1971, *22,* 282–294.

Conners, C. K., A teacher rating scale for use in drug studies with children. *American J. of Psychiatry,* 1969, *126,* 884–888.

Conners, C. K., Recent drug studies with hyperkinetic children. *J. of Learning Disabilities, 4* (9), 476–483.

Conrad, P., *Identifying hyperactive children.* Lexington, Mass.: Lexington, 1976.

Cytrin, L., Gilbert, A. and Eisenberg, L., The effectiveness of tranquilizing drugs plus supportive psychotherapy in treating behavior disorders of children: A double-blind study of 80 outpatients. *American J. of Orthopsychiatry,* 1960, *30,* 113.

Denney, D., Modeling effects upon conceptual styles and cognitive tempos. *Child Development,* 1972, *43,* 105–119.

Douglas, V., Are drugs enough? To treat or train the hyperactive child. *International J. of Mental Health,* 1975, *4* (1–2), 199–212.

Drabman, R., Spitalnik, R., and O'Leary, K. D., Teaching self-control to disruptive children. *J. of Abnormal Psychology,* 1973, *82* (1), 10–16.

Doubros, S. and Daniels, G., An experimental approach to the reduction of overactive behavior. *Behavior Research and Therapy,* 1966, *4,* 251–258.

Edelson, R. and Sprague, R., Conditioning of activitiy level in a classroom with institutionalized retarded boys. *American J. of Mental Deficiency,* 1974, *78,* 384–388.

Eisenberg L. and Conners, C. K., Psychopharmacology in childhood. In Talbot, N., Kagan, J. and Eisenberg, L. (Eds.), *Behavioral science in pediatric medicine.* Philadelphia: Saunders, 1971.

Eisenberg, L., Gilbert, A., Cytryn, L. and Molling P., The effectiveness of psychotherapy alone and in conjunction with perphenazine or placebo in the treatment of neurotic or hyperkinetic children. *American J. of Psychiatry,* 1961, *117,* 1088–1093.

Finch, A. and Kendall, P., Reflection-impulsivity: Implications and treatment strategies for child psychopathology. In Green, R. and Beutler, L. (Eds.), *Social and behavioral approaches to child and adolescent problems.* In preparation.

Firestone, P., The effects and side effects of timeout on an aggressive nursery school child. *J. of Behavior Therapy and Experimental Psychiatry,* 1976, *7* (1), 79–82.

Frazier, J. and Schneider, H., Parental management of inappropriate hyperactivity. *J. of Behavior Therapy and Experimental Psychiatry*, 1975, *6* (3), 246–247.

Freeman R., Drug effects on learning in children: A selective review of the past thrity years. *J. of Special Education*, 1966, *1*, 17–44.

Glass, G., Wilson. V. and Gottman, J., *Design and analysis of time series experiments*. Boulder, Colo : Colorado Associated University Press, 1974.

Goldiamond, I., Self reinforcement. *J. of Applied Behavior Analysis,* 1976, *9* (4), 509–514.

Grant, Q., Psychopharmacology in childhood emotional and mental disorders. *J. of Pediatrics,* 1962, *61* 626–637.

Hall, R. and Broden, M., Behavior changes in brain-injured children through social reinforcement. *J. of Experimental Child Psychology,* 1967, *5,* 463–479.

Hawkins, R., Peterson, R., Schweid, E. and Bijou, S., Behavior therapy in the home: Amelioration of problem parent-child relations with the parent in a therapeutic role. *J. of Experimental Child Psychology,* 1966, *4,* 99–107.

Henderson, A., Dahlin, I., Partridge, C. and Engelsing, E., A hypothesis on the etiology of hyperactivity, with a pilot study report of related non-drug therapy. *Pediatrics,* 1973, *52,* 625.

Hersen. M. and Barlow, D., *Single-case experimental designs: Strategies for studying behavior change.* New York: Pergammon, 1976.

Hochschild, R. and Levine, M., Rates of student maladjustment in open and traditional classrooms. Unpublished manuscript, 1977.

Hoffman H., *Der struwwelpeter: Oder lustige geschichten und drollige bilder.* Leipsig: Insel-Verlag, 1845.

James, C., Operant conditioning in the management and behavior of five hyperactive children: Five case studies. Unpublished manuscript, Orange State College, 1963.

Johnson, S. and Bolstad, O., Methodological issues in naturalistic observation: Some problems and solutions for field research. In Hamerlynch, L., Handy, L. and Mash, E. (Eds.), *Behavior changes: Methodology concepts and practice.* Champaign, Ill.: Research Press, 1973.

Kagan, J., Pearson L. and Welch, L., The Modifiability of an impulsive tempo. *J. of Educational Psychology,* 1966, *57,* 359–365.

Kuhn, T., *The structure of scientific revolutions.* Chicago: University of Chicago Press, 1962.

Lachman, R., Personal communication, 1976.

Laufer, M., Denhoff, E. and Solomons, G., Hyperkinetic impulse disorder in children's behavior problems. *Psychosomatic Medicine,* 1957, *19,* 38–49.

Lazurus, A. and Davison, G., Clinical innovation in research and practice. In Bergin, A. and Garfield, S. (Eds.), *Handbook of psychotherapy and behavior change: An empirical analysis.* New York: Wiley, 1971.

Leitenberg, H., The use of single-case methodology in psychotherapy research. *J. of Abnormal Psychology.* 1973, *82,* (1) 87–101.

Lipman, R., NIMH-PRB support of research in minimal brain dysfunction in children. In Conners, C. K. (Ed.), *Clinical use of stimulant drugs in children.* New York: Elsevier, 1974.

Lovaas. O. I., and Simmons, J., Manipulation of self-destruction in three retarded children. *J. of Applied Behavior Analysis,* 1969, *2* (3), 143–157.

Martin, G. and Powers, R., Attention span: An operant conditioning analysis. *Exceptional Children,* 1967, *33* (8), 565–570.

Masterman, M., The nature of a paradigm. In Lakatos, I. and Musgrave, I. (Eds.), *Criticism and the growth of knowledge.* London: Cambridge University Press, 1970.

Meichenbaum, D., Self-instructional methods. In Kanfer, F. and Goldstein, A. (Eds.), *Helping people change.* New York: Pergammon, 1975.

Meichenbaum, D. and Cameron, R., The clinical potential of modifying what clients say to themselves. In Mahoney, M. and Thoresen, L. (Eds.), *Self-control: Power to the person.* Belmont Calif.: Wadsworth, 1974.

Mercer, C. and Bower, K. Hyperactivity: Etiology and intervention techniques. *J. of School Health,* 1975, *45* (4), 195–202.

Miklich, D., Operant conditioning procedures with systematic desensitization in a hyperkinetic asthmatic boy. *J. of Behavior Therapy and Experimental Psychiatry,* 1973, *4,* 177–182.

Miller, R., Palkes, H. and Stewart, M., Hyperactive children in suburban elementary schools. *Child Psychiatry and Human Development,* 1973, *4,* 121–127.

Mulholland, T., Training visual attention. *Academic Therapy,* 1974, *10* (1), 5–17.

Nall, A., Alpha training and the hyperkinetic child — is it effective. *Academic Therapy,* 1973, *9* (1), 1–14.

Novy P., Burnett, J., Powers, M. and Sulzer-Azaroff, B., Modifying attending to work behavior of a learning disabled child. *Journal of Learning Disabilities,* 1973, *6* (4), 20–24.

O'Leary, K., Pelham, W., Rosenbaum, A. and Price, G., Behavioral treatment of hyperkinetic children: Adjunctive therapy or alternative to medication. *Clinical Pediatrics,* 1975.

Ozolins, D. and Anderson R., The effects of feedback on the vigilance performance of hyperactive and hypoactive children with learning disabilities. Unpublished manuscript, Texas Tech University 1976.

Palkes, H., Stewart, M., and Kahana, B., Porteus Maze performance of hyperactive boys after training in self-directed verbal commands. *Child Development,* 1968, *39,* 817–826.

Parks, A. L., Applied behavior analysis and hyperactivity: Focus on self-management. Presented at the annual American Psychological Association Convention, 1975.

Patterson, G. R., An application of conditioning techniques to the control of a hyperactive child. In L. P. Ullman and L. Krasner (Eds.), *Case studies in behavior modification.* New York: Holt, Rinehart & Winston, 1964.

Patterson, G. R., Jones, R., Whittier, J., and Wright, M. A., A behavior modification technique for the hyperactive child. *Behavior Research and Therapy.* 1965, *2,* 217–226.

Paul, G., Behavior modification research: Design and tactics. In Franks, C. (Ed.), *Behavior therapy: Appraisal and status.* New York: McGraw-Hill, 1969.

Pihl, R. I., Conditioning procedures with hyperactive children. *Neurology,* 1967, *17,* 424–428.

Price, R., *Abnormal behavior: Perspectives in conflict.* New York: Holt, Rinehart and Winston, 1972.

Quay, H., Werry, J., Sprague, R. and McQueen, M., Conditioning visual orientation of conduct problem children in the classroom. *J. of Experimental Child Psychology,* 1967, *5,* 512–517.

Ray, R., Shaw, D. and Cobb, J., The work box: An innovation in teaching attentional behavior. *School Counselor,* 1970, *18* (1), 15–35.

Reid, D., Hill, B., Rawers, R. and Montegar, C., The use of contingent music in teaching social skills to a nonverbal, hyperactive boy. *J. of Music Therapy,* 1975, *12,* 2–18.

Risley, T. The effects and side effects of punishing the autistic behaviors of a deviant child. *J. of Applied Behavior Analysis,* 1968, *1* (1), 21–34.

Rosenbaum, A., O'Leary, K. and Jacobs, R., Behavioral intervention with hyperactive children: Group consequences as a supplement to individual contingencies. *Behavior Therapy,* 1975, *6,* 315–323.

Rosenthal, R., Interpersonal expectations: Effects of the experimenter's hypothesis. In Rosenthal, R. and Rosnow, R. (Eds.), *Artifact in behavioral research.* New York: Academic Press, 1969.

Ross, D. and Ross, S., *Hyperactivity: Research, theory and action.* New York: Wiley, 1976.

Routh, D., Schroeder C. and O'Tauma, I., Development of activity level in children. *Developmental Psychology* 1974, *4,* 38–40.

Sachs D. A., The efficacy of time-out procedures in a variety of behavior problems. *Journal of Behavior Therapy and Experimental Psychiatry,* 1973, *4,* 237–242.

Safer, D. J. and Allen, R. P., Factors influencing the suppressant effects of two stimulant drugs on the growth of hyperactive children. *Pediatrics,* 1973, *51,*660–667.

Safer, D. and Allren, R., *Hyperactive children: Diagnosis and management.* Baltimore, Md.: University Park Press, 1976.

Salzinger, K., Feldman, R., Portnoy, S., Training parents of brain-injured children in the use of operant conditioning procedures. *Behavior Therapy,* 1970, *1* (1), 4–32.

Schrag, P., and Divoky D., *The myth of the hyperactive child.* New York: Pantheon, 1975.

Scott, T. J., The use of music to reduce hyperactivity in children. *American Journal of Orthopsychiatry,* 1970, *40* (4), 677–680.

Segal, E. and Lachman, R., Complex behavior or higher mental process: Is there is a pradigm shift? *American Psychologist,* 1972, *27* (1), 46–55.

Sidman M., *Tactics of scientific research: Evaluating experimental data in psychology.* New York: Basic Books, 1960.

Silver L., Acceptable and controversial approaches to treating the child with learning disabilities. *Psychiatry,* 1975, *55* (3), 406–415.

Simpson, D. D., and Nelson, A. E., Attention training through breathing control to modify hyperactivity. *Journal of Learning Disabilities,* 1974, *7,* 274–283.

Smith, B. S. and Phillips, E. H., Treating a hyperactive child. *Physical Therapy,* 1970, *50,* 506–510.

Sprague, R. L. and Sleator, E. K., Effects of psychopharmacologic agents on learning disorders, *Pediatric Clinics of North America,* 1973, *20,* 719–735.

Sroufe, L. A., Drug treatment of children with behavior problems. In F. Horowitz (Ed.), *Review of child development research, Vol 4,* Chicago: University of Chicago Press, 1975.

Stewart, M., Hyperactive children. *Scientific American,* 1970, *222,* 94–98.

Stewart, M. A., and Olds, S. W., *Raising a hyperactive child.* New York: Harper & Row, 1973.

Still, G. F., The Coulstonian Lectures on some abnormal physical conditions in children. *Lancet,* 1902, *1,* 1008–1012, 1077–1082, 1163–1168.

Strauss, A. A. and Kephart, N. C., *Psychopathology and education of the brain-injured child.* Vol. II, Progress in theory and clinic. New York: Grune and Stratton, 1955.

Strauss, A. A., and Lehtinen, L. E., *Psychopathology and education of the brain-injured child.* New York: Grune and Stratton, 1947.

Twardosz, S. and Sajwaj, T., Multiple effects of a procedure to increase sitting in a hyperactive, retarded boy. *Journal of Applied Behavior Analysis,* 1972, *5,* 73–78.

Ullman, L. P. and Krasner, L., *A psychological approach to abnormal behavior,* Englewood Cliffs, N.J.: Prentice-Hall, 1969.

Wahler R., Setting generality: some specific and general effects of child behavior therapy. *J. of Applied Behavior Analysis,* 1969, *2,* 239–246.

Wahler, R., Sperling, K., Thomas, M., Leeter, N. and Rupet, H., The modification of childhood stuttering: Some response-response relationships. *J. of Experimental Child Psychology,* 1970, *9,* 411–428.

Walker, H. and Buckley, N., The use of positive reinforcement in conditioning attending behavior. *J. of Applied Behavior Analysis,* 1968, *1* (3), 245–250.

Walker H. and Buckley, N., Programming gneralization and maintenance of treatment effects across time and across settings. *J. of Applied Behavior Analysis,* 1972, *5* (3), 209–224.

Weimar, W. and Palermo, D., Paradigms and normal science in psychology. *Science Studies,* 1973, *3,* 211–244.

Wender P. H., *Minimal brain dysfunction in children,* New York: Wiley-Interscience, 1971.

Werry, J. S., Studies on the hyperactive child IV. An empirical analysis of the minimal brain dysfunction syndrome. *Archives of General Psychiatry,* 1968, *19,* 9—16.

Werry, J. S., and Sprague, R. L., Hyperactivity. In C. G. Costello (Ed.) *Symptoms of psychopathology.* New York: Wiley, 1970, pp. 397—417.

Werry, J. S. and sprague, R. L., Methylphenidate in children — Effect of dosage, *Australian and New Zealand Journal of Psychiatry,* 1974, *8,* 9—19.

Whitman, T., Caponigri, V. and Mercurio, J., Reducing hyperactive behavior in a severely retarded child. *Mental Retardation.* 1971, *9* (3), 17—19.

Wiltz, N. A. and Gordon, S. B., Parental modification of a child's behavior in an experimental residence. *Journal of Behavior Therapy and Experimental Psychiatry,* 1974, *5,* 107—109.

Wolpe, J., Behavior therapy and its malcontents-I, II. *J. of Behavior Therapy and Experimental Psychiatry.* 1976, *7* (1—2), 1—6, 109—116.

MENTAL RETARDATION: AN EDUCATIONAL APPROACH

Richard Greene

In ancient times, the Spartans, Greeks, and Romans all treated the mentally retarded with great cruelty. Hippocrates, the "Father of Medicine," was the first to describe cretinism, a disorder of the thyroid gland causing mental retardation; from that time important figures in the early history of research in mental retardation have been Pinel, Jean Itard, Guggenbuhl, Downe, and Binet. The modern era of research started with Foling in 1939 and Barr and Moore in 1949 (Atkinson, 1968).

The prevalence of mental retardation is generally stated to be between 1 and 3 percent of the general population. Unfortunately, no large-scale epidemiological studies are available to support these figures. Seventy-five percent of mentally retarded children are only mildly retarded, having intelligence quotients over 50, and generally would be integrated into the regular school system. Approximately 15 percent of all retarded children are moderately retarded with an IQ rating of 20 to 49. These children will almost invariably be detected within the first two years of attendance at a regular school. The remaining 10 percent are seriously retarded and diagnosis would be made very early in life ... soon after birth in most cases

Attempts at classification have also shown much inconsistency beginning with Downe's Classification in about 1864, which was based on the supposed ethnic appearance of various groups of retarded children. Of this type of classification, the term "mongoloid" remains, and even this term today is being challenged.

Many centuries ago and in less complicated societies, the mentally retarded frequently held a position of importance, they were considered to be the children of God. At other times, the retarded were considered to be invested with special cultural attributes and were usually given the freedom of the community.

In the community, the educational system has now opened its doors to provide special education for the emotionally disturbed, the brain-damaged, the blind, and the hard-of-hearing. Many of the children in attendance at these classes today were previously considered "retarded" and frequently institutionalized. The mildly retarded are accepted as the responsibility of most boards of education. Auxiliary classes and vocational schools are providing special forms of education that allow handicapped children to develop to their maximum potential, and prepare them to take a place in the community. The moderately retarded, who were previously totally rejected by the educational systems, are now offered special facilities for training in retarded schools. Sheltered workshops are beginning to develop in many centers. They offer continued care beyond the school years, where the young adult retardate can make realistic contributions to society and to himself. The sheltered workshops are, at present, in their very early stages of development, and exploration of this type of facility is badly needed (Zarfas, 1962).

What is special education? Is it a special curriculum or a special teaching environment, or some combination wherein a teacher has fewer pupils, and can individualize instruction? Generally, the justification for having special education classrooms has been that many children are unable to profit from regular instruction and need an adapted curriculum and teaching assistance on a more individualized level. This justification of the special education classroom may be nothing more than a rationalization.

It is now fairly well agreed that special classes generally do not provide increased academic achievement for the educable mentally retarded (EMR). There have been suggestions that special education classes for the EMR have certain undesirable side effects. Zito and Bardon (1969) showed that the retarded children in special classes are impaired in (a) goal-setting behaviors and (b) expectations for achievement and growth when compared with retarded children in regular classes.

In any case, the special education classroom for the mentally retarded has not fulfilled the promise once perceived. While it is true that special classes frequently have limited enrollments, it should not be assumed that a reduction in the number of pupils in a class improves classroom instruction. There are two reasons why individualized instruction in special classes may be impossible. First, the number enrolled in a class is too great. One teacher can individualize work for one or even two children, but that teacher stands less of a chance with three. In some very rare and unusual cases, that same teacher may even be able to individualize work for four handicapped children. But no teacher, even one equipped with the best methods, techniques, and materials, can individualize work for five, ten, or fifteen. Second, the instructional homogeneity of categorically defined handicapped children is a faulty assumption. The same teaching approach to even five children at the same time would require a huge population-sampling procedure.

Special classes may be more aptly described as instructional nightmares. The special teacher's preparation includes perhaps the history of some aspects of special education. A superficial acquaintance with the need and characteristics of handicapped children, and a limited preparation in applying a few curricula to a person with an artificial disability are required. This training is irrelevant simply because the training fails to prepare the special teachers for their real task; to render meaningful educational programs while establishing realistic educational objectives, and to develop the method and materials to implement and validate these objectives.

The failure of special education classes for the EMR to show significant academic efficiency has prompted the special educators to reevaluate their position. One problem which exists is that the special educators have no say in the selection of students they will teach. Special placement depends upon IQ scores and neurological or psychiatric examinations.

RESOURCE ROOMS

Resource rooms in their many forms may be a first step in the development of a continuum of a special instructional environment. Reger and Koppman (1971) have made the most concise statements in thet literature regarding resource rooms. Resource room programs for children with problems are not new. However, there seems to be a large degree of variation among programs. Hillerich (1969) recommended the resource rooms as a "creative learning center" whose sole objectives are to increase language facility and improve the child's self-concept. Comparing the achievements of children served by resource rooms with those in special classes, Weiner (1969) concluded that the resource rooms serve handicapped children more effectively. Weiner emphasized the ineffectiveness of a widely varied approach as opposed to using any specific technique of instruction (Sabatine, 1972).

CLASS PLACEMENT

The topic of class placement for the educable mentally retarded has generated a wide scope of controversy in the field of special education. Some authorities support the notion that integration provides the best approach for educating EMRs, while other maintain that EMRs can obtain their optimum growth in a special class. There are still others who maintain that the main issue of controversy is not integration versus segregation, but whetherappropriate goals, instructional material, procedures, and supportive services exist for these children.

Integration

Considering the overall picture of research evidence supporting integration, the following guidelines would be useful:

First, it should be recognized that the adjustment of the retarded child to the normal world is unlikely to occur unless the retardate has frequent exposure to it and familiar interaction in it. The use of this interaction causing further maladjustment in the retardate is undesirable, yet adequate adjustment to the normal world by the retardate is dependent on taking such risks (Christopolos, 1969).

Second, a significant point used against special education classes by the proponents of integration is "labeling." There is some evidence that such grouping and labeling not only influences the student's perception of his own ability, but affects his actual abilities (Rosenthal and Jacobson, 1966).

Third, once segregation becomes institutionalized, it is most difficult to eliminate. The difficulty becomes magnified if current special education programs are administratively well entrenched and continue to multiply, introducing the real danger that the primary goal of special education may become self-perpetuation.

Segregation

Special class placement advocates maintain that the special class placement may save the retarded children from psychological damage; without special classes there would be no escape. Advocates of special class placement also maintain that the value judgments and attitudes of teachers and their efforts on pupils self-perception and performance are key questions in the issue of segregation versus integration.

They agree that research findings appear to indicate that grouping handicapped children together has no beneficial effect, but that the harmful effects of special class placement have not been demonstrated yet. It is agreed that the present methods of measurement are not sensitive enough to register change in placement. Therefore, the results supporting regular classes are inconclusive and not based on conducted or scientific principles.

CRITICAL ISSUES

Clearly stated educational goals for EMR children would certainly minimize the conflict. On the other hand, avoidance of clearly stated goals allows educators to support appropriate programs. While it is true that behavioral objectives of classroom instruction have now been fairly well defined in most areas of exceptionality, the objectives are vague for the retarded child. To achieve these goals, educators should have scientific objectives in mind as well as a plan for arranging steps or tasks that will lead to desired behaviors.

Critical issues in developing special education programs are the following: (1) understanding and categorizing the objectives of the school curriculum; (2) defining the objectives or goals in terms of expected behavior, based upon observable and measured data; (3) developing instruments, materials, and activities to assess, if desired, behaviors that have been met; (4) instituting changes at any point in the instructional process, if it appears that objectives are not being achieved; (5) arranging tasks so that retarded children can experience success (This will involve moving from the known to the unknown experiences and from the concrete to the abstract.); (6) developing more effective tools and new curricula to measure characteristics of retarded pupils, emphasizing need and characteristics, rather than placement; (7) recognizing individual differences and the program's scope when planning an instructional program for retarded children.

If proper supportive services are not provided for retarded children, no degree of placement will be successful. Special help teachers, itinerant or school-based, a resource room, and other well-known educational manipulation are needed if any plan is to be successful (Taylor, 1973).

In summary, it can be seen that special education cannot: (1) totally underrate environmental conditions which mold two students dissimilar to one another in values, learning styles, and attitudes (Hall, 1970, p. 19a); (2) underrate differences of the same curriculum which may not be implemented or reinforced identically in every classroom which employs it (Gallagher, 1967, pp. 442-446); (3) rely upon standard approaches or evaluation devices, which may be inappropriate or at least suspected of being unjustified for use with minority group students (Nilson and Schmidt, 1971, p. 382; Adelman, 1971, p. 529; Hall, 1971, p. 18a); (4) confuse the definition of terms so freely attached to learning disabilities of educable mentally retarded children (Iano, 1971, p. 309; Nilson and Schmidt, 1971, p. 384; Dunn, 1968, p. 8; Gallagher, 1972, pp. 528-529); (5) underrate special class placement whose stereotyping results in a negative stigma affecting the child throughout the remainder of his life (Young, 1970, p. 72; Dunn, 1968, p. 9; Simaches, 1970, p. 9; Blatt, 1972, pp. 541-542; Jones, 1972, pp. 554-555); (6) tolerate inappropriate curriculum programs which were not questioned, reevaluated or correctly implemented, causing further paralyzing of special education students (Dunn, 1968, p. 10; Iano, 1971, p. 307; Fine, 1967, p. 429; Simaches, 1970, pp. 12-13; Meyer and Hieronymus, 1970, p. 339; Vaughan, 1973).

Tyson (1969) feels that a syllabus of special education courses should be of use to the students, parents, teachers, and other school personnel in understanding the total program for slow learners in special classes.

RATIONALE

To facilitate the success of special education: (1) school personnel and teachers need to envision the total program from primary through secondary classes; (2) students need to have an overview of the content and purposes of special education to defend themselves from harassments and (3) parents need an overview of the curriculum for special education to insure cooperation and support.

PURPOSES AND OBJECTIVES

The purpose of special education programs is to provide a model philosophy for special education and a syllabus of courses taught in inspecial education classes.

The objectives of such programs are: (1) to increase student, parent, and school personnel acceptance of the total special education programs for slow learners through a model philosophy for special education; (2) to increase school administrator and teacher understanding of the total special education program for slow learners through a model outline of the total program for slow learners and (3) to increase parental and student understanding of the total special education program for slow learners through a model outline of the total program.

WHY STUDENTS ARE PLACED IN SPECIAL EDUCATION

Children are placed in the special or basic skills classes because they are slow in learning the subject matter taught in regular classes. By being placed in special classes, they may thereby: (1) avoid failure and frustration that would result from

313

regular classroom attendance; (2) postpone quitting school; (3) become self-supporting; and (4) learn basic skills.

If these children were to remain in the regular classroom they would experience failure and a feeling of frustration by not being able to keep up with their class-mates' work. When these students have experienced these problems throughout elementary and junior high school, they usually want to quit school as soon as possible and try to be successful by getting a job.

REASONS FOR SPECIAL CLASS SUBJECTS

The curriculum of the special classes covers the following twelve problem areas which affect the student after graduation. (Adapted from Stevens, 1958). (1) learning to keep healthy, happy, and in good shape; (2) learning to live safely at home, work or play; (3) learning to get along with himself; (4) learning to get along with other people; (5) learning to write and talk with other people; (6) learning to use spare time; (7) learning how to travel; (8) learning how to earn a living; (9) learning to take care of a home and family; (10) learning to enjoy life through art and music; (11) learning to cope with weather and other nature problems; (12) learning to manage money.

WHAT STUDENTS SHOULD LEARN IN THE SPECIAL CLASS

The students listed below explain the procedure of the following three categories: primary special, intermediate special, and secondary special classes.

PRIMARY SPECIAL

Reading: The students will learn the alphabet, simple words, and to describe what they see in pictures. They will tell stories about the pictures, the class, and themselves and must learn to listen to the stories and songs. Better reading skills, and an increase in vocabulary is learned. They will learn to take turns talking about events in the class.

Language Arts: The children learn to talk and listen while in a group and how to spell simple words that they are going to write. They will also copy simple sentences. They will learn to give information about themselves (e.g., where they live, full name, age, parents' address, etc.) They are taught how to follow directions and go on errands.

Arithmetic: Simple arithmetic skills will be taught: numbers, counting, writing numbers, recognizing money, and ideas about time and measures. Some children may learn simple addition and subtraction, and may begin to figure out simple problems.

Social Living: The children will practice skills in working and playing together as a class. They will learn about families, school, and community. They will also learn about school rules and safety at school and on the school bus. The children will study about work at home and at school and about their responsibility at home and school. In science, they will learn about such things as seasons, growing foods, and how plants and animals live and grow.

INTERMEDIATE SPECIAL

Reading: These students will continue to learn how to read better aloud and to themselves, and further increase their vocabulary. They will read and copy short stories which the class has written. Free reading time will allow them to really begin to enjoy reading, which will now become an important adjunct to the other subjects taught in the class.

Language Arts: The students practice listening to and following directions. They learn to speak in a group and to act out events in their lives in short plays. They learn how to write down what they want to say. Spelling and writing are also improved by writing short stories and filling out different kinds of forms. They learn to write down important information about themselves and to read and write people's first names. They learn to recognize common road signs, direction signs, information signs, and safety signs. The students will also begin to learn some words in catalogs, telephone books, menus, and other printed matter they will be using outside of school. The skill of letter printing is practiced so the students will be able to fill out applications and other business forms.

Arithmetic: Addition, subtraction, multiplication, and sometimes simple division are practiced by these students. They can now begin to learn simple problems of money, measurement, and time which will be practical when they finish school. Counting money, making change, and problems in buying various items are an important part of their arithmetic class.

Social Living: The students continue learning how to get along in a group. They learn how to do simple jobs in the classroom and have an opportunity to develop leadership. They learn about the working world and the kinds of jobs that they could do in the community. They begin to understand why it is important to work and what it takes to be a good worker. How to travel and get around in the community and the county are taught in this class. The students begin to study map reading, weather seasons, simple mechanics, and science in connection with home and work. Health and safety in the home, school, and at work are a part of the science course. The students will continue to study about food, clothing, and shelter.

SECONDARY SPECIAL

It is desirable to set up the class so that the students may graduate according to the policy of the local school boards. They are usually placed in a regular grade section for homeroom, art, music, physical education, shop, home economics, and sometimes other subjects. They often may take part in other school activities with regular class students.

Reading: For most students, reading skills must still be practiced. New words are learned which they must use on the job or in managing the home and finances.

Language Arts: The students continue to learn talking and listening skills for job interviews and telephone use. They will learn writing and spelling so as to be able to write and copy messages or letters to friends. They learn how to use a newspaper, radio, and television set and practice filling out various business forms.

Arithmetic: Most students must continue drilling in addition, subtraction, multiplication, and simple division. Actual life problems may now be learned in handling money, buying and selling, banking and borrowing, budget and savings, income and local taxes, measuring, and insurance problems.

Social Living: The working world will be the main consideration for the students. Food, clothing, and shelter will be used as a base to teach living problems. The county and state will be used as a model to learn about geography and making a living. The students will also learn how and when to buy various items, about Social Security, local and state laws, driver education, and how to buy a car.

Work Experience: Some school systems may have a work experience program in which senior high school students in special classes who are at least sixteen may participate. The students who want to be in the program are chosen if they are ready to work and if their parents and the school personnel approve their placement. The students will then attend school for one half day and work one half day at jobs in the community in which their school is located. They will work for eight weeks or more at one job and then change to a new work station. In most of these programs, the students are paid at least 25 percent of the minimum wage and are covered by workmen's compensation. These students will have special guidance classes to study jobs and job opportunities in the community. They will also learn which jobs they can do best as well as how to find and keep a job (Tyson, 1969).

LABELING THE "MENTALLY RETARDED"

The main trends and issues now confronting special education concern a serious reevaluation of its true mission, along with the assumptions underlying certain practices and their effectiveness in delivering the needed services to the handicapped child. "Six-Hour Retardates" refers to children who are labeled "mentally retarded" only in the schools; these children do not stand out as retarded in social situations and are unidentified before entering the class. The question is raised whether this practice is justifiable and whether the label affects the child's personal feeling and the behavior of others (peers and teachers) toward the child.

Whether a child's being labeled mentally retarded has a detrimental effect probably depends on a host of variables: (1) whether the child accepts or rejects the label as being accurate; (2) the extent to which the child has experienced informal labeling prior to formal labeling (being called stupid or dummy) by peers, teachers, and parents; (3) the age of the child at the time of labeling; (4) the presence or absence of physical stigma accompanying mental retardation; (5) ethnic status; and (6) the compounding effects of additional factors such as cultural deprivation.

Lacking, but necessary at the present time, is some high-quality research on the labeling issue to move it from one of rhetoric to one of empiricism. Until now seemingly no one has ever questioned decisions made by educators regarding what should be taught to children. Recent developments have led the public to hold the schools accountable. Schools are tax supported, and the public should be shown how the tax dollar is being spent. Most important to the educators is that the teacher show the public that he is accomplishing what he claims.

In the field of special education, teachers have been held less accountable. If a class of trainable mentally retarded did not learn anything within that year, the teacher when confronted with this fact could relate the failure to the characteristics of the children, which implies that the disability resides within the child and the failure to learn can be explained in terms of the child's mental capacities. Failures on the part of the educators now become teaching failures rather than failures of the children. Another major issue arising within the field of special education is the assessment procedures and the validity of instruments like the Stanford-Binet and the Wechsler Intelligence Scale for Children. Barnes (1972), and Mercer (1971), most critical of these instruments, state that the tests depend heavily upon performance at a given time. Another criticism leveled at intelligence testing is that the tests are only useful to classify children (retarded, average, or gifted), but do not diagnose areas of strength or weakness in a given child.

One argument is that information which pinpoints strengths and weaknesses, information which cannot be expected from intelligence tests is needed for educational programming. Another major issue arising within the assessment procedures concerns the interpretations now placed on test results. A distinction is made between performance and capacity (Bortner and Buch, 1970; Cole and Bruner, 1971). When a child gets an answer correct, one has little trouble in interpreting what is meant. When a child gets an answer incorrect, this may be due to limited capacity, but it may also be due to a host of other variables: motivation, anxiety, failure to understand what is being asked, feeling ill on the day of testing, etc. (MacMillan, 1973).

All across the educational scene we see evidence of dissatisfaction with many of the answers that have been given and until now accepted without question. Special education is no exception. Dunn (1968), in an article critical of the treatment of the mildly retarded in the United States, declared that, "In my view, much of our past and present practices are morally and educationally wrong (p. 5)." What is the source of this dissatisfaction? There is no one single research effort responsible; rather, it is due to a reappraisal of the evidence that has been slowly building up over recent years. Many of the practices instituted some time ago have been given their chance; they have been tried and tested and have failed to fulfill the expectations held for them.

In the process of classifying exceptional children, it is unusual to start looking at the way the child is different from other children. As special educators, we must ask the question: Will the classification we use facilitate the educational treatment of the child? On going a step further, we might ask: Does the classification system relate to variables that can be manipulated by the educator? Jordan (1967) notes that "Almost instinctively we emply terms such as 'brain-injury' and 'blindness' expressions with a clear medical or tissue-level connotation. These terms are indicative of disease rather than instructional handicap." The difference is that not all disease states of children are directly relevant to the instructional process" (p. 44).

The use of educationally relevant systems of classification is one of the trends evident in special education. There is a growing emphasis on the use of terms which relate to educational variables; such an approach would reject the term "brain-injury" but would approve of "deficiency in motor dexterity" because the latter term relates to a variable the educator can manipulate. This trend is also very evident in the approach proposed by Quay (1968). In this approach Quay uses a conceptual framework built around the learning process as it occurs in the classroom. The educational exceptionality is described in terms of input, response, and reinforcement. Quay says that, "What is needed to produce a truly effective special education is the development of a conceptual framework which permits the assessment of exceptional children on educationally relevant variables, their grouping according to similarities of dysfunction on these variables, and the development of a classroom teaching technology aimed at the correction of these deficiencies" (p. 26).

PRECISION TEACHING

Perhaps one of the most significant trends in special education is the concern for objectivity and precision in educational practices. Lance (1969) makes a plea for competency in determining precise needs of children; competency in preparing objectives as precisely stated outcomes; precision in preparing prescriptions; and precision in evaluating and recording. An example of the development of precision in stating educational objectives can be seen in the changing format of curriculum statements. Curriculum guides are being replaced by inventories of specific competencies to be taught. The language of the "guides" is changing. It is no longer acceptable to express educational objectives using terms such as "to appreciate" or "to grasp the significance of." Mager (1962) has stressed the importance of objectively defining the behavior that we expect from the child. The work of Lindsley (1964) in developing methods of direct measurement of classroom behavior is finding acceptance in many special education cases. Lindsley advocates that teachers adopt a research approach applicable to her own teaching. The teacher is trained to objectively define behaviors, record their rates of occurrence, and attempt to change the behaviors in order to assess the effects of the attempt. The desired change can be one of acceleration for appropriate behaviors or the reverse for inappropriate behaviors.

This trend toward precision in the statement and evaluation of educational objectives has far-reaching implications for all aspects of special education. This trend is not concerned with the promotion of a particular need, objective, or even philosophy, unless it is a philosophy of efficiency, reality, and truth. This trend is concerned with providing the machinery of improvement. No longer will we have to go for years with inconsistencies existing between what we say we are doing and what is being done, (Hofneister, 1969).

School demands are varied and far-reaching. First, the child must adjust to new feeling tones, behavioral blueprints and structures. He must try to fit into a new environment, both as an individual and as a member of a group. Secondly, the child is confronted with an entirely new array of learning symbols. Since far too little is known about his characteristic learning process, the rate of development of his various abilities, and the varieties of his motivations, absorption of all this new information may be hampered. Finally, the learning process is an active one produced by the voluntary participation of the child in interaction with objects and people in his environment. Learning is impeded if the individual is biologically incomplete (through genetic or acquired diseases). He is handicapped if deprived of opportunity, experiences, or the tools of learning. If his life is a series of failures and frustrations, motivation for further strivings will soon cease. Chronic environmental stress can hinder a child's learning as severely as polio can inhibit his walking. If he is not sure of himself, he cannot approach and interact adequately with the world of others, and consequently is unable to manipulate the symbols and abstract values within it to his own learning advantage.

Years ago when a child couldn't learn, we tended to say he was lazy, undisciplined, or deliberately resistant. In many instances punishment such as cutting his allowance, taking away his bicycle, or keeping him home from the movies was considered the cure-all. Educators, psychologists, and parents firmly held to discipline which, in some cases, worked. Many children were forced to alter their learning habits, but for others, forced learning was of no avail. The professionals tended to shake their heads, give up, or wait it out, hoping that in time things would work out. There is no doubt that in some cases learning took place. Perhaps because goals were not as high as at the present time, these children did manage to get through high school and subsequently made an adequate social adjustment. In more difficult cases, however, children left school basically illiterate.

SECONDARY EFFECTS AND "LABELING"

School achievements may be lowered as much by the consequences of secondary effects as by the cerebral dysfunction itself. The child's difference is often a source of embarrassment, anxiety and guilt for his parent. Trying to explain away his behavior as "psychological" only increases their anxiety since it implies their failure. The problem is either unsuccessfully avoided or extensive efforts are made to have it investigated, usually an equally fruitless task with the tremendous shortage of diagnostic and treatment facilities. The parents may either put extra pressure on the child to conform, or provide no limits or guidelines for him. With each case problems multiply. Inevitably, the child picks up the message of his parents' anxiety and reacts to it through insecurity, withdrawal, acting out hostility, etc. After many false starts, much self-analysis, and frantic searching among clinics and doctors for a favorable diagnosis, the parents eventually settle down to accept the truth about their child. The child will be "labeled." In a way, this is almost comforting after the frantic activity of the previous phase. After all, the child's brain impairment has been described as static and irrevocable. The only thing to do now is to love and care for him. This is how a labeled child gets deprived of an adequate life. The quite understandable resigned attitudes of the parents are soon reflected in the child. No wonder he is unable to advance. No wonder that he withdraws more and more into himself, being unable to escape his relegated position as "the dull one."

EVALUATING LEARNING DISABILITIES

Children with learning disabilities fail to exhibit such traits as the following: (1) absorbing information through one or more of the senses not necessarily related to sensory deficits per se; (2) organizing raw sensory data; (3) expressing knowledge through speech or writing; (4) remembering; and showing (5) readiness to meet the demands of home, neighborhood, and school.

In assessing a chld with learning difficulties, the following developmental factors need to be considered:

Auditory

1. Inefficient listening (with normal hearing)
2. Trouble distinguishing between speech sounds; e.g., "lecture" and "electric"
3. Transposition of sounds; e.g., "plasket" for "plastic"
4. Inability to follow rapid conversation or understand lengthy sentences
5. Inability to deal with timed auditory stimuli (reproducing rhythmic taps)
6. Inability to remember information told rather than seen

Visual (with normal vision)

1. Inefficient use of the eyes, such as, difficulty in converging on a word; inability to move eyes smoothly along a line of print

2. Little capacity for visual imagery; i.e., can't remember what words look like even after many exposures
3. Difficulty in discriminating between fine distinctions in shapes, as between letters: e.g.., c and e; or to perceive and learn directional differences: e.g., as between b and d.

Language

1. Inefficient listeners may confuse and disorganize language because of the distortions in their listening patterns.
2. Others may show little facility for language itself, as evidenced in their limited vocabulary, poor grammar, missing the point of a story or joke, or confusing complex directions. In addition, their understanding of reading materials may be poor.
3. Their language comprehension may be adequate, but they may be unable to express themselves easily, put ideas into words, or tell a story in logical sequences. This may be demonstrated in both speech and writing, or only in writing.

Movement

Illegible handwriting or laborious writing, caused by poor manual control, is often a major obstacle to success in school. Underlying this difficulty is a dim awareness of body parts, their position, and their potential for movement. The difficulty may stem from the following:
1. Poor integration of vision and movement; difficulty in prejudging the consequences of particular movements, such as when guiding their hands incorrectly
2. No consistent hand preference (do not develop skill in their dominant hand)
3. No awareness of right or left hand
4. Use of right hand for left-sided activities and left hand for right-sided activities.
    The observer should also alert himself to possible learning difficulties by considering the child's gait, general body management, and ability to execute skilled or rhythmic movements.

Concepts

One cannot take for granted that a child has mastered certain basic concepts of space, time, and number, as shown in the following examples:
1. The concept of top in two-dimensional surface; i.e., might know the top of a bottle but not the top of a page

Time and Number

2. Does not know which is longer — a month or a week.

3. Cannot remember days of the week or months of the year
4. Cannot recognize numbers

Remembering

5. Unable to profit from repetitive drill unless they understand what is being taught
6. Disorganized by competition
7. Unable to learn facts handed to them by authority, but can remember ideas they have figured out for themselves
8. Remember selectively; i.e., what is seen but not what is heard or vice versa
9. Remember what they have learned by doing, rather than by looking or listening (Smith, 1967).

Jaslow and Smith (1972) argue that the term "mental retardation" does not convey to the uninformed public an accurate picture of the person with this handicap. They have suggested that this term would be more accurately used in referring to the problem itself rather than in describing the nature of the person. They would prefer that the phrase "person with a mental retardation problem" rather than the "mentally retarded person" be used.

The term "mental retardation" can be criticized because it implies that the person's problem is in the "mental" area and specifically that the person himself is mentally retarded in some way or another. Mental retardation seems to imply an "area" or "entity" of retarded development. The term "mental retardation" very simply refers to the problem certain perople have in modifying behavioral patterns in accordance with the consequences of their responses. It is possible that changes in methodologies of teaching can modify certain of these behavioral patterns. Progress in this area cannot be considered advanced at present (McAllister, 1972).

If modern approaches to the problems associated with mental retardation and mental illness can be compared, one can characterize them as strikingly similar attempts at overcoming the unfruitful implications of these diagnostic labels. Characteristics which will contribute to the diagnosis vary from person to person. It is not surprising, for example, that (1) the diagnosis of schizophrenia is notoriously unreliable and (2) the label tells little about what we need to know in order to provide a rehabilitation and treatment program.

A similar line of reasoning applies to the label "mental retardation," which, in addition to the common label of maladaptive behavior, also denotes a score below some arbitary cut-off point on an intelligence test. Consider the following: (1) a variation in cut-off points occurs because of differing local usage; (2) large number of individuals are retarded on the basis of test scores, but never fully diagnosed as retarded because they do not come to the attention of the psychologist, the educator, or community at large; (3) significant numbers of people diagnosed as retarded have IQ scores which may, in fact, be approximately of average intelligence range. The label "mental retardation" obscures the more important differences and emphasize the similarities which draw attention to the mentally retarded person.

Retarded people are enormously varied in their cognitive and motivational profiles and in the level of adaptive behaviors displayed. The maladaptive behavior of a retarded person is not explained by his low IQ, any more than the adaptive behavior of a nonretarded person is explained by his high IQ. The term "mental retardation" focuses exclusively on the intellectual sphere and ignores the social-emotional factors. The retardation label leads us to think of a retarded person as an overgrown child. The bulk of problems which the retardates encounter in their lives as they reach adult status is more in keeping with their chronological age than with their psychometric mental age, while the mental age counterparts of the retarded adults are in the primary or secondary grades and occupied with sports and other recreational activities. The adult retardates are attempting to find and hold down jobs, seek out sexual compansionship, and considering the question of marriage and family. The adult retardate lacks the supporting environment of his mental age counterpart who continues to live with his parents (Milgram, 1972).

The present IQ 50–79 has been so long accepted for classes called "educable mentally retarded" that few people seem to seriously question it. What does "educable" mean? Why was this particular term attached to the classification system? Could it be that most of the children who fall within this classification could learn to "call words," sometime mistaken for reading, even though many could not effectively use the skill?

What happens to the mentally retarded child after leaving school? The retarded child, having remained in a special class for a number of years learning to read, eventually is dismissed with or without a certificate. Many of these children could not read well and had no chance of holding steady employment, while others made wonderful gains and even become sought-after workers. Would it not be logical, therefore, to reclassify the mentally retarded in terms of their future, rather than in terms of academic school grades and goals?

An IQ of 65–80 for the better group and below 65 for the lower group would appear to be a great improvement. Most of the more capable students will become literate at a certain level. Most of them can adapt to and profit from work-study programs. A core curriculum as well as appropriate social skills and motivational goals can be achieved. The individuals in this group will not be substantially different from the children in regular classes, so they can be more easily integrated.

The group having an IQ range of 50 to 60 will be quite small and from the standpoint of adulthood and vocational prospects can be handled with the below 50 IQ range or by themselves (Porter, 1970).

Between 1946 and 1966, the number of special education classes in public schools in Wisconsin increased from 142 to 972 (Bureau for Handicapped Children, 1967). Nationally, a similar pattern can be found. In some instances, special education classes have been established for emotionally disturbed or brain-damaged children; however, the vast majority of these classes have been for the mentally retarded. According to the policies of the Bureau for Handicapped Children, students are placed in such classes only after mental retardation has been clearly established by an individual intelligence test administered by a certified psychometrist or psychologist and by other evaluation procedures. The children in these classes are therefore seen by teachers, other students, and society at large as being mentally retarded, and the expectations for them have therefore been quite naturally limited. Similarly, most students in these programs are aware of the evaluations that have been made of them. The knowledge and placement in special education classes often leads to a negative self-image (Carroll, 1967). The accuracy of the evaluation procedures used in selecting students for special education classes is therefore of obvious importance. The following suggestions for modifying the evaluation procedures for special education placement do not seem unrealistic even given the limited number of personnel available.

First, annual regional institutes within each state should be established for individuals evaluating students for special education classes. At the institutes, these individuals should meet with clinical psychologists and other specialists in personality and intellectual evaluation to discuss ways of more effectively differentiating the basically retarded individual from the intellectually ineffectively functioning person whose low scores reflect emotional maladjustment or selective brain damage. The programs of these institutes should include the discussion of actual case material brought by the participants.

Second, it should be mandatory that the test protocols and all other pertinent information available on the case be examined by a qualified clinical psychologist in addition to the original examiner prior to the child's official placement in a special education program. Preferably this person would be a consultant from outside the school system. This consultant should have the authority to require additional evaluation materials on any child where significant evidence exists that his problem is not clearly one of mental retardation.

Third, at least once each year a consultant should visit all special education classes for the mentally retarded to observe the children, talk with the teachers, and examine the records to find any students who no longer appear appropriately placed in special education classes. This consultant should be a qualified clinical psychologist or someone with comparable training in psychological testing as well as personality development and evaluation (Barrington, 1968).

Special education, as a process, has the responsibility for helping the multihandicapped individual raise his levels of functioning in each of the domains of human abilities so that he may develop strategies to cope with a variety of life situations. The process of special education is directed toward the production of an adequately adjustable individual, not just an adjusted individual.

Special education is enrichment, providing a foundation upon which a child might forge ahead, giving him multisensory experiences, which he may not have had or may not have been able to interpret.

Special education is developmental, starting at the child's level of comfortable functioning and satisfaction, whatever it may be, recognizing the next step, however small, and assuring movement toward short- and long-range goals. Special education is evaluative (or diagnostic), seeking the impediments to learning; bringing to bear what is normal at certain stages in child growth and development (how children might be expected to respond to ordinary visual, auditory, and tactile stimuli); and raising questions rather than attaching labels. Educational activities and evaluation include the seeking of information through observation of the child functioning in selected school experiences. The teacher identifies assets and liabilities of the individual and draws conclusions upon which the program is based.

Special education is preventive, emphasizing the deletion of failure, boredom and time-wasting which leads to inactivity, malfunctioning, and secondary handicaps. The teacher is alert to the danger that children learn not to increase their knowledge because of the specimen provided for them; that they may develop behavior problems and emotional disturbances because teachers do not provide the necessary structure in selection of stimuli to guarantee successful response. Without clear-cut learning tasks and structure, educators may reinforce children's confusion and learning problems.

Special education is experimental, offering opportunity for applying research findings in small groups and selected populations; testing educational hypotheses and cutting new pathways.

Special education is preparatory, for varying degrees of satisfactors or independent living as well as for vocational placement. Not to be overlooked is the frequent need for preparing the community for the return of some of its citizens who have been living and learning in special residential settings.

Special education is highly individualized, assuming often the lack of clear concept of the nature of the disability and identification of distinct characteristics for common learning en masse. Reference is made constantly to the child's diagnosis, functioning, and prognosis for selection of school content, guidance, and programming.

Special education is mobile and continuous, providing for the child wherever he may reside, whether on a temporary or permanent basis.

One of the main functions of special education is to see that these objectives are implemented. Special educators resist decisions to reject individuals with disabilities and handicaps, and are busy developing resources within the schools to deal with those individuals who might easily be rejected and who, in the past, often were rejected.

Special education development emphasizes the responsibility of schools to allocate children to programs likely to be best for them. Traditionally, the only criteria for the placement in a given program was the paramount handicap of a child. It could be a physical disability, such as deafness, blindness, a crippling condition, impaired heart, etc. Another criterion could be the IQ of the individual. Thus, those with IQs below 50 were placed in one program; those with IQs between 50 and 75 in another program; and those above 75 found themselves in regular school classes. The paradox of this agreement is that discipline such as special education which has its principal aim, provisions for individual differences among school children should mistakenly assume that all children with deafness, blindness, IQ 50, or some other handicap are the same and need the same educational programs. As a result, in special education classes children are found who vary greatly in their abilities, interests, and handicaps (Goldberg, 1969).

EDUCATION

In a democratic society, the community assumes the responsibility for the education of all of its children. Special provisions must be made for those children who cannot adequately benefit from the instruction in the regular class.

Programming for the educable mentally retarded involves the development of special provisions for these students since they cannot benefit adequately from regular classroom instruction. To achieve this, several guidelines have been developed that will prove beneficial to school administrations in the planning of programs for the EMR. These guidelines are not exhaustive and should be considered only as one approach in providing quality education for retarded children

1. The mentally retarded child should be identified as early as possible by qualified experts. According to Dunn (1963), provisions should be made for a complete examination which would involve a variety of specialists including psychologists, psychiatrists, social workers, physicians, and nurses. The complete screening process should involve a medical, intellectual, social-emotional, and educational evaluation.

2. The EMR child should be assigned to special classes in accordance with his needs. Knowledge of the EMR child's strengths and weaknesses is required in order to develop a meaningful program. Care must be taken not to assign children to special classes for the EMR on the basis of physical handicaps, emotional disturbances, or behavior problems. Definite standards of eligibility should be established, such as chronological age, social maturity, mental age, educational achievements, and IQ.

3. The curriculum for EMRs should be based upon their needs, interests, and capacities and should, as much as possible, promote their personal and social growth. The curriculum should be extremely practical. A generous amount of time should be devoted to the teaching of hygiene, physical training, health care and habits, nutrition and safety. Adequate physical training is desirable. Physical training may include games and folk dancing. The EMR child can be taught simple reading and figuring, according to Taylor (1973). This will require considerably more drill and practice than what is given in regular class instruction. Taylor believes that long, involved sentences, abstract words and abstract numbers are definitely beyond the comprehension of the EMR child.

4. Facilities, equipment, and supplies should permit and foster the development of a functional curriculum for the mentally retarded. Kirk (1951) states that it is necessary for the teacher of a mentally retarded child to improvise, adapt, and adjust books and materials to the rate of learning of the child.

5. Teachers of the EMR should receive special training and be qualified to educate these children. Special class teachers, in general, should have instructional skills not normally required of regular class teachers. That is, they should have taken special courses in methods and materials needed to enable them to cope with the problems of the mentally retarded. Cain (1953) suggested that the prepration of special class teachers should contain certain essentials including (1) orientation and psychology courses dealing with the characteristics and needs of mentally retarded children (2) teaching and curriculum courses with materials and methods realistically related to the education of the mentally retarded; (3) actual observation, participation, and practice teaching with the mentally retarded. Teachers should be trained in using audio-visual materials.

6. There should be a well-defined guidance program for the mentally retarded. Slaughter (1964) indicated that for guidance programs concerning the mentally retarded to be most effective should be a continuous process that begins when the child enters school and is available for as long a period of time as is needed. A special class teacher is likely to find many handicaps and maladjustments among a group of mentally retarded children, including speech disorders, defective vision, poor reading ability, and behavioral maladjustment.

The following represent some common problems characteristic of mentally retarded children for which appropriate goals and guidelines should be established and a curriculum developed.

Goals and Guidelines for Curriculum

Language: Language development is of the utmost importance because it is highly related to successful academic achievement, to the facilitation of social interaction, and to the creation of an adequate self-concept. There is some basis for the belief that language can promote motor development.

Social Skills: Weak language development, poor social models by parents, overprotection by parents, and rejection by peers and members of the family are frequent inhibiters.

Self-Concept: The development of a strong positive self-concept is fostered when the child is able to interact successfully, but children who lag behind in language development have difficulty communicating their ideas to others. Too often, the mentally retarded child encounters failure in developing a positive self-concept because the special class teacher has not given due attention to what Hunt (1961) refers to as the "match," that is, providing the mentally retarded child with tasks compatible with cognitive development so that he can interact with others and complete tasks successfully.

Self-Help: One of the basic concerns of parents and teachers is that the mentally retarded child develop self-help skills. Immaturity, inappropriate training techniques which include overprotection, and the consequent lack of opportunity appear to be major reasons for the lack of self-help skills.

Motor Skills: Many handicapped children lack motor skills, A child with poorly developed motor skills tends to feel inadequate and is reluctant to attempt activities requiring well-developed motor skills.

Cognitive Skills: Development of cognitive skills influences all facets of a child's development. A child, retarded in cognitive skills, is usually retarded in other important facets of development: self-help, social, motor, and language development (Karnes and Lehrbach, 1973).

CURRICULUM

The curriculum may be said to be the organized implementation of an academic program. For it to be effective, the curriculum must be sequential so that there is orderly and systematic progress from one level of instruction to the next level. It must be flexible and developed in a way that meets individual as well as group needs. The following considerations must be given: (1) general goals of the educational program; (2) demands that society will make on each individual as worker and as social being; (3) skills, knowledge, and attitudes needed to enable each individual to meet expectations or society; (4) sequence to be followed in developing learning experiences so that there may be systematic and orderly progress.

Ninth Grade

Mathematics, English Review (or Reading Laboratory), Social Studies, Physical Education (or Adaptive P.E.)

Electives

Homemaking, Special Education I and II; Special Education Classes of Arts and Crafts, Metal Shop, and Woodshop; Regular Class for Beginning Band, Boy's Glee Club, Military Science, and Typing.

Tenth Grade

Health and Driver's Education added to curriculum.

Eleventh Grade

Students at this grade level have a choice of either an elective or Work-Experience; also, Civics, which is required, should be added to the curriculum.

Twelfth Grade

Work-Experience now becomes a requirement in addition to the regular curriculum (Blazoric, 1966).

CURRICULUM CONTENT AT EACH LEVEL

Primary Level

At this stage of instruction, there is a prereadiness and readiness level with emphasis on sensory and motor training and on the development of social competencies and language.

Intermediate Level

At this level of instruction, basic skills are begun along with broadening and strengthening of the social competencies.

Junior High Level

At this stage, the curriculum should consolidate social and academic learning and should make possible the application of this learning to prevocational training and homemaking skills.

Senior High Level

At this level, the emphasis should be on using and strengthening the basic skills and on helping each pupil develop the social and vocational competencies to become productive members of society.

Vocational Orientation of Program

A meaningful vocational program should emphasize the development of skills, attitudes, and competencies; it should begin at appropriate levels in the instructional program. Emphasis on attitudes and good work habits will begin at the preschool or primary level and continue through the secondary level. Emphasis on specific skills and competencies may begin at the junior high level.

A vocational program is concerned with more than the development of specific skills. Each individual needs to know the proper ways of behaving, and should have good attitudes and work habits and see the importance of his job.

Specific attributes are the following: (1) acceptable personal appearnce at all times; (2) promptness and regularity on the job; (3) compatibility with fellow workers and employees; (4) care of tools, machines, and materials on the job; (5) observance of safety rules in working situations; (6) skills necessary to perform assigned tasks.

The total educational program of the retarded individual must be geared toward helping him acquire those attitudes, skills, or competencies that will enable him to become a productive member of our society (Tennessee State Department of Education, 1970).

In the Detroit schools, the special education curriculum for the educable mentally retarded is divided into four classes. Special A Curriculum offers purposeful learning experiences and academic skills that will meet the children's need and capacities.

The Junior Special B Program is then considered a transitional step between the Special A and the Senior Special B Program. The curriculum usually offers a one-half day of academic work and a one-half day of prevocational training in a multipurpose room where experiences in cooking, woodworking, sewing, and crafts teach the students practical skills.

The Senior Special B Program includes a curriculum offering both prevocational and vocational experiences. The Special B Program may be terminal for some students; the opportunity for promotion to junior and senior high school special preparatory classes is available when certain standards are met. Special preparatory classes have selected students from Senior Special B. The criteria for special preparatory classes is as follows: (1) minimum chronological age of fifteen; (2) minimum average of 3.5 grade equivalent or better, based on standardized tests; (3) above average social adjustment.

A portion of the instructional time is under the direction of the special education teacher. In most instances, the pupils attend regular classes in shop and health education. After attending one of these classes for a year, the students can become eligible for promotion to a senior high school preparatory class under the following conditions: (1) minimum chronological age of sixteen; (2) at least one year of successful work in a junior high school preparatory class; (3) an average grade equivalent of 5.0 or better on standardized tests; (4) above average social adjustment.

These students have some of the basic subjects in special classrooms and other subjects such as vocational education, science, art, and music are provided in regular high school classes with nonhandicapped students (Detroit Board of Education, 1965).

VOCATIONAL EDUCATION IN SPECIAL EDUCATION

The term "occupational education" is not new in the education of the mentally retarded. Today, the newest concept in education stipulates that occupational education is needed by everyone and that schools "must provide for the world of work as an integral part of the curriculum from kindergarten through post high school years" (Smoker, 1971). Because occupational education soon will be extended to all students and since the unskilled labor category will be at an all-time low by 1975 (according to the Bureau of Labor Statistics, less than 5 percent), the mentally retarded can look forward to increased competition for the so-called "bottom-of-the-barrel" positions unless they receive intensive occupational training. The present EMR occupational program is an integral part of an overall program open to all students. It includes cooperative work study, distributive education, public services program (PL 90-576, Part H), dietary aide program, electromechanical program, health aide program, consumer education, human relations, on-the-job occupational seminar for 8th grade, occupational information for the 9th grade, preoccupational educational and vocational EMR classes in the junior and senior high schools.

EMRs in Standard Class

Currently a majority of EMR students are enrolled in one or more of the following courses: business, mathematics, typing, applied arts, shop, home economics, human relations, chorus, gym, and band.

EMRs in Occupational Programs

EMR students currently are enrolled in the following high school occupational programs: dietary aide, health aide, and the general cooperative work-study programs.

On-the-Job Supervision

Generally, the EMR teacher-coordinator is responsible for on-the-job supervision, the exception being those EMR students who are enrolled in the more intensive internship programs (for example, health aide, which is supervised by the respective teacher-coordinator of that program). The actual job development is the responsibility of the teacher-coordinator of the students' particular occupational program. Final decision for job placement of the EMR student is made in cooperation with the coordinator of the specific occupational program, the director of occupational education, and the EMR teacher-coordinator.

SUGGESTIONS FOR EFFECTIVE OCCUPATIONAL PROGRAMS

1. Sell the faculty; emphasize the positive academic ability of the students.
2. Sell the employer; emphasize the positive academic and specific abilities of the students.
3. Sell the students on their own abilities.
4. Implement a realistic curriculum; incorporate those academic skills which yield essential occupational skills for job success.
5. Define objectives for each student; write an individual training program for each student before the student is placed in a cooperative job.

6. Provide a socialization program; utilize not only classroom activities, but all community resources.
7. Convince the parents that they are the most important persons in a teenager's life.
8. Get other teachers involved.
9. Supervise and follow up; don't leave the EMR student in the world of work without constant support.
10. Remove the degrading special class label (Gardner, 1973).

EDUCATION AND WORK-STUDY PROGRAM

Vocationally oriented opportunities are available to many retarded public school students. In a work-study program, a student spend part of his time at school and part at a "work station" which can be a competitive job or workshop setting, depending on age, level of ability, and the availability of work. In general, the minimal age for acceptance is seventeen and the basic academic skill achievement criteria is included.

Some states, New Jersey, for example, involve high school age students on a half-day basis; others use an alternate day basis. New York prefers the alternate week format. With this arrangement on a competitive job, two students are placed to provide the employer with a worker each day (Borretti, 1972). Adjustment and success in a vocation by EMR students and others are dependent in part on pre-employment conditions which include these factors: (1) demonstration of substantial sophistication concerning appropriate vocational alternatives; (2) level of work motivation to sustain vocational goal-directed behavior; (3) emotional and intellectual readiness to meet the demands of employment.

One explanation for rehabilitation failure with retarded persons may be attributed to the counselor's limited understanding of the client's personality and potential. A program of vocational development initiated by a counselor or a school system may provide the retarded client with an understanding of his vocational development and adjustment problems and also with a motivation to participate meaningfully in a work-study program.

Because of changing industrial and business procedures, increasing worker production, expectations, and inadequate prevocational training, retarded individuals are less able to meet the demands of employers. The importance of a well-planned multidisciplined vocational education curriculum for retarded persons in institutions and in the community has been emphasized. The acquisition of job-related skills and development of awareness of the demands of the working world are essential for the retarded person, if job-seeking and job-holding efforts are to succeed.

Preparation of slow-learning (EMR) students for job-seeking and job-holding responsibilities must be carefully planned and carried out if such students are to become fully functioning citizens in today's society (Salomone, Lehmann, and Green, 1973).

Several recommendations for vocational training curricula designed to prevent failure would be the following:

1. Teaching and developing attitudes and concepts required in community development
2. Intensive study of job requirements and job opportunities in the community
3. Providing the retarded with knowledge of and familiarity with the various community agencies which could help in vocational, social, and personal problems
4. A course in driver's training
5. Counseling service within the school situation
6. Extended instruction in clothing care, laundering, pressing, food and cooking, child care, buying and budgeting, sewing, entertaining friends, home decorating, cleaning, simple home repairs, yard beautification and care, gardening, and other immediately practical abilities.

For the residential retardate, a five-phase vocational-training program must be in order:

1. There should be a prevocational evaluation in which the aptitudes, interests, and abilities in a variety of clerical, skilled, and semiskilled services and subprofessional occupations are tested. In this period, the students are to be assisted in developing acceptable work habits and achieving work confidence under simulated or actual work situations.

2. The second phase would consist of an on-campus training program for half-day.

3. The third phase would be a full-day work program.

4. There should be a day work program within the community with face-to-face situations in the competitive job market. Public utilities and transportation facilities are used. An increased awareness of agencies occurs. Incomes are budgeted. Ability of the student workers to perform in an independent fashion is observed.

5. The final phase includes an extended leave program with follow-up vocational counseling (Goldberg, 1963).

Wolfensberger (1967) has argued against the overrreliance on IQ scores as a criteria for vocational suitability. Rynbrandt (1947) and Bobroff (1956) found skilled tradesmen whose IQs ranged between 70–79.

Very little has been said about the low-moderate or severely retarded individual's vocational potential. Keith (1972) has noted that a moderately retarded person attains a "normal" rate of production as a consequence of the manipulation of reinforcement schedules.

A random selection was made of thirty-five employees who had worked at least three months at the Southeast Nebraska Community Sheltered Workshop. Individual IQ scores were obtained from existing psychological records and ranged from 26 to 82. Production scores were determined by averaging production in three different nonconsecutive weeks. The thirty-five retarded persons were then ranked on the basis of their IQ and production scores and analyzed via Kendall and Spearman relationship (r=-.01 p 145 p .05).

IQ then does not seem to be a requisite factor for vocational production or a valid predictor for it. Other experimentation was done on the IQ and vocational success. The results obtained seem to indicate that the vocational evaluation of an individual may be more valid when based on actual vocational behaviors, rather than on somewhat abstracted tests or checklists (Albin, 1973).

SELECTED SPECIAL EDUCATION INNOVATIONS

SMOCK PROJECT

The Smock Project[1] reflects a "marriage" of the schools with a community-based agency. This in itself is unique, not because of the difficulty to consummate, but because of the reluctance of the schools to become totally immersed in the social-economic problems of the community. The success of this venture and its relative ease of operation is adequate proof to assure others that this project can be replicated anywhere. The needs of the underprivileged and deprived are legion. Their deprivation should demand a greater involvement and awareness, not only in authorizing more funds to be allocated, but also, in a more meaningful manner, through enlisting the energies and efforts of people rather than dollars. In addition to providing an impact on the community through changing attitudes and life styles, the community and its problems should have an impact on the education of the students. In these experiences the students were mentally retarded, and their present state was as blighted and limited as that of the community.

It was agreed that the schools would provide teachers, students, tools, and transportation. The agency would provide the house to be renovated or a lot on which to build, the building supplies, adequate compensation insurance for the students, and be responsible for the sale of the property upon completion. There would be no charge for labor to the agency for either the students or the teachers, and there would be no completion date set or work schedule requirements demanded by the agency. The prime concern for the school would be to teach and develop skills, while for the agency, the major responsibility would be to provide low-cost and fixed-income housing.

The students selected for the class reflect those whom the school, the parents, and the students themselves wish to consider as applicants. No one is referred before the 10th grade since the program is regarded as a senior high school curriculum, and this training should be a culminating activity leading to graduation and employment. Teachers who have noted interests and abilities in junior high school shop classes refer students and confer about other applicants. Counselors and school psychologists can refer students and are also part of the team to confer about an applicant. Parents have submitted names as they have become more

---

[1] Intermediate Unit 1, 1148 Wood Street, California, Pennsylvania 15419

cognizant of the program and, as a result, desire to have their children considered. Also, the student himself is welcomed as an initial referral. Prior to a selection, each parent is contacted and the entire program and its significance to the student is discussed. Even with the selection of a particular individual there still exists some flexibility, permitting him to move into another program without being penalized or "held back" for graduation.

These students remain at the work site all day, but have their school day divided into half-day sessions. One half day is spent on the job and the other half day in the classroom. At the Smock Project there are two teachers, one a certified special education teacher and the other a vocational teacher. There are approximately twenty students assigned to the project. At any given period, half of them approximately ten, are in the classroom and the other half are with their vocational teacher engaged in the building trade activities. At noon, following lunch, the groups switch. Those in the classroom go to the work site as the others take up the classroom activities. The special education teacher and the vocational teacher must work together, perhaps more completely than teachers generally are expected to. The students' actual work exposure makes learning more meaningful, as the need for math skills and reading skills emerge. Problems which arise on the job often reflect unlearned basic skills associated with the elementary curriculum. As an example, when sawing boards on the job, the need to understand fractions and the motivation to learn about them could never be better attained. The classroom periods conducted by an experienced and certified special education teacher can translate the deficiencies noted by the vocational teacher into a most worthwhile lesson. The school provides a learning lab (trailer) as the classroom on the site because of the distance between the high school and the project and the obvious time lost in travel. The class size is held to ten students per teacher, so that neither safety nor the number of students one instructor can adequately teach are compromised.

The program is responsible for the placement of its graduates in gainful employment, and satisfied employers keep coming back and inquiring about future graduates. Finding employment for these students have proven itself less difficult than originally assumed. The graduates do have a skill to sell, and the building trades are presently among the nation's largest employers. It is felt that the graduates are more prepared for being good productive citizens than the average high school graduate and that they know what they want, feel a sense of confidence in having been trained, can present themselves well, and talk the "lingo" of the trade to prospective employers. The homes they have renovated stand as a monument to what they can do.

Philosophy of the Project

In order to effectively teach the mentally retarded, it must be recognized that these students are more like the so-called normal students than they are different. Actually, the major difference between retarded and normal students is one of time. Thus, given the necessary time to mature and to learn and develop skills, the retarded can reach heights heretofore considered unattainable.

After being involved with these students, it should become apparent to an instructor that he could teach more complicated skills, If a complete job and skill analysis is done, including the dexterities, coordinates, and attitudes required to perform the tasks, then the instructor can be relatively assured that the end result for the students will be the proficiency desired.

The teacher should accept the responsibility for his students' performance and therefore develop an attitude that if the students fail to learn, he has in some way failed to teach. Failure by the student should motivate the teacher to try other approaches, to rekindle the determination in both teacher and student to press on, and to make the student cognizant of the fact that the teacher shares his frustration. By no means should a teacher retain any of societies labeling of the mentally retarded as "failures" for not learning as much as expected. It is ridiculous to assume that the mentally retarded can become trained as skilled employees at the moment they are introduced to a particular trade. Therefore, the ultimate goal of being productive citizens begins in the primary special education class.

To assure the physical stamina and agility needed for a typical eight-hour day when the retarded reach adulthood, physical education and adaptive physical education, which should begin in the elementary school and continue, is essential.

An arts and crafts program introduced in the elementary grades can be imperative in those early developmental years when dexterity and hand and eye coordination are established. A total educational program for the mentally retarded which does not include arts and crafts in the formative years would penalize and interfere with expected trade-skill proficiencies at the senior high and adult level.

Occupational information, beginning no later than the intermediate levels and continuing into junior high school, would be most helpful in the development of attitudes, interests, self-images, and work habits. A segment of our mentally retarded do come from underprivileged and welfare homes where these attitudes and images could be quite limited and less than desirable. It becomes necessary for the school to take a positive role and, therefore, become involved and responsible for establishing them.

The industrial arts classes in junior high school should definitely introduce the students to the importance of shop safety and how to practice safety when using the tools and machinery. The curriculum would include how to properly use small amounts of hand and power tools and familiarize students with wood, nails, paints, varnishes, and stains. These teachers must be alert to any emerging interest areas as they consciously begin to instill enthusiasm in the students to take pride in what they are learning.

The age bracket (C.A. 16–21) assures the parent and the school that compensation and proper insurance coverage could be provided. Proper coverage is for the students' protection, as it should be for all vocational trainees, and is not to be construed as "protection" for the teachers and agencies involved. Contrary to what some public opinion might imply, these students are not accident prone. Therefore, with adequate training procedures and background, they can become as safety-conscious and establish safety records as impressive as the normal. Accident proneness in any individual, in part, reflects inadequate training, frustration, and anxiety, but never mental retardation.

The goal of the program is to expose the students in as many different facets of the building trades as possible by actually doing the work involved under close supervision. Those of us in education have accepted the philosophy that one can instruct the mentally retarded to become reasonably proficient in many areas if the skill is broken down into its simplest components, and each task is taught in strict sequence. It has become quite evident to me that most of the limitations placed on the retarded are due basically to society's understanding of the retarded. Therefore, as one becomes better acquainted with the retarded, one is enabled to penetrate this artificial facade of limitations. It is further evident, because of the program of prevocational training, that the student has been prepared emotionally and socially to enter into a satisfactory employee-employer relationship. He has also been acquainted with the basic tools, the language of the trade, and sufficient experiences in handling both so that he has developed employable skills on the apprentice level. The student has been sufficiently exposed to the trade, so that he can accept the demands and responsibilities of an apprenticeship program. Perhaps he can profit from some changes in the apprentice training cycle to better accommodate his individual differences and, therefore, make him more acceptable to union scale wages.

Job Placements for Smock Projects, Class of 1972

Hopefully, future plans of this program would include a staff member whose prime responsibility would be placement and follow-up. This teacher would be a liaison between prospective employers, unions, training programs, etc., and therefore enable the school to more completely develop essential skills and attitudes. Such an approach would also enable the program to engage in realistic continuous curriculum revision. Success for the program and the students can only be derived through exploring every effort for interaction between business, industry, unions, and education. Of the eight graduates in 1971, it is significant to note that not all of them are employed in the building trades. Proper employment is our main concern, and the Smock Project is but the vehicle to make employment a reality. The experiences at Smock simplify the opportunities to learn proper work habits, attitudes, develop skills, the use and care of tools and equipment, coordination, measurement, safety, etc. The factor of employment itself, is a result of having been in the program, and the caliber of job skills required where the graduates were hired were permeated and nutured through the same Smock involvement.

Two graduates employed in construction

One graduate employed in a glass manufacturing plant

One graduate employed in a lumber mill

One graduate employed in a coal mine

One graduate employed at a power plant

One graduate in the Armed Forces

One graduate took summer employment until called into the Armed Forces

The present hourly rate range is from $2.60 to $4.80 per hour (Sheetz, 1972).

PROJECT TOLD

Project TOLD (Tutors of Language Disorders) is an innovative program designed and operated under Title III, Public Law 89–10. Its primary purpose is to provide tutoring for students diagnosed as having a language disorder. Junior and senior year students from local colleges are employed as tutors.

In recent years there has been a growing awareness among educators, psychologists, pediatricians, and neurologists that there is a distinct syndrome frequently associated with children who are intelligent, yet underachievers. This syndrome has been characterized under such headings as "hyperkinetic disorders," "dyslexia," "learning disabilities," "language disorders," and many others. These children are thought by many specialists to have some dysfunction of the central nervous system which has interfered with their ability to receive or retain and reproduce visual, auditory or motor stimuli, as well as inducing a behavior syndrome. These children can often be identified in that they have short attention spans, are hyperactive, are easily distracted, and are readily overwhelmed by anything new or different.

These students were given individual psychological evaluations which revealed scores of at least average intelligence. In fact, many of the students were found to be very bright in certain areas. An educational assessment of each child's abilities was administered. These tests confirmed the fact that many students were underachieving approximately two grade levels in academic subjects such as reading, spelling, or mathematics. Some students were having extreme difficulty with handwriting.

The tutors were not all education majors or future teachers. Some of these were studying mathematics, religion, psychology, sociology, and other subjects. In a study comparing the effectiveness of these tutors, their major was not a significant factor.

Because of the lack of sophistication regarding teaching methods as well as the etiology and effect of language disorders, monthly in-service programs were conducted in the form of three-day workshop by the project director and leading authorities in the field of language disorders.

Project TOLD is surpassing the expectations hoped for in the initial planning of the project. An important aspect in the success of the plan is the advantage of the tutors having to report to the school to teach language disorder students. This arrangement not only provides extra help for the students while in a public school environment, but also provides the tutors with opportunities to observe and consult with the students' teachers.

Utilizing this approach to tutoring language disorder students, tutors, often used only the student's textbook but individualuzed methods, materials, workbooks, and worksheets. When called for, other materials such as basic sight vocabulary cards or phonetics drill cards were used. Programmed reading materials were available, and audio-visual aids, such as the controlled reader, were made available. Many students seem to respond favorably to any unique device designed to maintain interest. Methods were encouraged which utilized visual, auditory, and kinesthetic techniques. Typewriting was an exciting experience for the students who had a diagnosis of dysgraphia, or difficulty with handwriting. Learning to type not only helped the student a great deal with homework, but also aided in building self-concepts. For students having difficulty with mathematics because of the inability to copy problems legibly, learning to use a slide rule proved to be successful.

Children with learning disabilities often experience oral expressive difficulties as well as motor expressive problems. The tutors helped many of these students by making and using puppets along with other techniques of language development. Project TOLD provides for 100 tutors to teach boys and girls diagnosed as having a language disorder. In a study comparing the program of these pupils with similiar students receiving assistance through the Abilene (Texas) public schools special education language disorders class, Project TOLD students made approximately the same gains. It must be pointed out, however, that students who were more severely handicapped were assigned to special education classes where specially trained teachers worked with small groups of children, while the tutor's approach was a one-to-one situation with less severely handicapped students. Much of the success of Project TOLD cannot be measured by standardized tests, but measured only by observation and subjective evaluations of tutors, parents, teachers, and administrators (Gann, 1972).

PROJECT 3R

Project 3R: Reality, Reeducation, and Responsibility — is a cooperative education program for students with learning disabilities associated with behavior.

Project 3R set as one of its goals the regional cooperation of independent school systems to provide socially and emotionally maladjusted children with an educational program of high quality which cannot be provided by towns on an individual basis. These goals were to be evaluated according to the following criteria: (1) effort, (2) effect, (3) adequacy, (4) efficiency, and (5) process.

Richard Greene

The effort phase of the evaluation was divided up into two teams: a diagnostic team, which consisted of a psychiatrist, clinical psychologist, and a full-time social worker serving 513 children from 1969 to 1972; and an educational team, which consisted of a teacher-counselor, liaison teacher-counselor, teacher-aide, program coordinator, and ten graduate students serving 189 students from 1969 to 1972.

The effect of the project, which can be measured in terms of academic gains, was that twelve students who were served in the unit during 1971–1972 increased their reading achievement for each month in the unit by an average monthly gain of 1.7, 2.0, and 2.4 on reading comprehension, word discrimination, and word knowledge, respectively. These same students improved their mathematical achievement by making an average monthly gain of 1.5, 4.2, and 5.5 on arithmetic skills, arithmetic problem-solving, and arithmetic concepts, respectively.

The Metropolitian Achievement Test was used to measure the total effectiveness of the 3R program. The evaluation used a pre- and post-test design. The students who were served in the unit from 1969–1971 and who were followed up by pre- and post-measures on reading achievement maintained an average growth of one year, 2 months. Students served by the 3R diagnostic team and/or liaison teacher-counselor made an average monthly gain of 0.9 months in reading achievement.

Intelligence

The children enrolled in the unit in the first year increased their measured IQ by an average of 5.7 points over a two-year period. This was measured by pre- and post-administration of the program by a psychologist using an individual intelligence test — either WISC or Stanford-Binet.

Appropriate Behavior Improved

The students served by the unit were perceived by homeroom teachers to have some degree of inappropriate behavior in twelve out of the fourteen factors measured. When evaluated after their return, thse same students were found to have only one factor which was perceived to be inappropriate as measured by Devereux Elementary School Rating Scale. A very striking result was thus achieved.

Children Returned to Regular Program

Thirty-two of the thirty-three children served (over 95 percent) have been returned and maintained in an appropriate or augmented regular classroom program after an average of six months stay in the program (Gorman, Bondra, Camiros, and Gile, 1968).

PROJECT PLACE

Project PLACE means Personalized Learning Activity Centers for Educations. A component of this project is concerned with learning disabilities and is most appropriately called the early intervention program. This program is aimed at those six-year-old children in four specific schools who show evidence of becoming educational casualties as they move through the public school system. It is hoped that by early identification and diagnosis, strategies may be devised which will make it possible to keep these "high-risk" children in the regular classroom rather than relegated to "special ed" classes.

The learning disabilities encountered may be due either to academic or emotional factors and may demand a very wide range of treatment. Since the average classroom teacher is not equipped with sufficient strategies to cope with the many types of behavior exhibited, help is provided by two "strategists" — teachers trained in special education and working under the guidance of Dr. Gerald Wallace and Dr. James Payne of the University of Virginia. The disciplines of early childhood development and education have long shown the importance of working with primary-age children. Although it is generally accepted that early educational programs benefit all children regardless of race, color, creed or economic level, most current literature illustrates that traditional educational programs are not satisfactory for all children (Cruickshank, 1971; Cegelka and Tyler, 1970; and Dunn, 1968).

It is recognized that many children diagnosed early in life as being disabled in learning capacity, emotionally disturbed, educable mentally retarded, or just "problem children" are often labeled and placed in academic settings separate from their peers. The separation of young children from their peers for special educational services is being recognized by many (Engelmann, 1969) as a deterrent in the educational, psychological, and social development of these potentially handicapped children. Many handicapped children can be ameliorated and, in some cases, prevented by early detection and good personalized treatment by competent personnel within the regular public classroom setting. This is not to say that special class placement is unnecessary for many handicapped or high-risk children. It does imply that many children who have historically been placed in self-contained classrooms for the learning disabled, emotionally disturbed, and educable mentally retarded might well have profited more from a different kind of educational placement. It suggests also that the so-called normal child might profit from this association. To minimize or prevent behavioral problems and academic deficits, an effective intervention program should maximize individual ability to an optimum level of output. This intervention process can best be implemented when the specific behavior and deficits are identified in such a way that they can be measured over a period of time to determine the effectiveness of various modes of personalized instruction.

Project PLACE is designed to develop a model elementary school program of individual instruction. The program consists of the following components:

a. School organization for individualization, using the IGE (Individually Guided

Education) plan developed at the Institute for the Development of Educational Activities (I.D.E.A.) which features the Multi-unit School (M.U.S.E.) developed by the Wisconsin Research and Developmental Center for Cognitive Learning.

b. Mathematics skill and concept development, using the Individualized Mathematics System developed by the Regional Education Laboratory for the Carolinas and Virginia at Durham, North Carolina, and locally produced learning centers and modules.

c. Reading skill and concept development, using the Wisconsin Design for Reading Skill Development which was produced by the Wisconsin Research and Developmental Center for Cognitive Learning and locally produced learning centers and modules.

d. Attitude development and behavior modification through the creation of a warm supportive learning climate and emphasis on student responsibility and self-direction.

e. A locally developed physical education program built around the learning outcomes of Movement Education (M.E.) and designed to increase the performance of students on Virginia physical fitness tests and increase the number of President's Physical Awards earned by the students.

f. An early intervention program for the purpose of identifying, diagnosing, and treating six- and seven-year-old children with potential learning disabilities, which may be due either to academic or emotional factors. (Consultants, working along with three full-time strategists, help teachers develop more and better strategies for teaching those children within regular classroom.)

g. Teacher education through workshops, in-service training, demonstrations, observations, and teacher exchange.

h. Community involvement through a city-wide community council as well as individual school councils which act in an advisory capacity and assist in planning, evaluating, and disseminating information about the project.

i. Dissemination of information to patrons, the general public, and professional colleagues through tours, visits, newsletters, press releases, and staff presentations.

The Project PLACE represents a model in the field of individualized instruction. The project provides each student with a program appropriate for him, personalized to meet his needs, and furnishing the gratification of successful achievement.

IGE (INDIVIDUALLY GUIDED EDUCATION)

This program provides an instructional system in which each child is educated individually according to his own style of learning, his own level of ability, and what he can realistically be expected to learn. This is the IGE learning cycle:

1. Preassessment (What knowledge, attitudes, and skills each child learn? How does he best learn?
2. Design of a learning program for each child

3. Implementation of the learning program
4. Postassessment (Has the child achieved the goals set for him?)

The typical IGE school is organized with a principal and an Instructional Improvement Committee (IIC) composed of the principal and the four unit leaders who are responsible for planning and coordinating the instructional program of the entire school. Central planning through the IIC assures a greater instructional continuity from kindergarten through the sixth grade. The unit leader, a full-time teacher chosen by her co-workers or appointed by the principal, serves as a communicator between the 11C and her unit, as well as assisting and guiding the teachers and aides working with her.

Most IGE schools use instructional and clerical aides to allow certified teachers more time with students and more time to plan an individually instructionalized program. Students are grouped according to age, rather than grade, because IGE proponents feel it is unrealistic to assume that all students in a particular grade are at the same level of accomplishment in every subject. A more effective learning cycle can be designed if students are brought together by age range, by learning cycle, and by the objectives they are attempting to achieve.

IGE is a continually changing and improving concept. No school can ever say that it has fully implemented IGE because the in-service training program is designed to give teachers direction and momentum, but not specific goals that they might feel compelled to accomplish (Hutcherson, 1971, 1973).

Project PRIME (Programmed Reentry into Mainstream Education)

Project PRIME was initiated to investigate the effectiveness of alternatives for special education instructional programs. The principal questions addressed by the study is for whom and under what conditions is integration of handicapped children into mainstream education a viable alternative. In its broadest conceptualization, the study is concerned with identifying the determinants of an effective educational program for handicapped children in the public schools. Reflected in the study design is also the concern for isolating the determinants of effective education for normal children. The study seeks to determine the educational factors that promote children's growth in academic achievement, social competence, and emotional development.

Project PRIME is directed toward the anticipated information needs inherent in providing comprehensive and appropriate educational serves to handicapped children. The study seeks to provide answers to a variety of legal, social, economic, and educational concerns critical to special and general educational programming.

Studies such as Meyerowitz (1962) and Jones (1972) are illustrative of findings suggesting that where special self-contained classes are the primary means for providing educational services to mentally retarded children in public schools, stigmatization of the child associated with such placement occurs. The findings of sociological studies (Mercer, 1969) which generally characterize educational agencies as vestiges of mono cultural rather than pluralistic values are acting as catalytic agents requiring schools to reevaluate their abilities to assimilate and adapt to individual differences. Finally, the sociopolitical implications of state reports, such as Kaufman, Agard, and Vlasak (1973), reflect that a disproportionate number of minority children are being placed in special education classes for the educable mentally retarded. Concerns related to the efforts of labeling as a result of class placement, the realization of the deficiencies in a sociological theory of society as a "melting pot" rather than a nation, school systems reflecting a pluralistic culture, and the effects of an identification and placement process which results in disproportionate numbers of minority children being placed in classes for the mentally retarded, provide a sociological impetus for considering special education as a comprehensive continuum of educational services.

Historically, the field of special education has conceptualized the concern of special education programming for the educable mentally retarded as a dichotomous variable: services provided in a special class versus a regular class. It is improbable that useful information or valid inferences about educational programs can be obtained from the evaluation of such broadly conceptualized, loosely implemented administrative program arrangements. There is no comparability of results across the unit due to the enormous program variations. Thus, the program effectiveness cannot be determined.

Project PRIME was conceptualized in marked difference from previous studies and in anticipation of the information needs related to the legal, social, economic, and educational concerns. The study was designed to investigate for whom and under what conditions integration of mentally retarded children into mainstream education is a viable educable alternative. Integration is treated as a multidimensional variable including provision of services in the regular classroom with supportive instruction material or a helping teacher, provision of service in a regular classroom with special assistance in a resource room, or provision of service in a special education self-contained classroom. The study provides an opportunity to evaluate the correlation of the student's academic, social, and emotional growth as it relates to a comprehensive pattern of special and regular educational services.

The organizational structures developed for Project PRIME were designed to involve the collective excellence of current thinking and to maximize efficiency in processes and procedures. In effect, an adhorcracy (Tofler, 1970) was established which reflects federal, state, and local education agencies cooperating with institutions of higher learning, education, and private industry. It was expected that an adhorcracy would be a most effective and efficient organization for promoting diffusion and adaption of Project PRIME processes, products, and findings.

Project PRIME is unique in its wide-scale employment of direct observation of classroom interactions. The purpose for the extensive observation of classroom behavior was to determine the relevant dimensions of effective teaching as related to pupil growth. It was intended to describe a day of school activities based on inputs such as pupil behavior, teacher behavior, management techniques, cognitive demand levels in the class, pupil participation, and quality of classroom climate. Additional descriptive information was collected concerning classroom physical environment, personnel in class, classroom displays, academic activities, teacher tasks, pupil tasks, structure for classroom activities, and seating arrangement (Kaufman, Semmel, and Agard, 1973).

Career education is a vital concept that has now been developing for the better part of this century. It is based on the philosophy that all children deserve the chance for a relevant education that will prepare them for a satisfying and productive life in adulthood. It is the thread that permeates the entire curriculum. The community becomes the learning laboratory, with professional and lay representatives alike making up the teaching-learning team. The doors of the classroom are thrust open to make learning take on meaning and purpose.

In 1968, the Fullerton (California) Union High School District undertook to review its curriculum for exceptional students, age fourteen to nineteen. It was concluded that the programs offered were not benefiting students with special problems and that the current program offered a watered-down academic curriculum with token job placement being provided.

PROJECT WORKER: VIDEOTAPING WORK STATIONS IN INDUSTRY

Project Worker offers the following:
1. Workers trained for a specific job before being hired
2. Students available for work during school hours
3. Partially or fully trained workers upon request
4. Students working for credit
5. Students carefully evaluated and screened who enter into the program

The following steps were used in preparing the students:

1. The student's vocational potential is assessed through the use of extensive aptitude, interest, personality, and motor skills examinations. This testing is coupled with initial work experiences through on-campus employment.

2. The jobs are analyzed in detail, and training packages are constructed using video tapes and other media. Then simulations of the job are created in conjunction with the advice of the employers and industrial consultants.

3. The final tapes are edited and previewed prior to placement in the film library.

4. Now the student is trained by using the material packages in the classroom. The academics in school are not an end in themselves, but are related in every way possible to the training materials from the industrial world.

5. The students then work with each other to acquire knowledge and skills.

6. The locally concerned businessmen are now contacted and asked to employ

students in their industries once it is known and determined that the students have acquired the necessary skills for success on the job.

7. Finally, the students at work in the field are followed up by the work-experience counselor. Evaluations are made of the students' job performance, and the school work program is strengthened through programming school curricula to further necessary job skills (Retzlaff, 1973).

CAREER DEVELOPMENT CENTER

The underlying purpose of the Career Development Center (CDC) is to prepare adolescents to adapt to the environmental stress of daily living. The premise of the CDC is that deviant behavior is capable of change. Though the CDC is not an occupational training center, occupational training and programming assume major importance in the curriculum — the idea being that through success-oriented activities, students can be motivated to change. The CDC is a comprehensive secondary program for the handicapped which attempts to develop the student's interest in learning as well as a sense of future direction through its many offerings such as the performing arts, outdoor education, practical sciences, driver education, horticulture, and technical trades.

THE CLUSTER AND SUBJECT MATTER OF CDC

It is important to view the curriculum program:
1. Technical Building
    a. Automotive (small engines and combustion)
    b. Auto body repair (introduction to fundamentals)
    c. Auto mechanics (vehicle repair)
    d. Auto body repair (advanced application and auto painting)
    e. Electronics (radio TV repair, automotive, electrical system, assembly application)
    f. Building maintenance (woodworking, commercial electricity and plumbing)
2. Horticulture
    a. Floral design
    b. Greenhouse and landscaping
    c. Horticulture maintenance and equipment.
3. Distributive Occupations
    a. Health services
    b. Office occupations.
4. Food Trades
    a. Kitchen
    b. Service
    c. Short order preparation

d. Accounting aspects of small food business.

Since the students at the Career Development Center are given an opportunity to choose their course of study, electives can also be taken from among the following:
ceramics
personal grooming
science
art (sculpture, sketching, oils)
drama
swimming
skatemobile
typing
remedial math
individual study center (reading)
music (chorus, voice, band instruments — woodwind, string, percussion.

When a work experience counselor enters an industry setting, the counselor begins a plan survey which includes the following

1. An examination of the safety equipment
2. A determination of the ration of trained personnel available in order that supervision and additional job training be available exclusive of school supervision
3. A transportation system to make certain the retarded person can reach the place of employment and return home (The work experience counselor, after initial placement, takes the retarded person on a dry run to and from the place of employment to insure familiarization of route.)
4. An identification of a plant liaison to interact with the work experience counselor who then becomes a troubleshooter as well as a buffer for the retarded person
5. A job analysis to break down the components of a task in order to identify prerequisite skills needed for performance

PARENT INVOLVEMENT — OPERATION FACE

At the Career Development Center, a program is offered to the parents called the Family Activity Continuing Education (FACE). It is an attempt to involve families in an extension of the learning process of the day school program. The goal of FACE can best be stated as the assisting of students, parents, and staff in the following:

1. Developing an appreciation of learning as a process geared to the individual's pace and potential
2. Developing a new dimension of understanding among students by observing their parents in the role of their students
3. Making learning experiences enjoyable
4. Learning how to deal with their own problems

Richard Greene

5. Learning new skills, both manipulative and cognitive

6. Providing a unique opportunity for staff to observe family dynamics in prescribing assistance to the family

7. Providing parents with a new perspective in observing their child's behavior

8. Developing an informal nonthreatening line of communication with parents

The costs of meaningful secondary programming is high for the handicapped; the cost of not providing this continuum of education is incalcuable (Colella, 1973).

REFERENCES

Adelman, H. S., The not so specific learning disability population. *Exceptional Children,* 1971, *37,* 528–533.

Albin, T. J., Relationships of IQ and previous work experiences to success in sheltered employment. *Mental Retardation* (AAMD), 1973, *11* (3), 26.

Atkinson, D. I., Mental retardation research today (unpublished paper). C.P.R.I., 1968, 13 pages.

Barnes, E. J., Cultural retardation or shortcomings of assessment techniques. In Jones, R. L., and MacMillan, D. L. (eds.), *Special education in transition.* Boston: Allyn & Bacon, 1972.

Barrington, B. L., Special education students: How many are replaced? *Journal of Learning Disabilities,* 1968, *1* (12), 36–39.

Blatt, B., Public policy and the education of children with special needs. *Exceptional Children,* 1972, *38* 537– 46.

Blazoric, R. R., (ed.). *A curriculum guide for the educable mentally retarded* (rev.). Grossmont Union High School District, Grossmont, California, 1966, pp. 4–8.

Bobroff, A., Economic adjustment of 121 adults formerly students in classes for the mental retardate. *American Journal of Mental Deficiency,* 1956, *60* (3) 525–535.

Borretti, A. Occupational training for retarded persons. *Mental Retardation* (AAMD), 1972, *10* (5), 15–17.

Bortner, M., and Buch, H. G., Cognitive capacity and cognitive competence. *American Journal of Mental Deficiency,* 1970, *74* (6), 735–744.

Cain, L. F., Who makes the best teachers? *American Journal of Mental Deficiency,* 1953, *58,* 260–261.

Carroll, A. W., The effects of segreated and partially integrated school programs on self-concept and academic achievement of educable mental retardes. *Exceptional Children,* 1967, *34* (2), 93–99.

Christopolos, F., and Rentz, P., A critical examination of special education programs. *Journal of Special Education,* 1969, *3,* 371–379.

Cole, M., and Bruner, J. S., Cultural differences and inferences about psychological processes. *American Psychologist,* 1971, *26,* 867–876.

Colella, H. V., Career development center: A modified high school for the handicapped. *Teaching Exceptional Children,* 1973, *5* (3), 110–119.

Detroit (Mich.) Board of Education, *Special education for handicapped children,* 1965, pp. 18–21.

Dunn, L. M., *Exceptional children in the schools.* New York: Holt, Rinehart and Winston, 1963.

Dunn, L. M., Special education for the mildly retarded: Is much of it justifiable? *Exceptional Children,* 1968, *34,* 5–22.

Fine, M. J., Attitudes of regular and special class teachers toward the educable mentally retarded child. *Exceptional Children* 1967, *33,* 417–430.

Gallagher, J. J., New directions in special education. *Exceptional Children,* 1967, *33* 441–447.

Gann, L. N., Innovation: Project TOLD. From Aaronson, W. J. *Innovation in Special Education.* Title III. ESEA. Department of Health, Education, and Welfare, publication no. (OE) 72–30.

Gardner, D. C., and Gardner, P., Ten suggestions for an effective EMR occupation program. *Journal for Special Educators of the Mentally Retarded,* 1973, *9* (2), 90–93.

Goldberg, B., The ability of the mentally retarded to be vocationally successful. *Mental Retardation* (AAMD), *13,* 1963.

Goldberg, I. I., Multidimensional roles of special education teachers. *Rehabilitation in Australia,* 1969, *6* (5), 4–9.

Gorman, E.; Bondra, G.' Camiros, C.' and Gile, L. *3R — Reality, Reeducation, Responsibility.* Cooperating Connecticut School District, East Granby, East Windsor, Suffield, and Windsor Locks. July 24, 1968.

Hall, E., *The politics of special education: Inequality in education.* Harvard Center for Law and Education, III & IV, 1970, 17–22 (18@).

Hall, E., *The politics of special education: Inequality in education.* Harvard Center for Law and Education, III & IV, 1970, 17–22 (19@).

Hillerich, R. L., The creative learning center. *Elementary School Journal,* 1969, *69,* 259–264.

Hofmeister, A., Educational trends and special education. *Slow Learning Child,* 1969, *16* (2), 67–72.

Hungerford, R., The Detroit plan for the occupational education of the mentally retarded. *American Journal of Mental Deficiency,* 1941, *46,* 102–108.

Hunt, J. M., *Intelligence and experience.* New York: Ronald Press, 1961.

Hutcherson, B. S., Personalized learning activity centers for education, Title III. ESEA project. Section 306. Lynchburg (Va.) Public School System, 1971, 1973.

Iano, R. P., Learning deficiency versus developmental conceptions of mental retardation. *Exceptional Children,* 1971, *38,* 301–311.

Jaslow, R., and Smith, S. V., A proposal for a new conceptual use of the term "mental retardation." *Mental Retardation,* 1972, *10* (1), 36–37.

Jones, R. L., Labels and stigma in special education. *Exceptional Children,* 1972, *38,* 553–564.

Jordan, T. E., Persistent problems in the education of children with multihandicaps. In Lance, W. D. (ed.), *Special study institute for the multihandicapped.* Los Angeles: State Department of Education, 1967.

Karnes, M. B., and Lehrbach, R. R., Curriculum and methods in early childhood special education. *Focus on Exceptional chldren,* 1973, *5* (2).

Kaufman, M.; Agard, J.; and Vlasak, J., *The comprehensive special education program in Texas: Part III, Section B, Instructional arrangements,* 1973 (in press).

Kaufman, M.; Semmel, M.; and Agard, J., *Project PRIME: An overview,* May 1973. U. S. Office of Education, Bureau of Education for Handicapped, Division of Research. Intermural research programs in conjunction with Texas Education Agency, Department of Special Education and Special Schools, Division of Program Evaluation, pp. 1–9.

Keith, K., Ratio reinforcement schedules: Applications to a sheltered workshop. Unpublished paper, Beatrice State Home, 1972.

Kirk, S. A., *Educating the retarded child.* New York: Houghton Mifflin, 1951.

Lance, W. D., New trends paper presented at Troubled Child Conference, University of Oregon, January 1969.

Lindsley, O. R., Direct measurement and prosthesis of retarded behavior. *Journal of Education,* 1964, *147,* 62–81.

MacMillan, D. L., Issues and trends in special education. *Mental Retardation* (AAMD), 1973, *11* (2), 3–9.

Richard Greene

McAllister, E. W. C., Thoughts on the use of the term "mental retardation." *Mental Retardation* (AAMD), 1972, *10* (6), 40–41.

Mager, R. F., *Preparing instructional objectives.* Palo Alto: Fearon, 1962.

Mercer, J. R., The eligibles and the labeled: Books I & II. Public Health Service Research Grant No. MH-08667, NIMH. Public Health Service General Research Support Grant No. 1-501-FR-05632-02, HEW, 1969.

Mercer, J. R., The meaning of mental retardation. In Koch, R., and Dobson, J. (eds.), *The mentally retarded child and his family.* New York: Brunner/Mazel, 1971.

Meyer, E. L., and Hieronymus, A. N., The age placement of academic skills in cirriculum for EMR. *Exceptional Children,* 1970, *36* 333–339.

Meyerowitz, J. H., Self-derogations in young retardates and special class placement. *Child Development,* 1962, *33* 443–451.

Michal-Smith, H., Learning problems of children. *Canada's Mental Health.* Journal of the Department of National Health and Welfare (Ottawa), 1967, *16* (6), 10–20.

Milgram, N. A., MR and Mental illness: A proposal for conceptual unity. *Mental Retardation* (AAMD), 1972, *10,* (6), 29–31.

Nilson, C. C., and Schmidt, L. J., The question of the efficacy of special class. *Exceptional Children,* 1971, *37* 381–384.

Porter, R. B., Needed: A more realistic classification of mentally retarded children. *Training School Bulletin* American Institute for Mental Studies), 1970, *67,* 30–32.

Quay, H. C., The facets of educational exceptionality: A conceptual framework for assessment grouping and instruction. *Exceptional Children,* 1968, *35* (1), 25–32.

Reiger, R., and Koppman, M., The child-oriented resource room. *Exceptional Children,* 1971, *37* 460–462.

Retzlaff, W., Project worker: Videotaping work stations in industry. *Teaching Exceptional Children,* 1973, *5* (3), 134–137.

Rosenthal, R., and Jacobsen, L., Teacher expectations: Determiners of pupils' IQ gains. *Psychological Reports,* 1966, *19,* 115–118.

Rynbrandt, D. Sm., A study of the socioeconomic adjustment of people who have attended the auxiliary and upgraded class of the Grand Rapids Public School. Unpublished doctoral dissertation, Wayne State University, 1947.

Sabatine, D. A., Resource rooms: The renaissance in special education. *Journal of Special Education,* 1972, *6* (4), 335–347.

Salomone, P. R.; Lehmann, E.; and Green, A. J., Occupational exploration practices: A pilot study to increase the vocational sophistication of slow-learners. *Mental Retardation* (AAMD), 1973, *11* (4), 3–7.

Sheetz, A. C., Smock project. Director of Special Education, Intermediate Unit I, California, Pennsylvania, November 1972.

Simaches, R. F., The inside outsider. *Exceptional Children,* 1970, *37,* 5–16.

Slaughter, S. S., *The educable mentally retarded child and his teacher.* Philadelphia: F. A. Davis, 1964.

Stevens, G. D., An analysis of the objectives for the education of children with retarded mental development. *Exceptional Children,* 1958, 225–235.

Taylor, G. R., Programming for educable mentally retarded chldren. *Training School Bulletin,* 1970, *67* 183–188.

Taylor, G. R., Special education at the crossroads: Class placement for the EMR. *Mental Retardation* (AAMD), 1973, *11* (2), 30–34.

Tennessee State Department of Education. *Handbook for administration: A guide for programs for the mentally retarded,* 1970, pp. 18–22.

Toffler, A., *Future shock.* New York: Random House, 1970.

Tyson, K. L., A model guide to the special class, *Journal of Learning Disabilities,* 1969, *2* (5), 34–38.

Vaughan, R. W., Community, courts and conditions of special education today: Why? *Mental Retardation* (AAMD), 1973, *11* (2), 43–47.

Weiner, L. H., An investigation of the effectiveness of resource rooms for children with specific learning disabilities. *Journal of Learning Disabilities,* 1969, *2,* 49–55.

Wolfsenberger, W., Vocational preparation and occupation. In Baumeister, A. (ed.), *Mental retardation: Appraisal, education and rehabilitation.* Chicago: Aldine Publishing, 1967.

Young, Jr., W. M., Text of W. Young's keynote speech at CEC convention. *Exceptional Children,* 1970, *36,* 727–734.

Zarfas, D. E., Mental retardation today. *Canadian Medical Association Journal,* 1962, *87,* 479–485.

Zito, R. J., and Bardon, J. I., Achievement motivation among Negro adolescents in regular and special education programs. *American Journal of Mental Deficiency,* 1969, *74,* 20–26..

DEVELOPING COMMUNITY-BASED, SMALL-GROUP LIVING PROGRAMS IN REHABILITATION SERVICES

Ben P. Granger

This paper reports the findings of a two-year demonstration project (1971-1973) designed to develop a model for community-based, small-group living programs for persons who are mentally retarded. It is felt that these findings can be generalized to other client population groups in need of alternative living programs in such areas as rehabilitation, developmental disabilities, and corrections.

Objectives and Underlying Principles of the Project

This project was intended to emphasize the importance of one essential component of the continuum of rehabilitation services and programs. This was based upon the assumption that a major resource gap presently exists in the community; that of small-group living styles such as group homes, hostels, boarding homes, foster care, and supportive independent living arrangements. Thus, the project was designed to determine how and to what degree persons residing in one particular small-group living program could successfully function in the community while receiving a variety of social, occupational, educational, recreational, medical, and other supportive services from various community agencies and organizations.

This objective was put in operation through the planning, organizing, developing, directing, and evaluating of a coeducational model for eight adults who had varying degrees of mental, emotional, and physical disabilities, and who were all institutionalized for various lengths of time varying from several years to thirty years.

An additional objective was to mobilize and utilize a university's educational training and public service resources. Emphasis was given to establishing and enhancing an interprofessional approach to the project, stressing the need to both educate and practice in an interdisciplinary manner.

There were no formal hypotheses formulated for testing out; rather, the intent was to design a demonstration model and study, utilizing both qualitative and quantitative measures, in areas concerning: (1) the development, operation, and cost-effectiveness of this model; (2) the iterrelationship and impact with the community and other human service resources; and (3) the effect this program had on persons or residents participating in it. There was, however, the underlying assumption that alternative community-based, small-group living programs are not only desirable and essential in this continuum but that on the basis of legal and social justice, action has to be taken in this direction without further delay. This position is clearly supported by numerous reports, studies, and empirical research that points to the critical need to develop and validate effective alternatives to institutional or custodial care (i.e., Dybwad, 1964; Granger, 1972; Holland, 1973; Kugel, 1969; Morris, 1969; and Vail, 1969).

The project was guided by two basic principles of normalization and humanization. The essence of these principles is the emphasis upon assisting persons with disabilities to reside and function within their communities as normally and as self-dependently as possible, with emphasis on their worth, dignity, and potentiality. It means making available and incorporating patterns and conditions of everyday life that are as close as possible to the norms and patterns of the mainstream of society. It means having programs and services that are based upon social justice and the human aspirations of each person.

The Research Design

A research component was an integral part of the project since the inception. While a demonstration project is in itself research, the research component examined specific aspects in more depth. Two broad objectives were defined: descriptive research on the development of the project, and evaluative research on individual and group changes.

The descriptive research was designed to chronicle development and identify problem areas which may be common to small-group community living programs. A project such as this has to be viewed in terms of a process rather than as a static entity which can be examined after the fact. The focus, therefore, was on explaining the process of planning, implementing, and operating the facility while identifying significant problem areas. This could result in a guideline for other projects or programs.

This information was gathered using a participation-observation approach, and the administration of several interview schedules. The researchers recorded ongoing activities which involved preparing the facility, exploring insurance and zoning requirements, defining admissions criteria, planning programs, and other matters. Problem areas were identified. An interview schedule for assessing expectations and activities of staff members was devised and administrated. Interviews were conducted prior to the admissions of residents and approximately six months after they had been admitted. This effort was directed at ascertaining if staff had different expectations and if staff attitudes and behaviors changed.

In evaluating the development of the project, including problems, staff roles and operating procedures, continued effort was directed at assessing effects on the residents. Necessary modifications and replacements of rules and procedures were recorded. In observing this process of development, modification and change, the researchers had the opportunity to evaluate not only the resident reactions, but also effectiveness of certain rules and procedures. The resulting data should assist in establishing admission criteria for potential residents who might utilize this type of program.

Ben P. Granger

In evaluating resulting changes in the residents, the most obvious criteria was movement into the community. Research was focused on behavioral change and progress in independent living skills which could determine movement from the project to the community. A critical part of this effort was the identification of factors which prevented the person from attaining his or her highest level of independent living.

Originally, evaluation of the residents' progress was to be based on several psychological tests. However, it was soon apparent that these instruments were of little value in this situation. Numerous instruments were considered, but most of these seemed limited to the Vineland Scale of Social Maturity type items. The appropriateness of these scales was questioned for two reasons. First, the specific skills asserted did not logically appear to be ones which were necessarily critical for adequate independent functioning. Second, many of the skills asserted were easily mastered by the residents.

There were several important implications which were derived from the experience of trying to find an appropriate instrument. One implication was that little is known about the skills necessary for living in the community for an individual who is mentally retarded. The area of vocational training is a good example; programs such as the sheltered workshops operate on the assumption that the person who is disabled through mental retardation can do only minimal routine work. In reality, very little is known about job potential. Indications from the residents of the project suggested that these individuals get very bored with simple routine tasks and may be capable of much higher levels of work, contrary to popular belief.

Another important implication relates to the criteria used to assess the potential of these individuals for community living. Generally, intellectual functioning is the basis for assessment. Few other individuals in society are subject to any evaluation of intellectual functioning. In fact, most individuals, sixteen and above, are readily assimilated into the society. Thus, the question must be asked: Why should most individuals who are mentally retarded be treated differently? The conclusion drawn was that new criteria for assessing behavior or progress are needed.

Lacking appropriate instruments, the researchers initiated a system using a target-symptom approach. Project staff and researchers worked together in specifying what skills, attributes, or behavioral changes were necessary for movement to a higher level of independent living. For example, low self-esteem and expression of frustration-anger were identified consistently as interfering with community functioning as opposed to the skills which are generally assumed to be lacking. Therefore, a major thrust of the research effort was at specifying skills, attributes, and problem areas. By following through on this effort, it has been possible to begin to develop a scale for assessment.

Results

The data collected are not conclusive at present. However, it is possible to summarize several tentative results. These results are in three basic areas: development of the project, resident behavior, and functioning of the facility.

A. *Development:* The information gathered from the project provides a model for the development of other facilities. To implement other projects, a number of guidelines must be followed to avoid severe problems.

1. The very first step must be to engage existing human services and health-care agencies in supportive and cooperative relationships.

2. The lines of staff authority must be clearly defined. The project experience strongly indicates that development would have progressed more effectively with one individual exercising a position of leadership.

3. Prior to selection of residents, numerous operational requirements must be met (i.e., zoning, fire regulations, health department certification, license, insurance).

4. Admissions criteria and potential residents; participation in admissions decisions must be clearly defined.

5. Mechanisms for evaluating the residents' needs, and planning services must be specified in the development of the project.

B. *Residents:* Critical qualities for community living and of recurrent problems associated with movement from institutional to community living were identified.

1. The experience of the project suggests that a target-symptom approach is more appropriate than reliance on existing scales.

2. Evaluation of intellectual functioning should be deemphasized in favor of acceptable social functioning.

3. The most constant problems noted in these persons who were institutionalized were low self-esteem, inability to handle frustration-anger, and lack of adequate knowledge of sexuality. These factors were basic to almost every problematic situation encountered in the project.

C. *Functioning of the facility:* The daily operation of the project provided information about the feasibility of the philosophy, policy, and objectives upon which it was based.

1. The stated objectives of the projects are nearer realization. However, a deficiency does exist in participation by some of the university resources in research and service. A number of factors contributing to this deficiency can be identified.

2. The principles of normalization and humanization have not been fully developed in the literature. The research at the project can contribute to the operation of these concepts. The degree of structure in a group-home type program is a critical variable in examining these concepts. Variations in resident behavior to different implementation of these concepts offers some insight into practical application.

3. The policies of the project (related to 2 above) had a significant effect on

resident behavior. For example, the project had a policy of searching for "runaways," trying to discourage them and notifying all staff when this happened. The many threats, gestures, and absences suggested that this policy was ineffective. A policy which required a more mature response on the part of the residents was adopted. The concept of "running away" was discarded and replaced by a recognition of the residents' right to leave. Residents wre reminded that it is courteous to tell someone when they are leaving, or they should notify the staff of places they are moving to. This policy encouraged a higher level of rationality instead of reinforcing absences as a weapon for punishing self, staff, or other residents with whom the "runaway" was displeased. An immediate decrease in this problematic behavior occurred.

4. The coeducational living component of the project was important in realizing the goals of normalization and humanization. Exploration of the coeducational living experience implies such arrangements are feasible. While there have been problems in this area, efforts to cope with these have been moderately successful and the benefits are substantial. A problem area, for example, was that many of the residents knew little about sexuality. In addition to the counselors making themselves available to discuss the issue, a voluntary sex education course was initiated by social work, special education, and therapeutic recreation graduate students. The area of greatest benefit involved developing normal relationships with members of the opposite sex. As the residents came from institutions in which the sexes were segregated, this was a tremendous adjustment for many of them to make.

5. As the project was a community-based program, assessment of both the extent to which the project utilized the community and the extent that the community supported the project must be discovered to determine expectations of both community and residents. Factors in residents' use of community services include how quickly residents began to utilize community services, to what degree, for what purposes, and which services seemed most helpful. For example, residents very quickly learned to use city buses in order to get to work, but were slower to use the same service for shopping, medical appointments, or recreation. In general, residents were initially reluctant to move out of the neighborhood of the project. Staff had to become more forceful in encouraging residents' use of the community. Eventually most residents utilized several community services. Factors important in community support include volunteers, media coverage, purchasing discounts, police relations, contributions of material, job offers for residents, aids from social and medical services, etc. The issue of community support affects not only the day-to-day functioning of the facility, but also that of services for residents, and the morale of both

staff and residents. Community support started slowly, but picked up markedly. For example, the number of volunteers and student placements increased from one to sixteen. Utilization of agencies such as comprehensive care, the university medical center clinics, vocational rehabilitation, and public assistance has increased.

Obstacles to Program Development

At the beginning of this demonstration project, it was assumed that the most effective way to go about its develoment was in a rational and planned fashion. A problem-solving approach and a conscious use of both analytical and interactional skills were considered necessary. The author's views with regard to the basic requirements for reform were clearly stated in an earlier paper:

Reform of social welfare programs and service-delivery systems require an understanding of the past, a documentation of existing conditions, a theoretically sound base, a prevailing value structure based on social justice and human aspirations, a plan and implementation process that are both rational and participative, and an administrative climate that encourages change and innovation. (Granger, 1972) These requirements for change were essentially all met in the development of this particular project. Now, a year later, evaluation and reflection on this experience suggests that rationality was less significant and influential than were other factors, resistances, and unintended side effects of planned change efforts. In fact, the irrational aspects of the process appear to be more paramount. Obstacles, resistances, and frustrations that were unanticipated and unaccounted for were encountered throughout the project's existence. These were at times at the point of jeopardizing the project's vitality and continuation. Even though there are significant, important, and justifiable reasons for developing alternative living programs in the community for the mentally retarded, any number of major and petty impediments exist that blunt and prevent social justice from taking place. Some of these impediments or obstacles are enumerated.

A. *Personalities, Not Programs*

One of the most important single obstacles to developing this program was the overriding concern with the safety and security of one's own professional position within the various human service organization. This should be done whether there would be personal and agency gain or loss in the transactions taking place; and whether personal feelings were being hurt or adequately considered. Professional and nonprofessional staff in many of these organizations demonstrated little desire to "take a chance" in behalf of clients. For various reasons, from the top down, many persons were more preoccupied with themselves, with paper passing, with petty details, than they were with clients; a sad commentary on the socialization process to the human services and to the professions. Clients must come first. For example, one institutional administrator refused requests of persons in our program for inviting lifelong friends, who were currently residents in the institution, to be weekend guests in our project.

B. *Bureaucratic Blocking, Not Facilitating*

The proverbial "red tape" is in fact "red tape." In our demonstration project both the department of mental health and the university moved out in a painstakingly slow and arduous pace that even numbed the most exuberant and energetic students, let alone faculty and staff. It took months, for example, to acquire furniture through normal channels (we had to ignore standard operating procedures to purchase rugs, pots and pans, etc., or face weeks of frustrating delay). It took six months to get air conditioning in the winter, eight months to establish medical care benefits, and a year to establish working relationships with "cooperating" community programs. Every feasible need, from financing to furnishings, was delayed and frequently prevented by established procedure, and overlays of organizational structure upon organizational structure. The fear to deviate from established procedure and professional norms is in itself a form of deviancy that handicaps innovation. The large organizations involved were built for system stability, not for system change.

C. *Interorganizational and Professional Competition, Not Cooperation*

Zoning, fire, health, vocation, and educational regulations stifle most community-based, small-group living programs before they even get started. Certain standards are essential to prevent "back wards" from occurring in the community; yet existing regulations prohibit alternative living styles. We got around certain fire regulations by convincing the marshal that our program was a boarding home. Policies and regulations need to be modified to allow for different and better programs.

E. *The Psyche, Not the Social*

Emphasis continues to be placed on the psychological and intellectual, rather than on the social and functional. This is to a great deal cultural and societal; yet it has been clearly demonstrated, in our project as well as in others, that persons who have been placed for years in institutions or custodial systems can make it in the community, alone or with some supportive services. Attitudes about the "subhumans," the "children" and the need to "put away" or institutionalize these deviants continue to block new programs and living styles in the community. Our program employed persons who had a different view about people and their human aspirations.

F. *Consultation, Not Residential Services*

This subtitle might also be called "Who Wants to Do Direct Services?" From our experiences the trend of many state mental health programs is to get out of the business of providing residential services to clients. For years it was building large congregate institutions and "putting away" or "dumping in" as many deviants as was possible. Presently the trend is building community comprehensive care centers and for third-party contracts for various services with nonprofit and profit-making organizations. A problem with this is that little attention is given to the need for assuming the responsibilities for continuity, developing and evaluating the effectiveness and quality of these programs, follow-up and advocacy, for determining the effects of literally "dumping out" persons into the community without having adequate resources available, and determining where the program "gaps" are.

G. *Politics and Power, Not Values, Facts, and Issues*

When it comes right down to it, political power appears to frequently have the edge over values, facts, and issues. You may be morally and factually right, but if you do not have the power to reinforce this, you will more than likely end up a loser. Strategies for planned change require additional knowledge and skill in such areas as grant writing, the legislation process, budgeting, judicial review, administrative regulation, and political behavior.

Summary

Several points must be realized in developing alternative community-based, small-group living programs. From the project's experience, these kinds of programs are considerably more difficult and complicated to effectively operate than are institutions. For example, helping persons to become independent, to live and function as normally as possible within the community, to make gains and to make mistakes, and to experience the frustrations and joys of living are all factors which make community living programs more difficult to operate than custodial systems.

There appears to be a "drift" toward mediocrity in the ongoing operation of these small-group residential programs, with the essential requirement to countervail this drift with effective and ongoing professional supervision that will help to provide continuity, goal-directed and effective services.

In the foreseeable future, establishing these programs will be hard-fought, take persistance and dedication, require coalitions of staunch supporters, and a variety of strategies and tactics that will help to assure desired change. For example, this project would never have taken place if there had not been a firm commitment for action, and would have only been wishful thinking about things that need to be done.

Alternative small-group living programs work. With the allocation or reallocation of adequate resources, supportive community services, and goal-directed actions by professional and voluntary personnel, there is simply no need for the continuation of institutions for persons who are mentally retarded.

REFERENCES

Dybwad, G., *Challenges in mental retardation.* New York: Columbia University Press, 1964.
Dybwad, G., Roadblocks to renewal of residential care. In Menolascino, F. J. (Ed.), *Psychiatric approaches to mental retardation.* New York: Basic Books, 1971, pp. 204–221.

Granger, B. P., dilemmas of reorganizing institutions for the mentally retarded. *Mental Retardation,* August 1972, *10* (4), 3–7.

Granger, B. P., Alternatives to institutional care: Changing a service delivery system toward greater social justice for clients. Delivered at the third NASW National Professional Symposium, New Orleans, November 27, 1972.

Holland, T., Organizational structure and institutional care. *Journal of Health and Social Behavior* (in press), 1973.

Kugel, R. B., and Wolfensberger, W. (Eds.), *Changing patterns in residential services for the mentally retarded.* Washington, D. C.: President's Committee on Mental Retardation, 1969.

Morris, P., *Put away: A sociological study of institutions for the mentally retarded.* London: Routledge and Kegal Paul, 1969.

Vail, D. J., *Dehumanization and the institutional career.* Springfield, Ill.: Charles C. Thomas, 1969.

ALTERING THE TRADITIONAL INSTITUTIONAL MILIEU TO A CONTINUOUS TRAINING ENVIRONMENT VIA MINIMAL ALTERATIONS IN PHYSICAL DESIGN*

Bill J. Locke and Douglas C. Chatfield

The work described in this report was conceptualized in a context somewhat removed from the behavioral architecture movement. However, it was markedly influenced in the same vein by a 1964 address by Norman Ellis to the American Psychological Association. Despairing the prospect of ever securing sufficient personnel to effectively implement comprehensive learning-based training of the low-functioning retardate, Ellis affirmed the urgency of assigning major research priority to the development of comprehensive prosthetic features in every area of residential cottage life. He characterized a number of specific cottage design elements that could efficiently maximize productive self-direction and self-care by cottage residents while minimizing requirements for supervisory personnel. Many of the features involved physical constructions in which such functions as dispensing food and medication, shower controls, exercise and the like were not only automated but represented a substantial proportion of the residents' training programs. While the normalization principle was not yet in vogue, similar considerations tended to undermine attempts to implement recommendations such as those advanced by Ellis. For example, the peer review board of a federal grant agency rejected one such proposal because its thrust was deemed inimical to anything but a custodial, prosthetic environment in which normalized features were minimal. Clearly, such applications would be received in an even more critical vein today than in the early sixties.

Taking the above as an object lesson, yet recognizing the promise of such measures judiciously applied, we elected to attempt a similar but more circumscribed venture without marked alterations in the environs as designed or the introduction of features likely to be substantially at odds with the normalized setting. We reasoned that the vending machine, instrumentation designed to provide entertainment (jukeboxes, pinball machines, etc.), and even automated units designed to test and challenge our intellectual skills are sufficiently pervasive in ostensibly

---

*The authors are indebted to Dr. John Gladden and the staff of the Lubbock State School for their cooperation and assistance in the conduct of this project. The work was supported by a grant from the Institute of Human Resources, Texas Tech University. Portions of this report were presented at the Ninety-eighth annual meeting of the American Association on Mental Deficiency, Toronto, 1974.

normal environments so that similar units with more constructive functions should hardly compromise environmental integrity.

In our desire to attempt some design alteration that might productively impinge on institutional residents at severe and lower levels of retardation, we noted that most of these individuals' waking hours elapse in the day room or day hall, the institutional equivalent to a suburban living room, parlor, and game room. The room's formal accouterments typically consist of a number of durable furniture units, a few rudimentary toys or games, and a television set elevated toward ceiling level (and frequently out of adjustment). Scheduled activities for the residents as a group comprise only a portion of their time and many hours include no formal direction. Direct care personnel are often occupied with the implementation of housekeeping, medication, clothing, meals and record keeping with direct training activities relegated to time between other duties. In the resultant void, it is a reasonable premise that intellectual functioning is hardly stimulated and maladaptive behaviors may ensue. Stereotyped patterns of self-occupation, bizarre forms of self-stimulation, or active sets for aggressive behavior may be acquired. More likely, most residents simply lapse into a malaise of inactivity and become less and less responsive to an environment that is impoverished both programmatically and in physical stimulus features. As Ellis has suggested, an analysis of the problem from an engineering standpoint indicates this to be a case of inadequate behavior in an insensitive environment. To break the negative cycle, we must change one or both.

We had been impressed with the gains demonstrated in intense training efforts via systematic conditioning programs. However, such training often requires extensive personnel commitments in one-to-one exercises over a protracted period of time. Incremental units of learning are extremely small with such subjects while movement is slow and vast gaps occur between the repertoire of behavior presented and that toward which the program is directed. Little wonder then, that despite demonstrable gains under such procedures, their general application has either been limited in scope, poorly implemented, or heavily dependent upon extraordinary resources. While assistance from volunteers and other paraprofessional assistants is both feasible and productive, it lacks the precision and continuity that was offered by automated programming of instructional exercises. Thus, the project was one of instrumentation-mediated, programmed instruction introduced in the pivotal day room locale.

The system features that ultimately emerged were largely dictated by the following priorities. The units to be constructed must incorporate provisions for the essential elements of operant acquisition training, e.g., reinforcing stimuli and means for adjusting instructional step sizes. A second priority was that the frequency and duration of task-involvement be subject paced rather than assigned on some basis by an external agent. Moreover, even the earliest contacts with the task were to be based on adventitious interaction with the program. The common element to these concerns was the desire to avoid or at least minimize requirements for personnel or staff commitments. To achieve such functional ends, each of the units designed included provisions for autoshaping with extrinsic reinforcing consequences and lure-type promotion of subject-selected involvement with the program. Such goals were little different except in long-term value from those incorporated into the design of a pinball machine to be housed in the local teenager's haunts.

A variety of display units were designed ranging from systems concerned with motor behavior to those focusing on the acquisition of rudimentary concepts requisite for entry into more formal programs already available for the higher-functioning subject. One such unit, for example, involved a soft pad fixed directly under a series of bars mounted in columnar elevation and characterized by the property of vibrating when gripped. The subjects for whom this unit was designed were prone to spend much of their time lying on the floor, and we had determined that they responded to vibration as a reinforcing stimulus. The intent was to lure the subject into the vicinity of the instructional unit in seeking out the pad as a comfortable pillow on which to sit or lie. Once in that vicinity, the probability of adventitious contact with the lowest vibrating bar was quite high. As the rate of low bar contact increased, only the next highest bar was programmed to vibrate on contact. Thus, the subject was automatically shaped into a standing position with the highest bar ultimately becoming the functional response in a conceptual discrimination task, e.g., differentiation between alphanumeric symbols. Inherent in the development of these individuated shaping procedures was the continuing concern for reinforcing events capable of maintaining ongoing response differentiation and perceptual discrimination. Surprisingly, one of the most functional units designed was one with a single plunger-type manipulator with provisions for rear screen projection of slide displays and a column of clear pilot lamps whose activation was accompanied by a staccato-like series of auditory clicks. The unit is not too dissimilar from one recently offered commercially by Farrall Instruments.

These are representative of the systems designed and all were constructed so as to be housed in the facing of a locked closet door adjoining the day room. The unit was rear-programmed via electromechanical programming apparatus located inside the closet. Thus, there was no opportunity for subject contact with circuit voltage. Automated recording of manipulanda operations were secured via incorporation of digital counters in circuit with the manipulanda and a signal from an external observer indicating which of the alternate subjects was responding at any given time. The latter feature merits specific focus since the use of external observers violated our intent to obviate the necessity for personnel. A system to automate the identification of the subject responding at any given time had been designed for us by a team of NASA engineers. However, this work had only a small state research grant for its support and virtually all of our equipment was built out of parts cannibalized from state surplus purchases. Thus, we were forced to simulate such an application through external observers providing a circuit signal identifying the particular subject addressing the unit. In this case, graduate student observers came cheaper than the cost of automation, at least for the duration of this portion of the work. In effect then, the thrust of this work, perceived from the behavioral architecture vantage point, was to explore the positive potential of responsive closet doors in a day room.

The testing of these units was done in both field and simulated environments. A representative field application was an early one designed to examine the extent to which subjects could be shaped to address and master simple program requirements. A single cottage division of sixteen severely to profoundly retarded male adolescents constituted the locus of the work. Geographic areas of the day room were delineated and rate of subject entry noted in the respective areas prior to and during placement of the activity station in the day room closet facing. Two independent observers then monitored each resident on a time sampling basis while the total number of manipulanda operations of all subjects combined were automatically recorded. Relevant anecdotal data were also secured on a transactional basis. The stimuli were programmed in relation to manipulanda operations with pilot lamps scheduled on a continuous basis and an opaque color display and auditory clicks on an intermittent fixed ratio schedule. Experimental observations were taken over a thirty-day period during all waking hours in which the subjects were allowed access to the day room.

The general findings of this initial effort at field application included the following relationships. Prior to treatment, subjects exhibited no location preference within the day room, at least as a group. Subsequent to installation of the activity station, subjects tended to congregate in the immediately surrounding area. Thus, the lure properties of the unit did seem to have been operative. High initial response rates on the unit were obtained without staff mediation and autoshaping was clearly successful. High response rates were maintained throughout the course of operation suggesting that even the seemingly moderate reinforcing stimuli present seemed sufficient to maintain responding over a period of time. This probably would not occur in a more enriched environment where more powerful competing stimuli were present. The tendency of subjects other than the earliest operators to first observe and subsequently exhibit full-blown responding in their initial address to the manipulator strongly suggests that vicarious learning occurred. The most active and aggressive cottage residents tended to dominate operator time at the station. Frequent conflicts were noted among subjects attempting to assume the operator role, which was yet another indication that the station assumed substantial reinforcing value for these subjects. Finally, it was noted that a number of the attendants addressed the station on more than a few occasions, suggesting that it was not only the cottage residents who were responsive to a change in the day room properties.

These effects have been subsequently replicated, and much of the succeeding work has occurred in simulated settings. We are currently altering the focus from instrumentation and procedure to the range of content that may feasibly be incorporated. To date, the repertoire of symbols so acquired is rudimentary in conceptual level (i.e., simple two-choice discriminations) and erratic in production (error rates often approach chance levels for some subjects). Moreover, we have not demonstrated generalization to other contexts. Indeed, a substantial portion of our intervening efforts have involved attempts to reduce conflicts among subjects competing for use of the station in order to promote equitable access time among all subjects. We have not been too successful in this latter venture, and the work has often seemed in danger of becoming an examination of powerful territoriality phenomena. As a station is introduced in one area of the room, dominant subjects tend to establish territorial domain over that area and actively prevent other subjects from entering the area adjoining the station whether operating the station or not. It may be that the only effective means of handling this problem is the introduction of multiple units. The work is still ongoing and holds many challenges before the promise we imply can be met. Nonetheless, apart from the intersubject conflicts, we have noted no particular insult to the total ecology of the day hall environment and are inclined to facetiously suggest to you that, in pursuit of informed architectural design, you look to your closet doors as a heretofore untapped positive resource. A more serious inference is that simple and nonintrusive modifications in the physical design of virtually any environment can effect the introduction of autoinstruction and, therefore, pose the continuous opportunity for constructive training activities not otherwise available.

REFERENCE

Ellis, N. R., Behavioral engineering in mental retardation. Paper presented at American Psychological Association, Los Angeles, 1964.

IDEOLOGICAL, PROGRAMMATIC, AND ADVOCACY
FRONTIERS IN MENTAL RETARDATION

Frank J. Menolascino and Fred D. Strider

During the last twenty-four years, the National Association for Retarded Children (NARC) has had the courage to initially light some candles of hope for our retarded citizens. In the mid-fifties it converted to the kerosene lamp to help illuminate biomedical research interests and efforts, then switched to an electric flooding of the entire plight of the retarded in the early sixties. Now, in the seventies, it stands ready with its laser beam to bring the retarded out of the shadows of destructive folklore, mythology, and a non-human societal status, which make them the passive pawns of only temporarily interested professional groups Today we are in an exciting time and on the threshold of providing truly normalizing programs and expectations for the mentally retarded. I recently attended an annual convention of a state association for retarded citizens which is actively pushing itself past this threshold into some of the major ideological programmatic challenges of the seventies. On their program were the following topics: (1) preschool education for the retarded child at home; (2) special education dropout, the multiply handicapped children; (3) work and recreation for the mentally retarded programs for independence and risk; (4) sexual guidance; (5) community homes for the retarded — what should they be like and offer?; (6) the voice of the consumer -- the National Association for Retarded Citizens and the mentally retarded citizens themselves; and (7) advocacy — who will care and take care? These challenges concerning the future directions of ideology and programming were discussed at the *most* important level of change by the advocates of the actual consumer of current and future services for the retarded.

In this chapter, the modern ideology and models of service which will bring normalizing services for the mentally retarded — the concepts and programmatic implications of the developmental model and the principle of normalization will be reviewed. The major stumbling blocks which currently impede the active implementation of these concepts and their implications for professional morality will then be discussed at some length. Finally, this chapter will stress the future innovations of providing services for the mentally retarded which we feel can and must be attained in the near future.

Contemporary Services for the Mentally Retarded

Contemporary Western society places high social importance on such attributes as intelligent behavior, social adaptability, emotional in dependence, economic self-sufficiency, and physical attractiveness. Since the mentally retarded individuals do not meet one or more of these "expected" criteria, they are in dire need of normalization as part of their overall developmental programming so that they are able to meet or approximate these attributes and thus actively fit into the world around them. Yet, today we notice that most of the generic programs for the mentally retarded primarily reflect: (1) the retarded as a "sick" person; (2) the retarded as the perpetual child; (3) the retarded as a deviant from which society should be protected; and (4) similar derogatory assessments (Wolfensberger, 1969).

Therefore, future programs for the retarded must strongly embody the *twin principles* of the developmental model and normalization so as to fulfill both the societal and individual expectations of the mentally retarded. These two principles will be explored, reflecting on what modern trends and programs for the mentally retarded will encompass in the near future.

I. *The Developmental Model*

There are three fundamental aspects of the developmental model: (1) life as change—which means that all living beings are in a constant state of change and that to remain static is to cease to exist. Professional consideration must be focused upon the internal and external factors influencing the retarded individual, which means a concentration on the modification of both developmental expectations and social behavioral skills (Grossman, 1973). (2) Sequence of development, which means that all organisms progress from a simple state of structure and function to a complex one and that this process is an orderly growth. (3) Flexibility of development, which means that in addition to the general sequence of development, each individual is subjected to varying stimuli from the environment, cultural differences, and ongoing patterning from meaningful people — all of which combine to account for the variance in the rate and particulars of an individual's development. This last point is especially relevant in assessing the developmental potentials of children previously viewed as "inherently hopeless" or "genetic cripples." Professionals have become more cognizant of the numerous interrelationships of the environmental and inherited factors of retardation and, with this awareness their endeavors on behalf of the retarded have been more successful.

Programs for the mentally retarded, which are developmentally oriented, will of necessity focus on selected areas for *accelerating, decelerating,* or *modifying* both the direction and rate of learning and behavioral changes. The goal of the developmental model is an increased concentration on providing the retarded individual with effective coping devices for his interpersonal and physical environments; this is in sharp contrast to the past/current approaches of self-preservation (custodialism) and its associated concept of the "happy mentally retarded." How many of the current "lost generation" of the retarded have primitive behavior because they are "untutored" rather than "autistic," "psychotic," or "odd"?

These foci and goals of the developmental model will produce programs which allow the retarded individual to increase his control over his environment, increase the complexity of his behavior, extend his repertoire of interpersonal skills, and maximize his human qualities. Further, developmental maximization of the retardate's human qualities leads to the second basic concept of contemporary programs for the retarded normalization.

II. *The Implications of Normalization*

The concept of normalization embodies a philosophical position concerning the personal dignity and human rights of any individual, and a series of specialized service-program concepts. The direct application of both the philosophical position and the service-program concepts to a mentally retarded individual demands the full utilization of services which are in the mainstrain of society.

Normalization essentially refers to an *attitude* and *approach* to the retarded individual which stresses his having the opportunity to live a life as close to the normal as possible. The attitudinal dimension stresses that the retarded have a right to developmental opportunities as fellow citizens, period! They are not "vegetables," "mongolian idiots," or "low-level retardates," but rather, they are fellow humans who have a variety of special problems in coping with the world around them. The important aspect of this definition of normalization encompasses a positive posture of hope, challenge, and eyeball-to-eyeball honesty as to what can and must be done to help the retarded.

The National Association for Retarded Citizens has already moved from illustrating what the retarded can do by providing early pilot programs (e.g., Opportunity Centers) which became the spur for initiation and extension of developmental day-training programs for the young moderately severely retarded, to obtaining legislation for trainable classes for their developmentally older counterparts. Now the NARC is moving more actively toward monitoring the evolving service patterns so that they do not degenerate into baby-sitting operations. The NARC pushes the professionals to refocus their attention from singular preoccupation with the partial approaches of cure and treatment. These partial approaches are available to only a few, therefore, the NARC underscores future habilitation programs for *all* retarded citizens!

The following examples illustrate the application of both the attitudinal and programmatic aspects of the normalization principle in providing truly modern approaches to the mentally retarded.

1. Programs and facilities for the mentally retarded should be physically and socially integrated into the community. This implies that service facilities must not be placed in physical or social isolation. The large institutions for the retarded "up on the hill" or "out in the sticks" obviously are the antithesis of the normalization principle.

2. No more retarded persons should be congregated in one service facility than the surrounding neighborhood can readily integrate into its services, resources, and social life. Placing or maintaining an institution for the retarded of 1,000 patients in a rural town of 2,000 citizens does not permit integration of the retarded, and further, it continues the tragic model of the historical

"out of mind out of sight" posture of the past. Similarly, special education classes must be integrated into the neighborhood school to which the retarded child can go with his borhters and sisters — rather than to a large central facility.

3. Integration, and therefore normalization, can best be attained if the location of services follows population density and distribution patterns. This rather obvious dimension had been ignored in the era of institution building from 1900–1940. Similarly, it is being ignored in this decade as well.

4. Services for the mentally retarded often need to be dispersed, not only across the communities of a state but even within a community. Intracommunity dispersal is virtually mandatory if integration is to be attained in a larger population center. The disperal suggests that there must be multiple services and facilities rather than a single service or facility for a large population base; the clustering of these services (e.g., a developmental training center and a children's hostel in close geographical proximity to each other) will better serve neighborhoods within a community.

5. Services and facilities for the retarded must meet at least the same standards as other comparable services or facilities for the nonretarded; this means neither more standards or less. For example, developmental training centers must concentrate on scientifically sound methods for prescriptive teaching rather than baby-sitting. Residential facilities must have the fire safety and sanitary standards of a Holiday Inn. Unfortunately, the mention of mental retardation to the usual program-facility planner seems to close a thinking valve and produces only the fire-sanitary standards of a hospital type of institution; these are not the standards of a hospital type of institution; these are not the standards of the mainstream of our society, and hence are not normalizing.

6. The personnel who work with the retarded must have minimal qualifications just as those who work with comparable nonretarded groups have. Although forward in its intent, this aspect has been repeatedly ignored as unlicensed physicians, semiretired teachers, and similar borderline and/or other troubled individuals (who have typically not done too well in former community or institutional positions) have continued to be employed and permitted to ply their warped wares on the retarded.

7. To bring about the maximum degree of encouraging the retarded to *imitate* the nonretarded as well as in the perception of the retarded by the public, the retarded must have *maximal* exposure to nonretarded fellow citizens in their communities. The physical isolation of some community-based ("edge of town") residential facilities, and the self-imposed professional isolation of the staff members there are incongruent with the necessity to bring about normalization. The number of community-based programs that are located in the most lonely parts of the city, against a mountain, on a hill at the edge of town, or near the city dump is confounding.

8. The daily routines of programs and services for the retarded should be comparable to those of nonretarded persons of the same age. Yet how many institutionalized severely retarded persons are never permitted outdoors? How many of the moderately retarded leave their buildings only for the walk to the central dining room? The lack of daily normalizing routines for these retarded citizens is predicated on institutional policy not on developmental realities! Daily routines of school attendance, recreational activity, and bedtime should be made as normal as possible. Seasonal changes including vacations should also be programmed as a portion of expected activities.

9. Services for children and adults should be physically separated to reduce the probability that children will imitate the deviant behavior of their elders, and because services to adults and children tend to be separated in the mainstream of current society. Residential services for the retarded should be specialized for specific types of problems or groups, because specialization can be better attained by age separation and, in addition, congregation and dehumanization can be avoided. This approach is in sharp contrast to the omnibus (Procrustean bed) nature of the treatment programs of many current residential facilities for the retarded.

10. The retarded person is entitled to be dressed and groomed as any other person his age; he must be taught a normal gait, normal movements, normal expressive behavior patterns, and his diet should be so adjusted as to assure normal weight. The probabilities of identifying retarded persons on sight should be *minimized;* the sloppily dressed retarded children (poorly groomed and wearing out-of-date clothes), the barefoot (and often naked) institutionalized young adults, or the children with "bowl" haircuts and one-piece "monkey suits" are testimonials to our current widespread programmatic "retardation" and lack of caring.

11. As much as possible, the adult retarded, even if severely handicapped, should be provided the opportunity to engage in work that is culturally normal in type, quantity, and setting. Although it may occur in sheltered settings, work for adult retardates should approximate typically adult work (e.g., sheltered workshops should resemble industry) rather than activities and/or settings that are commonly associated with children, and with play, recreation, or leisure. This dimension demands a serious rethinking of the far too frequently noted occupational-recreational therapy activities which embody arts-and-crafts and fun-and-games approaches that keep the retarded occupied in the name of utilizing time, rather than focusing on meaningful work. This type of "diversional therapy" too often parades as recreational or vocational programming.

Normalization refers to concepts which are a cluster of ideas, methods, and attitudes toward the retarded as reflected in high standards of excellence in providing the needed human services, specialized programs which are integrated into the community, and high expectations of the retarded in keeping with that expected from all of us in the mainstream of our society. Utilization of the available social-family services whenever possible eliminate the notion of the retarded as a perpetual student and in need of overly unique types of service.

III. *Amalgamation of the Developmental Model and the Concept of Normalization*

The application of the concept of normalization to the mentally retarded requires the utilization of the developmental model for social-adaptive learning to enable the mentally retarded citizen to successfully cope with the outside world. Therefore, specific programs and techniques are needed for different challenges at differing developmental ages. The *child* needs developmental stimulation so as to attain a full repertoire of social-adaptive self-help skills. The *adolescent* principally needs socialization, positive peer group identity, and prevocational training. Finally, the *adult* principally needs specific vocational training and associated job placement so as to attain the dignity of work with associated minimal (if any) help in how to live an autonomous life in general society.

There are administrative implications of the amalgamation of the developmental model and the normalization principle into modern treatment programs for the retarded. Of vital importance is the administrator's orientation and attitude particularly with reference to what the retarded individual *can* do rather than the far too often voiced concern of what he *cannot* do! The administrator's attitude is far more important than his educational "stripes" or administrative experiences (e.g., ten years as an administrator of a large institution for the retarded is often a sign of a dedicated state employee but little else!). A positive administrative orientation toward sound and open staff-parent relationships is much more facilitating than the opposite — parents as "loudmouths who are never satisfied" or as "ignoramuses" because of their lack of training. The administrator must understand and utilize modern management approaches in establishing and operating a rather complex and interlocking system of services for the mentally retarded. This approach must encompass management techniques and objectives (e.g., the cost-benefit ratio rationale) so that a developmental prescription for each retarded individual can be outlined to meet his specific needs. It will be very beneficial in objectively demonstrating to the consumer what the current program has produced and will deliver in the way of specific human services. Lastly, the administrator must have a positive posture toward *change* itself — he must be flexible so as to evolve with the rapidly changing expectations and opportunities for mentally retarded citizens in our society. Application of the practical dimensions of the principle of normalization and the developmental model to the current-future programs for the retarded must permeate all service endeavors. In brief, the twin thrusts of the principle of normalization and the developmental model will permit forging of a new spectrum of opportunities for retarded citizens.

IV. *Implementation of Normalizing Services for the Retarded in the Seventies*

The first step in implementation can be accomplished by bringing together the confluent trends in the NARC and professional groups which serve the retarded, to demand superb services from general society. These trends have come because of: (1) instantaneous communication of events, their interpretations, and possible alternatives; (2) the emerging power of consumer groups, which is based on an increased awareness of the unrealized group potential for bringing about changes in major societal systems; (3) the rising costs of human services which are leading to an ever increasing sophistication of administrative and cost-service benefit approaches aimed at specific assessment of outcomes; (4) a new wave of humanism (especially in the young) which is blurring the lines of what is normalcy or deviancy; and (5) a deep and almost brooding national introspection about individual and societal *morality.* For example, in the recent past, the conscience of our country was deeply pricked by the Vietnam war, racial inequality, the despoiling of our physical habitat, and other problems, all within the context of a degree of openness and humility that permits this introspection to be actively pursued We will return to the dimension of morality as a major thrust of all of these confluent trends in our society toward a reaffirmation of respect for the dignity of the retarded.

Secondly, it is time to start new models of service for the retarded. A review of service models during the last forty years (Wolfensberger, 1969) reveals that virtually no new models have been initiated. During this period, the pattern has been to make mild variations on old models (i.e., regional centers), and to literally stumble over the better on the way to the best. In this last dimension parents have often unwittingly said, "At least a 650-bed institution is better than what we have. So why be against these new buildings, they are better than what we have now!" In this current period of change and increased public awareness of the retarded, by permitting these smaller institutions to be built as old wine in new bottles, there is spawning of a new wave of buildings that will haunt us for many years to come. The strengths of the NARC can be utilized as change agents for new programs and services for the retarded, rather than being cadres of thankful followers of endless dialogues that tend to mystify rather than clarify the models of care for retarded citizens. The change agent role of NARC must embody both new program models and new manpower utilization patterns, for either of these without the other has strongly contributed to the current lean offerings of services.

The Nebraska Plan for the Retarded (Wolfensberger and Menolascino, 1970) was the direct result of the activities and spurring of the Nebraska Association for Retarded Children. It started a new model of services which totally embodies the principle of normalization and the developmental model, and it has provided new vistas for manpower development and utilization. The plan synthesized the total needs of the mentally retarded, at all levels of retardation and chronological ages, into eleven types of programs facilities which provide the services that any retarded citizen may need during his lifetime. These eleven program facilities are as follows: (1) developmental maximation unit; (2) infant development; (3) child development; (4) prevocational; (5) habit-shaping services; (6) structured correctional services; (7) training hostels; (8) sheltered living settings; (9) minimal supervision settings; (10) crisis assistance unit, and (11) the five-day school (for rural settings). The Nebraska Plan represents a prototype of a contemporary regional service system (instead of a regional center) that can directly embellish the lives of all retarded citizens within their primary or extended family settings and within their home community. Since some of the currently unmet needs are those of severely-to-profoundly retarded children (with associated multiple handicaps), we would like to discuss the maintenance of life, infant development, and child development components of the above noted eleven-part total regional system of services for the retarded.

Residential Service Type 1 (Developmental Maximation Unit) — Some retarded individuals are so impaired as to require primarily those services necessary to sustain life. The profession most suited to offer these services is the medical profession and its related disciplines. Therefore, a residential service is needed that has a strong medical emphasis, that is administered by medical personnel, and that operates on the hospital model. Facilities to provide such service should be placed in close proximity to medical centers. Such a complex should be subdivided into a number of units, according to age and to some degree by sex. Care should be taken that individuals will be placed in this facility not merely because they are multiply handicapped, but because they do, in fact, require medical care more than other other single service.

While need for most residential services will decline as nonresidential services increase, the need for type 1 service is not likely to decline substantially as such a service is not readily rendered by nonresidential provisions. Also, if type 1 service is rendered in a quality medical context, present mortality rates of this group can be expected to decline considerably. Indeed, there is high expectation that many of these youngsters will "graduate" from this program to the Type 2 program.

Residential Service Type 2 (Infant Nursery) — Type 2 service is for presumably retarded infants and children up to the chronological ages of three to five who do not require maintenance-of-life types of care. Some conditions frequently associated with mental retardation (e.g. Down's Syndrome) can be diagnosed in newborn infants. Often, such children are likely to be multiply handicapped, but the extent of future handicaps and retardation can usually not be predicted with absolute confidence. Most such children can be adequately managed in the home if parents receive counseling and assistance. However, some such children are rejected, or are left homeless because of family disintegration and other causes. Unless foster homes can be found, or unless families or relatives can (with counseling) be persuaded to keep them, such children will require residential care. It is for these children that an infant nursery service is necessary.

The orientation of this service is toward nurturant development of infants and young children until basic self-help functions such as walking, feeding, some communication, and some toilet training have been accomplished. Accordingly, developmentally oriented nurses and child development personnel are the major staff personnel required. Eventually, these children must be transferred to other services such as child development and related residential components. A few of the beds of this service might, upon occasion, be used as a crisis-assistance function so as to accept retarded children whose families undergo severe stresses (e.g., illness, death, parents away from home, etc.).

In planning for the number of beds required, it should be kept in mind that for some of these children, the need for residential care may be temporary since (1) some families will reconstitute themselves; (2) some will accept the infant after initial rejection if they receive some counseling; and (3) foster care is increasingly found feasible with this group.

Residential Service Type 3 (Child Development) — This service is for children who are no longer infants and who do not require maintenance-of-life services. The anticipated age range here needs numerous units of six to ten children each, with some degree of specialization. We have found it prudent to think in terms of two subtypes: older chronological age higher-functioning children; and younger chronological age lower-functioning children. No division by sex appears to be necessary in this service.

Emphasis in this type of service is on child development. On the younger and/or lower levels, there is emphasis on completing mastery of self-help and social skills, to the degree that the children do not already have these skills upon entry into the program. Thus, the children are taught toilet use, feeding, dressing, speech, social courtesies, and other things. On the higher and/or older levels, many of the children are sent to local public school classes for the moderately or severely retarded. Special developmental programs have been established for those children who are not accepted by the public schools. Such programs are not operated in the living facilities, but at developmental day care centers which are adjacent to type 3 residential services.

The type 3 residential service is administered by a child development specialist, and various of the component units are headed either by child specialists or special educators. Some of the units in this residential type are operated by psychologists employing an operant behavior-shaping approach. However, this type of residence renders itself very well to the use of living-in houseparents who assume long-term and intensive parent-like functions under the administration of professionals. Houseparent assistants, who usually are college students that live in and are able to work odd hours, have been found to be most effective in these child development residential settings.

These three services are already running smoothly in Nebraska, and the first two services prompted the closing of a residential facility that was a shame to our state.

We are personally and professionally committed to bringing these services to full fruition, for we feel that their successful operation will be the "acid test" of the Nebraska Plan for the Retarded. The reader has undoubtedly recognized that it is the very lack of these three services (especially "maintenance of life" and "infant development") that has provided so much fuel for the current hopeless and helpless labeling of the severely and profoundly retarded and the monotonous "instant" solutions that keep being offered (e.g., a new wing added to an old institution and/or a "new" regional center). In this matter the personal and professional integrity of the advocates of the retarded in Nebraska will be fully tested to its limits!

The ideology and practical implementation of The Nebraska Plan for the Retarded has, to date, eventuated in a situation wherein the state of Nebraska has more locally based services for its retarded citizens than any other state in this country. More importantly, the new system is actively monitored by the local Associations for Retarded Citizens units, illustrating that ARC units must move their action efforts from *providing* services, to *obtaining* the services from local, state, and federal sources. Then, so as to assure their high quality, the ARC must successfully pass the monitoring hurdles such as cost-service benefit ratio considerations (e.g., the services range in cost from 84 cents a day for recreational-counseling services for a young adult in a job station in industry, to $22.60 a day for a full children's program including a specialized hostel for severely retarded older children with associated motor and/or special sensory handicaps). Similtaneously, the ubiquitous political hassels, such as public officials who had viewed the new locally based services as a threat to the active nurturing of their "local public works" (e.g., state residential facilities for the retarded and redirected state hospitals), have also been resolved by the sheer logic of programs which *actually work* to help the retarded in a direct fashion! Most importantly, the Nebraska Plan has become directly relevant to providing specialized and dispersed services of excellence to retarded citizens across Nebraska.

In the recent past, many of the prime movers of the Nebraska Plan were considered as, "dreamers when it comes to money. Why it will cost over $10,000 a year per client!". We were pushed to come up with specific cost-service benefit figures on our entire range of services. Rather than harm the new services, this request for "hard" economic guidelines and expenditures proved to be powerful documentation for the objective accountability of the services provided. Yet, the institutions' personnel do not have these figures and continue their "myths" of demanding more money while hiding larger costs (e.g., within separate state budgetary guidelines for renovation and construction), and blatantly amalgamate disparate costs such as the "client-employee" within the same leveling magic figure called the "per diem rate" for all residents. As one of our state legislators noted, "It doesn't take a superintendent to come before us to always ask for more and more money, since his secretary could easily do that! He has to be accountable for how much, where, and why, and the answers are always weak there." There are precious few indications that this traditional institutional posture, of "Give us more money, and don't bother us with accountability," has changed or will do so.

The questions and arguments that flow on and on across our country, about what are the "best" service approaches for the retarded, are researchable questions. Indeed, the NACR recently (1970) made a major policy decision relevant to this topic: NARC will re-balance its research thrust from biomedical research (with its prime focus on primary prevention) to operational—programmatic research (with its prime focus on embellishing the lives of our current retarded citizens via secondary and tertiary prevention approaches). A brief overview of this major redirection of NACR's research efforts may underscore the deep concern of this national organization of consumer representatives to be relevant to current and future trends. The early efforts of NARC's biomedical research support and efforts were the literal underpinnings of the current series of Mental Retardation Research Centers across our country. For example, an overview of research findings and challenges in mental retardation was commissioned by NARC in the mid-fifties and eventuated in *Mental Subnormality* (Masland, Sarason, Gladwin, 1958). This has been energetically followed through by NARC via ongoing efforts on the part of truly magnificent members of its Governmental Affairs Committee. Today, there are twelve Mental Retardation Research Centers that have been funded under P. L. 88-164 since 1964. The Congress has appropriated $26,000,000 of federal funds and the states and private sources supplied another $14,000,000 for construction of these Centers. The Centers, each located in a unviersity setting, have focused on the prevention of retardation in the unborn and/or new biomedical treatments for the very young retarded child (i.e., mostly primary prevention and some secondary prevention).

It should be noted that the overwhelming majority of these Centers are not mission oriented. They tend to focus on providing research personnel the freedom to inquire, and on technical excellence (highly prized in university settings), rather than on applied or nationwide coordinated research efforts, the latter being hallmarks of mission-oriented research. However, it appears that we currently need a more equitable balance between free inquiry and mission-oriented research endeavors in mental retardation; otherwise, the gap between the transmission of basic research into applied endeavors will continue its ten to fifteen year lag period — to the detriment of currently living retarded citizens.

The need for a balance between basic/applied research and financial considerations is not the prime rationale for the recent NARC research redirection from biomedical to operational-programmatic appraoches for the retarded. Instead it can become initiators and/or evaluators of research challenge. In contrast to biomedical research endeavors where an M.D. or Ph.D. degree "union card" seems to be needed as a qualification to discuss these matters, one notes that virtually all NARC members have had experiences concerning operational and programmatic dimensions of service systems for the retarded. We are stressing this point because we repeatedly winced upon reading a recent survey wherein NARC members disclaimed any competency to assess our past biomedical research activities, and uniformly requested that these matters be left up to "the experts." On the contrary, we vividly remember a wheat farmer from Montana reviewing for us the variety of options he felt were available for a work-study program for the retarded displaying in-depth operational-programmatic knowledge (replete with cost-service data!) about a topic very dear to his son and him. An attorney from New England completed a successful federal grant for a four-part residental model study that would shed evaluative and comparative light on current residential needs for the retarded in his area. His grant, in clearly presenting testable hypotheses, would put many masters and doctoral theses that we have reviewed to shame! Accordingly, this new redirection is properly in the area of expertise of NARC members so that they *can* evaluate (and utilize) the research efforts they will support.

What comprises operational-programmatic research and what guidelines can be utilized for this NARC research redirection? In brief, NARC has done research applicable to social-educational, behavioral, and service systems research that is directly relevant to the lives of the retarded (e.g. family support systems for needed services, different programs and designs for residential settings, which ones are best for what retarded citizens in differing geographical and social settings, at what ages, etc.) Similarly, sociological analyses of the planning process in the community leads to the questions, "What are the basic assumptions in community programs?" "What planning processes fail or succeed, where and why?" Other examples of possible operational-programmatic research include areas such as the following:

1. Ten years ago community-based hostels for the retarded were considered high-risk projects. If NARC had funded five to ten hostels at that time in different geographic areas for different age groups, levels, or types of mental retardation, it would have learned much and pushed others to follow. Similarly, today the concept of the "crisis assistance unit" is an example of a "high-risk" operational research challenge. We kick this residential component around, although we really don't know how well it will work. For example, will it really relieve individual family crises? What about program components such as costs involved and utilization rates? Can we or should we mix children and adults of both sexes therein? Should such a unit be in town, or in a vacation type setting at the edge of town (e.g., ease of transportation versus more resources and fun, such as a swimming pool? How should we architecturally design this crisis assistance unit?).

2. The history of the Holtner Valve for the clinical management of hydrocephaly suggests that past similar high-risk biomedical types of operational-programmatic research opportunities were and continue to be present. Mr. Holtner (an engineer who had a child with rapidly developing hydrocephaly) could have reached out to NARC and said, "I have two months to try and finalize this valve for my child. I need $2,000 to have a machinist turn my idea into reality." Or NARC could have aided him in establishing his eventual business to sell these valves by extending him a low-interest loan.

3. We need to translate currently available operational research into concrete

published guidelines (e.g., like the earlier NARC manual on how to organize a local NARC. We now need similar manuals such as "How To Plan a Community-Based Program of Residential Services" (or a regional network of services).

4. Similarly, operational research endeavors could harness what we already know about applicable techniques to help the retarded. A case in point would be a review of current deficit theory research on the learning process and its translation into concrete guidelines for teaching the retarded. The questions here are "What is mental retardation? Is it a global learning disability?" Are there specific deficits in attention, arousal, motivation, inhibition, or the organization of memor (long term versus short term)?" The deficit theory has spawned thousands of research proposals and reports. In turn they have yielded many practical recommendations for teaching the retarded (e.g., operant learning and transfer of learning principles). Yet, if you ask the usual special education teachers how they could maximize their teaching approaches to the retarded, they rarely know anything about these practical recommendations! Why? Because this body of information has not been pulled together as to its practical applications for teachers at the "front lines" in contrast to the yearly ("nonreadable") reviews for fellow scients. Lest we unduly pick on teachers, our residents in psychiatry are just recently becoming acquainted with operant learning-management techniques in their teaching curriculum, although Dr. Ogden Lindsey illustrated the application of operant learning to disordered and/or retarded behaviors almost fifteen years ago! An operational research project such as this one could be completed and help retarded individuals rather quickly (e.g., within three to five years).

5. A comprehensive cost-benefit analysis of the relative merits of community versus institutional programming could be initiated. We could help put to rest the ongoing arguments (on both sides) as to the relative service-cost relationships between different institutional settings and community systems of service (Balls, Butterfield, and Zigler, 1974). For example, there is rapidly developing in our country a "Scandinavian backlash" phenomenon concerning whether affluent America can "really afford" the approaches of the "socialists" in Scandinavia. These are issues to be further researched since they have direct reference to our local-state-national approaches and attitudes toward the retarded. Such a study should lean heavily upon the expertise available among many of our economist colleagues (Conley, 1973). We have mentioned our current Nebraska experiences on the cost-service benefit ratio and its relationship to accountability, but let's study it further to assess its strengths and weaknesses in differing socioeconomic populations and geographical settings.

6. There could be a study of representative systems for coordinating community services for the retarded, on the basis of which a model for an effectively coordinated system of services could be developed. This issue stems

from our experience that, in many instances, agencies purportedly established for the purpose of service coordination (e.g., regional mental health and mental retardation centers) primarily provide overly elaborate diagnostic procedures and tend to shunt parents from one service possibility to another. It is our opinion that such ineffective coordination has done much to unfairly contribute to the sterotype of the parent of the retarded as a diagnosis and/or service shopper.

7. A study of citizen advocacy programs (Wolfensberger and Zauha, 1973) could be aimed at determining their effectiveness in insuring the legal and personal rights of, and provisions of meaningful services to, our mentally retarded citizens.

8. There could be demonstration and investigation of a total developmental prosthetic environment, especially for the severely to profoundly retarded nonambulatory person. Though much has been written about this applied research challenge, few examples of it are present in our country today. Not only would this type of programmatic research directly aid the more severely retarded citizen, it would be an excellent example of what we could do for these citizens to spur societal changes in the current attitudes of hopelessness for this programmatic endeavor.

9. Lastly, we can try to focus on what operational-programmatic trends are now on the horizon. In other words, we would dedicate ourselves to selectively support (with "seed money") the work of current researchers and help them complete pilot programs before they go to state-federal sources to request funds for larger-scale operational-programmatic research endeavors. An example here could be the establishment of rigidly designed psychopharmacological studies to assess the effectiveness of some of the recently described purported memory and learning enhancers.

These general and specific types of operational-programmatic research efforts can have an immediate impact on the retarded citizen's current and future life. This new redirection of NARC's research efforts will give it the results needed to answer our current unanswered questions and stop our stumbling over the better along the way to the best services for our retarded citizens.

V. *Professional Morality*

"Am I mad that I should cherish that which
bear but bitter fruit?
I will tear it from my bosom, though my
heart be at its root."
Lord Tennyson, Locksley Hall

We have left to the end, though we have touched on it briefly earlier, a dimension of our current parental-professional efforts, which focuses on the issue of *morality*. We approach this dimension with some trepidation because; (1) morality is so often in the eye and soul of the beholder; and (2) it is a topic which has a high propensity for making "enemies." Yet, events of the past few months have made us ever more convinced that the morality of a man is measured by what he *stands for and does,* rather than the social graces that seem to lead to ever increasing numbers of "friends" who don't seem to disagree about anything! A year ago, some of our colleagues had begun to convince us that the slow, steady approach to changing the tragic plight of our institutionalized retarded citizens was the "cool way" to get the job done, and the "keep plugging away in a gentle fashion from inside the system" approach would change these large congregate mausoleums for the living dead. In other words, be tactful, and as surely as the day follows night our fellow professionals across this country would see the "Ford Light" of the new approaches to the retarded, and do what is right. After all, they *are* professionals! Even our friends said we were becoming more polite to those personal contacts who still mouth sweet emptinesses about, "Those hopeless retarded folks who belong out in the country with thier own kind so that they can't bother anyone."

Recently one of us (F.J.M.) attended a national meeting of an organization of professionals whose major vocational endeavor is in providing services for the retarded. Historically, this organization stems from the early meetings of superintendents of institutions for the retarded, and remains entrenched with these "old-and-not-so-old guard" professional personnel. I had been invited to present a paper on a panel concerning behavioral problems in the retarded. Since this dimension of the retarded is my favorite vocation-avocation, I readily agreed to attend and present a paper. I was the second speaker, the first being an experienced psychologist who presented a paper which was rather innocently listed in the program as, "Psychological Issues in Institutionalization of the Mentally Retarded." He prefaced his presentation by remarking that he had just changed jobs from an institution in the Midwest to a university setting in another region of our country. He stated that in the interval between the time he had agreed to present the paper and the day of the presentation he had: (1) deeply searched his reasons for being at this institution for the last six years, and his possible service value to the retarded citizens therein; (2) he wondered why the community programs (which he had both visited and studied) were not more actively accepted by his institutional colleagues; (3) rewritten his paper, and (4) decided to leave his institutional position.

It was a gut-level paper that succinctly questioned both the *validity* and *morality* of professionals who man institutional settings for the retarded which have lost their ideological underpinnings and are of minimal value to the retarded citizens therein, preparing them for a life of personal oblivion in a wasteland of humanity. He strongly recommended that institutions for the retarded be rapidly phased out while simultaneously a wide array of community-based programs were actively started, embellished, and brought to fruition. It was an excellent paper which was presented with gusto. Mindful of the admonitions of my friends to "play it cool," I inwardly decided not to partake in the rather heated discussion that followed. The audience, typical of this organization (i.e., mostly institutional-based professionals), threw their old rocks at this speaker: "Parents like the institutions — they don't want their retarded kids." "Community-based programs don't and can't work!" "We haven't failed the communities, they have failed us, no money!" "We have outstanding programs, it's just that no one appreciated them and we don't brag about them."

The presenter handled these "hack" statements which have lulled generations of institutionalized retarded citizens (and the professionals who serve as their gate-keeper) into oblivion, with ease. Expectedly, his detractors in the audience became more loud and abusive. Then, like a bolt out of the blue, a fellow in the second row got to his feet, pointed at me and said, "And you, Menolascino, you are one of those troublemakers that go around this country spreading lies about what can be done for the retarded. You lie to parents, and you use phony numbers and fancy cliches when you talk to legislators. Community programs cannot work, I know because the retarded have to be put away for their own sake and the sanity of their parents, so don't just sit there, say something!" Well, I did, for this man had recently been *removed* as a superintendent of an institution like those depicted in *Christmas in Purgatory,* (Blatt and Kaplan, 1976). Yet he had not learned, in the twilight of his professional career, that the parents of the retarded in his state have seen through this aimless and cruel warehousing of the retarded. Rather than talk about "lies," since there are none, past or present, I focused on the *morality* of any professional who does not actively utilize the knowledge which we do have to aid the retarded but, rather, continues his own personal mythology and its associated dehumanization of the retarded. In brief, I rather directly told this man to step aside and let the new wave of hope for the retarded revitalize our collective faith and trust that current ideologies (e.g., normalization and the development model) can bring new horizons of personal dignity to our fellow retarded citizens!

Yet the day had just begun and that afternoon there was a symposium on architectural challenges in providing residential settings for the retarded. One of the speakers began by discussing normalization, the "nonmedical" model, and special-ization of services. It sounded like a true haven from the old-guard powwow of that morning. Then a document which pertained to the speaker's topic was distributed to the audience. The document was a plan for a 400-bed institution out in the countryside in a large state. Like some cruel parody, the document effused modern concepts as a slick preamble to cover the dung heap of an institutional scheme! Excerpts were included, such as: "It was the belief of mental health experts that residents of state facilities for the mentally retarded have often been viewed as second-class citizens, subjected to a dehumanizing process, and denied their basic human and civil rights. Too often, state facilities have been 'make-believe' hospitals in their structuring, staffing and control, when in fact a large percentage of patients do not require medical care. The important needs of the mentally retarded (i.e., aid in language, social, emotional, and basic behavioral development) had been severely neglected. The philosophy of government is predicated on the belief that the men-tally retarded, as individuals and members of society, are entitled to the same rights and privileges due all citizens. It follows then that the state program for new residential centers should be based on the concept of 'normalization' that the

381

mentally retarded should have available to them the patterns and conditions of everyday life which are as close as possible to the norms and patterns of mainstream society."

Following this preface, there were a number of line drawings that depicted the retarded in a variety of "homelike settings." The drawings were embellished with accompanying vignettes such as "Come with me to touch, to taste, to feel the world: for this is what is real"; "Clustered homes amid the green of grass and trees. Walk with me. Enjoy the gentle breeze"; "Drink in the warm, the love, the sound you hear; where life is full of hope without fear." Are these the realities of life which you and I, presumably the "normals," experience in the normalizing mainstreams of our communities? More disturbing, and in my opinion grossly misleading, was an architectural rendering and its accompanying title narratives which commenced with the heading, "A Planned Community: Clusters of single-story condominiums set among green belts, playgrounds, winding walkways, overlooking a crystal lagoon"; "A complete community with medical, religious, educational, and recreational facilities"; "A community environment where the mentally retarded can experience the same rights and privileges as due all citizens where the exceptional are not an exception." One must ask, are these the standards of mainstream society? Who has the everyday luxury of a "crystal lagoon?" Doesn't a "complete community" sound like the sour old wine of current institutions for the retarded in a new bottle? The phrase "where the exceptional are not an exception," sounds like a modern-day rationalization to float a "colony for the deviants" whether they be "exceptional" via tuberculosis, leprosy, epilepsy, or *mental retardation.*

Rather than focus more on this tragic proof of Santayana's admonition, "He who does not know the past is committed to repeat its errors," we must ask: "Have we, the purported advocates of the retarded, learned so little these last fifty years? Are we really that 'retarded'?" Or has our courage toward challenging the professional morality of such schemes become of such low voltage that we accept these modern-day "solutions" which permit planners to enhance their "edifice complexes"? In our opinion, the price for us will be restless sleep and increasingly gnawing consciences for permitting the clarion call of St. Matthew — "Inasmuch as ye have done it onto one of the least of these My brethren, ye have done it unto Me" — to be muted. True, a 400-bed facility is "better" than two of the current institutions for the retarded in this particular state, which are among the largest institutions for the retarded in the world. True, this state is affluent and probably can afford the $35 a day per client projected cost at this "new" facility. True, the statement "They will receive up to four hours of programming a day" is far better than most current institutional programming schedules for the retarded. However, must we stumble over the "better" on our way to seeking and demanding the best for our retarded children and adults? The entire presentation and accompanying brochure bring clear validation to Samuel Gridley Howe's observation over 120 years ago: "As it is with individuals, so it is with communities; society moved by pity for some special form of suffering, hastens to build up establishments which sometimes increase the very evil which it wishes to lessen."

This type of presentation, which is aimed at mystifying rather than clarifying, *should* upset all professionals who purport to be knowledgeable about current programmatic needs for the retarded, and speak out against these "new" personifications of the tragic models of the past. Why? Because our morality demands that we directly challenge these "modern" planners who want to keep our retarded citizens out in the wasteland. It is they who, out of disrespect for the dignity of the retarded, send them out to the "new colony for the deviants." It is they who cause our children with, for example, Down's Syndrome (which is glibly referred to in this pamphlet as an example of "severe" retardation) to live out the professional's distorted value judgment of their minimal developmental expectancy (Menolascino, 1974), and to be viewed as ideal candidates for a tragic and often lifelong trip away from their loved ones, replete with minimal programming and growth opportunities.

Yet we *do* have viable alternatives for these children in their home communities! Lest the reader feels that I am side stepping the "real" issue of the severely to profoundly retarded (since the individuals with Down's Syndrome are not frequent inhabitants of this range of intellectual distribution), the previously noted "maintenance of life" and "infant Development" components of the Nebraska Plan for the Retarded are community-based services. Indeed, it is our opinion that the factors which have not permitted a more active implementation on a national scale of community-based alternatives for severely to profoundly retarded individuals are the professional myopia, laziness, and prevalent negative professional morality-value judgments concerning these citizens.

Normalization of the retarded takes place in our homes and in our communities — these are the mainstreams of our society. We must question the *morality* of those who prostitute modern concepts to crucify the retarded in their old and/or modern colonies for the deviants. As advocates of the retarded it is our moral obligation that we directly confront those people — at any level of our society — who say one thing and then do just the opposite. By not fearing reprisals, or caring whether we are termed "troublemakers" or "loudmouths," we can fulfill our true roles as advocates of the retarded. Indeed, as the advocates of the past-current-future consumers of these residential services, we owe it to those in planning policy positions to call a halt to these continuing fruitless efforts, and point out alternatives that will deliver the needed services in a manner which permits objective evaluation and accountability.

The sins of one generation have continued to haunt us in the areas of residential services for the retarded. Yet, if we do not utilize the knowledge we now have to seek and start new alternatives to these ongoing schizophrenic solutions to the needs of our retarded citizens, we shall all live to share our mutual guilt.

Community-based programs cannot possibly be the miserable failures that our human warehouses for the retarded have been these last fifty years! The evolving community-based programs need us on a people-to-people basis within the "glass bowl" of the community where all can see our efforts since there is nothing to hide, no humanity to deny. Above all there is a great joy in creating a system that we will all be proud to offer to those whose pathways in this world are uneven or stormy. We can then sleep soundly between our days of monitoring the new that we have created and can view without haunted consciences. To do less, such as in the numerous projected not-so-small institutions called regional centers which are being considered across our country, is in our opinion, to default and agree that NARC is powerless, its candles of hope have burned down, the developmental stimulation and normalization we have enjoyed is not "good" for the retarded, and our re-tarded citizens are less human and less deserving of the provisions for self-ful-fillment we have received. To us, these negative constructs hinge around a personal and professional moral crisis of values — a challenge which NARC has met these last twenty-seven years with direct action (and results!) Similarly, we must bring to full fruition the principles and practices embodied in the concepts of normalization and the developmental model to our fellow retarded citizens in the seventies. In this manner we *can* bring equal justice to the mentally retarded!

SUMMARY

We stand today just over the threshold of the seventies in our continuing com-mitment to provide developmentally oriented services within normalizing settings for our mentally retarded citizens. The principle of normalization for the retarded can only be denied if we feel that they are less than us — or nonhuman. Similarly, if the developmental model is applicable to even single-celled amoeba, then why not to the ever more complex (and interesting!) fellow citizen who just happens to be retarded? The confluence of current societal trends toward a new humanism that stresses the inalienable rights of all God's children, coupled with the change agent posture of NARC toward the future, can capture these two ideologies of human management, and start thereupon new models of superb community-based services for the retarded. Concomitantly, we can honestly research the *unquestioned answers* to *unanswered questions* via the newly redirected efforts of the NARC research thrust. This is the type of posture and commitment which will, in our opinion, permit us to go from our past and current scattering of candles of hope, to the utilization of modern "laser beam" technology that will cut through the cloud of "helpless and hopeless," and permit us to embellish the lives of retarded citizens across our country.

REFERENCES

Balla, D. A.; Butterfield, E. C.; and Zigler, E., Effects of institutionalization on retarded chiildren: A longitudinal cross-institutional investigation. *American Journal of Mental Deficiency,* 1974, *78* (5), 530–549.
Blatt, B., and Kaplan, F., *Christmas in purgatory.* Boston: Allyn & Bacon, 1976.

Conley, R. W., *The economics of mental retardation.* Baltimore: Johns Hopkins University Press, 1973.

Masland, R. L.; Sarason, S. B.; and Gladwin, T., *Mental subnormality: Biological, psychological and cultural factors.* New York: Basic Books, 1958.

Menolascino, F. J., Developmental attainments in Down's syndrome. *Mental Retardation,* 1974 (in press).

Mental Retardation News, 1971.

Wolfensberger, W., The origin and nature of our institutional models. In Kugel, R. B., and Wolfensberger, W., (Eds.), *Changing patterns in residential services for the mentally retarded.* Washington, D. C.: Government Printing Office, 1969, pp. 59–172.

Wolfensberger, W., and Menolascino, F. J., Reflections on recent mental retardation developments in Nebraska. *Mental Retardation,* 1970, *8* (6), 20–27.

Wolfensberger, W., and Zauha, H., *Citizen advocacy.* Toronto: National Institute of Mental Retardation, 1973.

BEHAVIORAL ARCHITECTURE:
EFFECTS OF THE PHYSICAL ENVIRONMENT
ON THE BEHAVIOR OF THE RETARDED*

James C. Griffin, William F. Landers and Earl T. Patterson

In the last decade, many writers have speculated about the effects of overpopulation and its possible adverse implications for the future (e.g., Ehrlich, 1968; Carson, 1969). Ehrlich (1968) has noted that if the current rate of world population growth continues, the population should double in approximately thirty-five years. The field of mental retardation is obviously affected by this prognostication. Conley (1973) reports that 5.6 million people or 3 percent of the current population of the United States under age sixty-five have IQs less than 70. Conceivably, 11.2 million individuals could need services within approximately three decades. Concomitant with increased instances of retardation as a result of natural population growth are other factors which may result in an even larger increment. The life span of the retarded has been greatly increased due to improved medical attention (Conley, 1973). In fact, the National Association for Retarded Citizens (1973) reports that the life expectancy of mildly retarded individuals is nearly equal to that of the nonretarded population. While it is considerably lower for the profoundly and severely handicapped at present, they too can expect longer lives in the future. Also, it appears that more cases of retardation have been discovered as additional services and programs have been developed. In other words, previously undetected needs have become obvious with the development of new agencies to serve the retarded. Finally, more people have become functionally retarded or unable to cope as society has become even more complex and technologically sophisticated.

If the demographic data just cited have not prompted reader concern about overpopulation in tomorrow's mental retardation facilities, perhaps recent court decisions will highlight the need for immediate concern. Litigation on the behalf of institutionalized retardates has produced landmark decisions. *Wyatt* v. *Stickney* provides an excellent example of the general national trend toward social advocacy on behalf of the retarded (Beerman, Bellamy, DiRocco, Friedland, Foss, and Steinbock, 1973). The *Wyatt* v. *Stickney* decision mandated that: (1) the number of individuals in a classroom shall meet minimum standards for a suitable education program; (2) all ambulatory residents shall sleep in a single room or in multiresident

*The authors' research and the writing of this manuscript was supported by the Social and Rehabilitation Services of the U.S. Department of Health, Education, and Welfare. Carol Sigelman is most gratefully acknowledged for her timely editorial assistance. Portions of this chapter were both presented at the annual meeting of the American Association on Mental Deficiency, June 4, 1974, in Toronto, Canada, and published in other manuscripts.

rooms of no more than six persons; (3) the number of nonambulatory residents in a multiresident room shall not exceed ten persons; (4) there shall be allocated a minimum of eighty square feet of floor space per resident in a multiresident room; (5) the minimum day room area shall be forty square feet per resident; (6) the minimum dining room area shall be ten square feet per resident. The intention here is not to pass judgment on the legal aspects of these decisions but, rather, to focus upon the absence of available information by which to formulate the court's decision. Objective information does not exist to either support or refute the assumptions of the decision and certainly neither the jurist writing the decision, nor the retardation specialists critical of the court order argue from a base of empirically derived optimal space requirements.

The design of physical plants for the mentally retarded has traditionally given primary consideration to durability, ease of maintenance cost, and the building patterns prevalent in comparable facilities. The design and construction of these facilities have been predicated on building codes and "voluntary guidelines" for which no empirical justification is available. In fact, facilities for the retarded are typically designed or renovated by the following process: (1) functional programmers draw a program for the building; (2) staff architects design the building based on the program; (3) the designs are circulated among ranking administrative figures; (4) revisions are made based on their comments; and (5) final approval is given for the design (Coniglio and Bussand, 1973). Apparently each new facility is a product of the idiosyncratic, nonobjective feedback provided by the planning committee. A desire to upgrade and standardize the properties of such facilities has been a significant element in efforts on behalf of the retarded of the Accreditation Council for Facilities for the Mentally Retarded. However, objective information on the basis of which meaningful guidelines could be developed has generally not been available, and reliance upon consensual judgment has been necessary in the absence of relevant empirical evidence (Crosby, 1973). Criticism is not directed toward those individuals involved in this process but, rather, to the deficient body of information utilized to establish these guidelines. An appeal to anecdotal evidence is insufficient since virtually any position can be so supported. Therefore, a major thrust of the present chapter is advocacy of an empirical data base more stringent than subjective experience.

This is by no means a new idea to mental retardation specialists. A decade ago, researchers and practitioners documented the pressing need for a prosthetic physical environment in all areas of residential life (e.g., Ellis, 1964). Our efforts in this sphere are truly embryonic. After ten intervening years of unprecedented emphasis on mental retardation research, the status of such a technology is essentially unchanged. This is not to say that the interaction of the physical environment and behavior has not been the subject of extensive professional concern. However, this concern has typically taken the form of descriptive, nonmanipulative demonstration projects or lectures by "authorities." It is not that all of the recommendations generated in these ways are invalid, but rather that the few empirical studies conducted to date raise serious questions about traditional assumptions (as will be evidenced in a subsequent section of this chapter).

Crowding and Behavior

In view of the forecast of the future outlined above, our attention must focus squarely on overpopulation. If most facilities for the retarded are not presently feeling the increasing demands, prognostications indicate that they soon will. Accordingly, in an attempt to alleviate current and forecasted difficulties, the authors chose to empirically examine the phenomenon of crowding. As noted by Stokols (1972), many authors have failed to discriminate between the physical condition *density,* involving spatial limitations, and the experimental state *crowding,* in which restrictive aspects of limited space are perceived by the individuals exposed to them. Density is viewed as a necessary antecedent, rather than a sufficient condition for the experience of crowding. Other papers have documented the lack of empirical knowledge germane to the effects of crowding on behavior (e.g., Freedman, 1970; McGrew, 1970; Zlutnick and Altman, 1972; Stokols, 1973). The majority of such work has been conducted with infrahuman populations (e.g., Christian, Fluger, and Davis, 1960; Calhoun, 1962, 1966; Clough, 1965; Marsden, 1970). However, social scientists in this area are fully cognizant of the difficulties associated with generalizing data from infrahuman to human populations (Hutt and Vaizey, 1966). Altman and Zlutnick (1972) have listed three major sources of information pertaining to crowding with humans: (1) laboratory research involving some form of loose controls; (2) correlational studies in natural settings primarily utilizing census tract data; and (3) contemporary speculations and guesses. Correlational studies are useful and necessary first steps but do not provide hard conclusions. Speculations and guesses, readily available in quantity, provide for stimulating leisure reading but are representative of the subjective approach to solving problems; and parametric laboratory studies involving manipulative procedures are practically nonexistent.

Reviews of the *Psychological Abstracts* and *Sociological Abstracts* and correspondence with interested parties have uncovered very few unpublished and published attempts to systematically assess the effects of crowding on human behavior (Zlutnick and Altman, 1972; Sommer, 1960). Of course, a large collection of empirical findings does not always produce clear and simple truths. If practitioners were forced to obviate all nonexperimentally verified treatment procedures from their repertoires, the resulting chaos would most likely be detrimental to effective programming. However, sound, replicable empirical conclusions should not be ignored simply because they oppose existing canons. If mental retardation specialists are to take advantage of the entire therapeutic milieu, effects of crowding on human behavior must be unraveled. The few new studies which do exist have used one of two procedures with the space held constant or manipulation of the space with the number of individuals held constant. (W. C. McGrew, 1970). Therefore, an investigator may manipulate either *social* density by observing groups of differing numbers in the same sized space or *spatial* density by observing same sized groups in spaces of differing sizes. P. L. McGrew (1970) empirically compared these two approaches and concluded that manipulations of social density had a more potent effect on behavior than did manipulation of spatial density. The importance of such a finding cannot be underestimated given the greater feasibility, in an applied sense, of varying the number of individuals in a space than of varying the size of the space.

The authors have been unable to discover any crowding research with the retarded population. However, Hutt and Vaizey (1966) used normal and brain-damaged children to examine, among other things, aggressive behavior and positive social interactions as a result of either small, medium, or large groups within the same spatial area (i.e., social density). They conclude that concurrent with increases in population density, both normal and brain-damaged children became more aggressive and normal children engaged in fewer positive social interactions, while brain-damaged individuals had the most positive interactions in the medium-sized group. According to Freedman, Klevansky, and Ehrlich (1970, the questionable procedures used in the experiment unfortunately make these conclusions suspect.

Moreover, these results are not completely consistent with the findings of two studies which manipulated spatial density. Hutt and McGrew (1967) found that concomitant with increases in population density, the social interactions of nursery school students with one another and with adults increased, in contradiction to Hutt and Vaizey (1966). As in the Hutt and Vaizey (1966) study, aggressive behavior increased. Yet a similar study with preschoolers discovered, in complete opposition to Hutt and McGrew (1967), less aggression and fewer positive social interactions in the high-density than in the low-density condition (Loo, 1972).

The results of the previously cited studies are equivocal. Although the question of how crowding affects the behavior of young children has not been answered, it is obvious that changes in behavior occurred. None of these investigations have examined the phenomenon of crowding with the retarded. Accordingly, we must ask this question: Do changes in the behavior of the retarded occur when social density is manipulated?

Research of the Effects of Crowding with Mentally Retarded Individuals

In order to answer empirically the question just presented, the authors of this chapter recently conducted a series of experiments with residents of the Lubbock State School for the Mentally Retarded. Finding no other published studies directly investigating the effects of crowding on the behavior of the mentally retarded, we hoped to provide the first evidence and compare it to other empirical findings concerning the relationship between crowding and human behavior.

Before embarking on our sequential research projects, several decisions had to be made. We elected to carry out our research in a specially constructed, fixed size (13' X 9' 6" X 8'), "clear space room" (i.e., an unfurnished room with all white or neutral colored walls, ceiling, and floor). This was done to reduce the possible contamination effects (Freedman et al. 1971) of other environmental variables (e.g., furniture, color, texture, lighting, etc.) and to give us a baseline for subsequent studies in natural environmental spaces. Our ultimate goal, however, was clearly the pragmatic one of providing data useful to architects and program planners.

The first study (Griffin, Landers, and Patterson, 1974 [a]) in our series asked, very simply, how the systematic manipulation of social density parameters influenced the behavior of the retarded. Specifically, we wanted to find out how three increasing levels of social density (e.g., two-, four-, and eight-person subject groups) were functionally related to the overt behavior of mentally retarded adolescent residents in our "clear space room." The positive social interactions, aggressive behavior and neutral behavior of the retarded subjects were recorded according to a time-sampling procedure — on videotape during four, thirty-minute sessions — in each density condition. After a consensus rating of the videotape data was achieved by a panel of four judges, statistical analyses indicated that there were reliable increases in positive social interactions and decrements in aggressive and neutral behavior concomitant with the increases in social density. In other words, we found that mentally retarded adolescents exhibited more positive social interactions and fewer aggressive and neutral behaviors when they experienced the higher levels of crowding. Furthermore, these increases in positive behavior as social density increased were linear. We were puzzled and intrigued by these results since the opposite would have been predicted from the majority of the published crowding studies.

Our findings in this first study were partially supported by Loo's (1972) study with preschool children, which reported significantly more aggressive acts in a less-crowded room. Yet they were inconsistent with those of Hutt and Vaizey (1966), who found a positive relationship between increases in crowding and aggressive behavior in hospitalized young children. However, these studies were not strictly comparable with ours since their subjects were younger and not mentally retarded. It is entirely possible that different types of subjects respond differently to crowding.

The present authors would discourage overgeneralization and feel compelled to state that our findings do not license crowding as a procedure to facilitate positive social interactions in institutions for the retarded. We believe that future research will establish a saturation point for social density beyond which negative behavior will predominate.

The second study (Griffin, Landers, and Patterson, 1974[b]) explored the relationship between objective behavior (i.e., overt behavior recorded on videotape) and subjective behavior (i.e., subjects' verbal responses to questionnaire items about their experiences) under these same three levels of increasing social density. As has previously been noted, a majority of the published studies of crowding with individuals of normal intelligence have presented data from surveys and questionnaires. It is conceivable that utilization of the subjective data collection format with retarded individuals could produce dubious findings (Guthrie, Butler, and Gorlow, 1961). When we analyzed our data from this second study, we found a high correlation between the subjects' verbal responses about their experiences in the "room" and their overt behavior in the same setting. However, this correlation was negative. In other words, the retardates' assessments of what occurred during the experimental sessions were diametrically opposed to their objectively rated overt behaviors during the same sessions. These results support the view that direct behavioral observations, and not a survey format alone, should be used when conducting research with a retarded population. Verbal reports from mentally retarded individuals should be considered with a great deal of caution, although they should not be ignored.

The Landers, Griffin, and Patterson study (1974), third in this series, represents somewhat of a departure from our previous studies. A multitude of experimental and anecdotal observations have been published pertaining to work settings (e.g., Nelson, 1971; Gold, 1972), but our review of the literature revealed no published investigations of how crowding affects the work performance of the mentally retarded. In order to explore the more practical implications of crowding for the rehabilitation of the mentally retarded, we investigated the affects of social density on the work performance of mentally retarded residents. However, since manipulation of crowding in an actual job setting would have been difficult, we devised a laboratory "job" which was an analogue of one or more types of jobs a mental retardate could perform in the actual work world. The retarded resident's job was to sort boxes of IBM cards and discard the defectives. Therefore, under four increasing levels of social density in the work area, we could observe the rate, accuracy, and efficiency of our subjects. The results of this study indicated that increases in social density led to highly reliable increases in rate of performance. However, the accuracy of our workers (i.e., the number of truly defective cards discarded) decreased as crowding increased. Analysis of our work efficiency measure (a function of accuracy and rate) indicated a trend toward more efficient work in pairs than when four and eight workers were in the area. The "questionnaire approach" utilized in the second study of this series once again revealed that the verbal responses of the workers were negatively related to their observed performance. In other words, our mentally retarded workers, under increasing conditions of crowding, increased their performance rate, decreased the quality of their work, and subjectively appraised their work as better than it actually was.

The somewhat unexpected findings from this third study were actually consistent with observations of the work performance of normal individuals in office settings published by Canter (1968). However, the fact that Freedman et al. (1970) found that the work performance of normal high school students was not affected by crowding partially contradicted our findings.

Cautiously, until the Landers et al. (1974) results are replicated or refuted, we would submit that the implications from this third study are most relevant to the rehabilitation and habilitation of the retarded population. Given that the task, schedules of reinforcement, and other variables are held constant, significant increments or decrements in work performance may occur as a consequence of manipulating crowding within the work environment of the mentally retarded.

Implications of Crowding Research with the Retarded

The ramifications of the authors' crowding research with the retarded are indeed numerous. The relevation that variations in population density can significantly enhance or detract from a retardate's behavioral repertoire or work performance could be useful in altering current modes of habilitation and rehabilitation in residential facilities. Many past studies of the behavior of the mentally retarded — which have influenced program decisions — may be misleading since they did not consider the effects of group size and space size on behavior. Moreover, our research suggests that it is simplistic to claim that problems will be solved if standards for floor space are set (e.g., *Standards for Residential Facilities for the Retarded,* 1971). It is not how much living space is available, but rather how many people occupy that space and what it is used for that is critical. Currently accepted guidelines (i.e., *Standards Manual for Rehabilitation Facilities,* 1973) germane to the retardate's working environment are actually in contradiction to the empirical findings. Authoritative sources have, by fiat, taken sixty or more square feet of floor space per individual as an essential hallmark of the optimally therapeutic work environment for retarded clients. However, when empirical research supplants historical precedent as the prevailing standard for such judgments, the critical variable appears to be the number of workers in a given space rather than the square footage per individual — especially when we know that workers are often clustered in small sections of a large work area. It is also very possible that normalization procedures which advocate a more secluded or private living environment (Wolfensberger, 1972), and necessarily more expense, may be inadvertently producing antitherapeutic effects. If positive social interactions are to be increased, sensibly sized groupings of individuals, and not privacy, may be essential. Such marked divergence in delineating elements germane to a productive environment demands our closest attention. We cannot afford to develop radically new environments for the retarded without knowing how these environments may affect these individuals.

An enormous amount of research is necessary to further delineate the effects of crowding on the behavior of the retarded. What densities of people elicit the most positive social interactions in a leisure enviornment? What are the retardate's subjective assessments of these manipulations? How do they compare with his overt behavior? Aside from the living environment, the characteristics of the work setting should be investigated further. Given varying degrees of complexity of the work task, what are the effects of density on the quality and rate of work performance? How many individuals should work in a given space to promote positive social interactions? The possibilities for such scientific inquiry are infinite. However, the prospective investigator should be forewarned that the effects of density are not simple. "They are complicated by many factors such as duration of the stimulation, number of subjects in each group, area per child, experimental versus naturalistic conditions, spatial versus social density, characteristics of the sample, the equipment and activities within, and the degrees of density studies" (Loo, 1972, p. 380). Zlutnick and Altman (1972), in their classic review of crowding, offer the following explanation: "It should be clear that the state of knowledge regarding the effects of crowding on human behavior is too sparse to permit any firm recommendations regarding ameliorative action. In fact, we do not appear to be in a scientifically defensible position to suggest the nature and magnitude of any effects. *The most honest statement is that we just do not yet know much about the psychological effects of crowding.*" [italics added, p. 55.] In other words, crowding does have strong effects on behavior but we are not able at this point in time to predict the direction of those effects. This statement appears to represent the most rational theoretical position until additional empirical knowledge has been accumulated.

Conclusion: Toward Behavioral Architecture

The Zeitgeist of the sixties and the seventies has been and continues to be ripe for the genesis of "humanistic" themes and "social advocacy" causes. Several of these parallel but independent movements seem to fit together and suggest the need for a more inclusive and coordinated thrust. The field which we envision emerging draws a number of environmental, behavioral, and social approaches into a holistic scientific field. We would arbitrarily label the area "behavioral architecture." Generically, behavior refers to the totality of overt and covert responses of an organism within his total environment. Architecture may be defined as the art and science of designing and building physical structures. The question is how to make behavioral and social psychological research affect architectural design outcomes, and how to intervene in the planning-design-construction-evaluation process to produce better living, working, and therapeutic environments. Specifically, we believe that behavioral architecture would significantly improve the habilitation and rehabilitation of retarded individuals.

The authors propose that behavioral architecture should be defined as the science of planning, designing, constructing, and evaluating physical structures in light of empirical data on the interrelationships of the characteristics and functions of the physical environment and the behavior-social characteristics of the user. A voluminous amount of rhetoric has been produced within the last decade concerning the relationship between human behavior and the physical environment, and this burgeoning field of interest crosses numerous disciplines such as ecology, ethology, psychology, and architecture (Cleland, Swartz, and McGavern, 1974). The focal area of concern remains constant across these disciplines, yet "inside" jargon, the lack of a common language, and divergent publication outlets have produced communication barriers that are difficult to circumvent. However, architects are now ready to interact with behavioral scientists, and vice versa. Since Howard's "Garden Cities" in the early 1900s, Gropius and the Bauhaus in the 1920s, and, most recently, the work of Aldo Van Eyck, Shadrach Woods, and Team 10, many planners have emphasized the social aspects of design (Zeisel, 1970). Zeisel also states that, unfortunately, "designers prefer to rely on personal experience and intuition — not on other people's research," in spite of the increasing number of publications which advocate the utilization of empirical research in architectural design. Zeisel further states that the "behavioral research already completed has never been used — is not even known. Although psychologists, sociologists, psychiatrists, and anthropologists for many years have been studying how man's social and physical environment affects him, and how he in turn adapts to and changes his surroundings, few design professionals have bothered to look into this research." Historically, psychologists such as Watson, Skinner, Kantor, and Piaget over the last fifty years have emphasized the interaction of organism and its environment as a key concept to the understanding of human behavior. However, "the inclusion of the physical environment as a variable in psychological research is unquestionably a fruitful and long overlooked endeavor" (Skaburskis, 1974). Apparently, cognizance of the interactive effects of the physical environment and behavior has spurred only token amounts of collaborative efforts. Although we coin the term "behavioral architecture," we are of the opinion that this holistic, scientific, multidisciplinary approach has not, as yet, achieved disciplinary status. Therefore, we must recognize that the perspectives in this manuscript are still in the process of emergence. We can only hope that others may join in the effort to generate a genuine discipline leading us toward behavioral architecture.

REFERENCES

Beerman. L.; Bellamy, T.; DiRocco, P.; Friedland, M.; Foss, G.; and Steinbock E., Civil rights of the retarded Working paper #69. Rehabilitation Research and Training Center in Mental Retardation, University of Oregon, Eugene, 1973.

Calhoun J. B., Population density and social pathology, *Scientific American,* 1962, *206,* 139–148.

Calhoun, J. B., The role of space in animal sociology. *Journal of Social Issues,* 1966, *22,* 46–59.

Canter, D., Office size: An example of psychological research in architecture. *The Architects Journal Information Library,* April, 1968, 881–888.

Carson D., Population concentration and human stress. In Rourke, B. F. (Ed.), *Explorations in the psychology of stress and anxiety.* Ontario: Longman Canada Limited, 1969.

Christian, J. J.; Fluger, V.; and Davis, D. C., Factors in the mass mortality of a herd of sika deer *Cervus nippon. Chesapeake Science,* 1960, *1,* 79–95.

Cleland C.; Swartz J.; and McGavern, M., Ecology, ethology, economics, and humanistic psychology in institutional architecture. Paper presented at the meeting of the American Association of Mental Deficiency Toronto, Canada, June, 1974.

Clough G. C., Variability of wild meadow roles under various conditions of population density and season and reproductive activity. *Ecology,* 1965, *46,* 119–134.

Coniglio, C., and Bussand E., A functional program for renovation of the children's building at a residential school for the mentally retarded. Unpublished manuscript, Newark State School, New Jersey 1973.

Conley W. R., *The economics of mental retardation.* Baltimore: Johns Hopkins University Press, 1973.

Crosby, K., *Personal communication,* 1973.

Ehrlich P. R., *The population bomb.* New York: Ballantine Books, 1968.

Ellis, N. R., Behavioral engineering in mental retardation. Paper presented at the American Psychological Association, Los Angeles, 1964.

Freedman, J. L., The effects of crowding on human behavior. Unpublished manuscript, Columbia University, 1970.

Freedman J. L.; Klevansky, S.; and Ehrlich, P. R., Effect of crowding on human task performance. *Journal of Applied Social Psychology,* 1971, *1,* 7–25

Gold, M., Research on the vocational habilitation of the retarded: The present, the future. In Ellis, M. R. (Ed.), *International Review of Research in Mental Retardation.* New York: Academic Press, 1972.

Griffin J. C.; Landers, W. F.; and Patterson, E. T., Systematic manipulation of crowding parameters with the retarded. Unpublished manuscript, Research and Training Center in Mental Retardation, Texas Tech University, 1974. (2)

Griffin, J. C.; Landers, W. F.; and Patterson, E. T., Retardate's subjective assessment of the physical environment in comparison to their overt behavior. Unpublished manuscript, Research and Training Center in Mental Retardation, Texas Tech University, 1974. (b)

Guthrie, G. M.; Butler A. J.; and Gorlow, Patterns of self-attitudes of retardates. *American Journal of Mental Deficiency,* 1961, *66,* 222–229.

Hutt, C., and McGrew, W. C., Effects of group density upon social behavior in humans. Paper presented at "Changes in behavior with population density," symposium at the meeting of the Association for the Study of Animal Behavior, Oxford, England, July 17–20, 1967.

Hutt, C., and Vaizey, M. J., Differential effects of group density on social behavior. *Nature,* 1966, *209,* 1371–1372.

Landers, W. F.; Griffin, J. C.; and Patterson, E. T., Effects of population density on retardates' work performance. Unpublished manuscript. Research and Training Center in Mental Retardation, Texas Tech University, 1974.

Loo, C., The effects of spatial density on the behavior of children. *Journal of Applied Social Psychology,* 1972, *2,* 372–381.

Marsden, H. M., Crowding and animal behavior. Paper presented at the meeting of the American Psychological Association, 1970.

McGrew P. L., Social and spatial density effects on spacing behavior in preschool children. *Journal of Child Psychology and Psychiatry,* 1970, *11,* 197–205.

McGrew, W. C., An ethiological study of social behavior in preschool children. Unpublished doctoral thesis, University of Oxford, 1970.

National Association for Retarded Children. *Facts on mental retardation.* 2709 Avenue E East, P. O. Box 6109, Arlington, Texas 76011, 1973.

Nelson, N., *Workshops for the handicapped in the United States.* Springfield, Ill. Charles C. Thomas, 1971.

Skaburskis, J. V., Commentary: Berkeley context. *Journal of Architectural Education,* 1974, *27,* 3–4.

Sommer, R., *Personal space: The behavioral basis of design*. Englewood Cliffs, N. J; Prentice-Hall, 1960.

Sommer, R., *Design awareness* (Rinehart ed.). New York: Ho H, Rinehart and Winston, 1972.

Standards for Residential Facilities for the Mentally Retarded. Joint Commission on Accreditation of Hospitals, 875 North Michigan Avenue, Chicago, Ill. 1971.

Standards Manual for Rehabilitation Facilities. Commission on Accreditation of Rehabilitation Facilities 6510 North Lincoln Avenue, Chicago, Ill., 1973.

Stokols, D., On the distinction between density and crowding: Some implications for future research. *Psychological Review,* 1972, *79,* 257–277.

Stokols, D., A social-psychological model of human crowding phenomena. *Journal of the American Institute of Planners,* 11973, *38,* 72–83.

Wolfensberger Wolf, *The principle of normalization in human services*. Toronto, Canada: National Institute on Mental Retardation, 1972.

Wyatt v *Stickney*. Civil Action No. 3195-N at 4, n. 7 (m. D. Alabama, March 13, 1972).

Zeisel, J., Behavioral research and environmental design: A marriage of necessity. *Design and Enviornment,* 1970, *1,* 50–51, 64–66.

Zlutnick, S., and Altman, I., Crowding and human behavior. In Wohlwill, J., and Carson, D. (eds.). *Environment and the social sciences: Perspectives and applications*. Washington, D. C.: American Psychological Association, Inc., 1972.

SUBJECT INDEX

A

ABA Research Design — 285, 288

Academic Achievement — 142—143, 149—151, 216—217, 297

Aggression — 200—201, 219—221, 389—390

Anxiety — 217

Attention — 142, 146, 148, 151—152

Attitude Change — 119—149

Autism (see Childhood Psychosis) — 229—230, 233—237, 248—249

Autoshaping — 220, 221

Aversive Conditioning — 172—174, 241—244

B

Balance — 344, 349

Basal Ganglia — 344

Baseline — 390

Behavioralism — 184—185

Behavioral Architecture — 218, 221—222, 387, 393—394

Behavioral Treatment — 285—303

Behaviorism — 160—185

Behavior Modification — 142, 147—150, 163—166, 170—171, 181—185,188—191, 255—258, 161, 190

Behavior Therapy — 237—249

Bender Visual-Motor Gestalt Test — 346, 347

Bimanual Dexterity — 347, 350, 353

Body Awareness — 341, 343

C

Catharsis — 209

Characteristics of — 196—197

Childhood Psychosis — 228—252

    Clinical features — 230—231

    Drugs — 249

    EEG's — 233

    Etiology — 231—232

E

F

G

H

I

Illinois Test of Psycholinguistic Abilities — 345
Imitation — 239—240, 244—246
Implosive Therapy — 169—170
Impulsivity — 142, 151—153
Individual Psychotherapy — 285
Insight — 209
Instigation Therapy — 183—184
Interpersonal Attraction — 166, 167—171
Interpersonal Similarity — 165, 167—171
Interpretation — 210

J

Jaundice — 346
Job Performance — 391—393

K

Kanners Syndrome — 229

L

Language — 133, 135—137, 230, 235—236, 238—240
Language, Cognition — 217—218, 219
Learning Disability — 246, 344—347
Locus of Conflict — 215—216
Locus of Control — 206, 139, 141, 143—145, 218—219

M

Matching Familiar Figures Test (MFF) — 215, 219—220
McCarron Assessment of Neuromuscular Development — 346, 347, 350—351
Mental Retardation — 218—222, 234—237, 352, 386—387, 389—393
Minimal Brain Dysfunction (see CNS Dysfunction) — 299—301
Misconceptions of — 198—200
Modeling — 148, 153—154; 202
Modeling (see imitation) — 206—208

T